Security and Diplomacy

Essential Documents

Security and Diplomacy

Essential Documents

Edited by

Arvind Gupta

Mukul Chaturvedi

and

Akshay Joshi

Published in collaboration with

National Security Council Secretariat

Manas Publications

New Delhi-110 002 (INDIA)

Manas Publications
(Publishers, Distributors, Importers & Exporters)
4858, Prahlad Street,
24, Ansari Road, Darya Ganj,
New Delhi - 110 002 (INDIA)
Ph.: 23260783, 23265523:, 27131660 (R)
Fax: 011-23272766
E-mail: manaspublications@vsnl.com
www.manaspublications.com

2004

ISBN 81-7049-202-5
Rs 995/-

Typeset at
Manas Publications

Printed in India at
RK offsets
and Published by Mrs Suman Lata for
Manas Publications,
4858, Prahlad Street,
24, Ansari Road, Darya Ganj,
New Delhi - 110 002 (INDIA)

Preface

The NSCS had brought out a compilation of select documents on security and diplomacy in 2003. Encouraged by the response, we are happy to present another compilation of speeches and documents covering important developments in the year 2003.

The compilation is divided into two parts. Part-1 (A&B) deals with India's bilateral relations. It contains joint statements and speeches made by the Indian leaders. Part-2 (A&B) contains select international documents and speeches of international leaders. To make it easy for the reader, a short abstract has been added before each document. The content page has also been made reader friendly. An exhaustive index at the end of the book will make referencing easier.

The year 2003 saw a major diversification of India's ties. The most significant development was the deepening of India's ties with China. The two countries signed a Declaration on Principles for Relations and Comprehensive Cooperation in which they declared that they are "not a threat to each other". The Indian side recognized that the "Tibet Autonomous Region is a part of the territory of the People's Republic of China". Each side appointed a "Special Representative" to "explore from the political perspectives" the framework of boundary settlement.

India's new "look east" policy was unveiled during Prime Minister Vajpayee's visit to Bali for the summit meeting with ASEAN. India and ASEAN agreed to established a Regional Trade and Investment Area (RTIA). The two sides agreed to conclude negotiations by 2007 in the area of Trade and Services.

During the year India followed active diplomacy on the bilateral front too. The press statement issued at the conclusion of the visit of Prime Minister Surya Bahadur Thapa of Nepal reflected the Indian Prime Minister's concerns over the serious security situation prevailing in Nepal. The India-Bangladesh joint statement issued after Foreign Secretary Kanwal Sibal's visit to Dhaka in April contained the commitment given by the Bangladesh side "not to allow its territory to be used for any activities inimical to the interests of India". King of Bhutan visited India in June 2003. Both sides, interalia, discussed the presence of Indian insurgent groups in Bhutan and agreed to "continue working closely" to resolve the issue. In December, the Royal Bhutanese Army took successful military measures to flush out the Indian insurgent groups from the territory of Bhutan.

The breadth of India's engagement with the world becomes evident from the wide variety of countries that India signed Joint Declarations/Framework Agreements with. India took initiative with Brazil and South Africa to establish a trilateral dialogue forum (IBSA) to revitalize south-south cooperation. It sought to use its strengths in information and communication technologies (ICT), biotechnology, human resources to improve bilateral relations and emphasized on establishing better connectivity through "transport corridors". to improve relations with Iran, Afghanistan and the CARs. Indian leaders also addressed a wide variety of international audiences on subjects like trade relations, information society, international relations, the knowledge economy, protection of sea lanes, counter-terrorism, UN reform, water security, elimination of trade barriers and the significance of the peace dividend. Documents covering these issues have been included in the book.

The Indian leaders expounded their vision for India and the world on several number of fora. Speaking at a symposium organised by the Hindustan Times in December, the Prime Minister dwelt on the theme of regional cooperation in South Asia and said that South Asian countries could eventually graduate to "mutual security cooperation, open borders and even single currency". At the 3rd SAARC, the PM asked members to overcome their apprehensions about the Indian economy and instead participate in its development to mutual benefit.

The External Affairs Minister Mr. Yashwant Sinha delivered a number of speeches throughout the year taking up a wide range of issues. In a speech at the Foreign Service Institute, he exhorted the Indian diplomats to make economic diplomacy "a mantra within the Ministry of External Affairs". He visualised India becoming a "soft power" in the world. He exhorted the SAARC countries to go beyond free trade and think of a South Asia union. Speaking at the 3rd India-Central Asia Conference in Tashkent in November, The External Affairs Minister underlined the threat posed by Hizb-ut-Tehrir, IMU and Lashkar-e-Toiba to both Central Asia and India. He spoke at length on Sino-Indian relations at the R.D. Katari Memorial Lecture in November in which he expressed his hope that India and China could eventually sign a Free Trade Agreement.

The war in Iraq dominated the headlines and attention of the world in 2003. The US case for war was kicked off with colin Powell's presentation to the UN Security Council in February 2003 that it was "irrefutable and undeniable" that Iraq remains in "material breach" of UNSCR 1441 (2002). Bush's speech declaring an end to major combat in Iraq on May 1, 2003 was followed by a gradual shift in US policy attempting to make it easy for international participation in the "reconstruction of Iraq" as it got bogged down with trying to "win the peace". The wordings of subsequent UNSC resolutions 1483 in May 2003, 1500 in August 2003, 1511 in October 2003 and finally the announcement of a "Timetable to Handover" on 15 November 2003 illustrate this shift.

Nuclear diplomacy between the EU and Iran led to the "voluntary suspension of Uranium enrichment" by Iran while LTTE's proposal for establishing an "Interim Self-Governing Authority for the Northeast of Sri Lanka" sparked off a major debate. The announcement of a "Roadmap" for "comprehensive settlement of the Israel-Palestine conflict by 2005" under the auspices of the "Quartet" (US, EU, UN, Russia); Putin's courting of the OIC; Europe's quest for a common "security strategy", and "Indo-Pak" and "US-UN" confrontation at the UNGA also made interesting reading.

Since the texts of the documents have been taken from various open sources, the NSCS does not take the responsibility for the accuracy of the contents.

Thanks are due to Shri S.S. Paul, Senior Systems Analyst, for the assistance rendered in compiling the documents.

We hope that this book will prove useful to researchers, analysts, and students of international affairs.

Arvind Gupta
Mukul Chaturvedi
Akshay Joshi

Contents

Part 2-B
Speeches delivered by the International leaders

Part 1-A

‹1›

Press Release of the Cabinet Committee on Security on Operationalization of India's Nuclear Doctrine (04.01.03)

Sharing the "operational arrangements governing India's nuclear assets" the CCS stated that the Nuclear Command Authority (NCA) comprised the Political Council and Executive Council. The Political Council chaired by the Prime Minister "is the sole body, which can authorize the use of nuclear weapons", while the Executive Council, chaired by the NSA, provided inputs for decision-making by the NCA and executed the diretives given to it by the Political Council. The CCS also approved the appointment of C-in-C, Strategic Forces Command, to manage and administer all Strategic Forces and approved "alternate chains of command for retaliatory nuclear strikes in all eventualities".

The Cabinet Committee on Security (CCS) met today to review the progress in operationalizing of India's nuclear doctrine. The committee decided that the following information, regarding the nuclear doctrine and operational arrangements governing India's nuclear assets, should be shared with the public.

2. India's nuclear doctrine can be summarized as follows:

(i) Building and maintaining a credible minimum deterrent;

(ii) A posture of "No First Use": nuclear weapons will only be used in retaliation against a nuclear attack on Indian territory or on Indian forces anywhere;

(iii) Nuclear retaliation to a first strike will be massive and designed to inflict unacceptable damage.

(iv) Nuclear retaliatory attacks can only be authorised by the civilian political leadership through the Nuclear Command Authority.

(v) Non-use of nuclear weapons against non-nuclear weapon states;

(vi) However, in the event of a major attack against India, or Indian forces anywhere, by biological or chemical weapons, India will retain the option of retaliating with nuclear weapons;

(vii) A continuance of strict controls on export of nuclear and missile related materials and technologies, participation in the Fissile Material Cutoff Treaty negotiations, and continued observance of the moratorium on nuclear tests.

(viii) Continued commitment to the goal of a nuclear weapon free world, through global, verifiable and non-discriminatory nuclear disarmament.

3. The Nuclear Command Authority comprises a Political Council and an Executive Council. The Political Council is chaired by the Prime Minister. It is the sole body which can authorize the use of nuclear weapons.

4. The Executive Council is chaired by the National Security Advisor. It provides inputs for decision-making by the Nuclear Command Authority and executes the directives given to it by the Political Council.

5. The CCS reviewed the existing command and control structures, the state of readiness, the targetting strategy for a retalliatory attack, and operating procedures for various stages of alert and launch. The Committee expressed satisfaction with the overall preparedness. The CCS approved the appointment of a Commander-in-Chief, Strategic Forces Command, to manage and administer all Strategic Forces.

6. The CCS also reviewed and approved the arrangements for alternate chains for command for retaliatory nuclear strikes in all eventualities.

New Delhi

❮2❯

Joint Declaration on the State Visit of Mr. Robert Kocharian, President of the Republic of Armenia to the Republic of India (31.10.03).

> Both sides agreed to intensify bilateral trade in areas of information technology, small and medium scale industries, textiles, food processing, pharmaceuticals and foodgrains. Armenia supported the resolution of differences between India and Pakistan "through bilateral dialogue in the spirit of the Shimla Agreement and Lahore Declaration" and reaffirmed full support for India's permanent membership of an expanded UNSC

At the invitation of the President of India, H.E. Dr. A.P.J. Abdul Kalam, the President of Armenia, H.E. Mr. Robert Kocharian, paid a State visit to India from October 29-November 1, 2003.

2. Within the framework of the visit, H.E. Mr. Robert Kocharian held fruitful discussions with H.E. Dr. A.P.J. Abdul Kalam, the President of India, and H.E. Mr. A.B. Vajpayee, Prime Minister of India. The Vice President of India, Mr. Bhairon Singh Shekhawat called on President Kocharian.

3. During the wide-ranging discussions held in a friendly and cordial atmosphere, both sides exchanged views on various bilateral, regional and international issues of mutual interest. The two Sides noted the high level of interaction and cooperation between Armenia and India at the United Nations and other multilateral fora and expressed their intention to further co-operate in this field.

4. Both sides noted with satisfaction that the close relations between India and Armenia, which have a cultural and historical basis, are marked by warmth and a high degree of understanding as well as shared interest in current principal issues. Both sides reiterated their desire to strengthen even further the bilateral relations and close ties between the two countries and peoples.

5. The two sides emphasized the continuing relevance of the Treaty of Friendship and Cooperation between the Republic of Armenia and the Republic of India signed in 1995. The Treaty has served both countries well and provided a solid foundation for further development of bilateral relations and cooperation on regional and international level in the years ahead.

6. While discussing possible ways of invigorating Indo-Armenian relations in trade, economic, scientific, technological and humanitarian spheres, the sides noted the considerable untapped potential of mutually beneficial cooperation between Armenia and India in these spheres. The two sides agreed to explore further, ways and means of increasing, intensifying and diversifying bilateral trade and investment to mutual benefit, in particular in the areas of Information Technology, small and medium scale industries, textiles, food processing sector, pharmaceuticals and foodgrains.

7. The sides marked with satisfaction the functioning of the Indo-Armenian Inter-Governmental Commission on Trade, Economic, Scientific and Technological, Cultural and Educational Cooperation which held its last meeting in May, 2003 in New Delhi. Both sides agreed to give high priority to intensifying cooperation in all areas identified during the last session of the Inter-Governmental Commission.

8. The two sides acknowledged the vital importance of the role of the United Nations in world peace, stability and development. They remained determined to continue their efforts in strengthening the UN system as the central mechanism for ensuring international peace and security as well as democratizing international relations. They reiterated their support for the need to reform the UN, particularly the expansion of the UN Security Council. They stressed, in particular, the need for equitable balance in the expanded Security Council to provide a constructive voice to the aspirations of the developing countries. They believed that piecemeal and discriminatory approaches to such expansion would be inconsistent with the objectives of that world body. Considering that India is the largest democracy in the world and in view of its past contributions to the promotion of peace and its role in advancing the interests and concerns of developing countries in international fora, Armenia reaffirmed its full support to India for permanent membership of an expanded UN Security Council.

9. The two sides expressed their concern over the increase in international terrorism, religious extremism, trans-border organized crime and illicit trafficking in arms and drugs. They viewed this upsurge as a serious threat to sovereign States, international peace, development, security and stability. They affirmed that terrorism was a grave violation of human rights and a crime against humanity and that no excuse could justify it in any form. They agreed that the fight against terrorism by the international community has to be global, comprehensive and sustained, with the ultimate objective of its total eradication from the world. Action should be taken against those States, entities and individuals who support, finance, harbour or abet terrorists or provide them shelter, safe havens or asylum to engage in cross-border terrorism. In that regard, it was essential that every State be made to refrain from organizing, instigating, assisting, training or participating in terrorist acts in another State or acquiescing in organized activities within its territories

directed towards the commission of such acts. In this context, they stressed the importance of strict, full and unconditional implementation of the UN Security Council Resolution on the fight against terrorism and reiterated in particular their commitment to the UN Security Council Resolution 1373. They stressed the need to strengthen the international legal regime to fight terrorism through the early finalization and adoption of the draft Comprehensive Convention on International Terrorism and the Convention for the Suppression of Acts of Nuclear Terrorism.

10. The Armenian side appreciated the evolving security concerns of India in the light of recent local, regional and global developments. It appreciated the initiatives taken by India to resume diplomatic relations with Pakistan. In this connection, the Armenian side supported the resolution of differences between India and Pakistan through bilateral dialogue in the spirit of the Shimla Agreement and the Lahore Declaration.

11. The Indian side appreciated the security concerns of Armenia in the light of local, regional and global developments. It welcomed the efforts undertaken by the Armenian side toward the establishment of lasting peace in the region. In this connection, the Indian side confirmed its support for finding peaceful and negotiated solution to the **Nagorno-Karabakh** problem.

12. The two sides reaffirmed their allegiance to the principle of peaceful and negotiated resolution of disputes as opposed to the use of force or the threat thereof, pursuant to the applicable rules of international law.

13. In the field of culture, the two sides reiterated the long standing historical ties between the two countries. They expressed satisfaction over the fact that they have the necessary framework for regular and diverse cultural exchanges. Both the Educational Exchange Programme and the recently concluded Cultural Exchange Programme are in place and would help to institutionalize cultural exchanges and ties. The two sides expressed their appreciation regarding the many and significant contributions made by the Armenian community in India to Indian national life.

14. On behalf of the Government and the people of Armenia, H.E. President Kocharian expressed sincere thanks to the Government of the Republic of India for all the hospitality extended to him and his delegation and the excellent arrangements made for their visit and stay in India.

❮3❯

Framework Agreement on Comprehensive Economic Cooperation Between the Republic of India and the Association of South East Asian Nations (08.10.03)

The "Parties" agreed to enter into negotiations to establish an India-ASEAN Regional Trade and Investment Area (RTIA) to facilitate trade in goods, services and investment. They identified non-tariff measures, customs, trade financing, agriculture, fisheries, forestry, services, ICT, biotechnology, HRD, Mekong Basin Development and intellectual property as some of the "areas of economic cooperation" and agreed to implement an "Early Harvest Programme" with a view to accelerate the implementation of the Agreement in respect of certain products

Preamble

We, the Heads of State/Government of Brunei Darussalam, the Kingdom of Cambodia (Cambodia), the Republic of Indonesia (Indonesia), the Lao People's Democratic Republic (Lao PDR), Malaysia, the Union of Myanmar (Myanmar), the Republic of the Philippines (the Philippines), the Republic of Singapore (Singapore), the Kingdom of Thailand (Thailand) and the Socialist Republic of Vietnam, Member States of the Association of Southeast Asian Nations (collectively, "ASEAN" or "ASEAN Member States", or individually, "ASEAN Member State"), and the Republic of India (India);

Recalling that in 2002, we had agreed on the importance of enhancing our close economic cooperation and to work towards an ASEAN-India Regional Trade and Investment Area (RTIA) as a long-term objective;

Desiring to adopt a Framework Agreement on Comprehensive Economic Cooperation (this Agreement) between ASEAN and India (collectively, "the Parties", or individually referring to an ASEAN Member State or to India as a "Party") that is forward-looking in order to forge a closer economic partnership in the 21st century;

Desiring to minimise barriers and deepen economic linkages between the Parties; lower costs; increase intra-regional trade and investment; increase economic efficiency; create a larger market with greater opportunities and larger economies of scale for the businesses of the Parties; and enhance the attractiveness of the Parties to capital and talent;

Recognising the important role and contribution of the business sector in enhancing trade and investment between the Parties and the need to further promote and facilitate their cooperation and utilisation of greater business opportunities provided by the ASEAN-India RTIA;

Recognising the different stages of economic development among ASEAN Member States and the need for flexibility, including the need to facilitate the increasing participation of Cambodia, Lao PDR, Myanmar and Viet Nam (the New ASEAN Member States) in the ASEAN-India economic cooperation and the expansion of their exports, inter alia, through the strengthening of their domestic capacity, efficiency and competitiveness;

Reaffirming the rights, obligations and undertakings of the respective parties under the World Trade Organisation (WTO), and other multilateral, regional and bilateral Agreements and arrangements; and

Recognising that regional trade arrangements can contribute towards accelerating regional and global liberalisation and as building blocks in the framework of the multilateral trading system,

have agreed as follows:

Article 1
Objectives

The objectives of this Agreement are to:

(a) Strengthen and enhance economic, trade and investment cooperation between the Parties;

(b) Progressively liberalise and promote trade in goods and services as well as create a transparent, liberal and facilitative investment regime;

(c) Explore new areas and develop appropriate measures for closer economic cooperation between the Parties; and

(d) Facilitate the more effective economic integration of the new ASEAN Member States and bridge the development gap among the Parties.

Article 2
Measures For Economic Cooperation

The Parties agree to enter into negotiations in order to establish an ASEAN-India Regional Trade and Investment Area (RTIA), which includes a Free Trade Area (FTA) in goods, services and investment, and to strengthen and enhance economic cooperation through the following:

(a) Progressive elimination of tariffs and non-tariff barriers in substantially all trade in goods;

(b) Progressive liberalisation of trade in services with substantial sectoral coverage;

(c) Establishment of a liberal and competitive investment regime that facilitates and promotes investment within the ASEAN-India RTIA;

(d) Provision of special and differential treatment to the New ASEAN Member States;

(e) Provision of flexibility to the Parties in the ASEAN-India RTIA negotiations to address their sensitive areas in the goods, services and investment sectors with such flexibilities to be negotiated and mutually agreed based on the principle of reciprocity and mutual benefits;

(f) Establishment of effective trade and investment facilitation measures, including, but not limited to, simplification of customs procedures and development of mutual recognition arrangements;

(g) Expansion of economic cooperation in areas as may be mutually agreed between the Parties that will complement the deepening of trade and investment links between the Parties and formulation of action plans and programmes in order to implement the agreed sectors/areas of cooperation; and

(h) Establishment of appropriate mechanisms for the purposes of effective implementation of this Agreement.

Article 3

Trade In Goods

(1) With a view to expediting the expansion of trade in goods, the Parties agree to enter into negotiations in which duties and other restrictive regulations of commerce (except, where necessary, those permitted under Article XXIV (8)(b) of the WTO General Agreement on Tariffs and Trade (GATT)) shall be eliminated on substantially all trade in goods between the Parties.

(2) For the purposes of this Article, the following definitions shall apply unless the context otherwise requires:

(a) "Applied Most Favoured Nation (MFN) tariff rates" shall refer to the respective applied rates of the Parties as of 1 July 2004; and

(b) "Non-tariff measures" shall include non-tariff barriers.

(3) Upon signing of this Agreement, the Parties shall commence consultations on each other's trade regime, including, but not limited to the following:

(a) Trade and tariff data;

(b) Customs procedures, rules and regulations;

(c) Non-tariff measures including, but not limited to import licensing requirement and procedure, quantitative restrictions, technical barriers to trade, sanitary and phytosanitary;

(d) Intellectual property rights rules and regulations; and

(e) Trade policy.

(4) The tariff reduction or elimination programme of the Parties shall require tariffs on listed products to be gradually reduced and, where applicable, eliminated in accordance with this Article.

(5) The products which are subject to the tariff reduction or elimination programme under this Article shall include all products not covered by the Early Harvest Programme (EHP) under Article 7 of this Agreement, and such products shall be categorised into two tracks as follows:

(a) Normal Track: Products listed in the Normal Track by a Party on its own accord shall have their respective applied MFN tariff rates gradually reduced or eliminated in accordance with specified schedules and rates (to be mutually agreed by the Parties) over a period from:

(i) 1 January 2006 to 31 December 2011 for Brunei Darussalam, Indonesia, Malaysia, Singapore and Thailand, and India;

(ii) 1 January 2006 to 31 December 2016 for the Philippines and India; and

(iii) 1 January 2006 to 31 December 2011 for India and 1 January 2006 to 31 December 2016 for the New ASEAN Member States.

In respect of those tariffs which have been reduced but have not been eliminated, they shall be progressively eliminated within timeframes to be mutually agreed between the Parties.

(b) Sensitive Track:

(i) The number of products listed in the Sensitive Track shall be subject to a maximum ceiling to be mutually agreed among the Parties.

(ii) Products listed in the Sensitive Track by a Party on its own accord shall, where applicable, have their respective applied MFN tariff rates progressively reduced/eliminated within timeframes to be mutually agreed between the Parties.

(6) The commitments undertaken by the Parties under this Article and Article 7 of this Agreement shall fulfill the WTO requirements to eliminate tariffs on substantially all the trade between the Parties.

(7) The specified tariff rates/tariff preferences to be mutually agreed between the Parties pursuant to this Article shall set out only the limits of the applicable tariff rates/preferences or range for the specified year of implementation by the Parties.

(8) The negotiations between the Parties to establish the ASEAN-India RTIA covering trade in goods shall also include, but not be limited to the following:

(a) Modalities, including detailed rules governing the tariff reduction and/or elimination;

(b) Rules of Origin;

(c) Treatment of out-of-quota rates;

(d) Modification of a Party's commitments under the agreement on trade in goods based on WTO Agreements;

(e) Non-tariff measures/barriers, including, but not limited to, quantitative restrictions or prohibition on the importation of any product or on the export or sale for export of any product, as well as sanitary and phytosanitary measures and technical barriers to trade;

(f) Safeguards based on the WTO Agreements;

(g) Disciplines on subsidies and countervailing measures and anti-dumping measures based on the existing WTO agreements; and

(h) Facilitation and promotion of effective and adequate protection of trade-related aspects of intellectual property rights based on existing WTO, World Intellectual Property Organisation (WIPO) and other relevant Agreements.

Article 4

Trade In Services

With a view to expediting the expansion of trade in services, the Parties agree to enter into negotiations to progressively liberalise trade in services on a preferential basis with substantial sectoral coverage. Such negotiations shall be directed to:

(a) Progressive elimination of substantially all discrimination between or among the Parties and/or prohibition of new or more discriminatory measures with respect to trade in services between the Parties, except for measures permitted under Article V(1)(b) of the WTO General Agreement on Trade in Services (GATS);

(b) Expansion in the depth and scope of liberalisation of trade in services beyond those undertaken by ASEAN Member States and India under the GATS; and

(c) Enhanced cooperation in services between the Parties in order to improve efficiency and competitiveness, as well as to diversify the supply and distribution of services of the respective service suppliers of the Parties.

Article 5
Investment

To promote investments and to create a liberal, facilitative, transparent and competitive investment regime, the Parties agree to:

(a) Enter into negotiations in order to progressively liberalise their investment regimes;

(b) Strengthen co-operation in investment, facilitate investment and improve transparency of investment rules and regulations; and

(c) Provide for the protection of investments.

Article 6
Areas of Economic Co-operation

(1) Where appropriate, the Parties agree to strengthen their co-operation in the following areas, including, but not limited to:

(a) Trade Facilitation:

(i) Mutual Recognition Arrangements, conformity assessment, accreditation procedures, and standards and technical regulations;

(ii) Non-tariff measures;

(iii) Customs co-operation;

(iv) Trade financing; and

(v) Business visa and travel facilitation.

(b) Sectors of Co-operation:

(i) Agriculture, fisheries and forestry;

(ii) Services: media and entertainment, health, financial, tourism, construction, business process outsourcing, environmental;

(iii) Mining and energy: oil and natural gas, power generation and supply;

(iv) Science and technology: information and communications technology, electronic-commerce, biotechnology;

(v) Transport and infrastructure: transport and communication;

(vi) Manufacturing: automotive, drugs and pharmaceuticals, textiles, petrochemicals, garments, food processing, leather goods, light engineering goods, gems and jewellery processing;

(vii) Human Resource Development: capacity building, education, technology transfer; and

(viii) Others: handicrafts, small and medium enterprises, competition policy, Mekong Basin Development, intellectual property rights, government procurement.

(c) Trade and Investment Promotion:

(i) Fairs and exhibitions;

(ii) ASEAN-India weblinks; and

(iii) Business sector dialogues.

(2) The Parties agree to implement capacity building programmes and technical assistance, particularly for the New ASEAN Member States, in order to adjust their economic structure and expand their trade and investment with India.

(3) Parties may establish other bodies as may be necessary to co-ordinate and implement any economic cooperation activities undertaken pursuant to this Agreement.

ARTICLE 7

Early Harvest Programme

(1) With a view to accelerating the implementation of this Agreement, the Parties agree to implement an EHP, which is an integral part of the ASEAN-India RTIA, for products covered under paragraph 3(a) below. The progressive tariff reduction under the EHP shall commence from 1 November 2004, and tariff elimination shall be completed by 31 October 2007 for ASEAN-6 and India, and 31 October 2010 for the New ASEAN Member States.

(2) For the purposes of this Article, the following definitions shall apply unless the context otherwise requires:

(a) "ASEAN 6" refers to Brunei Darussalam, Indonesia, Malaysia, the Philippines, Singapore and Thailand; and

(b) "Applied MFN tariff rates" shall refer to the respective applied rates of the Parties as of 1 July, 2004.

(3) The product coverage, tariff reduction and elimination, removal of non-tariff barriers, rules of origin, trade remedies and emergency measures applicable to the EHP shall be as follows:

(a) Product Coverage.

(i) Common products on which the Parties agree to exchange tariff concessions are listed in Annex A.

(ii) Products on which India accords concessions to the New ASEAN Member States are listed in Annex B.

(b) Modality for Tariff Reduction and Elimination.

The modality for tariff reduction and elimination for the products covered by the EHP shall be finalised under Article 8(2) of this Agreement.

(c) Removal of non-tariff measures.

In order to fully realise the potential benefits of the EHP, the parties shall promote and facilitate trade in all products listed in the EHP. The parties shall also endeavour to refrain from using non-tariff measures adversely affecting trade in Early Harvest products.

(d) Rules of Origin.

Products covered by the EHP shall qualify for tariff preferences in accordance with the Rules of Origin to be agreed under Article 8(2) of this Agreement.

(e) Application of WTO provisions.

The WTO provisions governing modification of commitments, safeguard actions, emergency measures and other trade remedies, including anti-dumping and subsidies and countervailing measures, shall, in the interim, be applicable to the products covered under the EHP and shall be superseded and replaced by the relevant disciplines negotiated and agreed to by the Parties under Article 3(8) of this Agreement once these disciplines are implemented.

(4) The Parties shall also explore the feasibility of cooperation in the areas listed in Annex C.

Article 8
Timeframes

(1) For trade in goods, negotiations on the Agreement for tariff reduction/ elimination and other matters as set out in Article 3 of this Agreement shall commence in January 2004 and be concluded by 30 June 2005 in order to establish the ASEAN-India FTA.

(2) The negotiations on Rules of Origin for trade in goods under Articles 3 and 7 and modality for tariff reduction and elimination under Article 7 shall be concluded no later than 31 July, 2004.

(3) For trade in services and investments, the negotiations on the respective Agreements shall commence in 2005 and be concluded by 2007. The identification, liberalisation, etc., of the sectors of services and investment shall be finalised for implementation subsequently in accordance with the timeframes to be mutually agreed: (a) taking into account the sensitive sectors of the Parties; and (b) with special and differential treatment and flexibility for the New ASEAN Member States.

(4) For other areas of economic cooperation, the Parties shall continue to build upon existing or agreed programmes set out in Article 6 of this Agreement, develop new economic cooperation programmes and conclude Agreements on the various areas of economic cooperation. The Parties shall do so expeditiously for early implementation in a manner and at a pace acceptable to all the Parties concerned. The Agreements shall include timeframes for the implementation of the commitments there in.

Article 9

Most-Favoured Nation Treatment

India shall continue to accord Most-Favoured Nation (MFN) Treatment consistent with WTO rules and disciplines to all the non-WTO ASEAN Member States upon the date of signature of this Agreement.

Article 10

General Exceptions

Subject to the requirement that such measures are not applied in a manner which would constitute a means of arbitrary or unjustifiable discrimination between or among the Parties where the same conditions prevail, or a disguised restriction on trade within the ASEAN-India FTA, nothing in this Agreement shall prevent any Party from taking action and adopting measures for the protection of its national security or the protection of articles of artistic, historic and archaeological value, or such other measures which it deems necessary for the protection of public morals, or for the protection of human, animal or plant life, health and conservation of exhaustible natural resources.

Article 11

Dispute Settlement Mechanism

(1) The Parties shall, within one (1) year after the date of entry into force of this Agreement, establish appropriate formal dispute settlement procedures and mechanism for the purposes of this Agreement.

(2) Pending the establishment of the formal dispute settlement procedures and mechanism under (paragraph 1 above), any disputes concerning the interpretation, implementation or application of this Agreement shall be settled amicably by mutual consultations.

Article 12

Institutional Arrangements for the Negotiations

(1) There shall be established an ASEAN-India Trade Negotiating Committee (TNC) to carry out the programme of negotiations set out in this Agreement.

(2) The ASEAN-India TNC may invite experts or establish any Working Group as may be necessary to assist in the negotiations of all sectors in the ASEAN-India RTIA.

(3) The ASEAN-India TNC shall regularly report to the Minister of Commerce and Industry of India and the ASEAN Economic Ministers (AEM-India Consultations), through the meetings of the ASEAN Senior Economic Officials and India (SEOM-India Consultations), on the progress and outcome of its negotiations.

(4) The Ministry of Commerce and Industry, Government of India, and the ASEAN Secretariat shall jointly provide the necessary secretariat support to the ASEAN-India Trade Negotiating Committee (TNC) whenever and wherever negotiations are held.

Article 13

Miscellaneous Provisions

(1) This Agreement shall include the Annexes and the contents therein, and all future legal instruments agreed pursuant to this Agreement.

(2) Except as otherwise provided in this Agreement, this Agreement or any action taken under it shall not affect or nullify the rights and obligations of a Party under existing agreements to which it is a party.

(3) The Parties shall endeavour to refrain from increasing restrictions or limitations that would affect the application of this Agreement.

(4) Any ASEAN Member State may defer its participation in the implementation of this Agreement provided that a notification is given to the other parties within twelve (12) months from the date of signing of this Agreement. Any extension of the negotiated concessions to such ASEAN Member State shall be voluntary on the part of the parties participating in such implementation. The ASEAN Member State concerned shall participate in the implementation of this Agreement at a later date on the same terms and conditions, including any further commitments that may have been undertaken by the other parties by the time of such participation.

Article 14

Amendments

The provisions of this Agreement may be modified through amendments mutually agreed upon in writing by the Parties.

Article 15

Depository

For the ASEAN Member States, this Agreement shall be deposited with the Secretary-General of ASEAN, who shall promptly furnish a certified copy thereof to each ASEAN Member State and India.

Article 16

Entry into Force

(1) This Agreement shall enter into force on 1 July, 2004.

(2) The Parties undertake to complete their internal procedures for the entry into force of this Agreement prior to 1 July, 2004.

(3) Where a Party is unable to complete its internal procedures for the entry into force of this Agreement by 1 July, 2004, the Agreement shall come into force for that Party upon the date of notification of the completion of its internal procedures. The Party concerned, however, shall be bound by the same terms and conditions, including any further commitments that may have been undertaken by the other Parties under this Agreement by the time of such notification.

(4) A Party shall upon the completion of its internal procedures for the entry into force of this Agreement notify all the other parties in writing.

In witness whereof, we have signed this Framework Agreement on Comprehensive Economic Cooperation between the Association of Southeast Asian Nations and the Republic of India.

Done at Bali, this 8th day of October, 2003 in duplicate copies in the English Language.

〈4〉

ASEAN-India Joint Declaration For Cooperation To Combat International Terrorism (08.10.03)

> The "Participants" committed to improve intelligence and terrorist financing information sharing including the development of effective counter-terrorism policies through liaison between law enforcement agencies; seminars, conferences and joint operations; border and immigration control. The Declaration called upon the Participants to comply with UNSCR's 1373, 1267, 1390 and become parties to all 12 of the UN conventions and protocols relating to terrorism.

The Governments of Brunei Darussalam, the Kingdom of Cambodia, the Republic of Indonesia, the Lao People's Democratic Republic, Malaysia, the Union of Myanmar, the Republic of the Philippines, the Republic of Singapore, the Kingdom of Thailand, the Socialist Republic of Vietnam, Member Countries of the Association of Southeast Asian Nations (ASEAN), and the Republic of India, hereinafter referred to collectively as "the participants";

Mindful of the 2001 ASEAN Declaration on Joint Action to Counter Terrorism, which, inter alia, undertakes to strengthen cooperation at bilateral, regional and international levels in combating terrorism in a comprehensive manner and affirms that at the international level the United Nations should play a major role in this regard;

Reaffirming their commitment to counter, prevent and suppress all forms of terrorist acts in accordance with the Charter of the United Nations, international law and all the relevant United Nations resolutions or declarations on international terrorism, in particular the principles outlined in United Nations Security Council Resolutions 1373, 1267 and 1390;

Viewing acts of terrorism in all its forms and manifestations, committed wherever, whenever and by whomsoever, as a profound threat to international peace and security, which require concerted action to protect and defend all peoples and the peace and security of the world;

Rejecting any attempt to associate terrorism with any religion, race or nationality;

Recognising the principles of sovereign equality, territorial integrity and non-intervention in the domestic affairs of other States;

Acknowledging the value of cooperation on security, intelligence and law enforcement matters, and desiring to entering into such a co-operation to combat international terrorism through the ASEAN Ministerial Meeting on Transnational Crime, as a leading ASEAN body for combating terrorism, and other mechanisms;

Recognising the transnational nature of terrorist activities and the need to strengthen international cooperation at all levels in combating terrorism in a comprehensive manner;

Desiring to enhance counter-terrorism cooperation between the relevant agencies of the participants' governments;

Solemnly declare as follows:

Objectives:

1. The participants reaffirm the importance of having a framework for cooperation to prevent, disrupt and combat international terrorism through the exchange and flow of information, intelligence and capacity-building.
2. The participants emphasize that the purpose of this cooperation is to enhance the efficacy of those efforts to combat terrorism.

Scope and Areas of Cooperation:

3. The participants stress their commitment to seek to implement the principles laid out in this Declaration, in accordance with their respective domestic laws and their specific circumstances, in any or all of the following activities:
   - i. Continue and improve intelligence and terrorist financing information sharing on counter-terrorism measures, including the development of more effective counter-terrorism policies and legal, regulatory and administrative counter-terrorism regimes.
   - ii. Enhance liaison relationships amongst their law enforcement agencies to engender practical counter-terrorism regimes.
   - iii. Strengthen capacity-building efforts through training and education; consultations between officials, analysts and field operators; and seminars, conferences and joint operations as appropriate.
   - iv. Provide assistance on transportation, border and immigration control challenges, including document and identity fraud to stem effectively the flow of terrorist-related material, money and people.
   - v. Comply with United Nations Security Council Resolutions 1373, 1267, 1390 and other United Nations resolutions or declarations on international terrorism.

vi. Explore on a mutual basis additional areas of cooperation.

Participation:

4. Participants are called upon to become parties to all 12 of the United Nations conventions and protocols relating to terrorism.
5. The participants are each called upon to designate an agency to co-ordinate with law enforcement agencies, authorities dealing with countering terrorism financing and other concerned government agencies, and to act as the central point of contact for the purposes of implementing this Declaration.

Disclosure of Information:

6. The participants expect that no participant would disclose or distribute any confidential information, documents or data received in connection with this Declaration to any third party, at any time, except to the extent agreed in writing by the participant that provided the information.

Implementation:

7. All the participants are urged to promote and implement in good faith and effectively the provisions of the present Declaration in all its aspects.

Adopted by the Heads of State/Government of ASEAN Member States and the Republic of India on this Eighth Day of October 2003 in Bali, Indonesia.

❮5❯

India-Bangladesh Joint Statement (29.04.03)

> The Foreign Secretaries discussed a range of outstanding issues including demarcation of the Indo-Bangladesh land boundary, exchange of enclaves, border management and economic cooperation in the IT sector through a project to provide Bangladesh with 650 computers for district schools and training of 250 teachers.

The Foreign Secretary of India, Mr. Kanwal Sibal visited Dhaka, Bangladesh from 28-30 April, 2003, at the invitation of the Bangladesh Foreign Secretary, Mr. Shamsher M. Chowdhury, for Foreign Office consultations. During his stay in Dhaka, the Foreign Secretary of India called on H.E. Begum Khaleda Zia, Hon'ble Prime Minister of Bangladesh, Mr. M. Saifur Rahman, MP, the Finance Minister, Mr. M. Morshed Khan, MP, Minister for Foreign Affairs and Mr. Reaz Rahman, State Minister for Foreign Affairs. While receiving the Indian Foreign Secretary, the Bangladesh leaders reaffirmed the importance attached by the people and the Government of Bangladesh to close ties with India. They stressed their keen desire and commitment to continue to work with India and to further strengthen the bonds of friendship between the two countries.

During the consultations, the Indian Foreign Secretary was accompanied by H.E. Mr. Manilal Tripathi, High Commissioner of India to Bangladesh, Ms. Neelam Deo, Joint Secretary, Ministry of External Affairs of India and other officials of the Ministry of External Affairs of India and the High Commission of India in Dhaka. The Bangladesh Foreign Secretary was assisted by the Bangladesh High Commissioner to India, H.E. Mr. Tufail Karim Haider, Mr. Liaquat Ali Chowdhury, Director General (South Asia) and representatives of the Ministries of Foreign Affairs, Commerce and Land. The two sides extensively discussed all issues of common interest in a candid and frank manner covering the entire gamut of their bilateral relations and important regional issues including SAARC.

Issues relating to the completion of demarcation of the Indo-Bangladesh land boundary, exchange of enclaves and of territories in adverse possession, peaceful management of the borders, cross-border illegal movement of people and specific security concerns of both India and Bangladesh and the larger question of economic co-operation between the two countries were discussed by the two Foreign Secretaries.

It was agreed that the Joint Boundary Working Groups would be revived and would meet soon to work towards early resolution of border demarcation and related issues. It was also agreed to strengthen and fully implement the existing agreed procedures to stop cross border illegal movement of people.

In response to Indian concerns regarding the activities of Indian insurgent groups in Bangladesh, the Bangladesh side reaffirmed the commitment not to allow its territory to be used for any activities inimical to the interests of India.

On the economic side, it was agreed to hold the sixth meeting of the Joint Economic Commission, co-chaired by the respective Foreign Ministers, in July 2003, where all areas of economic interest to the two countries would be comprehensively discussed. The two sides discussed issues relating to enhancement of rail and road connectivity. They expressed the hope that the Bilateral Investment Protection and Promotion Agreement and Agreement on Cooperation for preventing Illicit Trafficking in Narcotics and Psychotropic Substances, finalisation of which are at an advanced stage, will be signed soon marking a significant forward movement in the close relations between India and Bangladesh.

The Indian Foreign Secretary reiterated the importance of crafting innovative trading relationships such as a Free Trade Agreement in tune with global trends and which are working successfully in regional contexts.

The two Foreign Secretaries also welcomed the prospect of a visit by the Finance Minister of Bangladesh to India at a mutually agreed date in May 2003.

The Indian Foreign Secretary proposed cooperation in the IT sector through a project to provide Bangladesh with 650 computers for district schools and the training of 250 teachers in IT applications in India. He also proposed the commissioning of a Joint Storm Surge Disaster Reduction Project which can benefit both India and Bangladesh. The Bangladesh Foreign Secretary thanked the Indian Foreign Secretary for the offer.

The Indian Foreign Secretary invited the Bangladesh Foreign Secretary to visit New Delhi early next year for the next Foreign Office consultations which was accepted with thanks. The meeting concluded with an expression of desire by both the Foreign Secretaries to carry on constructive engagement and discussions at all levels to further enrich Indo-Bangladesh relations.

Joint Statement
Ministry of External Affairs, India

❮6❯

India-Bhutan Joint Press Statement (18.09.03)

> The EAMs of the two countries signed an MoU on the Punatsangchyu Hydroelectric Power Project and the Indian government agreed to an enhanced assistance package of Rs.1614 Crores during Bhutan's Ninth Five Year Plan. Both sides also discussed the measures being taken by the government of Bhutan to persuade militants and Indian insurgent groups in Bhutan to leave its territory.

At the invitation of H.E. Dr. A.P.J. Abdul Kalam, President of the Republic of India, His Majesty King Jigme Singye Wangchuck of the Kingdom of Bhutan paid a State Visit to the Republic of India from September 14 to 18, 2003.

2. His Majesty the King was accompanied by H.E. Lyonpo Khandu Wangchuk, Minister of Foreign Affairs, and other senior officials of the Royal Government of Bhutan.
3. During the visit, H.E. Dr. A.P.J. Abdul Kalam, President of the Republic of India held talks with His Majesty King Jigme Singye Wangchuck and hosted a State banquet at Rashtrapati Bhavan. Their Excellencies, Vice President Shri Bhairon Singh Shekhawat, Prime Minister Shri Atal Bihari Vajpayee, Deputy Prime Minister Shri L.K.Advani, Shri Yashwant Sinha, Minister of External Affairs, Shri Jaswant Singh, Minister of Finance, and other senior officials of the Government of India held separate talks with His Majesty the King.
4. Leaders from both countries recalled the strong historical ties of friendship and understanding between India and Bhutan. They noted with satisfaction the excellent state of relations and mutually beneficial cooperation that the two countries enjoy, and expressed their firm commitment to further strengthen India-Bhutan relations in the coming years.
5. The leaders welcomed the signing of the Memorandum of Understanding establishing the India-Bhutan Foundation during the recent visit to India of the Crown Prince of Bhutan, which will add a new dimension to the relations between the two countries by facilitating greater people to people contacts. The two sides noted that the Festival of India, currently underway in Bhutan provides an

opportunity for the people of Bhutan to experience the rich cultural heritage of India.

6. The two sides recognized the many years of successful economic cooperation, particularly the invaluable and substantial assistance that India continues to provide towards Bhutan's development efforts in all fields.
7. During the State Visit to India by His Majesty the King, the Government of India has agreed to an enhanced assistance package of Rs. 1614 crores during Bhutan's Ninth Five Year Plan.
8. It was agreed that India will continue to assist Bhutan's economic development programmes, including the harnessing of its water resources. It was also agreed that India will continue to purchase excess power generated by Bhutan's hydropower projects.
9. During the visit, a Memorandum of Understanding for the preparation of a Detailed Project Report on the Punatsangchu Hydroelectric Power Project was signed by the Foreign Ministers of the two countries, H.E. Shri Yashwant Sinha, Government of India and H.E. Lyonpo Khandu Wangchuk, Royal Government of Bhutan, in the presence of His Majesty the King, H.E. Dr. A.P.J. Abdul Kalam, President of India, and H.E. Shri Atal Bihari Vajpayee, Prime Minister of India.
10. There was a cordial exchange of views on wide-ranging issues of mutual interest and concern, including the presence of Indian insurgent groups in Bhutan, and the measures being undertaken by the Royal Government of Bhutan to persuade the militants to leave its territory. Both sides agreed to continue working closely for resolving the issue. The two governments reiterated that as close friends and allies they will not allow their territories to be used by anyone for carrying out activities that are harmful to each other's national interests.
11. The two sides agreed that the State Visit of His Majesty, the King of Bhutan to the Republic of India has contributed to further enhancing the mutual understanding, trust, and friendship between the Governments, leaders and peoples of the two countries. The visit is yet another milestone in the close and friendly ties between India and Bhutan, which stand out today as a model of good neighbourly relations.
12. On behalf of the Government and the people of Bhutan, His Majesty King Jigme Singye Wangchuck thanked the Government and the people of India for the warm welcome and gracious hospitality received by him and the members of his delegation during his visit.

New Delhi
September 18, 2003

‹7›

India - Brazil Joint Statement (20.06.03)

EAMs of India and Brazil expressed the view that both countries "have a natural claim to a permanent seat in the restructured Security Council" and stressed the need for developed countries to adopt "positions favouring the liberalization of trade on a fair and non-discriminatory basis, correcting the prevailing asymmetries". Both countries reiterated their commitment to conservation of biological diversity and cooperation in IT, biotechnology, health, agriculture and genomics.

At the invitation of the Minister of External Relations of Brazil, Ambassador Celso Amorim, the Minister of External Affairs of India, Mr. Yashwant Sinha, is visiting Brazil on June 4-8, 2003. During the visit, the External Affairs Minister held discussions with H.E. Mr. Celso Amorim, the Minister of External Relations and H.E. Mr. Humberto Costa, Minister of Health of the Government of Brazil. He also called on H.E. Mr. Luiz Inacio Lula da Silva, the President of the Federal of Republic of Brazil and handed over to him an invitation from H.E. Dr. APJ Abdul Kalam, President of the Republic of India, to visit India in early 2004.

2. The Ministers took note that the visit occurs very soon after the meeting of President of Brazil Luiz Inácio Lula da Silva and the Prime Minister of India, Atal Bihari Vajpayee, at Lausanne, Switzerland, on June 2.
3. The visit of Minister Sinha, which takes place amid profound changes in the realm of international relations, led to a very fruitful exchange of ideas between both Ministers concerning many issues pertaining to the international agenda. The visit also permitted them to explore new opportunities for bilateral cooperation.
4. Brazil and India are developing countries with large territorial expanses. They face similar challenges in terms of economic and social development. They share similar points of view with regard to the international system and aspire to participate more actively in the political, economic, commercial, and financial decisions that shape such system. Based on common views and aspirations, Brazil and India wish to develop and widen the close cooperation and consultations they already maintain in international fora.

5. Brazil and India are among the largest democracies in the world. At the same time as they endeavour to develop and improve internally their democratic institutions, they also aspire for democracy to prevail in the international order. In this context, the Ministers stressed the central role played by the United Nations in the preservation of international peace and security. They also stressed the need to ensure strict observance of the United Nations Charter and of the principles and rules of the International Law.
6. India and Brazil agreed that the functioning of the UN should be made more democratic and that the Security Council should be expanded so that it is truly representative of the membership of the UN. Developing countries, which account for the overwhelming majority of the UN General Assembly membership and play an increasingly prominent role in world affairs, should be fully represented in the Permanent Members category in the restructured Security Council. They also agreed that the reform and expansion of the Security Council should be an integral part of a common package. They expressed the view that countries such as that India and Brazil have a natural claim to a permanent seat in the restructured Security Council. They also felt that this would have a positive effect towards efforts to usher in a peaceful, just and equitable world order and make the Security Council more representative, effective and legitimate.
7. Brazil and India affirmed the need to respect the sovereignty and territorial integrity of Iraq. They agreed that the United Nations should play an important role and take early decisions concerning stability, security and reconstruction of the country. The humanitarian situation should be addressed expeditiously in order to meet the needs of the Iraqi people, who should be enabled to decide on a government of their choice at the earliest. In this context, they expressed their support for the role played by the U.N. Secretary General and his Special Representative to Iraq and to the multilateral efforts being made under the auspices of the U.N. to ensure the adoption of urgent measures to reduce the suffering of the Iraqi people.
8. The Ministers expressed their repudiation of all forms of terrorism, which constitutes a new and serious threat to international peace and security. They also expressed their willingness to fight the drug traffic and organised crime and pointed to the need of continuing to review measures to repress and prevent these phenomena, according to the specific features of each country and to International Law.
9. As regards economic development, the two Ministers expressed the need to adopt public policies aimed at fostering the modernisation of their respective economies while meeting the legitimate social demands of their peoples. They stressed the need for developed countries to

adopt, in trade negotiations carried out within the World Trade Organisation and in regional negotiations, positions favouring the liberalisation of trade on a fair and non-discriminatory basis, correcting the prevailing asymmetries. Likewise, they agreed that the resolutions approved at the International Conference on Financial Development, held in Monterrey in 2002, should be implemented.

10. The Ministers reaffirmed the commitment of their countries to sustainable development and, in particular, to the goals of Agenda 21, as agreed during the 1992 Rio Conference, as well as to the Plan of Implementation of the World Summit on Sustainable Development, held in Johannesburg, in 2002. They also expressed their hope that the Kyoto Protocol to the United Nations Framework Convention on Climate Change will enter into force soon, and that it will count upon the support of as many nations as possible.
11. Brazil and India reiterated their firm commitment to the full implementation of the principles contained in the Convention on Biological Diversity, namely the conservation of biological diversity, the sustainable use of its components and the fair and equitable sharing of benefits arising out of the utilization of genetic resources, and called for cooperation to enable all countries to protect and sustainably use their bio-diversity for the benefit of all mankind. They also emphasised the need to render the TRIPS Agreement compatible with the Convention on Biological Diversity, as well as the priority they give to the negotiation of an international regime to promote and safeguard the fair and equitable sharing of benefits arising out of the utilisation of genetic resources, within that same Convention, as agreed at the Johannesburg Summit. In this regard, the group of like-minded Megadiverse Countries, of which Brazil and India are founding members, should be also be strengthened.
12. Both Ministers expressed their satisfaction with regard to the approval of the World Health Organisation Framework Convention on Tobacco Use Control, on May 2003. They also committed themselves to accelerate the internal ratification process within their respective countries, as well the Convention´s entry into force internationally as soon as possible.
13. Concerning the bilateral agenda, they expressed satisfaction over the impressive increase in bilateral trade between the two countries in recent years, which totalled US dollar 1.2 billion in 2002. Trade estimates for this year are also encouraging. Exports have not only increased, but also diversified. The two Ministers envisaged the sale in the near future of aircraft manufactured by Embraer to the Indian Government, thus opening up new opportunities of cooperation in the

aerospace sector. They also took note with satisfaction of the contribution provided by the Indian drug industry to Brazil's National Health Program in the form of high-quality medicines at affordable prices, and mentioned the existence of joint ventures in the information technology sector established in Brazil. The presence of businessmen in the delegation of Minister Yashwant Sinha is indicative of the support that the Indian Government has been providing to these private-sector initiatives. The adoption by India of a program for mixing ethanol to gasoline that is similar to the PROALCOOL program enhances the possibilities for a bilateral cooperation in terms of goods and services.

14. The Ministers agreed that economic and trade relations will be further enhanced by two Agreements to be signed between the Mercosur and India in the very near future: the Framework Agreement and the Agreement on Fixed Tariff Preferences, the first to be signed next June and the other in the second half of 2003.
15. The Ministers expressed their commitment to continue the implementation of scientific and technological co-operation arrangements between Brazil and India in sectors already identified and in which both countries can provide relevant contributions. These areas are: information technology, biotechnology, especially in the fields of health and medicine, agriculture and genomics. In the space sector, they referred to the Agreement in force between both countries and to the possibility of the use of Indian launch vehicles to launch Brazilian scientific micro-satellites.
16. Considering the common need to foster social development for the Brazilian and Indian peoples, the two Ministers agreed to a regular and systematic exchange of national experiences in the areas of health, education, job generation, eradication of poverty, hunger and malnutrition, social work, and others.
17. The relationship between the two countries having achieved new importance and intensity, and with a view to providing it with structure and dynamism, the Ministers agreed to hold the 1st Meeting of the Brazil-India Joint Commission on Political, Economic, Scientific, Technological and Cultural Cooperation in India this year.
18. Minister Yashwant Sinha invited Minister Celso Amorim to pay an official visit to New Delhi in the second half of this year.

❮8❯

Memorandum Between the Government of the Republic of India and the Government of the People's Republic of China on Expanding Border Trade (23.06.03)

The two sides agreed to designate Changgu of Sikkim state and Renqinggang of the Tibet Autonomous Region as venues for border trade and to establish checkpoints to monitor and manage entry and exit through Nathula Pass.

The Government of the Republic of India and the Government of the People's Republic of China (hereinafter referred to as the two sides),

With a view to promote the development of friendly relations between the two countries and two people.

Pursuant to the Memorandum between the Government of the Republic of India and the Government of the People's Republic of China on the Resumption of Border Trade signed on 13 December 1991, and Protocol on Entry and Exit Procedures for Border Trade signed on 1 July 1992,

Desirous of opening another pass on the India-China border and setting up an additional point on each side for Border Trade,

Have agreed as follows:

Article I

The Indian side agrees to designate Changgu of Sikkim State as the venue for Border Trade market; the Chinese side agrees to designate Renqinggang of the Tibet Autonomous Region as the venue for Border Trade market.

Article II

The two sides agree to use Nathula as the pass for entry and exit of persons, means of transport and commodities engaged in Border Trade. Each side shall establish checkpoints at appropriate locations to monitor and manage their entry and exit through the Nathula Pass.

Article III

All the provisions of the Memorandum on the Resumption of Border Trade signed between the two Governments on 13 December, 1991 and the Protocol on Entry and Exit Procedures for Border Trade signed between the two Governments on 1 July, 1992 under the Memorandum shall also be applicable to the border trade through the Nathula Pass.

Article IV

This Memorandum may be amended or supplemented by Agreement in writing between the two sides.

Article V

This Memorandum shall come into force as from the date of its signature and shall be valid during the validity of the Memorandum on Resumption of Border Trade signed between the two Governments in New Delhi on 13 December 1991.

Done in Beijing on 23 June 2003 in two originals each in the Hindi, Chinese and English languages, the three texts being equally authentic.

For the Government of the Republic of India	For the Government of People's Republic of China

❮9❯

MEA's Press Release on other Documents Signed Between India and China During Prime Minister Vajpayee's Visit to China (23.06.03)

The two sides signed a number of documents for closer cooperation in drafting laws, exchange of teaching material, teacher training, application of phytosanitary requirements to facilitate exports of Indian fresh fruits and vegetables, ocean development and joint research in science and technology.

The Government of the Republic of India and the Government of the People's Republic of China (hereinafter referred to as the two sides),

With a view to promoting the development of friendly relations between the two countries and two people,

Pursuant to the Memorandum between the Government of the Republic of India and the Government of the People's Republic of China on the Resumption of Border Trade signed on 13 December 1991, and Protocol on Entry and Exit Procedures for Border Trade signed on 1 July 1992,

Desirous of opening another pass on the India-China border and setting up an additional point on each side for border trade,

Have agreed as follows:

Article I

The Indian side agrees to designate Changgu of Sikkim State as the venue for border trade market; the Chinese side agrees to designate Renqinggang of the Tibet Autonomous Region as the venue for border trade market.

Article II

The two sides agree to use Nathula as the pass for entry and exit of persons, means of transport and commodities engaged in border trade. Each side shall establish checkpoints at appropriate locations to monitor and manage their entry and exit through the Nathula Pass.

Article III

All the provisions of the Memorandum on the Resumption of Border Trade signed between the two Governments on 13 December, 1991 and the Protocol on Entry and Exit Procedures for Border Trade signed between the two Governments on 1 July 1992 under the Memorandum shall also be applicable to the border trade through the Nathula Pass.

Article IV

This Memorandum may be amended or supplemented by Agreement in writing between the two sides.

Article V

This Memorandum shall come into force as from the date of its signature and shall be valid during the validity of the Memorandum on Resumption of Border Trade signed between the two Governments in New Delhi on 13 December 1991.

Done in Beijing on 23 June 2003, in two originals each in the Hindi, Chinese and English languages, the three texts being equally authentic.

For the Government of the Republic of India	For the Government of the People's Republic of China

(1) Memorandum of Understanding on Cooperation between the Ministry of Law and Justice of the Government of the Republic of India and the Supreme People's Prosecution Service of the People's Republic of China.

(Signatories: Shri Yashwant Sinha, External Affairs Minister and Mr. Jia Chunwang, Procurator General on the Chinese side)

The MoU envisages facilitating closer cooperation in the judicial field between India and China, through the exchange of information, experience in legal matters, including drafting of laws and implementation of legal provisions, exchange of experience and best practices, mutual support for training public procurators and auxiliary judicial personnel, and cooperation in other legal and judicial matters of interest to both countries. The MoU also provides for setting up of expert working groups, facilitation of direct contacts, conduct of joint seminars and exchange of experts to meet the objective of cooperation in the judicial field. Seminars and Conferences on issues of mutual interest will also be organized.

(2) Executive Programme on Educational Cooperation and Exchange between the Ministry of Human Resource Development, Government of the Republic of India and Ministry of Education, the People's Republic of China.

(Signatories: Shri Yashwant Sinha, External Affairs Minister and Mr. Zhou Ji, Minister for Education of the PRC on the Chinese side)

Under this executive programme, both sides aim to consolidate and strengthen mutual cooperation in the field of education through sharing of experiences between the educational administrators and through the study of education systems and innovative education programmes in each country. The two sides agree to exchange views and conduct discussion on mutual recognition of academic degrees. They will also cooperate in such areas as the development of curriculam for primary and secondary school education, exchange of teaching materials, teaching methodologies as well as the feasibility of conducting joint research in various modes of pre-research and in-service teachers' training and will examine the possibility of jointly establishing a Demonstration Centre for Teacher's Training. They will also take measures to encourage higher education institutions from their respective countries to establish direct exchange and cooperation through exchange of lecturers, scholars, books, research materials and audio-visual aids, holding of joint seminars/ symposia etc. They have noted the importance of student exchange programmes in various areas including IT and have provided for 25 post-graduate scholarships to be offered annually by both countries. They have also agreed to exchange two language teachers in Hindi and Chinese respectively. This programme will be valid from June 2003 to 2006 and will be extended for another three years if both sides so agree.

(3) Protocol of Phytosanitary Requirements for Exporting Mangoes from India to China between the Ministry of Agriculture of the Republic of India and General Administration of Quality Supervision, Inspection and Quarantine of the People's Republic of China.

(Signatories: Shri Yashwant Sinha, External Affairs Minister and Mr. Li Changjiang, Head of AQSIQ on the Chinese side)

Under the India-China bilateral WTO accession Agreement of February 2000, both sides agreed to sign a Sanitary and Phyto-Sanitary (SPS) protocol to facilitate exports of Indian fresh fruits and vegetables to China. An umbrella MoU on the application of Phyto-Sanitary Measures was signed during the visit of Premier Zhu Rongji in January 2002. India proposed 17 categories of fruit and vegetables (including mangoes, guavas, grapes, papayas, melons, gherkins, cucumbers, beans, aubergines, capsicums, gourds etc) for coverage under this MoU. The Chinese side decided to deal with each item separately. The first item taken up for consideration under this procedure was the mango. After completion of a Pest Risk Analysis and detailed negotiations, agreement has now been reached on procedures relating to inspection, certification,packaging and labelling of all consignments of mangoes to be exported to China from India. Now that we have a basic understanding of the relevant procedures, it is hoped that Agreement on similar protocols for all the other identified fruits and vegetables can be concluded expeditiously.

(4) Memorandum of Understanding on Simplifying Visa Procedures Between the Government of the Republic of India and the Government of the People's Republic of China.

(Signatories: Shri Kanwal Sibal, Foreign Secretary, on the Indian side, and Mr. Wang Yi, Vice Foreign Minister of the PRC on the Chinese side)

This MoU lays down mutually agreed procedures for the issue of visas in various categories (business, employment, tourism, students, conferences and other short-term academic and cultural exchanges etc.) for private passport holders and on the Chinese side, also for holders of "ordinary passports for public affairs" who are mainly employees of State owned enterprises. This MoU provides clarity on the kind of documentation required for various visas and on the duration and validity of visas issued for different purposes. This will help streamline the process of obtaining visas for businessmen, tourists, students, academicians and other experts travelling to each other's countries and will serve to promote people-to-people interaction.

(5) Memorandum of Understanding for Enhanced Cooperation in the Field of Renewable Energy Between the Ministry of Non-Conventional Energy Sources, Government of the Republic of India and the Ministry of Water Resources, Government of People's Republic of China.

(Signatories: Shri Kanwal Sibal, Foreign Secretary, on the Indian side, and Mr. Wang Yi, Vice Foreign Minister of the PRC on the Chinese side)

This MoU seeks to establish cooperation in the field of small hydropower, wind power and other areas of renewable energy through joint research and development activities, exchange of technical expertise and information networking. The ultimate objective is to commercialise the result of such co-operation, create business opportunities and facilitate sustainable market development in an environmentally responsible manner. Areas of cooperation will be defined by mutual consent in accordance with the interest of experience of the scientific, technological and industrial institutions and personnel of the two countries and the facilities available. The MoU provides for exchange of scientific and technological problems, formulation and implementation of joint research and development and demonstration projects on application of renewable energy technologies for augmenting energy availability in a cost-effective manner, training of personnel and setting up of technical demonstration projects in areas of renewable energy.

(6) Memorandum of Understanding for Cooperation in the field of Ocean Science and Technology Between Department of Ocean Development, Government of the Republic of India and State Oceanic Administration, People's Republic of China.

(Signatories: Shri Kanwal Sibal, Foreign Secretary, on the Indian side, and Mr. Wang Yi, Vice Foreign Minister of the PRC on the Chinese side)

This MoU aims at promoting development and cooperation in areas such as integrated coastal zone management, sea-based resources exploration and exploitation technology, polar science, ocean energy, gas hydrate exploration and exploitation technology, marine resources assessment, sea-weed production and processing, satellite oceanography and other fields of marine science of mutual interest to both sides. Such cooperation would be developed through the exchange of scientists, research workers, specialists and scholars; exchange of marine data and information; organization of bilateral symposium, training courses and seminars; joint identification of marine problems, projects and planning and their formulation and implementation; exchange of experience and know-how gained through development and activities in marine science and technology; mutual supply of equipment; utilization of facilities for R&D and other such mutually agreed means of cooperation.

(7) Memorandum of Understanding Between the Department of Science and Technology of the Republic of India and the National Science Foundation of China.

(Signatories: Shri Shivshankar Menon, Ambassador of India and Mr. Wang Yi, Vice Foreign Minister on the Chinese side)

This MoU provides for maintenance and development of cooperative research activities in the field of natural sciences within the framework of the Agreement on Cooperation in Science and Technology between the Government of India and the Government of the People's Republic of China signed on 22 December, 1988 in Beijing. The objective will be to ensure that the cooperation will bring real benefits to the development of science and technology in both countries. Collaborative activities will be undertaken in the fields of natural sciences with emphasis on Physical Sciences, Mathematical Sciences, Chemical Sciences and Biological Sciences. It recognizes that as a first step, a practical means of initiating collaboration between scientists of the two countries is provided by holding meetings of equal numbers of researchers (to be known as N+N meetings) from each side alternatively in India and China. Other forms of collaboration, including individual outgoing and incoming visits by leading scientists and joint research in areas on subjects identified as a priority by scientists of both sides will be based on the relationship built by N+N meetings, or on other established relationships. Priority areas for cooperation will be identified as also a framework of cooperation for each selected area (key institutions, key persons, forms of cooperation, financing etc.). The MoU also provides for periodic reviews of on-going programmes and for the exchange of information.

(8) Memorandum of Understanding Between the Government of the Republic of India and the Government of the People's Republic of China on the Reciprocal Establishment of Cultural Centres in their Capitals.

(Signatories: Shri Kanwal Sibal, Foreign Secretary on the Indian side and Mme Meng Xiaosi, Vice Minister of Culture on the Chinese side)

This MoU reflects the Agreements reached in principle by both sides to establish independent cultural centres in each other's capital cities. Relevant details such as location, staffing patterns, broad consensus on activities to be undertaken by the centres and so on will be worked out through mutual negotiations in the near future.

(9) Executive Programme of Cultural Exchanges Between the Government of the Republic of India and the Government of the People's Republic of China for the years 2003-2005.

(Signatories: Shri Kanwal Sibal, Foreign Secretary on the Indian side and Mme Meng Xiaosi, Vice Minister of Culture on the Chinese side)

The Executive Programme of Cultural Exchanges (CEP) provides for exchange of cultural troupes, art exhibitions, and cultural festivals, cooperation in the fields of archaeology and library science, co-operation between the National Museum, national Gallery of Modern Art, National Library, Sangeet Natak Academy and their respective Chinese counterparts etc. It also provides for interaction in the fields of youth affairs and sports, social sciences and mass media, including exchange of radio and TV programmes and training of personnel in radio, TV and films. This is a programme valid for the period June 2003-2005. There is, however, a provision which states that after June 2005, this Agreement will remain operative till such time as a new CEP is negotiated and formalized.

Ministry of External Affairs, New Delhi

‹10›

Declaration on Principles for Relations and Comprehensive Cooperation Between the Republic of India and the People's Republic of China (23.06.03)

> The two sides agreed to set up a Joint Study Group (JSG) composed of officials and economists to examine the potential complementarities in expanded trade and economic cooperation and appoint a "Special Representative" to explore the framework of a boundary settlement. The Indian side reiterated its recognition of Tibet as an integral part of China while the two sides affirmed that they are not a threat to each other.

At the invitation of Premier of the State Council of the People's Republic of China H.E. Wen Jiabao, Prime Minister of the Republic of India H.E. Atal Bihari Vajpayee paid an official visit to the People's Republic of China from 22 to 27 June, 2003.

During this visit, Premier Wen Jiabao held talks with Prime Minister Vajpayee. Their Excellencies President Hu Jintao of the People's Republic of China, Chairman Jiang Zemin of the Central Military Commission, Chairman Wu Bangguo of the Standing Committee of the National People's Congress and Vice President Zeng Qinghong of the People's Republic of China held separate meetings with Prime Minister Vajpayee. The talks and meetings were held in a sincere and friendly atmosphere.

Leaders from both countries noted with satisfaction the progress made over recent years in bilateral relations. This is conducive not only to their respective development, but also to regional stability and prosperity. The two sides recalled the historical depth of their friendly contacts. India and China are the two largest developing countries of the world with centuries-old civilization, unique history and similar objectives. Both noted that the sustained economic and social development in the two countries, representing one-third of humanity is vital for ensuring peace, stability and prosperity not only in Asia but also in the whole world.

The two sides agreed that India and China have a mutual desire for good neighborly relations and have broad common interests. They agreed to fully utilize the substantial potential and opportunities for deepening mutually beneficial cooperation.

Friendship and cooperation between the two countries meets the need to:

- Promote the socio-economic development and prosperity of both India and China;
- Maintain peace and stability regionally and globally;
- Strengthen multipolarity at the international level; and
- Enhance the positive factors of globalization.

Both sides affirmed that they would abide by the following principles, promote a long-term constructive and cooperative partnership and, on this basis, build a qualitatively new relationship:

- Both sides are committed to developing their long-term constructive and cooperative partnership on the basis of the principles of Panchsheel, mutual respect and sensitivity for each other's concerns and equality;
- As two major developing countries, India and China have a broad mutual interest in the maintenance of peace, stability and prosperity in Asia and the world, and a mutual desire in developing wider and closer cooperation and understanding in regional and international affairs;
- The common interests of the two sides outweigh their differences. The two countries are not a threat to each other. Neither side shall use or threaten to use force against the other; and
- Both sides agree to qualitatively enhancing the bilateral relationship at all levels and in all areas while addressing differences through peaceful means in a fair, reasonable and mutually acceptable manner. The differences should not be allowed to affect the overall development of bilateral relations.

Both sides agreed to hold regular high-level exchanges between the two countries. This will greatly enhance mutual understanding and expand bilateral relations. With a view to deepening their co-ordination and dialogues on bilateral, regional and international issues, both sides agreed on the need for annual meetings between Foreign Ministers of the two countries. They also agreed that personnel exchanges and friendly contacts between Ministries, Parliaments and Political Parties of the two countries should be further enhanced.

The two sides welcomed the positive momentum of bilateral trade and economic cooperation in recent years and shared the belief that continued expansion and intensification of India-China economic cooperation is essential for strengthening bilateral relations.

Both sides shared the view that existing complementarities between their two economies provide an important foundation and offer broad prospects for further enhancing their economic relations. In order to promote trade and economic cooperation, both sides will take necessary measures consistent with their national laws and rules and international obligations to remove impediments to bilateral trade and investment. They reaffirmed the importance of the ministerial meeting of the Joint Economic Group (JEG) and agreed to hold the next (seventh) JEG meeting within the year.

The two sides will set up a compact Joint Study Group (JSG) composed of officials and economists to examine the potential complementarities between the two countries in expanded trade and economic co-operation. The JSG would also draw up a programme for the development of India-China trade and economic co-operation for the next five years, aimed at encouraging greater co-operation between the business communities of both sides. The Group should present a study report and recommendations to the two Governments on measures for comprehensive trade and economic cooperation by the end of June 2004.

The two countries will launch a financial dialogue and cooperation mechanism to strengthen their dialogue and co-ordination in this sector.

The two sides agreed to enhance co-operation at the World Trade Organization, which is not only to mutual benefit but also in the broader interest of developing countries. The two sides will hold dialogues on a regular basis in this regard.

Historical and cultural links between India and China will be strengthened, inter-alia, through the promotion of exchanges in culture, education, science and technology, media, youth and people-to-people relations. They agreed to set up Cultural Centers in each other's capitals and facilitate their establishment.

Both sides will work towards the enhancement of direct air and shipping links, tourism, exchange hydrological data in flood season on common rivers as agreed, co-operation in agriculture, dairy, food processing, health and other sectors.

They agreed on the need to broaden and deepen defence exchanges between the two countries, which will help enhance and deepen the mutual understanding and trust between the two armed forces. They confirmed that the exchange of visits by their Defence Ministers and of military officials at various levels should be strengthened.

The two sides exchanged views on the India-China boundary question and expounded their respective positions. They reiterated their readiness to seek a fair, reasonable and mutually acceptable solution through consultations on an equal footing. The two sides agreed that pending an ultimate solution, they should work together to maintain peace and tranquility in the border areas, and reiterated their commitment to continue implementation of the agreements signed for this purpose, including the clarification of the Line of Actual Control.

The two sides agreed to each appoint a Special Representative to explore from the political perspective of the overall bilateral relationship the framework of a boundary settlement.

The Indian side recognizes that the Tibet Autonomous Region is part of the territory of the People's Republic of China and reiterates that it does not allow Tibetans to engage in anti-China political activities in India. The Chinese side expresses its appreciation for the Indian position and reiterates that it is firmly opposed to any attempt and action aimed at splitting China and bringing about "independence of Tibet".

The Indian side recalled that India was among the first countries to recognize that there is one China and its one China policy remains unaltered. The Chinese side expressed its appreciation of the Indian position.

India and China recognized the primacy of maintaining international peace. This is a prerequisite for the socio-economic development of all developing countries, including India and China. The world is marked by diversity. Every country has the right to choose its own political system and path to development. As two major developing countries, India and China acknowledged the importance of their respective roles in the shaping of a new international political and economic order. The international community must help the developing countries to eliminate poverty and narrow the gap between the North and the South through dialogue and co-operation so as to achieve common prosperity.

The two sides acknowledged the vital importance of the role of the United Nations in world peace, stability and development. They are determined to continue their efforts in strengthening the UN system. They reaffirmed their readiness to work together to promote reform of the UN. In reform of the UN Security Council, priority should be given to enhancing representation of the developing countries.

Both sides stood for continued multilateral arms control and disarmament process, undiminished and equal security for all at progressively lower levels of armament and for multilateral negotiations aimed at nuclear disarmament and elimination of nuclear weapons. They are firmly opposed to introduction of weapons in outer space, use or threat of force against space-based objects and support cooperation in development of space technology for peaceful purposes.

The two sides recognised the threat posed by terrorism to them and to global peace and security. They resolutely condemned terrorism in any form. The struggle between the international community and global terrorism is a comprehensive and sustained one, with the ultimate objective of eradication of terrorism in all regions. This requires strengthening the global legal framework against terrorism. Both sides shall also promote cooperation on counter-terrorism through their bilateral dialogue mechanism.

India and China face special and similar challenges in their efforts to protect the environment while simultaneously forging ahead with rapid social and economic development of their countries. In this context, the two sides agreed to work together in a practical manner to cooperate on preserving the environment and ensuring sustainable development and to co-ordinate positions on climate change, biodiversity and other issues in relevant multilateral fora.

The two sides supported multilateral cooperation in Asia, believing that such cooperation promotes mutually beneficial exchanges, economic growth as well as greater cohesion among Asian countries. The two sides viewed positively each other's participation in regional and sub-regional multilateral cooperation processes in Asia.

The two sides stated that the improvement and development of India-China relations is not targeted at any third country and does not affect either country's existing friendly relations and cooperation with other countries.

The two sides agreed that the official visit of the Prime Minister of India to the People's Republic of China has been a success, has contributed to enhancing mutual understanding and trust between the Governments, leaders and peoples of the two countries, and marks a new step forward in strengthening the all-round cooperation between India and China in the new century.

Prime Minister Vajpayee invited Premier Wen Jiabao to visit India at a mutually convenient time and conveyed to President Hu Jintao an invitation from President Abdul Kalam to visit India. The Chinese side accepted the invitations with appreciation. The dates of the visits will be settled through diplomatic channels. On behalf of the Government and the people of India, H.E Prime Minister Atal Bihari Vajpayee thanked the Government and the people of China for the warm welcome received by him and his delegation.

Signed in Beijing on 23 June, 2003 in the Hindi, Chinese and English languages.

(Atal Bihari Vajpayee)	(Wen Jiabao)
Prime Minister	Premier of the State Council
The Republic of India	the People's Republic of China

‹11›

4th India-EU Summit-Joint Press Statement (29.11.03)

> The EU warmly welcomed PM Vajpayee's extending the hand of friendship to Pakistan in April 2003 and reiterated "the unacceptability of use of terrorism in pursuit of political goals". Both sides agreed to launch a "Trade and Investment Development Programme" and agreed to cooperate in developing the GALILEO Satellite Navigation System.

The 4th Summit between India and the EU was held in New Delhi, India, on 29th November, 2003. India was represented by Prime Minister, Mr. Atal Bihari Vajpayee. He was assisted by External Affairs Minister, Mr. Yashwant Sinha. The EU was represented by the Presidency of the European Council, Italian Minister of State for External Affairs, Mrs. Margherita Boniver, President of the European Commission, Mr. Romano Prodi, Secretary General/ High Representative for Common Foreign and Security Policy Mr. Javier Solana and the Commissioner [External Relations], Mr. Chris Patten.

The leaders sent the following message:

1. We reviewed developments since the last India-EU Summit in Copenhagen in October, 2002. We expressed satisfaction with the positive outcome of this Summit which has further reinforced the India-EU relationship. We are particularly satisfied with the successful conclusion of an Indo-EU Customs Cooperation Agreement, India's imminent participation in the development phase of Galileo Project and the launching of negotiations for an Indo-EU Maritime Agreement. We remain determined to develop this relationship further on the basis of equality and mutual benefit.
2. India and the EU, as global actors in the multi-polar world, remain committed to strengthening the role of the UN in the development field, as well as in the maintenance of international peace and security. We undertook to work towards strengthening multilateral institutions based on the principles of international law.
3. India and the EU are bound together by values of democracy and pluralism. We are willing to work together to promote pluralistic democracy in the world by laying special emphasis on democratic

principles and practice. We encourage greater exchanges between the Indian Parliament and the European Parliament. We will also promote cooperation between political parties, trade unions, universities and civil societies. This would give expression to our shared commitment to democratic values.

4. We affirmed that democracy provides a crucial safeguard for protection and promotion of Human Rights. All Human Rights including the right to personal, economic, social and cultural development are universal, indivisible, interdependent and inter-related. We believe in the equal importance of civil, political, economic, social and cultural rights and are committed to their full realization. International cooperation needs to be harnessed for the protection and promotion of human rights through dialogue and mutual understanding in a comprehensive global framework. We affirmed our willingness to discuss Human Rights in a comprehensive manner.
5. We agreed that terrorism is a global phenomenon that transcends border and region and can target any country. We expressed the belief that there can be no justification whatsoever for terrorism, and we support the fight against international terrorism, wherever it occurs and regardless of its motives. We affirmed our commitment to the universal ratification and implementation of all the UN Anti-terrorism Conventions. We called upon all States to fully implement their commitment under UNSC Resolution No. 1373 so as to ensure that their territories are not used for sponsoring terrorist activities against other States. We supported the early conclusion and adoption of the draft Comprehensive Convention on International Terrorism. As democracies founded on the rule of law, India and the EU remain committed to ensuring compatibility of counter terrorism measures with universally accepted Human Rights standards and norms. We also called for progress towards the establishment of cooperation between Europol and Indian agencies.
6. We expressed our common concerns about the link between cross border crimes particularly international drug-trafficking and terrorism and agreed to step up our common efforts to fight organized crimes, arms trafficking and money laundering, to combat drug abuse, international trafficking of illegal drugs and precursor chemicals.
7. We look forward to the early entry into force of the Kyoto Protocol and re-affirmed the continued validity of the UN Framework Convention on Climate Change. Recalling the New Delhi Declaration adopted at COP VIII, we agreed to work together for a successful outcome of COP IX, which will take place in Milan in next December.
8. In Afghanistan, we strongly support the efforts of President Karzai's

Government to promote national reconciliation and build a peaceful, united and independent Afghanistan. We expressed concern at the continuing threats to security and stability in Afghanistan and expressed support for all measures, including those contained in UNSC Resolution No. 1510, aimed at improving maintenance of peace and security and consolidation of authority in and outside Kabul. We remain committed to the re-construction and development of Afghanistan in partnership with the government and people of that country, while stressing that non-interference in the internal affairs of Afghanistan is a crucial factor in the return of peace and stability.

9. We reviewed the Middle East situation and expressed our deep concern for the resurgence of violence in Israel and the Palestinian territories. We called for the sincere implementation, in letter and spirit, of the Quartet Road Map provisions by both the parties concerned. In line with the Road Map provisions and the relevant UNSC Resolutions, we called for a just, comprehensive and lasting resolution of the conflict, envisioning a region where two States, Israel and Palestine, live side by side within secure and recognized borders. Such a solution must also encompass Israel-Syria and Israel-Lebanon tracks.

10. We reviewed the developments in Iraq and stressed the importance of the central role to be played by the UN in the restoration of peace and normalcy and the re-construction and re-habilitation of that country. We emphasized the urgency of the adoption of a clearly laid out political process within a realistic time-frame, in order to allow the Iraqi people to determine their own political future and retain an effective control of their economic resources. We welcomed the UNSC Resolution No. 1511 and its request to the Iraqi Governing Council to rcport to the UN Security Council by 15th December, 2003 on a time-table and a programme for the drafting of a new Constitution for Iraq and for holding of democratic elections under that Constitution. We are committed to contributing towards humanitarian assistance for the people of Iraq and re-construction and development of that country.

11. We support the process of seeking a negotiated settlement acceptable to all sections of Sri Lankan society, consistent with democracy, pluralism and respect for individual rights, within the framework of a united Sri Lanka and called for an early resumption of negotiations.

12. We shared a common analysis of the situation in Nepal, where we both support a settlement of the crisis, based on multi-party democracy and Constitutional monarchy.

13. The EU warmly welcomed Prime Minister Vajpayee's extending the hand of friendship to Pakistan in April 2003 and the latest peace initiatives through a series of wide-ranging steps taken and proposals

made for enhancing interaction between the people of the two countries which would be essential for creating an atmosphere of trust and cooperation. The EU welcomed the cease-fire recently agreed upon between both parties as a further step towards the normalization of India/Pakistan relations. The EU expressed the hope that the process could be continued and differences between the two countries resolved peacefully through dialogue. We reiterated the unacceptability of use of terrorism in pursuit of political goals. India stated emphatically that there could be no negotiations until cross border terrorism ends.

14. India welcomed the enlargement of the EU, and the ongoing discussions on its future evolution. We both affirmed that deepening and widening of EU would further strengthen relations between us. We have also agreed to remain in touch on the evolution of our respective Foreign, Security and Defence policies. Both sides also noted the draft EU Security Strategy paper and in this context the two sides agreed for further consultations as key partners for a strategic security relationship.
15. We remain committed to intensifying economic dialogue at all levels with a view to improving substantially market access and investment.
16. We expressed our resolve to facilitate and enhance trade by working together in a constructive manner in seeking speedy and amicable solutions to a number of specific trade issues including those relating to Sanitary and Phytosanitary Measures, Technical Regulations and Standards, and Conformity Assessment Procedures.
17. We called for continuation of the dialogue at experts level to promote better understanding of Trade Defence Instruments.
18. We welcomed the conclusions of the India-EU Business Summit and expressed our commitment to implement the Action Plans emanating from the 'Joint Initiative for Enhancing Trade & Investment'. We commended the study on the emerging opportunities from EU's Enlargement, and encouraged Industry to take full advantage of those opportunities. Both sides urged Industry to reflect on how to further develop their partnership.
19. We agreed to launch a "Trade and Investment Development Programme" with a view to enhance bilateral trade and investment through the strengthening and the simplification of the administrative and regulatory regimes and capacity building at the Government and Private sector level.
20. We reiterated our commitment to work towards further strengthening of the multilateral trading regime under the WTO. We affirmed that multilateral rules fairly agreed upon benefit every one. We reaffirmed that trade can play a positive role in development and that development should remain central to the ongoing negotiations in the WTO. We

welcomed the support of our business communities to our dialogue on these issues. We remain committed to driving forward all aspects of Doha Work Programme in a balanced manner including improved market access and the development of WTO rules, as well as the issues of Special and Differential Treatment and Resolution of Implementation Related Concerns of particular interest to developing countries. We are committed to the successful conclusion of the current Doha round of negotiations as also confirmed by the Ministers of the WTO Members at Cancun, and we invite all WTO Members to participate actively and constructively to the resumption of work in Geneva.

21. We remain committed to creating an appropriate economic environment for trade in services and especially in the growth of bilateral trade and investment including through the facilitation of the movement of skilled persons and professionals and enhancement of available infrastructure.

22. We expressed common commitment to promote shared values in education and culture by offering opportunities to the scholars to pursue academic activities. We agreed to launch an EU Scholarship Programme for the Masters and Doctoral level.

23. We reaffirmed our commitment to the fight against poverty and noted the progress made in preparatory activities for two new important development initiatives, namely, Disaster Preparedness Programme, and a Partnership for Progress in Social Development.

24. The vision of a vibrant Information Society and its fullest possible development is jointly shared by us. We decided to work together to further enhance bilateral cooperation in streamlining the regime for electronic communication services and designing an adequate regulatory framework for electronic commerce including digital signatures. We also agreed to jointly support the 2004 Euro-India Cooperation Forum on the Information Society that will be held in New Delhi on 24-26 March, 2004. We strongly recommended Indian and European industry, business and research bodies to grasp this unique opportunity.

25. We encouraged the scientific community to take advantage of the immense potential created by the Science & Technology Agreement and other available instruments.

26. We noted the successful implementation of the Indo-EU Civil Aviation Cooperation Project and the Indo-EU Maritime Project. We acknowledged the importance of efficient transport links to trade and economic growth. We noted the launching of negotiations for an Indo-EU Maritime Agreement covering issues of interest to both sides.

27. Recognising the vital importance of satellite navigation and positioning for our economies and societies, we agreed to cooperate in developing

the GALILEO programme. We expressed our willingness to open negotiations to conclude an Agreement between India and EU to formalize India's equitable participation in the Galileo programme, starting with participation in the GALILEO Joint Undertaking.

28. We expressed satisfaction at the successful conclusion of an Indo-EU Customs Co-operation Agreement.

Agenda for Action:

We agree on the following agenda for action;

1. Ensure in depth discussions on all aspects of bilateral relations between India and EU within the framework of our institutional architecture.
2. Discuss Democracy and Human Rights in a comprehensive manner.
3. Intensify cooperation to promote peace, stability and reconstruction of Afghanistan and Iraq.
4. Increase cooperation to counter international terrorism through implementation of the Declaration against International Terrorism adopted at the New Delhi Summit in 2001, and the UNSC Resolution No. 1373. Work towards early conclusion and adoption of the Comprehensive Convention on International Terrorism and the International Convention for the Suppression of Acts of Nuclear Terrorism.
5. Promote exchanges between the Indian Parliament and the European Parliament as well as Civil Society interaction.
6. Review the implementation of the Action Plans emerging from the sectoral studies conducted in the first two rounds of the "Joint Initiative for Enhancing Trade & Investment" and the study on implications of EU Enlargement.
7. Take steps to facilitate organisation of the first India-EC Steering Committee on S&T cooperation and secure its approval for (i) arrangements for the implementation of the agreed modes of cooperation and (ii) India-EU projects and other co-operative activities.
8. Continue high-level dialogue on multilateral trade issues.
9. Continue dialogue at the experts level to promote better understanding of the Trade Defence Instruments.
10. Enhance cooperation in the area of data protection and cyber security in the information society sector.
11. Find ways and means as to how best we can support and facilitate the movement of professionals and the enhancement of infrastructure.
12. Launch a Euro 14 million "Trade and Investment Development Programme" to enhance bilateral trade and investment.
13. Ensure an early launch of approximately Euro 30 million Scholarship Programme for the Masters and Doctoral level to promote academic

networking.

14. Launch a Euro 10 million Disaster Preparedness Programme and ensure an early launch of two State Partnership Programmes for a total commitment of Euro 160 million.
15. Ensure an early launch of the negotiations for an Indo-EU Maritime Agreement covering issues of interest to both sides.
16. Extend ongoing bilateral project in the Civil Aviation sector.
17. Collaborate in the development and operation of the Galileo Project.
18. Work for early entering into force of an Indo-EU Customs Cooperation Agreement.

❮12❯

The Republic of India and the Islamic Republic of Iran "The New Delhi Declaration" (25.01.03)

> The two sides affirmed that their growing "strategic convergence needs to be underpinned with a strong economic relationship" through measures like the conclusion of the Bilateral Investment Promotion and Protection Agreement, Double Taxation Avoidance Agreement and MoU on Energy cooperation. The two sides also expressed satisfaction with the agreement to develop the "North South transit arrangement" and the "Chahbahar route through Malak, Zarang and Delaram" to facilitate regional trade between India, Iran, Afghanistan and Central Asia.

Vision of a strategic Partnership for a more stable, secure and prosperous region and for enhanced regional and global cooperation The Republic of India and the Islamic Republic of Iran:

Conscious of the vast potential in the political, economic, transit, transport, energy, industries, science and technology and agricultural fields and of the benefits of cooperative endeavour,

Determined to build a strong, modern, contemporary and cooperative relationship that draws upon their historical and age-old cultural ties, the advantage of geographical proximity, and that responds to the needs of an inter-dependent world of the 21st Century,

Aware that their strengthened bilateral relations also contribute to regional co-operation, peace, prosperity and stability,

Recalling and reaffirming the Tehran Declaration issued on April 10, 2001 jointly by H.E. Shri A.B. Vajpayee, Prime Minister of India and H.E.Hojjatoleslam Seyyed Mohammad Khatami, President of the Islamic Republic of Iran, which resulted in further strengthening of dialogue aimed at strategic co-operation.

Declare as follows:

1. International developments since the adoption of the Tehran Declaration have reinforced their faith in and reconfirmed the values of pluralism, diversity and tolerance within and between societies.

2. International peace and stability, harmony between different religions,ethnic and linguistic groups, cultures and social systems can best be promoted through dialogue and acceptance of the right to ones' own beliefs and values expressed and exercised without injury or slight to those of others and without a desire to impose them on others. In this context, they positively assessed the contribution made by the concept of Dialogue Among Civilizations to address discord and differences in international relations.
3. They evaluate positively the consolidation of Indo-Iranian bilateral relations since the Tehran Declaration. Meetings of the Joint Commission, the Strategic Dialogue, interaction between the Security Councils of the two countries, discussions on energy and security, and cooperation based on existing complementarities and diverse possibilities, including supplies, exploration, investment, exchange of technical expertise, and other interaction at government and private sector levels have all contributed to deepening of mutual understanding and confidence, which has provided, in turn, the basis for further consolidation.
4. The two sides welcome the fresh impetus given to Science and Technology cooperation as also to cooperation in education and training since last year. They also note the potential of technologies, such as IT, to improve the lives of people in developing societies and agree to promote co-operation efforts to exploit this potential. They agree to promote fuler utilization of available capabilities for human resource development.
5. The two sides affirm that their growing strategic convergence needs to be underpinned with a strong economic relationship, including greater trade and investment flows. The Ministerial-level Joint Commission, the Joint Business Council and economic and commercial Agreements signed recently in this regard will play a critical role in this regard. They exhort the entrepreneurs in both countries to harness each other's strengths for mutual benefit and promote the process of economic rapprochement actively, including through expert studies on trade and investment facilitation, holding of exhibitions and seminars, promotion of business travel, and joint ventures.
6. They note that the enabling legislations to promote vigorous trade and economic exchanges are primary requirements to promote business confidence between the entrepreneurs of the two countries. Many arrangements have already been concluded in this field. To consolidate the bilateral business environment further, they agree on the need to undertake expeditious negotiations, inter alia, for the conclusion of the Bilateral Investment Promotion and Protection Agreement, Double Taxation Avoidance Agreement and MoU on Energy Cooperation.

7. India and Iran have a complementarity of interests in the energy sector which should develop as a strategic area of their future relationship. Iran with its abundant energy resources and India with its growing energy needs as a rapidly developing economy are natural partners. The areas of cooperation in this sector include investment in upstream and downstream activities in the oil sector, LNG/natural gas tie-ups and secure modes of transport.
8. They also decided to explore opportunities for cooperation in defence in agreed areas, including training and exchange of visits.
9. They agreed to explore mechanisms to preserve and maintain the common cultural heritage, rooted in history, of the two countries. As part of efforts dedicated to preservation of this heritage, they agreed to release a commemorative postage stamp.
10. Terrorism continues to pose serious a threat to nation States and international peace and security and should be eradicated. States that aid, abet and directly support international terrorism should be condemned. The international community should intensify its efforts to combat the menace of terrorism. They reiterate their resolve to strengthen the international consensus and legal regimes against terrorism, including early finalization of a Comprehensive Convention against International Terrorism. They agree that the combat against international terrorism should not be selective or based on double standards. Iran and India agree to continue joint cooperation to address the issues of international terrorism and trafficking in narcotic and psychotropic substances.
11. Both sides stressed that the interests of peace and stability in the region are best served by a strong, united, prosperous and independent Afghanistan. They assess highly the past and continuing cooperation between India and Iran in support of a united, sovereign and independent Afghanistan. They urge the international community to remain committed on long-term basis to the reconstruction and development of Afghanistan, to controlling re-emergence of terrorist forces, and spread of narcotics from Afghanistan. They agree that stability of Afghanistan is vital for the stability of the region. The recent trilateral agreement between the Governments of India, Iran and Afghanistan to develop the Chahbahar route through Melak, Zaranj and Delaram would facilitate regional trade and transit, including to Afghanistan and Central Asia, contributing thus to enhanced regional economic prosperity.
12. The two sides note with satisfaction the operationalisation of the North South transit arrangement and the growing interest among other States in the region to participate in it. They reaffirm their commitment to develop the full potential of the North South

arrangement, its infrastructure, desired certification and customs harmonization, expert studies and regular evaluation to aid its growth.

13. India and Iran support efforts to resolve the situation relating to Iraq peacefully through political and diplomatic means under the auspices of the United Nations.

14. The two sides reiterated their commitment to commence multi-lateral negotiations for nuclear disarmament under effective international control. They expressed their concern about restrictions imposed on the export of materials, technology and equipment to developing countries and acknowledged the right of these countries to research, production and use of technology, material and equipment for peaceful purposes.

15. The two countries are resolved to exploit the full potential of the bilateral relationship in the interest of the people of the two countries and of regional peace and stability, and recognizing that the 21st Century holds unbound promises of welfare and progress through peaceful application of science and technology, promoting knowledge based societies, and tackling fundamental problems such as disease, hunger and environmental degradation.

16. They directed that a time bound framework be worked out in agreed areas of cooperation, through the existing mechanisms of Joint Commission and Joint Working Groups, so that a firm and substantial economic and political underpinning would be provided for a strategic and long-term orientation to the bilateral relationship.

Signed on the 25th Day of January 2003, at New Delhi in two originals, each in Hindi, Persian and English languages.

Prime Minister Republic of India **President Islamic Republic of Iran**

❮13❯

Delhi Statement on Friendship and Cooperation between India and Israel (10.09.03)

The two sides emphasized the need to enhance cooperation in areas like hi-tech and infrastructure and explore the possibility of R&D in bio-technology, IT, telecom, agricultural research and civilian use of outer space. Both sides also paid tributes to the contribution of the Jewish community in India and the Indian community in Israel in strengthening the ties of culture and trade between the two countries.

1. At the invitation of the Prime Minister of India, Atal Bihari Vajpayee, the Prime Minister of Israel, Ariel Sharon, paid a State visit to India from September 8-10, 2003, the first-ever by an Israeli Prime Minister.
2. Prime Minister Sharon was accompanied by Deputy Prime Minister and Minister of Justice, Yosef Lapid, Minister of Culture, Education and Sport, Limor Livnat (together with a cultural delegation) and Minister of Agriculture, Israel Katz. The large accompanying business delegation underscored the importance the two countries attach to expanding their economic relations.
3. During the visit, Prime Minister Sharon called on President Dr. APJ Abdul Kalam, and held talks with Prime Minister, Vajpayee. He also held separate meetings with Deputy Prime Minister and Minister for Home Affairs, Lal Krishna Advani, Minister of Defence, George Fernandes, Minister of Finance Jaswant Singh, Minister of External Affairs, Yashwant Sinha and Leader of the Opposition, Sonia Gandhi.
4. As ancient cultures and societies, India and Israel have left their mark on human civilization and history. As democratic countries since their inception, both nations share faith in the values of freedom and democracy. Both countries gained independence during the same period and embarked on a course of nation building to advance the well being of their respective people and to build modern democratic States able to face difficult challenges.
5. The two Prime Ministers discussed a range of important bilateral, regional and international issues. They reiterated their commitment to further advance the bilateral relations between the two countries and increase the scope of trade and economic exchanges.

6. The shared ideals draw both peoples into a natural amity in pursuit of common goals. Since the establishment of diplomatic relations in 1992, there has been rapid expansion and deepening of bilateral relations. Both sides attach great importance to strengthening their long-term cooperation in the political, defence, economic, commercial, cultural and science and technology areas.
7. In the presence of the Prime Ministers, Ministers from both sides signed the following Agreements:
   a. An Agreement on Environment Protection.
   b. An Agreement on Cooperation in Combating Illicit Trafficking and Abuse of Narcotic Drugs and Psychotropic Substances.
   c. An Agreement on Visa Free Travel for Diplomatic, Official and Service Passport Holders.
   d. An Agreement on Cooperation in the fields of Health and Medicine.
   e. Exchange Program on Cooperation in the field of Education
   f. Exchange Program on Cooperation in the field of Culture.

   These Agreements will further enhance the institutional framework created by those which have already been signed between the two countries.
8. Both sides agreed to increase the frequency of bilateral visits by Ministers and officials and to consolidate the ties between business communities of the two countries. People-to-people relations will also be encouraged, in order to increase and deepen understanding between the societies.
9. Both sides expressed their satisfaction with the impressive growth in bilateral economic relations. They believe that there is considerable untapped potential to enhance these relations, particularly in fields such as hi-tech and infrastructure where there are synergies, in order to encourage the private and public sectors to expand the scope of mutual trade and investments. Israel expressed its interest in and willingness to participate in key national Indian Projects. Indian companies were invited to expand their activities in Israel-to encompass the field of investment-and to participate in the process of privatization in Israel. Both sides will explore together the best ways to strengthen and implement these goals.
10. Both sides noted the scientific and technological cooperation between the two countries and expressed willingness to enhance participation in the joint fund for scientific research established in 1994, as well as explore the possibility of the establishment of a bi-national research and development fund in the industrial fields, particularly in bio-technology, information technology, telecommunication, agricultural research and the civilian use of outer space.

11. Both sides expressed satisfaction with the relations between the countries in the field of tourism, and called for the expansion of these relations as an additional tool for strengthening the bond of familiarity between their peoples.
12. Israel and India expressed their desire to work together, along with other countries and the international community, to create a new and better world- a world of peace, prosperity and welfare, for the benefit of all peoples and nationals.
13. Terrorism undermines the very foundation of freedom and democracy, endangers the continued existence of open and democratic societies and constitutes a global threat; therefore, cannot be any compromise in the war against terrorism. Together with the international community and as victims of terrorism, Israel and India are partners in the battle against this scourge. In line with their adherence to UNSCR 1373, they strongly condemn terrorism in all its forms and manifestations and call upon the international community to take decisive action against this global menace, and condemn States and individuals who aid and abet terrorism across borders, harbour and provide sanctuary to terrorists and provide them with financial means, training or patronage.
14. India and Israel called for the establishment of a just and durable peace in the Middle East. The two sides expressed their respective views, and called for a complete cessation of violence, so that a conducive environment is created for continuation of the dialogue.
15. India and Israel share the goal of advancing peace, security and stability in their own region and respect for democracy in the entire world, and will continue efforts to encourage this trend.
16. Both sides paid tribute to the contribution of the Jewish community in India and the Indian community in Israel in providing a bridge of understanding and in strengthening the ties of culture and trade between the two countries. The shining example of the freedom always given to the Jews of India to practice their religion and give expression to their culture is a tribute to India's religious tolerance and secularism and sends a vital message of co-existence and harmony to the international community.
17. Prime Minister Sharon invited Prime Minister Vajpayee to visit Israel. Prime Minister Vajpayee accepted this invitation with pleasure.
18. India and Israel believe that the State visit of Prime Minister, Ariel Sharon, will further expand and enhance the framework of bilateral cooperation in various fields, and will contribute to strengthening the friendship between the two countries.

‹14›

India-Mauritius Joint Statement (02.07.03)

> The EAMs expressed satisfaction with the development of a "strategic partnership in information technology" characterized by the construction of a Cyber City in Mauritius with Indian collaboration and the proposal for a Bio-Informatics Institute in Mauritius. India welcomed the Mauritian initiative to convene a conference of political leaders from countries with a large community of PIOs and affirmed support for the Meeting in Mauritius on the Review of the "Barbados Programme" for the Sustainable Development of Small Island Developing States (SIDS). Mauritius also extended support for India's claim for permanent membership of an expanded UNSC.

Official Visit of H.E Mr. Yashwant Sinha, Minister of External Affairs, Government of the Republic of India to the Republic of Mauritius 1-3 July, 2003

At the invitation of the Hon. Anil Kumarsingh Gayan, Minister of Foreign Affairs & Regional Cooperation of the Republic of Mauritius, H.E Shri Yashwant Sinha, Minister of External Affairs of the Republic of India paid an official visit to Mauritius from 1-3 July 2003.

2. During the visit, the Hon. Minister of External Affairs of India called on H.E Karl Auguste Offmann, President of the Republic of Mauritius, H.E Abdool Raouf Bundhun, Vice President of the Republic of Mauritius, the Rt. Hon. Sir Anerood Jugnauth, Prime Minister and H.E Paul Raymond Berenger, Deputy Prime Minister of the Republic of Mauritius.
3. H.E Shri Yashwant Sinha, the Minister of External Affairs of the Republic of India visited the Mahatma Gandhi Institute, Moka, Indira Gandhi Centre for Indian Culture and the CyberCity being constructed with Indian collaboration. He also interacted with a wide cross-section of the Mauritius business community and the people of Indian origin.
4. Both sides expressed satisfaction that action had already been initiated to implement cooperation in areas such as renewable energy, anti-narcotics, counter terrorism, oil exploration, handicrafts, etc, which were identified during the visit of the Rt. Hon. Sir Anerood Jugnauth, Prime Minister of the Republic of Mauritius, to India in January 2003.

5. The following Agreements were signed during the visit of the Minister of External Affairs of India:
   (i) MoU on Foreign Office Consultations Mechanism.
   (ii) MoU in the field of Social Defence including the Welfare of the Elderly, Programme of Demand Reduction with regard to Drug Abuse, Welfare of Street Children, Juvenile Justice System and other areas in the general field of Social Defence.
   iii) Extension of MoU on Training of Small and Medium Enterprises run by Women in Mauritius.
6. Both sides also agreed that the following MoUs should be concluded at the earliest possible:
   - MoU in the Field of Non-Conventional Energy Sources.
   - MoU on the Exchange of Airport Personnel, Information on Search and Rescue Emergency, and Consultancy Service in Air Traffic Management and Civil Aviation Regulations.
   - MoU on Environment Matters between the Ministry of Environment of Mauritius and the Ministry of Environment and Forestry of India.
   - MoU including Concept Paper in respect of the World Hindi Secretariat and its staffing.
   - MoU on Cooperation in the field of Prospection and Exploration of Oil and Gas Resources in the Mauritius EEZ.
7. The Hon. Minister of External Affairs of India held official discussions with the Hon. Minister of Foreign Affairs & Regional Cooperation of Mauritius. The talks were held in a friendly and cordial atmosphere and covered a wide range of issues pertaining to bilateral, regional and global matters of mutual interest.
8. The two Ministers reiterated that Indo-Mauritian relations were characterised by the deep and abiding bonds based on common friendship, culture, and a shared civilisational heritage. They reaffirmed the vision for a closer and stronger relationship between the two countries and stressed that the traditional and historical ties between India and Mauritius should be further strengthened.
9. Both Ministers expressed satisfaction that the strategic partnership between the two countries in information technology was taking shape with the establishment of the Cyber City in Mauritius. They agreed that this project is a pointer to the way ahead in the bilateral economic relations between the two countries. It was agreed in this context that the Mauritian proposal for a Bio-Informatics Institute in Mauritius to strengthen cooperation between the two countries, which are rich in bio diversity, and resources need to be implemented

expeditiously. Both sides are happy to note that a Joint Advisory Committee is being established.

10. They reaffirmed their commitment to democracy and secularism and emphasized on the importance of harmonious co-existence in multi-racial, multi-ethnic, multi-religious and multi-lingual societies, and stressed on the concept of unity in diversity.

11. Both sides felt that the bilateral relations have reached a stage at which strengthening of existing institutional mechanism was necessary. In this context, it was agreed that the scope of Joint Commission between the two countries would be expanded to set up Joint Working Groups on trade and investment, terrorism, science and technology (including IT), culture and textiles under the umbrella of the Joint Commission. It was further agreed that the Joint Commission should meet at the earliest possible.

12. Both Ministers recognised the potential of increased flow of investment between the two countries. During the last decade, Indian investment amounted to US$ 90 million approximately representing nearly 20% of total foreign direct investment inflows in the Mauritius EPZ sector. More Indian investments with a value of more than approximately US$ 335 million, in electronics, cables, ICT, spinning and light engineering products are in the pipeline. In the wake of developments in the regional integration process, Mauritius, as member of COMESA and SADC offers opportunities to attract investors from India to tap preferential markets in the member State countries. In this context, Mauritius has agreed to set up a high level group to study the proposal for a Comprehensive Economic Cooperation Agreement.

13. India welcomed suggestion of Mauritius to convene a Conference of political leaders from countries with large community of Persons of Indian Origin (PIO) on the sidelines of the UN General Assembly meeting in New York or CHOGM this year. It was agreed that Mauritius would take initiative in this regard. India offered its assistance to facilitate this Conference.

14. Both sides expressed satisfaction about the level of bilateral cooperation in the defence and security areas. India reiterated its commitment to provide assistance to Mauritius in the defence sector, including training. India would provide assistance in conducting hydrographic surveys of the harbours, ports, and outer islands of Mauritius and update existing navigational charts. The Indian navy would also assist in the surveillance of the exclusive economic zone of Mauritius. The procurement of equipment such as Dornier aircraft is under active consideration of the Mauritian authorities.

15. India and Mauritius affirmed that no cause or reason could justify terrorism. Both sides reiterated their firm belief that the fight against terrorism has to be global, comprehensive and sustained so as to totally eliminate terrorism everywhere. In this context, they reaffirmed their commitment to UN Security Resolution 1373. Both sides underlined the need for the global fight against terrorism to address those who instigate, support or assist terrorism, as much as those who perpetrate terrorism. The Mauritian side appreciated India's efforts to promote peace and to counter cross border terrorism in the Indian sub-continent. It welcomed the recent initiative taken by the Prime Minister of India aimed at fostering friendship and good neighbourly relations between India and Pakistan. To create an appropriate atmosphere for a sustained dialogue, cross border terrorism must end and its sources should be dismantled. Mauritius supports resolution of India-Pakistan issues through bilateral dialogue based on the Simla Agreement of 1972 and the Lahore Declaration of 1999.
16. Both Ministers welcomed the Agreements reached on the plan of implementation at the World Summit on Sustainable Development held in Johannesburg in August 2002, reaffirming the Rio principles, in particular, the principle of common but differentiated responsibilities. The Ministers expressed their concern about the adverse effect of climate change and its implications and highlighted the vulnerabilities of both countries to this problem. In this regard, they expressed their desire for an early entry into force of the Kyoto Protocol of the United Nations Framework Convention on Climate Change. Both sides highlighted the importance of the initiation of negotiations within the framework of the Convention on Bio Diversity towards an international regime for promoting and protecting the just and equitable sharing of benefits derived from the utilisation of genetic resources.
17. The two sides recalled the specificities of Small Island Developing States (SIDS) and welcomed the holding in Mauritius in August/ September 2004 of the International Meeting on the Comprehensive Review of the Barbados Programme of Action for the Sustainable Development of SIDS. India affirmed her support to Mauritius in this endeavour.
18. The two sides reaffirmed their faith in the Non-Aligned Movement. They agreed that the NAM can play an important role in addressing global issues such as poverty alleviation, financing for development, food security, issues of international peace and security, terrorism and disarmament as well as environmental protection.
19. India and Mauritius share the belief that the emerging world order should be just, equitable, multi-polar and based on the principles of

democracy, sovereign equality, territorial integrity, non-interference in the internal affairs of states and respect for human rights and principles of the United Nations.

20. Both sides agreed to co-ordinate positions in the international fora. It is imperative to expanding the UN Security Council to make it more representative and efficient. The External Affairs Minister of India conveyed the appreciation of Indian government for the Mauritian support to India's candidature to the permanent membership of an expanded UN Security Council.

21. The External Affairs Minister of India, Shri Yashwant Sinha expressed his deep gratitude to the Government of Mauritius for the warm welcome offered to him and his delegation. He extended invitation to H.E. Anil Kumarsingh Gayan, Minister of Foreign Affairs of Mauritius to visit India. He also extended invitation to H.E. Paul Raymond Berenger, Deputy Prime Minister of Mauritius, on behalf of the Hon'ble Deputy Prime Minister of India, Shri L.K Advani. The invitations were accepted with pleasure and it was agreed that mutually convenient dates would be finalized through diplomatic channels.

(Yashwant Sinha)	(Anil Kumarsingh Gayan)
Minister of External Affairs	Minister of Foreign Affairs
Republic of India	& Regional Cooperation

July 2, 2003

❮15❯

Ministry of External Affairs' Press Statement on Visit of Mr. Surya Bahadur Thapa, Prime Minister of Nepal (25.11.03)

> Both sides agreed to advance regional economic cooperation agenda at the SAARC Summit in January 2004, including the adoption of the framework treaty for SAFTA. The Indian Prime Minister also expressed concern at the serious security situation in Nepal and reaffirmed India's consistent position that a national consensus needs to be evolved based on the principles of multi-party democracy and constitutional monarchy.

The Prime Minister of Nepal, H.E. Mr. Surya Bahadur Thapa, paid a working visit to India in his capacity as the Head of Government of the outgoing SAARC Chairman country, Nepal. During the visit, His Excellency the Prime Minister of Nepal, called on the President of India and Vice-President of India on November 25, 2003. The Prime Minister of India received the visiting dignitary and hosted a lunch in his honour at 7, Race Course Road on Monday, November 24, 2003. The External Affairs Minister, Shri Yashwant Sinha and *Raksha Mantri*, Shri George Fernandes also called on Prime Minister Thapa at his suite in the hotel.

In the discussions held between the Nepali PM and Indian PM, the two sides reviewed the progress achieved in SAARC since the 11th Summit was held in Kathmandu in 2002. The Indian side appreciated the skillful manner in which Nepal exercised leadership of SAARC and imparted momentum to a number of items of co-operation on the SAARC agenda. Both sides agreed on the need to advance the regional economic cooperation agenda at the forthcoming summit to be held at Islamabad in January 2004, including the adoption of the framework treaty for SAFTA.

The two sides expressed satisfaction over the progress achieved on a number of issues in our bilateral relations and pledged their determination to raise the level of our relations and bilateral cooperation to even higher level, reflecting the very close and cordial relations existing between the two neighbouring countries.

The Prime Minister of India expressed concern over the serious security situation prevailing in Nepal and stressed the need to take urgent broadbased measures to deal with it. In this context, Prime Minister reaffirmed India's consistent position that a national consensus needs to be evolved based on the principles of multiparty democracy and Constitutional monarchy. This would require both the institution of monarchy as well as the political parties to demonstrate flexibility and reach a consensus to address the challenges posed by the Maoist insurgency. A representative Government, with the participation of all Parliamentary parties, working in close co-operation with the monarchy, would assist in evolving such a national response to the situation.

India would, as always, continue to extend its support to Nepal in the spirit of the longstanding and traditional friendship between our two countries.

New Delhi
November 25, 2003.

❮16❯

India - Peru Joint Statement on the Occasion of the Official Visit of the External Affairs Minister of India, Shri Yashwant Sinha (05.06.03)

> EAM discussed a number of issues like cooperation in peaceful uses of nuclear energy, climate, bio-diversity, protecting traditional knowledge, etc. He also met the foreign Ministers/ Representatives of the Rio Group Troika (Peru, Brazil, Costa Rica) who briefed him regarding the "Cusco Consensus"approved at the XVII Summit of the Rio Group in May 2003 that highlighted the for "innovative financial mechanisms" for attending to social needs and overcoming poverty. Peru also extended support for India's claim for permanent membership of an expanded UNSC.

On the invitation of the Foreign Minister of Peru, H.E. Ambassador Allan Wagner, the External Affairs Minister of India, Shri Yashwant Sinha paid an official visit to Peru from 3rd to 4th June, 2003. This visit coincides with the 40th anniversary of establishment of diplomatic relations between both countries.

2. During his visit, the External Affairs Minister of India had a special meeting with the President of the Republic of Peru, H.E. Dr. Alejandro Toledo. Shri Sinha conveyed the greetings of the President of the Republic of India, Dr. A. P. J. Abdul Kalam and of the Prime Minister of India, Shri A. B. Vajpayee.

3. The External Affairs Minister of India, Shri Sinha, held an official meeting with the Foreign Minister of Peru and met and held discussions with the First Vice President and Minister of External Trade and Tourism, H.E. Mr. Raul Diez Canseco, the Minister of Education, H.E. Mr. Gerardo Ayzanoa del Carpio and the Secretary General of the Andean Community, H.E. Dr. Guillermo Fernandez de Soto. In addition, he also had a meeting with Foreign Minister Wagner in his capacity as the President of the Rio Group, and with Ambassador Andre Amado, Representative of Brazil, and Ambassador Julio Suñol, Representative of Costa Rica, being the countries that make up the Rio Group Troika.

4. The External Affairs Minister visited Peru accompanied by an important delegation of Indian businessmen interested in exploring the possibilities of investment and trade.
5. The talks were held in a friendly and cordial atmosphere and covered a wide-range of issues pertaining to bilateral, regional and global matters of mutual interest. The two sides noted with satisfaction that India-Peru relations are marked by a high degree of mutual understanding and similarity of views on almost all current issues of international importance. Both sides reiterated their desire and commitment to further strengthen their bilateral relations based on mutual friendship and understanding.
6. The Indian side noted with satisfaction the efforts of the people and Government of Peru, under the leadership of President Toledo, to consolidate democracy, maintain the supremacy of rule of law and respect for human rights, and to work for social reconciliation. The Indian side also noted the appreciable performance of the Peruvian economy in the recent past.
7. The two sides noted with satisfaction the increase in bilateral trade that was around US$ 80 million in the year 2002. At the same time, both sides stressed the need for the private sector as well as the chambers of Commerce and Industry in both countries to work closely towards promoting trade, investment and economic development. They also expressed their desire to continue exploring new opportunities for augmenting bilateral trade.
8. The Ministers expressed their interest in the early conclusion of the negotiations for signing an Agreement on Promotion and Protection of Investments. They also highlighted the importance of initiating negotiations towards the adoption of a Preferential Tariff Agreement and an Agreement on Avoidance of Double Taxation, all as part of a supportive and stable legal framework for the promotion of investment between both countries.
9. Both countries agreed to work together in taking common positions on issues of interest to developing countries in the WTO, with the aim of ensuring liberalization of international trade in goods and services while strengthening development.
10. India and Peru recognised the need to reactivate and renew the Agreements already signed in the fields of agriculture, space, information technology, Antarctica and culture with the objective of consolidating political, trade, economic, scientific and technological linkages. Both sides agreed on the necessity of continuing to explore potential areas of cooperation for mutual benefit.

11. Both sides recognized the potential of trade and co-operation between the two countries in the Communication & IT sector and the need to tap capabilities and opportunities in this sector in a more focused and comprehensive manner. The Indian side agreed to examine the possibility of cooperation and participation in the Huascaran Project of the Peruvian Government.
12. Being members and Consultative Parties of the Antarctic Treaty, both sides agreed to encourage their respective national Antarctic Institutes to strengthen their mutual co-operation through the exchange of experts, participation in studies and scientific programmes and the examination of possibilities of developing joint projects in the Antarctic continent.
13. Both sides agreed to promote the early conclusion of the Joint Work Plan between the Peruvian Agricultural Research Institute (INIA) and the Indian Council for Agricultural Research (ICAR), the signing of a new co-operation Agreement between the Peruvian National Council for Science and Technology (CONCYTEC) and the Indian Council for Scientific and Industrial Research (CSIR). In addition, they agreed to work for the renewal of the cooperation Agreement for peaceful uses of nuclear energy between the Peruvian Institute of Nuclear Energy (IPEN) and the Indian Atomic Energy Commission (AEC), as well as exploring the possibility of cooperation in the fabrication of composite material for low-cost housing.
14. The Peruvian side thanked India for providing technical training to several persons from Peru under the Indian Technical and Economic Cooperation Program (ITEC).
15. Both Ministers welcomed the Agreements reached on the Plan of Implementation at the World Summit on Sustainable Development held in Johannesburg, reaffirming the Rio principles, in particular, of common but differentiated responsibilities. They also welcomed the commitments adopted at the Millennium Summit and noted the resolve of the world community at the Conference on Financing for Development held in Monterrey in March, 2002 to eradicate global poverty.
16. The Ministers expressed their concern about the adverse effects of climate change and its implications and highlighted the vulnerabilities of both countries to this problem, one of the effects of which is the phenomenon of "El Niño". In this regard, they expressed their desire for an early entry into force of the Kyoto Protocol of the Framework Convention of the United Nations on Climate Change.
17. India and Peru being Mega Bio-diverse countries, both sides welcomed the "Cusco Declaration on Access to Genetic Resources, Traditional Knowledge and Intellectual Property Rights of the Group of Like-minded Megadiverse Countries", adopted at Urubamba on November

29, 2002. In this regard, both sides highlighted the importance of the initiation of negotiations within the framework of the Convention on Bio-Diversity towards an international regime for promoting and protecting the just and equitable distribution of benefits derived from the utilisation of genetic resources. At the same time, both sides agreed to work together towards protecting traditional knowledge and the rights and interests of the people who possess such traditional knowledge.

18. Both Ministers expressed their satisfaction at the signing of the Agreement for the "Establishment of a Mechanism of Political Consultation and Cooperation between India and the Andean Community", which would permit the strengthening and diversification of the ties of friendship, understanding and cooperation, as also the development of commercial relations, investment, cultural, scientific and tourism exchanges between India and the members of the Andean Community. In this regard, they committed themselves to promote necessary actions to achieve these objectives. The Indian side expressed deep appreciation at Peru's role in facilitating the above agreement.

19. The External Affairs Minister of India, Shri Yashwant Sinha, also met with the Secretary General of the Andean Community, H.E. Dr. Guillermo Fernandez de Soto. Among other issues, they held discussions on the implementation of "Mechanism of Political Consultation and Cooperation between India and the Andean Community", as also on the possibilities of negotiating in future a Preferential Tariff Agreement or a Free Trade Agreement between India and the Andean Community.

20. The Ministers expressed their satisfaction at the meeting of the External Affairs Minister of India and the Foreign Ministers/Representatives of the Rio Group Troika. In this regard, they reiterated their commitment to the further strengthening of the linkages between India and the Rio Group. The Indian side expressed special appreciation at the efforts of Peru as Pro-Tempore Secretary of the Rio Group to forge closer ties between India and the Rio Group.

21. During his meeting with the Foreign Ministers/Representatives of the Rio Group Troika, the External Affairs Minister of India noted the importance of the XVII Summit of the Heads of State and Government of the Rio Group held on May 23–24, 2003. In this regard, the Troika Foreign Ministers/Representatives briefed the External Affairs Minister of India regarding the "Cusco Consensus", approved at that Summit, highlighting the need for innovative financial mechanisms for attending to the social needs as a way of supporting democratic governance and for overcoming poverty, as well as the role of political parties in the strengthening of institutionalised democracy.

22. The two sides reaffirmed their faith in the Non-aligned Movement. They agreed that the NAM can play an important role in addressing global issues such as poverty alleviation, financing for development, food security, issues of international peace and security, terrorism and disarmament as well as environmental protection.
23. India and Peru share the belief that the emerging world order should be just, equitable, multi-polar and based on the principles of democracy, sovereign equality, territorial integrity, non-interference in the internal affairs of States and respect for human rights and principles of the United Nations.
24. They reiterated their commitment to work for the achievement of the objectives agreed to at the Second Ministerial Conference of the Community of Democracies, held in Seoul from November 10–12, 2002.
25. Both countries reiterated their support for the democratisation and reform of the United Nations, particularly the expansion of the UN Security Council. They especially stressed the need for an equitable balance in the expanded Security Council to provide a constructive voice to the aspirations of the developing countries. They agreed that piecemeal and discriminatory approaches to such expansion will be inconsistent with the objectives of the world body. Keeping in mind that India is the largest democracy in the world and in view of its past contributions to the promotion of peace, Peru extended its support for India's claim for permanent membership of an expanded UN Security Council. At the same time, India extended its support to the Peruvian candidature for the non-permanent membership of the Security Council for the period 2006-07.
26. India and Peru affirmed that terrorism cannot be justified in any form for any cause or for any reason. They agreed that the fight against terrorism has to be global, comprehensive and sustained with the objective of achieving total elimination of terrorism worldwide with full respect of international law and human rights. To this end they stressed the need to strengthen the international legal regime to fight terrorism through the adoption of a Comprehensive Convention against International Terrorism. In this context, the two sides reiterated their commitment to the UN Security Council Resolution No.1373.
27. Both countries reiterated their rejection of drug trafficking and transnational organized crime, and reaffirmed their commitment to mutual cooperation in the fight against these problems.
28. Both sides noted with satisfaction the high-level contacts that had been facilitated between the Parliaments of both the countries. The Indian side noted with satisfaction the re-activation of the India – Peru Parliamentary Friendship League in the Peruvian Congress and

welcomed the visit of Peruvian Congressmen to India in January 2003. Both sides agreed to encourage a sustained dialogue between the Parliaments of the two democracies.

29. The Foreign Ministers signed an agreement on the "Abolition of visa requirement for holders of diplomatic and official/service passports".

30. The External Affairs Minister of India extended an invitation on behalf of the President of India, Dr. A. P. J. Abdul Kalam to the President of Peru, H.E. Dr. Alejandro Toledo to visit India. The Minister also extended an invitation to the Minister of Foreign Affairs of Peru, H.E. Ambassador Allan Wagner to visit India. The invitations were accepted with pleasure and it was agreed that mutually convenient dates would be finalized through diplomatic channels.

31. At the end of the visit, the Indian side expressed sincere thanks to the Government of the Republic of Peru for the hospitality extended to them and the excellent arrangements made for their visit to Peru.

❮17❯

India - Russia Joint Statement (13.11.03)

> Both sides expressed satisfaction at the setting up/working of various bilateral initiatives like the JWG's on terrorism, Joint Business Council, North South Transport Corridor Project, Business Dialogue Forum on Energy, Construction of Kudankulam nuclear power plant and the signing of MoU between ISRO and Rosaviakosmos. They also emphasized the need for Pakistan to "implement in full its assurances to prevent infiltration of terrorists across the LoC......as well as to dismantle terrorist infrastructure in Pakistan......".

The Prime Minister of India, Mr. Atal Bihari Vajpayee, paid an official visit to the Russian Federation from November 11-13, 2003.

The Prime Minister of India held detailed discussions with the President of the Russian Federation Mr. Vladimir Putin. Deputy Prime Minister of the Russian Federation Mr. Boris Alyoshin, Foreign Minister of the Russian Federation Mr. Igor Ivanov and Defence Minister of the Russian Federation Mr. Sergei Ivanov called on the Prime Minister of India.

The Prime Minister of India and the President of the Russian Federation discussed a wide range of issues of bilateral, regional and international importance. The talks took place in an atmosphere of warmth, friendship, openness, trust and mutual confidence that characteristically mark the strategic partnership between the two countries.

The visit of the Prime Minister of India to the Russian Federation provided continuation to the practice of holding of regular annual Summits between the two countries since the year 2000, when the Declaration on Strategic Partnership between India and the Russian Federation was signed. This visit saw the fourth meeting between Prime Minister Vajpayee and President Putin within twelve months. After President Putin's successful visit to India in December 2002, the Prime Minister of India had visited St. Petersburg in May 2003 at the invitation of President Putin to attend the Tercentenary celebrations of the city of St. Petersburg. The two leaders also met in New York during the 58th Session of the UNGA in September this year.

During his present visit to Russia, the Prime Minister of India was accompanied by Ministers and senior officials, besides a 90-member high-profile and well-represented business and industrial delegation from India comprising prominent members and leadership of the apex Indian industry and trade chambers, such as Federation of Indian Chambers of Commerce and Industry, Confederation of Indian Industry, Associated Chamber of Commerce and All India Association of Industries.

The Prime Minister of India addressed a meeting of distinguished scientists and intellectuals at the Russian Academy of Sciences.

A 'Joint Declaration on Global Challenges and Threats to World Security and Stability' was signed by the Prime Minister of India and the President of the Russian Federation during the visit. Based on the profound understanding of each other's interests and concerns, the document has further reinforced the commitment of the two countries to work closely together in meeting the new threats and challenges faced by India, Russia and the world as a whole. A number of other bilateral Agreements were also signed to further augment the development of Indo-Russian cooperation in a wide variety of areas of mutual interest.

Both sides expressed satisfaction over the useful practice of holding regular annual Summits, as also the frequent and regular exchanges and interactions at Ministerial and other levels. Both sides recognised the significant contribution that intense bilateral interaction at all levels makes to further developing their strategic partnership and wide-ranging dialogue to mutual benefit. The two sides reiterated the need to further continue, expand and consolidate the excellent political contacts between the two countries. They agreed that focused, detailed and regular bilateral Foreign Office level consultations at regular intervals on a large number of regional and international issues have been particularly meaningful and productive.

Both sides reaffirmed the centrality of a vibrant and robust economic and commercial engagement to their strategic partnership. Both sides agreed that the Joint Declaration on Strengthening and Enhancing Economic, Scientific and Technological Cooperation, signed during the last summit in December 2002, provided a broad framework as well as a roadmap towards revitalisation of trade and investment ties. The two countries took note of the important developments since the signing of the Joint Economic Declaration. They welcomed the revival and meeting of the Joint Business Council and the holding of an Indian Trade Exhibition, with participation of more than 200 Indian companies, in Moscow in February 2003.

The Joint Economic Declaration had acknowledged the essential central role of the Indo-Russian Inter Governmental Commission (IRIGC) in overseeing and co-ordinating the implementation of the provisions of the Joint Declaration. Through its nine Plenary sessions and a number of functional meetings of its 12 specialised Working Groups, the IRIGC has proved to be an important vehicle to initiate and promote bilateral cooperation in diverse areas. The two sides welcomed the results of the Commission's 9th

Session held in Moscow in May 2003. They positively assessed the developments in various areas of cooperation including rough diamonds, agricultural products and ferrous and non-ferrous metallurgy.

The two sides emphasized the need to jointly find new ways and means to further strengthen bilateral trade and economic relations, including by promoting investments and trade as well as removing trade barriers. The leaders agreed to accord high priority to discussing and formulating policies to encourage and facilitate mutually beneficial interaction between the private sectors of the two countries. To this end, the sides agreed to devise a long-term strategic approach taking into account the mutually complementary strengths of the two countries, the changes anticipated in the nature of bilateral economic ties and the emerging trends at the global level.

Hope was expressed that more frequent interaction between the business communities of the two countries would lead to an enhanced level of understanding between them on each other's existing potential and emerging capabilities. The sides agreed to consolidate the practice of organising and participating in exhibitions in each other's countries on a regular basis, especially in key areas of bilateral economic interaction including textiles, leather, information technology and telecommunication, tourism, food processing, tea and tobacco, automobile components, power, construction, etc. Both sides expressed the hope that the visit of a high level Russian Business Delegation at the invitation of Federation of Indian Chambers of Commerce and Industry during the India International Trade Fair in November 2003 will further catalyse bilateral economic interaction. The two sides also welcomed the re-opening of the office of the Confederation of Indian Industry in Moscow.

Both sides reiterated their decision to hold at an early date the first meeting of an Inter-Governmental Task Force which will study the issue of utilisation of Rupee debt fund payable to the Russian Federation for the credit of the former USSR and the Russian Federation for investments in both countries in mutually beneficial and priority sectors and the issue of Settlement of mutual financial obligations. Utilisation of the debt funds for investment purposes will give a new impetus to bilateral Indo-Russian economic cooperation.

Both India and Russia represent expanding market economies that have achieved high growth rates in recent years. Economic growth and rapid globalisation have led to emergence of new capabilities as well as new avenues for meaningful collaboration. In order to enable the business sectors of both countries to grasp new possibilities for cooperation, the sides considered it essential to ensure sharing of information on a regular basis. To this end, the sides agreed to facilitate early establishment of an Indio-Russian Business Centre during 2004 with the assistance of the Joint Business Council and their other apex trade and industry bodies.

The bilateral trade basket has shown encouraging signs of expansion. While both sides have striven to consolidate existing trade in traditional items, there has been growing interest in trading in new items such as engineering goods, automobile and components, plastic products, chemicals, IT and telecom goods. Consolidation and expansion of trade requires understanding of national standards and certification regulations. Such an understanding is also important for encouraging investment. Both sides, therefore, agreed to schedule a joint meeting of the concerned statutory bodies of both countries during 2004 for discussing and harmonising national standardization and certification regulations relevant to trade and investment, with a view to removing technical barriers to trade between the two countries.

The North South Transport Corridor Project has the potential to radically transform the existing connectivity between India and the Russia Federation. Both sides noted with satisfaction the effort exerted towards effective operationalisation of this project during 2003, and underlined their commitment towards acceleration of this process through improvement of infrastructural links and harmonisation and standardisation of procedures. Both sides agreed to strive to actively involve their business sectors in this endeavour.

Enhancement of contacts between the businessmen requires establishment of a mutually co-ordinated visa regime. Both sides agreed to consider liberalising travel laws for businesspersons of each other's country accredited with their nationally recognised trade bodies. The two sides emphasised the importance of increased people-to-people exchanges in the process of sustaining economic growth and development of their bilateral relations. In this context, they recognised the vast potential to build on the significant increase in the flow of tourists from Russia to India during the past year. Both sides agreed to encourage greater contacts between the tourism and hospitality sectors to sustain the growing interest.

Both sides acknowledged that increased cooperation between financial institutions was crucial to facilitating growth in investment and trade. The setting up of a commercial bank in Moscow by State Bank of India and Canara Bank was welcomed. Both sides expressed their readiness to facilitate the setting up of at least one branch of a commercial bank of India and Russia in each other's markets by the year 2005. They also underlined the need for effective and expeditious use of Lines of Credit extended to the Russian Banks by EXIM Bank of India.

The Indian side reaffirmed its support for early accession of Russia to the World Trade Oraganisation (WTO). The first Indo-Russian Inter-Ministerial Consultations on economic issues and WTO held in New Delhi in March 2003 marked a good initiative and both sides agreed to continue with such consultations in Geneva and in each other's capital. The two sides agreed to strengthen their co-ordination and cooperation in this regard and to share experience on economic reform and liberalisation in the two countries. Both sides also agreed to continue the process of consultations on various tariff and non-tariff issues relating to bilateral trade.

Both sides reiterated that mutually beneficial cooperation in energy was an area of good potential. In this regard, they welcomed the initiative to set up a Business Dialogue Forum on Energy, which will enable the two countries to regularly exchange views on this vital area of economic activity with the view to, inter alia, evolving a comprehensive joint approach to foster a sustainable and reliable energy future in mutual interest.

Both sides expressed satisfaction over the progress of the project of construction of the nuclear power plant at Kudankulam. Their discussions in this area explored the possibilities of expanding cooperation in peaceful uses of nuclear energy.

The sides expressed satisfaction at the ongoing co-operation in the field of space. Given the existing potential, both sides reiterated their commitment to further expand cooperation for the development of space technology for peaceful purposes. A Memorandum of Understanding was signed between the Indian Space Research Organisation and the Russian Aviation and Space Agency (Rosaviakosmos) on Cooperation in the Exploration and Use of Outer Space for Peaceful Purposes, which charts out future areas of cooperation in this field.

Both sides noted with satisfaction the progress being made in expanded bilateral military technical cooperation, including joint research, development and training, as well as inter-services exchanges. Such co-operation is mutually beneficial and meets the national interests of the two countries, besides promoting peace and stability at regional and international level. They also expressed confidence that the visit of the Indian Defence Minister to the Russian Federation in January 2003, during which he co-Chaired the 3rd Session of the Indo-Russian Inter-government al Commission on Military-Technical Cooperation, and the forthcoming visit of the Russian Minister of Defence to India, expected to take place towards the end of November 2003, will further strengthen their cooperation in this vital area of bilateral interaction. Both sides also welcomed holding of the joint naval exercises by India and the Russian Federation in 2003 and agreed that such exercises and service-to-service interaction should be held on a regular basis.

Both sides expressed satisfaction at the progress of bilateral cooperation in the field of science and technology within the overall framework of the Integrated Long-Term Programme (ILTP). In the series of establishment of joint science and technology centres, they welcomed the signing of the MoUs on the establishment of joint centres on gashydrates and seismology in India. Signing of the Protocol on further cooperation between Russian Academy of Sciences (RAS) and Government of India's Department of

Science and Technology and an Agreement between RAS and Indian National Science Academy will further bolster co-operation in this sphere. It was agreed to keep the focus on specific projects and objectives and to strive for promoting commercial benefits from joint endeavours in the area of science and technology.

Both sides reiterated the contribution and importance of the traditional cultural and people-to-people contacts in consolidating the long-standing and deep-rooted civilisational ties between the two countries. They welcomed the successful organisation of the Days of Russian Culture in India from 1-8 November 2003 and hoped that this event and the organisation of Days of Indian Culture in Russia in 2004 will serve as means of bringing the two peoples further closer. The significance of inter-governmental framework of support for facilitating intense interaction in this sphere, including through Cultural Exchange Programmes, was underlined.

Both sides reaffirmed their keen interest to implement the decision to jointly publish documents on Indo-Russian relations and welcomed the signing of a Protocol between Ministry of External Affairs of India and the Ministry of Foreign Affairs of the Russian Federation in this regard.

The two sides had an in-depth exchange of views on regional and international issues of mutual interest and concern. They noted a high degree of mutual understanding and close identity of views.

India and the Russian Federation are convinced that their strategic partnership has served as a factor in global peace and security. India and Russia, as strategic partners, reaffirmed their commitment to cooperate bilaterally and at international fora towards the establishment of a multipolar and just world order based on sovereign equality of all States, their territorial integrity and non-interference in their internal affairs. Threats to global security and strategic stability should be dealt with taking into account the legitimate security considerations of all States.

Both sides supported the continued disarmament process and multilateral negotiations aimed, inter alia, at nuclear disarmament. Both sides reiterated their commitment to further strengthen their systems of export controls without adversely affecting the peaceful application of dual use materials and technologies.

The two sides acknowledged the importance of the central role of the United Nations in the preservation of world security and stability in accordance with its Charter. They confirmed their opposition to unilateral use or threat of use of force in violation of the UN Charter. Both sides emphasized the need for reform of the UN system to further strengthen it and agreed to work towards promoting an early consensus in this regard.

Both sides agreed on the need to expand the UN Security Council to make it more representative and more effective. Assessing India as an important and influential member of the international community, the Russian Federation reaffirmed its support to India as a deserving and strong candidate for the permanent membership in an expanded UN Security Council.

There was a complete identity of views of India and the Russian Federation on the acute threat posed by international terrorism to the two countries and to international peace, stability and security. Both sides noted with deep concern the growing transnational linkages of terrorist organizations and also the role of transborder organized crime and illicit trade in arms and drugs in supporting terrorism, particularly by financial means.

The sides strongly condemned terrorism everywhere and called upon the international community in accordance with UNSCR 1373 and 1456 to take decisive action against this global menace, and against those who aid and abet terrorism across borders, harbour and provide sanctuary to terrorists and provide them with financial means, training or patronage. They reiterated that international action against terrorism cannot be selective, but has to be uniform, comprehensive, continuous and multifaceted.

Russia expressed support for India's initiative at the UN General Assembly on "measures to prevent terrorists from acquiring weapons of mass destruction". Both sides expressed their deep concern on the growing risk of the use of weapons of mass destruction by terrorists and emphasised the need for wide international cooperation in combating it.

The sides agreed to further develop mutual cooperation and assistance in meeting the threats and preventing acts of international terrorism. They positively assessed the growing cooperation and dialogue between their concerned agencies, including the National Security Council of India and the Security Council of the Russian Federation. They also underlined their resolve to promote cooperation in this area at the United Nations and other international organizations and fora, including the efforts to move further ahead with the draft International Convention for the Suppression of Acts of Nuclear Terrorism and the draft Comprehensive Convention against International Terrorism.

Both sides noted that cooperation in combating international terrorism is an important aspect of their strategic bilateral ties. In this context, they appreciated the continued exchange of views and further consolidation of their close cooperation against international terrorism at the recently held meetings of the Joint Working Group on Global Challenges (which has as its precursor the Joint Working Group on Afghanistan) and the Joint Working Group on Combating International Terrorism, established under the provisions of the MoU signed during the visit of the President of the Russian Federation H. E. Mr. Vladimir Putin to India in December 2002.

The Russian Federation supported the steps taken by India in the Indian State of Jammu & Kashmir in combating international terrorism. India reiterated its support to the measures taken by the Russian Federation in the Republic of Chechnya for the protection of Russia's territorial integrity and Constitutional order. Having noted the recent Presidential elections in the Republic of Chechnya, an integral part and constituent unit of the Russian Federation, on 5 October 2003, India expressed the hope that their results will lead to the return of complete normalcy in Chechnya.

The two sides discussed the situation in Afghanistan and expressed full support to all international efforts aimed at reconstruction, and emergence of Afghanistan as a peaceful, strong prosperous, united and independent nation. They expressed support for the broad based government led by Mr Hamid Karzai, the President of Transitional Islamic State of Afghanistan. Stressing that non-interference in the internal affairs of Afghanistan is a crucial factor in the return of peace and stability, they called upon the neighbouring States of Afghanistan to adhere to their commitments as outlined under the Kabul Declaration on Good Neighbourly Relations signed on 22 December 2002. The two sides expressed concern at the escalation of subversive and terrorist activity by the remnants of Taliban and Al-Qaida. The regrouping of Taliban with support from outside was seen as a most worrisome development. Concern was also expressed at the large increase in production of narcotics in Afghanistan and illegal drug trafficking.

They reiterated support to the continued important role of the UN in the post-Bonn Agreement processes in Afghanistan, including constitutional and democratic institution building. The two sides agreed that Afghan ownership must be accorded fundamental importance in Afghanistan's reconstruction and institution building efforts. They agreed to continue coordinating their efforts on Afghanistan in international forums.

Both sides reviewed the situation in Central Asia and noted that security and stability in that region is of vital interest to both of them. They supported further progress of Central Asian states along the path of democracy. India and Russia emphasised the importance of the consultations between their Foreign Offices, including in the context of the region's traditional ties and contemporary significance for both of them as regards economic cooperation and challenges and threats to security and stability in the region from phenomena such as extremism and illicit drug trafficking.

Both sides discussed in detail the situation in South Asia. They emphasized the need for Pakistan to implement in full its assurances to prevent infiltration of terrorists across the Line of Control into the State of Jammu and Kashmir and at other points across the border, as well as to dismantle the terrorist infrastructure in Pakistan and Pakistan controlled territory as a prerequisite for a purposeful dialogue between the two countries to resolve all outstanding issues in a bilateral framework as envisaged in Simla Agreement of 1972 and the Lahore Declaration of 1999. The Russian Federation appreciated and supported the peace initiative made by the Prime Minister of India in

April 2003 under which High Commissioners have returned to each other's capitals, the Delhi-Lahore-Delhi bus service has been resumed and people-to-people contacts are taking place at non-governmental and business levels. Russia also welcomed further measures announced by India's External Affairs Minister on 22 October 2003 and hoped that Pakistan will come out with a positive response.

Both sides noted the ever-increasing importance of Asia-Pacific Region and stressed the significance of the bilateral and multilateral relations, including in the framework of ASEAN Regional Forum, with the countries of this region in the interest of stability and security in this vast region.

Both sides emphasized the urgent need to restore peace, security and stability in Iraq and to safeguard its unity and territorial integrity. They called for an early transfer of sovereignty to the Iraqi people and need for continued efforts of the international community to ensure a central role for the UN in political and economic reconstruction of Iraq.

Both sides expressed their concern over the developments in the Middle East. They described the present situation as critical and called upon all concerned for de-escalation and ending the cycle of violence. The sides firmly advocated a negotiated settlement between Palestine and Israel on the basis of the Quartet Road Map to bring about a just and durable peace where both Palestine and Israel live side by side in peace and security.

Both sides reiterated that the strategic partnership between India and the Russian Federation was based on mutuality of interests and shared perceptions. It is aimed at the further development of mutually beneficial bilateral co-operation in diverse areas, and at strengthening international peace, stability and security through joint efforts.

The Prime Minister of India invited the President of the Russian Federation to visit India. The invitation was accepted with gratitude. The dates for the visit will be decided through diplomatic channels.

Moscow,

13 November 2003

❮18❯

Joint Declaration of the Republic of India and the Russian Federation on Global Challenges and Threats to World Security and Stability (13.11.03)

> As "strategic partners" the two sides discussed a arrange of issues including Middle East Peace Process, reform of the UNSC, international terrorism, drug-trafficking, and emphasized the need for "adoption of a time-bound plan of action under UN aegis" for restoration of Iraq's sovereignty. Both sides emphasized that "success of efforts aimed against contemporary global challenges and threats largely depends on adequately addressing social and economic issues………" including access to "high technology – a driving force of globalization"

The Republic of India and the Russian Federation,

Guided by noble purposes and principles of the United Nations Charter,

Relying on the provisions of the United Nations Millennium Declaration of 8 September 2000 concerning shared responsibility of States for managing threats to international peace and security and for promoting principles of human dignity, equality and justice at the global level,

Noting the United Nations General Assembly Resolution 57/145 entitled "Responding to Global Threats and Challenges" of 16 December 2002,

Recognising globalisation and interdependence in the world as natural processes in evolution of mankind, which offer both opportunities and challenges,

Taking into account the fact that uneven distribution of benefits and costs of globalisation have resulted in growing disparities among countries of the world,

Determined to cooperate in countering global challenges and threats, which emanate from international terrorism in all its forms and manifestations, transnational organized crime, illicit drug trafficking, money laundering and environmental and developmental challenges,

Proceeding from an urgent need to consolidate efforts of the international community and the role of the United Nations in eliminating these global challenges and threats,

Conscious of their common values and responsibilities as pluralistic democracies,

Desiring to continue to closely cooperate in contributing to world peace and progress,

Confirming their obligations in accordance with the Treaty of Friendship and Co-operation between the Republic of India and the Russian Federation of 28 January 1993, Moscow Declaration on Protection of Interests of Pluralistic States of 30 June 1994, the Declaration on Strategic Partnership between the Republic of India and the Russian Federation of 5 October 2000, the Delhi Declaration on Further Consolidation of Strategic Partnership between the Republic of India and the Russian Federation of 4 December 2002, the Moscow Declaration by the Republic of India and the Russian Federation on International Terrorism of 6 November, 2001 and the Memorandum of Understanding between the Government of the Republic of India and the Government of the Russian Federation on Cooperation in Combating International Terrorism of 4 December 2002,

Hereby declare:

India and the Russian Federation recognise that the aim of promoting global peace, security and stability through dialogue, consultation and cooperation among countries concerned is essential. As strategic partners, India and the Russian Federation reaffirm their commitment to co-operate bilaterally and at the multilateral level on strategic issues, and to evolve a universal effective system of countering global challenges and threats of the 21st Century. The UN should continue to play a leading role in this regard.

India and the Russian Federation as two large and influential democracies are to play a significant role in this context. Both countries are committed to promoting to the maximum extent, democratic values in international relations. India and the Russian Federation affirm that the future international order based on multi-polarity, should be determined by collective and multilateral processes rather than unilateral ones. Both countries stand for building a unified, just and democratic world order and a comprehensive system of collective security based on respect for rule of law and international norms, reciprocal trust, mutual benefit, equality and cooperation.

India and the Russian Federation stress that the United Nations Organisation has a vital role in tackling major international issues. The United Nations can and should be reformed to reflect the current realities, with a view to preserve and enhance its efficacy and efficiency. India and the Russian Federation proceed from the idea that the reform of the UN should include an early expansion of the UN Security Council. The UN should continue to play an important role in the prevention and peaceful settlement of conflicts in conformity with the UN Charter and international law.

* * * * *

India and the Russian Federation are convinced that greater interaction and mutual respect among diverse societies and cultures will lead both to enrichment of these cultures as well as to enhanced harmony and security in the world. In this era of globalisation, it is by preserving pluralism that true multipolarity–in its political and economic as also social and cultural dimensions–will be attained. India and the Russian Federation also resolutely affirm that there is no place in today's pluralistic and diverse global village for any type of extremist ideology and intolerance. They will resist with their full might all forms of extremism, including religious extremism, which has proved to be a hot bed of terrorism in their common neighbourhood.

* * * * *

India and the Russian Federation are united in their fight against the evil of international terrorism. They actively cooperate with each other and with other countries in anti-terrorist activities. Both countries resolutely declare that international terrorists, whatever be their stated objectives and the causes they espouse, will never succeed in bringing the world to its knees.

India and the Russian Federation believe that most urgent and essential steps in effectively and comprehensively dealing with the threat of international terrorism should be:

- Creation of environment for total rejection of terrorism and absolute unacceptability of any of its forms;
- Consistent and uncompromising approach to terrorism and giving up "double standards";
- Preventing the flow of funds for terrorist activities;
- Effective implementation of the UNSC Resolution 1373 aimed against those who support, fund, or abet terrorists or provide them shelter or asylum to engage in cross-border terrorism;
- Promotion of confidence between members of the anti-terrorist coalition by, *inter alia,* due consideration of interests of each one of them and ensuring that the fight against terrorism is strictly based on rules of international law and principles of the UN Charter;
- Reinforcing national and international legal instruments for countering terrorism, making the existing anti-terrorist Conventions genuinely universal, and earliest completion of negotiations on the draft Conventions in the UN, including the Comprehensive Convention against International Terrorism submitted by India and the International Convention on Suppression of Acts of Nuclear Terrorism submitted by the Russian Federation;
- Steadfast cooperation to prevent terrorists from acquiring weapons of mass destruction, their means of delivery and materials and technology related to their manufacture;

- Improvement of mechanisms of legal assistance and extradition in order to ensure the inevitability of punishment for terrorist crimes;
- Efforts to promote co-existence of different religions, cultures and civilizations by stressing greater mutual understanding and respect amongst them, especially the idea that terrorism cannot be identified with any particular religion or ethnic group.

India and the Russian Federation are concerned that trafficking in illegal drugs, psychotropic substances and their precursors is assuming ever more threatening dimensions. Strong and effective measures are required by the international community to handle this threat, especially as narco-business serves as a source of financing to international terrorism. Both countries are taking specific practical steps to counter traffic in illegal drugs, psychotropic substances and their precursors, especially in their common neighbourhood.

* * * * *

India and the Russian Federation believe that one of the most urgent challenges today is strengthening multilateral cooperation for countering the global narcothreat. India and the Russian Federation underline the urgency of the need for the development of a comprehensive strategy, under the auspices of the UN, to effectively counter this problem and reiterate their commitment for close cooperation with the United Nations and other international organizations within the framework of UN Drug Control Programme.

* * * * *

India and the Russian Federation support the efforts by Transitional Islamic State of Afghanistan to rebuild the nation and express full support to all international efforts aimed at promoting peace, stability, national reconciliation and economic reconstruction. It is important to adhere to the time-table, as envisaged in the Bonn Agreement, in implementation of its provisions leading to the holding of democratic elections next year. India and the Russian Federation strongly believe that Afghanistan should emerge as a peaceful, strong, prosperous, united and independent nation that would be free from external interference and living in peace and harmony with its neighbours.

* * * * *

India and the Russian Federation are convinced that a concrete and time-bound plan of action under the UN aegis should be adopted for the earliest restoration of Iraq's sovereignty, stabilization of political and humanitarian situation in the country, and ensuring its economic growth, through broad international efforts.

India and the Russian Federation call for the prevention of the failure of the Road Map drawn to settle the Israeli-Palestinian conflict. The failure of the Road Map may result into the situation in Israel and Palestine, as also in the entire Middle East, spiraling beyond control. This may have adverse consequences not only for the region but for the whole world.

* * * * *

India and the Russian Federation support the efforts of the countries concerned and the international community for a peaceful settlement of the nuclear issue on the Korean Peninsula and maintaining its non-nuclear status. They also support all efforts including the continuation of six-party talks, started at Beijing, to bring about mutually acceptable solution, as well as further development of the inter-Korean dialogue and cooperation.

* * * * *

India and the Russian Federation are convinced that success of the efforts aimed against contemporary global challenges and threats largely depends on adequately addressing social and economic issues, such as elimination of poverty, mass unemployment, illiteracy, and racial, ethnic and religious discrimination. Both countries believe that it is essential to promote steady and sustainable development of the world economy to ensure prosperity of all countries. One of the ways to achieve this goal, as they see it, is to ensure access of the majority of people around the world to high technology-a driving force of globalization. Wider reach of scientific and technological achievements and benefits will bring more prosperity to a larger number of people, reduce the gap between the developed and the developing world and neutralize some of the impulses which trigger conflicts.

India and the Russian Federation, which are important partners in science and high technology, possess a vast potential for joint development of alternative technologies. They are convinced that multi-polarity in the world of high technology will make an immense contribution to the enhancement of political and economic multi-polarity in the modern world.

* * * * *

India and the Russian Federation declare that through their longstanding relationship as reliable, predictable and responsible strategic partners, they are dedicated to strive for finding effective and long-term solutions and appropriate responses to the aforementioned new global challenges and threats to humanity, basing their efforts on the UN Charter and principles of international law.

Prime Minister of the Republic of India **The Kremlin, Moscow**	President of the Russian Federation **12 November 2003**

❮19❯

India - Seychelles Joint Statement (10.09.03)

The two sides identified pharmaceuticals, IT, agro-based industries, plastic technology and production of paper-related products as focus area for joint ventures. India agreed to provide assistance in conducting hydrographic surveys, updating navigational charts and providing defence technology, ammunition and equipment while Seychelles stressed on early adoption of the draft Comprehensive Convention on Terrorism and supported India's claim for permanent membership of an expanded UNSC.

1. At the invitation of the Vice-President of the Republic of Seychelles, Mr. James Alix Michel, who visited the Republic of India in March 1999, the Vice President of the Republic of India, H.E. Shri Bhairon Singh Shekhawat, paid an official visit to the Republic of Seychelles from 8th to 12th September 2003.
2. The Vice-President of India was accompanied by the Minister of State for External Affairs of India, Shri Digvijay Singh and other high level officials.
3. During his visit, Vice President Shekhawat met with Vice President Michel. The Minister of Health and the Minister of Environment called on the Vice President of India. The Indian delegation also met with the Minister of Foreign Affairs as well as with the Chief of Staff of the Seychelles Peoples Defence Forces. The Hon'ble Vice President of India addressed a special session of the National Assembly and later interacted with its Members. He visited the Seychelles Defence Academy.
4. During the visit, the following Memoranda were signed:-
   - Cultural Exchange Programme between India and Seychelles for 2003-2005.
   - Memorandum of Understanding on Cooperation in Science and Technology.
   - Memorandum of Understanding on Health Cooperation.
   - Memeorandum of Understanding on Defence Cooperation.

5. The two sides agreed to finalise a Bilateral Investment Promotion and Protection Agreement (BIPPA) at an early date.
6. Discussions at the delegation level talks focused on areas relating to trade, commerce, investment, technical assistance, oceanography, health, manpower development, culture, defence cooperation, regional and international issues.
7. Following a presentation by the Seychelles side on trade and investment opportunities in Seychelles both sides agreed that there was a need to strengthen trade and investment possibilities between the two countries. Both sides agreed that the Joint Trade Committee Meeting between the two countries should meet at an early date for this purpose. The focus areas for joint ventures were identified in the fields of pharmaceuticals, information technology, agro-based industries, plastic technology and production of paper and paper-related products.
8. Both sides expressed satisfaction that bilateral co-operation in various fields was governed by the Joint Commission on Economic and Technical Co-operation which has been meeting regularly.
9. Given India's varied experience in high technology and industrial areas, India is willing in a spirit of South-South Cooperation, to share its expertise in priority areas identified by Seychelles with a view to enhancing the current programme of cooperation in the areas of economic, commercial and human resources development. To this end, the Indian side agreed to consider extending the scope of ongoing co-operation under the India Technical & Economic Co-operation. The possibility of deputing Indian ITEC experts in key sectors identified by Seychelles would be considered favourably.
10. The two sides reiterated that Indo-Seychelles relations were characterized by deep and abiding bonds based on common friendship and a shared cultural heritage. They reaffirmed their commitment towards a closer and stronger relationship between the two countries and stressed that the traditional and historical ties between India and Seychelles should be further strengthened.
11. Both sides expressed satisfaction about the level of bilateral cooperation in the defence and security areas. India reiterated its commitment to provide assistance to Seychelles in the defence sector, including training. India agreed to provide assistance in conducting hydrographic surveys of the harbours, ports, and outer islands of Seychelles and update existing navigational charts as well as in provision of defence technology, ammunition and equipment.
12. The two sides expressed their concern over the increase in international terrorism, religious extremism, trans-border organized crime and illicit trafficking in arms and drugs. They viewed their upsurge as a serious

threat to sovereign States, international peace, development, security and stability. They affirmed that terrorism was a grave violation of human rights and a crime against humanity and that no excuse could justify it in any form. They agreed that the fight against terrorism by the international community has to be global, comprehensive and sustained with the ultimate objective of its total eradication from the world. Actions should be taken against States, entities and individuals who support, finance, harbour or abet terrorists or provide them shelter. In this context, they stressed the importance of strict, full and unconditional implementation of the UN Security Council Resolution on the fight against terrorism and reiterated in particular their commitment to the UN Security Council Resolution 1373. They stressed the need to strengthen the international legal regime to fight terrorism through the early finalization and adoption of the draft Comprehensive Convention on International Terrorism and the Convention for the Suppression of Acts of Nuclear Terrorism.

13. In this connection, the Seychelles side appreciated the evolving security concern of India in the light of recent local, regional and global developments. It appreciated the initiatives taken by India to resume diplomatic relations with Pakistan. In this connection, the Seychelles side supported the resolution of differences between India and Pakistan through bilateral dialogue.

14. Both sides welcomed the Agreements reached at the World Summit on Sustainable Development held in Johannesburg in September 2002, reaffirming the Rio Principles, in particular, the principle of common but differentiated responsibilities. Both sides expressed their concern about the adverse effect of climate change and its implications. In this regard, they expressed their desire for an early into force of the Kyoto Protocol of the United Nations Framework Convention on Climate Change. Both sides highlighted the importance of the initiation of negotiations within the framework of the Convention on Bio-diversity towards an international regime for promoting and protecting the just and equitable sharing of benefits derived from the utilization of genetic resources.

15. Seychelles and India agreed to explore the possibility of concluding a Memorandum of Understanding on Environment Issues.

16. With regard to the world trading system, both sides underscored the need for international trade negotiations to obtain balanced and equitable results. In regard to the developing countries in particular the small vulnerable economies, the size and differences in levels of economic development should be taken into account for special and differential treatment.

17. The two sides acknowledged the vital importance of the role of the United Nations in world peace, stability and development. They remained determined to continue their efforts in strengthening the UN system as the central mechanism for ensuring international peace and security as well as democratizing international relations. They reiterated their support for the need to reform the UN, particularly the expansion of the UN Security Council. They stressed, in particular the need for equitable balance in the expanded Security Council to provide a constructive voice to the aspirations of developing countries.
18. The Hon'ble Vice President of India conveyed his appreciation for the support extended by the Government of Seychelles to India's candidature to the permanent membership of an expanded Security Council.
19. Seychelles welcomed India's growing engagement through NEPAD and other regional fora in Africa's development and India's concern for the well being, particularly of Small Island Developing States (SIDS) to which Seychelles belongs. The two sides agreed that the needs of Small Islands Developing States should be fully addressed to enable them to effectively participate in the globalization process.
20. The two sides reaffirmed their faith in the Non-Aligned Movement. They agreed that the NAM could play an important role in addressing global issues such as poverty alleviation, financing for development, food security, issues of international peace and security, terrorism and disarmament as well as environmental protection.
21. India and Seychelles share the belief that the emerging world order should be just, equitable, multi-polar and based on the principles of democracy, sovereign equality, territorial integrity, non-interference in the internal affairs of states and respect for human rights and principles of the United Nations.
22. The Hon'ble Vice President of India expressed his deep gratitude to the Government of Seychelles for the hospitality and excellent arrangements made for him and his delegation. He extended on invitation to His Excellency James Alix Michel, the Vice President of the Republic of Seychelles to pay on official visit to India. The invitation was accepted with pleasure. The dates of the visit would be finalized through diplomatic channels.

Done in Victoria on Wednesday 10th September 2003.

❮20❯

Joint Declaration by India and South Africa On the Occasion of the State Visit to India by H.E. Mr. Thabo M.Mbeki, President of South Africa (16.10.03)

Both sides hoped that negotiations between India and Southern African Customs Union (SACU) towards a Free Trade Agreement would be concluded by end 2004 and the recently constituted India, Brazil, South Africa (IBSA) dialogue forum would "contribute to the revitalization of South-South cooperation". They reiterated their commitments towards advancing the agreements reached at World Summit on Sustainable Development (WSSD) in September 2002 and called for implementation of international conventions on climate change and bio-diversity.

1. During this visit, which takes place on the tenth anniversary of the establishment of diplomatic relations between India and the new South Africa, both countries reaffirm their commitment towards a strategic partnership, based on their shared values: democracy, economic development with social justice, and a just and equitable global order.
2. Both countries recall that their freedom struggles were linked intrinsically through Mahatma Gandhi whose ideals and vision continue to inspire the two countries. They, furthermore, agreed that this had created a unique historical bond between them.
3. Recalling the Red Fort Declaration on a Strategic Partnership between India and South Africa, signed in March 1997, both countries note with satisfaction the consolidation of this partnership over the years. A high degree of understanding, mutual trust and confidence mark India-South Africa cooperation which has extended to every sphere of human endeavour including, in particular, political, economic, defence, scientific, technological and cultural matters. This has made the bilateral relationship strong, broad-based and vibrant. Both countries reiterate their desire to further strengthen and diversify bilateral relations and take their partnership from strength to strength for the benefit of both.
4. Taking note of the commendable progress made by both countries towards the goal of growth with equity and justice, addressing poverty

and under-development, India and South Africa agree that their bilateral cooperation should contribute to empowerment of the marginalized and disadvantaged citizens, which is a common priority.

5. The two countries note that the economies of India and South Africa have certain comparative advantages and complementarities, which offer a wide range of potential opportunities for cooperation in trade, investment and transfer of technology. For example, India has valuable experience in Human Resource Development, Information and Communication Technology, and the Pharmaceutical Sector. South Africa has world-class skills and technology in Mining, Power Generation and Infrastructure Development, and a vast reservoir of mineral resources. Both countries agree on the need for creating better awareness of each other's strengths within their respective private sectors.
6. Both countries note with satisfaction that negotiations between India and Southern African Customs Union (SACU) towards a Free Trade Agreement have shown substantial progress. It is hoped that the matter will be concluded by the end of 2004. Such an Agreement will provide a significant incentive to the business communities of the two countries to explore mutually beneficial commercial opportunities and contribute to the growth of bilateral trade.
7. Both agree that the recently constituted tripartite IBSA dialogue forum, comprising India, Brazil and South Africa, is a significant addition to the architecture of South-South dialogue. These three likeminded countries from three continents represent large vibrant democracies with strong economies and rich human and natural resources. By providing an avenue for utilizing the potential synergies among the members, IBSA will contribute to the revitalization of South-South cooperation.
8. Both countries reaffirm their faith in the Non-Aligned Movement (NAM). They agree that the NAM can play an important role in addressing global issues such as sustainable development, poverty alleviation, financing for development, food security, issues of international peace and security, terrorism and disarmament, as well as environmental protection.
9. Furthermore, they welcome the Agreements reached at the World Summit on Sustainable Development (WSSD) held in Johannesburg in September 2002, reaffirming the Rio Principles, in particular, the principle of common but differentiated responsibilities. Both sides reiterate their commitment towards advancing the Johannesburg Plan of Implementation. Both express concern about the adverse effect of climate change and its implications. In this regard, they express their desire for an early entry into force of the Kyoto Protocol of the

United Nations Framework Convention on Climate Change. Both countries stress the importance of the initiation of negotiations within the framework of the Convention on Bio-diversity towards an international regime for promoting and protecting the just and equitable sharing of benefits derived from the utilization of genetic resources.

10. India appreciates the role being played by South Africa in promoting peace, development, democracy and good governance in Africa. Reiterating the historical links that bind India and Africa, the two countries agree to work closely and actively to make India's engagement with Africa even more meaningful. South Africa notes with appreciation that the Afro Asian Games will be held in India (Hyderabad) from October 24 to November 1, 2003.
11. South Africa values India's determination to support the transformation of Africa. The two countries noted that both the establishment of the African Union and the adoption of the New Partnership for Africa's Development (NEPAD) as the regeneration programme of the African continent, hold tremendous promise for the development of Africa. India has already taken many steps in order to engage fruitfully with NEPAD, including allocation of US$ 200 million for projects that contribute to realization of NEPAD's objectives. The two countries welcome the opportunity of enhancing cooperation with each other in identifying and implementing these projects.
12. The two countries recognize that international economic relations continue to be characterized by inequities and inequalities. Large sections of the world are yet to reap the benefits of globalization, which has led to economic crises and instability in several developing countries. The two countries agree that globalization must not perpetuate existing inequalities and call upon the countries of the North and of the South to continue their dialogue towards establishing a more equitable global economic environment. Both counties reiterate their commitment towards ensuring the success of the WTO Doha Development Round.
13. Both countries reiterate the need to reform the United Nations to make it more effective and truly representative of the contemporary international community. They acknowledge the vital importance of the role of the United Nations in promoting world peace, stability and development. They remain determined to continue their efforts in strengthening the UN system as the central mechanism for ensuring international peace and security as well as democratising international relations. They reiterate their support for the need to reform the UN, particularly the expansion of the UN Security Council. They stress, in particular, the need for an equitable balance in an expanded Security Council to provide a decisive voice to developing countries. They

believe that piecemeal and discriminatory approaches to such expansion would be inconsistent with the objectives of that world body. India and South Africa share the belief that the emerging world order should be just, equitable, multi-polar and based on the principles of democracy, sovereign equality, territorial integrity, non-interference in the internal affairs of states and respect for human rights and principles of the United Nations.

14. Both countries stress their concern over the increase in international terrorism, religious extremism, trans-border organized crime and illicit trafficking in arms and drugs. They view this upsurge as a serious threat to sovereign states, international peace, development, security and stability. In this context, they stress the importance of strict, full and unconditional implementation of the UN Security Council Resolution on the fight against terrorism and reiterate in particular their commitment to the UN Security Council Resolution 1373. They stress the need to strengthen the international legal regime to fight terrorism through the early finalisation and adoption of the draft Comprehensive Convention on International Terrorism and the Convention for the Suppression of Acts of Nuclear Terrorism. They affirm that terrorism is a grave violation of human rights and a crime against humanity, and that no cause or pretext can justify it. They agree that the fight against terrorism by the international community has to be global, comprehensive and sustained, with the ultimate objective of its total eradication from the world. Action within the ambit of the UN system should be taken against those states, entities and individuals who support, finance, harbour or abet terrorists or provide them shelter, safe havens or asylum to engage in any acts of terrorism. In that regard, it is essential that every State be made to refrain from organizing, instigating, assisting, training or participating in terrorist acts in another state or acquiescing in organized activities within its territories directed towards the commission of such acts.

15. Both countries note the existence of global threats and challenges including trafficking in narcotic drugs, human beings and small arms; hunger and malnutrition; diseases like malaria and tuberculosis that grip developing countries; the pandemic of HIV/AIDS; and the degradation of our common environment. In this regard they reiterate the need to fully implement the Millennium Development Goals.

16. To concretize cooperation between India and South Africa, both countries agree that the following bilateral Agreements, signed during the visit, are an important step forward.

- Extradition Treaty;
- Agreement on Mutual Legal Assistance in Criminal Matters;

- Cultural Exchange Programme for the years 2004-2006.
- Agreement on cooperation in the field of power;
- Agreement on cooperation in the field of hydro-carbons;

17. The strategic partnership between India and South Africa is guided by the common vision of a global order marked by peace, security and equity. Both countries emphasize the multi-dimensional nature of poverty. It extends beyond income to education, health care, capacity building and skill enhancement, political participation at all levels, advancement of indigenous culture and social organization and access to natural resources, clean water and air for all. To tackle these multiple challenges, they agree to consolidate their cooperation bilaterally as well as multilaterally, including at international fora such as the United Nations, the World Trade Organization, the Non-Aligned Movement, the Commonwealth and through the IBSA dialogue forum, to build a better world for the present and future generations.

Prime Minister	President
The Republic of India	The Republic of South Africa

‹21›

India - Sri Lanka Joint Statement (21.10.03)

> The two sides urged the early conclusion of the proposed Additional Protocol to the SAARC Convention on Suppression of Terrorism and agreed to commence discussions with a view to concluding a defence cooperation agreement at the earliest. India also supported a negotiated settlement in the peace process "within the framework of a United Sri Lanka and consistent with democracy, pluralism and respect for individual rights".

Hon. Ranil Wickremesinghe, Prime Minister of Sri Lanka, visited India from 19-21 October 2003 at the invitation of the Government of India. He was accompanied by Tyronne Fernando, Minister of Foreign Affairs; Milinda Moragoda, Minister of Economic Reforms, Science and Technology and other senior officials.

The Prime Minister of Sri Lanka held wide-ranging discussions with Prime Minister Shri Atal Bihari Vajpayee. Deputy Prime Minister and Ministers of External Affairs, Commerce & Industry, Civil Aviation and Petroleum & Natural Gas called on Prime Minister Wickremesinghe. The discussions were substantive and held in a cordial atmosphere, reflective of the close relations between the two countries.

The two Prime Ministers expressed their happiness that the Free Trade Agreement, which became operational in December 2001, had enabled bilateral trade to cross the US$ 1 billion mark in the financial year 2002-03.

A decision to go beyond the Free Trade Agreement was taken during the last visit of the Prime Minister of Sri Lanka in June 2002. An India-Sri Lanka Joint Study Group was set up to make recommendations for the establishment of a Comprehensive Economic Partnership Agreement. The Co-Chairmen of the Joint Study Group presented their recommendations to the two Prime Ministers on 20th October 2003. Expressing their satisfaction on the speed with which the Joint Study Group prepared its comprehensive report with its far-reaching recommendations, the Prime Ministers congratulated the members of the Group and directed that negotiations begin immediately, with the target of concluding the Comprehensive Economic Partnership Agreement by the end of March 2004. This would enable the two countries to reap the early benefits of freer trade in goods and services and enhanced investment and economic cooperation.

The two Prime Ministers noted the successful holding of the 5th session of the Joint Commission Meeting, co-chaired by the Foreign Ministers, in Colombo on 15th October 2003 and the signing of the Agreement to release the second tranche of US$ 30 million out of the US$ 100 million Line of Credit extended to Sri Lanka. They agreed that further Lines of Credit for infrastructure projects could be discussed.

The two Prime Ministers expressed satisfaction that existing understandings on dealing sympathetically and humanely with fishermen who stray into each other's maritime zone were working well. It was noted that a number of Indian fishermen had been released by the Sri Lankan side and several Sri Lankan vessels detained at Nagapattinam had been released for repair and escorted back to Sri Lanka. It was agreed that while it was important that the fishermen should be released early, the boats may be held till the judicial processes in the two countries are completed. The Prime Ministers agreed on the need to undertake enhanced surveillance to minimize incursions, institutionalize assistance for salvage operations of released vessels, pay attention to ecological and conservation aspects and consider licensed fishing within a bilateral Memorandum of Understanding on Fisheries.

The two Prime Ministers expressed their satisfaction at increased civil aviation links between India and Sri Lanka. They noted that Sri Lankan Airlines had increased the number of its weekly flights to Indian destinations from 29 to 44 since their last meeting. Without prejudice to already existing arrangements, India offered to Sri Lanka the facility of daily air services by its designated airlines between Colombo and the metropolitan cities of Delhi, Mumbai, Chennai, Bangalore, Hyderabad and Kolkata. In addition, unlimited access would be available for air services to and from 18 tourist destinations in India. It was agreed to do away with the existing requirement of Commercial Agreements between designated airlines of the two countries for asymmetrical operations. With a view to increasing tourist flow and connectivity, it was also decided to encourage private scheduled airlines of India, who operate only in the domestic sector at present. to extend their operations to airports in Sri Lanka. The Sri Lankan Prime Minister agreed to reciprocate in terms of the access that airlines from India could have to Sri Lankan airspace.

The Sri Lankan Prime Minister proposed commencement of a ferry service linking Colombo with Kochi (Kerala).

The Prime Ministers noted with satisfaction the significant contribution made by the India-Sri Lanka Foundation towards fostering exchanges in cultural, educational, scientific and technological areas and announced a further contribution of Rs. 1 crore each to enable the Foundation to sustain its diverse activities.

Taking note of the continuing acts of terrorism worldwide and in our region, the two Prime Ministers emphasized the need for concerted opposition to terrorism in all its forms and manifestations. They agreed that there can be no justification for terrorism, be it political, religious or ideological. They recalled the obligations devolving on States, inter alia, under Security Council Resolution 1373 and the International Convention on the Suppression of Financing of Terrorism. The Kathmandu Declaration adopted at the 11th SAARC Summit held in Kathmandu on 6 January, 2002 on criminalization of financing for terrorist purposes and the need to prevent the abuse of financial systems of States was also recalled. They reaffirmed the need to finalize and adopt, at the earliest, the proposed Comprehensive Convention on Terrorism, which would send a strong signal that the international community was united and determined in its efforts to eliminate the scourge of terrorism. Furthermore, they also urged the early conclusion of the proposed Additional Protocol to the SAARC Convention on Suppression of Terrorism.

The two Prime Ministers discussed the ongoing cooperation in training and the supply of equipment to the Sri Lankan defence forces and agreed that the two sides will commence discussions with a view to concluding a defence cooperation Agreement at the earliest.

The Sri Lankan Prime Minister apprised the Indian leadership of recent developments in the peace process and proposals made by his Government for the establishment of an Interim Administration. India expects that the response to the proposals made by the Sri Lankan Government in July 2003 will be reasonable and comprehensive. India supports the process of seeking a negotiated settlement acceptable to all sections of Sri Lankan society within the framework of a united Sri Lanka and consistent with democracy, pluralism and respect for individual rights. It believes that an enduring solution has to emerge purely through internal political processes.

India will maintain an abiding interest in the security of Sri Lanka and remains committed to its sovereignty and territorial integrity. India would welcome a resolution of the current impasse in the peace process and an early resumption of negotiations. Any interim arrangement should be an integral part of the final settlement and should be in the framework of the unity and territorial integrity of Sri Lanka.

New Delhi

October 21, 2003

‹22›

India - Sudan Joint Statement (22.10.03)

Both sides expressed satisfaction with the cooperation in the oil sector and "the landmark entry of the Indian ONGC-OVL into the GNPOC". Sudan agreed to offer the project of Portsudan Oil Refinery, expansion and Khartoum-Portsudan petroleum products pipeline to ONGC-OVL. Indian extended an EXIM Bank line of credit of US$50 million to Sudan while Sudan supported India's candidature to a permanent seat in the UNSC.

1. At the invitation of H.E. President Omar Hassan Anmad al-Bashir, Yashwant Sinha resident of the Republic of the Sudan, H.E. Dr. A.P.J. Abdul Kalam, President of the Republic of India, accompanied by a high-level delegation, paid a State visit to Sudan during 20-22nd October, 2003. H.E. the President, Dr. A.P.J. Abdul Kalam was warmly received by the Sudanese leadership and people, who described his visit as historic and a reaffirmation of the centuries-old and time-tested relations between the two countries and their peoples.
2. During the visit, H.E. President Abdul Kalam held discussions with H.E. President Omar Hassan Ahmed al-Bashir. He also received in separate meetings, Their Excellencies Professor Moses Macar, Vice-President of the Republic of the Sudan, Sayed/Abdalla Ahmed Alhardalo, Deputy Speaker of the National Assembly, Dr. Mustafa Osman Ismail, Minister of Foreign Affairs and Dr. Awad Ahmed Al-Jaz, Minister of Energy and Mining. H.E. President Abdul Kalam addressed the National Assembly and visited educational, cultural and economic sites of importance and interacted with the Indian Community in Sudan as well as with the Sudanese Alumni of Indian Universities.
3. During the visit of H.E. Dr. Abdul Kalam, and in the presence of the two Presidents the following Agreements were signed:
   a) Bilateral Agreement on the Promotion and Protection of Investment.
   b) Agreement on the Avoidance of Double Taxation.
   c) A Memorandum of Understanding on Cooperation in Communications and Information Technology.

4. Relations between Sudan and India have always been cordial and friendly. The two sides reiterated that the Indo-Sudanese relations were characterized by deep and abiding bonds based on friendship, culture and a shared civilizational heritage. They affirmed their vision for closer and stronger relationship between the two countries and stressed that the traditional and historical ties between India and Sudan should be further strengthened and expanded.
5. The two sides discussed a wide range of important bilateral relations, and exchanged views on various regional and international issues of mutual concern.
6. India and Sudan expressed their satisfaction with the recent impressive evolution of their bilateral relations. Both sides expressed satisfaction that the strategic partnership between the two countries in the oil sector has taken shape with the landmark entry of the Indian ONGC-OVL into the GNPOC. Both sides underscored the need for further Indian involvement in the oil and energy sectors and related industries. In this connection, the two sides also took note of the fact that the Sudanese Ministry of Energy and Mining agreed to offer the project of Portsudan oil refinery expansion and the project of Khartoum – Portsudan petroleum products pipeline to ONGC-OVL in view of their good performance and excellent relationship existing between them and expressed their hope that these contracts be signed expeditiously.
7. Both sides recognized the potential of increased flow of investment between the two countries. They expressed their conviction that there is considerable untapped potential in major sectors including, information technology, agriculture, food security and agro-processing, small-scale industries, human resource development, science and technology and pharmaceuticals. To that end, the two sides reiterated their commitment to further enhance and increase the scope of their economic, investment, trade and cultural exchanges. They noted also, in this regard, that the 2nd Session of the Joint Business Council would be held in New Delhi next November, 2003.
8. Both sides felt the need to strengthen existing institutional mechanisms to cope with their expanding bilateral relations. In this connection, the two sides expressed the hope that the forthcoming meeting of the Joint Commission in New Delhi co-chaired by the two Foreign Ministers will give added dynamism commensurate with the aspirations and interests of their respective peoples. In this context, India extended an EXIM Bank Line of Credit of US $ 50 million to contribute to the economic development of Sudan. India also announced a grant of US$ 50,000 worth of Indian medicines to meet the humanitarian requirements of victims of recent floods in Kasala region of Sudan.

9. Sudanese side briefed its Indian Counterpart on the positive and far-reaching developments in the Peace Process in Sudan including the recently signed Agreement on Security Arrangements, which represented its commitment to lasting peace and stability. The Indian side reiterated its position in support of Sudan's unity and territorial integrity. The two sides affirmed that both India and Sudan were multi-religious and multi-ethnic societies committed to pluralism, harmonious co-existence and the concept of unity in diversity. The Sudanese side called upon its Indian counterpart to share and participate in the consolidation of peace and in the reconstruction efforts in the various parts of the country. Indian side promised to do everything possible.
10. The two sides exchanged views on India's vision as a developed country by 2020 and Sudan's 25-year strategic plan for development. Both commended the on-going efforts to realize those lofty goals and need to share experiences and insights.
11. On the situation in Africa, the two sides expressed satisfaction over the positive developments in the continent represented by the establishment of the African Union, with NEPAD as its economic arm. The Sudanese side expressed its appreciation of India's commitment to work closely with Africa in the context of NEPAD, pursuant to the traditional ties of cooperation and solidarity that have always characterized Indo-African relations and appreciated, to that end, the recently launched "Focus Africa Programme" by the Government of India aimed at enhancement of those historic ties.
12. On the situation in the Middle East, the two sides called for an early establishment of a Palestinian State in accordance with relevant UN Security Council Resolutions so as to end the Israeli occupation.
13. Sudan welcomed the initiative taken by the Prime Minister of India aimed at fostering friendship and good-neighbourly relations between India and Pakistan, and supports resolution of India-Pakistan issues through dialogue and peaceful means.
14. On the developments in the International scene, both Sudan and India share the conviction that the emerging world order should be just, equitable, multi-polar and built on the principles of democracy, sovereign equality, territorial integrity, non-interference in the internal affairs of States and the peaceful settlement of disputes. They share the imperative of a comprehensive reform of the U.N. system including an expanded Security Council to make it more representative and responsive to the needs and aspirations of the developing countries. In this context Sudan supported India's candidature to a permanent seat in the UN Security Council. Both sides agreed to closely co-ordinate positions in the international fora.

15. The two sides in line with their commitment to the UNSC Resolution 1373 affirmed their condemnation of terrorism in all its forms and manifestations. They re-affirmed their conviction that terrorism knows no religion or geographical boundaries and stressed the need to combat this global menace.
16. The two sides reaffirmed their faith in the Non-aligned Movement and stressed the importance of its revitalisation to address global issues such as poverty alleviation, sustainable development, food security, as well as issues of International peace and security. The two sides hailed the position taken by developing countries during the recently concluded WTO Ministerial meeting in Cancun.
17. Sudan and India strongly believe that the State visit of H.E President Abdul Kalam to Sudan will undoubtedly consolidate further and expand the framework of bilateral cooperation in all fields. They both agreed on the importance of increasing the frequency of bilateral visits at all levels including by dignitaries, ministers, officials, experts as well as the people-to-people contacts.
18. H.E. President Abdul Kalam, on behalf of the Indian delegation and his own behalf, expressed deepest thanks and appreciation to the Sudanese Government and people for the warm welcome and generous hospitality extended throughout their stay in the Republic of the Sudan.
19. H.E. President A.P.J. Abdul Kalam, President of the Republic of India invited H.E. President Omar Hassan Ahmed al-Bashir, President of the Republic of the Sudan to visit India.
20. H.E. President al-Bashir accepted, with pleasure, the kind invitation, the date of which will be decided through diplomatic channels.

Khartoum, Sudan
22nd October, 2003.

❮23❯

India - Surinam Joint Statement (17.03.03)

The two sides identified a number of projects involving Indo-Suriname cooperation including the setting up of an electrical transmission line from Paranam to Paramaribo and sharing of Indian expertise in the Health sector. The Indian side expressed pleasure that Suriname will be venue for the Seventh World Hindi Conference in June 2003 while Suriname extended support for India's claim for permanent membership of an expanded UNSC.

1. The President of Surinam, H. E. Mr. R. R. Venetiaan undertook a State Visit to India from March 16-20, 2003 upon the invitation of the President of India H. E. Dr. A.P.J. Abdul Kalam.
2. Within the framework of the visit H. E. Mr. Venetiaan held fruitful discussions with H. E. Dr. A.P.J. Abdul Kalam, the President of the Republic of India, and H.E. Mr. A.B. Vajpayee, Prime Minister of India.
3. During bilateral discussions held in a friendly and cordial atmosphere, both sides exchanged views on various bilateral, regional and international issues of mutual interest.
4. Both sides noted with satisfaction that India-Surinam relations, which have a strong cultural and historical basis, are marked by cordiality and a high degree of understanding and close proximity on current principal issues. Both sides reiterated their desire to strengthen bilateral relations based on the traditionally close ties between the two countries.
5. India noted the efforts of Surinam to increasingly integrate with regional organizations such as, CARICOM, ACP, OAS and also the global economy. In this connection, both sides recognized that considerable potential exists for India to undertake mutually beneficial cooperation with Surinam in various sectors.
6. Surinam is a country with rich untapped natural resources and emerging infrastructural requirements. Given India's varied experience in high technology and industrial areas, India could, in a spirit of South-South cooperation, share expertise in priority areas identified by Surinam.

7. To these ends, the Indian side agreed to consider suitably extending the scope of ongoing cooperation under the Indian Technical & Economic Cooperation. India also agreed to double the quota of ITEC scholarships offered to Surinam from 15 to 30 slots. Possibility of deputing Indian ITEC experts in key sectors identified by Surinam would also be considered.
8. With a view to giving fillip to ongoing cooperation in the economic and commercial area, the Indian side agreed to extend a concessional line of credit of US $ 10 million to Surinam through the Exim Bank of India for undertaking developmental projects and activities in Surinam jointly identified by the two sides and requiring Indian products and services.
9. The two sides noted that besides projects already identified for the US $ 10 million Credit Line being extended by India to Surinam, some Surinamse companies had requisitioned for the technical services of Indian companies e.g. EBS of Surinam had signed an MoU with M/s. P.E.C. and L & T of India for setting up an electrical transmission line from Paranam to Paramaribo. In connection with all such developmental projects requiring application of Indian products and expertise in Surinam, Indian side agreed to give best possible consideration for extending similar concessional credit line facilities through Exim Bank of India.
10. As a gesture of its commitment to further strengthening India-Surinam bilateral relations, the Indian side agreed to waive in entirety, all pending payments due by Surinam to India against the first Credit Line of Rs. 50 million extended by India in 1992.
11. Both sides noted that a high-level Surinamse delegation, led by Health Minister of Surinam and including representatives of the private sector had participated in an India–Latin American Health Summit held in India in September 2002. During the visit, possibilities of sharing Indian expertise in the areas of hospital management services, deployment of Indian medical doctors and specialists in Surinamse hospitals, the public health sector, for control of malaria and other infectious tropical diseases and sourcing of Indian medicines at economical costs, were identified. In order to give impetus to such cooperation, the Indian side agreed to donate Indian medicines worth US $ 100,000/- to Surinam for treatment of different diseases.
12. Although the bilateral Joint Commission meeting could not take place in 2001 in India due to constraints in both countries, both sides agreed to give high priority to intensifying cooperation in all the agreed sectors of cooperation and to consider the possibility of convening a meeting of the Joint Commission in New Delhi this year on mutually convenient dates.

13. The following Agreements were signed during this State Visit:
    a) MoU on Agriculture;
    b) Cultural Exchange Programme
    c) Agreement on extending a new US$10 million Line of Credit by India to Surinam

Possibility of signing Agreements/MoU in the field of civil aviation; in the area of technical cooperation and in Information Technology would be given high priority by both sides.

14. Both sides emphasized the need for creating better awareness of each other's strengths within the private sector of the two countries. Trade missions would be undertaken and participation in trade/ commercial exhibitions in both countries would be encouraged. In keeping with these objectives, they welcomed the decision of the apex Indian industry association, FICCI (Federation of Indian Chamber of Commerce & Industry) to sign an MoU with its Surinamse counterpart KKF (Surinamse Chamber of Commerce & Industry) during the visit. They also welcomed the proposal to establish a Joint Business Council between the two countries.
15. The two sides reiterated their support to the need to reform the UN, particularly the expansion of the UN Security Council. They stressed, in particular, the need for equitable balance in the expanded Security Council to provide a constructive voice to the aspirations of the developing countries. They believed that piecemeal and discriminatory approaches to such expansion will be inconsistent with the objectives of that world body. Considering that India is the largest democracy in the world and in view of its past contributions to the promotion of peace, Surinam expressed support for India's claim for permanent membership of an expanded UN Security Council.
16. India and Surinam affirmed that terrorism cannot be justified in any form, for any cause or for any reason as an excuse. They agreed that the fight against terrorism has to be global, comprehensive and sustained for the objective of total elimination of terrorism worldwide. In this context, they reiterated their commitment to the UN Security Council Resolution 1373. They stressed the need to strengthen the international legal regime to fight terrorism through the adoption of the comprehensive convention on international terrorism.
17. The Surinamse side appreciated the evolving security concerns of India in the light of recent local, regional and global developments. It appreciated the restraint and responsibility shown by India despite its varied defence capabilities. In this connection, Surinamse side supported the resolution of differences between India and Pakistan through bilateral dialogue. It also recognized that cross-border infiltration and

terrorism had to end to encourage resumption of dialogue. It called on concerned countries to dismantle the infrastructure of support to terrorism and to stop serving as a platform for international terrorism.

18. Both sides noted with satisfaction that in the recent past, high-level contacts had been facilitated between the Parliaments of both countries. The Hon'ble Speaker of the Surinam led a Parliamentary delegation to India in August 2002 and also graced the Golden Jubilee celebrations of the Indian Parliament in January 2003. Likewise, the Hon'ble Speaker of the Lok Sabha (Lower House of the Indian Parliament) had accepted the invitation of the Hon'ble Speaker of the Surinam National Assembly to visit Surinam as per mutual convenience. Both sides welcomed such contacts and agreed to maintain a sustained dialogue between the Parliaments of the two democracies.

19. The Indian side expressed pleasure that Surinam will be the next venue for the Seventh World Hindi Conference in Paramaribo from June 5-9, 2003.

20. The Indian side welcomed the invitation by the Government of Surinam for India to participate as a guest country in the mega CARICOM cultural event (CARIFESTA) being hosted by Surinamese in August 2003 and agreed to send an Indian cultural contingent to perform in the event.

21. The Surinamese side expressed sincere thanks to the Government of the Republic of India for all the hospitality extended to them and the excellent arrangements made for their visit to India.

❮24❯

India - Syria Joint Statement (16.11.03)

Both sides decided to set up a Joint Hydrocarbon Committee and the establishment of Syrian National Biotechnology Centre at the University of Damascus with Indian assistance. Syria supported resolution of India-Pakistan issues through dialogue based on the Shimla Agreement of 1972 and the Lahore Declaration of 1999 while India reiterated support for the legitimate rights and aspirations of the Palestinian and Syrian causes in the framework of UNCR's 242,338,1397, 497 and the "Land for Peace" principle.

1. At the invitation of the President of Syria H.E. Dr. Bashar Al-Assad, the Prime Minister of India H.E. Shri Atal Bihari Vajpayee, paid a State visit to Syria on November 14-16 2003. The visit helped in establishing deeper understanding between the leaderships and renewed old historical links between the two countries.
2. Prime Minister Shri Vajpayee was accompanied by Minister of External Affairs of India, the National Security Advisor and a delegation comprising of senior officials from important Ministries.
3. During the visit, Prime Minister Shri Vajpayee had one to one meeting with President Dr. Bashar Al-Assad and held talks with Prime Minister Eng. Mohammad Naji Al-Otri and Cabinet Ministers.
4. In his meeting with President, Prime Minister had a cordial and comprehensive exchange of views on a wide range of important bilateral, regional and international issues, in a way that reflects the deep historical relations between India and Syria.
5. During the discussions, both sides expressed their satisfaction at the steady and comprehensive growth in bilateral relations. They, however, emphasized that enormous potential for further bilateral cooperation needed to be tapped for mutual benefit. They committed themselves to further strengthening and expanding their bilateral cooperation, especially in political, economic, commercial, cultural and science & technology sectors.
6. In the presence of the President Dr. Bashar Al-Assad and Prime Minister Shri Vajpayee, the following documents were signed:

i. Executive Programme for Cultural Cooperation,
ii. Memorandum of Understanding for Cooperation in Information Technology and Services,
iii. Memorandum of Understanding on Cooperation in the field of Agriculture and Allied Sectors,
iv. Memorandum of Understanding on Technical Cooperation,
v. Exchange Programme in the field of Education,
vi. Cultural Cooperation Agreement between the Arab Writers Union in Syrian Arab Republic and the Sahitya Academy in India,
vii. Agreement of Mutual Cooperation between National Small Industries Corporation, India and Ministry of Industry of Syrian Arab Republic,
viii. Executive Work Plan: Department of Bio-technology, Govt. of Republic of India and the Ministry of Higher Education, Syrian Arab Republic, and
ix. Programme of Cooperation in Science & Technology.

The two sides hoped that these documents would further enhance the bilateral legal and institutional framework and boost their cooperation in respective sectors.

7. Both sides agreed to hold periodic consultations between the two Governments on topical issues. Both sides also agreed to increase the frequency of bilateral visits by Ministers and officials and to consolidate the ties between business communities of the two countries. People-to-people relations will also be encouraged, in order to increase and deepen understanding between the societies.
8. In view of the potential for cooperation in the Hydro-carbon sector, both sides decided to set up a Joint Hydro-carbon Committee, having three representatives from each side. This Committee will be mandated to suggest specific projects for joint cooperation in the Hydro-carbon sector within a specified timeframe. The two sides agreed to consider setting up an Institute of Petroleum with the assistance of the Government of India.
9. Both sides reviewed their economic and commercial cooperation and identified fields such as Biotechnology, Information Technology, hydro-carbons, Railways, Education and Agriculture where existing complementarities could be exploited for mutual benefit. They agreed to encourage the private and public sectors to expand the scope of mutual trade and investments.
10. Prime Minister of India also announced a Credit Line of US$ 25 million (US Dollar twenty five million) for development of bilateral trade. The announcement of credit line by India for the purpose of

boosting bilateral trade was welcomed by Syria. Both sides agreed to double the bilateral trade by 2005 and decided to identify priority areas for this purpose.

11. Both the governments noted with satisfaction the progress achieved in bilateral cooperation in bio-technology sector. The establishment of Syrian National Bio-technology Centre at the University of Damascus with Indian assistance will further enhance their peaceful cooperation in this vital field. Both sides will undertake joint projects for mutual benefit. Indian Prime Minister announced a special grant of US$ 1 million to assist implementation of the agreed programme of co-operation and make the Centre an institute of excellence.

12. The two delegations held an in-depth exchange of views on the emerging international and regional security environment. Both sides condemned all acts of terrorism, of which they have been victims. Both delegations agreed that terrorism should not be linked to any religion and no attempt be made to tarnish any religion in the name of terrorism.

13. Syria welcomed the initiative taken by the Prime Minister of India aimed at fostering friendship and good-neighbourly relations between India and Pakistan. Syria supported resolution of India-Pakistan issues bilaterally through dialogue based on the Simla Agreement of 1972 and the Lahore Declaration of 1999. Both sides supported strong co-operation for combating international terrorism according to the international law and the stand of the Non Aligned Movement taken in this regard.

14. India and Syria called for the establishment of a just, comprehensive and durable peace in the Middle East. The Prime Minister reiterated India's principled support for the Palestinian and Syrian causes and for the legitimate rights and aspirations in the framework of the UN Security Council Resolutions No. 242, 338, 1397 and 497 as well as the "land for peace" principle. The Prime Minister also reiterated India's view that the cycle of violence and counter-violence must end. In this context, he emphasized that action against the sovereignty and territorial integrity of Syria, as happened last month, is not acceptable.

15. Both sides had a convergence of view on Iraq and felt that it was imperative that the people of Iraq should be empowered to determine their own future to rebuild their nation. Both sides also agreed that the UN had a crucial role to play in the process of political and economic re-construction of that country. The immediate priorities in Iraq are ensuring security and stability, restoration of basic facilities and infrastructure, and a road map for the political process towards a representative Government.

16. Prime Minister Shri Vajpayee thanked President Dr. Bashar Al-Assad for the cordiality and hospitality extended during the State visit and conveyed his good wishes to the leadership and people of Syria on the occasion of the holy month of Ramadan. Prime Minister Shri Vajpayee invited President Dr. Bashar Al-Assad to visit India. President Dr. Bashar Al-Assad accepted this invitation with pleasure.

❮25❯

Joint Declaration on Friendship and Cooperation Between the Republic of India and the Republic of Tajikistan (14.11.03)

> The two sides expressed satisfaction on the formation of a Joint Working Group to combat terrorism, opening of a cultural center and IT institute in Dushanbe and the placement annually of scholarships for 70 Tajik students and professionals in India. The Tajik side supported India " as an appropriate candidate for permanent membership in the expanded UNSC" and expressed its belief "that India's membership of SCO would add to the strength of that organization when it decides to take a new member".

"The Republic of India and the Republic of Tajikistan, hereinafter referred to as the sides,

Recalling the historical affinity between the cultures and the traditions of their people,

Recognising that they share the ideals of peace, democracy and secularism,

convinced that cooperation between India and Tajikistan would further the cause of peace and security in Asia and globally,

Seeking to establish qualitatively new and mutually beneficial relations in the political, economic, military, development cooperation and in other areas,

Agree that :-

The sides shall develop bilateral cooperation based on the universally recognized principles and norms of international law; respect for the sovereignty, independence and territorial integrity of the both states; non-interference in each other's internal affairs and commitment to democratic values.

The sides affirmed that strengthened cooperation between the two countries is a positive factor for the maintenance of peace and stability. They also reaffirmed the importance of settling issues through peaceful dialogue.

The sides noted with satisfaction the formation of a Joint Working Group to combat international terrorism. They expect the group's work will aid co-operation in combating organized crime, money laundering, illegal trafficking in weapons, ammunitions and explosives, international terrorism and other trans-national threats. In this context, they reiterated that terrorism cannot be justified on any ground whatsover. Terrorism is an attack on the human rights and civil liberties of the citizens of the world. It must be condemned unambiguously and eradicated wherever it exists. The sides also condemned the supporters of terrorism and those that finance, train or provide support for terrorists.

The sides were pleased to note the steady progress in defence exchanges and the intent to further intensify relations in this area in the future.

The sides noted with satisfaction the increased bilateral contacts and the frequency of exchanges at political and senior official levels between the two countries. The sides were pleased to note that India has opened cultural centre in Dushanbe and that its functioning since January 2003 has re-established the cultural bridges between the two countries. They also noted with satisfaction the commencement for the first time of direct flights between Dushanbe and New Delhi from 18 February, 2003. The sides welcomed the establishment of the diplomatic mission of Tajikistan in New Delhi in October 2003. These measures are indicative of the mutual desire to promote greater people to people contact and bilateral exchanges.

The sides noted that the humanitarian cooperation has shown steady increase. They recalled the delivery of food aid worth US$ 5 million by India to Tajikistan is September-October 2003 and the placement annually on medium to long-term scholarships of nearly 70 Tajik students and professionals in India. They took note of the substantial progress in the plans to set up under Indian aid a Fruit-processing plant and an institute for Information Technology in Dushanbe.

The economic cooperation between the two sides is on increase. It was decided to help and promote this further though institutional encouragement. Considering the vast hydro-electric potential of Tajikistan, it was felt that a beginning should also be made to cooperate in this sector. To encourage joint ventures and investment in Tajikistan, the Government of India has decided to extend a new package of economic assistance, including a line of credit.

The sides expressed readiness to widen cooperation in the fields of culture, mass media, sports and tourism. They also placed importance on cooperation in the fields of science and technology.

The Republic of India reiterates its support to the Republic of Tajikistan and its Government in its efforts at strengthening democracy and in promoting economic development.

The Republic to Tajikistan re-affirms its support to the efforts of the Republic of India, and its Government to promote and strengthen international peace and security, including mutual understanding and co-operation in South Asia.

The sides acknowledged the vital importance of the role of United Nations in promoting world peace, stability, and prosperity. They agreed that there is an urgent need to restructure and strengthen the UN Security Council to reflect the new international realities. The Tajik side, noting the role India plays in international affairs, supports India as an appropriate candidate for permanent membership in the expanded UN Security Council.

The sides also noted the progress being made by the Shanghai Corporation Organisation (SCO) as a regional body. Noting India's geographical proximity and historical links with Central Asia, and its active participation on regional and global matters of cooperation, the Tajik side expressed its belief that India's membership of SCO would add to the strength of that organization when it decides to take a new member.

The sides noted the positive development since the Bonn Agreement of December 2001, including the establishment of the Transitional Administration and the efforts towards a new Constitution and a strong, united, independent and sovereign Afghanistan free from interference from outside. They expressed concern at the challenges to security being mounted by the former Taliban and Al Qaida elements with support from outside. They reiterated their determination to continue providing economic and other assistance to contribute to peace, stability and reconstruction in Afghanistan.

The Prime Minister of India thanked the President of Republic of Tajikistan for the warmth of reception and the hospitality extended to his delegation and to him. The Prime Minister of India invited the President of Republic of Tajikistan to visit India at an early date. The invitation was accepted with pleasure."

‹26›

India-U.S. Global Issues Forum Joint Statement, (04.02.03)

The two sides discussed a number of issues like international agreements on Persistent Organic Pollution, sea turtles, fisheries; health issues like treatment and care for HIV/AIDS and other infectious diseases; and ways to advance human rights and democracy in international fora.

Following is the text of a joint statement issued by the United States and India upon the conclusion of the U.S. India Global Issues Forum Meeting in Washington, DC.

Begin Text:

"Senior United States and Indian government officials participated in the second meeting of the Global Issues Forum at the Department of State in Washington, DC, February 3-4, 2003. The first meeting of the Global Issues Forum was held in New Delhi on October 30, 2002.

The U.S. delegation was led by Under Secretary of State for Global Affairs Paula Dobriansky, and included representatives from the Bureau of Oceans and International Environmental and Scientific Affairs, Science and Technology Adviser to the Secretary of State, and the Bureau of Democracy, Human Rights and Labour. The Government of India delegation was led by Foreign Secretary Kanwal Sibal, with the participation of other senior officials from the Ministry of External Affairs.

The objective of the Global Issues Forum is to strengthen current areas of cooperation between the U.S. and India on issues of global interest and explore new avenues of cooperative endeavour. This session focused on a range of issues including environment; health and infectious diseases, with an emphasis on HIV/AIDS; and human rights and democracy-related issues. In addition, there was discussion of the Indo-U.S. Science and Technology Forum, with both sides expressing strong interest in substantially expanding science and technology cooperation. In the area of environment, the two sides discussed a range of global issues such as the forthcoming session of the Commission on Sustainable Development and the United Nations Environment Governing Council/GMEF, international Agreements on Persistent Organic Pollution (POPS), sea turtles, and fisheries issues. The health segment concentrated on action taken for the prevention, treatment and care for HIV/AIDS and other infectious diseases. These discussions were a prelude to full interagency discussions expected later this year in New Delhi on those issues.

The segment on multilateral issues was led by Assistant Secretary of State for Democracy, Human Rights, and Labour Lorne Craner and explored ways to advance human rights and democracy in multilateral fora. In addition, the two sides discussed the issue of trafficking in persons (TIP) and policies on population.

The two governments agreed to continue their dialogue on all three sets of issues more extensively in New Delhi later in 2003. These discussions all fall under the umbrella of the Global Issues Forum, adding a new dimension to the steadily broadening and deepening U.S.-India partnership. Cooperation in the Global Issues Forum is another important step toward completing the process of transforming U.S.-India relations to which President Bush and Prime Minister Vajpayee pledged the commitment of both governments in their November 2001 Joint Statement. Both delegations expressed their deep regret on the deaths of Dr. Kalpana Chawla and her fellow crew members in the Columbia space shuttle tragedy this weekend."

‹27›

Joint Statement Meeting of the US-India Defense Policy Group Washington, D.C., (06.08.03)

> The two sides decided to hold a missile defence workshop in India in the next six months and agreed to enhance capabilities to combat terrorism and increase interoperability between the armed forces of the US and India. The two delegations approved a range of activities for the coming year including possible sale of P-3 Maritime Patrol aircraft and specialized equipment to support India's peacekeeping training capabilities.

The U.S.-India Defense Policy Group (DPG) met 6-7 August, 2003 in Washington, DC. U.S. Under Secretary of Defense for Policy Douglas Feith hosted the meeting and Defence Secretary Ajay Prasad led the Indian delegation.

The strategic situation in the world has changed dramatically in recent years. Global terrorism, state sponsors of terrorism, and the proliferation of weapons of mass destruction are the key threats to international peace and security. The United States and India are drawn together in an effort to deal with these new circumstances. As a result, President Bush and Prime Minister Vajpayee have re-defined the U.S.-India relationship. Democracy, common principles, and shared interests are the foundation of our new strategic partnership.

Since the last meeting of the DPG in May 2002, the U.S. and Indian defense establishments have continued to expand cooperation. The past year's accomplishments include:

- Combined special forces counterinsurgency exercise in Northeast India;
- Combined Air Force exercise in Alaska;
- Complex Naval exercises on the East Coast of India;
- Delivery of "Firefinder" radars to India;
- Senior-level missile defense talks; and
- Conclusion of a Master Information Exchange Agreement to facilitate cooperation in research and development of defense technologies.

During this year's DPG, the delegations emphasized the long-range strategic concepts that guide the new approach to the U.S.-India relationship. They agreed that the work of the two countries together during the past year and planned activities for the next year are translating that strategic vision into action.

The delegations discussed the threat posed by the proliferation of weapons and technologies of mass destruction, including the risk that terrorists will acquire such weapons. They also discussed measures to combat proliferation.

The two sides agreed to establish a high-level dialogue on defense technology security issues.

The two sides reaffirmed the shared view that missile defense enhances cooperative security and stability. They decided to hold a missile defense workshop in India in the next six months as a follow-on to an international workshop attended by U.S. and Indian delegations at the June 2003 Multinational Ballistic Missile Defense Conference held in Kyoto, Japan. The Indian delegation also accepted invitations to the July 2004 Multinational Ballistic Missile Defense Conference in Berlin and the 2005 Roving Sands missile defense exercise.

The two sides welcomed the improved prospects for freedom and security in the Middle East. They underlined their commitment to furthering stability and security for the people of Iraq and the contribution that international co-operation could make to that process. They agreed to continue to seek ways for the United States and India to work together to support the people of Iraq. They also welcomed the establishment of Iraq's Governing Council and noted the important role of the UN Special Representative in addressing the needs of the Iraqi people.

They discussed the success of Operation Enduring Freedom and reaffirmed the ongoing commitment of both countries to the future of Afghanistan. They agreed that a permanent end to terrorism is critical to ensuring a future of peace and stability in South Asia.

The United States and India have continued to work together to enhance their capabilities to combat terrorism and increase interoperability. The two delegations highlighted the importance of the ongoing series of Joint and Combined exercises in building interoperability between U.S. and Indian armed forces and agreed to continue this interaction. They also agreed to continue to review counter terrorism equipment requirements for India's special operations forces.

The two delegations welcomed the reports on the recent meetings of the Military Cooperation Group (co-ordinating military exercises and exchanges), Security Cooperation Group (co-ordinating sales and licensing), and Joint Technical Group (co-ordinating research and development). These groups will meet again in the coming months.

In addition to the above-areas, the two delegations approved a range of activities for the coming year, including:

- Specialized training programs and joint exercises to be carried out by the armed services of the two countries, including an air combat training exercise.
- India will host in co-ordination with the United States a multinational planning exercise to develop standard operating procedures.
- Continued development of a defense supply relationship, including through the Government-to-Government Foreign Military Sales program. A U.S. team will travel to India in September to discuss the details of a possible sale of P-3 maritime patrol aircraft.
- U.S. sale to India of training materials and specialized equipment to support India's peacekeeping training capabilities.
- A Defense Planning Exchange to permit U.S. and Indian defense experts to conduct discussions on defense strategy and planning.

Secretary Prasad also met with U.S. Secretary of Defense Donald Rumsfeld, U.S. Deputy Secretary of State Richard Armitage, and Chairman of the Joint Chiefs of Staff General Richard Myers. These meetings emphasized the importance both sides place on the growing bilateral relationship.

Next year, the DPG will hold its meeting in New Delhi.

❮28❯

Joint Declaration on the Framework of Comprehensive Cooperation Between the Republic of India and the Socialist Republic of Vietnam as they enter the 21st Century (01.05.03)

> The two parties agreed to implement a "Comprehensive Cooperation Programme" in the next 15 years with the major thrusts being regular high-level meetings, cooperation in international fora , implementation of UNSC resolutions against terrorism and raising economic cooperation. India also committed to continue concessional credits and grants for import of equipment by Vietnam and provide 120yearly scholarships to Vietnamese students to study in India while Vietnam supported India's entry as a permanent member of an expanded UNSC.

The Republic of India and the Socialist Republic of Vietnam (hereinafter referred to as the 'Parties') are bound by traditional and long-standing ties of friendship which have been continuously nurtured by President Ho Chi Minh and Prime Minister Jawaharlal Nehru and succeeding generations of leadership of the two countries. The historic visits of Pandit Jawaharlal Nehru to Hanoi in October 1954, immediately after liberation of Hanoi and of President Ho Chi Minh to India in February 1958 opened a new chapter in the history of close and time-tested relationship between the two countries and constituted a strong inspiration for our two peoples in their struggle for independence and freedom and in the building of a new life, thus contributing to the preservation of peace in Asia and the world.

Building upon this tradition, the leaders of both sides have exchanged State visits and established a firm foundation for mutual understanding and trust and comprehensive cooperation between the two peoples. After establishment of full diplomatic relations on 7 January 1972, and particularly after the reunification of Vietnam, the two countries have cooperated closely and effectively to build a comprehensive, long-term and reliable partnership. The bilateral relationship has been increasingly deepened in each other's interest as well as for peace, stability, cooperation and development in the region and beyond. Through mutual support for each other in times of adversity, the relationship between the two countries has become an abiding factor amidst the changing currents and cross-currents of international affairs.

Entering the 21st century, the two Parties are resolved to bring into full play this traditional and friendly relationship and raise their cooperation to new heights to meet the new challenges posed by globalisation, the menace of international terrorism and the significant challenges to the international system. Both sides endeavour to develop a strategic dimension to their partnership for the mutual benefit of their peoples, and to contribute to peace, stability, cooperation and prosperity in the Asia-Pacific region and the world at large.

The two Parties reaffirm their respect for the fundamental principles of the United Nations Charter and international laws, particularly those of mutual respect for independence, sovereignty and territorial integrity, non-interference in each other's internal affairs, doing no harm to each Party's relations with a third country, equal and mutually beneficial cooperation, and mutual support and assistance in the spirit of fraternity. In this context, the Socialist Republic of Vietnam always highly values India's traditional role in the United Nations and supports its entry as a permanent member of an expanded UN Security Council.

Pursuant to the above-mentioned objectives, guidelines and principles, the two Parties agree to implement a Comprehensive Cooperation Program in the next 15 years with the major thrusts as follows:

(i) The two Parties undertake to conduct regular high-level meetings with the aim of further cementing the existing political ties and creating new momentum for bilateral multi-sided cooperation. Aware of the strategic importance of their bilateral cooperation, Ministries, Parliamentarians, agencies, local authorities, business communities and mass organizations of the two Parties will increase friendly exchanges and contacts in order to further consolidate their partnership.

(ii) The two Parties agree to closely cooperate in the UN and other international fora. Recognizing the importance of the regional dimension in their bilateral relations, the Parties reaffirm their intention to coordinate their positions in the regional and sub-regional organizations, especially in ASEAN, ARF and Mekong-Ganga Cooperation.

(iii) The two Parties also undertake to assist each other in protecting their respective interests in the international arena and to contribute to the common efforts for democratizing international relations. They condemn terrorism in all its forms and manifestations and agree to strengthen cooperation in the implementation of relevant UN Security Council resolutions against terrorism and for opposing all forms of violence and terror, attempts to force one's will on others or interfere in internal affairs of sovereign nations. To these ends, the Foreign Ministries of the two countries shall hold annual political consultations on international political developments, measures to help each other fully integrate into regional and international arrangements, and on co-ordination in international fora.

(iv) The two Parties shall endeavour to maintain and improve the efficiency of the biennial meetings of the Vietnam-India Joint Commission to make it more responsive to the economic reforms in the two countries and set new directions in keeping with the needs of each country's developmental goals.

(v) The two Parties resolved to raise their economic cooperation, inter alia, in the following areas:

1. In trade, the two Parties are committed to diversify the content of their bilateral imports and exports and promote trade promotion activities so as to reach a trade turnover target of US$ 1 billion by 2015. They also agree to take measures to grant tariff preferences to each other in conformity with their international obligations so as to promote a balance in their trade exchanges;
2. In investment and management consultancy, the two Parties pledge to create every favourable condition for their investors and consultants, including small and medium sized enterprises, to expand investment and business management and consultancy activities in the areas such as oil and gas, chemicals, petro-chemicals, fertilizer, power, pharmaceuticals, information technology, agricultural processing and light industries, telecommunications, ship-building and seaports, railways, steel and mining;
3. In order to facilitate trade and investment relations between the two countries in a fraternal spirit, the Republic of India is committed to continue providing the Socialist Republic of Vietnam, to the maximum extent possible, concessional credits and grants to import equipment from the former. The latter is committed to use these resources effectively and to give preferences, in other non-credit/grant financed requirements of its industry, to import similar equipment from India on the basis of competitive price offers.

(vi) The two Parties view cooperation in science and technology as driver of their bilateral cooperation. They will promote R&D co-operation in the areas of agriculture, biotechnology, new material technology, information technology, remote sensing and other space applications, hydrography, meteorology, oceanography, peaceful uses of nuclear energy and other areas of frontier technologies.

(vii) The two Parties agree to take gradual steps to expand cooperation in security and defence, anti-piracy measures, preventing terrorist acts targetted at each other and early signing of a bilateral Agreement on

countering crime. They will encourage exchange of delegations and sharing of information and experience on combating international terrorism and its support mechanisms, particularly organized crime, illicit arms and drug trafficking.

(viii) The two Parties recognise that cooperation in human resource development constitutes a pillar of their bilateral cooperation and undertake to further expand and diversify such cooperation. The Republic of India pledges to continue providing on a yearly basis 120 short-term and long-term scholarships for Vietnamese undergraduate and post-graduate students to study in the Republic of India. The two Parties shall also work closely to facilitate Vietnamese students to study in the Republic of India with scholarships provided by the Socialist Republic of Vietnam and funded by themselves. The Socialist Republic of Vietnam will create every favourable condition for establishment of branches of Indian high educational institutions and for Indian undergraduate and post-graduate students to study in Vietnam.

(ix) The two Parties undertake to increase exchange of and co-operation in culture and information, archaeology, conservation, museology, tourism, public health and sports at the central and local levels. The two Parties will also encourage and create favourable conditions for youth and mass organisations to foster people-to-people contacts to consolidate their mutual understanding and eternal friendship.

Done in Hindi, Vietnamese and English, all texts being equally authentic. In case of divergence in interpretation, the English text shall prevail.

At New Delhi on 1 May 2003,

For the Republic of India India	For the Socialist Republic of Vietnam
Yashwant Sinha Minister of External Affairs	Nguyen dy Nien Minister of Foreign Affairs

[illegible]

[illegible]

For the Republic of [illegible] [illegible] For the [illegible]
India [illegible] [illegible]

[illegible] Sinha [illegible]
Minister of External Affairs [illegible] Minister of Foreign Affairs

Part 1-B

‹29›

Address to the Nation by the President Dr. APJ Abdul Kalam on the Eve of Independence Day, 2003 (14.08.03)

The President emphasized that "core competencies, resources and safety consciousness" should be the basis on which the country should embark on a "national mission of transformation". He discussed five specific missions: networking of rivers, quality power, Providing Urban Amenities in Rural Areas (PURA), information and communication technology and tourism that "will provide the thrust for the realization of a developed India". All issues except national development, according to him, should be considered as "non-issues" if India is to achieve the mission of a developed country.

What should we be remembered for?

My dear Citizens of India,

On the eve of the 57th Independence Day, I extend to you my best wishes for your happiness and prosperity. My salutations to all of you at home and abroad. Let us on this occasion remember with gratitude, the selfless service rendered by the personnel of the armed forces and also those of the para-military forces, who guard our frontiers on the land, at sea and in the air.

Let me dedicate this Independence Day broadcast to those great souls who pioneered the Independence Movement. We remember them with reverence and gratitude, not for their religious, political, language, caste and creed affiliations, but for the ninety-year saga of sacrifices to realise the singular and noble vision of heralding an Independent India.

What should we be remembered for?

Let us for a moment pause to reflect what it is that for which we would like to be remembered for by future generations. Will we be remembered for how many churches our generation has added, will we be remembered for how many mosques our generation has added, will we be remembered for how many temples our generation has added or will we be remembered for how many gurudwaras our generation has added? No, not at all. We will be remembered only if we give to our younger generation a prosperous and safe India, resulting out of economic prosperity coupled with our civilisational heritage.

At this point of time, I would like to share with you an experience which I had at Raj Bhavan, Srinagar during my recent visit to the three regions of Jammu and Kashmir. A number of children from different schools of the city and the neighbourhood interacted with me and sang with me the National Anthem. At the end of our interaction, three students approached me and introduced themselves. One was a Hindu girl, the second a Muslim boy, and the third a Sikh boy. They asked me - "Mr. President, please tell us now, when will we become prosperous, free from poverty and from the fear of terrorist attacks? Allow us to go on a mission to penetrate the minds of the extremists and bring about unity of minds." These children represent the 300 million strong youth of the nation. The questions of the students engulfed me, resulting in a poetic verse:

"Oh Almighty, create thoughts and actions in the minds of the people of my nation, so that they live united.

Light the minds of the religious leaders of my country to evolve a bridge among religions with compassion and love.

Embed the thought 'Nation is bigger than the individual or party' in the minds of the leaders.

May God, bless my people to work hard and transform the country into a prosperous nation in a decade."

Aspirations of the people

In one year's time, I visited 23 States and three Union Territories. I interacted with various cross sections of people and had an exclusive dialogue with Members of Parliament and Legislators of certain States and also presented the Developed India Plan to the Joint Session of Parliament in February 2003.

The dialogue with the people, and written responses from many citizens gave me an insight into the aspirations of the people to get into the action of transforming India into a developed nation, in less than two decades. Whether it was a remote village in Kerala, or a far away rural set-up in Nagaland or Uri in Jammu and Kashmir, the area close to the Line of Control, I would like to emphatically state that the feelings and aspirations for a prosperous India are the same.

Our Strengths

For India to become a developed nation, we must give thrust to the Nation's core competencies. The GDP has to grow annually by 8 to 10 percent with consistency over years instead of the current 5 percent. This year, it is reassuring that our economy in three sectors - agriculture, manufacturing and services is in the ascent phase. If we put in united efforts to keep up the momentum we can reach an 8 percent growth rate in about a year. We should ensure that the benefits of this growth should reach the economically weaker sections of society.

We should reinforce our gains in the Agriculture, Power, Information and Communication Technology, Industrial and Education Sectors, Space, Nuclear, and Defence Technologies, Chemical, Pharmaceutical and Infrastructural Industries, Oil Exploration and Refining, and more importantly in critical technologies.

When we are consolidating our strengths, we should develop increased safety consciousness to prevent loss of valuable human and material resources in road, rail, air, power, industrial and other accidents. The relief mechanisms have to reach accident sites at the right time.

The core competencies, resources and safety consciousness should be the basis on which the country can embark on a national mission for transformation.

Vision to Mission

We need to evolve and develop specific integrated missions sector-wise to take the country forward on the path to self-sustaining development. These missions will provide the thrust for the realisation of a developed India in a time bound manner. They will also provide large-scale employment opportunities for the youth, through the creation of various types of industries and enhancement of national infrastructure. I would like to discuss five specific missions.

Networking of Rivers

The first mission on the Networking of Rivers is under active consideration of my Government and from the task team evolving the plan of action, we must move on to a mission mode programme including an ecological enhancement plan for executing the project. This mission will eliminate the periodical problem of droughts and floods experienced in a number of river basin States and provide both water and power security. In addition, the nation has to embark on water harvesting and desalination of seawater as national missions.

Quality Power

Availability of quality uninterrupted power should be ensured at an affordable price, which is a key to economic growth. This is our second mission. The existing capacity of about one lakh Megawatts would need tripling by the year 2020. To achieve it, apart from hydel, thermal and nuclear power systems, we need to give thrust to sustainable energy resources like bio-mass, wind and solar farms of 800 to 1000 Megawatts capacity and to efficient transmission and distribution.

Providing Urban amenities in Rural Areas (PURA)

Providing urban facilities to rural areas is another important mission about which I have talked to you earlier. In the long term interest, it is necessary for us to make living in villages an attractive proposition for our people by reinforcing the rural habitat and providing modern economic linkages. To achieve this, an economically viable cluster of villages have to be created through a mission mode programme into physical, electronic, and knowledge connectivities, leading to self-sustained economic prosperity for groups of villages. It is essential that PURA has to become a business proposition to be run by small scale industrialists, entrepreneurs, and societal establishments.

Information and Communication Technology (ICT)

The mission of Information and Communication Technology (ICT) and related services is one of the wealth generators for the nation. We should aspire to increase business volume by 15 to 20 times in a ten year duration. The benefit of ICT must reach all parts of the country through tele-medicine, tele-education and e-governance. We have to embark on creating ICT infrastructure and developing knowledge products to promote selective self-reliance in the ICT sector, thus achieving a competitive edge globally.

Tourism

The vast civilisational heritage of the country, from the Himalayas to Kanyakumari, Jammu and Kashmir, Central India, the North Eastern States, Bihar, the Western States, the large coastal line, the Andaman and Nicobar Islands and Lakshadweep Islands have a lot to attract tourists. After my visit to almost all the regions of the country, I have realised that the tourism industry has a tremendous potential for wealth generation and should operate as our fifth mission with higher targets. To succeed in this mission, infrastructural requirements are very essential and are to be improved. Thrust is required to be given for inland water navigation, hotels, communications and tourist promotion. If we promote sustainable tourism, it will become India's core competence.

These mission areas need action and will provide a multiplier effect and give the necessary momentum to all sectors of the economy.

Enriching village life

During my visit to rural areas in certain States, I realised that the hard earned money of rural people, instead of being deployed for education of children and environmental improvements including their habitat, was being wasted in undesirable practices like alcoholism and other addictions. In certain States, I realised that the ratio between males and females was not proportionate. This prompted me to evolve a declaration in consultation with the rural population for administering it to village citizens. They participated in it with enthusiasm. The oath for enriching village life is as follows:

- Children are our precious wealth.
- We will give equal importance to male and female children in providing education and rights for growth of our society.

- Earnings come out of hard work. We will not waste it in gambling and liquor. We will become role models for our children.
- We need to tell our children about the importance of education as learning gives knowledge and knowledge makes children succeed.
- We need to jointly protect our forests and prevent pollution.
- We will plant at least five trees or saplings.

It is essential that reputed leaders and social workers while visiting rural areas can administer this oath in a similar way. Social workers, women self-help groups and non-governmental organisations have to take-up this task as a mission. For India to develop we need vibrant villages.

Challenges

Divisive forces use terrorism as a tool in the name of ethnic groupism, religious fundamentalism and sometimes political ambitions as a rationale for terrorism, leading to conflicts among nations. People are used as war tools. Within the next two decades, we will encounter a totally new situation of acute shortages of water, energy and minerals. No single nation will be able to handle this situation by itself. Humanity will require mega-missions for harnessing solar energy, drinking water from sea-water through the de-salination process and bringing minerals from other planets. In such a situation, the present reasons for conflict will become insignificant and unwarranted. I call upon the neighbouring countries to see this perspective and have a bigger vision. India has definitely taken a significant peace initiative with all its neighbours. The recent visit of our Prime Minister to China definitely paves the way for resolving certain outstanding issues.

The recent terrorist attack in Jammu and Kashmir through a suicide bombing, resulting in a number of casualties, of both service and civilian personnel, is a cause for serious concern. No religion has mandated killing others as a requirement for its sustenance or promotion. These cowardly acts borne out of utter frustration deserve severe condemnation and actions for preventing recurrence of such events.

Tasks before us

I am convinced that the developed India 2020 vision transforming into a mission is a national challenge and requires nationwide participation. While my Government is committed for such missions, every citizen of India should ask in what way he or she can contribute to these missions directly or indirectly. It is difficult to spell out all specific possibilities of tangible contribution by our citizens. I would like to mention a few here, as examples:

Educationists should build the capacities of the spirit of inquiry, creativity, entrepreneurial and moral leadership among students and become their role model. Today, professional education is becoming a commercial venture. It is not affordable for even middle class people, what to talk of people below the poverty line. State governments, universities and the managements of educational institutions should review and streamline the admission process and bring down the cost of education without sacrificing quality. Education is enlightenment; it is not trade.

In the health sector, the major challenge is to develop an Anti-HIV/AIDS vaccine to prevent the further spread of this disease. Another humane issue is to ensure that HIV affected children are not discriminated in schools and hospitals. It is essential that voluntary organisations and religious leaders of localities provide a humane touch to these members of society, by removing fear from the minds of the people. Can we dream and act for a HIV free India?

The farming community needs to increase its productivity through the mission of the Second Green Revolution, using technological advances. Dry land cultivation also needs a thrust. Large-scale industries have to increase their productivity and quality so that their market share can be increased for economic growth and the GDP. They should aim to become multinational companies and global leaders.

The judiciary is a prime pillar in our democratic set-up and should be able to administer natural justice with speed and nobility.

The media has to become a partner and positive critic in national development and celebrate individual successes and collective efforts of rural India.

Governmental tasks

The Government, with the support of R&D labs, can provide technological

அரசியல் பிழைத்தோர்க்கு அறம் கூற்றாவதும்

- சிலப்பதிகாரம்

upgradation to small-scale industries and remove procedural and systemic bottlenecks in executing missions. Actions emanating from the Government in all its public dealings should become fully transparent through e-governance.

Parliamentarians and Legislators belonging to each constituency should become mission facilitators for their Constituency and also resolve inter and intra - Constituency conflicts. I am reminded of a Tamil epic which provides the code of conduct for people in high and responsible positions:

It means, people who are in high and responsible positions, if they go against righteousness, righteousness itself will get transformed into a destroyer. Whoever deviates from righteousness, whether they are an individual or States, are responsible for their own actions.

If a country is to be corruption free and become a nation of beautiful minds, I strongly feel there are three key societal members who can make a difference. They are the father, the mother and the teacher. Let us join together and launch this movement from the home and the school to eradicate corruption.

Conclusion

We are a large country, we are also blessed with natural resources and a highly motivated young human resource. We have to prioritise our thoughts on national development and make all other issues as "non-issues". This will ensure focus and thrust for the development process. And it will prevent dissipation of energy and resources on non-productive issues.

I appeal to political leaders, religious leaders, opinion makers, media personnel and all Indian citizens to place a moratorium on all issues which are impediments to the development of the nation, from now and pledge ourselves to make the missions of Developed India a reality.

This will be the greatest legacy that we can proudly leave behind for our next generation. Let us sacrifice our today so that our children can have a better tomorrow. I pray to the Almighty to provide us the wisdom, knowledge, physical resources and ability to work hard to succeed in our missions. Allow me again, my dear citizens to wish you a very purposeful and happy Independence Day tomorrow.

Jai Hind.

❮30❯

Banquet speech by President Dr. A.P.J Abdul Kalam in Honour of His Majesty Jigme Singye Wangchuk the King of Bhutan (15.09.03)

The President highlighted that in addition to cooperation in the field of water resources and hydro-electricity, India and Bhutan could cooperate "in the field of traditional medicine by adding value to the... herbal medicines and convert them into marketable drugs". He also expressed India's appreciation for His Majesty's efforts at strengthening participatory democracy and addressing the issue of extremist activities emanating from Bhutan.

Your Majesty, Jigme Singye Wangchuck, the King of Bhutan
Excellencies,
Distinguished Guests,
Ladies and Gentlemen,

It gives me immense pleasure to welcome you and your delegation to India. We welcome you as the Monarch of the friendly neighbouring country of Bhutan and as a dear friend. The people of India have great admiration for Your Majesty, your wisdom and leadership in guiding the destiny of your people in pursuit of happiness and harmony with a focus on material progress, spiritual well-being and preservation of the environment.

Our relationship is based on the firm foundations of shared historical and cultural linkages. It is also a dynamic and progressive relationship constantly searching for new avenues of cooperation, new complementarities and new opportunities to strengthen itself. Cooperation in the field of water resources between our two countries sets an example which other countries would do well to emulate. Harnessing our rivers to mutual benefit is a good economic proposition. Bhutan has harnessed and managed nature's bounty well. While protecting the fragile ecology of the Himalayas by judiciously using the vast potential for generation of hydro-electricity, you have contributed to the well being of your people. India has benefited from this cooperation with an assured supply of power. Indeed, this is a win-win situation for both countries.

Chukha, Kurichu and Tala are symbols of Indian assistance, friendship and partnership for mutual benefit. Today, we have added Punatsangchu to this list and we look forward to undertaking several more such projects in the future. Bhutan also has a rich bio-diversity. We could cooperate in the field of traditional medicine by adding value to the rare and varied herbal medicines and convert them into marketable drugs.

Open borders and free trade provide the backdrop for our mutual relationship. The Festival of India in Bhutan, which began in June this year is an opportunity for the Bhutanese people to get a glimpse of the varied culture of India. I am glad that the celebrations are not limited to Thimpu alone but are being held in other towns as well. India is always happy to host the many Bhutanese pilgrims who visit major sites of Buddhist heritage in different parts of India. The India-Bhutan Foundation, which has been recently established, will contribute to a greater degree of people-to-people contact as well as civil society interaction. I am glad that the Crown Prince, as a patron of the India-Bhutan Friendship Association is taking keen interest in promoting an ever-closer friendship amongst our two peoples. It is a pleasure to see his commitment to the cause of India-Bhutan friendship.

Your Majesty, we are happy to note that the institutions and processes of participatory democracy are being strengthened. Power and authority are being increasingly devolved to the grassroots level. A written Constitution is being drafted, debated and discussed in the councils of state and amongst the ordinary people. All this is happening under Your Majesty's guidance and direction. We are aware of the tremendous love and affection with which the people of Bhutan look up to Your Majesty.

We are all aware that recent years have witnessed an upsurge in terrorism, insurgency and extremist activities globally as well as in our region. A strong global compact is being forged to combat this menace. Democratic societies cannot succumb to violence and terror unleashed by disgruntled elements. I am glad that our two countries are cooperating closely in addressing these issues.

In your brief stay in India, Your Majesty, you are meeting a wide cross-section of our leadership and our people. You will find a clear message in all your interactions - a message of India's total commitment to an ever-lasting friendship and cooperation with Bhutan, based on mutual trust and understanding. Together, we are working for a better future for our two peoples and indeed our whole region.

Excellencies, ladies and gentlemen, may I now invite you to join me in a toast: -

- to the health and happiness of His Majesty the King of Bhutan;
- to the prosperity and happiness of the friendly people of Bhutan;
- and to ever closer and warmer relations between India and Bhutan.

❮31❯

Address of the Hon'ble Vice-President of India, Shri Bhairon Singh Shekhawat to the Indian Community during the Indian High Commissioner's Reception at India House in seychelles (09.09.03)

The Vice-President said that Seychelles was "uniquely placed to play a role" in India's efforts to integrate its policies with Africa as part of its "Focus Africa" policy. He also appreciated Seychelles support on the issue of "cross border terrorism" and India's candidature for a permanent seat of an expanded UNSC.

Our High Commissioner, Mr. Mishra, Brothers and Sisters,

It is great to be here in your company. I feel at home in the India House. I hope you also share the same feelings.

I am happy that Indian community has a substantial presence and diverse spread in this beautiful island country. Many of you are occupying important positions in Secychelles and contributing substantially to the development and prosperity of this country, strengthening its beautiful pluricultural fabric. It is a matter of great pride that the Indians here are respected and loved by the local people and there has been a great degree of cross-cultural fertilization over the 200 odd years since the first bath of Indian immigrants reached these islands.

The Indian diaspora in recent times has been engaged in forging a constructive and symbiotic relationship with the motherland. Our Government encourages their active participation in all areas of national development. Overseas Indians are presently over 20 millions, dispersed over more than a hundred countries all over the world. Many have excelled in their adopted countries. Together they constitute a formidable force, both in themselves as well as in holding potential for ploughing back their resources and acumen toa the motherland. You are well aware that our Government organised the first Pravasi Bharatiya Divas (PBD) in January this year which will now be an annual feature. We value the participation and views of all our brothers and sisters living abroad. I am aware that the Indian community here has evinced interest in seeking dual citizenship. As you know, this has been considered for a few countries in the first stage and legislation on the subject is being brought by the Government.

India has fascinated the rest of the world since time immemorial. The cultural ethos of our country has the capacity to stay deep-rooted in the minds of its people, no matter where they live. It is the Indian way of life, all embracing, tolerant, multi-cultural, spiritual, which is our heritage and strength. This has been augmented by the Indian thirst for knowledge which has today found expression in our country being among the foremost in the knowledge revolution.

Friends, today, India's growth impulses are vivid and evident to everyone. India is developing fast. Our economy is steadily growing with a sense of confidence and abiding optimism. I am happy to inform you that Indian economy is resilient and is on fast track of growth. It is among top ten economies in the world and sixth largest reservoir of technical and professional manpower. GDP is growing at over 6 percent. GDP growth target in next five years is 8 percent. Inflation is very low, at present it is only 3.72 percent. We are not only self-sufficient in food production which is over 200 million tonnes, we have also become exporters of food grains and we have food stocks of over 35 million tonnes. Total, annual exports from India amounts to 50 billion dollars. The country has foreign exchange reserves to the tune of 85 billion dollors. India is a growing world force in Information Technology and Software. Our achievements in the fields of Atomic Energy, Space and Defence have also been spectacular.

I take this opportunity to compliment you all in Seychelles for having integrated themselves so well into the local milieu and for making significant contribution to the growth of the island nation, which is indeed the pivot on which Indo-Seychelles cooperation stands. Everyone of you is India's overseas ambassador and also an inheritor of our shining legacy. With your unwavering commitment to the country in which you are living, you are the bridge of understanding on which the cordial relations between India and Seychelles should continue to flourish.

I extend to you heartiest greetings on the auspicious occasion of Onam, the festival of harvest, which was celebrated yesterday with much gaiety and enthusiasm in Kerala and other parts of the country. Here also you must be filled with the spirit of Onam. May this festival bring happiness and prosperity to all of you.

Jai Hind.

‹32›

Statement by PM, Shri in AB Vajpayee in Lok Sabha on His Two Day Visit to Jammu & Kashmir (22.04.03)

PM Vajpayee informed the Lok Sabha that he had extended a "hand of friendship" to Pakistan during his two-day visit to J&K and insisted that "talks can take place on all issues, including that of Jammu & Kashmir". He also insisted that "stopping cross-border infiltration and destruction of terrorist infrastructure can open the doors for talks".

Following is the text of the Prime Minister, Shri Atal Bihari Vajpayee's statement in the Lok Sabha on his two day visit to Jammu & Kashmir :

"I went to Jammu & Kashmir on a two-day visit on April 18-19, 2003.

I had five programmes in Srinagar. The first had to do with the Foundation Stone laying ceremony for modernization of Srinagar Airport. This project would double the capacity of the airport. We would like international air services to start from Srinagar.

The second programme related to the National Highway Development Project. Under this, work on a four-lane highway from Srinagar to Kanuyakumari was launched. The newly elected Chief Minister of Jammu & Kashmir, Shri Mufti Mohammed Sayeed, had been insisting that work on this project in the Kashmir Valley should start as early as possible.

In my public rally, I congratulated the people of Kashmir on participating in the Assembly elections in large numbers. They exercised their franchise defying the threat of bullets. I assured them, "We have come here to share your pain and suffering. Whatever complaints you have, try to address them collectively. Knock on the doors of Delhi. Delhi will never close its doors for you. The doors of our heart will also remain open for you".

I assured the people of Jammu & Kashmir that we wish to resolve all issues – both domestic and external – through talks. I stressed that the gun can solve no problem; brotherhood can. Issues can be resolved if we move forward guided by the three principlies of *Insaniyat* (Humanism), *Jamhooriyat* (Democracy) and *Kashmiriyat* (Kashmir's age-old legacy of Hindu-Muslim amity).

In my speech, I spoke of extending our hand of friendship to Pakistan. At the same time, I also said that this hand of friendship should be extended by both sides. Both countries should resolve that we need to live together in peace.

My last programme was about the start of work on the construction of Udhampur-Srinagar- Baramulla railway line. It is our resolve to ensure that train services start in Kashmir Valley before August 15, 2007.

Unemployment is the greatest problem facing the youth of Jammu & Kashmir. We have decided to facilitate creation of one lakh opportunities for employment and self-employment over the next two years. For this, a special Task Force would be set up with representatives from the Central Government, State Government industry, Commerce, Banking and Financial Institutions. The Task Force will present its report by June 30 and implementation would commence from August 15 this year.

At a Press Conference before returning to Delhi, I expressed the hope that a new beginning can take place between India and Pakistan. I said that we have extended our hand of friendship. Let us see how Pakistan responds to this. Stopping cross-border infiltration and destruction of terrorist infrastructure can open the doors for talks. Talks can take place on all issues, including that of Jammu & Kashmir.

Thank You

April 22, 2003

❮33❯

Speech by Prime Minister Shri AB Vajpayee at Peking University (23.06.03)

The PM highlighted that the "combined strength" and "complementarities" of India and China in areas like economic development, knowledge based industries, and common positions on international issues like "multipolarity" and "authority of international organizations" formed the basis of an India-China partnership. To dispel fears of "rivalry" he suggested that the two countries should focus on the simple truth that there is "no objective reason for discord" between India and China.

Mr. Minister,
President of Peking University,
Distinguished Faculty Members,
Friends,

I thank you for inviting me to speak today at this renowned centre of learning. This premier University of China has had an eventful history, including migrating over 3000 kilometres during the Second World War to maintain its uninterrupted academic tradition.

You also have a special connection with India. We are grateful to your University for having sent Professor Tan Yun Shan to Shantiniketan many decades ago. It was he who inspired our great poet Rabindranath Tagore to set up the famous "Cheena Bhavan" in Vishwa Bharati University, of which I have the honour to be the Chancellor.

Today, we repay this debt in some measure by pledging our support for a Centre for Indian Studies in this University. I have just had the privilege of inaugurating that Centre and of making a symbolical initial donation to its library. My government is prepared to depute two faculty members from India to the Centre. We have pledged to contribute an amount of one million rupees annually for the first five years towards its running costs. We can fund an annual scholarship at an appropriate institute in India for a student of the Centre. We are also offering an annual prize of a three-week visit to India for the first-ranked student of the centre. I propose we call this the Tan Yun Shan Award in memory of that modern-day pioneer of India-China cultural understanding. We would be happy to extend any other form of support, which the Centre may require.

Friends,

Initiatives like the Centre for Indian Studies are specially welcome as part of our current effort to enrich the interaction between the India and China of today. We are, of course, two of the world's oldest civilizations with contacts over at least two millennia. The Silk Route connected us through commerce, but also by facilitating the free flow of our music, our scriptures and our literature. The message of the Buddha, transmitted from India, was received by millions in China. Our maritime trade links kept us in close contact and also created a confluence of our cultures with that of South-East Asia.

But there were periods in history when our civilizations went into an introspective phase and lost regular touch with each other. In a later era, both countries suffered from colonial invasions and deprivations, which accentuated this trend. The shadow of the Cold War and the consequent distortions of global international relations had its impact also on India and China. From relative isolation from each other, we went into a state of estrangement.

We have emerged decisively from this dead-end of mistrust, already a few decades ago. We have vigorously set about recovering our mutual understanding, building a broad base for our cooperation and redeeming the promise of our complementarities.

It is in this task of recovering mutual understanding that the Centre for Indian Studies can make a significant contribution. You have built up an impressive scholarship in Indological studies, focussing mainly on history, languages and literature. I would suggest that you also strengthen your scholarship on modern Indian political, economic and sociological studies. Distance encourages caricatures and stereotyped images, based on old experiences. Academic exchanges and contemporary studies help to bridge the gap of information and perceptions. You can make your centre fulfill Lao Zi's ideal of knowledge and understanding:

> "Without stirring abroad
> One can know the whole world;
> Without looking out of the window
> One can see the way of heaven."

We know where we have come from. Let us better understand each other as we are today, and comprehend where we can go together in the future. The better we understand each other, the more we can do together.

No objective analysis can deny the combined strength and complementarity of an India-China partnership:

- We are the two most populous countries of the world,
- We have the two fastest growing economies in the world–yours faster than ours. In any economic forum in the world these days, the focus is on India and China.
- Both of us have continent-sized markets, with the advantages of huge economies of scale.
- We also have the problems of continent-sized countries–unequal development, a wide spread of income disparities, and a potential digital divide. Exchange of developmental experiences can be valuable.
- We are both at the forefront of developing and applying the technologies, which drive the Knowledge Economy.
- We have a harmonious balance of strengths. India's strengths in Information Technology, software engineering, management and financial services are well matched by the Chinese expertise in hardware, construction and industry.
- Both India and China were present at the broader dialogue of developing countries with the G-8 countries in Evian earlier this month. I was struck by the congruence in our positions. If we acted in concert, it would be very difficult for the world to ignore us.
- India and China have frequently reiterated their commitment to the development of a cooperative multi-polar world order. In the complex international situation of today, we have a role to play in helping to restore the authority of the international organisations, which have been undermined in recent months.

Our two countries have been taking steps towards increasing mutual trust and understanding, through more intensive interaction. In recent years, our cooperation has greatly expanded and diversified. Our bilateral trade has shot up from around 200 million dollars in the early nineties to around 5 billion dollars. Indian business and industry have overcome their initial cultural and commercial apprehensions of Chinese business and are strengthening their linkages. The conclusive proof of this is the size and variety of the business delegation, which is here in China to coincide with the visit. It is also noteworthy that Indian investment in China is nearly 65 million dollars.

The India-China dialogue already transcends bilateral relations to encompass international issues such as terrorism, security, environment and sustainable development. We have an increasing commonality of interests within the World Trade Organization and overlapping concerns on globalization. Our co-ordination and collaboration in various multilateral institutions is expanding into newer and newer areas. A small, but important, example of such effective joint action is our cooperative effort to make the infrastructure lending policies of the World Bank more rational.

But, as I have said before, for two countries of our human resources, economic strengths and technological skills, we have only scratched the surface. Your senior leader Mr. Deng Xiaoping once said that the 21st century can only be the Asian century if India and China combine to make it so. To do so effectively, we should be conscious of our complementary strengths, resist contradictory pulls, and deploy our resources in a mutually reinforcing manner. Our trust and understanding should be able to withstand forces which seek to divide us.

I would like to dwell in this context on what is frequently described as "rivalry" between India and China. As two large developing countries at roughly the same stage of development, sharing the same neighbourhood, pursuing similar growth trajectories, with comparable economic priorities and similar political ambitions, it is inevitable that comparisons will be made between India and China. It is also an unavoidable characteristic of human nature that there is always a sense of competition between two close and equal neighbours.

But we need to clearly understand the difference between healthy competition and divisive rivalry. Even in the present-day world, you can find examples of countries which have maintained close political co-ordination, strengthened their economic complementarities and harmonized their international objectives, even while maintaining a healthy and good-natured economic and commercial competition. The developing world in general, and our two countries in particular, can benefit greatly by absorbing the lessons from these experiences. We should focus on the simple truth that there is no objective reason for discord between us, and neither of us is a threat to the other. These simple, but profound, principles should form the bedrock of the future India-China partnership.

One cannot wish away the fact that before good neighbours can truly fraternize with each other, they must first mend their fences. After a hiatus of a few decades, India and China embarked on this important venture a few years ago. We have made good progress. I am convinced that, with steadfast adherence to the Five principles of peaceful co-existence, with mutual sensitivity to the concerns of each other, and with respect for equality, our two countries can further accelerate this process so that we can put this difference firmly behind us. I am encouraged after my discussions with Premier Wen Jiabao that both our countries see an opportunity to proceed along this path.

It is a tryst with destiny, which beckons to us. When we redeem it, we can truly fulfill the ideal of close cooperation, described so colourfully by Gurudev Rabindranath Tagore :

"When daylight breaks, we are free from the enclosure and the exclusiveness of our individual life. It is then that we see the light, which is for all men and for all times. It is then that we come to know one another, and come to cooperate in the field of life."

India and China can create this destiny.

Thank you.

❮34❯

Speech by PM, Shri AB Vajpayee at the Asia Society in the U.S.A. (22.09.03)

In his speech PM Vajpayee dwelled upon the "irrefutable logic of the India-US partnership" while examining the main features of the emerging global environment. Giving the details of the present status of Indo-US relationship, the Prime Minister noted the role of the Indian American community in bringing the two countries together.

India-US Relations in the Emerging Global Environment

Ambassador Holbrooke,

Mr Menezes,

Distinguished Guests,

It is a pleasure to be here with Asia Society again. Five years ago, I addressed you on India-US relations. India was then facing a difficult international environment; and that included our relations with USA. Even then, I described India and USA as natural allies. I would like to return to that theme today, to reflect on the transformation in India-US relations, and on the global environment in which this transformation has taken place.

The end of the Cold War encouraged hopes of a rare era in history, when international relations would no longer be defined by great power rivalries. There may be differences on issues and disagreements on approaches, but conflict and confrontation do not overshadow the relations among great and emerging powers. There are debates on whether the international order will be unipolar or multipolar. There are questions about the balance between national interest and international responsibility; about national sovereignty and international obligations. These debates are inevitable, since we are still in the process of shaping the contours of the post-Cold War era.

Another dominant theme of our times is the interdependence of nations, accentuated by technological changes and economic inter-linkages. Globalization has touched every sphere of our activity.

The end of the Cold War had kindled hopes of an enduring era of security and stability. This has not happened. Instead, new political problems and security challenges have been thrust upon us.

Many newly independent countries still suffer from weak political institutions, economic stagnation and a deficit of democracy and modernity. This threatens the security of their people and that of their neighbours.

Globalization has promoted development and prosperity in some countries, but the uneven spread of its benefits has also created new disparities. The communications revolution has also resulted in the globalization of crime and terror, and even of epidemics and diseases.

Through all these uncertainties, we still have a unique opportunity today to shape global politics and international relations within a framework of plurality and equality, based on consensus, compassion, co-existence and cooperation. This cooperative world has to be development-oriented, to accommodate the interests of all.

To achieve this goal requires cooperation among democracies of the world to tackle the challenges, which have survived the Cold War, and those which have arisen more recently.

Continued terrorist attacks around the world remind us that the global war against terrorism, which commenced after the tragedy of 9/11, is far from over. Our long-term strategy to combat it should have four broad elements:

One, a concert of democracies acting in cohesion. A threat against one should be seen as a threat against all.

Two, Consistency of approach in demanding from all countries, the same high standards in combating terrorism.

Three, continuity of resolve, and clarity of purpose. We should not be drawn into the grey zone of conflicting policy objectives, which condone ambiguous positions on terrorism.

Four, to win the war against terror, we have to win the war of ideas. We have to expand the constituency of democracy by promoting the ideals of freedom, democracy, rule of law and tolerance, which are our defining strengths.

The post cold war age has also seen a significant proliferation of weapons of mass destruction and their delivery systems. Today, the threat of their falling into terrorists' hands looms large. The existing regimes for non-proliferation rigorously audit the performance of responsible states, but do not touch the proliferators. An honest reappraisal is required.

The structure of international political, security and economic institutions, established nearly sixty years ago, needs to be reviewed from the perspective of today's realities and future needs. Our international trade negotiations should place the development agenda at the centre of attention. We should not let status quo tendencies sabotage the long-term gains of genuine change.

Iraq and Afghanistan are two immediate test cases of our efforts to build a world order based on cooperation and partnership. In both cases, the way we address these challenges will have far-reaching implications for our common future.

In Iraq, we have to develop an international consensus, which accelerates the political, economic and security transformation in that country. In Afghanistan, we need to complete the work commenced by the Bonn process, and help its government to completely wipe out the remnants of Taliban, to establish full control over the entire country and to progress as scheduled towards national elections.

The future of Iraq and Afghanistan is vital for their citizens, but will equally have far-reaching implications for the region and for the world.

Distinguished Guests,

On many of these global challenges, India and USA share similar perspectives. We see our growing partnership with the United States of America as an important element in our efforts for a dynamic and cooperative multipolar world order. India-USA relations have undergone a major transformation in recent years. The strength of this relationship derives from a greater understanding of our basic commonalities. The end of the Cold War has enabled us to enhance our engagement, based also on a convergence of many geo-political perspectives.

In March 2000, President Clinton and I agreed that India and USA would be partners in peace in the new century, and share a common responsibility for ensuring regional and international security.

In November 2001, President Bush and I affirmed our commitment to transforming our bilateral relationship. We agreed that we should try to give this partnership the inherent strength to survive all future political changes in our democracies.

In India, my government's commitment to building this relationship enjoys support across the political spectrum. In fact, people often remark that progress is not fast enough! They seek immediate, dramatic results and media-friendly symbols of friendship. I tell them that one lesson I have learnt from four decades on the Opposition benches in Parliament is the virtue of patience! The transformation of our ties takes place after years of doubt and indifference. We have to guide it carefully, with a vision which extends beyond our immediate horizon.

The range and frequency of the India-US dialogue has increased considerably in recent times. It covers global and regional matters, as well as long term and near-term issues. But most significantly, it is the atmosphere of our dialogue that has changed. We now address each other with the confidence and candour of friends. This dialogue, based on respect and equality, is successful precisely because we have recognized that there is no fundamental conflict of interest between us. We work together on areas of Agreement, and frankly discuss our differing perceptions, without this affecting our relationship. This reflects the growing maturity of our friendship.

We have, for the first time, entered into substantive defence cooperation. Our Armed Forces have established contact, and there are regular exercises and exchanges of growing complexity. Our common concerns on terrorism, transnational crime and cyber crime have led us to establish ties in these areas as well.

India and USA are jointly exploring frontier areas of science and technology, including medicine, environment-friendly energy and advanced materials. We are working to re-establish ties in civilian space applications and in civilian nuclear safety. Information technology and the new knowledge economy are increasingly defining the story of our bilateral relationship. Our growing partnership in developing technologies of the future should take our bilateral relations to a qualitatively new level.

It is not only at government and official levels that our two countries are deepening and widening linkages. In educational institutions, scientific laboratories, offices and homes, and even in cyber space, Indians and Americans are discovering new identities of interest.

The Indian American community has played – and will continue to play – an important role in bringing us together. Through talent, hard work and enterprise, Indian Americans have risen to become one of the wealthiest minorities in this country. Their achievements – especially in IT, financial services, management and medicine – have contributed to America's progress. They have also created greater awareness in this country of the opportunities in the India-US partnership.

Distinguished Guests,

The Indian economy continues to grow. It has doubled in the last ten years, and we hope to redouble it in less than a decade. We are today the fourth largest economy in the world in terms of purchasing power parity. Our external reserves are about US $ 90 billion and are increasing by a billion dollars every two weeks. Our foreign trade is growing at double-digit rates. We are rapidly reducing our external debts. Our inflation rate is low and interest rates are on a declining curve. There is a strong increase in business confidence in recent months. Our reserves of food stock stands at over 30 million tonnes. Starting from scratch a few years ago, Indian software exports have reached US$ 10 billion per annum.

I have no doubt that the fundamentals of a rapidly developing India will strengthen our partnership with the world's largest economy. Our economic links will strengthen rapidly as India's economic growth creates new opportunities for investment and joint ventures. On both sides, there is recognition of the strong strategic value of the economic partnership.

Naturally, the vision of a new India-US relationship for the 21st century cannot be realised overnight. We still need to overcome internal resistance, old habits and traditional perspectives on both sides. Mindsets have to be changed in some quarters. We have to address vestiges of our past differences on security and proliferation issues. We must also ensure that the long term perspective of the India-US engagement is not diluted by short term exigencies.

In dealing with these hurdles, our two countries need the wisdom and foresight to recognize the irrefutable logic of the India-US partnership. We have laid the foundations of such a relationship. Our governments will sustain their commitment to it. Political, economic and strategic convergences will generate their own momentum to accelerate the pace of the transformation. An India-US relationship of maturity. substance and strength can have a major impact on the emerging world order in this century.

Thank you

‹35›

Speech by PM, Shri AB Vajpayee at the UNGA (25.09.03)

The PM said that the UN had a "crucial role to play in the political and economic reconstruction" of Iraq and in ensuring "compliance by member-states of their obligations under UNSCR 1373 and 1456" for combating global terrorism. In response to President Musharraf's offer to "encourage a general cessation of violence within Kashmir" in return for "reciprocal obligations and restraints", he stated that India "refuses to let Pakistan-sponsored terrorism become a tool of blackmail".

Mr. President,

We congratulate you on your election to the Presidency of the 58th session of the UN General Assembly. We wish you every success in our shared endeavours. You will have our fullest cooperation in your efforts.

As we gather here, in the wake of many momentous events over the past year, it is inevitable that we ponder on some fundamental questions about the role and the relevance of the United Nations.

The United Nations was charged by its Charter 'to save succeeding generations from the scourge of war'. The Charter also speaks of our collective determination *'to unite our strength* to maintain international peace and security'. There was an implicit conviction that the UN would be stronger than the sum of its constituent member-States. Its unique legitimacy flows from a universal perception that it pursues a larger purpose than the interests of one country or a small group of countries.

This vision of an enlightened multilateralism has not materialized. There have been difficulties and deficiencies in ensuring a world free from strife, a world without war. The United Nations has not always been successful in preventing conflicts or in resolving them.

During the past year, the United Nations encountered further new challenges. We saw the extraordinary inability of the five permanent members of the Security Council to agree on action in respect of Iraq, in spite of complete Agreement on basic objectives. Most recently, the brutal terrorist attack on the UN Office in Baghdad struck a body blow at the UN's humanitarian efforts there.

Looking back at events over recent years, we can analyze the successes and failures of the UN in this or that crisis. But it would be more purposeful to reflect on our own commitment to multilateralism, the extent of its applicability in the real world of today, and the manner in which it can be exercised through the UN. The reality is that international institutions like the UN can only be as effective as its members allow it to be.

Our reflections on the UN should focus on three key aspects:

- First, we need to introspect on some of the assumptions that have been made over the years on the will and reach of the United Nations. In the euphoria after the Cold War, there was a misplaced notion that the UN could solve every problem anywhere. Its enthusiasm and proactive stance on many issues reflected laudable intentions. But we soon realized that the UN does not possess magical powers to solve every crisis in all parts of the globe, or to change overnight the motivation of leaders and communities around the world. We need to clearly recognize, with a sense of realism, the limits to what the UN can achieve, and the changes of form and function required for it to play an optimal role in today's world.
- Second, the Iraq issue has inevitably generated a debate on the functioning and the efficacy of the Security Council and of the UN itself. Over the decades, the UN membership has grown enormously. The scope of its activities has expanded greatly, with new specialized agencies and new programmes. But in the political and security dimensions of its activities, the United Nations has not kept pace with the changes in the world. For the Security Council to represent genuine multilateralism in its decisions and actions, its membership must reflect current world realities. Most UN members today recognize the need for an enlarged and restructured Security Council, with more developing countries as permanent and non-permanent members. The permanent members guard their exclusivity. Some states with weak claims want to ensure that others do not enter the Council as permanent members. This combination of complacency and negativism has to be countered with a strong political will. The recent crises warn us that until the UN Security Council is reformed and restructured, its decisions cannot reflect truly the collective will of the community of nations.
- Third, even after such reform, the Security Council would have to evolve suitable decision-making mechanisms, which ensure better representation of the collective will of the international community. How can multilateralism be genuinely implemented? A single veto is an anachronism in today's world. On the other hand, the requirement of unanimity can sabotage imperative actions. A simple majority vote

may not be sufficiently representative for major issues bf gravity. Should we aim for the highest common factor, or should we settle for the lowest common denominator? National experiences in democratic countries provide usable models of mechanisms, which could specify the extent of support required, depending on the impact of action to be taken.

The Secretary General has rightly emphasized the urgency for reform of the institutions and processes of the United Nations. We encourage his efforts in this direction. We should seek to implement these reforms within a specified time frame.

Mr. President,

The Iraq issue continues to present a major challenge to the United Nations. At this point in time, it is not very productive to linger on the past. Our thoughts and concerns should be about the suffering of the people of Iraq. It is imperative that the people of Iraq should be empowered to determine their own future, to rebuild their nation.

The immediate priorities are ensuring security and stability, restoration of basic facilities and infrastructure, and a roadmap of political processes for a representative Iraqi government. It is clear that the UN has a crucial role to play in this process of political and economic reconstruction of that country. This has been acknowledged both by those who had opposed military action and by those who did not seek specific UN endorsement for it.

Mr. President,

One issue on which the UN showed remarkable unanimity after 9/11 was global terrorism. Security Council Resolutions 1373 and 1456 were unequivocal in condemning all forms of terrorism and in calling for united action against support, shelter, sponsorship, arming, training and financing for terrorism or terrorists.

Unfortunately, the solidarity in words has not translated into coherent and effective action. Terrorist acts continue to shatter our peace: from Mombassa to Moscow; from Baghdad to Bali. India has had more than its share in various parts of the country. The global coalition against terrorism has registered successes in Afghanistan, but has not been able to extend this elsewhere. Some of its members are themselves part of the problem. We are sometimes led into semantics about the definition of terrorism. The search for "root causes" or imaginary "freedom struggles" provides alibis for the killing of innocent men, women and children.

There is a lot that the UN can do to carry forward the war against international terrorism. Its Counter Terrorism Committee should develop measures to ensure compliance by member-States of their obligations under UNSCR 1373 and 1456. We should have credible multilateral instruments to identify States that contravene these Resolutions. Multilateral mechanisms must be created to detect and choke off international financial flows to terrorists and terrorist organizations.

A much better international system of information exchange and intelligence sharing needs to be devised to prevent terrorists from evading capture, simply by crossing national borders. No State should be allowed to profess partnership with the global coalition against terror, while continuing to aid, abet and sponsor terrorism. To condone such double standards is to contribute to multiplying terrorism.

Yesterday, the President of Pakistan chose this august assembly to make a public admission for the first time that Pakistan is sponsoring terrorism in Jammu & Kashmir. After claiming that there is an indigenous struggle in Kashmir, he has offered to encourage a general cessation of violence within Kashmir, in return for "reciprocal obligations and restraints".

We totally refuse to let terrorism become a tool of blackmail. Just as the world did not negotiate with Al-Qaida or the Taliban, we shall not negotiate with terrorism.

If we do so, we would be betraying the people of Jammu & Kashmir, who defied a most ferocious campaign of violence and intimidation sponsored from across our borders, and participated in an election, which has been universally hailed as free and fair. This was an unequivocal expression of both determination and self-determination.

When the cross-border terrorism stops-or when we eradicate it-we can have a dialogue with Pakistan on the other issues between us.

While on this subject, I would also like to point out to the President of Pakistan that he should not confuse the legitimate aspiration for equality of nations with outmoded concepts of military parity.

Mr. President,

We should be particularly concerned at the various recent revelations about clandestine transfers of weapons of mass destruction and their technologies. We face the frightening prospect of these weapons and technologies falling into the hands of terrorists. Surely, something needs to be done about the helplessness of international regimes in preventing such transactions, which clearly threaten international security. The same regimes expend considerable energy in imposing a variety of discriminatory technology-denial restrictions on responsible States.

Mr. President,

Our pre-occupation with terrorism should not dilute our commitment to tackle the non-military threats to human and international security. We have to sustain the fight against trafficking in narcotic drugs, human beings and small arms; the pandemic of HIV/AIDS; diseases like malaria and tuberculosis that grip developing countries and the degradation of our common environment. Food security, energy security and health security are important goals.

The countries of the North and of the South - the developed, developing, and transition economies-must resume their dialogue to build a better world for the present and future generations. For the agenda of globalization, Cancun was a disappointment. Significant progress was made at Johannesburg towards realization of sustainable development, but the entry into force of the Kyoto Protocol on climate change remains stalled. The Bio-diversity Convention has not yielded any tangible benefits to the world's poor.

International economic relations continue to be characterized by inequities and inequalities. Globalization has helped sections of the international economy, including some developing countries. However, large communities have been left outside its pale. It has engendered economic crises and instability in several developing countries, which have sharply increased poverty.

Poverty is multi-dimensional. It extends beyond money incomes to education, health care, skills enhancement, political participation at all levels from the local to the global, access to natural resources, clean water and air, and advancement of one's own culture and social organization.

Poverty alleviation requires resources on a far greater scale than now available. Globalization itself constrains developing country governments in raising public resources for poverty alleviation. The promise of the climate change and bio-diversity treaties to raise significant resources for investment and technology transfer is yet unrealized. The resources of multilateral and bilateral development agencies are limited by the failure of industrialized countries to enhance development budgets.

Therefore, if the current regimes of globalization and sustainable development are to be expanded-or even to survive-they must be directly harnessed to provide the necessary resources for poverty alleviation. In fact, all international Agreements and initiatives affecting developing countries have to be evaluated by their impact on poverty.

Developing countries need to coordinate their positions in international negotiations to promote the adoption of regimes, which would help poverty alleviation. The India-Brazil-South Africa Dialogue Forum, which was established earlier this year, is an effort in this direction.

Mr. President,

We in the developing countries do not have the luxury of time. Political compulsions force us to meet the aspirations of our people quickly even as we subject ourselves to newer and more rigid international standards and norms. We owe it to our future generations to make strong efforts to meet the Millennium Development Goals. There is a mutuality of interest in this between the developed and the developing countries. Global interdependence today means that economic disasters in developing countries could create a backlash on developed countries. We hope the world will act in this spirit of enlightened self-interest.

Thank you.

‹36›

Statement to the Indian Media by PM, Shri AB Vajpayee at the Conclusion of his visit to Bali and Thailand (12.10.03)

> The PM informed the media that ASEAN leaders underlined the potential for cooperation with India in "public health including joint research for medicines to deal with HIV/AIDS, TB and Malaria" and agreed to submit a "Vision 2020" document at the next India-ASEAN Summit in Laos. He also said that the Thai PM Thaksin and he had agreed to expedite the implementation of the Free Trade Area Agreement for elimination of trade barriers between the two countries.

"We will return to India after a rewarding visit to Bali and Thailand.

The 2nd India-ASEAN Summit in Bali marked the institutionalisation of our annual summit level dialogue with ASEAN. It enabled us to review the substantive progress in several areas of common interest to India and ASEAN since our first Summit meeting in Phnom Penh last year. We also discussed the future directions of our cooperation.

ASEAN leaders appreciated the fact that we have made remarkable progress on the substantive agenda that we spelt out at Phnom Penh.

Our Framework Agreement on Comprehensive Economic Cooperation was finalized within a year of our announcing that we would be aiming for it. Through this, India also demonstrated its ability and political will to deliver on its economic linkages within the region. We made it clear that we can proceed at a pace at which ASEAN is comfortable.

India reiterated its willingness to support new projects for training, education and capacity building to hasten the process of integration of the new ASEAN members.

ASEAN leaders welcomed our new offers for additional flight services from airlines of ASEAN countries to our major metropolitan cities and other tourist destinations. They shared our ideas for strengthening India-ASEAN road links. We agreed to join with ASEAN countries in efforts to liberalize the air cargo services sector. Our idea of an India-ASEAN Motorcar Rally to demonstrate our geographical links, drew an enthusiastic response from many ASEAN leaders. Here in Thailand also, Prime Minister Thaksin strongly supported the idea.

Several ASEAN leaders underlined the potential for cooperation with India in the field of public health, through pharmaceutical imports from India and joint research for medicines and measures to deal with diseases like HIV/AIDS, TB and Malaria.

I put forward the idea that ASEAN needs to be more closely integrated with India, China, Japan and Korea. An Asian Economic Community, including the 14 countries of ASEAN + 3 + 1, would more efficiently exploit our synergies.

We agreed to ask our thinktanks to submit to the next (Laos) India-ASEAN Summit a "Vision 2020" document, which would lay out the road map for future development of our relations with ASEAN.

By acceding to the Treaty of Amity and Cooperation in South East Asia, we have initiated a new level of political cooperation with ASEAN.

Our Joint Declaration on Cooperation in Combating International Terrorism is an important step forward in promoting cooperation to eliminate the scourge of terrorism from the region.

During my stay in Bali, I also had meetings with the Presidents of Korea, Philippines and Indonesia, and with the Prime Ministers of Vietnam, Singapore and China.

President Megawati and I welcomed the development of bilateral ties in recent times. We agreed to expand cooperation in combating terrorism. Ways of increasing trade between our two countries were also discussed. We expressed interest in undertaking railway projects in Indonesia. India was invited to invest in existing palm oil plantations of Indonesia or those now coming up.

In my meeting with the President of Korea, we agreed that our two countries should work to strengthen existing economic links. Korean companies have recently expanded their activities in India, using it as a manufacturing base for their global exports. President Roh and I agreed that we would strengthen the political aspects of our friendly relations. We have invited President Roh Moo-hyun to visit India in the first half of next year.

The President of Philippines expressed her country's keenness to deepen relations with India. She made a special mention of the contributions of the people of Indian origin to the Philippines' economy. I invited President Arroyo to visit India.

The Prime Minister of Vietnam and I agreed to maintain the momentum of our recent high-level exchanges, in keeping with our traditionally close ties. We talked about our cooperation bilaterally and within ASEAN.

In my meeting with Singapore Prime Minister Goh, we discussed the progress in other negotiations for our bilateral Comprehensive Economic Cooperation Agreement. We have set the target for finalization of the agreement in the first half of 2004.

My meeting with Chinese Premier Wen Jaibao touched on the substantive forward movement in our bilateral relations since our last meeting. To continue this process, we have agreed to expedite the establishment of the Joint Study Group on economic cooperation. The Special Representatives of the two governments will have their first meeting on the border question in the near future. :Premier Wen agreed to make a return visit to India s as early as possible.

Although it has been ten years since the last visit of an Indian Prime Minister to Thailand, our bilateral relations have developed rapidly, particularly in recent years. I was particularly touched by the Prime Minister of Thailand's attentive and warm hospitality, going well beyond normal protocol requirements. We also greatly appreciated Prime Minister Thaksin's commitment to developing our bilateral relations in all areas, and his support for India's dialogue with ASEAN.

In our discussions, Prime Minister Thaksin and I expressed our commitment to intensify our security cooperation and our joint efforts against terrorism. India and Thailand also agreed to work together against drug trafficking, and in joint naval patrolling against narcotics and piracy. We underlined the further scope for our economic cooperation and collaboration in areas like science & technology, tourism and civil aviation. We agreed to set up cultural centres in each other's country to reinvigorate our age-old cultural affinities.

The Framework Agreement for a Free Trade Area is the first between India and an ASEAN country. Through its Early Harvest Programme, India and Thailand can shortly reduce tariffs on 84 items of our trade. Prime Minister Thaksin and I agreed hat we would expedite the implementation of the Agreement, for the elimination of tariff and non-tariff barriers to the free movement of goods, capital and services within agreed time frames.

The other Agreements signed in Bangkok cover cooperation in tourism, biotechnology, agriculture and exemption of visa requirements for certain categories of passport holders.

Our decision to jointly work out a liberalized visa regime for business travellers between India and Thailand will have a positive impact on our economic exchanges.

Thailand has agreed to reciprocate our offer of increased flight services to Indian destinations, by offering daily flights to Bangkok and the freedom of operation to other cities in Thailand.

We agreed to set up a twinning arrangement between Port Blair and Phuket in Thailand and to develop combined India-Thailand tourism destination packages.

The Prime Minister of Thailand and I also discussed our close cooperation in various regional and multilateral institutions. Both sides underlined the importance of making early progress on trilateral transportation projects between India, Myanmar and Thailand. Prime Minister Thaksin responded positively to several of our initiatives in ASEAN.

My address to a specially-convened joint session of the Thai National Assembly, the first by a foreign leader, was a unique honour for India. I also addressed a meeting of Indian and Thai businessmen organized by the apex chambers of commerce and industry of the two countries.

I had the pleasure of an audience of an hour and a half with His Majesty the King at his palace in Hua Hin. Deputy Prime Ministers Korn Dabbaransi and Somkid Jatusripitak, Commerce Minister Adisai and Foreign Minister Surakiart called on me during my stay in Bangkok.

I was impressed by the Huai Hong Krai Royal Study Centre here in Chiang Mai. It is a striking demonstration of afforestation and sustainable development.

Both the India-ASEAN Summit and my bilateral visit to Thailand illustrated the depth and versatility which our relations with ASEAN and its countries have acquired. The development of closer political and economic linkages between India and ASEAN is in consonance with our efforts for a multipolar world order and for expanding our economic opportunities. The response of ASEAN to our initiatives has been unequivocally positive in all aspects".

Chiang Mai
October 12, 2003

❮37❯

Inaugural Speech by PM, Shri AB Vajpayee at the Third SAARC Information Ministers' Conference (11.11.03)

The PM invited all SAARC neighbours "to participate in India's economy, rather than be apprehensive about it". He also exhorted them to use the revolution in communications technology to ensure free flow of information and to "consider constructively, India's suggested guidelines on Trans-national Satellite Broadcasting in the region".

"It is a great pleasure to be here with you. As our Information & Broadcasting Minister has just said, I have somewhat delayed my departure for my tour abroad to share some thoughts with you on this important occasion.

Meetings of SAARC forums are welcome opportunities for exchange of views and perspectives among various strata of our societies, contributing to greater mutual awareness and better understanding. A Conference of Information Ministers is particularly valuable, since they frame our national policies on dissemination of news, views and perceptions through our mass media.

I have recently returned from an India-ASEAN Summit meeting in Bali, where we took many momentous decisions about closer integration between India and ASEAN. We concluded a framework Agreement on comprehensive economic cooperation–including free trade–barely a year after commencement of negotiations. We advanced towards an open skies policy for passenger traffic and for cargo services. We also discussed some significant sub-regional cooperation initiatives for BIMSTEC and the Mekong Ganga Initiative. Later this month, we will host an India-European Union Summit in Delhi, where similarly many new proposals for economic co-operation are on the anvil. In Moscow this week, I will also be discussing the multi-modal North-South transport corridor linking India, Iran and Central Asia with Russia.

I am mentioning all this, because such experiences in regional and sub-regional cooperation hold a lesson for SAARC.

Since its inception in 1985, SAARC has been struggling to emerge from the concept to the practical reality of close regional cooperation. The concept is to harness our abundant natural resources, our talented human energies and our industrial synergies to accelerate growth and development in our countries. We are yet to achieve this.

Post Cold War alignments and the technology revolution, have set in motion trends which we can ignore only at our peril. ASEAN is, of course, an old example of the triumph of economic organization over political differences. We can also see how post Cold War Europe has forgotten its former political divisions and accepted differential economic development, while expanding the European Union. Innovative regional and sub-regional arrangements are being launched in Africa, Latin America and the Caribbean region–including countries, which have a history of bitter hostility towards each other.

This is a dominant trend in today's globalising world. It is time that we recognize what it means for all of us in South Asia. If SAARC cannot organize itself, it will simply miss the boat. Other alignments will develop, to seize the economic opportunities offered by closer integration. We cannot forever be challenging logic and mocking economics.

I would like to take this opportunity to re-affirm that India is fully committed to the effort to build on our commonalities and shared aspirations for equitable development. I often hear the argument that our unequal physical sizes and economic strengths inhibit equal cooperation. I believe these very factors can be turned to mutual economic advantage by creating inter-linkages, which can enhance confidence and trust. The collective size of our markets creates economies of scale with obvious impact on costs of production and competitiveness.

We invite all our SAARC neighbours to participate in India's economy, rather than be apprehensive about it. We have repeatedly expressed our willingness to enter into preferential trading arrangements and free trade agreements within the SAARC framework. We are equally willing to do so with SAARC countries individually. With Nepal and Bhutan, we have had such special trading arrangements for decades. With Sri Lanka, we have gone a considerable distance down that road. We are making a beginning with Bangladesh also. As I said at the Kathmandu SAARC Summit, we are also willing to have special and differential treatment for the least developed SAARC countries.

All this has immediate relevance to Information Ministers, since the media today plays a crucial role in moulding opinions and shaping public attitudes. Technology changes have today led to an explosive expansion in media platforms–including newspapers and magazines, TV channels and radio stations, and the Internet. The mass media can no longer remain the monopoly of governments. Private initiative has permeated every sphere of media activity. There is a surge in the flow of information, education, entertainment and culture among the peoples of the world. At the same time, it has become economically viable to develop platforms for dissemination of programmes of special interest to specific communities.

This revolution in communications presents great opportunities to SAARC countries. We need to use the technologies, rather than try to suppress them. We should try to ensure that our populations have free access to all the media platforms in our region, so that they remain completely up-to-date, not only about major political events, but also economic, cultural and sociological trends in all our countries. In this way, the media can be a powerful force for information rather than propaganda, for education rather than prejudice, for awareness rather than misinformation. We can carry regular SAARC news programmes on national TV and radio channels. We should properly publicise and project SAARC activities within and outside the region. Information on developmental programmes and cultural events in individual SAARC countries should be aired in all the other countries of the region. This free flow of information, news, views and perspectives can do more for regional cooperation than any political exhortation. Since we are committed to SAARC, let us try this method.

For this Information Ministers' Conference, you have a rich agenda. It includes the evolution of a SAARC-recognised Regional Media Forum, annual conferences of editors from SAARC countries, training facilities for media persons and a SAARC Media Development Fund. I hope you will also consider constructively India's suggested guidelines on Trans-national Satellite Broadcasting in our region. I hope you will approach this agenda with the objective of genuinely strengthening all-round regional co-operation in information and media. To show India's commitment to this process, we would be willing to offer-under our technical and economic assistance programme–12 seats to SAARC countries in training institutions for various media disciplines.

I will conclude by extending my best wishes for your discussions at this Conference. Your deliberations should open new windows of cooperation. There is an overwhelming desire for friendship and cooperation at the level of the people of our region. We, as politicians, should respond to this demand."

‹38›

Address by PM, Shri AB Vajpayee at the Russian Academy of Sciences (12.11.03)

Prime Minister Vajpayee expressed concern that the level of economic ties between India and Russia did not conform to the excellent level of their political relationship. He highlighted that the two countries could pursue their similar goals of economic prosperity "through a synergy between scientific endeavours and business enterprises" as India's success in the pharmaceutical industry with Russian cooperation demonstrates.

"I am deeply honoured to be addressing this eminent gathering today. The Academy has played a significant role in the expansion of human knowledge, which has benefited not only Russian society, but, indeed, the entire world.

We in India have always admired the spirit of enquiry and the search for excellence that have marked the activities of the Academy. This is evident from the steady stream of internationally renowned scientists, including many Nobel Laureates that Russia has produced. I am happy that some of them are in our midst today.

I often wonder what accounts for the extraordinary stability and warmth of the relations between India and Russia. What nourishes the enduring goodwill between our two peoples? One thing is certain. The tree of our friendship does not have its roots in the thin topsoil of politics and ideology. For it has continued to grow inspite of the political upheavals and structural changes in our two countries.

Perhaps, a deeper reason lies in the spiritual and cultural affinity between India and Russia, which manifested in the extraordinary resonance between the best minds of our two countries. They were men who represented the "soul" of our two great nations. They were towering names in culture and arts, literature and poetry, science and technology who gave voice to the universal concerns and aspirations of mankind.

For example, we know what an immense influence the great Russian writer Leo Tolstoy had on Mahatma Gandhi in his formative years in South Africa. It inspired the Mahatma even to establish a Tolstoy Farm near Johannesburg for his early experiments in truth, non-violence and self-realisation through community service. Similarly, Rabindranath Tagore, the great Indian poet, was widely admired and revered in Russia for his passionate appeal for universal peace, love and harmony. Shortly before his death in 1941, which were the darkest days of World War II, he predicted that your country would be victorious against the forces of fascism. That prediction came true, thanks to the unparalleled heroism of your people.

This mutual resonance is also seen in the long tradition of intellectual interaction between our two countries in the various disciplines of the humanities and sciences that comprise the totality of human knowledge. The legendary Gerasim Lebedev, one of the first Russian scholars to write on India, learnt Sanskrit, Hindi and Bengali, and published his grammar of Indian languages in the late 18th century. F.I Sherbatsky was one of Russia's most well known specialists on Indian religions, philosophy and literature. A.P. Barannikov translated Saint-Poet Tulsidas' *Ramacharitamanasa* into Russian. I.P. Minayev, well known for his rich library of Sanskrit and Pali manuscripts, had established close friendship with Bal Gangadhar Tilak and Bankim Chandra Chatterji, two of the most respected names in India's Freedom Struggle. I am glad that this rich tradition of Indology, nurtured by the Institute of Oriental Studies and other institutions, has continued upto the present day.

The Roerich family occupies a unique place in the artistic, intellectual and philosophical interaction between India and Russia. Nikolai Roerich, one of the greatest painters in the 20th century, not only traveled to India, but made the Himalayas his home. His older son and fellow-explorer George Roerich has left behind scholarly work on Tibetan Buddhism. Next year marks the birth centenary of his younger son, Svetoslav Roerich, the great artist who lived in Bangalore. We are taking steps to restore his beautiful estate and turn it into a befitting cultural park. We are also planning to establish an International Roerich Art School in India. I am particularly glad that during my Prime Ministership, we have been able to make significant contributions to safeguarding the precious legacy of the Roerichs, which is our common heritage.

Today, I applaud the seminal work produced by the Indo-Russian Joint Commission on Social Sciences, in which your Academy participates with its counterpart institution in India, the Indian Council for Historical Research. Perhaps in no other foreign language has so much of great Indian literature, both ancient and modern, been translated as in Russian. It is a matter of pride for us that today more than 1400 Russian scholars and students are studying Hindi in Russia. Two years ago, during my visit to St. Petersburg, I had announced the establishment of chairs for the study of India at various institutions and universities in Russia. I am happy to hear that these chairs have since been activated, and are arousing great interest among the younger generation.

It is a matter of immense satisfaction for us that Indo-Russian co-operation in science and technology has evolved continuously. Today it represents perhaps the most dynamic aspect of our overall relationship. The Integrated Long Term Programme of cooperation in science and technology (ILTP) is one of the most elaborate bilateral programmes in the world. More than 2,500 scientific exchanges have taken place during the 15-year existence of ILTP.

Keeping with the challenges of modern times, our scientific cooperation now extends to the frontier areas of scientific research including bio-technology, informatics, nano technology, environmental protection, drugs, and development of new materials. This is in addition to the traditional area of cooperation in space, atomic energy and defence technologies.

Thus, what defines Indo-Russian relations is their all-sided and ever-growing character. During the past few years, dialogue and summit level meetings have become more frequent and productive than ever before. This has helped us evolve a comprehensive vision of Indo-Russian ties for the 21st century, reinforcing our conviction that the strategic partnership between India and Russia is a reliable factor in promoting peace, security and stability both in Asia and the world. Our current efforts are dedicated to enhancing this partnership to even higher levels. We are confident that this can be achieved with ease.

The reason for this optimism is that we have a long tradition of stable and continuous relationship unaffected by the tumultuous changes that have taken place in the world. There are no divisive issues in our relationship. Neither India nor Russia perceives a threat from the strength of the other. On the contrary, each sees a benefit for itself in the increased political and economic strength of the other. This is best illustrated by Russia's public and unambiguous support to India's permanent membership of the United Nations Security Council. Both countries have a common interest in the evolution of a multipolar world based on a cooperative security order. We are both opposed to unilateralism in international matters.

The fundamental factor behind the stability of Indo-Russian ties is the exemplary sensitivity both countries have shown to each other's concerns, including security concerns. We in India deeply appreciate Russia's consistent and strong support to our campaign against terrorism, inspired by religious extremism. This dangerous phenomenon is rapidly spreading its tentacles, posing a threat to the entire civilized world. Specifically, it is threatening the unity, territorial integrity and sovereignty of both India and Russia. President Putin minced no words in his address to the Indian Parliament three years ago, when he said that the same individuals, the same terrorist and extremist organizations are involved in terrorist acts from the Philippines to Kosovo, including in Kashmir, Afghanistan and Chechnya.

Both India and Russia are multi-ethnic, pluralistic, democratic countries. Therefore, intellectuals, scientists and all public figures have an important role to play in the fight against the forces of intolerance and violence. Our two countries have established a sound legal basis and a useful institutional mechanism for cooperation in the struggle against international terrorism.

The only area where our bilateral relations have made less than desired progress is economic cooperation. It is also that area whose importance in international relations has grown tremendously in recent times. Both President Putin and I have been concerned that the volume and quality of our economic ties does not conform to the excellent level of our political relationship. We need to convert the extraordinary goodwill between India and Russia into a thriving, visible, vigorous and mutually beneficial economic relationship. In this endeavour, we need to show both innovation and a sense of urgency.

We in India have followed with much admiration Russia's strong economic revival, overcoming the transitional difficulties your country faced a few years ago. In the same period, India has emerged as one of the fastest growing economies in the world, and become the world's 4th largest economy in terms of purchasing power parity. The world has begun to take note of India's rapid strides towards developing a knowledge-based economy.

Perhaps the most well-known of Indian achievements in the last few years have been the emergence of our software industry and India's preeminent position in IT and IT-enabled services. An Indian made supercomputer PARAM is being used at the Institute for Computer-Aided Design of this Academy. Today India is the fastest growing telecom market in the world. The information and communication revolution in India is closely followed by the emerging bio-technology revolution. We are expanding and modernizing our physical infrastructure–roads, railways, ports, airports and the energy assets–in a determined manner.

Although many economic and social problems persist, any visitor can see that India is now a nation on the move–stronger, more prosperous and more self-confident than ever before. We have now set before ourselves the goal of transforming India into a Developed Nation by 2020. President Putin is likewise committed to making Russia one of the world's great economic powers. Thus, both India and Russia are pursuing a similar goal, relying on our enormous human and natural resources.

How can we achieve this goal? I think that one of the most efficient ways would be through a synergy between scientific endeavours and business enterprises of our two countries. Such a synergy can bring rewards not only to business corporations, but also to scientists. More importantly, commercially sound application of science and technology will benefit millions of common people in their daily lives, both in our countries and around the world. India and Russia have already experienced this in the past. For example,

India's pharmaceutical industry, which is today globally recognized for its cutting edge R&D and its success in the low-cost development of new drugs, was established largely through our bilateral cooperation with Russia several decades ago. I see no reason why such an example cannot be emulated in the widest possible range of opportunities that can be identified in the regular interaction between the Academy and its partner institutions in India.

I have brought with me a 95-member business delegation from India on this visit. I am confident that our captains of trade and industry, and their Russian counterparts, would contribute to our reaching this goal.

Thus, I see a bright future for Indo-Russian relationship. However, I would like to inject here a note of realism. We should not rest on past laurels. Otherwise, stagnation would set in. We must follow a determined course towards continuous strengthening of political, economic, scientific and cultural ties. The Russian Academy of Sciences has a major role in this regard. We are ready to work with you.

I conclude by recalling the words of Nikolai Roerich, which are very apt for this occasion: *"The Indian heart is drawn irresistibly to the boundless spaces of Russia and India too has a great magnetism for the Russian heart. There is great beauty in this magnetism between India and Russia. Heart speaks to heart."*

I wish each and every one of you good health, prosperity and success in your endeavours.

Pust Vsigda bujdit Indiiskaya-Rossiskaya druzba!

Long-Live Indo-Russian Friendship!"

❮39❯

Extracts of the speech by PM, Shri AB Vajpayee at the Combined Commander's Conference (1.11.03)

The PM emphasized that "as we grow in our international stature, our defence strategies should naturally reflect our political, economic and security concerns." In this context, our war fighting doctrines must take into account the advances in IT, cyber and no-contact warfare, the RMA and the need for R&D establishments to make use of the talents and skills available in the private sector.

I am happy to be here with senior representatives of the Armed Forces, the civilian defence institutions and the political leadership of the country. On a day-to-day basis, we exchange information and discuss policy on important defence and military issues. This annual exercise provides us an opportunity to exchange strategic and security perspectives. It adds value to the process of governmental consultations.

In the twelve months since we last met, the world has been through some extraordinary experiences. The Iraq war opened up new post-Cold War divisions, with heated debates on the meaning and viability of a cooperative multi-polar world order. We saw the inability of the UN structures to deal with current world realities. A new acrimony developed among members of the P-5. There has also been a steep escalation of violence and terrorism in Asia, Europe and Africa.

We need to understand the true significance of these events and to draw from them the right political and strategic lessons for our long-term security.

Everyone knows that we live in a globalizing world, undergoing many simultaneous technology revolutions. But the evolution of the post-Cold War world and its impact on our political, diplomatic, strategic and security equations are not so well understood.

The end of the Cold War and disintegration of the Soviet Union gave a strong jolt to many of India's strategic and security assumptions of nearly five decades. The changed circumstances of the Indo-Soviet strategic alliance greatly affected India's room for diplomatic manoeuvre in the world.

The quality of many of our other relationships and alliances also suffered from the realignment of world forces.

All of you know how badly the collapse of the USSR disrupted our defence cooperation with that country.

Simultaneously, our security environment also deteriorated rapidly. The Russian retreat from Afghanistan released thousands of armed Mujahideens and Jehadis, whom Pakistan could re-direct into J & K. The present phase of cross-border terrorism began then.

I have mentioned these developments in detail, because I often wonder whether we have really comprehended their implications. The recent national discussions on events in Iraq showed that many in our country are still caught up in the time warp of a Cold War mindset and strategic assumptions of an earlier era.

Of course, we have emerged from these turbulences with many positive achievements. India exploited the fluidities in the emerging World Order to forge new links with democratic societies on the basis of shared values, common objectives, convergent worldviews and – more recently – a coalition against terrorism. We have experienced an economic resurgence by developing and using skills in the knowledge-based technologies, and by pragmatically accepting the consequences of globalization. The opening up of our billion-strong market to imports and investment has put India prominently in the global economic mainstream. The Pokharan nuclear tests and our ambitious missile development programme showed our determination to respond decisively to our security environment, inspite of all external pressures.

Without undue modesty, we can say that the combination of diplomatic repositioning, economic resurgence and military firmness has given India a new importance in the international league. We have re-established our cordiality with USA, while strengthening our strategic partnership with Russia. We have established Summit-level dialogues with the European Union and ASEAN. We have strategic dialogues, counter-terrorism linkages and other political and security interaction mechanisms with a large number of European and Asian countries........... The number of Heads of State and Government visiting India these days can be seen from the regularity with which Vijay Chowk is blocked off to traffic on two or three mornings virtually every week!

We have played an important role in the G-20 efforts at Cancun. We have had discussions on India-Russia-China trilateral cooperation, and – on an entirely different plane – an India-Brazil-South Africa dialogue. We are developing other regional and sub-regional linkages in Asia, Latin America and Africa.

Again, the magnitude of these developments is not fully grasped, as our foreign policy debates show. Too many of us are caught up in limiting ideologies and a limited vision of what India is doing and where it should be going.

As we grow in our international stature, our defence strategies should naturally reflect our political, economic and security concerns, extending well beyond the geographical confines of South Asia. Our security environment ranges from the Persian Gulf to the Straits of Malacca across the Indian Ocean, including Central Asia and Afghanistan in the North-west, China in the North-east and South East Asia. Our strategic thinking has also to extend to these horizons.

The relentless march of technology drives war-fighting doctrines and defensive strategies today. Information technology, cyber techniques and other elements of 'no-contact' war have revolutionized modern day military thinking. Operation Enduring Freedom and the recent war in Iraq again reminded us of this truth. Our defence strategists have to work closely with defence research and development establishments to ensure a smooth two-way interflow between technology and strategy. Since both technologies and strategies mutually transform each other, it is essential that the users of the technology – the field units – should also be in the loop. It is my impression that some streamlining may be required in this area.

Indian scientists and engineers, in India and abroad, are powering much of the technology explosion that the world is witnessing today. Many of them are in research laboratories in the private sector. In today's competitive world, it would be inefficient for our defence R&D establishments and equipment manufacturers not to make use of the talents and skills available in the private sector. This again is an area on which our defence establishments should focus more intensively.

In the recent past, I have been stressing the need to develop technologies to counter actions of terrorists and insurgent groups. This would also have to include WMD terrorism and cyber terrorism emanating from non-state actors. Given India's continuous exposure to the proxy war from across our borders, it is important that we evolve a comprehensive counter-terrorism doctrine backed by suitable capabilities of manpower and high technology equipment.

Friends,

We have regular discussions in the Cabinet Committee on Security and in security groups at other levels on the national security situation in our immediate neighbourhood. I will therefore touch on them only very briefly.

The use of neighbouring countries by various insurgent groups has helped to prolong insurgency in our North-eastern states, retarding their development. Deliberate efforts to inhibit access to these states also create hurdles to rapid economic growth. We have to adopt a two-pronged strategy to counter this:

- **One**, to use various means of persuasion with our neighbouring countries to choke off support to the terrorist groups;
- **Two**, to focus strongly on economic development and improved connectivity of the North East.

The activities of Maoist groups in Nepal cause us considerable concern especially because of their links with ultra leftist groups in India. Again, we need to devise innovative security measures to curb the mobility of Maoists and other insurgent groups across the India-Nepal border without inhibiting the people-to-people and commercial traffic between the two countries.

Our border with China has remained largely peaceful for the last few decades. During my recent visit to China, we agreed to raise our bilateral and other economic cooperation to a qualitatively higher level. The decision of the two Governments to appoint Special Representatives to discuss the boundary question from a political perspective was a particularly significant measure. A final resolution of the boundary question would release considerable military energies and finances for other more purposeful activities. It is therefore a strategic objective. To achieve it, we should be willing to take some pragmatic decisions.

In the larger picture of our regional interests, including energy security, Afghanistan and Central Asia are of great importance to us. We cannot accept Pakistan's implied claim to Afghanistan as an expansion of its strategic space. We will firmly withstand the crude threats that are being made against our Consulates in Kandahar and Jalalabad. Our economic assistance and other cooperation initiatives with Afghanistan will continue. We will similarly expand our cooperation in all areas with Central Asian countries.

I will also say a few words about our western neighbour, Pakistan. We have yet again announced some measures a few days ago to promote greater people-to-people interaction, cultural exchanges and economic cooperation. Our constant effort is to encourage those elements in Pakistan, who recognise the folly of permanent hostility towards India.

By our recent measures, we have also silenced the whispering campaign that the requirements of forthcoming elections dictate a harsh Pakistan policy. The political leadership of this country is well aware that the constituency for peace with Pakistan is much larger than that which favours hostility.

At the same time, we will continue to deal firmly with cross border terrorism and to insist that a meaningful dialogue with Pakistan is only possible when we see sincerity in the effort to stop cross-border infiltration and to dismantle the infrastructure of terrorism.

Friends,

We have talked about our security perspectives, specific security threats and the situation in our immediate neighbourhood. In the globalized world of today, every strategy is inter-disciplinary. It is, therefore, imperative to develop a close synergy between our security agencies, our armed forces, our diplomats and our Finance, Commerce, Energy and other Ministries. In the 21st century, war in whatever form can be won only through multiple levers of power.

I will conclude with my best wishes to the Senior Commanders of our Armed Forces present here. Through you, I send good wishes to your officers and men. India will remain proud of your patriotism and professionalism. I also compliment the three Service Chiefs for their exemplary commitment.

Thank you.
Jai Hind.

‹40›

Speech by PM, Shri AB Vajpayee at the Hindustan Times Symposium on the Peace Dividend: Progress For India And South Asia (12.12.03)

> The PM highlighted that "the investment inputs required to reap the peace dividend for South Asia are pragmatic policies, rational economics and popular participation". He stated that once we reach a stage where we can put aside our mutual rivalries and inadequate coordination, "we would not be far from mutual security cooperation, open borders and even a single currency".

The Prime Minister inaugurated Conference "Hindustan Times Leadership Initiative—The Peace Dividend: Progress for India and South Asia", here today.

Following is the text of the Prime Minister's inaugural address on the occasion:

"When the Hindustan Times Leadership Initiative invited me to this Conference, what really attracted me was the powerful imagery of the peace dividend as the engine of progress in our region. At the same time, I must confess to some sadness that–over half a century after all the countries of our region attained independence–this truth still needs to be emphasized.

The peace dividend for South Asia is the creation of new hope and opportunity for its billion and a half people. We need no stronger justification for peace than this simple statement. The investment inputs required to reap this dividend are pragmatic policies, rational economics and popular participation.

There can be no argument about our inherent advantages, common interests and complementary strengths, which present a tremendous opportunity for our region to realize its full potential:

- First and foremost, our rich and varied human resources. Our citizens have created waves around the world with their technical, financial and managerial expertise. Their energies and talents can find greater application in regional co-operative enterprises.
- Second, our populations are younger than the world average, and will therefore constitute an increasing proportion of the global workforce in the future.

- Third, our technological advances have put us at the vanguard of today's Knowledge Economy, enabling us to accelerate our development process.
- Fourth, the size and increasing purchasing power of our collective market create economies of scale for cost-effective production.
- Fifth, efficient exploitation of our synergies can vastly enhance intra-regional trade, even as we work towards a rule-based international trading regime.
- Sixth, the region has massive untapped capacities for hydropower and unexploited hydrocarbons, which can more than meet its huge energy deficit.
- Seventh, the rich diversity of our bio-resources – in the Himalayan region and elsewhere–are yet to be exploited for our common benefit.
- Eighth, our combined political weight and economic strength can give us considerable leverage in pursuing our shared objective for a co-operative multi-polar world order.

The peace dividend lies in converting this exciting potential into vibrant reality. Our region is heir to a centuries old tradition of tolerance, pluralism and creative interaction. We need to re-capture this ethos in the modern context.

In the post-Cold War world of globalisation, countries around the world are increasingly focusing on regional economics. Political disputes have been resolved diplomatically or quietly deferred for tackling at a more opportune time. Conflict has given way to cooperation; dialogue moderates differences. There is a clear recognition that hostility only stunts economies, inhibits trade and retards progress.

This realization has dawned not only in the developed world, but also in developing regions that have experienced bitter differences and violent conflicts in the past. It encompasses Mercosur and the Andean Pact, COMESA and SADC, NAFTA and APEC. Nearer home, we have the outstanding example of ASEAN. South Asia needs the wisdom to heed these lessons.

By most estimates trade within regions accounts for nearly three-fourths of global trade. Yet, inspite of our geographical proximity, shared economic characteristics and similar development infrastructure intra-South Asia trade is under 5% of our total foreign trade.

We must discard the myth that, because of the asymmetries in our economies, the smaller countries do not benefit from closer economic integration within South Asia. Our Free Trade Agreements with Nepal and Sri Lanka have resulted in narrowing the trade deficit of both these countries with India. In fact the success of the India-Sri Lanka Free Trade Agreement has inspired us to expand its scope to cover services and investment in a comprehensive economic partnership agreement.

Energy is one area with the greatest promise of mutually enriching partnerships. Nepal and Bhutan today have an estimated potential of 100,000 MW of environmentally clean hydro-power. Bangladesh has similarly promising reserves of natural gas. They need to sell these energy sources. India is the only viable buyer and its energy demands are expanding exponentially. There is obvious scope for win-win arrangements. The hydroelectric projects in Bhutan illustrate this dramatically. Bhutan's per capita income of $ 600 today is expected to double by the end of 2005, when the 1020 Megawatt Tala power plant is completed.

The optimum management of our regional water resources for irrigation, navigation and flood control can have a multiplier effect on infrastructure, development and growth in our entire region. This requires not only financial investments, but also maturity of policy. We should recognise that an enduring partnership can only be built on the basis of each country wisely exercising the rights of a lower riparian, and responsibly fulfilling the obligations of an upper riparian.

Our region sits astride the land routes and sea lanes that connect the worlds' big energy sources of the Middle East to the expanding energy markets of East and Southeast Asia. With our extended neighbourhood of Iran and Afghanistan, our land mass also links the new energy sources of Central Asia with the warm water ports of the Indian Ocean in the South. It does not require much imagination to envisage how close regional co-operation can cash in on the strategic importance of our location.

Our most important common war today is against poverty, disease, hunger and under-development. We can share experiences and promote intra-regional linkages for economic and social development. A small, but significant, beginning has been made by our SAARC Experts Group on Poverty Alleviation. The Group, drawn from all SAARC countries, has extensively documented best practices in poverty alleviation programmes across the region. It has made detailed recommendations for regional dissemination of information on these practices and for regional capacity building. We have to show dedication in implementation of these recommendations and multiply such examples of regional experience sharing.

As we develop greater economic stakes in each other, we can put aside mistrust and dispel unwarranted suspicions. We will also develop mutual sensitivity to each others' concerns and promote more of our common interests. If we provide legitimate avenues of free commercial interaction, we can eradicate the black market and underground trade. We could jointly tackle smuggling, drug trafficking, money laundering and other trans-national crimes, which today flourish in our region because of our mutual rivalries and inadequate co-ordination. Once we reach that stage, we would not be far from mutual security cooperation, open borders and even a single currency.

If this seems unrealistic and utopian, perhaps we are being unnecessarily cynical. Let us remember that the world did not anticipate the sudden end to the Cold War or the collapse of the Berlin Wall. No one thought Apartheid South Africa could be transformed bloodlessly into Mandela's Rainbow Country. Not many political analysts would have predicted that the hostile suspicion between Russia and China could be converted in such a short time into a strategic partnership.

Each one of these developments flowed from objective factors in the global environment, but actually occurred because of some enlightened and responsible decisions by people at the helm of affairs.

I would suggest that the demands of globalisation and the aspirations of our people provide the objective bases for our energetic pursuit of a harmoniously integrated South Asia. Our people, businesses and organisations are waiting to interact more closely with each other. This includes producers and consumers, investors and markets, doctors and patients, artists and audiences, students and universities. They are all part of the supply and demand dynamics of a vast sub-continent. They see the unexploited potential in their own neighbourhood. They have waited for over an half-century for its fulfilment and are now impatient to move ahead.

We can sense this impatience in the outpouring of popular sentiment after our initiatives. The increased travel between India and Pakistan of Parliamentarians, businessmen, artists and sportsmen show the intense desire for amity and goodwill. We have to respond to this desire by seeking every possible way to banish hostility and promote peace.

If we in South Asia look back objectively at the experiences of our freedom struggles and of our nation-building, the one stark lesson that stands out is the imperative of forging a unity based on our commonalities. Whenever we have dissipated our energies in internal squabbling, external forces have come in to sort out our differences and stayed on to exploit our resources. We should never create the possibility of reliving these historical experiences in new forms and on different fronts

All these are aspects which your Conference could discuss as it exchanges ideas on the economic, strategic and geopolitical future of India and South Asia, ahead of the forth coming SAARC Summit. Our search for pragmatism, maturity and wisdom will have to involve both Governments and civil society. It will also require a wide-spread understanding that in today's context, collective regional interest is an expression of enlightened self-interest.

New Delhi

December 12, 2003

❮41❯

Inaugural Address by by Shri Yashwant Sinha, External Affairs Minister of India on "Diplomacy in the 21st Century" Organized by the Foreign Service Institute (03.01.03)

> The EAM made a distinction between diplomacy and foreign policy and gave a brief history of the transformation of diplomacy from the ancient to modern times. He listed several challenges before Indian diplomacy in the 21st century: "Upgradation of Foreign Service"; proficiency in the use of latest "communication and information technology"; making economic diplomacy as the "mantra within the Ministry of External Affairs"; developing the instruments to enhance India's "soft power" and building a sound "foreign policy establishment".

Shri Santosh Kumar, members of the Indian Foreign Service Batch 2001, distinguished colleagues from the past, ladies and gentlemen,

I am extremely happy to be here today to deliver the First Distinguished Persons Lecture organized by the Foreign Service Institute and to attend the Valedictory function of officer trainees of the 2001 batch. I wish the young officers of the Foreign Service the very best in their careers. I am sure they have a bright future ahead of them and that all of them will do India proud in the years to come.

Friends, I chose the topic of today's talk – "Diplomacy in the 21st Century" with some deliberation. I have already spoken on the topic of India's Foreign Policy in other fora. I thought I should focus today on diplomacy as distinct and different from 'foreign policy'.

Many people use diplomacy and foreign policy interchangeably. It is, therefore, important to clarify the difference between the two at the very outset. Harold Nicholson (I discovered his book with great difficulty because I have read it in my university days), the well known author of many books on diplomacy describes diplomacy as the executive aspect as compared to foreign policy which is the legislative aspect. Diplomacy is the means by which foreign policy is implemented. Foreign Policy is therefore the larger framework and strategy which countries evolve to advance their national interests. It is formulated by the political leadership of each country on the basis of inputs from various sources such as the Foreign Office and Embassies abroad, other Ministries, State Governments in our case, experts and think tanks, the Parliament, media etc. Diplomacy on the other hand is the principal tool or set of tools by which Foreign Policy is executed and given shape to.

To proceed then to the substance of today's topic, it is important to begin with some history. What is striking about the transformation of Diplomacy from ancient to modern times is the fact that it has been marked by both continuity and change. I am sure many of you would have seen a recent article in the 'Economist' on life of Ambassadors in London towards the end of the 15th Century when the institution of permanent and resident Ambassadors was still in its infancy. The article titled "Sent abroad to lie" reflects the popular myth which has prevailed for centuries that diplomats are persons sent abroad to lie for their country. At the same time, it also describes how precarious the life of Ambassadors was in those days. How they appeared to live in great luxury and splendour but in reality had a tough time making two ends meet, how the state of communications forced them to make up their briefs as they went along. Apparently, Ambassadors even used to hover around Royal Courts to get a free meal. I wonder if this is how the much talked about diplomatic entertainment had its origins. Much of the complaints our Foreign Office receives from various Missions regarding inadequate foreign allowance, problems relating to security of Missions and its personnel, lack of timely instructions from Headquarters etc. even today echo the travails of Diplomats in the 15th Century.

Diplomacy has evolved and transformed with the changing nature of the world and global problems. Yet, some basic problems and practice remains the same. Scholars of diplomacy tend to divide diplomatic history into 'Old Diplomacy', 'New Diplomacy', 'Total Diplomacy' etc. Old Diplomacy is of the variety we discussed above when Ambassadors had powers to even declare war on behalf of States they represented. New Diplomacy is characterized by the practices of the democratic age where negotiations are conducted in public and there is popular participation in decision-making. Total Diplomacy describes the age where the scope and expanse of diplomacy covers virtually every aspect of contacts between nations and their people.

We, in India, can trace the evolution of our diplomacy on similar lines as the above. For example, there are references to diplomatic practice in our great epic *Mahabharata*. The episode of Krishna going as an emissary of the Pandavas to negotiate with the Kauravas is well known. This story reflects how the use of emissaries to engage in political negotiations was prevalent in ancient India. It highlights the importance attached to resolution of disputes through dialogue and peaceful means. It advocates the need for concessions and compromise from both sides in any dispute. It also refers to the principles of diplomatic immunity and the danger of horrendous war when negotiations collapse. The *Arthashastra* of Kautilya contains similarly a large section on policy between kingdoms.

India, after independence made a signal contribution to diplomacy by ushering in the "Non-Aligned Movement". India can be considered a pioneer in "Developing Country Diplomacy" which involved efforts to place issues such as development, de-colonization, racism etc. on the international agenda. Even today in the UN and other multilateral fora, India retains its image as a country which is in the forefront of putting across developing country perspectives on international issues. We, in India, have proved by our talent and contributions that skills in diplomatic practice are not the monopoly of rich and the powerful or exclusive to the Western world.

Speaking from my personal experience of the last six months as Minister of External Affairs, let me emphasize four points. Firstly, the Indian Foreign Office and our Missions abroad are today truly in an age of Total Diplomacy. Foreign relations is defined and interpreted by us in the broadest possible fashion. There is no issue pertaining to contacts between India and other countries that the Foreign Office is not interested in or concerned about. For example, the Ministry of External Affairs is actively engaged in promoting Free Trade Areas between India and other parts of the world. It is part of decision-making process on WTO matters. It closely works with CBI and MHA on issues such as extradition. It interacts closely with the Ministry of Defence and National Security Council on security related issues. It engages the United States on matters of high technology commerce. It is the lead agency for the India-Russia Inter-Governmental Commission which deals with all issues of economic, commercial and scientific interaction. It is organizing in the next few days from now the first ever *Pravasi Bharatiya Divas*.

The pace and intensity of diplomatic activity that India is engaged in today is the second factor that deserves special mention. In the last six months, I have interacted with over 80 Foreign Ministers. The list of visitors to India in 2002 fills over three pages and include all important nations of the world. (Zhu Rongji in January 2002, Putin in December 2002, Khatami in January 2003 and a large number of senior visitors from the U.S., EU and our extended neighbourhood).

Thirdly, technology has transformed our diplomacy. I had an important conversation with Foreign Minister Ivanov of Russia even when I was in Cape Town. Secretary of State Collin Powell is a person I am frequently in touch with over telephone irrespective of where I am and where he is. In fact, he is going to talk to me when I get back from here today. The mobile phone thus transcends barriers of space and geography. It enables instantaneous communication at the highest levels. Similarly, internet and e-mail is bringing increasing information to us on an instant basis and enabling us to put across India's message effectively to the rest of the world.

Fourthly, non-state actors are playing an increasingly important role in the advancement of India's foreign policy interests. This includes 'Track II' exchanges, Joint Business Councils, activities of organizations like CII and FICCI, the media and others.

Some have argued that the change in the nature of diplomacy has rendered the diplomat or the permanent Ambassador in foreign countries irrelevant. The speed of communications and active involvement of principals such as the Foreign Minister and the Prime Minister have reduced the role of our Missions abroad. The above arguments, in fact, remind me of the situation of District Magistrates in our country when confronted with law and order problems such as riots, communal tensions etc. Philip Mason in his book called "The Men Who Ruled India" talks about how a Divisional Commissioner left the district at the time of a riot so as to give the District Magistrate a free hand in handling the problems. I can well imagine the difficulties faced by some of our Ambassadors who have Headquarters and delegations from India constantly breathing down their necks. When I was Consul General in Frankfurt, I had a similar experience.

It is true that today political leaders are directly involved in negotiations and are in frequent touch with each other. Moreover, the growing complexity of issues dealt with by nations such as trade, disarmament, environment, terrorism etc. have expanded the role of specialists as compared to the traditional Diplomat whose primary expertise is in negotiations and in cross-cultural understanding. Today, there is even talk of "Virtual Missions" which exist in cyber space emerging in the future. However, I still cannot visualize a situation where our Missions abroad or our Ambassadors become irrelevant. 'Our man on the spot' continues to play a critical and invaluable role as the eyes, ears and the voice of the Indian Government and people. A good example is the recent incident involving Mr. Arun Jain of Polaris who was detained in Indonesia. Our Ambassadors in key stations such as Washington, Beijing, Moscow, Islamabad, Colombo, Dhaka and others provide vital inputs into making policy. The understanding they contribute to the making of policy based on their local knowledge and understanding of events as well as personal interaction with policy makers in the host country is something irreplaceable by anyone or anything else.

What are the principal challenges that are likely to confront us in the 21st Century? There are many issues that can be listed. Terrorism will continue to remain a primary concern. Mobilization and management of the forces of globalization will be another priority. We need to enhance our comprehensive national strength and in particular speed up efforts in the field of economic development. We must, however, accomplish this without aping the western model of development with its disastrous impact on environment and natural resources. We need to evolve new patterns of not only sustainable development but also sustainable consumption.

As an emerging economic power, we have to work hand in hand with Indian industry and business to expand India's presence to all parts of the world. Assuring energy security will be a key goal of the future. We need to preserve and protect our culture as well as indigenous systems of knowledge. Developing our high-tech capabilities including in the field of defence and defence production will be another important task. We need to pursue our candidature for permanent membership of the UN Security Council. In short, India's Foreign Policy in the 21st Century will be aimed at enabling and facilitating India's rapid emergence on the world stage as a major player through the building of both its domestic strength as well as global influence.

I believe that our practitioners as well as practice of diplomacy have served us well in the past. There is, however, need for continuous introspection and constant refinement. In a rapidly changing world, the Ministry of External Affairs and its Missions must be ahead of times.

Secondly, our Foreign Service needs to be upgraded both in terms of manpower as well as quality of human resources. (I am not saying this simply because some former members of the service are present here. But I have no hesitation in saying that the batch of 2001 should remember that you are joining a Foreign Service that has upheld the best traditions of diplomatic service anywhere in the world.) As an emerging world power, 600 and odd Officers are not sufficient to provide the sinews for Indian diplomacy. Simultaneously, there must be greater and more systematic training. Language training is important and essential. But, that alone will not suffice. We need to train our officers in counter terrorism, WTO matters, global economics and finance, the intricacies of nuclear command structures, concepts of deterrence, missile defence, environment etc. In this connection, I compliment the FSI for the initiative it has taken to develop 'on line training' for Diplomats and would encourage it to become more ambitious in its efforts.

Thirdly, our Diplomats should be at the vanguard of using the latest of communication and information technology to advance India's interests. For example, I have directed that a programme to computerize the issue of visas in all key Missions across the world be completed as quickly as possible.

Fourthly, economic diplomacy should become a *mantra* within Ministry of External Affairs. We need to expand our outreach to State Governments as well as to the Chambers of Commerce and Industry within India. Our ITEC programme must be revamped, if necessary with the help of private consultants. Co-ordination with other economic Ministries must be institutionalized with a view to ensuring maximum impact for our investment and trade promotion efforts. With these goals in mind, the Commerce and Industry Minister and I recently led a high level review involving senior officials of both Ministries to look at what steps needed to be taken in this regard. A special inter-Ministerial task force has been constituted at the behest of the Ministry of External Affairs to examine what can be done to strengthen economic relations with our immediate neighbours in South Asia. Instructions have been issued to Missions in Africa and Latin America to actively explore the possibility of preferential and free trade arrangements with them. India's diplomacy will further need to develop expertise in facilitating the expansion of India's industrial and commercial presence overseas. It will also need to be equipped to provide to our companies support when incidents such as the one involving the Polaris Chief occurs.

Fifthly, India has always exercised a great amount of 'soft power' in the world and a large number of soft power instruments are available to us today. We need to develop and perfect them. For example, Indian culture and cuisine continue to grow in popularity across the world. Bollywood is growing in its strength and global reach. Indian intellectuals who live abroad like Amartya Sen and Jagdish Bhagwati have a distinct impact on the influential academic communities in which they work. Indian writers like Rohington Mistry are bringing us new friends every day. Moreover, Non Resident Indians and People of Indian Origin are extremely important sources of support for the Indian Government in the execution of its policies through the influence and respect they command in the countries in which they live.

Finally, we must build a sound 'foreign policy establishment' within India to supplement and contribute to the efforts of the Government in the field of foreign and security policy. While several think-tanks exist and are undertaking important work, much more remains to be done in terms of institution building in this field. A major step has been taken with the constitution of the National Security Council and the National Security Advisory Board. Proposals for setting up a National Defence University is also under consideration. We need to do much more to build expertise on our immediate neighbourhood, China, Central Asia, ASEAN, Gulf and other countries in our extended neighbourhood. Needless to say, the interface between our academic community and Government also must be streamlined.

To conclude, India has the ability to emerge as a great power and the will and determination to achieve this goal. During the first decade and a half of our independence, India played a stellar role in world diplomacy. We were trouble-shooters for the world. Our involvement in the resolution of disputes was sought after by others because we were seen as genuinely independent and effective interlocutors. We attained status and honour in the international community at that time by the sheer dint of our conviction, our sincerity, our intellectual abilities and because our policies were right. It was also because we were led by men of vision like Nehru. Our capabilities at that time were extremely limited. Our hard power was minimal. But, we ascended tremendous heights.

In contrast, we today have both the capabilities as well as the opportunities. We have built significant national strength in every sense of the term. We have averaged 6% growth rate over the last decade and are now targeting 8%. Our foreign exchange reserves are nearly US$ 70 billion. From a food shortage country, we have become an exporter and donor of food grains. Our software industry is envy of the world. We are a nuclear power. We also possess significant conventional capabilities. We have an advanced defence production industry. Our space, nuclear science, bio-tech and other high-tech capabilities are a matter of pride. Most of all, our human resources are among the best in the world.

The need of the hour, therefore, is simply for us to 'get our act together'. India's diplomacy in the 21st Century should become a force that brings together all the elements of soft power and hard power that are at her disposal today and converts them into a powerful tools for advancing India's interests and global peace. Indian diplomacy in 21st Century should guide and lead India to her promised tryst with destiny. And, let me affirm with confidence, I am certain that we shall succeed in this endeavour.

Thank you very much.

❮42❯

Inaugural Address by Shri Yashwant Sinha, External Affairs Minister At the Seminar on South Asian Cooperation Organised by the South Asian Centre for Policy Studies, Dhaka (10.01.03)

The EAM expressed his disappointment at the slow progress in SAARC on trade issues, analyzed the reasons and went on to suggest that "we move forward from SAARC and think of a South Asian Union", which in due course, will acquire a political dimension as well.

Thank you Mr. Vohra, Shri Gujral, Dr. Sobhan, Shri Dubey, Ladies and Gentlemen.

I am very grateful to the organizers for having invited me to this function this morning. Mr. Vohra was quite right in saying that I had been approached some time in December, I don't remember the exact date, to be present here today. The programme was uncertain at that point of time and I hope it has been noted, I said the programme was 'uncertain'. I had said that I will try and come if we don't go to Islamabad. Unfortunately, the Summit has been postponed. But just as there is a silver lining to every cloud, it has given me an opportunity to be present here today.

I have listened very carefully to what Mr. Vohra and Dr. Sobhan had to say. I note that both of them referred with a degree of both nostalgia and regret to an occasion 20 years ago led by Trilok Singhji in which Dr. Sobhan was also present. As we sit here today and discuss issues, we have to perhaps look at those 20 years and why we have not reached where we should have reached during this period.

The Seminar being organised today is from the point of view of policy extremely important. That is the reason why I am here. I shall look forward to a report of the day long discussions which is going to take place and the conclusions which you will be arriving at. I am sure that not only in India but in all countries of South Asia they will become an important input for policy.

Dr. Sobhan was referring to the festival of People of Indian Origin which is going on in Delhi and which was inaugurated by the Prime Minister yesterday. He is quite right in saying that there is a great deal of similarity between what is happening there and what we are trying to do here. We have a shared history. We have so much in common. We are joined together by geography and, therefore, there is no way we can either ignore each other or not afford to be friendly and cooperative. We must live with each other.

But there is an element of geography which is beyond our control -the element that India is a large country and that we have a billion or over a billion people. Just as there is a reality of seven sovereign countries in South Asia, similarly, there is a reality of the size and population of India. Therefore, my first point is that our size and our population need not be held against us. There is nothing we can do about it. It is there. I notice that it arouses some suspicions. It arouses some apprehensions. I hasten to add that these suspicions and apprehensions are not well founded. We have no other desire or intention than to be able to live in peace and friendship with our neighbours and join in the common task of improving the quality of life of our people.

It is with that desire and it is not a new desire that our Prime Minister Mr. Vajpayee when he was the Foreign Minister in 77-79 made a conscious effort to evolve a good neighbourhood policy. He is the one who encouraged me to follow this policy when I took my present assignment. We are lucky today that we have Mr. Gujral amidst us. It was in 1996 in a Chatham House speech that we heard of the famous Gujral Doctrine. India remains committed to the good neighbourhood policy of Mr. Vajpayee. India remains committed to the Gujral Doctrine and today, I would like to say that we are prepared to move further ahead also in the direction of peace, friendship and prosperity with all our neighbours.

I am going to make some suggestions today which I hope SACEPS will take notice of. SAARC was created in 1985 if I am not mistaken. Under the leadership of people like Trilok Singhji, we have been discussing this for over two decades. But unfortunately, we have not been able to make progress under SAARC, the kind of progress which was perhaps necessary, desirable, even inevitable.

Now, when we think of the future, we perhaps have to forget the past. If you want to pick anything from the past, it is perhaps the mistakes that we have made and how we can avoid making those mistakes in future. I am extremely disappointed that after having come formally into existence 17 years ago, SAARC has not been able to move or make progress with regard to its primary objective of economic cooperation between the members of SAARC. With Pakistan, we have a list of only 18 items where we give each other preferential tariff. Just 18 items out of over 7000 tariff lines. With Bangladesh, we have 2672 items where India gives preferential tariff to Bangladesh and we have 484 items where we get preferential tariff from Bangladesh. And as we all know, this is not good enough.

So what should we do? My specific suggestions are India is ready to enter into a free trade arrangement in SAARC, in South Asia tomorrow. I am aware of what happened in Kathmandu at the end of December when we all met to discuss the framework arrangement for a free trade area. Let us make the preferential tariff arrangement irrelevant. There is no point in discussing SAPTA which we have gone on discussing without making any progress. Let us look in concrete terms at a free trade arrangement in South Asia. And, as I said, we will be more than willing to do it tomorrow.

There is a consultant who is going to advice on this matter. The report will be available sometime in March. I think there are too many reports and too many Committees which have gone into this in the past. What we need is not another consultant's report. What we need is political will to be able to move forward. And I am trying to demonstrate that political will on behalf of the Government of India here. We are for a free trade arrangement.

Now there can be two approaches to this: one is the 'positive' list approach and the other is the 'negative' list approach. I am suggesting the negative list approach. We will not tell each other these are the items or these are the tariff lines where we shall give you a free trade arrangement or a preferential tariff arrangement. I am advocating a 'negative' list approach where we shall cover all items except those items where we have reasons to worry about the injury aspects of the domestic industry. If there are any such items, then let us sit down and exchange details of those items on the negative list. I think discussions should be about the negative list. We could look at it as carefully as possible in as I said, a spirit of friendship and accommodation. We should try and keep the negative list as limited as possible. Even within the negative list, we could think in terms of the 'tariff rate quota' which is a term well understood in WTO. We can only have so much imports and not anymore until we are able to move forward and remove the 'tariff rate quotas'. Along with a free trade arrangement for goods and merchandise, we should also have free flow of investment and services within the SAARC area. We cannot have a full-fledged free trade arrangement without free flow of investment and free flow of services. We are making that offer. We are prepared to enter into an arrangement where services and investments will be allowed to move freely. We also need to work carefully on the concept of 'value added'. We are prepared. On behalf of India, let me tell you that we are prepared to work at a reasonable level of 'value added' which will be uniform for all countries in South Asia. The next step will be the harmonization of tariffs where we could sit down. It is going to take time. It cannot happen overnight but harmonization of tariffs is an essential aspect of a free trade area so that we don't create disadvantages for each other through a discriminatory tariff regime for imports from third countries from outside the free trade area.

You have already suggested that we work together in the World Trade Organization. This is very important if we are knit together as a trading bloc. Then, we should have a commonality of approach to international trade issues and let us work seriously. I share your optimism that when the

Trade Ministers meet during the course of this month, they will be able to evolve a common position for the Cancun meeting in Mexico. I am also suggesting that we move forward from SAARC and think of a South Asian Union. If Africa can think in terms of a Union, if the Economic Community in Europe could become an European Union, if ASEAN could make progress, if the countries in Latin America could make progress, there is no reason why we in South Asia cannot become a Union of South Asian States. So, I am putting this idea on table. We will be interested in negotiating a new agreement which will create a South Asian Union and in course of time, the South Asian Union - the SAU will not merely be an economic entity. It will acquire a political dimension in the same manner which the European Union has come to acquire a political and strategic dimension. That is the direction in which I suggest we move. I am not suggesting an end to SAARC but an upgradation of SAARC into a South Asian Union.

All this, as I said, could become possible if were to give up, suspecting each other's intentions all the time. When I was in Dhaka, I noticed a feeling with regard to the natural gas which Bangladesh has. There is a view that India wants to exploit Bangladesh by asking for that gas. Now, I am referring to it because it appeared to me as an outstanding example of misunderstanding. What is the situation today? We are discovering gas within our own territory. We have offers of gas from the Gulf and from Central Asia. The Indian market will not remain static. There is a dynamics to market forces. Therefore, if we establish trade in gas, it need not necessarily mean exploitation. It will be exploitation of natural resources and not exploitation of one country by another. When I was in Dhaka and when I was meeting with Editors, someone pointed out to me how we could even think in terms of importing Bangladesh gas and sending it back in cylinders to them . Gas is not merely cooking gas as we all know, and it is not merely packaged in cylinders. It has large industrial use and this was envisaged as a major area of cooperation. Something has held it up.

The final point which I would like to make in all humility is the second point of the Gujral Doctrine. We have to be aware and sensitive to each other's security concerns. We have to be sensitive to the security concerns of South Asia as a whole. But within the overall approach to the security concerns of South Asia, we have to be aware and sensitive of the security concerns of each other. Quite clearly, this is one of the least of friendly things that one would expect. Bangladesh will expect that from India. India will expect that from Bangladesh, and similarly from all our neighbours. And it is quite clear that if those security concerns become overpowering, then many other areas of cooperation are lost sight of temporarily or in the long run. So, sensitivity to each other's security concerns is an issue which we have to keep in mind.

We must promote people to people contact. But once trade starts moving in the manner in which I am envisaging, then people to people contact will become easier. Connectivity is an extremely important aspect of trade exchanges. You cannot have trade flourishing between nations if there is no connectivity. Therefore, the land route, the sea route, the air route, telecommunications, all these are aspects of connectivity which have to be looked at.

On behalf of India, let me tell you that whatever strengths we have built over the years in terms of technology, in terms of human resource development and in terms of capacities, we are prepared to put at the disposal of our neighbours in South Asia. Whatever we have, can be yours, just for asking.

I am quite sure that if we take this road and I am talking of the whole of South Asia. I am not making any distinction between the countries of South Asia. If we take this road, I am quite sure, the misunderstandings of the past will automatically vanish and it will be possible for us to move ahead on the road to prosperity and a good quality of life for our people.

Thank you very much.

‹43›

Inaugural Address By Shri Yashwant Sinha, External Affairs Minister At The Fifth Asian Security Conference Organised By The Institute For Defence Studies And Analysis, New Delhi (27.01.03)

The EAM sought to debunk theories that foresee in Asia a "coming battle for supremacy between India and China" and stated that "India's approach to relations with China will be infused with a sense of optimism.... and will be based on the conviction that a prosperous India is inevitable". He admitted that while differences existed, India-China relations had diversified to include subjects like counter terrorism, security, policy planning and the boundary question.

Theme: "Asian Security And China In 2000-2010"

Dr. Santhanam, Ambassador Bhutani, distinguished ladies and gentlemen,

I am happy to be here today to inaugurate this fifth Asian Security Conference being organized by the Institute for Defence Studies and Analysis (IDSA). I commend the IDSA for organising this seminar on an annual basis. It is important that we look at the big picture in Asia and decipher long-term trends and their implications for the world as well as for us. I am delighted that a large, diverse and distinguished panel of scholars from India and abroad are joining this effort and I am certain these discussions will prove fruitful for all those gathered here today as well as for the Governments of the region.

Ladies and gentlemen, it is widely accepted that the 21st century will be an Asian century. Let me, therefore,. begin by asking what is it that makes Asia special. What makes Asia unique?

Asia is the largest continent in the world both in terms of population as well as territory. It encompasses extraordinary diversity in terms of religion, race, ethnicity and culture. Each of its regions, whether they be the Gulf and West Asia, Central Asia, South Asia, South East Asia and North East Asia, all have distinctive characteristics that separate them from the others. Yet Asia has civilizational commonalties that seeks unity in its diversity.

In 1940, Asia accounted for 60% of the world's population and 19 percent of the world's GDP. This changed to 57% of the world's population and 37% of the world's GDP by 1995. It is estimated that the Asian population will account for 55% of the world population and 57% of global GDP by 2025. Asia accounts for the world's largest energy resources. The world's fastest growing economies and markets are also within Asia.

It is evident, therefore, that the fulcrum of political and economic activity is shifting in an inexorable manner towards Asia and away from the traditional centers of North America and Europe.

What are the challenges which confront Asia today? Which of those are likely to persist in the coming decade?

Poverty and disparity among and within nations is the fundamental challenge faced by Asia. Asian diversity is most acutely reflected in these differences in economic development within countries and in different parts of the continent. Nearly two thirds of the world's poor live in Asia. Yet, several Asian countries have become middle income or even developed countries in terms of per capita income. How to overcome economic backwardness and remove disparities remains the primary concern of most Asian countries.

Similarly, the need to stem the overall rate of population growth and manage demographic changes, particularly phenomena such as migration and refugee flows is a priority for many countries. Some scholars have pointed out that the battles of the future may be battles over water. How to harness the water resources of the region to meet the requirements of its huge population is another issue of concern.

Terrorism, as all of us are aware today is a global phenomenon. Its roots, however, lie in Asia and there is virtually no corner of Asia unaffected by this scourge. Asia is the only part of the world which has been the victim of a nuclear attack. Yet, there are nations in Asia who resort to nuclear blackmail and openly brandish threats that they will use nuclear weapons. Proliferation is another major challenge that Asia confronts. Some of the most deliberate and well documented instances of nuclear and missile transfers have taken place in this region. It could be said that the risk of nuclear weapons falling into the hands of terrorist groups is the greatest in Asia, particularly in the immediate neighbourhood of India where it is possible to find the conjunction of authoritarian rule, religious fundamentalism, terrorism, drug trafficking and weapons of mass destruction.

In much of the world, war between States has been replaced by war within States. Asia too mirrors this broad trend. Intra-state conflicts and proxy war has taken the place of open war and inter-state conflict. Non state actors, some with the direct backing of States and some operating on their own form important figures on Asia's security landscape. By spreading violence and terror, they actively seek to undermine democracy, civil society and rule of law. Narco terrorism and trafficking in small arms is also a rapidly spreading and disturbing phenomenon.

The Asian Security Conference this year focuses on China which carries the world's largest population and is India's biggest neighbour. The timing of this Conference is particularly opportune for it follows the convening of the 16th Party Congress in China last November and the publication thereafter of the fourth Chinese White Paper on national defence last December. The distinguished scholars present here today will no doubt carefully assess the import of the deliberations of the Party Congress and analyse the contents of the White Paper.

The rise of China is a phenomenon which has engaged the attention of scholars in many parts of world. There have been negative scenarios as well as positive scenarios outlined and I am sure that these will be discussed in the next few days. Often the conclusions drawn reflect personal convictions of the scholars concerned. In general, academics of the Realist school tend to see China as a potential hegemon in Asia-a country which seeks to throw the United States out of the region and declare a new Monroe Doctrine. Liberal scholars on the other hand see China as a positive force within Asia-a China which through its economic strength and constructive diplomacy contributes to the overall peace and stability of the region.

The rise of India is similarly an issue which has attracted academic debate. There are many who see the emergence of India on the world stage as part of an inevitable and inexorable process of history. They look to India's history and tradition of commitment to peace and non-violence, her success in institutionalizing democracy in the face of unparalleled challenges, her commitment to fostering a secular, diverse and plural society even as she strengthens her national unity, her rapidly growing economy, world class human resources and her leadership of developing countries as positive factors which would contribute to peace, stability and prosperity in the world. There are, however, others who see India as an ambitious and non status quo power seeking to break into the private club of major powers.

Some analysts foresee in Asia a coming battle for supremacy between India and China. They talk of the inevitability of conflict owing to overlapping areas of influence between India and China and the determination of both countries to emerge as major powers on the world stage. Let me debunk these theories completely and state with full conviction that India neither pursues nor makes policy towards China based on the belief that conflict between the two is inevitable.

It is true that there are important differences between India and China. Some of the wounds inflicted by the conflict of 1962 have been slow to heal and the scars have not fully disappeared. Reliable and widespread reports of Chinese nuclear and missile proliferation to Pakistan cause deep concern. The Chinese position on issues such as Sikkim and India's candidature to a permanent seat in the UN Security Council sows doubts. There is also a sense of disappointment over the pace of improvement in the relationship.

Let me, however, assure everyone gathered here that India's approach to relations with China is and will remain forward looking and infused with a sense of optimism. India's policies will not be based on fear of Chinese power nor envy of China's economic achievements. They will be based on the conviction that a prosperous India is inevitable. So is a strong and prosperous China. It is, therefore, logical, reasonable and in the enlightened self-interest of both that the two countries learn not just to live with each other but also address differences and build on what is common. Further, both India and China are too large and too strong to be contained or cowed down by any country, including each other.

A substantial measure of success has been achieved by now in the endeavour to establish mutual understanding between India and China. Despite the fact that the India-China border spans thousands of kilometers of territory and there exist material differences in perception, the two countries have been successful in maintaining relative peace and tranquility for over twenty-five years. This achievement should in no way be underestimated. Moreover, the process of clarifying the Line of Actual Control along the India-China border based on the institutional framework provided by the important agreements of 1993 and 1996 is making progress.

India-China relations have diversified and a series of dialogue mechanisms are in place including on subjects such as counter terrorism, security issues, policy planning and the boundary question. Functional delegations to learn from each other's experiences are criss-crossing each other's countries. High level visits are also being regularly exchanged. Premier Zhu Rongji visited India early last year and Prime Minister Vajpayee will visit China this year. Both countries realize, however, that much more ground remains to be traversed.

The civilisational and cultural ties between the two countries provide India and China with the foundation to build a strong relationship. India seeks to develop relations with China on the basis of the principles of Panchsheel, mutual sensitivity to each other's concerns and equality. We have agreed at the highest level to move ahead in diverse areas of co-operation while simultaneously finding ways and means of addressing our differences through dialogue and peaceful means.

An important consequence of the above has been the remarkable transformation that has taken place in India–China economic relations. Trade and economic cooperation between India and China has grown rapidly in the last decade from US$ 264.8 million in 1991 to US$ 4.3 billion for the period January-November, 2002.

Many of you will recall the fact that in 2001 when India removed the last of its quantitative restrictions, there was great fear of cheaper Chinese goods swamping the Indian market. A popular news magazine even described it as a second invasion by China. However, producers and manufacturers in India over the last two years have more than stood their ground. Far from being swamped by imports, India-China trade figures reflect a relative balance in India's exports and imports. There is an important lesson to be learnt here. India can be globally competitive if it continues to strengthen its efforts in this regard. The Indian business community should face the world as well as China with confidence.

I am convinced that the future of Asia rests in expanded economic interaction. The logic of economics is bound to inevitably overwhelm Asia just as it has happened in Europe. The key to enhancing Asian security lies in our collective ability to build mutual economic stakes in each other. This is a process which is already happening throughout the region. Regional infrastructure linkages in the form of roads, railway lines and pipelines are rapidly becoming a reality. They hold the potential to knit Asia together in a manner never before seen. On its part, India too has been contributing to this process by expanding connectivity with its neighbours towards the east as well as the west.

Ladies and Gentlemen, power in the 21st century will flow from the pores of a well run economy. India and China have shown the wisdom to move ahead in their bilateral relations even as contentious issues such as the border dispute are separately addressed. Economic integration and an overall improvement in relations has not been held hostage to differences over specific issues, however, important those issues are. The wisdom of adopting such an approach to India-Pakistan relations is self evident. I hope our neighbour will not keep its eyes forever shut to this truth.

To conclude, Asian security can be visualized in terms of concentric circles comprising West Asia, Central Asia, South Asia, South East Asia and North East Asia. India is part of them all. Each one affects India's security and India proposes to play an active role in promoting security within Asia in collaboration with fellow Asian countries.

Asia is today and will continue to be the most dynamic, rapidly changing and modernizing region of the world. Asian countries have already begun to apply themselves to addressing the whole array of security issues of concern to the continent ranging from arms control, terrorism, confidence building mechanisms, security of sea-lanes, greater economic integration, security of energy supplies, greater connectivity. As these efforts develop and coalesce, we will have established a co-operative architecture that guarantees peace, security, stability not only in Asia but also in the whole world.

A strong and confident India is ready to contribute to this process.

Thank you

‹44›

Address by Shri Yashwant Sinha, External Affairs Minister at the Kyrgyz National State University (31.01.03)

The EAM identified a range of fields of Indo-Kyrgyz cooperation including training in IT, mass media, management, diplomatic and administrative training, energy and hydroelectricity. He also proposed the development of various "transport corridors" through Iran, Afghanistan and the CARs to usher in a "new era of trade relations and people to people contacts between India and Central Asia".

Excellencies, Distinguished Rector, Members of the Academic Council, Ladies and Gentlemen,

I am pleased to be here today amongst some of the finest minds of Kyrgyzstan. I also bring with me good wishes of the people of India for you. We have for long admired your great epic 'Manas'. Delhi boasts of a road named after 'Manas'.

Historically, our links with Kyrgyzstan have been strong since the time of Silk Route, and even before. It is said that two major branches of the Silk Route travelled through Central Asia and came down to India. Moreover, Central Asia also provided the meeting point for China and India. Great names of history travelled between the two countries through Central Asia. It is said that at one point, the trade between India and China through the Silk Route was one of the highest in the World. So, your region has for a long time been India's connection with the West and with the North. And in doing so, Central Asia has truly been at the confluence of civilizations.

Because it was not just trade which travelled down these roads. The teachings of Buddha also took this route and spread the message of peace all over Central Asia.

Later, through most of the twentieth century, culture also played an important role. Indian films and Indian artists became household names everywhere. But it was not only culture which was our calling card during this twentieth century. Our leaders like Mahatma Gandhi and Jawaharlal Nehru were known throughout Central Asia.

We have rejoiced in your Independence. We were amongst the first to recognize the independence of Kyrgyzstan, as also other countries in Central

Asia. We were also amongst the very first to set up Embassies in Central Asian countries. Now, a decade later, the time has come for us to make an assessment of how much we have achieved, and what remains to be done.

India's first focus during these past ten years has been to increase the reach of our cooperation programme. In Kyrgyzstan alone, this programme is providing training every year for about 300 man months in different fields. Information Technology, Mass Media, Management, Diplomatic and Administrative Training, are just a few of them.

A Dairy Plant was set up near Bishkek. I believe it is running well. Recently, the Prime Minister of India had announced the gift of 10 four-wheel drives for the Mountain Summit, which was held late last year in Bishkek. I am glad that these vehicles could arrive in time for the Summit.

Now, we are considering setting up an Institute for Information Technology and a Food Processing Plant, as a part of our cooperation programme.

Last year, for the first time, India had organized an Industrial Exhibition in Bishkek. Encouraged by the response received then, we are thinking of having a second exhibition. This time, a consumer goods show, with perhaps as many as 100 Indian businessmen.

All these are a part of our effort to reach out to Central Asia. We have already put to test the new transport corridors. The Trilateral Agreement between India, Iran and Turkmenistan, has started working. Faster clearances at Bandar Abbas and then at other check points have meant a reduction in transit and travel time from India to Central Asia. Similarly, the North-South Corridor is another attempt at making the flow of goods to Central Asia faster. But we are looking beyond these routes.

Recently, India, Iran and Afghanistan, have agreed to develop a new route. This will utilize the Chah Bahar Port of Iran to send goods through Afghanistan and to Central Asian countries. It is being estimated that this new route will cut distances by 1500 kms. India is going to construct 200 kms of this new road, and this might usher in an entirely new era of trade relations and people-to-people contacts between India and Central Asia. This new Silk Route of prosperity is India's wish for its relations with Central Asia. As in the past, we hope that our cooperation would once again bring the best of cultures, prosperity and friendship to Central Asia. Once again, let us make this new Silk Route the lifeline of our friendship.

The areas of energy and hydro-electricity are two other areas where we can achieve a lot together. India would have one of the highest rates of growth of energy requirements over the next few decades. Central Asia is virtually sitting on lakes of oil and gas. There is, therefore, a lot that can be done together for import of oil and gas into India. We can also work together for new pipe-line routes and additional refineries.

Nature has blessed Kyrgyzstan with bountiful charms. It has also given it immense hydro electric potential. This is an important area where Indian technology and Kyrgyz resources could work together for mutual benefit.

We must think of innovative ways to tap the traditional goodwill and our resources to best advantage. It is with that hope that I came to your beautiful country. And, it is in confidence of fulfill ment of that hope that I bid goodbye to you. I do so with my best wishes.

Thank you.

❮45❯

Inaugural address by Shri Yashwant Sinha, External Affairs Minister at the Third Meeting of India-Pakistan Chambers of Commerce and Industry (07.07.03)

Shri Yashwant Sinha opined that Indo-Pak bilateral trade could be increased from the current US $ 200-250 million to $ 6-8 billion. He lamented the slow progress in "SAFTA and SAPTA" and assured his listeners that there was no need to "harbour any special fears about India". He felt that India's "neighbours must become full partners" in its economic progress and reiterated that India intended to pursue the twin objectives of "peace and economic cooperation" without "swamping Pakistan markets".

Dr. A.C. Muthiah, President, FICCI, Jenab Ilyas Ahmed Bilour, President, India-Pakistan Chamber of Commerce and Industry, Jenab Iftekar Malik, Immediate Past President, Federation of Pakistan Chambers of Commerce and Industry, Jenab Aziz Ahmad Khan, High Commissioner-designate of Pakistan, Dr. Amit Mitra, Secretary General of FICCI, Ladies and Gentlemen.

A very warm welcome to our friends from Pakistan.

I am happy to have this opportunity to participate in this third meeting of the India-Pakistan Chambers of Commerce and Industry. It is a reminder of the historic initiative that was taken through the Lahore Bus journey of Prime Minister Vajpayee in 1999. The hope for the future that had been rekindled by the Lahore process was quickly seized by your two Chambers to create this common platform for pursuing mutually benefiting endeavours.

The fact that this meeting is taking place today and the overwhelming participation here from both sides are clearly a reflection of the hitherto unfulfilled yearnings of the people of our two countries to find ways to contribute to enhanced trade and economic exchanges, and the resulting employment and income generation benefits for our respective peoples.

Ladies and Gentlemen,

Figures show clearly, and they have been mentioned here by speaker after speaker, that we have not fully exploited our common potential. Our bilateral trade recorded officially has hovered, over the past several years, in the range of US$ 200-250 million. Our exports to each other constitute a very small proportion of the overall exports of each of our countries, namely, a mere 1%. It is also much lower than India's trade figures with other countries in the SAARC region. With Bangladesh our total trade is almost US$ 1 billion, with Sri Lanka it was close to US$ 1 billion in 2002, with Nepal it is around US$ 600 million. The level of trade with Pakistan is clearly not natural, since Pakistan's economy, as has been mentioned, is much bigger, much larger. Let us not forget that at the time of independence more than 50% of Pakistan's exports and 30% of its imports were accounted for by India.

A comparison would be relevant in this regard. The US has strong trade relations with its neighbours Canada and Mexico. In both these cases, although US is the stronger economy, trade balances are in favour of Canada and Mexico. Apprehensions, therefore, that the larger economy will inevitably swamp the smaller neighbouring economies are not borne out by reality. Balance of trade is a reflection of complementarities in the economies. The challenge is to exploit the potential that exists to mutual benefit. With Nepal, for example, India generally imports more than it exports.

I would like to compliment FICCI for its excellent "Status Paper on India-Pakistan economic relations". It has shown that with a normal trade relationship, our trade will easily reach the level of US$ 3-4 billion, and Dr. Muthiah just mentioned that it could even reach $6-8 billion. You can visualise the impact that this will have on employment and incomes in both our countries. There would also be the resulting need for further investments in communications and infrastructure to support this, a point which has been made here, which would have its own spin-off benefits. Government revenues would benefit from the tax incomes generated and business persons of Pakistan would also benefit from the more than one billion strong Indian market, with a middle class of over 300 million people with increasing purchasing power, which is much larger than the total population of many industrialised countries. Normal trade relations will therefore expand the potential for foreign direct investment in Pakistan considerably.

The FICCI study that I just referred to points out that many of Pakistan's exports would benefit and become even more competitive, a point which has been made by both sides, through cheaper raw material and intermediate inputs from India. This would apply to the plastics, leather and textile industry. The Pakistani domestic and industrial consumer would also benefit from lower prices in several sectors including engineering industry and transport equipment.

Goods from other neighbourhood economies with whom Pakistan has normal trade relations have not swamped Pakistani markets. For example, out of US$ 1.8 billion worth of trade with China in 2002, Pakistan's exports are quite substantial and to the tune of US$ 750 million. There is no need, therefore, to harbour any special fears about India. The wide range of products of potential trade such as chemicals, industrial machinery, cement, tyres, tea, pharmaceuticals, etc. clearly show the complementarities that exist between our two economies.

Bilateral trade between India and other SAARC countries has not been to the disadvantage of the other SAARC countries nor has it been to the sole advantage of India. For example, there has been a remarkable increase in the level of trade with Sri Lanka, and this is a point I would like to particularly emphasise, following the Free Trade Agreement signed in 2001. In 2002 alone, exports of Sri Lanka to India grew by around 137%. Consequently, we have now created a Joint Study Group which is studying how to take us into the next generation of economic partnership with a focus on trade in services and investments in each other's countries. Similarly, we also hope to commence negotiations on a Free Trade Agreement with Bangladesh before the end of this year. Let me assure you that we in India have no intention to overwhelm Pakistan's economy through trade. Our aim is only to have a normal trade relationship, and promote trade in a manner that people of both countries benefit.

Friends, it is also unfortunate that not enough progress has been made in SAFTA and SAPTA so far. SAARC came into being in 1985. Almost 18 years later, very little progress has been made with regard to its primary objective of economic cooperation. After eight years and four rounds of SAPTA negotiations, intra-SAARC trade forms only 4% of the total trade of South Asia. The number of products on which Preferential Tariffs have been exchanged with Pakistan is in particular, minimal.

As early as 1997, there was also a decision at the summit level to have a South Asian Free Trade Area by the year 2000. However, till the beginning of 2002, only one meeting had taken place, and efforts continue to be made to delay this process. We are now in the second half of 2003, and not a single meeting has taken place this year on SAFTA despite the Kathmandu Summit mandate for a speedy conclusion of the talks to finalise the Framework Treaty. I know that your group needs no convincing of the immense benefits that would accrue from such an arrangement.

In fact, I believe that along with a free trade arrangement for goods and merchandise, we should also have free flow of investment and services within the SAARC area. We are also prepared to work for reasonable levels of uniform value addition norms for all countries in South Asia, and for harmonisation of tariff regime.

In a globalizing world, regional trade is increasingly seen as a protective measure against external shocks. According to some estimates, intra-regional trade between ASEAN countries is over 40 percent of its total trade. The European Union, too, trades over 65 percent within itself. And these figures have been achieved because both ASEAN and the EU have not allowed political differences amongst member countries to hamper trade within the region.

There is much that we can achieve together. Our representatives have worked successfully and productively in international fora including the WTO, and on discussions in UN fora on issues of poverty alleviation, access to better healthcare, ensuring education for all, and solutions to problems of environmental degradation.

Ladies and Gentlemen,

India is today one of the fastest growing economies of the world, ranking fourth in terms of purchasing power parity. India remained relatively unscathed from the 1997-98 Asian financial crisis and maintained a healthy growth rate despite recession in major world economies over the past several years. We have built external foreign exchange balances of around US$ 82 billion. From a food grains importing country, we are net exporter of good grains today. Our rate of inflation has also been well under control over the last five years. A Morgan Stanley Dean Witter report felt that were it not for the resilience of China and India, the world economy would have been in deep recession in 2002.

We are proud of our achievements and confident of the future. At the same time, we are also clear that if we want to secure this future, our neighbours must become full partners in this endeavour and make equal if not more economic progress. We wish to celebrate together as we purposefully move forward. It is for this reason, I recently suggested that even as we implement fully the SAARC Charter, we should also start thinking of a South Asian Union. If other regions could achieve this kind of Union, despite political, social and economic differences, there is no reason why we should deprive our people of this opportunity. I repeat this here today to show India's commitment to the concept of a South Asian Union. We are prepared to enter into discussions on this issue from tomorrow, if other countries of the region are willing.

My intention is not in any way to wish away or to underplay the differences that exist between us. We must, at the same time, exploit the potential for cooperation that exists. I am confident that this would increase the political and economic space to create and exploit additional areas of cooperation and deal with differences. This is the approach that we have successfully adopted and productively followed in our relations with others.

Friends, the challenge faced by India and Pakistan is whether we can truly live together as good neighbours. Till now, we have witnessed the simple logic of mutual economic benefits being overwhelmed by political and other differences between our two countries. I believe that the time has come for us to reverse this trend and for economics to attain a dominant role in our bilateral interaction. It is businessmen such as you and Chambers of Commerce and Industry of the two countries who can play a critical role in this regard.

In conclusion, the most important objective that India seeks to achieve in the next decade or so is to completely banish poverty from our land and to provide our people with a better quality of life. This objective would naturally benefit from peaceful and cooperative relations in the region and the rest of the world. We intend to continue to pursue the twin objectives of peace and economic progress with determination.

I would like to once again thank the Federation of Indian and Pakistani Chambers of Commerce and Industry for the initiative they have taken to convene this meeting and for this very important contribution to the improvement in relations between our two countries.

I wish you success in your deliberations. I would also urge you to work out specific joint recommendations to both Governments for taking the trade and economic relationship significantly forward.

Let me assure you that the Government of India would not be found wanting in implementing these joint recommendations.

Thank you very much.

‹46›

Remarks by Shri Yashwant Sinha, External Affairs Minister at The Plenary Session Second India - ASEAN Business Summit (04.09.03)

According to the EAM, Phase-II of India's "Look East" policy "marks a shift in focus from exclusively economic issues to economic and security issues" like protection of sea lanes, counter-terrorism, etc. He also drew attention to the "growing importance of 'soft' areas of cooperation like culture, entertainment and the media" and initiatives like the India-Myanmar-Thailand highway and Delhi-Hanoi rail line to improve connectivity.

Let me begin by extending to all of you a hearty and warm welcome to this Ministerial Session of the 2nd India-ASEAN Business Summit. I am particularly grateful to our Ministerial colleagues from the various ASEAN countries who have come to India to participate in this event and are with us this morning. I would like to recognize the distinguished Ministers from Malaysia, Myanmar and Singapore, the Chief Minister of Malacca who are with me on the dias, as well as the large number of senior officials from all ASEAN countries. Let me also extend cordial greetings and a warm welcome to all the business delegates.

It is gratifying that this event has become an annual feature. I am glad that this year, the Confederation of Indian Industry, has joined hands with the Federation of Indian Chambers of Commerce and Industry, the organizers of the First India-ASEAN Business Summit, in organizing this event. I also welcome the keen interest shown by ASEAN business in this event, symbolized by the participation of the Chairman of the ASEAN Business Advisory Council in our gathering this morning.

India's 'Look East' policy has now entered its Phase - II. Phase- I was focused primarily on the ASEAN countries and on trade and investment linkages. Phase- II is characterized by an expanded definition of 'East' extending from Australia to China and East Asia with ASEAN as its core. Phase - II marks a shift in focus from exclusively economic issues to economic and security issues including joint efforts to protect sea lanes, co-ordination on counter terrorism etc. On the economic side, Phase - II is also characterized by arrangements for FTAs and establishing of institutional economic linkages between the countries of the region and India.

The world is today integrating very fast and every country is forced to face the challenge of globalization. Since the process of globalization is inevitable, the challenge is to manage its effects and to ensure that its benefits are appropriately assimilated and internalized. Special steps are also required to ensure that globalization does not have an adverse impact on the weakest sections of society. The Asian financial crisis in 1997 holds valuable lessons for the rest of the world. This crisis demonstrated that globalization can be faced more effectively through collective efforts rather than singly and it is in this context that evolution of ASEAN and India-ASEAN relations should be viewed.

Friends, as was mentioned in the inaugural address by our Prime Minister, we are delighted that the Economic Ministers of ASEAN and India yesterday finalized the text of the Framework Agreement on Economic Cooperation that our leaders will sign at the Second India-ASEAN summit at Bali next month. This is truly a major breakthrough in economic cooperation that should significantly contribute towards the evolution of an increasingly integrated India-ASEAN economic space over the next 15-20 years. Some of our ASEAN friends have had some hesitations and reservations about this Agreement, but we hope that they would be convinced that this initiative is a long-term win-win initiative for all parties.

India is currently also engaged in negotiations with Thailand for an FTA and with Singapore for a Comprehensive Economic Cooperation Agreement. Both sets of negotiations are proceeding well and we hope to bring them to an early conclusion. I am convinced that these Agreements along with measures we are undertaking to improve physical connectivity such as the India-Myanmar-Thailand trilateral highway and Delhi-Hanoi rail line will together usher in a new era in our relationship.

Prime Minister Vajpayee called upon us today to aim high and target a turnover of US$ 15 billion over the next two years and US$ 30 billion by 2007. Trade and investment between India and ASEAN is far below potential considering that we have a combined population of 1.5 billion, a GDP of US$1.5 trillion, and share the huge advantage of geographical proximity. The share of ASEAN in India's foreign trade has shown only a modest rise from about 6% in 1991 to 9% in 2002. The share of India in ASEAN's foreign trade has remained at a negligible 1%. There are obviously latent strengths in India and ASEAN that we have not fully tapped.

In the decade 1991-2000, there was a nearly three-fold increase in trade turnover (from US$3.5 billion in 1991 to US$10.1 billion in 2000), with the most rapid increase in the five-year period between 1991 and 1996. Trade between India and ASEAN grew by 22.6% from US$ 9.88 billion in 2001 to US$ 12.11 billion in 2002. However, the 1997 Asian financial crisis led to an understandable decline in trade. Despite the fact that the economic situation has improved over the last 5 years, India-ASEAN trade hasn't really picked up significantly over this period. We need to work harder to get India-ASEAN trade grow at the impressive rates it registered in the first half of the 90s.

There are also some other features of India-ASEAN trade that need to be looked at seriously. While the composition of India's exports to ASEAN is quite diversified, ASEAN's exports to India are dominated by two items viz. electronic goods and edible oils. Secondly, there is need to diversify the direction of India-ASEAN trade. Currently, about 85 to 90% of India-ASEAN trade is with three or four ASEAN countries. While seeking to increase the trade with existing partners, Indian and ASEAN exporters must also actively explore possibilities of greater mutually beneficial trade with the other ASEAN countries.

Creating greater awareness about one another plays a vital role in creating new opportunities for business. Let me, therefore, draw attention to the growing importance of the 'soft' areas of cooperation like culture, entertainment and the media. There is tremendous potential for cooperation and collaboration in the fields of tourism and entertainment industry. Bollywood films are now shot all over the world, including increasingly in Asian locales. Films can be a powerful medium to explore the richness in art, architecture, nature, culture, religion and civilizations of Indian and South-East Asia. Such collaborative efforts, whether in cinema or other forms of art and culture, will make a tremendous contribution to spreading greater mutual awareness about India and ASEAN among our people. They will also showcase our part of the world to people beyond the region, and promote tourism and business into India and ASEAN.

The media of our respective countries has an important role to play in creating greater awareness not only about the opportunities for business between India and ASEAN, but also about the life and culture of the people. We need to use all the catalysts at our disposal to generate an irreversible momentum in the flywheel of our relationship. It is gratifying that a number of journalists from the ASEAN region have come to India to cover this Business Summit. This morning, we also saw the inauguration of the India-ASEAN Business Portal. I am confident that this portal will play an important role in creating greater awareness about the opportunities of doing business between India and ASEAN.

With ASEAN engaged in negotiating free trade arrangements with India, China, Japan and South Korea, we stand today on the threshold of an Asian economic community for the first time. I am convinced that the future of Asia rests in expanded economic interaction between the countries of the region.

An environment of security, predictability and peace is essential for business to flourish and development to take place. Enhancing co-operation in the field of security is critical to our larger efforts aimed at building lasting economic ties. Today, the principal threats to peace and stability in the world are not from wars between nations but from the threat of trans-national terrorism. That is why, as we jointly work towards an intensification of our economic and other ties, India and ASEAN should not lose sight of the overarching importance of working purposefully and in cooperation to combat the menace of terrorism. The recent incidents of bombing in Jakarta a few weeks ago and in Mumbai last week are a reminder to us all that we have to stand united in our war against the spreading tentacles of terrorism. The Joint Declaration on Cooperation in Combating International Terrorism and other Trans-national Crimes that India and ASEAN propose to sign at Bali reflects our determination to effectively combat this menace.

In today's globalising world, economic cooperation is at the heart of relations between countries. It is the foundation on which the entire edifice of relations has to be built. India looks forward to a comprehensive engagement with all ASEAN countries. We would like to share our strengths for the development of the region and for mutual benefit.

Let me conclude by pointing out that ten plus one constitutes a full team. Whether it be cricket, football or hockey, eleven is a team. India is delighted to complete the team of the ASEAN ten.

‹47›

Inaugural Address by Shri Yashwant Sinha, External Affairs Minister of India at the 21st Meeting of the Health Ministers of WHO South East Asia Region (08.09.03)

The EAM emphasized that experience showed that "rapid social progress could be achieved..., if priority is given to social development in education and health". He called for greater South-South cooperation in the field of health and pharmaceuticals to overcome problems of market access in fellow developing countries.

Madam Chairperson, Smt. Sushma Swaraj,

Chairman of the Health Ministers' Forum, Dr. Achmad Sujudi, the Health Minister of Indonesia,

Honourable Ministers of Health from other countries of the WHO South East Asia region,

Regional Director, WHO SEARO

Distinguished delegates,

Ladies and Gentlemen,

It is an honour for me to address this distinguished gathering of Health Ministers of the South East Asia Region of the World Health Organisation. Let me at the outset welcome Timor L'este, the new addition to our family.

2. Ours is a region with challenging statistics in the realm of health. But equally, it is a region united by a mission to bring about change. It is India's conviction that countries of the world, especially developing countries, can bring about the required change through collective efforts and cooperation.

3. Meetings such as these provide therefore invaluable opportunities for bringing about greater synergy of human resource capital and technological capacities available within the region, exchange of best practices and experiences, and to strategise joint action to tackle health related problems.

4. I wish all of you a productive meeting and pleasant stay in New Delhi.

5. The membership of this grouping is interesting as it does not strictly conform to the principle of geographical contiguity, pointing to the self-evident truth that health epidemics are not contained by political or geographical boundaries. The recent months have been testimony to this as the outbreak of SARS raged across the world, affecting all aspects of life – political,

economic and social. It brought home the stark message of human vulnerability to disease, and the downside of living in a global village where no one can be untouched by the suffering of the other. But the containment of the epidemic, through vigilance and early warnings, transparent exchange of information and concerted public action, also showed that such challenges can be overcome successfully when we act together.

6. India, inspite of its very large population remained a SARS-free country. This was possible entirely due to prompt preventive action, personally supervised by our very able and dynamic Minister of Health, Smt. Sushma Swaraj.

7. Health occupies a pre-eminent position when we speak of human development and global prosperity. At the Millennium Summit of the UN General Assembly in 2000, world leaders pledged to work together to "uphold the principles of human dignity, equality, and equity at the global level", and set themselves eight goals with quantifiable and monitorable targets to measure progress of humankind – three of these are directly related to human health – viz. reducing child mortality, improving maternal health and combating the "globalized" scourges of HIV/AIDs, malaria and other diseases. Four of the remaining eight have a tangential but vital link with health – eradication of poverty and hunger, universal primary education, empowerment of women and sustainable development, which includes access to safe drinking water.

8. It is now accepted widely that international endeavours to improve global health have a direct bearing on the economic development of countries, in particular developing countries, which lag behind in key indicators. The Commission on Macro-economics and Health set up under the aegis of the WHO to examine this link came up with some telling conclusions. It showed that with interventions costing as little as US$ 34 per head, infectious and nutritional deficiencies could be brought down, saving eight million lives per year. The economic spin-off of better health, thus, achieved would amount to an increase of global wealth by US$ 186 billion per year. This was seen to be a 6:1 return on investment. For this Utopian situation, health related assistance would need to rise six fold from present figures of around US$ 6 billion per annum. With global political will, particularly of our developed country partners, this should not be impossible to achieve given that health expenditure of OECD countries is to the tune of US$ 3 trillion per year, and their total GDP, US$ 30 trillion.

9. However, while calling for international cooperation, we should take heed of the fact that the primary responsibility for improved health of our people vests with national governments. The experience of some developing countries, and parts of my own country, have shown that rapid social progress can be achieved, inspite of a low level of economic development, if priority is given to social development in education and health. Our own

experience in India in this regard is worth sharing with countries in the region. Through a systematic programme of political empowerment of women at the grassroots level through reservation of seats in elected local bodies and by making large catalytic investments in education and health, particularly of women and children, we have been able to effect significant change within the span of a single generation. There has been a breakthrough in reduction of maternal and child mortality, malnutrition and diseases related to poor hygiene. Fertility rates have also been moderated.

10. While looking at health related statistics in isolation can draw a picture of gloom, there are also positive indicators in many key areas which point to progress achieved. But much more is yet to be done. Thus, while immunization has helped to prevent 85% of measles deaths and ensure a near eradication of polio, eleven million children continue to die every year across the world of preventable causes. There has been significant progress in the consciousness of the need to combat the HIV/AIDs pandemic with virtually all countries having adopted multi-sectoral HIV/AIDs strategic plans. At the same time, almost 25 million people have been lost to the disease world wide.

11. Developing countries have reasons to take pride, however, from the success notched by our combined efforts in the context of the WTO. We have won a hard-fought battle for recognition of the need for access to medication at affordable prices for the people of developing counties. It is now accepted that such access is among the most effective elements of public health policy aimed at reducing mortality and infection rates of scourges such as HIV/AIDS. Combined action by developing countries has brought a human-face to the debate on trade policies and public health needs.

12. The war is, however, not yet over. Governments of developing countries must consult each other on their policies, pool technical expertise and exchange best practices. R&D in the Pharma sector has hitherto been primarily the preserve of resource-rich MNCs of the developed world. As a result, only around 10% of R&D in health spending is directed at the health problems affecting 90% of the world's population. Search for legitimate profit has in some instances, sadly, given way to profiteering. Health should be a commitment and not merely a matter of money. Suffering innocents should not be exploited but supported.

13. Strangely, sometimes cheaper and better medicines manufactured by countries like India are also confronted with problems of market access in fellow developing countries. Procedures relating to drug registration, testing etc. are used to shut our products out of the market. This situation should change. There is a crying need for greater South–South cooperation in the field of health and pharmaceuticals. The interests of the large majority of the people in our countries demands that we not only sustain existing cooperation but also rapidly strengthen it. Developing countries need to

draw up effective strategies to ensure greater market access for generic and patented drugs which they are able to produce at competitive prices. Where appropriate, we must evolve common platforms in international fora, including the WTO and enter into bilateral as well as regional arrangements.

14. The South East Asian region of WHO which we represent, unfortunately accounts for 40% of the world's poor, 40% of global maternal and neo-natal deaths, 40% of the world's cases of tuberculosis and 40% of deaths due to infectious diseases. These are thresholds which need to be brought down if we are to ensure human centred development in the region. We can take heart from the fact that the human development indices related to average life expectancy and basic health care have shown substantial improvement in the last two-three decades. But clearly there are miles to go before any of us can rest. The key to ensuring a disease-free region quite obviously rests in greater cooperation among ourselves. It is also my view that the since the basic responsibility for fighting disease is that of the Government, R & D in the pharmaceuticals sector should also become an important duty of Governments. I say this not to discourage the private sector but to assert that Governments should not abdicate their responsibilities in this regard.

15. Let me also emphasize in this connection, the need to promote indigenous medicines as well as strengthen cooperation in this field. Many of us have strong traditions of indigenous medicines which derive from our rich resources of bio-diversity. Indigenous medicines are relatively cheap and normally, have few side effects. It will be useful for countries of this region to take up research into indigenous medicines and their popularization as a priority.

16. The Pandava King Yudhisthira, who in our ancient traditions is associated with righteousness, as *Dharmaraja*, expressed his vision of leadership as:

Quote

> "I seek no kingdoms nor heavenly pleasure nor personal salvation, I seek only to relieve humanity from its manifold pains and sufferings as this is the supreme objective of mankind." Unquote

17. We, as Ministers, representing at once the leadership of our governments, and the aspirations of our peoples, have an onerous responsibility to ensure the human dignity of each of our citizens, central to which is their physical well-being. Let me, therefore, wish you all success in your deliberations–may you learn from each others successes and failures–and use the combined experience and talent of the region to achieve the goal of 'Health for all'.

18. With these words, I declare open the 21st Meeting of Ministers of Health of the South East Asia Region of the WHO.

❮48❯

Speech by Shri Yashwant Sinha, External Affairs Minister on 'Resurgent India in Asia', at Harvard University (29.09.03)

The EAM identified "fiscal deficit and elimination of poverty as areas of special concern" for India as it marches ahead because of its "comparative advantage in knowledge driven areas like development of high-technology, roads and ports". He asserted that favourable trends of demographics and economic indicators of countries like India and China show that "Asia will be the fulcrum of economic activity in the 21st century"

Members of the Harvard faculty,
Distinguished guests and friends,

I

I am happy to be here and to share my views with you on 'Resurgent India in Asia'. I propose to cover this subject in four parts - an introductory part, a part on why I think India is resurgent, thirdly, India and Asia and fourthly, a concluding part.

The United States has been heavily invested in Asia, especially since the end of the Second World War. But its deeper engagement with India is of more recent vintage.

According to conventional wisdom prevailing in the United States at the beginning of the twentieth century, the Mediterranean was considered the sea of the past, the Atlantic, the sea of the present and the Pacific, the sea of the future. The Indian Ocean, providing the link between the, past and the future, was not in the reckoning, nor was the littoral landmass above it.

During the Cold War years, the strategic dimensions of India-U.S. relations were dictated by John Foster Dulles's dictum: 'if you are not with us, you are against us'. India's refusal to join the anti-communist military alliance systems and commitment to non-alignment set limits to our relationship at that time. This may explain why interest in India in the U.S. had been limited in the past, compared to US interest in other parts of Asia. Happily, all this is changing now. The largest democracy and the most powerful democracy in the world are coming together as never before.

II

Over the past fifty-six years since our independence in 1947, India has established a sound and stable liberal democracy. It has done so by successfully conducting free and fair elections, by ensuring repeatedly peaceful transfer of political authority, by empowering women and by devolving powers to elected local authorities. The dynamics of coalition politics that has come to dominate the central government over the past decade has further strengthened governance by consensus. The manner in which India has kept the flame of democracy burning bright is unparalleled in the developing world.

An independent judiciary and a lively, thriving media buttress democratic institutions in India. Delhi alone has 25 daily newspapers, 13 published in English and the remaining in Hindi and Urdu, besides ten 24-hour television news channels. Other major cities and states capitals have their own newspapers and television channels, many of them in regional languages. This effervescence is reflected also in the development and blossoming of the Indian arts, including literature, and the energy of the Indian entertainment industry.

Although a relative latecomer in initiating economic reforms, India quickly outstripped its traditional 'Hindu rate of growth'. Since 1991, India has recorded an average growth of over 6 percent. The size of the economy had doubled since then, and we hope to re-double it now in less than a decade, with a target growth rate of 8 percent. Already, India is the fourth largest economy in the world in terms of purchasing power parity. Poverty levels have dramatically declined and the feel-good factor is high, with business confidence showing the most optimistic outlook since 1995, according to a July 2003 survey.

The Latin American crisis of the 1980s and the Asian crisis of 1997 taught India the virtue of maintaining healthy foreign exchange reserves. These currently stand at around US$ 90 billion and are going up by a billion dollars every two weeks. At 28 percent, for the five-year period up to September 2003, India has had the highest cumulative annual growth rates in reserves accumulation in Asia. This provides India a self-insurance against the vicissitudes of the International financial systems, as also flexible options for exchange rate management. Besides, India has a healthy current account surplus. Short-term debt has declined steadily during this period. India's external debt to GDP, at 17%, is substantially lower than Asia's average. India has paid back its IMF loans ahead of schedule and has also prepaid some World Bank and ADB loans. In fact, India has now become a net lender to IMF. In the last six months, India contributed US$ 355 million in cash to IMF, which was in turn lent by IMF to Brazil and Burundi.

The successful management of the external sector has, in turn, led to the stabilization of the Rupee. Lower inflation, in the low single digit, has led to a decline in interest rates. From a 'ship-to-mouth' existence in the mid-1960s, India is now a food-grain exporter, with national buffer stocks at over 30 million tones, despite a bad monsoon year in 2002. We exported, in the current year, close to US$ 7 billion of agricultural produce and our assistance to Afghanistan includes a million tones of wheat, being supplied in part in the form of high-protein biscuits.

It is interesting that Indians are also now investing abroad. We have invested in oil fields in several countries including Russia, Sudan and Vietnam. Aggregate Indian investments in the United States in the past three years, according to some estimates, is close to a billion dollars, almost keeping pace with U.S. foreign direct investment into India since the year 2000, which has averaged only about US$ 300-350 million each year.

Two areas of special concern to India are the fiscal deficit and elimination of poverty. The consolidated fiscal deficit, at 10% of the GDP, is unsustainable. The Fiscal Responsibility and Budget Management Act will help government bring down its borrowing in phases and buttress government efforts to raise tax revenues. The recent gains in poverty reduction, by pulling up 60 million people from below the poverty line in a period of six years, requires to be accelerated both by promoting growth and improving the implementation of special schemes directed towards poverty elimination.

We are heartened by the optimistic prognostication of two young Cambridge-based scholars, Yasheng Huang of the Harvard Business School and Tarun Khanna of MIT, published in Foreign Policy last month, that while India is not outperforming China overall, it is doing better in certain key areas, and that such success may enable India to catch up with and perhaps even overtake China. It is true that a number of Indian companies compete internationally with best that Europe and the United States have to offer and that India has the potential of becoming the world's technology lab. India's 250 universities, 1500 research institutions and over 10,000 higher education centres produce 200,000 engineers and 300,000 non-engineering Post graduates every year, including 5,000 Doctors of philosophy (PhDs), besides over 2 million undergraduates.

India's comparative advantage in knowledge-driven areas of economic activities has made it both attractive for outsourcing of IT enabled services and an R&D hub. 190 Fortune-500 companies already outsource to India. The IT segment of the Indian economy is expected to grow from US$ 1.5 billion in 2002 to US$ 17 billion in 2008, according to a recent NASSCOM-McKinsey study. Export of software services from India grew by 26 perent last year, and together with electronics hardware exports, account now for 18 percent of India's total exports. Efforts are on to replicate this achievement in the areas of biotechnology, biogenetics and pharmaceuticals.

Development of high technology, such as satellite applications, have led to a telecommunications revolution and the establishment of long-distance telephony, TV broadcast, radio networking and bringing connectivity to remote parts of the country. Data and voice carrying capacity in India are increasing exponentially as also are phone and internet-connections. The meteorological cameras on INSAT have helped us monitor cyclones and save lives and property, while the IRS remote-sensing satellites have helped us build a National Natural Resources Management System, including crop monitoring and wasteland mapping for reclamation. Other achievements in high technology include our success in indigenously building super-computers and the complete nuclear fuel-cycle facilities and to placing geo-synchronous satellites in orbit. Prime Minister Vajpayee just announced, during the course of his Independence Day address on 15th August, that we shall send a Spacecraft to the Moon within the next five years.

A similar transformation is taking place in the areas of roads and ports. The turn around time in Indian ports has been halved in the past few years and further improvements are under way by upgrading existing facilities and building new terminals ports. India is now executing the world's biggest single project, in 13,000 kilometers of four lane roads linking the four corners of India as also its four major cities. The project is already generating daily employment for quarter million construction workers and 10,000 supervisors and engineers. This is supplemented by equally important rural roads development schemes to improve the infrastructure of India's interior. Another large infrastructure project for the moment at a conceptual stage, is on linking of India's major rivers as part of an effective long-term strategy to prevent droughts and floods and to better harness India's fresh water resources for irrigation.

III

Our performance so far has revealed our strengths as well as future areas of growth. It has demonstrated where we can provide leadership and how we can integrate into the global economy. As India's economic development accelerates, India's association with Asia will only widen and deepen further.

Asia's challenge lies in its immense political, economic and social diversity, as also the seemingly unique dynamics of its different regions. A co-operative future global order will inevitably require full Asian participation. With its increasing weight in world economy, Asia holds the key to collective global prosperity and security. Asia's contribution to world output has doubled since 1950. Both IMF and the World Bank consider that Asia will continue to power global growth in the coming years. We require, therefore, to advance the principles of democracy, development and dialogue, on the basis of respect for pluralism and national sovereignty, as the guiding principles of Asian and global progress.

The primary impulse for this has to come from within the Asian countries themselves. But others, including the United States, have a strong stake in it too. If all major powers in Asia and beyond work together, in a spirit of co-operation rather than competition, to smoothen its fault lines, combat terrorism, counter proliferation of weapons of mass destruction and advance free commerce and political freedoms, we would create a basis for a stable and prosperous Asia that will have a salutary effect on the rest of the world. Guided by this vision, India is working vigorously to strengthen its relations with its Asian partners - with China, Japan, Southeast Asia, West Asian countries and Central Asian neighbours. We have a similar vision of South Asia unshackled from historical divisions, and bound together in collective pursuit of peace and prosperity.

India seeks to promote in Asia in general, and in South Asia in particular, its ethos of pluralism, tolerance, democracy and human rights and by promoting the idea of societies that are multiethnic, multilingual, multi-religious and multicultural.

Eighteen years of the existence of the South Asian Association of Regional Cooperation (SAARC) has so far failed to catalyse significant exchanges among its Constituents in the social or economic domains. To shake SAARC from this relative torpor, earlier this year I called for a movement toward a South Asian Union. I believe that a South Asia, with one currency, one tariff regime and free movement of goods, services and people, is well within the realm of possibility. South Asia should emerge as a region with comprehensive air, rail, road and sea linkages. Movement in this direction would lead to softer national boundaries, and eventually, the seven South Asian countries can constitute a single economic space within one system and a single market.

Reaching beyond South Asia, East and Southeast Asia have remained a natural focus of India's foreign and trade policy. China is a contiguous country and we share land or maritime boundaries, not just with our South Asian neighbours and China, but also with several ASEAN countries such as Myanmar, Thailand and Indonesia. Our historical and civilizational ties also extend to Japan.

In the past, India's engagement with much of Asia, including Southeast and East Asia, was built on an idealistic conception of Asian brotherhood, based on shared experiences of colonialism and of cultural ties. The rhythm of the region today is determined, however, as much by trade, investment and production as by history and culture. That is what motivates our decade-old 'Look East' policy. Already, this region accounts for 45% of our external trade.

The first phase of India's 'Look East' policy was ASEAN-centred and focussed primarily on trade and investment linkages. The new phase of this policy is characterised by an expanded definition of 'East', extending from Australia to East Asia, with ASEAN at its core. The new phase also marks a shift from trade to wider economic and security issues, including joint efforts to protect the sea-lanes and co-ordinate counter-terrorism activities.

Last year, the first India-ASEAN Summit was held at Phnom Penh, Cambodia. The Prime Minister of India suggested in this meeting that India and ASEAN should enter into a free trade Agreement. It is a matter of great satisfaction to us that the Framework Agreement for this purpose has already been finalized between India and ASEAN and will be signed at the Second India-ASEAN Summit at Bali in a few days from now. This major breakthrough should contribute significantly to an increasing integration of the India-ASEAN economic space over the coming years, including a free trade Agreement. India is simultaneously negotiating an FTA with Thailand and a Comprehensive Economic Cooperation Agreement with Singapore. Both these negotiations are well advanced. These, along with measures to improve physical connectivity and transportation links such as the India-Myanmar-Thailand trilateral highway and the Delhi-Hanoi railway line, as part of the Ganga-Mekong project, will improve India-ASEAN linkages even further. With ASEAN engaged in parallel negotiations on free trade arrangements with India, China, Japan and South Korea, we are now perhaps at the threshold of an Asian economic community.

India's relations with China are following a positive course. Both sides have made a steady effort to overcome past differences and build a forward-looking relationship. Our bilateral trade has shot up from under US$ 200 million in the early 1990s to nearly US$ 4.5 billion in 2002, and current trends might carry this figure to US$ 6 billion this year, with the balance of trade markedly in India's favour, which is not the case with many other of China's trading partners. The apprehensions of Indian business in dealing with Chinese competition is slowly withering away. Our trade with Japan, a country that accounts for 40 percent of Asian GDP, is at a disappointing $ 3.6 billion, but the two sides are now taking pro-active steps to spur our commercial and economic interaction.

The Gulf region and the wider Middle East is of great importance to India. It is a major source of our energy supplies. Some 3.5 million Indians are employed in the region, over 1.5 million in Saudi Arabia alone. Iraq in the pre-1990 days once provided 30 percent of our oil imports and was home to 100,000 Indians. Given the growth trends, India's dependence on energy supplies from the area is only going to increase.

We also have traditional links with Central Asia and are exploring new trade and transportation connections to provide a strong economic dimension to our relations with countries of the region. The Central Asian republics could be an alternative source for India's energy supplies. India is actively engaged in the reconstruction of Afghanistan. Besides food support, we have provided buses, civilian aircraft and human resource training in a variety of areas through our $270 million assistance programme, which extends also to agriculture, irrigation and the education and health sectors.

IV

I have attempted a quick sketch of Indian involvement with Asia as a whole, stretching beyond our extended neighbourhood, from the Gulf of Hormuz to the Straits of Malacca and between West and Central Asia to Southeast and East Asia. While the world economic outlook continues to be fragile, Asia continues to progress. India, by all accounts, is set to post robust growth in the coming decade. As statistics show, the dragons, tigers and elephants within the Asian landmass have begun to move, with the hiccups of the late 1990s behind them.

It is estimated that by 2010, 60 percent of the world's population in the 20-35 age group will be Asian, contributing a vast pool of producers of goods and services and driving global demand. Together with strong growth in India and China, and favourable trends in demographics and increasing intra-Asian trade, Asia is set to contribute over 50 percent of global GDP by 2025, surpassing the GDP of North America and Europe combined. By virtue of their population, size and growth rates, India and China will play a significant role in the demand and use of technology, FDI flows and in the new equilibrium of economic power. Asia will thus be the fulcrum of economic activity in the twenty-first century, which is seen by many now as an Asian century.

This, however, is predicated on an environment of peace, predictability and security. India has, therefore, not only an interest but a stake in the stability of Asia, which is what we share with the United States. It follows that we, therefore, also have a common interest in dealing with any potential threats to Asian security, whether prompted by non-State actors or by adverse political or economic developments in the region.

What are the most important threats facing Asia today? Terrorism continues to stalk Asia as never before. The bombings at Bali and Mumbai testify to that. Terrorist networks have spread across many Asian countries. Al Qaida and Taliban have regrouped in Afghanistan and Pakistan, aided and abetted by elements within the State structure in Pakistan. The intersection between weapons of mass destruction and terrorism is another major threat, again fostered through dangerous and deliberate nuclear and missile transfers in the region.

Peace, thus, is under the greatest threat in Asia. From the stand-off in North Korea to the violence in Philippines and Aceh in Indonesia to the renewed threats to the Karzai regime in Afghanistan and the senseless violence in Iraq and Middle-East. These threats to peace will have to be dealt with and dealt with effectively and quickly so that violence subsides and peace reigns. I have no doubt that this will happen and that Asia shall fulfil its destiny in the 21st century for the betterment of its people and the rest of the world. India will play an ever increasing role in this journey.

* * * * *

‹49›

Keynote address by Shri Yashwant Sinha, External Affairs Minister at the Third India-Central Asia Conference, Tashkent (06.11.03)

The EAM emphasized that with its oil, gas, gold, silver, mineral wealth and water resources, Central Asia "can become a new silk road of prosperity once again". He also announced that from this year the IDSA and the ICCR would be providing 10 and 30 scholarships respectively every year to students from Central Asia in addition to the setting up of IT education institutes in the CARs.

Your Excellency, Mr. Sadik Salikhovich Safayev, Minister of Foreign Affairs, Excellencies and Distinguished Guests,

It gives me great pleasure to be with you at this third and the most ambitious India-Central Asia Conference. I would like to commend the Institute of Strategic and Regional Studies, Tashkent and the Institute for Defence Studies and Analysis, New Delhi, for their efforts in organising this Conference at short notice. The participation from more than 20 countries is a tribute to the growing ties between India and Central Asia. I am delighted to see that Indian industrialists are also here. Their participation should provide a useful, new dimension to the deliberations.

I propose to divide my talk today in four broad parts – an introductory portion on the history and the range of our relations with Central Asia, a second part on the energy and economic potential of Central Asia, a third on the new bilateral initiatives and a concluding part on the international security situation.

I have been in Tashkent for just a few hours, but already I can see why this beautiful city was chosen by the Indian organisers as the venue for the Conference. Great cities like Tashkent, Bukhara and Samarkand are daily reminders to the world of the kind of civilisations that have flourished here.

India's connection with these splendid cities, indeed entire Central Asia, has deep roots in history. Trade between us pre-dates the Silk Road by at least three thousand years. And Aryans provide a link between Central Asia and India. Some scholars maintain that the Vedas are a blend of the adventurous 'Central Asian' spirit and the cultural genius of the Indus Valley

Civilisation. We, in India, still use the Saka Calendar as a sort of daily reminder of the deep bonds between Central Asia and India.

During the so called great game, Napoleon and later the imperial ambitions of Russia and Britain, were engaged in a tournament of shadows where Central Asia was the chess board and the prize was India. But a lesser known and less commented upon effect of this great game was to cut off Central Asia, for nearly 150 years, from its cultural neighbours to the south.

In more recent times, few regions have changed as dramatically as Central Asia has since 1990s. The transition from communism to democracy has been made without major convulsions. It will be fair to say that this was expected of a region where the literacy rate is over 98 percent and where the constitutional liberty carries with it secularism as an article of faith. India and Central Asia share these national strengths.

There are new developments in international economic environment too. Thanks to dramatic changes in technology, transportation and communication systems, Central Asia is bound to wield far more influence in global economy, than it ever did earlier. If Central Asia was once famous for its good horses, it was also known for men of substance like Al Baruni, Olog Bek and Ibn Sina. In my view, Central Asia is once again poised for greatness.

In so far as Central Asia and India are concerned, greater economic engagement is needed. We have taken some steps already, there are now sound institutional linkages in place. India was one of the first countries to set up Embassies in each of the Central Asian countries. After Tajikistan has opened its mission in Delhi in October 2003, all the Central Asian countries are represented in India. And after Tajikistan commenced direct flights to India from February this year, we are connected by air with all of the Central Asian States. For some years now, we have also been paying attention to land and sea connectivity. The trilateral arrangement, and the North-South Corridor have made the flow of goods to Central Asia faster.

Earlier this year, India, Iran and Afghanistan decided to open a new sea and road route through the port of Chahbahar. India hopes to construct 200 kms of the road linking Zaranj and Delaram. Once this road is complete, it will reduce by 1500 kms the distance from India to Central Asia.

Our desire for multiple transport links with Central Asia is in tune with our economic progress. Over the last decade, India has transited from a mixed to a largely market economy. During this momentous period of change, the GDP has grown at around 6 percent annually. The foreign exchange reserves are nearly $ 90 bn. Technologically too, it has been a period of achievement. India has become a major centre for outsourcing. Its manufactured products compete with the best in the world. Two years ago we launched a satellite into geo-stationary orbit, and we propose to send a spacecraft to Moon within the next five years.

Indian companies have also become major investors abroad. They are investing in oilfields too - in Sakhalin in Russia with an investment of $ 2 bn; in Sudan with an investment of $ 1 bn; in Vietnam, Libya, Syria and other countries. And they are looking keenly to invest in oilfields in Central Asia.

It is remarkable that while the energy resources are getting increasingly scarce in rest of the world, new oilfields are being discovered with great regularity in Central Asia. Some experts maintain that Central Asian Resources may be difficult to reach, because it is the largest landmass in the world which is landlocked. But this is both a challenge and an opportunity, because in the technology driven world of today it is not always necessary to transport material. That is the logic of investment abroad and organising production facilities there. Therefore, no part of the world today can remain on the margins, every part is capable of becoming the centre of the world. Central Asia, with its rich resources, has definite potential to become so.

Moreover, Indian companies are also interested in setting up refineries and new pipelines. The presence at this conference of the representatives of Indian energy industry is proof that they wish to participate and develop the energy infrastructure in the region.

Our cooperation with Central Asia includes cultural, economic, defence and security relations. For us Central Asia is our *'immediate and strategic neighbourhood'* .

Thus, we are currently engaged in setting up, with our aid funds, Institutes of Excellence in IT education in Kyrgyzstan, Tajikistan and Uzbekistan. A Fruit Processing plant is being set up by India in Tajikistan. Earlier this year, a complete Industrial Training Centre was commissioned and handed over to Government of Turkmenistan. Currently India provides 1000 man-months of training to senior Central Asian professionals every year.

I am happy to announce that from now onwards, we will also be providing at the Institute of Defence Studies and Analyses (IDSA) ten scholarships every year. Two senior researchers from each Central Asian state would be invited to undertake projects on regional cooperation and security related issues. I hope this new dimension to our cooperation would provide a diverse and long term perspective to India's relations with Central Asia.

I would also like to announce that from this year, thirty full scholarships will be provided by the Indian Council for Cultural Relations to students from Central Asia.

Our cultural links need constant attention. Therefore, we are currently engaged in finalising with Central Asian states a major cultural project. We propose to host "A Festival of Central Asia" in major cities of India in 2004.

There are a number of new economic initiatives under way. On 1st April 2003, the Government of India announced that the year 2003 would be the 'Focus CIS Year'. Central Asia is, therefore, the centrepoint of Indian exhibitions, buyer-seller meetings, seminars and special studies. To give just one example, there are three exhibitions being planned in Tashkent over the next three months. A total of hundred Indian businessmen will be participating in these events.

Friends, ours has never been a one-sided relationship. We want to export, but we want even greater exports from Central Asia to India. And in that spirit, we would welcome and support in India a 'Made in Central Asia' exhibition at a time of their convenience.

I am convinced that Central Asia, with its oil, gas, gold, silver, other mineral wealth and water resources, can become a new silk road of prosperity once again.

But we need peace and stability for full economic progress. Unfortunately, both India and Central Asia have been victims of terror for a long time. Hizb-ut-Tahrir, IMU, Lashkar-e-Toiba and others who threaten Central Asia or India, represent a transnational threat. They have no interest in bargaining. They seek to cripple nations, it is impossible to imagine them apologising for mass destruction.

Terror-trained, financed and sponsored-is now striking globally with no desire to negotiate. The current circumstances are even more alarming when one considers the bumper drug crop and resurgence of Al Qaida and others. For us in the region, the concern is even greater because the epicentre of terror lies in our common neighbourhood. These trends are worrying, and a more determined and co-ordinated fight against terrorism is needed by the international community. Ladies and Gentlemen, India is ready to stand shoulder to shoulder with its Central Asian neighbours in confronting and overcoming this menace.

If our neighbourhood is peaceful and stable, if the only interference from outside is one of economic inputs, then Central Asia can once again be a bridge between East and West. That bridge can contribute to peace, prosperity and energy security in the wider world too. India's increasing engagement with Central Asia is aimed at promoting peace and mutual prosperity. We are civilisational partners, we want our ancient links to have contemporary colour.

I am sure the deliberations of this Conference will point us towards that direction and I take great pleasure in wishing your efforts success.

‹50›

Admiral RD Katari Memorial Lecture by Shri Yashwant Sinha, External Affairs Minister on "The Emerging India-China Relationship and its Impact on India/South Asia" (22.11.03)

The EAM stated that while the basic paradigm of the Indo-China relationship was to improve relations at all levels and in diverse areas, it was important to deal with some of the outstanding issues in a determined manner. In this regard, India and China had agreed to take principled positions on issues like Tibet, Taiwan and Sikkim and had agreed to develop the economic partnership.

It is a privilege for me to be invited here today to deliver this lecture in memory of Admiral Ramdas Katari, a distinguished sailor, strategist and diplomat. The first Indian to become the Chief of the Naval Staff, Admiral Katari envisioned a modern navy for the country and did a lot to translate that vision into reality. A highly decorated soldier, he moved effortlessly to the world of diplomacy and served with distinction as India's Ambassador to Burma (now Myanmar) for four years. I would like to compliment the Indian Navy for carrying forward the fine traditions initiated by visionaries like Admiral Katari.

I have been asked to share a few thoughts with you on one of the most important bilateral relationships we have. Let me begin on a somewhat provocative note by saying that the title of this lecture–"The Emerging India-China Relationship and its Impact on India/South Asia"–represents a particular mind-set that is no longer valid. This is because first, I think that the relationship between India and China today is mature enough to be seen as having "emerged" rather than "emerging", though in a sense the relations between these two large countries will always remain a work in progress. Secondly, the impact of our relationship is global and to restrict the canvas to South Asia is to limit the scope of our understanding of India-China relations.

Let me substantiate my first contention regarding the maturity of the relationship between India and China. In recent years, relations between India and China have progressively developed and diversified. This is a process that both Governments have consciously promoted. Our Prime Minister's visit to China marked the beginning of a new phase in the India-China relationship. It was a historic visit, the results of which have surprised many. During the visit, the leaders of the two countries agreed that we should qualitatively enhance the bilateral relationship in all areas, while addressing differences through peaceful means in a fair, reasonable and mutually acceptable manner. We agreed that the common interests of the two sides outweigh their differences, and that they are not a threat to each other. For the first time, the two Prime Ministers signed a Joint Declaration. It is an important document, which outlines the principles and shared perspectives that will guide the future development of our bilateral relations. The Declaration sends a signal to Asia and the world that our two countries are committed to working more closely together, including through our common desire to strengthen the trend towards multi-polarity.

I will illustrate the maturity of the present state of our relations with China with a few observations, which do not attempt to present a comprehensive picture. First, India and China have today extensive dealings in bilateral, regional and multilateral forums. We are seeking improved relations with each other without pre-conditions. We continue to have differences, including an unresolved boundary issue, but over the years, we have, together, evolved a remarkable matrix of relations, under which we have consciously decided to "compartmentalise" our differences and address them without letting them come in the way of the development of relations in other areas. We have not allowed our differences to define our relationship. It is a pragmatic model of inter-state relations, which has obvious relevance in other situations, including in our dealings with Pakistan.

Secondly, it is a relationship that is characterised by a strong political commitment, and indeed investment, by the leaderships of the two countries. This is evident in the pattern of high-level exchanges. There is no objective reason for discord between us. We also believe that mutual exclusion or containment is not a valid policy choice. At the same time, we are fully aware that there is a deficit of trust, which must be addressed as the two countries move towards their shared vision of a constructive and cooperative partnership. Our Prime Minister's visit to China represented a major step forward in that direction.

Thirdly, the level of mutual understanding that has been achieved is exemplified by our success in maintaining peace and tranquillity along the border. It is no mean achievement considering that we have a common border that extends for almost 3500 kilometres and where there are clear differences of perception, both in terms of the boundary and the Line of Actual Control (LAC). You are aware that in the late 1980s, there was tension along the border, particularly after the Wangdung incident, but the two countries responded in a sensible manner and have over the years carefully put in place an edifice of CBMs, of dialogue and interactions at the diplomatic and border commanders levels, of service-to-service exchanges, including the first-ever joint search and rescue exercise conducted by our

Navies only a week ago. This has helped preserve and reinforce peace, tranquillity and indeed amity in border areas. We are engaged in clarifying the LAC, a process that must be expedited. During the Prime Minister's visit to China, the two Prime Ministers appointed their Special Representatives to explore the framework of a boundary settlement from the political perspective of the overall bilateral relationship. It is an issue I will return to a little later in my talk.

Fourthly, bilateral economic and commercial interactions have acquired an altogether new dimension now. Possibly for the first time in the exchanges between India and China since our independence, we have now a significant economic aspect to this relationship. Our bilateral trade has shot up from around US $ 200 million in the early nineties to around US $ 5 billion in 2002, and this year we hope to reach US $ 7 billion. Indian business and industry have overcome their initial cultural and commercial apprehensions of Chinese business and are strengthening their linkages in a pro-active manner. Enhanced trade and investment linkages not only make great economic sense but also provide ballast to the political relationship; mutual economic stakes will be a factor of stability in a relationship, which has seen many ups and downs in the past.

Finally, the India-China dialogue already transcends bilateral relations to encompass international issues such as security, environment and sustainable development. These are being discussed through dialogue mechanisms which have recently been extended to new subjects such as counter terrorism and policy planning. Our deliberations in these forums have revealed a growing convergence of views on key issues, including on terrorism. We have an increasing commonality of interests within the WTO and overlapping concerns on globalisation, as was evident at the recent ministerial meeting at Cancun. Our co-ordination and collaboration in various multilateral institutions is expanding into newer and newer areas. Both countries, seek to reinforce multilateralism and multi-polarity. The concept of multi-polarity must not, however, be mistaken for creating poles in opposition to each other. We do not want to reinvent the confrontationist model of the Cold War. Both India and China look upon the next twenty years as a window of strategic opportunity to raise the living standards of their peoples.

It is clear that as in India, there is also a need felt in China to improve the bilateral relations. This is not only because together we represent one-third of humanity. This has much to do with the changing perceptions about India, her economic success, her achievements in the field of science and technology, and global reach and dynamism of her foreign policy. It is also a factor of our steadily improving relations with the United States, the continued strategic partnership with Russia, our comprehensive partnership relations with the EU and its constituents, and our initiatives in West Asia, CIS countries, Africa and Latin America. It also has to do with our improving relations with other Asian countries, particularly ASEAN. It has to do with the increasing scope of potential cooperation between India and China in regional and multilateral forums, as we face new global challenges such as terrorism, drugs and piracy, as well as dangers in the fields of public health, environment, etc. It has to do with the fact that we are both in the forefront of developing countries and have similar approaches to many global and regional issues. It is clear that both India and China respect each other's independent foreign policies and are adjusting their relationship to take into account the new global realities, each other's growth as vibrant nations and economies and also in response to the dynamics operating regionally and globally.

Let me also clarify here what does not drive our relations with China. There are some who argue that India's relations with the United States could be used as a counterforce against China. We categorically reject such notions based on outmoded concepts like balance of power. We do not seek to develop relations with one country to 'counterbalance' another. We value our relations with both China and the USA and both relationships have their own compelling logic. We must also debunk the theory that India's 'Look East' policy of greater engagement with ASEAN is somehow aimed at containing China. Indeed, as I have stated at other forums recently, we have now entered Phase-II of the 'Look East' policy, which encompasses not only the ASEAN Ten but also China, Japan, and other countries of East Asia, including Australia and New Zealand.

I would also like to reiterate, what I have said earlier, that we reject the theory that a conflict between India and China is inevitable. India neither pursues nor makes policy towards China based on the belief that the conflict between the two is inevitable. India's approach to China is and will remain forward-looking and full of optimism. It will not be driven by a sense of either fear or envy. We are convinced that both countries can grow strong and prosperous in partnership rather than in conflict, and maintain their independence and national character in the process. While it is undeniable that China and India are in some sense competitors, it is also clear that, just as the US and Europe, we can be both partners and competitors at the same time. All that is required is, that this competition be healthy. This also relates to the level and rate of success achieved by the different development paradigms followed by India and China. While China may be seen by some as currently being ahead in this competition, India's success is clearly recognised and better understood now nationally and internationally than before. The management of this competition is the challenge and the Joint Declaration signed during Prime Minister's visit to China provides an agreed via media for that.

Likewise, the argument that the dominant theme of China's South Asia policy is to prevent the rise of a potential rival or competitor in the form of India is a defeatist argument. There are probably some in our neighbourhood who seek to play their "China connection" or "China card" to "counter" or even "contain" India. The bankruptcy of this approach is, however, becoming increasingly evident. China cannot objectively be a competitor for India in South Asia. Destinies of the countries of South Asia are interlinked by the overwhelming logic of History, Geography and Economics. I believe the current relationship between India and China is certainly beneficial for each other and for South Asia. That India and China have succeeded in maintaining peace and tranquillity on their borders, and are steadily increasing the lines of communication between them, brings a large measure of stability to the region. We do not and should not judge our relationship with China in the context of our bilateral relations with any other country, whether in the region or outside the region. It also means that other countries need to adjust their own equations with both India and China to factor in the reality that it is no longer a matter of playing one against the other. It must also be recognised that increasing cooperation between India and China in the multilateral arena, which is a sub-set of our current relationship, will also have a positive cascading effect on the region, especially on issues relating to the interests of developing countries.

As I have stated earlier, during Prime Minister's visit to China in June this year, both countries agreed to qualitatively enhance their bilateral relationship in all areas and also charted out a road-map for doing so. Let me share with you some of my thoughts on what can be done by India and China to bring about a quantum jump in the relationship.

While the basic paradigm of the relationship–of seeking improved relations at all levels and in diverse areas while addressing differences–remains valid, the time has perhaps come to deal with some of those outstanding issues in a determined manner, without postponing tough decisions for the next generation. We believe the relationship has reached a level of maturity where we can discuss those issues with a greater sense of urgency. This updated paradigm of relationship is both desirable and sustainable. The initiative on the appointment of the Special Representatives flows from such an assessment. As Prime Minister stated recently, a final resolution of the boundary question is a strategic objective and both countries should be ready to take some pragmatic decisions to achieve it. While India and China agree that their differences should not be allowed to affect the overall development of bilateral relations, there is little doubt that a boundary settlement will give a major boost to the relationship. It will also send a powerful signal to the rest of the world that India and China have broken out of the shackles of the past.

Secondly, the two countries must pay closer attention to each other's sensitivities and aspirations. This has been agreed to in the Joint Declaration signed by the two Prime Ministers. We have taken a principled position on issues like Tibet and Taiwan, and our position is appreciated by China. We are happy that the understanding reached during Prime Minister's visit to China started the process by which Sikkim will soon cease to be an issue in India-China relations. Some aspects of China's relations with Pakistan, including their nexus in nuclear and missile proliferation, however, continue to cause serious concern in India as they have a direct and negative bearing on our national security environment. We regard China as a friend and we expect friends to show greater sensitivity to our security concerns. It is also important that both countries acknowledge each other's strengths and aspirations, and try to ensure that each has sufficient strategic space in keeping with the principle of multi-polarity to which both India and China subscribe.

Thirdly, we must be far more pro-active and ambitious in developing our economic partnership by exploiting more fully our complementarities and the new opportunities created by globalisation. Though our bilateral trade has shown an impressive increase in recent years, the turnover is still less than 1% of China's overall trade, which is expected to reach US $ 800 billion this year. India-China trade is quite inadequate when compared to the complementarities that exist. For the first time, the business communities of the two countries are seriously looking at each other, with optimism and not with anxiety, and the two Governments must encourage this process with appropriate policy initiatives. Our economic engagement must be commensurate with the fact that India and China have two of the fastest growing economies in the world. A recent report by Goldman Sachs projects that India's economy will overtake that of France, Germany and Japan in less than thirty years and emerge as the third largest economy in the world in US dollar terms (and not just in Purchasing Power Parity), next only to that of the USA and China.

I believe that we in India must be ambitious, and not excessively cautious. Our experience during the last two-and-a-half-years has shown how our apprehensions regarding Chinese goods overwhelming our manufacturing sector, following the lifting of quantitative restrictions on imports, were greatly exaggerated. This is a matter of some personal satisfaction to me because, as Finance Minister, I was at the receiving end of all this criticism. I do expect that the India-China Joint Study Group, agreed upon during Prime Minister's visit, will examine the feasibility of an upgraded bilateral framework for relationship, including a Free Trade Area. I know that some will receive this suggestion with disbelief and regard it as premature, as they did when Prime Minister proposed a framework Agreement for a Free Trade Area between India and ASEAN just over a year ago. But the fact is that we have already concluded a framework FTA with ASEAN. An Asian FTA, including China, Japan and South Korea, apart from ASEAN and India should therefore be within the realm of possibility. Indeed, I am also inclined to believe that in the years to come, India and China will be key partners in regional economic arrangements transcending Asia.

Finally, it is in the interest of both India and China to continue to raise the level of mutual trust and understanding. We must upgrade the quality of our dialogue and continuously address each other's concerns in a frank but constructive manner, not as adversaries but as friends, convinced that there is no fundamental contradiction in our basic interests. The degree of positive or negative influence which the actions of other countries can have on the bilateral relationship between India and China is proportional to the level of mutual trust and understanding that exists between us. It is important to continue in the conflict resolution mode that now exists between India and China, and indeed accelerate this process, not only because it is beneficial to us but also because it is beneficial to the region, and to the world. The risk of conflict or even divisive rivalry, open or covert, between two of the largest countries in the world, with huge and steadily growing economies, with nuclear weapon capabilities, with geographical contiguity and unresolved territorial issues, is a spectre that should never be allowed to haunt us or affect our search for peace and stability in this world.

Friends, India's fundamental national goal is the pursuit of a better quality of life for its people. What we seek the most is, economic progress and prosperity, the development of art, culture, literature and sports, and the emergence of a plural and multifaceted society that utilises the natural talents and versatility of our people to the full. I believe China also has a similar motivation. Peace and stability in the neighbourhood is of critical importance to both of us, in order to be able to pursue these goals and it is in this context that we must see India-China relations over the long term.

‹51›

Statement by Shri Arun Shourie, Minister for Communications, Information Technology and Disinvestment, at the World Summit for Information Society, Geneva (11.12.03)

Mr. Arun Shourie stated that the "four projects worthy of this gathering are: .... the use ICT to abolish illiteracy; development of a Universal Networking Language; bringing text-to-voice and voice-to-text software to perfection for print disabled; and completing research to enable wireless signals to go to a multiple of the 50/60 kms." He mentioned that "each of these was a doable task....each of these will spell untold benefit to millions....we should join hands so that they are accomplished before we meet in Tunis."

Mr. President, Distinguished Participants,

As a result of detailed and intensive exchanges, valuable declarations have been agreed upon. They set out important principles. They set out a sound work programme.

As a country that has secured many gains from Information Technology-India earns around $ 11 billion from the export of IT services and products every year; as a country that has contributed significantly to the growth of this field -one-third of the start-ups in Silicon Valley were by Indians; as a country that is one of the principal knowledge-generators in this field over 100 of the Fortune–500 companies have set up R&D centers in India; as the country that today has three-fourths of the world's CMM Quality level V companies; as a country that is expanding the infrastructure for an Information Society rapidly -we are adding 1.3 million subscribers to mobile telephony every month, we have already laid out 500,000 kilometers of fiber optic network; India will participate vigorously in the work programme that you are adopting.

You are instituting a Working Group to ascertain the feasibility and effectiveness of setting up a Fund for advancing Information Society. Should such a Fund be set up, India will contribute financially in accordance with the formula that collective deliberations yield. To be of even greater assistance, we will contribute in kind -by training and equipping people for this new society, by sharing the substantial experience that we have acquired in spheres such as e-Governance, Telemedicine, imparting literacy, Information

Security, language technologies. Indian firms today equip people in over 55 countries for the Information Society. Our Government is itself setting set up Cyber cities and training centers in other countries. I am delighted to report that just day before yesterday, the Prime Minister of India and the President of Ghana, opened the Kofi Annan Center for Excellence that India has established in Accra for West Africa. Friends, the inauguration itself was a token of a new world -the Indian Prime Minister was in Dejhi, the President in Accra; they inaugurated the Center via a video teleconference! We will redouble such initiatives.

Sir, one of the gains of your deliberations has been that important issues such as Intellectual Property, Internet Governance, and freedom of speech have been subjected to close examination. The declarations that you are adopting are carefully modulated, they embody a fine balance between several competing objectives.

Freedom

In India, we value freedom for itself -in regard to the subject of your deliberations, Knowledge and Information Societies, we believe that they are predicated on creativity, and it is in freedom that creativity flourishes best. For the same reason, we are deeply committed to freedom of speech: on the rarest of rare occasions when a hand has been raised to curtail it, the people have singed that hand. Moreover, we recognize that the right to information is the foundation of freedom to speak one's mind.

Internet Governance

You are requesting the Secretary General to set up a Working Group to think through issues concerning Internet Governance. India has considerable experience in this regard, and we will contribute in whatever way the Secretary General deems appropriate. I have two suggestions. In going through the deliberations that you have held on this matter, I feel that, the preliminary technical points having been discussed at length, we should now look farther afield. Consider just one example. As we modernize, our economies, our financial systems, our power grids, our rail and air traffic control systems get progressively integrated. A vast literature is already available -it is available on the Internet itself!—on how Information Technology can—and *should!*—be used to disrupt such progressively integrating systems. All of us together have to devise ways to prevent terrorists and other adversaries from doing so. I am, therefore, confident that the Working Group will examine the issue more comprehensively than has been possible in the run-up to this Summit.

I would also urge that even as the Group examines issues relating to Internet Governance, it scout for impedances that are created in fact. This will ensure that the next time we deliberate on the matter we are dealing with actual misuse of servers and the like rather than warding off miasmas and hypothetical possibilities.

Felt needs

Sir, as you know this is a sphere in which technological change occurs at lightning speed, in which the technological possibilities are beyond what we can imagine today. In such spheres there is often the temptation of plenty. Everything seems worth doing. Someone in Government or in a firm hears of something that has been done somewhere-sometimes he even thinks up some bright application! As he has the position or resources, work on that idea commences. Substantial sums are spent developing and then installing that application. But when after a few years it is seen that such pursuits did not yield any concrete benefit to people, they discredit the new technologies, they compound cynicism.

Therefore, we should, through the new technologies, address specific, and urgent needs of our people.

There are many fancy applications for e-Governance, for instance. In India a few hundred applications have been developed and adopted. But the one that has brought immediate, tangible benefit to ordinary farmers is that in some States all land records have been digitized-so that the farmer can secure title documents etc. without having to wait upon the village official.

Similarly, by installing telemedicine infrastructure and software, we have enabled patients in distant, isolated communities to receive the best medical diagnosis and advice in the foremost of our hospitals.

Eighteen languages are recognized as official languages under our Constitution. To enable people to access these new technologies, software has been developed that transforms text -and will soon convert speech - automatically from one language to another.

The script of Indian languages is phonetic. That of English is not. Therefore, software has been developed by which, while I type on a standard English keyboard, the computer transcribes and prints the text in the script of the Indian language.

Many of us cannot read print -either because we are visually impaired or because we are illiterate. We have, therefore, developed software that transforms text into speech. This has already been done for anything available in electronic form -for instance, a person who is blind can by just a click or two get to his favourite newspaper on the Internet. and the computer reads out the paper to him.

Yesterday, Mrs. Kicki Nordstrom, President of the World Blind Union, drew our attention to the fact that she could not read the papers of this conference -they are not available in Braille. Let us reflect on that reproach for a moment. The papers of this Summit are available in print. In India we already use software to convert printed text into electronic form, and then print the text in Braille. As this Summit is about the Information Society, we can be confident that the papers will soon be available on the Internet. That is where we come in. I give you my assurance, Mrs. Nordstrom, that within three months I will personally send you text-to-voice software that will read aloud all the papers the moment they are accessed on the website of the Summit. Imagine the liberation that such steps spell for a blind child, for the aged parent who has lost sight because of macular degeneration.

Similarly, one of the doyens of the IT industry in India, Mr. F. C. Kohli, has developed methods for making people literate using IT that are bound to spell a revolution. Instead of teaching the person to read by first getting him to learn the alphabet, the method exposes her or him to the word as a whole; simultaneously, the person hears the sound and sees a depiction of what the word connotes. Through this "total immersion", and capitalizing on the fact that a vocabulary of just 500 to 700 words is sufficient for reading the average, daily newspaper, almost 40,000 persons who were totally, but totally illiterate have been brought to a level that they can now read newspapers on their own. This has been done through instruction ofjust 1 to 1 1/2 hours a day for just 10 weeks.

I could readily give scores of examples of this kind. My suggestion is that even as, and specially because the new technologies make so many things seem attractive, we should sharpen our focus, and concentrate efforts on those projects that will spell immediate benefits to vast numbers, and which will lift them into this new Information Society.

Six areas for focused effort

Permit me, Sir, to suggest six areas concentration on which will yield immediate benefits:

- Abolishing illiteracy;
- Upgrading existing educational institutions-for instance, engineering and medical colleges -by connecting them with the best institutions in the country or region so that students in the less advantaged ones can share the teaching material, the lectures etc. of the best;
- Distant diagnosis and prescription of those who are not well,
- Enabling the disabled -specially the print disabled:
- Codifying traditional knowledge -for instance. household, indigenous remedies for common ailments.

Sir, I have one final suggestion, and I will conclude.

After a great deal of sustained effort, declarations have been finalized. They will soon be adopted. The Summit should now go beyond declarations. We should agree on a few actual programmes that we will execute in mission mode-so that when we meet in Tunis two years from now, we are not just deliberating on the next declaration but are celebrating actual accomplishments.

In the coming months we should adopt a few specific projects of global reach and global significance, and organize co-ordinated research on them. Of the many projects that occur to one, I commend four for your consideration:

- Use ICT to abolish illiteracy;
- Develop the Universal Networking Language -so that a person in India can put his data or message on to the Net in any of our 18 languages, the machine should translate it into the Universal Networking Language, and my friend in Iran should be able to receive it in Persian;
- Bring text-to-voice and voice-to-text software to perfection so that worlds from which they are today shut out are opened to the print disabled;
- Today one of the severest impediments to enabling people to avail the benefits of the Information Society is the expense of laying the infrastructure to their doorstep; we should complete research that would enable wireless signals to go to a multiple of the 50/60 kilometers they traverse at present.

Each of these is a do-able task.

Each of these will spell untold benefit to millions.

Together, they are worthy of a gathering as exalted as this one.

We should join hands so that they are accomplished —*before* we meet in Tunis. Thank you.

❮52❯

Speech by Shri Brajesh Mishra, National Security Adviser of India, at the Council of Foreign Relations, New York (07.05.03)

Shri Brajesh Mishra highlighted the features of the New World Orders that emerged at the end of World War II, then after the fall of the Berlin Wall and now after the terrorist attacks of September 11, 2001. He felt that the challenge for the US was not to demolish the "multilateral global architecture" comprising the UN, WTO, World Bank and IMF but to address their shortcomings. Reconfiguration of the UNSC, the reform of "restrictive regimes like the NPT" and legitimizing "extraordinary measures" to deal with international terrorism are some of the strands on which a new world order should be woven.

India, United States and the New World Order: Prospects for Cooperation

Ladies and Gentlemen,

It is a privilege to be here today with you to exchange views on India-US relations.

At the same time, you have put me in a bit of a spot by asking me to talk about the New World Order! Frankly, I think it is still very much an evolving process. Are recent events a continuation of the post-Cold War readjustment of the world order, or do they signal a re-ordered "post-9/11" world order? The jury is still out on this, and the verdict will emerge only in the future.

I will, therefore, make some brief remarks on what I see as elements of the emerging world order and then talk about the India-US relationship in that framework.

History tells us that after a great war, the victorious forces seek to redesign the world order. But history also warns us that unexpected events and the interplay of diverse forces can divert or derail this effort.

Just look at the previous world order. At the end of World War II, the victorious Allies sought to guarantee collective security through the United Nations and its specialized agencies.

This blueprint for a New World Order did not last for even a decade. The UN Security Council was paralysed by the confrontation between the Eastern and Western blocs. Instead of multilateral cooperation within the UN, the Cold War became the world's strategic paradigm for four decades after World War II.

With the fall of the Berlin wall came the next quest for a New World Order. Political leaders across the globe spoke about a new window of opportunity for peace and cooperation.

But optimistic hopes for the end of conflict were soon belied. Countries disintegrated under the onslaught of ethnic nationalism and religious extremism. The myth of self-correcting market forces was exploded by the East Asian financial crisis and similar afflictions in parts of Europe and Latin America. Conflicts claimed more casualties during the decade of the 1990's than during the entire Cold War. Terrorism was beginning to announce itself on the world stage as a non-state actor of worrying proportions.

And then came September 11, 2001, demonstrating the reach of global terrorism and its ability to bridge the asymmetry in power and strength between the terrorist and his victims. The coalition, formed to fight this scourge, achieved its immediate purpose of restoring a popular government in Afghanistan, but its composition does not enable it to tackle global terrorism comprehensively since not all its members have a firm commitment to this objective. The military action in Iraq involved another "coalition of the willing", and in the process opened up divisions within the UN Security Council, European Union and NATO.

Today, we hear two prognostications of the evolving new world order. The first is of a unipolar world with the United States taking the principal decisions on international political and economic issues. According to this theory, the dominance of U.S. power would drive the impulse to unilaterally shape the world in its image, brushing aside any dissenting opinion. The other model is one of a world comprising multiple political poles, suggesting that a certain level of tension between the poles will maintain an equilibrium in which the dominant pole can be kept in some check.

While pondering on the viability of the model of a unipolar world, we need to recognize that the post Cold War order has been profoundly influenced by globalisation. Inspired by – and now itself driving – the technologies of the information age, it affects every aspect of human and group activity – political, economic and social. No country or society has remained immune from this phenomenon. The consequences of globalisation cannot be localised within national boundaries.

Demographic changes and migration patterns; the movement of natural resources – particularly energy and water; and issues like climate change pose challenges transcending national boundaries. Even States with the most advanced technical means are increasingly unable to fully control international flows of disease, illicit drugs, funds and weapons. The international information networks of terrorism and the proliferation of weapons of mass destruction among its State and non-State practitioners can only be countered by close cooperation between democratic societies through regular information exchanges and intelligence sharing.

Today, a regional epidemic like SARS becomes a global problem overnight. The ongoing arguments about whether more real-time information might have halted its spread prove the point of global interdependence.

Such global inter-dependence means that even a unipolar power needs cooperative action in pursuit of its various objectives. The current crisis over North Korea is an example.

The question is also one of resources. If a terrorist network is smashed in a failed or failing state – as Afghanistan was under the Taliban – there would obviously be costs for the reconstruction of the State. The external assistance for Afghanistan's reconstruction is now about $250 million a year; it would need to be increased and sustained over many years. The cost of restoration after the last Gulf War was higher, and that of Iraq's reconstruction is expected to be much, much higher. No single world power, however rich, would want to take on this kind of financial burden, at the expense of its taxpayers.

On the second model, we should realize that in the real world, an arrangement not in conformity with geo-political realities cannot be sustained. It is an unquestionable fact that USA is the pre-eminent power in the world today. The American commentator, Fareed Zakaria, recently pointed out that USA spends as much on defence as the entire rest of the world put together; and this amount is only 4 percent of its GDP. The US economy is as large as those of Japan, Germany and Britain put together.

It would make poor political or economic sense for a country – or a group of countries – to set itself up as an alternate pole in opposition to USA. Most countries advocating a multi-polar world also affirm that they attach great importance to relations with USA. What they seek is an ethic of plurality and consensus which would ensure that collective decisions give due weightage to their legitimate interests and concerns. It is a non-confrontationist model, not based on outmoded concepts of balance of power, spheres of interest and military blocs.

Nearly sixty years ago, after the end of World War II, America was in a similar position of political, military and economic pre-eminence. Then, a mature American communitarian impulse inspired the creation of a multilateral global architecture. The United Nations, the World Trade Organisation, the World Bank and the IMF are all products of this internationalism.

The challenge today is not to demolish these edifices, but to address their shortcomings, some of which are serious. The United Nations system of collective security has not always functioned effectively. It needs reform. The Security Council needs reconfiguration. But we should not throw out the baby with the bathwater. As I pointed out earlier, even a powerful unipolar power requires multilateral agencies, which can maintain political, financial and economic order.

A reform is also required in the current non-proliferation architecture to make it serve the real purpose for which it was created. Restrictive regimes deny access of several countries to dual-purpose goods and technologies, without either rewarding responsible behaviour or punishing irresponsible proliferators.

Deterrence, prevention and defence are accepted elements of a national security strategy. But today, the international terrorist is often an irrational individual, ready to sacrifice his and innocent lives for an extremist cause, acquiring weapons of mass destruction and using unorthodox techniques to overcome asymmetries of strength. There can be no deterrence against irrational behaviour. Prevention and defence are also almost impossible. In such cases, extraordinary measures have to be taken in the interests of security. This is where a smoothly operating world order with a functioning consultative mechanism can help to provide legitimacy.

It is from these strands that a new world order would be woven. What we need is a constructive and continuing dialogue on the management of global inter-dependence.

In the world order defined by the Cold War, India and US were not really allies though, to be fair, nor were they enemies. India-US relations reflected a lack of engagement, coupled with wariness and a periodically recurring suspicion whenever the shadow of the Cold War fell over our region.

In the post-Cold War world (and even in the post-9/11 world order), the situation is dramatically different. We have shared geo-political interests and economic opportunities, which can bind an enduring partnership. This was the perception that led Prime Minister Vajpayee to declare, nearly five years ago, that the two countries could be "natural allies", which have yet to fulfill the promise of their cooperation.

We know that President Bush fully shares this vision for an enduring India-US partnership. The US National Security Strategy released by the President last September states, "The United States has undertaken a transformation in its bilateral relationship with India based on a conviction that US interests require a strong relationship with India. We are the two largest democracies, committed to political freedom protected by representative governments. India is moving towards greater economic freedom as well. We have a common interest in the free flow of Commerce, including through the sea-lanes of the Indian Ocean. Finally, we share an interest in fighting terrorism and in creating a strategically stable Asia." This is a succinct statement of our complementarities and convergences.

It is particularly refreshing that our two countries are now looking at the full scope and breadth of the Indo-US relationship. To speak very frankly, what really stunted the growth of our bilateral relations in past years was the tendency to look at India's role only within a South Asian canvas and to see South Asia solely as the theatre of an India-Pakistan zero sum game.

India has broken free of these limiting confines, which the Cold War ideologies sought to impose. It has land borders of well over 3000 km with China and Southeast Asia. It has maritime borders with Indonesia and Thailand. Its exclusive economic zone spans the waters almost from the Persian Gulf to the Straits of Malacca. As your National Security Strategy recognizes, it straddles the commercial sealanes and the oil routes from the West to all of East Asia.

Our cultural and trade connections have historically extended along the Silk Route through Central Asia into Europe; and along what could be termed the Buddhist trail through Myanmar, Indo-China, China and Southeast Asia to Japan.

Today, India has a population of over a billion people, upwardly mobile on the economic ladder. In terms of purchasing power parity, it is the world's fourth largest economy, averaging an annual growth rate of over 5 percent since 1980 – the highest ever achieved over a comparable period by any democracy in the world. I might also mention that this growth rate was maintained through the turbulent period a few years ago when the so-called "Asian crisis" seized a few Asian economies.

Our economic fundamentals remain strong. Inflation is within the reasonably low single digits. Over the last few years, India has been attracting foreign direct investment at an annual rate of nearly 1.7 percent of GDP. American companies in India sometimes complain about operating conditions, but statistics show that they all have very healthy balance sheets. The inflow of American investments into India has grown significantly in the last few years. The case of Enron's Dabhol Project is *sui generis*. It is not so well known that the financial exposure of Indian entities exceeds the foreign funds deployed in the project. It is more a case of an economically unviable project than a foreign investment venture turned sour.

I have set out these facts in some detail, illustrating India's wider political, economic, security and strategic interests, to reiterate that to view India solely through a South Asian prism would be an analytical error. In our view, the world made this mistake in May 1998, in its reactions to India's nuclear tests. Our security concerns, which prompted that decision, are better understood today.

We must acknowledge that USA was among the first countries to temper its reservations about our nuclear tests with an understanding of the larger picture of India's political concerns and economic potential. The visit of

President Clinton to India in March 2000 – less than two years after the tests – was in that sense a landmark event. After this opening, President Bush has personally led the effort for a complete transformation in relations.

Given its past history, the Indo-US relationship needs to liberate itself from a number of misconceptions and prejudices of past years. I think we have made considerable headway on this path with good impact on our relations. Our leaders are in regular touch with each other on the phone and through letters. Regular exchanges of visits at the political and senior official levels have resulted in a harmonisation of our position on a number of issues.

Nowhere is this engagement more visible than in defence and security. Indian naval vessels took on the responsibility of escorting US vessels through the Malacca Straits last year. Joint exercises involving US Special forces and Indian paratroopers in India and Alaska, largest ever combined naval exercise in the Malabar series, institutional linkages between civilian, military and defence institutions of our Ministries of Defence, discussions on missile defence, purchase of defence equipment etc are some new developments. Working groups have been set up on counter-terrorism, the Defence Policy Group has been revived and a joint forum on cyber-terrorism established to pursue defence and infrastructure protection projects.

India was one of the first countries to declare support to the USA in its global war against terrorism after the horrendous events of September 11, 2001. We extended unwavering support to operation 'Enduring Freedom'. We worked closely with our American and other colleagues in the Bonn process for restoration of representative government in Afghanistan and continue to participate in Afghan reconstruction efforts. On a diverse range of other subjects, India's interactions with USA and its reactions to US statements or actions have been governed by a pragmatic understanding of realities, rather than doctrinaire ideologies. I might mention our prompt and positive reaction to the New Strategic Framework unveiled by President Bush in May 2001, our support to the many welcome elements in the energy and climate change policies enunciated by the President and our convergent positions on the International Criminal Court. There are a number of other areas where we have been able to find common ground for joint action.

This does not imply that there are no longer any differences between our two countries, but there is certainly a realisation that there is far more that unites us than divides us. We have had differences including over issues like our nuclear programmes, but a sustained bilateral dialogue with a frank exchange of concerns has led to a far better mutual understanding on these issues.

I have been saying very candidly that a trinity of issues – high technology commerce, civilian nuclear energy cooperation and collaboration in space can take the Indo-US relationship to a qualitatively new level of partnership.

India has consistently followed responsible policies on non-proliferation of nuclear and missile technologies and has strict export control regimes for dual-use technologies. The sharp contrast with others in our near and extended neighbourhood is evident for all to see. We believe that our discussions with our American partners on this subject are on the right path and hope that the road to free high technology commerce will soon be cleared of the hurdles of misconceptions.

We have to cover the same path for civilian nuclear cooperation and collaboration in space. Here again, I have to say that the obstacles come from remnants of cold war thinking and are not in consonance with our mutual interests. India has repeatedly asserted – and this is acknowledged internationally – that its nuclear and missile development programmes are entirely indigenous. We have not violated any of our bilateral commitments or international obligations. We will continue to restrict the development of these programmes to the minimum levels required for our national security.

When the world has recognized this reality, it defies logic to place obstacles on civilian applications of our nuclear programme and developmental projects of our space programme. These are areas where there are huge commercial possibilities for American companies (and companies from other countries).

We have, ofcourse, undertaken that we would put all nuclear power projects of foreign collaboration under safeguards. I am aware that some US regulations and laws are constraining factors, but rules and legislation can be amended to respond to changed situations.

Let me also put the nuclear energy issue in an environmental perspective. If the huge additional power required for India's ambitious development plans is to be generated from fossil fuels, the consequent drastic increase in carbondioxide emissions could have disastrous effects on the global environment. This is, in fact, the logic for our decision to increase the percentage of nuclear power in our energy output.

In sum, therefore, the political leadership in both countries sees value in building upon the natural links between our two democracies in a globalising world. The India-U.S. relationship is not a single-issue relationship. Our friendship is based on a broad range of shared values, beliefs and interests. Societies of this size and complexity, by their very nature, cannot agree on all issues. Our disagreements are now increasingly discussed with the candour and confidence injected by the recent transformation of our bilateral relationship. Both combating terrorism and forging a new world order demand close and solid partnerships among democratic societies, which value freedom, pluralism and entrepreneurship. These are the values that unite India and the United States.

To fulfill this potential, we have to ensure that the firm broom of cold logic decisively sweeps out the cobwebs of Cold War misconceptions and blinkered mindsets. We are working hard at it.

Thank you.

‹53›

Address by Shri Brajesh Mishra, National Security Advisor of India at the American Jewish Committee Annual Dinner (08.05.03)

Shri Brajesh Mishra argued that stronger India – US relations and India – Israel relations have a "natural logic" in view of their "common vision of pluralism, tolerance and equal opportunity". He debunked the theory of "root causes" of terrorism as "nonsense" and called for the gradual emergence of a "viable alliance" of democratic countries having "political will and moral authority to take bold decisions in extreme cases of terrorist provocation".

Your Excellencies,
Ladies and Gentlemen,

It is an honour to be invited to this distinguished gathering at the AJC Annual Dinner. The people of India admire the pioneering work of AJC, particularly in promoting human rights and combating religious discrimination. We also value your contribution to promoting US-India relations and India-Israel relations.

India has a historical affinity with the Jewish people. It is one of very few countries in the world with no history of anti-Semitism. Until the early 1990's, the constraints of the Cold War prevented this cordiality from extending to India's relations with Israel. Now we have full diplomatic relations, and a broad range of economic and, defence cooperation. We have increased the tempo of our high-level visits. We hope to receive Prime Minister Ariel Sharon soon in India on an official visit.

The end of the Cold War also ushered in a major transformation in India's relations with USA. Our Prime Minister has referred to the two countries as 'natural allies'. The US National Security Strategy report, released last September by President Bush, asserts that the two countries have common strategic interests.

India, the United States and Israel have some fundamental similarities. We are all democracies, sharing a common vision of pluralism, tolerance and equal opportunity. Stronger India-US relations and India-Israel relations have a natural logic.

I am pleased to see so many distinguished members of the United States Congress here today. They are friends of Israel. They are also friends of India. The Caucus on India and Indian-Americans in the House of Representatives has nearly 160 members. It is perhaps the largest single country-Caucus in the House, testifying to the growing bonds of friendship between the world's oldest democracy and its largest.

The increasing contact between the AJC and Indian-American community organizations is another positive reflection of shared values of our peoples.

Ladies and Gentlemen,

Our principal theme here today is a collective remembrance of the horrors of terrorism and a celebration of the alliance of free societies involved in combating this scourge. The US, India and Israel have all been prime targets of terrorism. They have to jointly face the same ugly face of modern day terrorism.

This is a common challenge. Global terrorism did not start on September 11, 2001. But that date marks a global awakening to its reach.

The international coalition against terrorism has scored some successes. Terrorism needs to be rooted out wherever it exists.

After over a year and a half of the global fight against terrorism, it is far from over. The leaders of the Al-Qaida remain at large. We keep hearing that they have the know-how and the material to build at least a crude radiological device. This is naturally a matter of extreme concern. We cannot ignore this spectre of globalization of terror and its intersection with WMD.

We see worrying signs of a re-grouping of Taliban elements in southern and southeastern Afghanistan. And this is only a segment of the international terrorist network. It will, therefore, be a long haul and its success would require a genuine commitment to its objectives by every member of the International coalition.

It is most unfortunate that some diversionary arguments are still preventing a consensus on important anti-terrorist conventions. An agreed definition of terrorism still eludes the International community. Distinctions sought to be made between freedom fighters and terrorists propagate a bizarre logic, which glorifies massacres of one set of innocent civilians, while condemning killings of others.

Another fallacy motivatedly propagated is that terrorism can only be eradicated by addressing its 'root causes'. This is nonsense. Terrorist attacks against innocents have no justification. Democratic societies, which address the 'root causes' of alienation and anger through pluralism and socio-economic justice, are precisely the targets of terrorism.

As the main targets of International terrorism, democratic countries should form a viable alliance against terrorism and develop the multi-lateral mechanisms to counter it. Such an alliance would have the political will and moral authority to take bold decisions in extreme cases of terrorist provocation. It would not get bogged down in definitional and causal arguments about terrorism. Blocking financial supplies, disrupting networks, sharing intelligence, simplifying extradition procedures - these are preventive measures which can only be effective through international cooperation based on trust and shared values.

A core, consisting of democratic societies has, therefore, to gradually emerge from within our existing coalition, which can take on international terrorism in a holistic and focused manner. It would ensure that the global campaign against terrorism, is pursued to its logical conclusion, and does not run out of steam, because of other pre-occupations. We owe this commitment to our future generations.

Thank you.

❮54❯

Address by Shri Brajesh Mishra, National Security Advisor, to the 43rd Course of the National Defence College (24.11.03)

The NSA emphasized that "the traditional concept of national security as signified by large armies and potent weapons is incomplete". Today, the threat posed by non-state actors, security of the individual, technology and demography were some of the other dimensions of national security. The roadmap to better security incorporates faster economic growth and enhancement of technological capability.

India's Perspectives on National Security

Friends,

I welcome this opportunity to share some thoughts with you on India's national security perspectives. What I would like to do is to spell out some broad considerations; I can then respond to any specific questions you may have.

2. Today, it is well recognized that the traditional concept of national security as signified by large armies and potent weapons is incomplete. Of course, the military dimension of security remains important. But it is not a complete picture. The 9/11 attacks showed that the citizens of even the most powerful nation in the world are not secure. Today, the threat posed by non-State actors – particularly terrorist groups with access to modern technology and weapons of mass destruction – is the most pervasive threat to individual nations and to world peace. Democratic societies are the most vulnerable to this threat, since terrorists exploit the freedoms and openness of our societies. The spate of recent terrorist attacks – from our Parliament in Delhi, to a nightclub in Bali, synagogues in Istanbul, a threat in Moscow and against targets in many other countries – proves this point.
3. Another consequence of the relentless march of globalization and the rapid spread of democracy is the vastly increase emphasis on the security of the individual, as a factor of national security. Therefore, issues such as economic security, energy security, food security, clean environment, decent healthcare, protection of individual life and property, etc. have become extremely important. More people die in internal conflicts around the world than in military confrontation. Civil

wars, ethnic conflicts, religious extremism, poverty, disease, organized crime, and narco-trafficking create more insecurity than enemy attacks. Good governance and equitable economic development make almost as great a contribution to security as military weapons.

4. Technology is a major determinant of security. In the modern world, technology drives multiple socio-economic revolutions, which together constitute globalization. It has empowered the individual and made our lives better. But it is a double-edged weapon. Technology accelerates the pace of change to a level where it can create new disparities within and among nations. The denial of technology, through discriminatory international technology control regimes, can accentuate disparities by slowing down development. Non-state actors – including terrorists and organized crime – can misuse technology to victimize societies. A more enlightened regime of equal access to, and equitable dissemination of technology would enhance the comprehensive security of nations.
5. Some countries have harnessed technology to integrate land, oceans, air and space in their battle plans. Others have been unable to keep pace with new revolutions in military affairs. Overwhelming technological superiority of a single country – or a group of countries – would naturally strengthen the trend towards unilateralism of action.
6. Demography is yet another dimension of national security. Population growth; trans-border migrations; regional, ethnic and religious differentiation are all key issues impinging on security. Human resource development and balanced regional development are issues getting increasing attention in national security debates.
7. No security policy can be crafted in a vacuum. The extraordinary developments of the last few years have transformed the strategic environment in the world. The end of the bi-polar world, with the collapse of the Soviet Union, has ushered in an era of extraordinary flux and transition.
8. The unipolar world naturally raises the specter of Unilateralism of the dominant power. But the complexities of today's security challenges, and their trans-national character, make it practically difficult and unacceptably expensive for even the most powerful to dictate global events unilaterally. At the same time, the United Nations structures have been found wanting in dealing with the contemporary security challenges. An equally disturbing recent manifestation was the absence of consensus in the international community on major security issues of today. The establishment of a cooperative multi-polar world order, in which he interests and aspirations of the various poles would be harmoniously accommodated and decision-making by broad consensus

would be institutionalized, is the major security challenge before the world today. India's security interests also lie in realization of this objective.

9. This is the broad context in which we see the security of India. I will deal with some specific security challenges before us.

10. Since India's nuclear tests in 1998, and the Kargil war in 1999, India's security environment has changed significantly. India faces the modern day threats from WMD proliferation, religious extremism, ethnic conflicts, proliferation of small arms, narco-terrorism and environmental degradation. These pose challenges to the Indian endeavour to build and sustain a modern, democratic, plural, multi-ethnic, multi-religious and multi-cultural State comprising more than one billion people. It is incumbent upon us to ensure that we succeed against all such threats.

11. The instability in our neighbourhood naturally has an obvious impact on our security. India is linked with its neighbours through intimae historical, cultural, economic and political ties. Our borders with neighbours are porous.

12. With Nepal, we have an open border, which can be traversed by citizens of Nepal and India without visa requirements. A large number of Nepali citizens work in India; many Indian citizens have businesses in Nepal. Therefore, instability in Nepal caused by the activities of Maoist groups, causes us great concern. It has upset the equilibrium between constitutional monarchy and multiparty democracy in Nepal. Maoists also have links with violent ultra-left groups in India. We maintain close contacts with the King, the Government and the political parties in Nepal on the restoration of stability and calm.

13. We also have a long and porous border with Bangladesh. We face the problem of illegal immigration from Bangladesh. Indian insurgent groups have also been using Bangladeshi territory to carry out their activities in our Northeast. We have been in constant touch with the Bangladesh government on the peaceful management four borders and on the wider question of bilateral economic cooperation, which will–in the medium to long term–tackle the problem of economic migration.

14. The ethnic conflict in Sri Lanka has also affected us deeply over the last twenty years. It was a fall-out of the conflict, which resulted in the tragic assassination of Prime Minister Rajiv Gandhi in 1991. India, therefore, welcomed the peace process, which promised a negotiated settlement acceptable to all sections of Sri Lankan society, while preserving the territorial integrity of Sri Lanka. Our concern about recent developments in Sri Lanka is that this process should not be derailed by internal political differences. We hope the differences will

be resolved and that solutions to the impasse will emerge through internal political processes.

15. With our western neighbour, Pakistan, we have made every effort to establish a peaceful and cooperative relationship. We have done so in the face of sustained State-sponsored cross-border terrorism over the last two decades, which has taken thousands of lives in Jammu & Kashmir alone. This terrorism has spread to other parts of India and seeks to impede our economic development.

16. Our Prime Minister has frequently reiterated that we are willing to resolve all our bilateral differences with Pakistan through peaceful discussions, but only when cross border terrorism ends. Unfortunately, we are up against an obsessive anti-India mindset, which promotes Jehadi fundamentalism and justifies its export to India in terms of a so-called freedom struggle in Kashmir. This cannot be the basis of peaceful and durable ties with India.

17. We have taken initiatives to promote economic cooperation, cultural exchanges and people-to-people contacts with Pakistan. By this, our consistent effort is to encourage those elements in Pakistan who recognize the folly of permanent hostility towards India. They will eventually have to counter those, who see their political future as depending on confrontation with India. In the long run, peace and friendship between Indian and Pakistan have to be based on an objective realization that current global trends are moving towards economic integration, rather than political and military confrontation.

18. It is this realization which also drives India's commitment to SAARC. SAARC was conceived as a forum to promote multifaccted cooperation among south Asian countries, irrespective of political differences. Unfortunately, the South Asian Free Trade Agreement (SAFTA) and South Asian Preferential Trading Arrangements (SAPTA) have not made sufficient headway, because irrelevant political obstacles have been put in the way. We remain committed to SAARC, but simultaneously we have also pursued economic cooperation measures sub-regionally in South Asia and with other regions. By 2010, India would have a free trade area with ASEAN. We are actively participating in sub-regional co-operation initiatives like BIMSTEC, Mekong-Ganga Cooperation, and other linkages with Iran, Afghanistan and Central Asia. These economic integration measures should contribute to peace and stability and hence to enhanced security. As our Prime Minister said recently at a SAARC Information Ministers' Conference, if SAARC cannot organize itself, it will simply miss the boat, because we will move ahead with alternative arrangements.

19. In the larger picture of our regional interests, including energy security, Afghanistan and Central Asia are of great importance to us. We have invested considerable resources in the reconstruction of Afghanistan. Reports of the regrouping of Taliban and resurgence of Al-Qaida in Afghanistan are of fundamental security consequence for us. We work closely with the Government of Afghanistan to counter such trends, which threaten the unity and territorial integrity of Afghanistan. Similarly, we are expanding and intensifying our cooperation with Central Asian countries to promote stability in our common neighbourhood.
20. Conflict, tension and instability in the Gulf region and West Asia affect India's interests. We have committed financial assistance for re-construction activities in Iraq, but we have also been emphasizing that re-construction can only go hand in hand with a political process, leading to an early return of sovereignty to the Iraqi people. Millions of Indians live and work in West Asia. They remit about US$6 to 7 billion to India annually. We source about 80% of our oil from the region. It is, therefore, obvious that we maintain a close engagement with all courtiers of the region.
21. China is our largest neighbour. Sino-Indian relations have seen tensions in the past and we continue to have differences over our boundary. But over the past 15 years or so, India and China have taken measured steps to reduce tensions and to make their borders peaceful and tranquil. We have strengthened our political ties and deepened our economic cooperation. We have agreed to tackle all contentious issues in a pragmatic manner. During our Prime Minister's recent visit to China, we agreed to raise our economic and other bilateral co-operation to a qualitatively higher level. The decision of the two Governments to appoint Special Representatives, to discuss the boundary question from a political perspective, was a particularly significant measure. A final resolution of the boundary question would release considerable military energies and finances for other more purposeful activities. We consider this a strategic objective and are willing to take pragmatic steps to achieve it.
22. On a global scale, our broad-based foreign policy is aimed at integration India into the global political and economic mainstream. As a country of one billion plus people, located in a critical geo-strategic region of the world, India's foreign policy has to reflect its multi-dimensional security concerns. Our strategic partnership with Russia, based on close political understanding, traditional cultural bonds and intensive defence cooperation, has a strong geopolitical logic. It is also an important element in our efforts for a cooperative multi-polar world order. In recent years, our relations with USA have developed into a

mature engagement, with a healthy dialogue on all issues and an increasingly diverse cooperation. We have also strengthened our ties with the EU countries, emphasizing our shared values of democracy and pluralism. The combating of international terrorism and the strengthening of multilateral trade regimes are common strands in our engagement with all these countries. The articulation and pursuit of developmental concerns of the developing countries in an element, which in parallel cements our relationship with countries of the South. We, therefore, have an abiding interest in the emergence of a rule based, non-discriminatory international order. This requires a fundamental reform of the UN system to make it more representative of contemporary relativities and responsive to modern needs.

23. India is conscious of the fact that the road map to better security incorporates faster economic growth and enhancement of technological capability. The Indian economy is now largely integrated into the global mainstream. The knowledge-based economy, which has emerged in India, will create beneficial linkages between India and other countries. Our competitiveness will be enhanced. Our effort is now focused on leveraging our economic technological and human assets to enhance our security.

24. A few years ago, we undertook a detailed review of our security structures. A Group of Ministers presented its report to the Government on Reforming the National Security System. This was the first time in independent India's history that comprehensive review of the national security system in its entirety was undertaken. The recommendations looked at the challenges to the management of national security and made suggestions with regard to the overhaul of our intelligence apparatus, internal security structures, border management and the management of defence. The Government is at present involved in implementing these recommendations, and we hope that as a result of this overhaul, India will have the necessary structures to meet modern-day challenges to security. As a result of this review not only will the management of security improve, we also hope to have a better civil-military interface, better information dissemination and better media relations.

25. To sum up, therefore, India faces multiple challenges to its security but it is fully prepared to meet them. While we maintain adequate military force to safeguard our borders, our primary thrust in improving our security environment is through balanced and rapid economic growth, good governance and strengthening our network of international relations.

Thank you

❮55❯

Address by Shri Satish Chandra, Deputy to the National Security Advisor on Water in Global Security, Moscow (29.06.03)

The Deputy to the NSA warned that global water shortage represented a "full scale emergency" that underlined the potential for "water wars". In addition to the use of water harvesting, recycling and extensive use of drip irrigation and sprinklers for "water conservation", he suggested that "the riparians in internationalized basins should enter into cooperative arrangements for integrated basin management".

Introduction:

Like any other scarce resource, water too impinges on global security. Its impact on regional and global security in a scarcity situation arises essentially from three factors:

(i) It is the basis of life – no living organism can survive without it.

(ii) There is no substitute for it in the multiplicity of its uses: domestic, agricultural, industrial etc.

(iii) Passing often through more than one state its control and utilisation can become a matter of dispute.

Accordingly, a water stressed environment is likely to see increasing competition for water both within and among states. The potential for conflict is aggravated by the fact that unlike other scarce resources, whose location is clear and stable within one or another State, that of water bodies is often dynamic and extending to more than one state. In such situations, there can be more than one interpretation on the extent to which and manner in which each riparian can utilize it.

Water Scarcity: A Reality

2. While most of us are aware that the days of water plenitude are over, as it is our generation which has made the transition from water for free to water pricing, from hosing the drive way to mopping the same and most painful from sinfully wasteful showers to bucket baths, yet we are perhaps not fully conscious of the severity of water scarcity which confronts us. The following data places the situation in a proper perspective:

- Global freshwater consumption rose six-fold between 1900 and 1995 – more than twice the population growth rate.[1]
- Since 1950, per capita global renewable fresh water supply has fallen by 58% as world population has increased from 2.5 billion to 6 billion.[2]
- It is projected as per a CIA study that by 2015 over 3 billion people – or about 40 percent of the world's population at that time – will live in countries that are water stressed[3] i.e. having less than 1700 cu meters of water per capita per year. As per capita water availability falls below 1700 cu meters (defined as water stress level) and particularly if it falls below 1000 cu meters (defined as water scarce level), it would be difficult or impossible for such countries to mobilize enough water to satisfy the food, industrial and domestic needs of their citizens.
- It is estimated that today more than 2 billion people are affected by water shortages in over 40 countries[4]. As per some data culled from 'Water Resources 1991-92', as many as 18 countries were facing severe water scarcity with per capita availability of 1000 cu meters or less. The number is projected to increase to 33 by 2025. Most of these countries are in Africa and the Middle East.
- By 2025, water scarcity could cause annual global losses of 350 million tons of grain production – slightly more than the entire US grain crop and grain prices could sky rocket.[5]
- In parts of western US, China, India, Egypt, West Asia and North Africa water supplies will be threatened as ground water is being pumped faster than aquifers can recharge. In parts of China water tables are already falling five feet a year and in parts of India between three and ten feet.[6]
- India will face serious fresh water shortages. With 16 percent of the world's population, it has only 4 percent of global water resources. Its per capita fresh water availability has dropped from a comfortable 5177 cu. Meters in 1951 to 1869 cu meters in 2001. By 2025, it will be 1341 cu meters and by 2050, 1140 cu meters.[7]

It is in the backdrop of the foregoing that the UNEP report of 2000 warns that the global water shortage represents a full-scale emergency.

2.1. Many of the above projections on impending global water shortages have been made without taking into account the impact of global warming. The latter is bound to distort global weather patterns, which in turn will produce new stresses and strains on water availability. Some areas, which today are not water stressed, could become so under the impact of global warming leading to additional tensions.

Water Wars: Increased Possibility

3. Differences over water at the local, national and regional levels are as old as history given the fact that water, in the words of a former Israeli PM, is "life itself". In fact, the first water war was fought some 4500 years ago between two Mesopotamian city-states – Lagash and Umma – in Southern Iraq. Since then, while there has been no outright water war between nation States, use of water and it's sharing has been a matter of much discord between States[8]. In a seminal study undertaken by Prof. Aaron T Wolf, Shira B. Yoffe and Mark Giordana on water related exchanges between nations in the period 1948-2000, it was found that out of a total of 1831 events, 507 or 27 percent were conflictive in nature. Although the bulk of these exchanges did not go beyond verbal antagonism, in as many as 37 cases, they resulted in some form of military action. It is submitted that as more and more countries and people become water stressed, the potential for conflictual situations will increase. As per Peter Gleick's estimates, over 30 countries received more than one-third of their surface water from across national borders[9]. It is indeed this grim situation that led UNSG Kofi Annan to warn on the occasion of World Water day in March 2002 that "fierce national competition over water resources has prompted fears that water issues contain the seeds of violent conflict". In a similar vein, at the inauguration of the International Year of Fresh Water in 2003, he said: "Water is likely to become a growing source of tension and fierce competition between nations, if present trends continue, but it can also be a catalyst for cooperation".

4. Water scarcity in internationalized basins constitutes an explosive mix, which can well lead to the eruption of conflict. The trans boundary movement of water in such basins raises thorny and complicated questions of water rights, allocation, management, control etc. which in a scarcity situation can lead to major differences and even conflicts. Questions such as the rightful share of each riparian in the context of its catchment area and the water contributed by it, its manner of utilization, whether optimal or sub-optimal, its needs on the basis of its population and historic patterns of utilization etc. are open to interpretation.

5. In Africa alone, more than eighty rivers and lakes are shared by two or more countries. All countries in sub-Saharan Africa share atleast one river basin or lake. Guinea is the upstream riparian of fourteen shared rivers and Mozambique the downstream riparian of eight shared rivers. The Nile is shared by ten countries: Congo and Niger by nine, Zambezi by eight, Volta by six, Orange, Okavango, Senegal and Limpopo by four countries each[10]. Few of these rivers and lakes are governed by agreements regulating their use and protection that encompass all the riparian States. Consequently, the riparians excluded from those treaties do not recognise them and downstream/ upstream tensions dominate a number of basins.[11]

6. The foregoing has been mentioned merely to underline the potential for conflict amongst States across which water flows naturally in an environment of increasing scarcity. It is estimated that there are today somewhere between 260 to 300 trans-boundary water basins. Approximately, one-third of these basins involve more than two countries and nineteen involve five or more sovereign States. The Danube has eighteen riparian states. Five basins - Congo, Niger, Nile, Rhine and Zambezi -are shared between nine and eleven countries.

7. The UNESCO in its 2003 report "Water for People, Water for Life" has identified as many as twenty-one basins[12], with potential for conflict in the next five to ten years, notably Aral, Ganges-Brahmaputra, Han, Incomati, Jordan, Kunene, Kura-Araks, Lake Chad, La Plata, Lempa, Limpopo, Mekong, Nile, Ob [Ertis], Okavango, Orange, Salween, Senegal, Tigris-Euphrates, Tumen and Zambezi. These basins have been so identified on the basis of the following criteria:

- They fall across more than one country and indeed often across several.
- In one or more countries in each of these basins, unilateral developmental activities are being planned by one or more country in the absence of cooperative regimes.
- Some of the basin States have adversarial relationships on other issues.

The short point is that the potential for water wars is considerable and is on the increase.

International Law: No Solution

8. The situation is aggravated by the fact that current International law does not provide clear-cut positions on how to manage, share and utilize waters of Internationalized basins. The 1997 UN Convention on the **Law of Non-Navigational Use of International Water Courses** is yet to take effect as it has only been signed by a handful of countries. In any case, it is controversial, as at the time of its adoption, over eighty countries did not vote for it. In this background, the 1966 Helsinki Rules alone provide some guidelines on the sharing of waters in internationalized basins. These guidelines embody principles like equitable utilization, prevention of significant harm to other states, obligation to notify and inform other nations of activities being undertaken etc. Each of these principles is hedged in by extensive qualifiers, which lend the guidelines to multiple interpretations. For instance, 'equitable utilisation' does not mean equal use; rather, it implies that many factors such as population, geography, availability of alternative resources etc. can be considered in determining allocation of water rights. International law today, thus, does not provide all the answers and will not be able to handle the stress and strain of current and future problems. Accordingly, it is

evident that the possibility of serious conflicts erupting between states due to increasing water scarcity in internationalized basins is real. We need to take note of it and devise methodologies to avert it.

The Way Out

9. First, given the fact that mankind is condemned to live in a water stressed world, we must rigorously conserve water and ensure its optimum utilization. Water conservation should be extended to all aspects of its utilization through water harvesting, recycling, reuse of wastewater, water thrift appliances etc. Attention must particularly be focused on agriculture, which accounts for nearly seventy percent of water use worldwide. In this context, more efficient irrigation systems must be devised, entailing a more extensive use of drip irrigation and sprinklers. Cropping patterns may need to be altered. Indeed, some water stressed countries, who presently export food grains, may well decide to curtail their production levels and become importers from countries better endowed with water resources. The shift from grain production, if possible, would be particularly helpful in reducing water stress given the fact that it takes about one thousand tons of water to produce half a ton of rice or one ton of other cereals. Ground water depletion should be averted by ensuring that its use is proportionate to the recharge level. Both conservation and increase in productivity of water should be encouraged by introduction of judicious price mechanisms. Indeed, there is a good case to consider the establishment of an *International Fund to promote Water Conservation* designed both to prevent its abuse and encourage more effective utilisation. The Fund should be channeled to develop technologies for doing so and the same should be made available to countries facing water stress situations.

10. Second and even more important, as a means of avoiding conflict, is that the riparians in internationalized basins enter into cooperative arrangements for integrated basin management. This would not only address the issue of water allocation but also help ensure optimal basin development. Accordingly apart from resolving issues like the sharing of waters for industrial, domestic and agricultural use, issues like flood control, hydropower generation, water transport, etc., would also be addressed. This is all the more necessary as there can be no hard and fast rules for the just allocation of waters amongst riparians. It is only through a process of give and take that States in an Internationalized basin can come to mutually beneficial arrangements on their respective water rights as well as understanding on the control, allocation and utilization of the available waters. Such a cooperative approach would lead to a 'win-win' situation for all concerned. One riparian may benefit more than another on allocation of waters but the sum total of the benefits accruing to each through a mutually agreed cooperative approach would far outweigh what each could hope to derive through a unilateralist approach.

Indian Experience

11. As pointed out earlier, India is on the verge of becoming a water stressed country. It would therefore be instructive to examine as to how it has acted, particularly as many of its river systems are shared with neighbours. It is with much satisfaction that one can say that India has evolved a cooperative bilateral relationship with all its neighbours on the utilization of river waters. The nature of this cooperative relationship varies from neighbour to neighbour. With Pakistan, the rights and obligations of each of the two countries on the three Eastern and three Western Rivers forming part of the Indus basin have been defined. As per these rights and obligations, India enjoys unrestricted use of the three Eastern Rivers whereas Pakistan gets the bulk of the flows of the three Western Rivers, with India having some defined rights for domestic, non-consumptive and agricultural use of these waters as well as for generation of hydel power. With Bangladesh, it has entailed a sharing of dry season scarcity in the Ganges downstream of Farakka and with Nepal and Bhutan, it has entailed extensive assistance for irrigation and hydro-electric projects. All the arrangements entered into by India have been considered not merely in the context of mutual and equitable benefit but in a wider frame and with the hope that they would promote friendly ties. Accordingly, there has been more 'give' than 'take' on the part of India in these cooperative bilateral arrangements.

12. In respect of water sharing with Pakistan, it may be mentioned that the **Indus Waters Treaty** of 1960 provides that out of the six rivers which pass naturally through India to Pakistan, the former has unrestricted use of the three eastern rivers while the latter has use of the three western rivers. While seemingly an equitable arrangement, it is in fact weighted heavily in favour of Pakistan as the eastern rivers carry only 32.8 MAF of water while the western rivers carry more than four times this quantity (135.6 MAF). The icing on the cake as far as Pakistan is concerned is that apart from the generous settlement made by India, the latter also paid over £62 million to Pakistan for construction of replacement works in the Indus basin. It is quite clear that the many concessions made by India were predicated on the hope that the Treaty would pave the way for better ties between the two countries. While it is unfortunate that these expectations have been belied, what is even more regrettable is that Pakistan has sought to misuse many of the provisions of the Indus Water Treaty to slow down or block several upstream ongoing developmental projects, notably the Tulbul Navigational Project, Baglihar Hydel Project, Kishan Ganga Hydel project etc.

13. In respect of Bangladesh, India has entered into a Thirty-year treaty in 1996 on the sharing of the Ganges waters at Farakka. While recognizing the need for a "solution to the long-term problem of augmenting the Ganges flows", pending such a solution, it puts in place allocations for each country in the dry season. It envisages that when flows are 70,000 cusecs or less,

water will be shared equally between the two countries. When these flows are between 70,000 – 75,000 cusecs, Bangladesh will receive 35,000 cusecs with the balance for India and when they are 75,000 cusecs or more, India will receive 40,000 cusecs with the balance for Bangladesh. These allocations are subject to the condition that India & Bangladesh each shall receive a guaranteed 35,000 cusecs of water in alternate three 10-day periods during the period March 11 to May 10. As would be evidenced from the foregoing, the Agreement envisages an element of sacrifice on the part of India, as it does not meet India's requirements of a minimum of 40,000 cusecs of water, which is essential for the flushing of Calcutta port. It was nevertheless agreed to, keeping in mind the broader objective of forging friendly ties with Bangladesh. The gesture made by India is all the more notable given the fact that while it is on the verge of being water stressed, Bangladesh is rich in water with a per capita availability of 19,600 cu meters – over ten times India's per capita water availability.

14. India has over the years assisted Nepal in several important irrigation projects of which the notable ones are the Kosi and Gandak Barrages as well as some hydroelectric projects such as **Trisuli** and **Devighat**. As a result about 300,000 hectares of land in Nepal has been brought under irrigation with Indian assistance and hydropower generating capacity created. With the signing of the **Mahakali Treaty** between India and Nepal, the two countries are poised to undertake the **Pancheshwar Multipurpose Project** designed to generate 5600 MW of power and irrigate 130,000 hectares of land in Nepal and 220,000 hectares of land in India. Under the Treaty, both countries are committed to share water and electricity from the projects envisaged on the Mahakali River and also the costs on the basis of benefits received. It is significant that the Treaty provides that the water requirements of Nepal "shall be given prime consideration in the utilization of the waters of the Mahakali River".

15. India has been assisting Bhutan mainly on generation of hydel power. The most significant project to-date in Bhutan has been the 336 MW Chukha Hydroelectric Project, which went on stream in 1988. Seventy percent of the energy generated by this project is exported to India. Yet, another important project is the 60 MW **Kurichhu Hydroelectric Project** which was completed in 2002. Nearly fifty percent of Bhutanese Government revenue comes from sale of energy to India and this has contributed to the enhancement of Bhutans per capita GDP from around $230 to $640. India is currently assisting Bhutan in the 1020 MW **Tala Project**, which would be completed by 2004-2005. Once this project is fully commissioned, the revenues generated through export of electricity to India would result in a doubling of Bhutan's per capita GDP to a level of about US $1200-1300.

16. India also has bilateral co-operation arrangements with Bangladesh, Bhutan, China and Pakistan on exchange of data for flood and flood forecasting.

17. Apart from a cooperative bilateral relationship with its neighbours, India has also developed a National Perspective Plan designed to inter-link its rivers for transferring water from surplus to deficit basins. This exercise would be undertaken with a view to enhance the country's irrigation potential, mitigate floods and droughts and reduce regional imbalances in the availability to water. The exercise would be undertaken on a consensual basis after consulting not only all our states but also concerned neighbours. The scheme is expected to cost Rs.5,60,000 crores ($120 billion), irrigate 150 million hectares, produce 35,000 MW of power, save Rs.5000 crores ($1.06 billion) in diminishing annual flood losses and add 70 million tons to food grain production and provide employment to a million people annually for the next ten years.

18. In conclusion, I would like to reiterate that water scarcity is a timebomb posing a serious threat to global security. Defusing the time bomb demands the efficient management of available water resources. This, in turn, calls for an end to the abuse of water and a readiness to cooperate in order to ensure its optimal utilization and management.

Notes

1 World Water Development Report.

2 Postel, Sandra L & Wolf, Aaron T. – "Dehydrating Conflict", Foreign Policy, Sept – Oct. 2001.

3 "Global Trends 2015: A Dialogue About the Future with Non-Government Experts" – Paper of US National Intelligence Council: http://www.cia.gov/nic/speeches/speeches/army-war-college-htm.

4 WHO/UNICEF-2000 Report (page 10 UN World Water Development Report: "Water for People, Water for Life")

5 Global Water Outlook to 2025 (Food Policy Report – International Food Policy Research Institute and International Water Management Institute: Rosegrant, Mark W., Cai, Ximing, Cline, Sarah A.).

6 Global Water Outlook, ibid.

7 World Water Development Report, The Ministry of Water Resources of India.

8 Postel, Sandra L. & Wolf, Aaron T. – "Dehydrating Conflict", Foreign Policy, Sept – Oct 2001.

9 Gleick, Peter H. "Water and Conflict, Fresh Water Resources and International Security", International Security Vol. 18, No.1(Summer 1993).

10 Gleick, 2000 - The World's Water 2000-2001: The Biennial Report on Freshwater Resources.

11 SMA Salman - The Abuja Ministerial Declaration on Water: A Milestone or Just Another Statement?

12 UN World Water Development Report: "Water for People, Water for Life" Page 319.

❮56❯

Address by Shri Kanwal Sibal, Foreign Secretary of India on 'Indian Foreign Policy: Challenges and Prospects', at Geneva Forum (23.01.03)

> Mr. Kanwal Sibal shared candidly his perceptions about the challenges and prospects for India's Foreign Policy. He highlighted India's security concerns with neighbouring countries like Nepal, Sri Lanka, Bhutan, Myanmar, Pakistan and China. Expressing concern at the re-emergence of Al Qaida and Taliban, the Foreign Secretary described Pakistan as the "nerve-centre" of this activity. He also articulated India's nuclear doctrine comprising, inter alia, of a "credible nuclear deterrent", "no-first use", "moratorium on nuclear tests" and "commitment to the goal of a nuclear weapon free world".

I am delighted to be here amongst you today to share what my perceptions are about the challenges and prospects for India's foreign policy in the months and years ahead. The challenges are manifold. Peace and security in our neighbourhood and in our region as a whole are uppermost in our mind. The combat against international terrorism presents an immense challenge. Energy security, creating favourable conditions for our economic development, coping with the consequences of instability or military conflict in the middle east, the reform of the Security Council, promoting multi-polarity, finding an adequate response to doctrines diluting the principles of sovereignty and seeking to establish the right to intervene, promoting a more equitable equation between the developed and the developing world in the political, economic and technological domains are some of the challenges facing Indian foreign policy. The prospects by definition are a function of our success in meeting the challenges. On the whole, given India's geographical and demographic size, a huge and growing market, our human resources, the advances we are making in the knowledge economy, our steady economic growth, our desire to integrate ourselves more fully into the global market, our democracy which gives us enormous resilience, our prospects, I would like to believe, are bright.

2. India has to give priority to safeguarding its security interests in its neighbourhood. Nepal is currently being wracked by the Maoist insurgency and its political system is under strain. In Sri Lanka the

Peace Process with the LTTE is showing some hopeful signs but its ultimate success will depend on Sinhala unity and the real transformation of the LTTE from a terrorist organization to a peace partner. Our largest border is with Bangladesh. This porous border creates problems of insurgency and illegal migration which can be dealt with effectively only in conditions of acceptance of each others' legitimate concerns. The problem of Indian insurgent groups misusing Bhutan's territory for launching terrorists operations against India has to be resolved within the framework of India's excellent relations with Bhutan.

3. With Myanmar, with which India shares its borders in the troubled eastern region infested with violent insurgency, a cooperative relationship is being steadily built around a commitment to stabilize the area, cooperate in economic projects and create multi-model transport links extending to Thailand and prospectively beyond. Myanmar is keen to balance its external relationships and India has vital long term interest in increasing Myanmar's strategic options.
4. The rapid growth in understanding between India and Iran will be symbolized by President Khatami's presence in Delhi on January 26 as Chief Guest at India's Republic Day celebrations. Both countries are interested in forging a long term strategic relationship built around energy security and transit arrangements. Iran is ready to work with India to provide viable and rapid access to Afghanistan, Central Asia and Russia and some projects have already been agreed upon. India and Iran have shared geo-political interests in the pursuit of which this part of Asia can be knit into networks of economic co-operation with increased stability as a consequence.
5. The biggest challenge and a prospect worthy of realization would be the emergence of Pakistan as a moderate Islamic State in the true sense, with "moderation" being evaluated not merely in terms of the pro and anti-West orientation of Islamic regimes. Pakistan was born on the basis of extremist muslim demands and the roots of its identity lie in ideologically confrontational Islam. Indeed, Pakistan's emergence was a "clash of civilizations" in action long before the West discovered this frightening concept. Political Islam, as opposed to pious Islam, which the West began to fear after the Khomeini Revolution in Iran because of its perceived anti-West orientation has long been used against India, first to break it up and now to continue wounding it through recourse to terrorism. The military, which has ruled Pakistan for large periods of its existence, has become the custodian of Pakistan's Islamic hostility towards India, not the least because under that cover it can continue to preserve its enormous privileges within the system. Pakistan was fully involved in the creation and unleashing of the Taliban on the hapless Afghans. The Al-Qaida networks were

built under its nose. Together with Afghanistan, Pakistan became the epicenter of international terrorism. So long as this activity promoted Pakistan's strategic interests and was directed against India, it was ignored by the West. Now we know at what cost. Big tragedies have big lessons to offer and for the sake of the victims all of us should learn them. Today the forces behind the Taliban and Al-Qaida, displaced from Afghanistan have re-emerged in the North West Frontier Province and Baluchistan in Pakistan. What was removed by force in Afghanistan has re-emerged legally in adjoining areas waiting for patience and time to run out before the politics of fundamentalism and destabilization is resumed. The nerve-centre of all this remains in Pakistan.

6. International terrorism is our common challenge today and how we deal with it holds out common prospects for all of us. Political expediency, short term gains, considerations of geo-politics, the difficulties in making a choice between one's own immediate priorities and the global good, nurturing of old constituencies, faulty analysis, double standards, all these and other reasons unfortunately blur the moral clarity and political focus on how this terrorism should be dealt with. Pakistan is today being rewarded for its cooperation with the West against terrorism with political and financial oxygen. The military leader of Pakistan has been allowed to manipulate the political system by weakening mainstream political parties and creating space for fundamentalists. From the margins these fundamentalists have moved into the mainstream. While deep concerns are mounting about the nexus between fundamentalism, terrorism and weapons of mass destruction, the spotlight is not on Pakistan which has all the three ingredients of concern, plus the additional one of fears of it becoming a "failed State". We have seen how there is a remarkable lack of curiosity about Pakistan's nuclear connection with North Korea in exchange for missile technology, which poses grave challenges to our security.

7. One of the major challenges facing India today is the one posed by terrorism from across its borders. In fact, it is not a challenge that appeared in the context of today; the country has been seeing its innocent citizens victimized for the last two decades. It has evolved from being a mere law and order problem because of Pakistan's deliberate policy of relying on terrorism as a form of proxy war and an instrument of foreign policy. This has made terrorism a major security threat and countering it a predominant foreign policy challenge for us. India has successfully met this challenge earlier in Punjab. Cross-border terrorism in Jammu & Kashmir has assumed greater dimensions partly because the success that Pakistan had in foisting the Taliban in Afghanistan provided it with extensive experience of

using terrorism as policy. According to conservative estimates, the extensive cultivation of opium in Afghanistan provided the Pakistani establishment with between US $ 90 million to US $ 136 million of money per annum for at least seven years. This money has been used to finance its proxy war in J&K, equip, train and arm terrorists and infiltrate them into India with weapons and modern communication equipment.

8. The evolution of the situation in Afghanistan presents a complex and enormous security and political challenge to India's foreign policy. Afghanistan is more peaceful but not stable yet. The political vacuum in the Pashtun areas, the absence of any anti-Taliban cohesive Pashtun force, the failure to curb Pakistan's ambitions in south and eastern Afghanistan and the likelihood that the situation in the middle east may further divert attention from the danger of pro-Taliban Pashtuns being backed by Pakistan filling this vacuum is real and present. There are reports that Taliban and Al-Qaida elements are regrouping along its southern and eastern borders and continue to receive support, both moral and material from Pakistan. Early economic reconstruction of Afghanistan is one of the most important requirements for the return of peace and stability to that country. India has provided extensive humanitarian, financial and project assistance to Afghanistan. The governing philosophy of India's assistance to Afghan reconstruction has been to respond to Afghan felt and priority needs. India regards this as crucial for regional peace and stability and views her relationship with Afghanistan as direct and bilateral.

9. Our close historical links with Central Asia provide an asset for building important relationships with the Republics that emerged in the region following the collapse of the Soviet Union. Today we are exploring new avenues of cooperation, new routes – land, air and sea routes. Statistics suggest that thirty percent of the medicines consumed in Central Asia are of Indian origin. Indian information technology is becoming a part of their system. There is a cultural revival of traditional warmth. The essence of this new emerging relationship is the new way in which we address each other and the absence of any "game", great or otherwise. The conceptual definition of our relations recognizes that Central Asia has always been the land bridge between India and Europe. India's view of its neighbourhood has always had a trans-Himalayan dimension. That vision carried trade and culture across the Pamirs, through the silk route. More recently, we have participated in the CICA (Conference on Interaction and Confidence Building Measures in Asia) process from the beginning. It had an impressive Summit meeting in June 2002 in Almaty. We also hold equal interest in the Shanghai Cooperation Organisation. The menace of Islamic

fundamentalism facing these countries is internationally recognized as a problem that needs to be collectively dealt with, to enable them to fully benefit from their new-found independence and to allow them full use of their resources for development. We were amongst the first to establish diplomatic missions in all the Central Asian States and the area would continue to receive significant focus in the coming years as we seek to forge multi-faceted ties to this important region.

10. Moving eastwards, East Asia has been a natural component of India's foreign policy priorities. India is an Asian country, the second largest both demographically and geographically. Developments in Asia impinge directly on our security and strategic interests. China is a direct neighbour as are ASEAN countries such as Myanmar and Indonesia. The Indian Ocean straddles the most important sea routes that connect the oil producing region of the Gulf with the consumer countries of East Asia. Increase in maritime trade is another reality today. Cooperation between India and these countries is a necessary pre-requisite for the 21st century to become the century of Asia. India's look east policy starts from North East Asia and not simply the ASEAN region. Yet, India is excluded from APEC as also ASEM. We have, however, a sound framework for meeting the challenges ahead – India has become a member of the ASEAN Regional Forum and a summit partner with the ASEAN. The ASEAN countries themselves have realized the value of engaging India for greater political, security and economic balance in the region. India has engaged in an effort to craft special trade and investment arrangements through an India-ASEAN Free Trade Area to be brought about in ten years, a BIMST-EC FTA as also bilateral arrangements such as the India-Thailand FTA and India-Singapore Comprehensive Economic Cooperation Agreement. BIMST-EC and Mekong-Ganga Cooperation are other structural frameworks for India's "Look-East" policy. We are working on a trilateral highway project between India, Myanmar and Thailand. Connectivity, canalizing resources and policy co-ordination among India and the countries in the region are the tasks ahead.

11. Our relations with the United States have entered a phase of unprecedented improvement. India and the United States are, respectively, the world's most populous and the most powerful democracies, having clear commonalities in shaping a new democratic and pluralistic world order. The US with its belief that it is right to be good and India with its belief that it is good to be right can together promote what is both good and right, in the one case bringing power to the enterprise and in the other case numbers. Our Prime Minister has described India and the US as natural partners. Our relationship with the US is being transformed. There is an intensive

dialogue covering a broad agenda, seeking new possibilities for cooperation. Besides regular political dialogue, India and the United States have established over fifteen institutional forums that meet regularly. Notwithstanding the chill of May 1998, dramatic progress has been seen in security and defence cooperation, and trade and investment – the US is our largest trading partner(US $ 23 billion in goods and services last year), the predominant destination of our IT services exports(US $ 5.7 billion last year) and the major source of foreign investments. Areas for dialogue include energy and environment, science and technology, biotechnology and health, information technology and cyber security, combating terrorism and missile defence. Yet, the challenges remain for better management of relations, given the different geo-strategic and economic contexts, and occasional differences in perspectives. Our approach seeks to deal with these differences in a transparent, positive manner, according to enduring principles of our foreign policy that sought never to define relations with any one country through the prism of any other country or regional equations or alliance systems. The investment that both sides have made in the relationship is predicated as much on mutual benefit as on its global significance.

12. India's foreign policy has conserved its very close strategic relationship with Russia. Our challenge, as of others, has been to manage the consequences for us of the collapse of the Soviet Union. The close political contacts that have existed at the highest levels, the regular dialogue through the years, the recent coming together of both countries against the global menace of international terrorism are elements of strength in the relationship. The challenge lies in the field of bilateral trade which has failed to keep pace with the political relationship. India and Russia have identified high value and hi-tech items for cooperation like information technology, diamonds, energy etc. The Oil and Natural Gas Corporation of India is investing nearly US $ 1.7 billion in the **Sakhalin-I Project**. This is the highest ever overseas investment by an Indian company. Under the framework of energy security, India and Russia are also cooperating in nuclear energy. The ongoing construction of the Kudankulum Nuclear Plant with Russian participation is an example. The historical perspective to defence relations between our countries is being taken further by the successful development of the Brahmos cruise missile. These activities will be expanded further in the future. We also seek to bring about greater synergy between the scientific capabilities and potentialities of both countries.

13. Our relations with China are following a positive course and a steady effort to overcome past differences and build a growing convergence

of interests is being made. The challenge that we face vis-à-vis China is to sustain the steady expansion and strengthening of the relationship in diverse fields even as we attempt to together resolve the border issue. India and China are amongst the fastest growing economies in the world, the two largest developing countries and two major Asian powers with a recognized capacity to play major roles in shaping the future of the continent. The challenge is to balance legitimate interests of all the other players – Japan, the ASEAN bloc and the US - in a co-operative framework. Bilateral trade between India and China this year will equal four and half billion US dollars. Compared to the three and a half billion dollars trade with Japan, this illustrates the progress in efforts to normalize relations. But the unresolved border issue as also elements of China's own internal and external policies, the impact of its growing strength on the region and beyond, the extent of its sensitivity to concerns about proliferation of nuclear and missile technology in the region and the degree to which its economic success would translate into a more democratic, transparent system, would be a subject of intense interest to India as also to the international community as a whole.

14. Our foreign policy towards Japan is based on economic complementarities and developing strategic convergences. In August 2002, both countries agreed on a Global Partnership in the 21st century, at a time when economic sanctions imposed by Japan on India following our nuclear tests of May 1998 were still in force. During her recent visit, Japanese Foreign Minister Kawaguchi spoke of Japan's strategic partnership with India and India's pivotal role in the vision to create a pan Asian economic area extending from East to South Asia. In the second quarter of 2002, Japan, Korea, China and India were among the second, fourth, sixth and eighth largest importers of oil in the world. Cooperation amongst our countries to ensure the security of sea lanes has become another priority. India's achievements in the software sector and those of the East Asian countries in the hardware sector offer natural synergies that are currently in the process of being jointly exploited to mutual benefit. India and Japan are also candidates for permanent membership of the UN Security Council.

15. Europe is a key trading partner of India and a very important investor of capital. It is important, however, that the levels bilateral trade between India and Europe be improved. At Euro 25 billion today, it is far below its potential. Ambitious but realistic targets were set at the third India-EU Business Summit in October 2002 at Copenhagen for raising the current level to Euro 35 billion by 2005 and Euro 50 billion by 2008. Further transformation of the India-EU relationship

would require a two-pronged strategy of sustaining traditional links and also exploring new linkages, for instance, in knowledge industries i.e. information technology, biotechnology, pharmaceutical etc. In political terms, the relationship has already seen steady institutionalization, with Summit-level interaction between India and the EU. The strategic partnership between India and the EU is based on shared values such as democracy, pluralism and liberalism – all values of open, inclusive societies.

16. A few words on a country which today is under great international focus. Iraq was once the source of 30 percent of India's oil needs and home to ninety thousand Indians working in that country until the Gulf War. We support Iraq's compliance with the UN Resolutions and elimination of weapons of mass destruction there. We also maintain that if Iraq complies with UN Resolutions, then sanctions should be lifted in tandem for humanitarian considerations. With 3 million Indian expatriates in the Gulf region and a population of over 140 million Muslims in India, we are concerned about military action in Iraq sparking turmoil and creating more bitterness and violence, aggravating an already unstable and volatile situation. In Iraq, the international community is caught in the middle between wish and expectation. No one wishes a military conflict but most expect it.

17. Arms limitation and Disarmament through proper multilateral negotiation has been central to India's world view. India continues to stress for a cooperative thrust to reduce the salience of nuclear weapons, by subscribing to political measures such as no-first-use, non-use against non-nuclear weapon states and a move away from deployment in hair trigger alert. India, as the only country to commit to no-first-use, believes that restraint on use of nuclear weapons will reduce their salience in strategic calculus and over time pave the way for their reduction and elimination.

18. For us it is also a conviction that the idea of comprehensive security requires not just security from war or threat of war, but also food security, energy security and a sustainable environment. This necessitates sustained economic development which, in turn, is today increasingly dependent on the technological prowess of a country. Technology - nuclear, space, hi-technology - are critical tools for development and comprehensive security. Ironically, regimes of technology denial, created in the name of nonproliferation, but which have outlived their relevance, are still being maintained even in the face of mounting evidence of their failure to prevent proliferation. The case of North Korea's nuclear development programme and Pakistan's involvement is the most recent illustration; Pakistan's own clandestine acquisitions of nuclear technology and missiles and related

technology were earlier instances. These denial regimes that have proved ineffective in preventing proliferation to irresponsible regimes are inimical to our interests when used to deny developmental tools to states such as India with impeccable nonproliferation credentials. There is a pressing demand for energy to fire the engine of rapid economic growth. Given the limitations of fossil fuels, the global concerns about climate change and ecological degradation, nuclear power generation provides a clean, viable alternative. International cooperation in the civilian nuclear power generation remains hostage to denial regimes insisting on "club" rules rather than genuine nonproliferation. India, with its indigenous nuclear technology capability demonstrated, its huge market and nonproliferation credentials views nuclear power generation as the need and task of the immediate future. In a sense, it is comparable to our quest for space technology, driven by socio-economic needs, demands of weather forecasting, communications and disaster management. It is a travesty of truth to perceive this quest in narrow terms of missile proliferation in India's case. That is why India rejects controls on transfer of technology related to peaceful uses of outer space.

19. Let me say a few words on India's nuclear doctrine and share with you information that our Cabinet Committee on Security has also made available to the Indian public regarding operational arrangements governing India's nuclear assets. The basic principles of India's nuclear doctrine can be summarized as follows:

- Building and maintaining a credible nuclear deterrent;
- A Posture of ' No-First Use': This implies that nuclear weapons will only be used in retaliation against nuclear attack on Indian territory;
- Deterrence strengthened by maintaining capacity for retaliation;
- Nuclear retaliatory attacks can only be authorized by the civilian political leadership through the Nuclear Command Authority;
- Non- use of nuclear weapons against non-nuclear weapon States;
- A continued observance of the moratorium on nuclear tests, participation in the FMCT negotiations and continuance of strict controls on export of nuclear and missile related materials and technologies;
- Continued commitment to the goal of a nuclear weapon free world, through global, verifiable and non-discriminatory nuclear disarmament.

20. This doctrine that has been spelt out forms part of a responsible and restrained approach to the security challenges of the future. It provides for transparency and predictability and should, therefore, serve the purpose of deterrence and stability.

21. In the days ahead, we will continue to place emphasis on multilateral efforts to establish instruments and norms that will enhance respect for international law rather than perpetuate the concept of unilateral advantage, whether in the field of security or trade or other areas of international interaction. Whenever the United Nations is ready to expand the permanent membership of the Security Council to reflect the global realities of the new century, it is evident that India will stake a rightful claim for a place in it.
22. Cooperation among the countries of the Indian Ocean Rim is another concept that India would pursue with greater momentum, with the active participation of African states. India has a creditable record of supporting liberation movements in Africa and the anti-apartheid struggle. There has been, and still is, significant movement in terms of people between India and that continent. A large number of students from Africa have studied in Indian technical and other institutions. There is considerable potential for economic and commercial co-operation, for promoting small-scale industries in the continent with technological support from India.
23. There are 20 million persons of Indian origin living beyond the shores of India, making creditable contributions to the countries that they live in. India has only recently begun to give serious consideration to the resources, entrepreneur skills and goodwill that they could contribute to India in a variety of ways. Early this month, representatives of the Indian diaspora gathered in New Delhi for the first **Pravasi Bharatiya Diwas** tos explore such possibilities. The decision to offer dual citizenship to Persons of Indian Origin in seven countries to begin with will have far reaching impact on the future development of India.
24. I'll end here. This has been a long statement, covering a broad-range of issues. I will be happy to respond to questions, if any.

‹57›

Keynote Address by Shri Kanwal Sibal, Foreign Secretary, at the Centre for United Nations Peacekeeping, New Delhi (21.08.03)

In this speech the Foreign Secretary outlined India's approach to UN Peacekeeping. He said that while "our basic approach has been to uphold the principle of sovereignty and of supporting assistance from outside, including the UN only at the explicit request and consent of the State", India nevertheless cannot ignore the "reality around us" and, therefore, in such cases where "the sovereignty cannot be exercised effectively at all", India can "countenance the question of the role of international community including the UN, in peace operations". He also outlined in detail the factors which are relevant in determining India's response for the quest for assistance. These, in his view, are: "the involvement of the UN", "the goodwill of the countries served by our peace keepers", "the bilateral relations and the regional equations", "the national sentiment in India", "the issue of command and control", "the professionalism of our armed forces" including their "international exposure and experience".

National Seminar on "Complex Peace Operations: Traditional Premises and New Realities" (August 21-22, 2003)

General Nambiar, Director of the United Service Institution of India, Distinguished Participants and Guests,

2. It gives me great pleasure to be amidst you today in the Centre for United Nations Peaekeeping(CUNPK), at the inaugural session of the National Seminar. This is my first visit to this institution. In the short span of three years since its inception, the Centre has attained stature and has evolved into a well recognized institution. I congratulate Gen. Satish Nambiar, under whose able leadership the CUNPK has grown, for the meticulous planning and dynamism that he has imparted to the institution.

3. The Centre has been set up as a joint endeavour of the Ministry of External Affairs, the Ministry of Defence and the Armed Forces. I am particularly happy to see this vibrant example of active cooperation

and to see that such concepts can be concretized. We all know that collective pooling of our experiences and expertise, a sharing of our perceptions and perspectives in the different wings of the Government, is a *sine qua non* for the successful management of critical issues of national interest, especially issues of war and peace. This Centre is an example of how such cooperation and synergy can be achieved. I have been told about what the CUNPK has done so far – visits including by the UNSG, an impressive list of seminars – national and international, training capsules and a building of data and case studies. I am told that in October this year, CUNPK is gearing up to co-host along with the U.N., a training capsule for emerging Troop Contributing Countries. This event, the first of this kind, is yet another step. May I use this opportunity, to express my Ministry's continued commitment to make CUNPK a Centre of excellence on Peacekeeping issues.

4. It is necessary for India to have such a Centre. India is among the longest serving and the largest troop contributors to UN peacekeeping activities. Our credentials in this regard are second to none. We have a formidable track record of having more than 67,000 personnel who have participated in thirty seven out of the fifty six U.N. peacekeeping missions established so far. We have emerged as one of the most dependable and sought-after Troop Contributing Countries in the world. What is more, we have taken up difficult challenges. Starting with Korea in 1950, we have been participating in difficult missions such as in Cambodia, Angola, Rwanda, Somalia etc and now, once again the IAF is in Congo. None of this is without risks. Only two weeks ago, Shri Satish Menon, the Deputy Commandant in the BSF tragically laid down his life while serving in the U.N. Mission in Kosovo. We solemnly salute this brave officer and also 108 others before him who have made this supreme sacrifice under the U.N. flag.

5. Apart from being a leading troop contributor, we have also been an energetic and influential participant in the U.N. debates on peacekeeping, and have helped in shaping current thinking on many conceptual issues. India has played an important role in the deliberations in the UN on the recommendations of the **Brahimi Report**, and supported efforts to make the UN more efficient and effective in its peacekeeping functions. It is eminently appropriate therefore that this National Seminar has as its theme the contemporary issue under the title "Complex Peace Operations – Traditional Premises and New Realities". Let me express some thoughts on the theme, in the light of our recent preoccupations and experiences.

6. I would like to emphasize that this is no longer an innocuous, theoretical debate, confined to academic circles. It is a timely issue for discussion also in the public domain. This became abundantly clear during the

extensive and animated national debate that took place recently on the question of deploying our troops in Iraq. The debate involved practically all sections of people: parliamentarians, policy makers, analysts, defence forces and the general public. While the advantages and disadvantages of sending our troops to Iraq as a part of the stabilization force were hotly debated, there were some who sought to see the whole issue only in terms of so-called "U.S. pressure" on India. There has been no US pressure on India. US would, of course, like India to contribute to the stabilization force but to say that a request amounts to pressure would be a reflection of an undue sense of vulnerability. We value our relations with the US and whenever possible we should explore issues on which we can work together. I would like to emphasize, however, that to see India as bending to pressure is not to do justice to ourselves. The strength and stature of our country has been demonstrated time and again in the independent stance we have adopted on important global issues and the independent decisions we have taken in matters that concern us. We cannot be pushed into taking any decision that is not of our own making. Our decisions will always be arrived at after careful consideration of all relevant aspects of issues under examination, and will be guided, in the final analysis, solely by our national interests. So was it in this case.

7. Let me share some reflections on the broader theme: "traditional premises and new realities". Our standard approach to 'peacekeeping' is well known to most of you and can be summarized briefly. We believe that the UN has a major responsibility for the maintenance of international peace and security, and that peacekeeping continues to be one of the key tools or instruments available to the UN. We view peacekeeping in the traditional sense of the term as an effort to assist in 'keeping peace' and facilitating a return to normalcy, preferably within a finite, well defined timeframe. We have believed that peacekeeping follows a 'peace accord' between parties to a conflict and a commitment by them for a peaceful settlement. Peacekeeping operations should strictly adhere to the principles of the UN Charter, in particular, the principles of full respect for the sovereignty and territorial integrity of States and non-intervention in their internal affairs. We have also insisted that peacekeeping operations should be considered only at the request of the Member States involved, and should be under the command and control of the UN. It is also our belief that Chapter VI operations, based on consent of the parties are more likely to succeed and Chapter VII operations which are in the nature of an enforcement operation should be viewed as exceptions.

8. While the above has constituted our approach to peacekeeping, we are nevertheless fully alive and sensitive to the reality of the changing nature of peacekeeping, and the growing complexity and scale of these operations. In the last ten years the principles and practices in peacekeeping have undergone something of a revolution.
9. These changes have been described and commented upon variously. Let me merely identify a few elements:
   - Peace keeping, an operation relevant to keeping peace between two or more states has also moved to keeping peace within a State. There is involvement of the UN not only in situations of inter-state conflict but also in the intra-State conflicts.
   - The objectives pursued in operations have enlarged from assisting in the maintenance of ceasefire to the increasingly detailed stabilization, humanitarian, and civilian police components. UN operations have widened and peace keeping is seen as one element in a larger process of managing a 'post-conflict' situation. Examples: East Timor or Afghanistan. The nature of 'Peace operations', itself a new term instead of the conventional 'Peacekeeping Operations' has, therefore, changed from being uni-dimensional to multi-dimensional involving a wide spectrum of activities – humanitarian assistance, refugee returns, provision of interim State services, establishment of rule of law, assistance to international criminal tribunals, facilitation of political process, monitoring of elections, and even establishment of transitional governments, etc.
   - The use of civil police and other civilians is increasing in these operations. We ourselves are getting more and more requests for policemen and have had police contingents in Bosnia and Kosovo.
   - There are also varying mandates under the UN: from classical UN peacekeeping operations, to UN-authorised multinational operations as in the case of Afghanistan and operations outside the ambit of the UN such as the coalition forces in Iraq.
   - Another significant evolution is the UN's reliance on regional and sub-regional organizations to support and even carry out missions on its behalf. The recent example is of ECOWAS in Liberia.

This is not an exhaustive but an indicative listing of some of the changes that we see around us today. It is clear that there are new realities. Indeed it is bound to be so since the structure and features of international relations have undeniably changed since the 1990s. India recognizes the changes and the new realities. The question then is how do we respond to them?

For a country like India – with its size, population, resources, a rich and successful experience of handling internal dissensions and problems, well established institutions, a proud record of independence of judgement and action-some of these precepts and practices amounting to erosion of sovereignty and dependence on others for even the essential tasks of governance cannot be but a matter of concern. Our basic approach has been to uphold the principle of sovereignty and of supporting assistance from outside, including the UN, only at the explicit request and consent of the State. Having said this, nevertheless we cannot shut our eyes to the reality around us and of the needs, the vulnerabilities and even the demands of weaker or smaller States which may seek international involvement in the resolution of their conflicts or in the protection of civilian populations. In some cases the Government is simply not functional, in others the institutions have collapsed or are non-existent: in other words the sovereignty cannot be exercised effectively at all. I would not name examples, but these should be clear to you. It is in such cases and only in such cases that we can countenance the question of the role of the international community including the UN, in peace operations in its larger sense as a component of nation-building.

In recent months we have pondered on some of these issues as we have looked at the situations in Afghanistan, in Congo, in Liberia and in Iraq. All these are different situations and let me say that India's interests are also different. Let me identify a few points, which in our view are relevant in determining India's response for requests for assistance.

- To start, India's policy on involvement in peace keeping operations continues to be shaped by a commitment to UN, its objectives and a commitment to Peace. The involvement of the UN implies a certain legitimacy, an international recognition and acceptability. In saying this, I am not implying that all decisions of the Security Council are necessarily objective or wise or fair. In the real world we are well aware that the decisions of the Security Council could also be a product of the power politics. Nevertheless, they do confer a certain international legitimacy as distinct form adhoc or unilateral decisions.
- We also are influenced by both the goodwill of the countries served by our peacekeepers and by the prospect of minimizing the civilian suffering which is a concomitant to peace.
- We should however be failing in recognizing the realities that I described, if each and every of our decisions on peacekeeping is an automatic response to a UN request (and only to a U.N. request). There are too many conflict situations, too many requests and too few resources for India to so respond.

Therefore, the bilateral relations and the regional equations and an assessment of India's interests broadly defined have to be a part in determining our response.

- The perception about India's involvement in a country or in a region where our troops might go, the public sentiments about the role that India would play and the national sentiment in India about such involvement are also undoubtedly factors which would influence a decision.
- Operational questions such as the issue of command and control, the resources for meeting the costs, the nature of the risk and the functions that the peacekeepers are expected to carry out are all relevant factors.
- The professionalism of our armed forces, the international exposure and experience that they would get by successfully carrying out a peacekeeping assignment in different parts of the world is no doubt also an input in the Government's decision-making.
- Therefore, an assessment of India's overall national interests in a given situation has to be undoubtedly the major determinant in deciding on our response.

10. I see from the programme that there are a number of eminently qualified experts who would debate and deliberate on these important issues at greater length. I congratulate the Centre on organizing this seminar on an eminently topical and useful theme. I wish your deliberations all success.

Part 2-A

❮58❯

Extracts from UNSC press release regarding Security Council's briefing on Iraq by US Secretary of State (05.02.03)

In his presentation to the UN Security Council, US Secretary of State Colin Powell stated that it is "irrefutable and undeniable" that Iraq remains in "material breach" of UNSC Resolution 1411 (2002). He indicated that Saddam Hussein retained "a few dozen SCUD-Variant Ballistic Missiles with a range of 650-900 kilometres" and that Iraq's record on chemical weapon was "replete with lies".

Several Council Members Call for More Time For Inspections; France Proposes Strengthening of Inspection Regime

"Clearly, Saddam Hussein and his regime will stop at nothing until something stops him", Secretary of State of the United States Colin Powell warned the Security Council today in his briefing intended to convince members that Iraq had failed to disarm.

Through the use of satellite photographs and intercepted telephone conversations in a presentation entitled "Iraq: Failing to Disarm", Mr. Powell promised that that evidence plus that which had been gathered by people who had risked their lives would let the world know "what Saddam Hussein was really up to". Saddam Hussein was determined to keep his weapons of mass destruction and to make more, he said. For him, possession of the world's most deadly weapons was the ultimate trump card, the one he must hold to fulfill his ambition.

Underlying all the facts and patterns of behaviour was Saddam Hussein's contempt for the will of the Council, his contempt for the truth, and most damning of all, his utter contempt for human life, Mr. Powell said. His use of mustard and nerve gas against the Kurds in 1988 was one of the twentieth century's most horrible atrocities. He had also conducted ethnic cleansing against the Shia Iraqis and the Marsh Arabs. His police State ruthlessly eliminated anyone who dared to dissent. Nothing pointed more clearly to Saddam Hussein's dangerous intentions than his calculated cruelty to his own citizens and neighbours.

Mr. Powell then declared that the United States would not – could not- – run the risk to the American people that Saddam Hussein would one day use his weapons of mass destruction. Council members must not shrink from whatever lay ahead or fail in their responsibility to their citizens. Iraq still posed a threat and it still remained in material breach. By failing to seize its one last opportunity to "come clean" and disarm, it had put itself in deeper material breach and closer to the day when it would face serious consequences for its continued defiance.

Security Council resolution 1441 (2002) was written, not in order to go to war, but to try and preserve the peace and give Iraq one last chance, he said. Iraq so far is not taking that one last chance. It was "irrefutable and undeniable" that, by the standard set out in operative paragraph 4 of resolution 1441 (2002), which defines a further material breach as false statements oromissions in declarations and failure to cooperate fully in the implementation of the resolution, Iraq was now in further material breach.

Mr. Powell cited several examples of obstruction of the inspections, including the falsification of a death certificate for one scientist forced into hiding, and disclosed evidence of biological and chemical weapons, and longer-range missiles. The United States had also learned that Saddam Hussein's son Qusay had ordered the removal of all prohibited weapons from Saddam's palace complexes. While the Council was debating resolution 1441 (2002) last fall, a missile brigade outside Baghdad was dispersing rocket launchers and warheads containing biological warfare agent to various locations in western Iraq.

Concerning the missiles capable of delivering prohibited weapons, he said that while inspectors had destroyed most of the prohibited ballistic missiles, numerous Intelligence reports over the past decade from sources inside Iraq indicated Saddam Hussein retained a covert force of up to a few dozen SCUD-Variant ballistic missiles with a range of 650 to 900 kilometers. Iraq had programmes intended to produce ballistic missiles that flew over a thousand kilometers, for which it had built an engine test stand larger than any it had ever had.

One of the most worrisome things that had emerged from the thick Intelligence file of the United States on Iraq's biological weapons programme was mobile production facilities for biological agents, he said. The United States had first-hand descriptions of at least seven sophisticated mobile biological weapons factories on wheels and rails, which were designed to evade detection by inspectors. In a matter of months, those could produce a quantity of biological poison equal to the entire amount that Iraq claimed to have produced in the years prior to the Gulf War. Iraq had also developed ways to disperse lethal biological agents, widely and indiscriminately, into the water and air.

Mr. Powell said that Iraq's record on chemical weapons was "replete with lies". It took years for Iraq to finally admit that it had produced four tons of the deadly nerve agent VX. A single drop of VX on the skin would kill in minutes. The United Nations Special Commission (UNSCOM) had also gained forensic evidence that Iraq had produced VX and had put it into weapons for delivery. Yet, to this day, Iraq denied it had ever weaponized VX, and on 27 January, the United Nations Monitoring, Verification and Inspection Commission (UNMOVIC) told the Council that it had information that conflicted with the Iraqi account of its VX programme.

Terrorism and Iraq went back decades, but today there was a potentially more sinister nexus between Iraq and Al-Qaida, he said. Iraq harboured a deadly terrorist network headed by an associate and collaborator of Usama Bin Laden. After the Taliban had been ousted from Afghanistan, the Zarqawi network helped establish another poison and explosive training centre in northeastern Iraq. A detained senior Al-Qaida terrorist had described Iraq as offering chemical or biological weapons training for two Al-Qaida associates, beginning in December 2000. The nexus of Iraq and terror was old, but the nexus of poisons and terror was new. The combination was lethal, Mr. Powell said.

Speaking after the presentation, Council members agreed that Iraq must comply with all relevant Council resolutions in their entirety and completely eliminate its weapons of mass destruction. Several States suspected that Saddam Hussein's regime was withholding relevant information and concealing military capabilities, but urged more time to allow the inspectors to do their work before resorting to war.

Minister for Foreign Affairs of France, Dominique de Villepin, said that, for now, the inspections regime should be strengthened. Given the choice between military intervention and an inspections regime that was inadequate for lack of cooperation on Iraq's part, the international community should choose to strengthen decisively the means of inspection. For example, the number of inspectors could be doubled or triped and their monitoring capabilities increased. An information processing centre could be established, and a United Nations co-ordinator for disarmament could be assigned to the country.

The Russian Federation was convinced that maintaining unity in the international community, the context of the Council, and concerted actions in compliance with the United Nations Charter and Security Council resolutions were the most reliable ways of solving the problem in Iraq through political means, its Foreign Affairs Minister Igor Ivanov said. Resolution 1441 (2002) was geared towards speedy and practical results, but time frames were absent. Only the inspectors could determine how much time was needed for their task.

Following the statements by Council members, the representative of Iraq said the clear goal of the meeting today and of Mr. Powell's presentation had been to sell the idea of war against Iraq, without any legal, moral or political justification. He reiterated Iraq's commitment to continue proactive cooperation with the inspection teams, so they could verify, as soon as possible, that Iraq was free of weapons of mass destruction. Then, sanctions could be lifted and regional security ensured. His country would provide a detailed and technical explanation to the allegations made by Mr. Powell.

Also speaking at today's meeting were: Vice-Chancellor and Minister for Foreign Affairs of Germany, Joschka Fischer; Minister for Foreign Affairs of China, Tang Jiaxuan; Secretary of State for Foreign and Commonwealth Affairs of the United Kingdom, Jack Straw; Minister of State in charge of External Relations of Cameroon, Francois-Xavier Ngoubeyou; Minister for Foreign Affairs of Mexico, Luis Ernesto Derbez; Bulgaria's Minister for Foreign Affairs, Solomon Passy; Foreign Minister of Pakistan, Khurshid M. Kasuri; Minister for Foreign Affairs of Spain, Ana Palacio; Minister for Foreign Affairs of Chile, Soledad Alvear Valenzuela; Vice-Minister for Foreign Affairs of Angola, Georges Rebelo Chikoti; as well as the permanent representatives of Syria and Guinea to the United Nations.

Also attending today's meeting were Secretary-General Kofi Annan, and Hans Blix, Executive Chairman of UNMOVIC and Mohamed ElBaradei, Director-General of the International Atomic Energy Agency (IAEA).

The meeting began at 10:35 a.m. and was adjourned at 2:10 p.m.

Statement by United States

COLIN POWELL, Secretary of State of the United States, said that, by the time the Council had adopted resolution 1441 (2002) on 8 November 2002, Iraq had already been found guilty of material breach of its obligations stretching back over sixteen previous resolutions and twelve years. Resolution 1441 was not dealing with an innocent party, but a regime that the Council had repeatedly convicted over the years. The resolution gave Iraq one last chance to come into compliance or to face serious consequences. No Council member present and voting on that day had any illusions about the nature and intent of the resolution of what serious consequences meant if Iraq did not comply.

To assist in Iraq's disarmament, he said, the Council called on Iraq to co-operate with returning inspectors. The Council laid down tough standards for Iraq to meet to allow the inspectors to do their job. It placed the burden on Iraq to comply and disarm, and not on the inspectors to find that which Iraq had gone out of its way to conceal for so long. "Inspectors are inspectors. They are not detectives", he said. He asked for today's session for two purposes: to support the core assessments made by Drs. Blix and Elbaradei. As Dr. Blix reported to the Council on 27 January, "Iraq appears not to have come to a genuine acceptance—not even today—of the disarmament, which was demanded of it..."

He said his second purpose today was to provide additional information, to share what the United States knew about Iraq's weapons of mass destruction, as well as its involvement in terrorism, which was also the subject of resolution 1441 (2002). The material to be presented today came from a variety of sources, including from other countries. Some were technical, such as intercepted telephone conversations and photos taken by satellites. Other sources were people who had risked their lives to let the world know what Saddam Hussein was really up to. He could not tell the world everything he knew, but what he could share, when combined with what had been learned over the years, was "deeply troubling". What the Council would see was an accumulation of facts and disturbing patterns of behaviour.

The facts and Iraq's behaviour demonstrated that Saddam Hussein and his regime had made no effort to disarm, as required by the International community, he continued. Indeed, the facts and Iraq's behaviour showed that Saddam Hussein and his regime were concealing their efforts to produce more weapons of mass destruction. He began by playing a tape-recorded conversation, monitored by his Government. It took place on 26 November 2002, on the day before United Nations teams resumed inspections in Iraq. The conversation involved two senior officers: a Colonel and a Brigadier General from Iraq's Elite Military Unit, the Republican Guard.

(That tape was played, over which a transcript of the remarks was projected on a screen.)

Focusing on a few key elements of that conversation, Mr. Powell said that, clearly, the two officers had not gotten rid of everything they were so anxious to hide. On the day before Dr. ElBaradei arrived, they were anxious to hide something. What was it? Under resolution 1441 (2002), they were supposed to tell us. The conversation referred to items received from *Al-Kindi*, a company known to have been involved in prohibited weapons systems activity.

(A second tape was played of a voice of an officer of the Republican Guard Headquarters issuing an instruction to an officer in the field.)

Mr. Powell explained that the conversation took place just last week, on 30 January. He recalled that the inspectors had found twelve empty chemical warheads on sixteen January. On 20 January, four days later, Iraq promised the inspectors it would search for more. After the tape, he said he did not know what the Iraqi regime intended to do with any "forbidden ammunition". But, he could be sure they had not intended to present it to the inspectors. And, why destroy the evidence that would prove that Iraq was fulfilling its promise to inspectors to find more munitions? It made no sense unless Iraq's intention was to keep concealing the munitions, yet claim to the inspectors that they had looked for them and found nothing.

The effort to hide things from the inspectors was not an isolated event, he went on. That was part and parcel of a policy of evasion and deception that dated back twelve years-- a policy set at the highest levels of the Iraqi regime. Think about the fact that Iraq had a high-level committee to monitor the inspectors who were sent in to monitor the country's disarmament. Not to cooperate with them, not to assist them, but to spy on them and keep them from doing their job was the reason why. General Amir Al-Sa'di was the Iraqi regime's primary point of contact for Drs. Blix and ElBaradei. It was the General who publicly pledged last fall that Iraq was prepared to cooperate unconditionally with inspectors. Quite the contrary—Sa'di's job was to deceive, not to disarm; to undermine the inspectors, not to support them.

Turning to the declaration that Iraq had submitted to the Council on 7 December 2002, he said that Iraq had never intended to comply with the Council's mandate. Instead, it had planned to use the declaration to overwhelm the international community and the inspectors with useless information about Iraq's permitted weapons, so that there would be no time to pursue Iraq's prohibited weapons. Iraq's goal was to give everyone in this room the false impression that the inspection process was working. The result was a 12,200-page declaration "rich in volume" but "poor in information and practically devoid of new evidence". "Could any member of the Council honestly rise in defence of that false declaration?" he asked.

Everything he had seen and heard indicated that Saddam Hussein and his regime were busy doing all they possibly could to ensure that inspectors succeeded in finding absolutely nothing, he said. His statements today were not assertions, but backed up by solid sources. Citing some examples from human sources, he said: orders were issued to Iraq's security organizations, as well as to Saddam Hussein's own office staff, to hide all correspondence with the Organization of Military Industrialization. That organization oversaw Iraq's weapons of mass destruction activities.

Also, he said he knew that Saddam's son Qusay had ordered the removal of all prohibited weapons from Saddam's numerous palace complexes. He knew that Iraqi government officials, members of the ruling Ba'ath Party, and scientists had hidden prohibited items in their homes. Other key files from military and scientific establishments had been placed in cars that were being driven around the countryside by Iraqi Intelligence agents to devoid detection. Thanks to the Intelligence that had been provided, the inspectors recently found dramatic confirmation of those reports when they searched the home of an Iraqi nuclear scientist, uncovering roughly 2,000 pages of documents. Some of that material was classified and related to Iraq's nuclear programme.

Other sources had told him that, in some cases, the hard drives of computers at Iraqi weapons facilities had been replaced, he added. Who took the hard drives? Where did they go? What's being hidden? he asked. While the Council was debating resolution 1441 (2002) last fall, a missile brigade outside Baghdad was dispersing rocket launchers and warheads containing biological warfare agent to various locations in western Iraq. Most of the launchers and warheads had been hidden in large groves of palm trees, and were to be moved every one to four weeks to escape detection. The United States also had satellite photos that indicated that banned materials had recently been moved from a number of Iraqi weapons of mass destruction facilities.

(He proceeded to show various photographs.)

He said that the first was a close-up image of Taji Bunker, on the left of which was a close-up of one of the four chemical munitions bunkers. The arrows indicated the presence of sure signs that those bunkers were storing chemical munitions-enhanced security and a chemical de-contamination vehicle. The photo on the right, taken on 22 December 2002 when the inspectors were arriving, showed two of the chemical munitions bunkers above the convoy of United Nations vehicles—no security, no de-contamination vehicle. The weapons were gone. The bunkers were clean. The inspectors found nothing, he said. That sequence of events raised the worrisome suspicion that Iraq had been tipped off to the forthcoming inspections at Taji.

As it did throughout the 1990s, he said he knew that Iraq today was actively using its considerable intelligence capabilities to help hide its illicit activities. From other sources, he knew that the inspectors were under constant surveillance by an army of Iraqi Intelligence operatives. Iraq was relentlessly attempting to tap all their communications, both voice and electronic. He then turned to an example of what he called the type of concealment activity Iraq had undertaken in response to the resumption of inspections. Just when the inspections were about to resume, that type of activity spiked.

As examples, and with accompanying images, he said that, at a ballistic missile site on 10 November 2002, he saw a cargo truck preparing to move ballistic missile components. At a biological weapons-related facility on 25 November 2002, just two days before inspections resumed, a truck caravan appeared—something almost never seen at that facility. At a ballistic missile facility, again two days before inspections began, five large cargo trucks appeared, along with the truck-mounted crane to move missiles. The United States had seen that kind of "housecleaning" at close to thirty sites.

He said that Iraq had also refused to permit any U-2 reconnaissance flights that would give the inspectors a better sense of what was being moved before, during and after inspections. That refusal was in specific violation of operative paragraph 7 of resolution 1441 (2002). Saddam Hussein and his regime were not just trying to conceal weapons; they were also trying to hide people. The basic facts were known. Iraq had not complied with its obligation to allow immediate, unimpeded, unrestricted and private access to all officials and other persons as required by resolution 1441 (2002).

Also, Saddam Hussein had directly participated in the effort to prevent interviews with scientists, he went on. In early December, Saddam Hussein had all Iraqi scientists warned of the serious consequences that they and their families would face if they revealed any sensitive information to the inspectors. They were forced to sign documents acknowledging that divulging information was punishable by death. He also said that scientists should be told not to agree to leave Iraq; doing so meant they would be treated as spies.

He noted that, in mid-November, just before the inspectors returned, Iraqi experts were ordered to report to the Headquarters of the Special Security Organization for Counter-Intelligence for training, which focused on evasion methods, interrogation resistance techniques, and how to mislead inspectors. Among other points: weapons at a facility in mid-December were replaced by Iraqi Intelligence agents who were to deceive inspectors about the work being done there; on order from Saddam Hussein, Iraqi officials issued a false death certificate for one scientist, and he was sent into hiding. That list went on and on, he said.

By the standard set out in operative paragraph 4 of resolution 1441 (2002), he said he believed that Iraq was now in further material breach. That conclusion was "irrefutable and undeniable". Iraq had now placed itself in danger of the serious consequences called for under that resolution. At the same time, the Council placed itself in danger of irrelevance if it allowed Iraq to continue to defy its will without responding effectively and immediately. The issue before that body now was not how much more time it was willing to give the inspectors to be frustrated by Iraqi obstruction, but how much longer it was willing to put up with Iraq's non-compliance before it said "Enough!", he said.

Turning to biological weapons, he recalled that it had taken the United Nations Special Commission (UNSCOM) four long and frustrating years to pry an admission out of Iraq that it had biological weapons. When it finally admitted having those weapons in 1995, the quantities were vast. Less than a teaspoonful of dry anthrax in an envelope had shut down the United States Senate in the fall of 2001. That had forced several hundred people to undergo emergency medical treatment, and killed two postal workers. Iraq had declared 8,500 litres of anthrax, but UNSCOM estimated that Saddam Hussein could have produced 25,000 litres. If concentrated in dry form, that amount would be enough to fill tens of thousands of teaspoons, and Saddam Hussein had not verifiably accounted for even one teaspoon of that deadly material.

Continuing, he said that one of the most worrisome things that emerged from the thick Intelligence file the United States had on Iraq's biological weapons programme was mobile production facilities for biological agents. His country had first-hand descriptions of biological weapons factories on wheels and rails, which could be easily moved and were designed to evade detection by inspectors. In a matter of months, they could produce a quantity of biological poison equal to the entire amount that Iraq claimed to have produced in the years prior to the Gulf War.

He said that, during previous inspections, the United Nations inspectors had had only vague hints of that programme. The confirmation had come only in 2000, from an Iraqi Chemical Engineer who supervised one of those facilities. His account had been corroborated by other sources. Iraq had at least seven of those sophisticated mobile biological weapons factories. In fact, they could produce enough dry biological agent in a month to kill thousands upon thousands of people. From Iraq's past admissions, it was known that it had successfully weaponized not only anthrax, but also other biological agents, including aflatoxin and ricin.

Iraq had also investigated dozens of biological agents causing diseases, he continued, such as gas gangrene, plague, typhus, cholera and haemorrhagic fever. It had developed ways to disperse lethal biological agents, widely, indiscriminately, into the water supply and into the air. In 1995, an Iraqi military officer, Mujahid Salh Abdul Latif, had told inspectors that Iraq intended the spray tanks to be mounted onto an MIG-21 that had been converted into an unmanned aerial vehicle, or UAV. Iraq had also admitted to producing four spray tanks, but to this day it had provided no credible evidence that they had been destroyed. There could be no doubt that Saddam Hussein had biological weapons and the capability to rapidly produce more. It also had the ability to dispense those lethal poisons and diseases in ways that caused massive death and destruction.

Turning to chemical weapons, he said that it was important to keep in mind that Saddam Hussein had used those horrific weapons on another country and on his own people. In fact, in the history of chemical warfare, no country had more battlefield experience with chemical weapons since the First World War than Iraq. Saddam Hussein had also never accounted for vast amounts of chemical weaponry—550 artillery shells with mustard, 30,000 empty munitions and enough precursors to increase his stockpile to as much as 500 tons of chemical agents. Considering just one category of missing weaponry—6,500 bombs from the Iran-Iraq war—the United Nations Monitoring, Verification and Inspection Commission (UNMOVIC) had said that the amount of chemical agent in them would be on the order of 1,000 tons. The United States had evidence that those weapons existed, but there was no evidence from Iraq that they had been destroyed.

Iraq's record on chemical weapons was replete with lies, he said. It had taken years for Iraq to admit that it had produced four tons of the deadly nerve agent VX. To this day, Iraq was denying that it had ever weaponized VX. Yet, on 27 January, UNMOVIC had told the Council that it had information that conflicted with the Iraqi account of its VX programme.

Iraq had embedded key portions of its illicit chemical weapons infrastructure within its legitimate civilian industry, he continued. Even to experts, that infrastructure looked like an ordinary civilian operation. The inspectors would be unlikely to turn up anything prohibited, especially if there was warning that they were coming. "Call it ingenious—or evil genius —but the Iraqis deliberately designed their chemical weapons programme to be inspected", he said.

Presenting evidence related to the "delivery end of Saddam's chemical weapons business", he said that in May 2002 his country's satellites had photographed unusual activity at the Al-Musayyib chemical complex. In the photograph before the Council, cargo vehicles were accompanied by a decontamination vehicle associated with biological or chemical weapons activity. What made the picture so significant was that a human source had corroborated that movement of chemical weapons.

To support its deadly biological and chemical programmes, Iraq procured needed items from around the world using an extensive clandestine network. What the United States knew came largely from intercepted communications and human sources who were in a position to know the facts. Iraq's procurement efforts included equipment that could filter and separate micro-organisms and toxins involved in biological weapons and to concentrate the agent, as well as growth media that could be used to continue producing anthrax and botulism toxins, sterilization equipment for laboratories, class-lined reactors and specialty pumps, large amounts of a precursor for nerve and blister agents — thionyl chloride, and other chemicals, including sodium chloride, an important mustard agents precursor.

Of course, Iraq would argue that those items could also be used for legitimate purposes, he said, but if that were true, why did the United States have to learn about them by intercepting communications and risking the lives of human agents? His conservative estimate was that Iraq today had a stockpile of between 100 and 500 tons of chemical weapons agent, which was enough to fill 16,000 battlefield rockets. Even 100 tons of agent would cause mass casualties across more than 100 square miles of territory—an area nearly five times the size of Manhattan. In that connection, he reminded the Council that the 122-millimetre chemical warheads that United Nations inspectors had found could very well be, as had been noted, "the tip of a submerged iceberg".

Other sources testified to the fact that, since the 1980s, Saddam's regime had been experimenting on human beings to perfect its biological or chemical weapons. A source said, for example, that 1,600 death-row prisoners were transferred in 1995 to a special unit for such experiments. An eyewitness saw prisoners tied down to beds, blood oozing around their mouths, and autopsies performed to confirm the effects on the prisoners. Saddam Hussein's inhumanity had no limits.

Turning to nuclear weapons, he said that there was no indication that Saddam Hussein had ever abandoned his nuclear programme. On the contrary, there was more than a decade of proof that he remained determined to acquire nuclear weapons. While in 1991 the inspectors had found nothing to conclude that Iraq had a nuclear weapons programme, based on defector information, in May of 1991 Saddam Hussein's lie was exposed. In fact, he had a massive clandestine nuclear weapons programme that included several techniques to enrich uranium, including electromagnetic isotope separation, gas centrifuge, and gas diffusion. If Saddam had not been stopped, Iraq could have produced a nuclear bomb by 1993. In 1995, another defector had reported that, after his invasion of Kuwait, Saddam Hussein had initiated a crash programme to build a crude nuclear weapon in violation of Iraq's United Nations obligations.

Saddam Hussein already possessed two of the three key components needed to build a nuclear bomb. He had a cadre of nuclear scientists with the expertise, and he had a bomb design. Since 1998, his efforts had been focused on acquiring the third and last component—sufficient fissile material to produce a nuclear explosion. He had made repeated covert attempts to acquire high-specification aluminum tubes from 11 different countries, even after the inspection resumed. Those tubes were controlled by the nuclear suppliers group precisely because they could be used as centrifuges for enriching uranium. While there was a lot of controversy about those tubes, most United States experts thought they were intended to serve as the rotors in centrifuges used to enrich uranium.

The United States also had Intelligence from multiple sources that Iraq was attempting to acquire magnets and high-speed balancing machines, he said. Both items could be used in a gas centrifuge programme to enrich uranium. Intercepted communications from mid-2000 through last summer showed that Iraqi front companies sought to buy machines that could be used to balance gas centrifuge rotors. People would continue to debate that issue, but there was no doubt in his mind. Those illicit procurement efforts showed that Saddam Hussein was very much focused on putting in place the key missing piece from his nuclear weapons programme—the ability to produce fissile material.

Mr. Powell then turned to the systems he said Iraq was developing to deliver weapons of mass destruction, in particular, Iraq's ballistic missiles and unmanned aerial vehicles (UAVs). While inspectors had destroyed most of the prohibited ballistic missiles, numerous Intelligence reports over the past decade from sources inside Iraq indicated Saddam Hussein retained a covert force of up to a few dozen SCUD-Variant ballistic missiles with a range of 650 to 900 kilometres. Iraq's alleged "permitted" ballistic missiles, the *Al-Samoud* 2 and the *Al-Fatah*, violated the 150 kilometres limit and were prohibited systems. The UNMOVIC had also reported that Iraq had illegally imported 380 SA-2 Rocket engines, some acquired as late as December last year, after resolution 1441 had been adopted.

While showing a map and a photo, he said that Iraq had programmes intended to produce ballistic missiles that fly over a thousand kilometres. As part of the effort, Iraq had built an engine test stand that was larger than any it had ever had. The missiles were intended to project power, to threaten and to deliver chemical, biological and, "if we let him", eventually, nuclear warheads.

Iraq had been working on a variety of UAVs for more than a decade. The UAVs were well suited for dispensing chemical and biological weapons, and there was ample evidence that Iraq had dedicated much effort to developing and testing spray devices that could be adapted for UAVs. Intelligence collected on 27 June last year indicated that Iraq's newest UAV went five hundred kilometres non-stop on autopilot. Not only was the test well in excess of the 150-kilometre limit, the test was left out of Iraq's 7 December declaration. That declaration had claimed that its UAVs had a range of only eighty kilometres. Iraq could use UAVs to deliver biological agents to its neighbours or, if transported, to other countries, including the United States.

Turning to the subject of terrorism, he said Iraq and terrorism went back decades. Baghdad trained Palestine Liberation Front members in small arms and explosives, and Saddam used the Arab Liberation Front to funnel money to the families of Palestinian suicide bombers. It was no secret that Saddam's own Intelligence service was involved in dozens of attacks or attempted assassinations in the 1990s. There was, however, the potentially more sinister nexus between Iraq and the Al-Qaida network. Iraq today harboured a deadly terrorist network headed by Abu Musab Al-Zarqawi, an associate of Osama Bin Laden. After the Taliban had been ousted from Afghanistan, the Zarqawi network helped establish another poison and explosive training centre in north-eastern Iraq.

Baghdad had an agent in the most senior levels of a radical organization, Ansar Al-Islam, that controlled that corner of Iraq, he continued. In 2000, that agent had offered Al-Qaida safe haven in the region. Zarqawi travelled to Baghdad in May 2002 for medical treatment, and during his stay nearly two dozen extremists converged on Baghdad and established a base of operations there. Those Al-Qaida affiliates now coordinated the movement of people, money, and supplies into and throughout Iraq for his network and had been operating freely in the capital for more than eight months. Denials on the part of Iraqi officials were not credible. Last year, an Al-Qaida associate had bragged that the situation in Iraq was "good", that Baghdad could be transited quickly.

Last year, two suspected Al-Qaida operatives were arrested crossing from Iraq into Saudi Arabia. The captured assassin of Laurence Foley, murdered in Amman, Jordan, last October, had said his cell received money and weapons from Zarqawi. After the attack, Mr. Powell said, an associate of Mr. Foley's killer left Jordan for Iraq to obtain weapons and explosives for further operations. The United States had asked a friendly security service to approach Baghdad about extraditing Zarqawi. That service had contacted Iraqi officials twice and had passed details that should have made it easy to find him. The network remained in Baghdad, and Zarqawi still remained at large. His network's terrorism was not confined to the Middle East. Zarqawi and his network had plotted terrorist actions against countries, including France, Britain, Spain, Italy, Germany and Russia.

When Bin Laden was based in the Sudan, in the early and mid-1990s, an Al-Qaida source had said that Saddam and Bin Laden had reached an "understanding" that Al-Qaida would not longer support activities against Baghdad. Early ties between Iraq and Al-Qaida had been forged by secret high-level Iraqi Intelligence service contacts. Members of both organizations had met repeatedly and had met at least eight times at "very senior levels" since the early 1990s. A foreign security service had told the United States that Bin Laden had met with a senior Iraqi Intelligence official in Khartoum and later with the Director of the Iraqi Intelligence service. He said he was not comforted by the belief of some that the contacts did not amount to much, as Hussein's secular tyranny and Al-Qaida's religious tyranny did not mix. Ambition and hatred were enough to bring Iraq and Al-Qaida together.

A detained senior Al-Qaida terrorist had described Iraq offering chemical or biological weapons training for two Al-Qaida associates beginning in December 2000. A militant known as Abu Abdallay Al-Iraqi had been sent to Iraq several times between 1997 and 2000 for help in acquiring poisons and gases. That militant had characterized his relationship with Iraqi officials as "successful". None of that should come as a surprise to any. Terrorism had been a tool of Saddam for decades. The nexus of poisons and terror was new. The nexus of Iraq and terror was old. "The combination is lethal", Mr. Powell said. "When we confront a regime that harbours ambitions of regional domination, hides weapons of mass destruction, and provides haven and active support for terrorists, we are not confronting the past. We are confronting the present—and unless we act—an even more frightening future."

He said underlying all the facts and patterns of behaviour described was Saddam Hussein's contempt for the will of the Council, his contempt for the truth, and, most damning of all, his utter contempt for human life. His use of mustard and nerve gas against the Kurds in 1988 was one of the twentieth century's most horrible atrocities. He had also conducted ethnic cleansing against the Shia Iraqis and the Marsh Arabs. His police State ruthlessly eliminated anyone who dared to dissent. Iraq had more forced disappearance cases than any other country. "Nothing points more clearly to Saddam Hussein's dangerous intentions—and the threat he poses to all of us—than his calculated cruelty to his own citizens and to his neighbours", he said. "Saddam Hussein and his regime will stop at nothing until something stops him."

In conclusion, Mr. Powell said that, for more than twenty years, Saddam Hussein had pursued his ambition to dominate Iraq and the broader Middle East, using intimidation, coercion and annihilation of all those who might stand in his way. Saddam Hussein was determined to keep his weapons of mass destruction and make more. "Should we take the risk that he will not someday use these weapons at a time and a place and in a manner of his choosing—at a time when the world is in a much weaker position to respond?" he asked, and continued, "The United States will not—and cannot—run that risk to the American people. Leaving Saddam Hussein in possession of weapons of mass destruction for a few more months or years is not an option. Not in a post-September 11 world."

He said over three months ago, the Council had recognized that Iraq continued to pose a threat to international peace and security and that Iraq had been and remained in material breach of its disarmament obligations. Today, Iraq still posed a threat and still remained in material breach. "Indeed, by its failure to seize its one last opportunity to come clean and disarm, Iraq has put itself in deeper material breach and closer to the day when it will face serious consequences for its continued defiance of this Council." Resolution 1441 was not written to go to war, but to preserve the peace. Iraq was not taking the last chance it had been offered. "We must not shrink from whatever lies ahead of us. We must not shrink from our duty to the citizens of our countries", he concluded.

Statements by Other Members

TANG JIAXUAN, Minister for Foreign Affairs of China, said that the Council had basically maintained unity and cooperation on the issue before it today, which was critically important. He welcomed the United States' effort to provide the United Nations with its information and evidence on mass destruction weapons in Iraq, which was consistent with the spirit of resolution 1441 (2002) and could help increase transparency. He hoped the various parties would hand over their information and evidence to UNMOVIC and the International Atomic Energy Agency (IAEA) to help them achieve more effective inspections. The inspections had been going on for more than two months, and everyone should respect the views of the two agencies and support the continuation of their work.

He hoped, he said, the upcoming trip to Baghdad by Dr. Blix and Dr. ElBaradei on 8 February would yield positive results. The Council had a common stand on the elimination of mass destruction weapons in Iraq. It was also the universal desire of the international community to see a political settlement to the issue within the United Nations framework, and to avoid any war. At present, the most important issue was full implementation of resolution 1441 (2002). As long as there was still the slightest hope for political settlement, the utmost effort should be exerted to achieve it. China was ready to join others in working in that direction.

JACK STRAW, Secretary of State for Foreign and Commonwealth Affairs of the United Kingdom, said that the Council had just heard a most powerful and authoritative account of Iraq's practices by Mr. Powell, which demonstrated the great danger that Iraq's regime represented. Three months ago, the Council had united to send Iraq an uncompromising message: cooperate fully with weapons inspections or face disarmament by force. Resolution 1441 was a powerful reminder of the importance of international law and the authority of the Security Council itself. United and determined, the international community had given Iraq a final opportunity to rid itself of weapons of mass destruction, of gases that could poison thousands of people; of bacteria and viruses that could disable and kill by the tens of thousands; of the means to make nuclear weapons, which could kill by the million.

Without Iraq's immediate, full and active cooperation, however, inspectors in a country as huge as Iraq could never be sure of finding all weapons of mass destruction, he continued. Sadly, the inspectors' report last week and Mr. Powell's presentation today left no illusions—Iraq held resolution 1441 in the same contempt as previous resolutions on the matter. Saddam Hussein was gambling that the international community would lose its nerve, rather than impose its will.

Resolution 1441 had set two clear tests for further material breach by Iraq, he said. First, it must not make "false statements" or "omissions" in its declaration. However, the documents that Iraq had submitted in December, while long on repetition, were neither full nor accurate, nor complete. The declaration's central premise that Iraq possessed no weapons of mass destruction was a lie, which had been repeated yesterday on television by Saddam Hussein. The declaration also had obvious omissions, not least a failure to explain what had happened to the large quantities of chemical and biological weapons materiel and munitions unaccounted for by United Nations inspectors in 1998. And there was no admission of Iraq's extensive efforts to develop weapons of mass destruction since the last round of UNSCOM inspections ended in December 1998.

Regarding a second test for a further material breach, namely, "a failure by Iraq at any time to comply with and cooperate fully in the implementation" of resolution 1441, he said that it was clear that Iraq had failed that test. Last week's briefing and today's presentation had confirmed the worst fears: that Iraq had no intention of relinquishing its weapons of mass destruction and no intention of following the path of peaceful disarmament set out in resolution 1441. "Instead of open admissions and transparency, we have a charade, where a veneer of superficial cooperation masks wilful concealment, the extent of which has been devastatingly revealed this morning by Secretary Powell", he said.

He said that among the questions remaining were: why was Iraq refusing to allow UNMOVIC to use a U-2 plane to conduct aerial imagery and surveillance operations; when would it account for 6,500 bombs which could carry up to 1,000 tons of chemical agent; and how would Iraq justify having a prohibited chemical precursor for mustard gas? There could be only one conclusion: Iraq was in further material breach, as sset out in resolution 1441.

Given what had to follow, and the difficult choice now facing the Council, it would be easy to turn a blind eye to the wording of the resolution and hope for a change of heart by Iraq, he continued. Easy, but wrong, because in doing so the Council would be repeating the mistakes of the past twelve years and empowering a dictator who believed his diseases and poison gases were essential weapons to suppress his own people and to threaten his neighbours.

"Saddam must be left in no doubt as to the serious situation he now faces", he said. The United Kingdom did not want war. It wanted the United Nations system to be upheld. But the logic of 1441 was now inescapable: time was now very short. If non-cooperation continued, the Council must meet its responsibilities. Now was a moment of choice for Saddam and the Iraqi regime. It was also a moment of choice for the United Nations. The League of Nations—the United Nations' pre-war predecessor—had failed because it could not create actions from its words. "We owe it to our history, as well as to our future, not to make the same mistake again", he said.

IGOR S. IVANOV, Minister for Foreign Affairs of the Russian Federation, said his country viewed today's meeting through the prism of the consistent United Nations efforts to find a political settlement of the situation on the basis of complete and scrupulous compliance with its resolutions. The deployment of international inspectors in Iraq had demonstrated the ability of the international community to act together. He was convinced that maintaining the unity of the international community, within the context of the Council, and concerted actions in compliance with the United Nations Charter and Security Council resolutions were the most reliable way of solving the problem of weapons of mass destruction in Iraq through political means.

The Council, and through it the international community, must have all of the necessary information it needed to answer the question about whether weapons of mass destruction remained in Iraq, he said. The information given today required further and serious study and had to be immediately handed over to UNMOVIC and the IAEA for on-site verification. The inspectors must answer the questions asked by the United States. He appealed to all States to immediately hand over to inspectors any information that could help them discharge their mandate. Information provided today indicated that the activities of the inspectors in Iraq must continue. They alone could help the Council work out the best possible and balanced decision.

Mr. Blix's and Mr. ElBaradei's statements showed that in Iraq a unique inspection system had been deployed which had everything it needed to ensure compliance with resolution 1441. The Council must do everything possible to support the inspection process. His country was prepared to provide an airplane for aerial monitoring and additional inspectors. It was obvious that the work of UNMOVIC and the IAEA could be effective only with full cooperation, in good faith, by Iraq. That would be the only way towards a political settlement, including the lifting of sanctions. Iraq should realize how crucial that was and do everything possible to allow the inspectors discharge their mandate. Resolution 1441 was geared towards speedy and practical results, but timeframes were absent. Only the inspectors could determine how much time was needed for their task.

He said the international community in the twenty-first century was confronting new global threats, requiring a unified response from all States. The creation of the broad coalition combating international terrorism was an example of that. It was obvious that a difficult battle with terrorism lay ahead, and the information provided today was further corroboration of that. Unity in the world was pivotal in approaching that, or any problem. Tactical differences might arise, but must not overshadow the strategic goals in the interest of common security and stability.

FRANÇOIS-XAVIER NGOUBEYOU, Minister of External Relations of Cameroon, said that the information presented today was certainly troubling. It was now up to the Council to make the best use of it, in the spirit of the process provided by resolution 1441 (2002). The data just produced could facilitate the inspections. Would it not be wise to provide the inspectors with that information and give them more time to do their job? he asked. It was undoubtedly the first time since the Cuban missile crisis that the peoples of the world were assessing two options—diplomatic or peaceful; or a war which, in its wake, had grave consequences for Iraq, the Middle East and the world.

He said the Council did not act on the basis of public opinion, but the disarmament of Iraq clearly divided people into two schools of thought. Both sides had assuredly assessed the role and the mission of the Council, which was today considered a decisive player from which the world expected a solution. Cameroon recommended the continuation and implementation of forceful and robust action to compel Iraq to cooperate fully with the inspection teams. He appreciated the commitment of the United States to the eradication of all mass destruction weapons in Iraq.

At the same time, he went on, the Council's central role must be preserved, reaffirmed and respected, as it took a decision, in one direction or another. War was not inevitable; the inspectors should be given time to study and verify the information just presented. The UNMOVIC and the IAEA must continue their delicate mission, with strengthened resolve and in a more robust manner. He asked the Secretary-General to go to Iraq to speak with Saddam Hussein about that urgent problem.

DOMINIQUE DE VILLEPIN, Minister for Foreign Affairs of France, said that the report presented to the Security Council by United States Secretary of State Colin Powell contained information, indications and questions that deserved to be explored further, but it would be up to the inspectors to assess the facts in accordance with resolution 1441 (2002). Already, the report brought a new justification to the path chosen by the United Nations, which should strengthen the international community's common resolve on the disarmament of Iraq.

He noted that there were still "gray areas" in Iraq's cooperation with the inspections, such as the unresolved questions in the ballistic, chemical and biological areas. Those uncertainties were unacceptable. As a priority, the focus must be on the biological and chemical domains, since it was there that presumptions about Iraq were most significant. "So, it is a demanding démarche, anchored in resolution 1441, that we must take together." If that path failed and led into a dead end, then France ruled out no option, including the use of force as a last resort, to ensure Iraqi compliance.

But, he added, in such a hypothesis, the entire world needed to be provided with answers to several questions in order to limit the risks and uncertainties. To what extent did the nature and scope of the threat justify the recourse to force? How could the considerable risks of such an intervention actually be kept under control? That, obviously, required a collective responsibility on the part of the world community.

For now, he continued, the inspections regime, as outlined in resolution 1441, should be strengthened since it had not been explored to the end, and the use of force could only be a final recourse. "Why go to war if there still exists an unused space in resolution 1441?" he asked. Consistent with the logic of that resolution, efforts had to be made to move on to a new stage and further strengthen the inspections. Given the choice between military intervention and an inspections regime that was inadequate for lack of cooperation on Iraq's part, the international community should choose to strengthen decisively the means of inspection, he said. For example, the international community could double or triple the number of inspectors, increase the monitoring capabilities, and establish an information-processing centre to supply the needed intelligence resources. Such an enhanced regime could be complemented by having a permanent United Nations coordinator for disarmament in Iraq.

In that regard, he urged Iraq to cooperate actively. That should include permitting meetings with Iraqi scientists without witnesses and agreeing to U-2 observer flights, among other demands. Iraqi authorities must also provide inspectors with answers to the new information presented by Secretary of State Powell, between now and the inspectors' next report on 14 February. The upcoming trip to Baghdad by Mr. Blix and Mr. ElBaradei would have to be the occasion for clear results to that end.

The Minister for Foreign Affairs of Mexico, LUIS ERNESTO DERBEZ, said that today's presentation clearly contained valuable information to help determine and guide the Council's decisions. It would also provide the Council with additional elements of judgement in determining the extent to which Iraq had complied with its resolutions.

Mr. Powell's presentation had reinforced Mexico's firm belief in the need for progress towards effective and verifiable elimination of weapons of mass destruction in Iraq, as well as the facilities for developing them, he continued. Mexico's position had been unequivocally aimed at achieving the disarmament of Iraq in the most effective way possible and by peaceful means, while ensuring at all times that that goal was achieved at the lowest cost in terms of human suffering and economic instability, without undermining the urgent battle against international terrorism.

Consistent with that position, his Government had made direct approaches to the Iraqi authorities, urging them to cooperate without delay in the manner required by the inspectors. Mexico had also shared the content of those initiatives with other members of the Council so that the message could be conveyed to the Iraqi authorities as forcefully as possible and through the greatest possible number of channels. In the presence of Iraq's representatives at the Council table, he wanted to repeat his call for that country to concretely translate its declared intentions into active cooperation and genuine collaboration with the inspection process, as provided for in resolution 1441, he said.

Concluding, he reaffirmed his country's confidence in the inspection activities as the best possible way to detect, destroy and verify the elimination of weapons of mass destruction in Iraq. He was in favour of intensifying and strengthening those inspections, as well as the assistance that members of the Council and the international community, in general, could provide to UNMOVIC and to the IAEA to successfully accomplish their delicate mission.

It was in that context that Mexico recognized the importance of today's presentation to the Council by the United States, he said. It reiterated its willingness to continue to make a constructive contribution to the work of the Security Council, in the conviction that cooperation and the search for multilateral solutions would give greater weight to the decisions of that body.

SOLOMON PASSY, Minister for Foreign Affairs of Bulgaria, said his country had aligned itself with the position taken by the European Union. The compelling evidence presented today shed additional light on the realities in Iraq as far as the implementation of resolution 1441 and other Council resolutions was concerned. He hoped that the data made public could still be used by UNMOVIC and the IAEA. Resolution 1441 had unanimously been adopted as a last chance for the disarmament of Iraq by peaceful means. Today's Council meeting would carry a compelling message to the international community.

He said Iraq's cooperation had not been satisfactory on substantive issues identified by the inspectors. He insisted that Iraq provide all additional and complete information confirming the destruction of any available weapons of mass destruction. It was paramount that Iraq change its attitude to proactive cooperation with the inspectors. So far, Iraq had been in material breach of relevant Council resolutions, including resolution 1441. He expected Iraq to comply fully with its disarmament obligations by the next briefing by inspectors, scheduled for 14 February.

Effective and peaceful disarmament of Iraq was still possible through the implementation of 1441, he said. At the same time, the international community should assume its responsibilities for ensuring the implementation of the respective Council resolutions. In the event that in the near future inspectors did not report that Iraq had changed its attitude, the Council would have to take all necessary and appropriate action for implementation of relevant resolutions adopted since 1990.

KHURSHID M. KASURI, Minister for Foreign Affairs of Pakistan, said he welcomed the United States' initiative to work through the United Nations in seeking the elimination of mass destruction weapons in Iraq. The extensive presentation made by Secretary Powell would add to the knowledge base of Council members, and, even more importantly, enhance the ability of the inspectors to identify areas of concerns and to pursue more specific lines of action. The presentation, therefore, was a significant step forward in responding to the challenge facing the Council in securing full implementation of its resolutions regarding Iraq's disarmament.

He said that, following the presentations last week by Drs. Blix and El-Baradei, the majority of Council members felt that full verification of the Iraqi declaration would require more active cooperation from that country. In particular, Dr. Blix asked the Iraqi Government to take three steps in the context of his forthcoming visit to Baghdad: allow free and unrestricted aerial surveillance, including manned and unmanned reconnaissance vehicles; agree to private interviews of Iraqi scientists; and adopt legislation prohibiting the acquisition and local production of weapons of mass destruction. Iraq should move swiftly towards meeting those requirements.

The briefings by the head inspectors were not meant to be conclusive, he said. Their conclusions—positive or negative—should be awaited. The inspectors' report in the future would constitute an indispensable element in the judgement that the Council was supposed to make regarding Iraqi compliance, as envisaged in resolution 1441 (2002).

While the international community was justified in bringing about the earlier possible compliance by Iraq with its resolutions, he said it could not ignore other elements that arose in the context of security, namely: ameliorating the suffering and ensuring the welfare of the Iraqi people; preserving the unity and territorial integrity of Iraq; and preserving the political and economic stability of the region.

ANA PALACIO, Minister for Foreign Affairs of Spain, expressed gratitude to Secretary Powell for the information provided to the Council today. The fact that the United States had presented the evidence to the United Nations was a recognition of the importance of keeping the question of Iraq within the framework of the Organization. The data presented today led to a conclusion that Iraq was deceiving the international community and violating its obligations established under resolution 1441. The presentation had also demonstrated the links of Saddam Hussein's regime to terrorism.

Iraq should not be allowed to accumulate weapons of mass destruction, she continued. The lack of co-operation by Iraq could be explained by the fact that Saddam Hussein had not given up his plans to develop biological, chemical and nuclear weapons. The IAEA and UNMOVIC had full confidence in their ability to uncover the truth, but inspections were not an end in itself. The inspections could only bear fruit with active cooperation by Iraq. So far, that was not the case. The question remained, of the lack of will on behalf of the regime to fulfil its disarmament obligations. The Council could and should demand full cooperation from Iraq, which should disarm without delay and without any concealment.

She went on to say that at stake was the credibility of the Security Council, which had become an invaluable instrument of maintaining international peace and security. Yet, for twelve years, it had witnessed consistent non-compliance on behalf of Iraq. It was time to send a message that accumulation of weapons of mass destruction by that country was a threat to international peace and security.

Spain continued to maintain as a fundamental principle the need for compliance with Council resolutions, she said. Iraq must face the most serious consequences for its non-compliance. In spite of continued non-compliance by Iraq, however, there was a still a chance for that country if it radically modified its behaviour. Now, the international community was offering the last chance to Saddam Hussein, and she hoped he would not miss that opportunity.

SOLEDAD ALVEAR VALENZUELA, Minister for Foreign Affairs of Chile, expressed concern at the serious information just received, which pointed to a pattern of defiance by Iraq in fulfilling its obligation of unconditional and immediate disarmament. Resolution 1441 gave Iraq a last opportunity to fulfill its disarmament obligations, but the Iraqi regime was now bringing its people into greater suffering. Attempts at partial compliance and attempting to deceive or obstruct the process were violations of the resolutions. Such an attitude no doubt derived from the authoritarian attitude of the regime.

She said the inspections process must be continued so that the process could lead to conclusions the Council could use for its decisions. The inspections could lead to the goal of peace only if pressure was kept upon Iraq. It was up to the head of UNMOVIC, in accordance with paragraph 11 of resolution 1441, immediately to inform the Council of any non-compliance on the part of Iraq, including that related to Iraq's obligation of cooperation with inspections. She demanded action and information from Iraq without any delay or hesitations, and the accusations levelled today required urgent and precise clarification by Iraq.

The Council must use the mechanisms of multilateral cooperation, she said. The adoption of resolution 1441 had demonstrated the unity of which the Council was capable, and it must persevere in efforts to maintain a shared position. A crucial stage was being entered in a situation involving many fears concerning the region and the world, and she was concerned at the consequences of ending the use of diplomatic channels. She appealed to Iraq to consider its responsibilities to the Council and the preservation of international peace and security.

GEORGES REBELO CHIKOTI, Vice-Minister for Foreign Affairs of Angola, thanked Secretary Powell for sharing with the Council that compelling evidence. The information presented today by Mr. Powell introduced new elements, strengthening the view that it was important to continue to monitor the situation and be prepared to take a decision within the framework of the Council. The importance of cooperation should not be minimized. He strongly urged Iraq to do much more, especially given that its substantive cooperation was an obligation. Only through such co-operation could Iraq prove, beyond any doubt, that it was ready to embark on a programme for the elimination of its missiles, and chemical and biological weapons.

He said the Council needed clear and unambiguous answers from Iraq to the outstanding questions raised by the inspectors. Strengthening and enlarging the scope of the inspections were important developments and were another chance to enhance their efficiency. If the inspections enjoyed the full political support of the Council and the international community, and if those were given adequate time, they could be a powerful tool in the common endeavour to disarm Iraq, avert war, and reinforce international peace and security.

The overall picture reinforced the need to continue the inspections, he stressed. In that respect, he urged Iraq, the United Nations inspectors and countries with the means to do so, to pursue urgently, and more aggressively and cooperatively, decisive information leading to an accurate identification of weapons of mass destruction and their elimination, in accordance with the relevant Council resolutions. Iraq threatened international peace and security, but he still believed that a peaceful solution could be found. His own country was living testimony of the disastrous consequences of war.

MIKHAIL WEHBE (Syria) said that in order to ascertain the data presented by Secretary Powell, it was necessary to refer the facts to UNMOVIC and the IAEA. He urged all Member States, which had accurate information regarding Iraq's weapons of mass destruction, to submit it to the inspectors, who could assess their accuracy and report to the Council accordingly.

While the Council had unanimously adopted resolution 1441, it was no secret that Syria had joined the consensus after receiving clarifications and guarantees that the international community would seriously proceed with the investigation, refraining from the use of the resolution as a pretext for war against Iraq. The fact that some Council members were now speaking about adopting a second resolution testified to the seriousness of that approach.

The inspections had achieved some progress, he said. They had also not encountered serious obstacles. The Council could still make an effort to arrive at a peaceful solution to the question of Iraq. Syria still believed in the possibility of avoiding war, which would bring serious consequences for the whole region and endanger numerous lives. Several days ago, the Council had addressed the issue of protecting civilians and children in conflict. While making such efforts to protect civilians, how could it speak about going to war against a country that remained within its boundaries, while Israel continued to occupy Arab territories in violation of relevant Security Council resolutions?

It would be incorrect to believe that inspections in any part of the world could be free from obstacles and problems, he continued. Also, from hearing the inspectors' reports last week, it was important to ask if the difficulties encountered in Iraq were serious enough to warrant war. Iraq had expressed its readiness to cooperate with inspections and arrive at a peaceful solution. Iraq and the inspectors should work out a common denominator of cooperation in order to clarify the situation, as soon as possible. The continuation of the work of the inspectors would definitely lead to building confidence in the region. Syria was calling on the Council to continue to endorse the work of the inspectors and give them sufficient time to carry out their mandate under resolution 1441.

He added that the Council should also lift the sanctions imposed on the Iraqi people and activate the provisions of its resolution calling for the declaration of the Middle East as a zone free of all weapons of mass destruction, without any exceptions. Those provisions should include Israel, which was the only country in the region possessing such weapons. It was important to arrive at a peaceful solution of the Iraqi crisis. Iraq's neighbours had expressed a readiness to cooperate with the Council towards that end. A peaceful settlement would save the thousands of lives that would be lost through military action outside of the legitimacy of the Council.

MAMADY TRAORE (Guinea) said the information and Intelligence provided by Mr. Powell would be transmitted immediately to the competent authorities for evaluation. He hoped other States would also put information at the disposition of the inspectors. That was one of the recommendations of resolution 1441 that, had it been implemented, would have allowed the inspectors to have made more progress in the field. The 27 January reports of Mr. Blix and Mr. ElBaradei had shown that, from the point of view of procedure, progress had been made. Thanks to cooperation of Iraqi authorities, for instance, inspectors had had easy access to more than two hundred sites, including presidential sites and private residences. That had helped UNMOVIC and the IAEA to make a partial evaluation of the Iraqi arsenal.

Turning to substantive questions, he said there was still work to be done, particularly in the biological, chemical and ballistic missiles area. The inspectors had reported that the 7 December declaration of Iraq had been inadequate, that interviews with scientists did not proceed satisfactorily and that reconnaissance flights by U-2 airplanes were not possible. Iraqi cooperation had been more forthcoming on matters of procedure than on substance. He, therefore, appealed to Iraq to scrupulously conform to its obligations under resolution 1441. Among other things, Iraq must give precise responses to numerous questions not addressed, including convincing proof of unilateral destruction of certain biological and chemical weapons. Iraq should also provide without delay a credible and updated list of scientists involved in arms programmes.

While the promise of better cooperation was encouraging, Iraqi authorities must translate that promise into verifiable action. The possibility of the suspension or lifting of sanctions should encourage Iraq to fully cooperate with inspectors. The existence of gray areas, on the one hand, and progress made, on the other, indicated that inspections must go on. His country had always stressed peaceful settlement of the matter. There were still chances for a peaceful settlement, and those chances must be grasped. "Today, we are witnessing a crucial stage for maintenance of international peace and security. We must work in unity to build a world of peace and cooperation", he said.

JOSCHKA FISCHER, Vice-Chancellor and Minister for Foreign Affairs of Germany, said that the place and timing of today's detailed account underlined, once more, that the Security Council remained the centre of decision-making on the Iraq crisis. It was now decisive that the inspectors were also provided with that extensive material, in order to be able to clarify the unresolved questions, quickly and fully. He had no illusions about the inhuman and brutal nature of Saddam Hussein's dictatorship. Under his rule, Iraq had attacked its neighbours, Kuwait and Iran, fired missiles at Israel, and deployed poison gas against Iran and its own Kurdish population.

He said that several States suspected that Saddam Hussein's regime was withholding relevant information and concealing military capabilities. That strong suspicion must be dispelled beyond any doubt. At the same time, the dangers of military action were plain to see. A peaceful solution must continue to be sought. The instruments of inspection and control should be toughened. The French delegation made some very interesting proposals on that matter, which deserved further consideration. Moreover, diplomatic efforts under way by States in the region to bring the Iraqi Government to fully implement the resolutions should be supported. Iraq should disarm openly, peacefully and in cooperation with the inspectors, without any delay.

Statement by Iraq

MOHAMMED A. ALDOURI (Iraq) said his country would provide detailed and technical explanatory answers to the allegations made in Mr. Powell's statement. What had been mentioned in the presentation was utterly unrelated to the truth. No new information had been provided, except for sound recordings that could not be ascertained as genuine. What had been presented contained incorrect allegations, unnamed and unknown sources, as well as assumptions in line with the American policy towards one known objective.

He said President Hussein had reiterated in his interview yesterday that Iraq was free of weapons of mass destruction, a statement repeated by numerous Iraqi officials for more than a decade. Mr. Powell could have spared himself, his team and the Council the effort by presenting his allegations directly to UNMOVIC and the IAEA in accordance with resolution 1441. He could have left the inspectors to work in peace and without pressure.

At any rate, the forthcoming visit of Mr. Blix and Mr. ElBaradei on the eighth and ninth of this month would be another opportunity to verify the validity of those allegations, he continued. The ongoing inspections had proven the falsity of previous allegations and reports issued by the United States and the United Kingdom. Iraq had submitted an accurate, comprehensive and updated declaration of 12,000 pages, he continued. It included detailed information on previous Iraqi programmes, as well as updated information on the country's industries in various fields.

The inspectors had begun their activities in Iraq as of 27 November, he said. By 4 February, the inspection teams had conducted 575 inspections all over Iraq covering 321 sites. The sites referred to by President Bush and Prime Minister Blair in their September reports, as well as the Central Intelligence Agency (CIA) report of October 2002, topped the list of the sites inspected by the United Nations teams. The inspections had ascertained that all the allegations contained in those reports were not true. That confirmed Iraq's declaration that it was free from weapons of mass destruction. It was well known that the inspectors had taken samples of water, soil, plants, air, factory and production remnants throughout Iraq. The analysis of those samples conducted by UNMOVIC and the IAEA confirmed the absence of any indication of proscribed chemical, biological or radiological agents, or any proscribed activities in any part of Iraq.

In his statement to The New York Times on 30 January, Mr. Blix had confirmed that the inspectors had not ascertained any of the scenarios alleged by Mr. Powell, including movement of proscribed materials aiming at concealment. He had confirmed that he had not found enough reasons to believe that Iraq was sending scientists out of the country to prevent them from being interviewed. He also had no reason to believe what President Bush had said in his State of the Union address regarding Iraqi Intelligence agents posing as scientists for the interviews. Iraq was encouraging its scientists to participate in the interviews requested by UNMOVIC and the IAEA.

As for the mobile laboratories, he said that Mr. Blix had stated that UNMOVIC to date had found no proof of those laboratories' existence. His country did not object to overflights of U2 planes. The obstruction to those overflights stemmed from the presence of United States and United Kingdom warplanes in the illegally imposed no-flight zones. It would be sufficient if those flights were suspended during the U2 overflights. Allegations that trucks had left sites before the arrival of inspection teams were unfounded. Inspection teams, after all, arrived unannounced, and UNMOVIC and the IAEA had their own resources for surveillance.

Programmes for weapons of mass destruction were not like an aspirin pill easily hidden. Such programmes required huge facilities which could not be concealed, and inspectors, criss-crossing the country had not found them. Regarding the sound recordings, he said scientific and technical progress had allowed for fabrication of such allegations. As for the alleged relationship between Iraq and Al-Qaida, he said that, recently, Saddam Hussein had said that if such relationship had existed, he would not have been ashamed to admit it. Such a relationship did not exist, he had said.

Analysts at the CIA had complained that administration officials had exaggerated reports on that issue, he said. Mr. Straw of the United Kingdom had set aside Intelligence reports from his own Government asserting that such a relationship did not exist. Mr. Powell's assertion that Iraq had used chemical weapons against his own people was surprising. A CIA official had recently stated that the United States Administration had known since 1998 that Iraq had not used such weapons for the simple reason it did not have the weapons used in the mentioned incident.

The clear goal of the Council meeting today and Mr. Powell's presentation was to sell the idea of war against Iraq without any legal, moral or political justification, he said. He reiterated Iraq's commitment to continue proactive cooperation with the inspection teams so they could verify as soon as possible that Iraq was free of weapons of mass destruction in order for unjust sanctions to be lifted. Regional security could be ensured by disarming weapons of mass destruction in the Middle East, including the huge arsenal of weapons of mass destruction in Israel, in accordance with the provisions of paragraph 14 of Council resolution 687 (1991).

❮59❯

Declaration on Continuing the Revitalisation of the Non-aligned Movement, at the NAM XIII Summit, Kuala Lumpur (25.02.03)

> The HOS/HOGs of the NAM decided that "the continued relevance of the movement will depend" on how its Members adapt to the changes in international relations like the end of the Cold War, the emergence of unipolarity, globalization and the revolution in information technology. There was need "to be proactive rather than reactive..., enhance South-South cooperation..., cooperate through regular meetings of the Coordination Bureaus at international institutions and utilize effectively the non-aligned caucus of the UNSC."

We, the Heads of State and Government of the Non-Aligned Movement, gathered in Kuala Lumpur, Malaysia on 24 – 25 February 2003 for the XIII Summit Conference, reaffirmed our abiding faith in, and strong commitment to, the ideals, principles and purposes of the Movement, as laid out at the Bandung Conference of 1955, and the Charter of the United Nations, in our common and continuing pursuit of establishing a peaceful, prosperous, and a more just and equitable world order.

The Movement had played an active, even central role, over the years, on the issues of concern and vital importance to its members, such as decolonisation, apartheid, the situation in Palestine and the Middle East, disarmament, poverty eradication and socio-economic development, among others. After more than forty years of its founding, and having undergone many challenges and vicissitudes, it is timely and appropriate to comprehensively review the role, structure and work methods of our Movement in keeping with the times and the new realities, aimed at the further strengthening of our Movement. With the end of the Cold War, the emergence of unipolarity, the trend towards unilateralism and the rise of new challenges and threats, such as international terrorism, it is imperative for the Movement to promote multilateralism, better defend the interests of developing countries and prevent their marginalisation.

With increased globalisation and the rapid advance of science and technology, the world has changed dramatically. The rich and powerful countries exercise an inordinate influence in determining the nature and direction of international relations, including economic and trade relations, as well as the rules governing these relations, many of which are at the expense of the developing countries. It is imperative, therefore, that the Movement respond in ways that will ensure its continued relevance and usefulness to its members.

Globalisation presents many challenges and opportunities to the future and viability of all States. In its present form, it perpetuates or even increases the marginalisation of developing countries. We must ensure that globalisation will be a positive force for change for all peoples and will benefit the largest number of countries and not just a few. Globalisation should lead to the prospering and empowering of the developing countries, not their continued impoverishment and dependence on the wealthy and developed world.

The revolution in the Information and Communications Technology is changing the world at a rapid speed and in a fundamental way, and is already creating a vast and widening digital divide between the developed and developing countries, which must be bridged if the latter are to benefit from the globalisation process. This new technological innovation must be made more easily available to the developing countries in their efforts to modernise and revitalise their economies in pursuit of their developmental goals.

The achievement of these developmental goals requires an enabling international environment and the honouring of commitments and pledges made by States, including our partners in the developed world.

The future presents as many challenges and opportunities as the past and the Movement must continue to remain strong, cohesive and resilient. The continued relevance of the Movement will depend, in large measure, on the unity and solidarity of its members as well as its ability to adapt to these changes. In this regard, the process of the revitalisation of the Movement, begun at its previous Summit Meetings, must be given further impetus.

Consistent with our desire to translate our rhetoric into action, and in re-dedicating ourselves to the fundamental principles, purposes and goals of the Movement of Non-Aligned Countries, we resolve to make every effort to:

Enhance our unity, based on our common interests and history of shared struggles, and persevere with our efforts to ensure that these interests are continuously promoted and our concerns are fully addressed;

Uphold and adhere to the fundamental principles of the Movement and the Charter of the United Nations in the preservation and promotion of world peace through dialogue and diplomacy among states and the avoidance of the use of force to resolve conflicts;

Promote and strengthen the multilateral process as an indispensable vehicle in safeguarding the interests of member states of the Movement as well as those of the United Nations;

Promote the democratisation of the system of International governance in order to increase the participation of developing countries in International decision-making;

Be pro-active, rather than reactive, to international developments, especially those that impact on the members of the Movement, so as to ensure that the Movement is not sidelined but be at the forefront of the International decision making-processes;

Strengthen our national capacities in order to enhance our individual and collective resilience;

Enhance South-South Cooperation in all areas of our relations, particularly in the political, social, cultural, economic and scientific fields;

Promote a more dynamic and cooperative relationship with the developed and industrialised countries, based on constructive engagement, broad partnership and mutuality of benefits;

Promote closer interaction and cooperation with organisations of our civil society, the private sector and Parliamentarians on the recognition that they can play a constructive role towards the attainment of our common goals;

In pursuit of these goals, Member States of the Movement shall strive to implement the following concrete measures:-

- Undertake a sound review and analysis of the positions of the Movement on international issues, with a view to consolidating the common denominators among member States by focusing on issues that unite rather than divide us, thereby strengthening the unity and cohesion of the Movement.
- Review and redefine the role of the Movement and improve its structure and methodology, including the need for a more focused and concise documentation, in order to make it more effective and efficient.
- Enhance our coordination and cooperation through regular meetings of the Co-ordinating Bureau in New York, as well as in Geneva, Vienna, Nairobi and other centres, if necessary, with a view to responding, on a timely basis, to international developments affecting the Movement and its members.
- Utilise fully and effectively all exisiting mechanisms and institutions, such as the Troika, the Coordinating Bureau and all existing working groups, committees, the Non-Aligned Caucus of the Security Council, and establish new ones, as appropriate.
- Utilise more effectively the regular NAM Foreign Ministers Meetings through more interactive sessions as well as encourage the interaction and involvement of other relevant Ministers towards enhancing the effectiveness and profile of the Movement.

- Strengthen the role of the Chair, as spokesman of the Movement, through the establishment of appropriate mechanisms as part of the necessary backup system.
- Strengthen co-ordination and cooperation, and formulate common strategies on socio-economic and development-related issues, with the Group of 77 through regular and more frequent meetings of the Joint Co-ordinating Committee (JCC).
- Follow up on decisions made at the United Nations Millennium Assembly and other international fora, such as the Doha Meeting on international trade, the Monterrey Conference on Financing for Development and the Johannesburg World Summit on Sustainable Development as imperatives in addressing the urgent concerns of developing countries, such as poverty eradication, debt relief, capacity building and HIV/AIDS.
- Expand, deepen and enrich South-South cooperation through enhanced regional and inter-regional cooperation, undertaking concrete projects and programmes, pooling of resources, and tapping the contributions of eminent personalities and institutions of the South.
- Promote and develop mechanisms, including at relevant Conferences, for international cooperation and solidarity in efforts to bridge the digital divide based on a partnership involving States, civil society and the private sector.
- Continue to strongly support international programmes for Africa, particularly through NEPAD, as well as the Least Developed Countries, Landlocked Developing Countries and Small Island Developing Countries.
- Promote constructive dialogue and interaction with our development partners, particularly the G-8, through existing and appropriate new mechanisms, including institutionalised contacts, so as to bring about greater understanding between the North and South and to ensure that the views of the Movement are fully taken into account before important decisions affecting developing countries are made.

In realising our goal of revitalising the Non-Aligned Movement, we must exert every effort towards the promotion of a multipolar world through the strengthening of the United Nations, as an indispensable international organisation for the maintenance of international peace and security, the promotion of human rights, social and economic development and respect for international law, as enshrined in its Charter.

❮60❯

A Performance-Based Road Map to a Permanent Two-State Solution to the Israeli-Palestinian Conflict (30.04.03)

"The performance based and goal-driven roadmap" under the auspices of the Quartet (US, EU, UN and Russia) stated that a two-state solution will only be achieved through an end to violence and terrorism, when the Palestinian people have a leadership acting decisively against terror...and through Israel's readiness to do what is necessary for a democratic Palestinian state. Phase-I of the roadmap would entail ending violence and building Palestinian institutions while Phase-II would create an independent Palestinian state and Phase-III would consolidate Palestinian institutions.

The following is a performance-based and goal driven roadmap, with clear phases, timelines, target dates, and benchmarks aiming at progress through reciprocal steps by the two parties in the political, security, economic, humanitarian, and institution-building fields, under the auspices of the Quartet. The destination is a final and comprehensive settlement of the Israel-Palestinian conflict by 2005, as presented in President Bush's speech of 24 June, and welcomed by the EU, Russia, and the UN in the 16 July and 17 September Quartet Ministerial statements.

A two state solution to the Israeli-Palestinian conflict will only be achieved through an end to violence and terrorism, when the Palestinian people have a leadership acting decisively against terror and willing and able to build a practicing democracy based on tolerance and liberty, and through Israeli's readiness to do what is necessary for a democratic Palestinian State to be established, and a clear, unambiguous acceptance by both parties of the goal of a negotiated settlement as described below. The Quartet will assist and facilitate implementation of the plan, starting in Phase I, including direct discussions between the parties as required. The plan establishes a realistic timeline for implementation. However, as a performance-based plan, progress will require and depend upon the good faith efforts of the parties, and their compliance with each of the obligations outlined below. Should the parties perform their obligations rapidly, progress within and through the phases may come sooner than indicated in the plan. Non-compliance with obligations will impede progress.

A settlement, negotiated between the parties, will result in the emergence of an independent, democratic, and viable Palestinian State living side by side in peace and security with Israel and its other neighbors. The settlement will resolve the Israel-Palestinian conflict, and end the occupation that began in 1967, based on the foundations of the Madrid Conference, the principle of land for peace, UNSCRs 242, 338 and 1397, Agreements previously reached by the parties, and the initiative of Saudi Crown Prince Abdullah - endorsed by the Beirut Arab League Summit - calling for acceptance of Israel as a neighbour living in peace and security, in the context of a comprehensive settlement. This initiative is a vital element of international efforts to promote a comprehensive peace on all tracks, including the Syrian-Israeli and Lebanese-Israeli tracks.

The Quartet will meet regularly at senior levels to evaluate the Parties' performance on implementation of the plan. In each phase, the Parties are expected to perform their obligations in parallel, unless otherwise indicated.

Phase I:

Ending Terror and Violence, Normalizing Palestinian Life, and Building Palestinian Institutions Present to May 2003

In Phase I. the Palestinians immediately undertake an unconditional cessation of violence according to the steps outlined below; such action should be accompanied by supportive measures undertaken by Israel. Palestinians and Israelis resume security cooperation based on the Tenet work plan to end violence, terrorism, and incitement through restructured and effective Palestinian security services. Palestinians undertake comprehensive political reform in preparation for Statehood, including drafting a Palestinian Constitution, and free, fair and open elections upon the basis of those measures. Israel takes all necessary steps to help normalize Palestinian life. Israel withdraws from Palestinian areas occupied from September 28, 2000 and the two sides restore the status quo that existed at that time, as security performance and cooperation progress. Israel also freezes all settlement activity, consistent with the Mitchell report.

At the outset of Phase I:

- Palestinian leadership issues unequivocal statement reiterating Israel's right to exist in peace and security and calling for an immediate and unconditional ceasefire to end armed activity and all acts of violence against Israelis anywhere. All official Palestinian institutions end incitement against Israel.
- Israeli leadership issues unequivocal statement affirming its commitments to the two-state vision of an independent, viable, sovereign Palestinian State living in peace and security alongside Israel, as expressed by President Bush, and calling for an immediate end to violence against Palestinians everywhere. All official Israeli institutions end incitement against Palestinians.

Security

- Palestinians declare an unequivocal end to violence and terrorism and undertake visible efforts on the ground to arrest, disrupt, and restrain individuals and groups conducting and planning violent attacks on Israelis anywhere.
- Rebuilt and refocused Palestinian Authority security apparatus begins sustained, targeted, and effective operations aimed at confronting all those engaged in terror and dismantlement of terrorist capabilities and infrastructure. This includes commencing confiscation of illegal weapons and consolidation of security authority, free of association with terror and corruption.
- GOI takes no actions undermining trust, including deportations, attacks on civilians; confiscation and/or demolition of Palestinian homes and property, as a punitive measure or to facilitate Israeli construction; destruction of Palestinian institutions and infrastructure; and other measures specified in the Tenet Work Plan.
- Relying on existing mechanisms and on-the ground resources, Quartet representatives begin informal monitoring and consult with the parties on establishment of a formal monitoring mechanism and its implementation.
- Implementation, as previously agreed, of U.S. rebuilding, training and resumed security co-operation plan in collaboration with outside oversight board (U.S. - Egypt - Jordan). Quartet support for efforts to achieve a lasting, comprehensive cease-fire.
  - All Palestinian security organizations are consolidated into three services reporting to an empowered Interior Minister.
  - Restructured/retrained Palestinian security forces and IDF counterparts progressively resume security cooperation and other undertakings in implementation of the Tenet work plan, including regular senior-level meetings, with the participation of U.S. security officials.
- Arab states cut off public and private funding and all other forms of support for groups supporting and engaging in violence and terror.
- All donors providing budgetary support for the Palestinians channel these funds through the Palestinian Ministry of Finance's Single Treasury Account.
- As comprehensive security performance moves forward, IDF withdraws progressively from areas occupied since September 28, 2000 and the two sides restore the status quo that existed prior to September 28, 2000. Palestinian security forces redeploy to areas vacated by IDF.

Palestinian Institution-Building

- Immediate action on credible process to produce draft Constitution for Palestinian statehood. As rapidly as possible, Constitutional committee circulates draft Palestinian Constitution, based on strong Parliamentary democracy and cabinet with empowered Prime Minister, for public comment/debate. Constitutional committee proposes draft document for submission after elections for approval by appropriate Palestinian institutions.
- Appointment of interim Prime Minister or cabinet with empowered executive authority/decision-making body.
- GOI fully facilitates travel of Palestinian officials for PLC and Cabinet sessions, internationally supervised security retraining, electoral and other reform activity, and other supportive measures related to the reform efforts.
- Continued appointment of Palestinian Ministers empowered to undertake fundamental reform. Completion of further steps to achieve genuine separation of powers, including any necessary Palestinian legal reforms for this purpose.
- Establishment or independent Palestinian Election Commission. PLC reviews and revises elections law.
- Palestinian performance on judicial, administrative, and economic benchmarks, as established by the International Task Force on Palestinian Reform.
- As early as possible, and based upon the above measures and in the context of open debate and transparent candidate selection/electoral campaign based on a free, multiparty process, Palestinians hold free, open, and fair elections.
- GOI facilitates Task Force election assistance, registration of voters, movement of candidates and voting officials. Support for NGOs involved in the election process.
- GOI reopens Palestinian Chamber of Commerce and other closed Palestinian institutions in East Jerusalem based on a commitment that these institutions operate strictly in accordance with prior Agreements between the parties.

Humanitarian Response

- Israel takes measures to improve the humanitarian situation. Israel and Palestinians implement in full all recommendations of the Bertini report to improve humanitarian conditions, lifting curfews, and easing restrictions on movement of persons and goods, and allowing full, safe, and unfettered access of international and humanitarian personnel.

- AHLC reviews the humanitarian situation and prospects for economic development in the West Bank and Gaza and launches a major donor assistance effort, including to the reform effort.
- GOI and PA continue revenue clearance process and transfer of funds, including areas, in accordance with agreed, transparent monitoring mechanism.

Civil Society

- Continued donor support, including increased funding through PVOs/NGOs, for people to people programs, private sector development and civil society initiatives.

Settlements

- GOI immediately dismantles settlement outposts erected since March 2001.
- Consistent with the Mitchell Report, GOI freezes all settlement activity (including natural growth of settlements).

Phase II:
Transition June 2003 - December 2003

In the second phase, efforts are focused on the option of creating an independent Palestinian State with provisional borders and attributes of sovereignty, based on the new Constitution, as a way station to a permanent status settlement. As has been noted, this goal can be achieved when the Palestinian people have a leadership acting decisively against terror, willing and able to build a practicing democracy based on tolerance and liberty. With such a leadership, reformed civil institutions and security structures, the Palestinians will have the active support of the Quartet and the broader international community in establishing an independent, viable, state.

Progress into Phase II will be based upon the consensus judgment of the Quartet of whether conditions are appropriate to proceed, taking into account performance of both Parties. Furthering and sustaining efforts to normalize Palestinian lives and build Palestinian institutions, Phase II starts after Palestinian elections and ends with possible creation of an independent Palestinian State with provisional borders in 2003. Its primary goals are continued comprehensive security performance and effective security co-operation, continued normalization of Palestinian life and institution-building, further building on and sustaining of the goals outlined in Phase I, ratification of a Democratic Palestinian Constitution, formal establishment of office of Prime Minister, consolidation of political reform, and the creation of a Palestinian State with provisional borders.

- **International Conference**: Convened by the Quartet, in consultation with the parties, immediately after the successful conclusion of Palestinian elections, to support Palestinian economic recovery and launch a process, leading to establishment of an independent Palestinian State with provisional borders.

- Such a meeting would be inclusive, based on the goal of a comprehensive Middle East peace (including between Israel and Syria, and Israel and Lebanon), and based on the principles described in the preamble to this document.
- Arab states restore pre-intifada links to Israel (trade offices, etc.).
- Revival of multilateral engagement on issues including regional water resources, environment, economic development, refugees, and arms control issues.

- New Constitution for democratic, independent Palestinian state is finalized and approved by appropriate Palestinian institutions. Further elections, if required, should follow approval of the new Constitution.
- Empowered reform cabinet with office of Prime Minister formally established, consistent with draft Constitution.
- Continued comprehensive security performance, including effective security cooperation on the bases laid out in Phase I.
- Creation of an independent Palestinian state with provisional borders through a process of Israeli-Palestinian engagement. Launched by the international conference. As part of this process, implementation of prior agreements, to enhance maximum territorial contiguity, including further action on settlements in conjunction with establishment of a Palestinian state with provisional borders.
- Enhanced international role in monitoring transition, with the active, sustained, and operational support of the Quartet.
- Quartet members promote international recognition of Palestinian state, including possible UN membership.

PHASE III: PERMANENT STATUS AGREEMENT AND END OF THE ISRAELI - PALESTINIAN CONFLICT 2004 – 2005

Progress into Phase III, based on consensus judgment of Quartet, and taking into account actions of both parties and Quartet monitoring. Phase III objectives are consolidation of reform and stabilization of Palestinian institutions, sustained, effective Palestinian security performance, and Israeli-Palestinian negotiations aimed at a Permanent Status Agreement in 2005.

- **Second International Conference:** Convened by Quartet, in consultation with the parties, at beginning of 2004 to endorse Agreement reached on an independent Palestinian State with provisional borders and formally to launch a process with the active, sustained, and operational support of the Quartet, leading to a final, permanent status resolution in 2005, including on borders, Jerusalem, refugees, settlements; and, to support progress toward a comprehensive Middle East settlement between Israel and Lebanon and Israel and Syria, to be achieved as soon as possible.

- Continued comprehensive, effective progress on the reform agenda laid out by the Task Force in preparation for Final Status Agreement.
- Continued sustained and effective security performance, and sustained, effective security cooperation on the basis laid out in Phase I.
- International efforts to facilitate reform and stabilize Palestinian institutions and the Palestinian economy, in preparation for Final Status Agreement.
- Parties reach final and comprehensive Permanent Status Agreement that ends the Israel - Palestinian conflict in 2005, through a settlement negotiated between the parties based on UNSCR 242, 338, and 1397, that ends the occupation that began in 1967, and includes an agreed, just, fair, and realistic solution to the refugee issue, and a negotiated resolution of the status of Jerusalem that takes into account the political and religious concerns of both sides, and protects the religious interests of Jews, Christians, and Muslims worldwide, and fulfills the vision of two states, Israel and sovereign, independent, democratic and viable Palestine, living side-by-side in peace and security.
- Arab State acceptance of full normal relations with Israel and security for all the States of the region in the context of a compressive Arab-Israeli peace.

‹61›

UN Resolution 1483 (2003) on Iraq Adopted by the Security Council at its 4761st Meeting (22.05.03)

The Security Council adopted the resolution 14-0 with Syria not participating, to extend the "oil for food" programme for six months and appoint a special representative of the Secretary General to coordinate UN activities in post-conflict processes in Iraq. The Council supported the formation of an Iraqi Interim Administration with the help of the Authority (the occupying powers under unified command) until a representative government is established by the people of Iraq.

The Security Council,

Recalling all its previous relevant resolutions,

Re-affirming the sovereignty and territorial integrity of Iraq,

Re-affirming also the importance of the disarmament of Iraqi weapons of mass destruction and of eventual confirmation of the disarmament of Iraq,

Stressing the right of the Iraqi people freely to determine their own political future and control their own natural resources, *welcoming* the commitment of all Parties concerned to support the creation of an environment in which they may do so as soon as possible, and *expressing* resolve that the day when Iraqis govern themselves must come quickly,

Encouraging efforts by the people of Iraq to form a representative government based on the rule of law that affords equal rights and justice to all Iraqi citizens without regard to ethnicity, religion, or gender, and, in this connection, *recalls* resolution 1325 (2000) of 31 October 2000,

Welcoming the first steps of the Iraqi people in this regard, and *noting* in this connection, the 15 April 2003 Nasiriyah Statement and the 28 April 2003, Baghdad Statement,

Resolved that the United Nations should play a vital role in humanitarian relief, the re-construction of Iraq, and the restoration and establishment of national and local institutions for representative governance,

Noting the Statement of 12 April 2003 by the Ministers of Finance and Central Bank Governors of the Group of Seven Industrialized Nations in which the members recognized the need for a multilateral effort to help rebuild and develop Iraq and for the need for assistance from the International Monetary Fund and the World Bank in these efforts,

Welcoming also the resumption of humanitarian assistance and the continuing efforts of the Secretary-General and the specialized agencies to provide food and medicine to the people of Iraq,

Welcoming the appointment by the Secretary-General of his Special Adviser on Iraq,

Affirming the need for accountability for crimes and atrocities committed by the previous Iraqi regime,

Stressing the need for respect for the archaeological, historical, cultural, and religious heritage of Iraq, and for the continued protection of archaeological, historical, cultural, and religious sites, museums, libraries, and monuments,

Noting the letter of 8 May 2003 from the Permanent Representatives of the United States of America and the United Kingdom of Great Britain and Northern Ireland to the President of the Security Council (S/2003/538) and recognizing the specific authorities, responsibilities, and obligations under applicable international law of these States as occupying powers under unified command (the "Authority"),

Noting further that other States that are not occupying powers are working now or in the future may work under the Authority,

Welcoming further the willingness of Member States to contribute to stability and security in Iraq by contributing personnel, equipment, and other resources under the Authority,

Concerned that many Kuwaitis and Third-State Nationals still are not accounted for since 2 August 1990,

Determining that the situation in Iraq, although improved, continues to constitute a threat to international peace and security,

Acting under Chapter VII of the Charter of the United Nations,

1. *Appeals* to Member States and concerned organizations to assist the people of Iraq in their efforts to reform their institutions and rebuild their country, and to contribute to conditions of stability and security in Iraq in accordance with this resolution;
2. *Calls upon* all Member States in a position to do so to respond immediately to the humanitarian appeals of the United Nations and other international organizations for Iraq and to help meet the humanitarian and other needs of the Iraqi people by providing food, medical supplies, and resources necessary for reconstruction and rehabilitation of Iraq's economic infrastructure;

3. *Appeals* to Member States to deny safe haven to those members of the previous Iraqi regime who are alleged to be responsible for crimes and atrocities and to support actions to bring them to justice;
4. *Calls upon* the Authority, consistent with the Charter of the United Nations and other relevant international law, to promote the welfare of the Iraqi people through the effective administration of the territory, including in particular working towards the restoration of conditions of security and stability and the creation of conditions in which the Iraqi people can freely determine their own political future;
5. *Calls upon* all concerned to comply fully with their obligations under international law including in particular the Geneva Conventions of 1949 and the Hague Regulations of 1907;
6. *Calls upon* the Authority and relevant organizations and individuals to continue efforts to locate, identify, and repatriate all Kuwaiti and Third-State Nationals or the remains of those present in Iraq on or after 2 August 1990, as well as the Kuwaiti archives, that the previous Iraqi regime failed to undertake, and, in this regard, *directs* the High-Level Co-ordinator, in consultation with the

International Committee of the Red Cross and the Tripartite Commission and with the appropriate support of the people of Iraq and in co-ordination with the Authority, to take steps to fulfill his mandate with respect to the fate of Kuwaiti and Third-State National missing persons and property;

7. *Decides* that all Member States shall take appropriate steps to facilitate the safe return to Iraqi institutions of Iraqi cultural property and other items of archaeological, historical, cultural, rare scientific, and religious importance illegally removed from the Iraq National Museum, the National Library, and other locations in Iraq since the adoption of Resolution 661 (1990) of 6 August 1990, including by establishing a prohibition on trade in or transfer of such items and items with respect to which reasonable suspicion exists that they have been illegally removed, and *calls upon* the United Nations Educational, Scientific, and Cultural Organization, Interpol, and other international organizations, as appropriate, to assist in the implementation of this paragraph;
8. *Requests* the Secretary-General to appoint a Special Representative for Iraq whose independent responsibilities shall involve reporting regularly to the Council on his activities under this resolution, co-ordinating activities of the United Nations in post-conflict processes in Iraq, co-ordinating among United Nations and international agencies engaged in humanitarian assistance and reconstruction activities in Iraq, and, in co-ordination with the Authority, assisting the people of Iraq through:

(a) Co-ordinating humanitarian and re-construction assistance by United Nations agencies and between United Nations agencies and non-governmental organizations;

(b) Promoting the safe, orderly, and voluntary return of refugees and displaced persons;

(c) Working intensively with the Authority, the people of Iraq, and others concerned to advance efforts to restore and establish national and local institutions for representative governance, including by working together to facilitate a process leading to an internationally recognized, representative Government of Iraq;

(d) Facilitating the re-construction of key infrastructure, in co-operation with other international organizations;

(e) Promoting economic re-construction and the conditions for sustainable development, including through co-ordination with national and regional organizations, as appropriate, civil society, donors, and the international financial institutions;

(f) Encouraging international efforts to contribute to basic civilian administration functions;

(g) Promoting the protection of human rights;

(h) Encouraging international efforts to rebuild the capacity of the Iraqi civilian police force; and

(i) Encouraging international efforts to promote legal and judicial reform;

9. *Supports* the formation, by the people of Iraq with the help of the Authority and working with the Special Representative, of an Iraqi interim administration as a transitional administration run by Iraqis, until an internationally recognized, representative Government is established by the people of Iraq and assumes the responsibilities of the Authority;

10. *Decides* that, with the exception of prohibitions related to the sale or supply to Iraq of arms and related materiel other than those arms and related materiel required by the Authority to serve the purposes of this and other related resolutions, all prohibitions related to trade with Iraq and the provision of financial or economic resources to Iraq established by Resolution 661 (1990) and subsequent relevant resolutions, including Resolution 778 (1992) of 2 October 1992, shall no longer apply;

11. *Re-affirms* that Iraq must meet its disarmament obligations, *encourages* the United Kingdom of Great Britain and Northern Ireland and the United States of America to keep the Council informed of their activities in this regard, and *underlines* the intention of the Council to revisit the mandates of the United Nations Monitoring, Verification, and Inspection

Commission and the International Atomic Energy Agency as set forth in Resolutions 687 (1991) of 3 April 1991, 1284 (1999) of 17 December 1999, and 1441 (2002) of 8 November 2002;

12. *Notes* the establishment of a Development Fund for Iraq to be held by the Central Bank of Iraq and to be audited by independent public accountants approved by the International Advisory and Monitoring Board of the Development Fund for Iraq and looks forward to the early meeting of that International Advisory and Monitoring Board, whose members shall include duly qualified representatives of the Secretary-General, of the Managing Director of the International Monetary Fund, of the Director-General of the Arab Fund for Social and Economic Development, and of the President of the World Bank;
13. *Notes further* that the funds in the Development Fund for Iraq shall be disbursed at the direction of the Authority, in consultation with the Iraqi interim administration, for the purposes set out in paragraph 14 below;
14. *Underlines* that the Development Fund for Iraq shall be used in a transparent manner to meet the humanitarian needs of the Iraqi people, for the economic reconstruction and repair of Iraq's infrastructure, for the continued disarmament of Iraq, and for the costs of Iraqi civilian administration, and for other purposes benefiting the people of Iraq;
15. *Calls upon* the International Financial Institutions to assist the people of Iraq in the re-construction and development of their economy and to facilitate assistance by the broader donor community, and *welcomes* the readiness of creditors, including those of the Paris Club, to seek a solution to Iraq's sovereign debt problems;
16. *Requests* also that the Secretary-General, in co-ordination with the Authority, continue the exercise of his responsibilities under Security Council resolution 1472 (2003) of 28 March 2003 and 1476 (2003) of 24 April 2003, for a period of six months following the adoption of this Resolution, and terminate within this time period, in the most cost effective manner, the ongoing operations of the "Oil-for-Food" Programme (the "Programme"), both at Headquarters level and in the field, transferring responsibility for the administration of any remaining activity under the Programme to the Authority, including by taking the following necessary measures:

    (a) To facilitate as soon as possible the shipment and authenticated delivery of priority civilian goods as identified by the Secretary-General and representatives designated by him, in co-ordination with the Authority and the Iraqi interim administration, under approved and funded contracts previously concluded by the previous Government of Iraq, for the humanitarian relief of the people of Iraq, including, as necessary, negotiating adjustments in the terms or conditions of these contracts and respective letters of credit as set forth in paragraph 4 (d) of Resolution 1472 (2003);

(b) To review, in light of changed circumstances, in co-ordination with the Authority and the Iraqi interim administration, the relative utility of each approved and funded contract with a view to determining whether such contracts contain items required to meet the needs of the people of Iraq both now and during reconstruction, and to postpone action on those contracts determined to be of questionable utility and the respective letters of credit until an internationally recognized, representative Government of Iraq is in a position to make its own determination as to whether such contracts shall be fulfilled;

(c) To provide the Security Council within 21 days following the adoption of this resolution, for the Security Council's review and consideration, an estimated operating budget based on funds already set aside in the account established pursuant to paragraph 8 (d) of resolution 986 (1995) of 14 April 1995, identifying:

(i) All known and projected costs to the United Nations required to ensure the continued functioning of the activities associated with implementation of the present Resolution, including operating and administrative expenses associated with the relevant United Nations agencies and programmes responsible for the implementation of the Programme both at Headquarters and in the field;

(ii) All known and projected costs associated with termination of the Programme;

(iii) All known and projected costs associated with restoring Government of Iraq funds that were provided by Member States to the Secretary-General as requested in paragraph 1 of Resolution 778 (1992); and

(iv) All known and projected costs associated with the Special Representative and the qualified representative of the Secretary-General identified to serve on the International Advisory and Monitoring Board, for the six month time period defined above, following which these costs shall be borne by the United Nations;

(d) To consolidate into a single fund the accounts established pursuant to paragraphs 8 (a) and 8 (b) of Resolution 986 (1995);

(e) To fulfill all remaining obligations related to the termination of the Programme, including negotiating, in the most cost effective manner, any necessary settlement payments, which shall be made from the escrow accounts established pursuant to paragraphs 8 (a) and 8 (b) of Resolution 986 (1995), with those parties that previously have entered into contractual obligations with the Secretary-General under the Programme, and to determine, in co-ordination with the Authority and the Iraqi interim administration, the future status of contracts undertaken by the United Nations and related United Nations agencies under the accounts established pursuant to paragraphs 8 (b) and 8 (d) of Resolution 986 (1995);

(f) To provide the Security Council, 30 days prior to the termination of the Programme, with a comprehensive strategy developed in close co-ordination with the Authority and the Iraqi interim administration that would lead to the delivery of all relevant documentation and the transfer of all operational responsibility of the Programme to the Authority;

17. *Requests further* that the Secretary-General transfer as soon as possible to the Development Fund for Iraq 1 billion United States dollars from unencumbered funds in the accounts established pursuant to paragraphs 8 (a) and 8 (b) of Resolution 986 (1995), restore Government of Iraq funds that were provided by Member States to the Secretary-General as requested in paragraph 1 of Resolution 778 (1992), and *decides* that, after deducting all relevant United Nations expenses associated with the shipment of authorized contracts and costs to the Programme outlined in paragraph 16 (c) above, including residual obligations, all surplus funds in the escrow accounts established pursuant to paragraphs 8 (a), 8 (b), 8 (d), and 8 (f) of Resolution 986 (1995) shall be transferred at the earliest possible time to the Development Fund for Iraq;

18. *Decides* to terminate effective on the adoption of this Resolution the functions related to the observation and monitoring activities undertaken by the Secretary-General under the Programme, including the monitoring of the export of petroleum and petroleum products from Iraq;

19. *Decides* to terminate the Committee established pursuant to paragraph 6 of Resolution 661 (1990) at the conclusion of the six month period called for in paragraph 16 above and *further decides* that the Committee shall identify individuals and entities referred to in paragraph 23 below;

20. *Decides* that all export sales of petroleum, petroleum products, and natural gas from Iraq following the date of the adoption of this

Resolution shall be made consistent with prevailing international market best practices, to be audited by independent public accountants reporting to the International Advisory and Monitoring Board referred to in paragraph 12 above in order to ensure transparency, and *decides further* that, except as provided in paragraph 21 below, all proceeds from such sales shall be deposited into the Development Fund for Iraq until such time as an internationally recognized, representative Government of Iraq is properly constituted;

21. *Decides further* that 5 percent of the proceeds referred to in paragraph 20 above shall be deposited into the Compensation Fund established in accordance with resolution 687 (1991) and subsequent relevant resolutions and that, unless an internationally recognized, representative Government of Iraq and the Governing Council of the United Nations Compensation Commission, in the exercise of its authority over methods of ensuring that payments are made into the Compensation Fund, decide otherwise, this requirement shall be binding on a properly constituted, internationally recognized, representative Government of Iraq and any successor thereto;

22. *Noting* the relevance of the establishment of an internationally recognized, representative Government of Iraq and the desirability of prompt completion of the restructuring of Iraq's debt as referred to in paragraph 15 above, further *decides* that, until December 31, 2007, unless the Council decides otherwise, petroleum, petroleum products, and natural gas originating in Iraq shall be immune, until title passes to the initial purchaser from legal proceedings against them and not be subject to any form of attachment, garnishment, or execution, and that all States shall take any steps that may be necessary under their respective domestic legal systems to assure this protection, and that proceeds and obligations arising from sales thereof, as well as the Development Fund for Iraq, shall enjoy privileges and immunities equivalent to those enjoyed by the United Nations except that the abovementioned privileges and immunities will not apply with respect to any legal proceeding in which recourse to such proceeds or obligations is necessary to satisfy liability for damages assessed in connection with an ecological accident, including an oil spill, that occurs after the date of adoption of this Resolution;

23. *Decides* that all Member States in which there are:

(a) Funds or other financial assets or economic resources of the previous Government of Iraq or its state bodies, corporations, or agencies, located outside Iraq as of the date of this Resolution, or

(b) Funds or other financial assets or economic resources that have been removed from Iraq, or acquired, by Saddam Hussein or other senior officials of the former Iraqi regime and their immediate family members, including entities owned or controlled, directly or indirectly, by them or by persons acting on their behalf or at their direction, shall freeze without delay those funds or other financial assets or economic resources and, unless these funds or other financial assets or economic resources are themselves the subject of a prior judicial, administrative, or arbitral lien or judgement, immediately shall cause their transfer to the Development Fund for Iraq, it being understood that, unless otherwise addressed, claims made by private individuals or non-government entities on those transferred funds or other financial assets may be presented to the internationally recognized, representative Government of Iraq; and *decides further* that all such funds or other financial assets or economic resources shall enjoy the same privileges, immunities, and protections as provided under paragraph 22;

24. *Requests* the Secretary-General to report to the Council at regular intervals on the work of the Special Representative with respect to the implementation of this resolution and on the work of the International Advisory and Monitoring Board and *encourages* the United Kingdom of Great Britain and Northern Ireland and the United States of America to inform the Council at regular intervals of their efforts under this Resolution;
25. *Decides* to review the implementation of this Resolution within twelve months of adoption and to consider further steps that might be necessary;
26. *Calls upon* Member States and international and regional organizations to contribute to the implementation of this Resolution;
27. *Decides* to remain seized of this matter.

❮62❯

Extracts from the Draft Treaty Establishing a Constitution for Europe (18.07.03)

The EU offered its citizens an area of freedom, security and justice without internal frontiers, and a single market where competition is free and undistorted. It also agreed to respect the national identity of the member states inherent in their fundamental structures, political and constitutional, inclusive of regional and local self-government.

Preface

Noting that the European Union was coming to a turning point in its existence, the European Council which met in Laeken, Belgium, on 14 and 15 December 2001 convened the European Convention on the Future of Europe. The Convention was asked to draw up proposals on three subjects: how to bring citizens closer to the European design and European Institutions; how to organise politics and the European political area in an enlarged Union; and how to develop the Union into a stabilising factor and a model in the new world order.

The Convention has identified responses to the questions put in the Laeken declaration:

- it proposes a better division of Union and Member State competences;
- it recommends a merger of the Treaties and the attribution of legal personality to the Union;
- it establishes a simplification of the Union™s instruments of action;
- it proposes measures to increase the democracy, transparency and efficiency of the European Union, by developing the contribution of national Parliaments to the legitimacy of the European design, by simplifying the decision-making processes, and by making the functioning of the European Institutions more transparent and comprehensible;

- it establishes the necessary measures to improve the structure and enhance the role of each of the Union's three institutions, taking account, in particular, of the consequences of enlargement.

The Laeken declaration also asked whether the simplification and reorganisation of the Treaties should not pave the way for the adoption of a Constitutional text. The Convention's proceedings ultimately led to the drawing up of a draft Treaty establishing a Constitution for Europe, which achieved a broad consensus at the plenary session on 13 June 2003.

That is the text which it is our privilege to present today, 20 June 2003, to the European Council meeting in Thessaloniki, on behalf of the European Convention, in the hope that it will constitute the foundation of a future Treaty establishing the European Constitution.

Valéry Giscard d'Estaing

Président de la Convention

Giuliano Amato Jean-Luc Dehaene

Vice-Président

PREAMBLE

Our Constitution ... is called a democracy because power is in the hands not of a minority but of the greatest number. Thucydides II, 37

Conscious that Europe is a continent that has brought forth civilisation; that its inhabitants, arriving in successive waves from earliest times, have gradually developed the values underlying humanism: equality of persons, freedom, respect for reason,

Drawing inspiration from the cultural, religious and humanist inheritance of Europe, the values of which, still present in its heritage, have embedded within the life of society the central role of the human person and his or her inviolable and inalienable rights, and respect for law,

Believing that reunited Europe intends to continue along the path of civilisation, progress and prosperity, for the good of all its inhabitants, including the weakest and most deprived; that it wishes to remain a continent open to culture, learning and social progress; and that it wishes to deepen the democratic and transparent nature of its public life, and to strive for peace, justice and solidarity throughout the world,

Convinced that, while remaining proud of their own national identities and history, the peoples of Europe are determined to transcend their ancient divisions and, united ever more closely, to forge a common destiny,

Convinced that, thus "united in its diversity", Europe offers them the best chance of pursuing, with due regard for the rights of each individual and in awareness of their responsibilities towards future generations and the Earth, the great venture which makes of it a special area of human hope,

Grateful to the members of the European Convention for having prepared this Constitution on behalf of the citizens and States of Europe,

[Who, having exchanged their full powers, found in good and due form, have agreed as follows:].CONV 850/03 5

PART I

TITLE I: DEFINITION AND OBJECTIVES OF THE UNION

Article 1: Establishment of the Union

1. Reflecting the will of the citizens and States of Europe to build a common future, this Constitution establishes the European Union, on which the Member States confer competences to attain objectives they have in common. The Union shall coordinate the policies by which the Member States aim to achieve these objectives, and shall exercise in the Community way the competences they confer on it.
2. The Union shall be open to all European States which respect its values and are committed to promoting them together.

Article 2: The Union's values

The Union is founded on the values of respect for human dignity, liberty, democracy, equality, the rule of law and respect for human rights. These values are common to the Member States in a society of pluralism, tolerance, justice, solidarity and non-discrimination.

Article 3: The Union's objectives

1. The Union's aim is to promote peace, its values and the well-being of its peoples.
2. The Union shall offer its citizens an area of freedom, security and justice without internal frontiers, and a single market where competition is free and undistorted.
3. The Union shall work for the sustainable development of Europe based on balanced economic growth, a social market economy, highly competitive and aiming at full employment and social progress, and with a high level of protection and improvement of the quality of the environment. It shall promote scientific and technological advance. It shall combat social exclusion and discrimination, and shall promote social justice and protection, equality between women and men, solidarity between generations and protection of children's rights. It shall promote economic, social and territorial cohesion, and solidarity among Member States. The Union shall respect its rich cultural and linguistic diversity, and shall ensure that Europe's cultural heritage is safeguarded and enhanced.
4. In its relations with the wider world, the Union shall uphold and promote its values and interests. It shall contribute to peace, security,

the sustainable development of the earth, solidarity and mutual respect among peoples, free and fair trade, eradication of poverty and protection of human rights and in particular children's rights, as well as to strict observance and development of international law, including respect for the principles of the United Nations Charter.

5. These objectives shall be pursued by appropriate means, depending on the extent to which the relevant competences are attributed to the Union in the Constitution.

Article 4: Fundamental Freedoms and Non-Discrimination

1. Free movement of persons, goods, services and capital, and freedom of establishment shall be guaranteed within and by the Union, in accordance with the provisions of the Constitution.
2. In the field of application of the Constitution, and without prejudice to any of its specific provisions, any discrimination on grounds of nationality shall be prohibited.

Article 5: Relations between the Union and the Member States

1. The Union shall respect the national identities of the Member States, inherent in their fundamental structures, political and constitutional, inclusive of regional and local self-government. It shall respect their essential State functions, including those for ensuring the territorial integrity of the State, and for maintaining law and order and safeguarding internal security.
2. Following the principle of loyal cooperation, the Union and the Member States shall, in full mutual respect, assist each other in carrying out tasks which flow from the Constitution. The Member States shall facilitate the achievement of the Union's tasks and refrain from any measure which could jeopardise the attainment of the objectives set out in the Constitution.

❮63❯

Brasilia Declaration (on Cooperation between Brazil, India and South Africa) (06.06.03)

India, Brazil and South Africa (IBSA) announced the formation of a dialogue forum that would contribute to the "revitalization of South-South cooperation". In addition to identifying a number of areas of cooperation like S&T, ICT, Defence and Civil Aviation, the three countries reiterated their efforts for effective implementation of the convention on biodiversity, especially the rights over their own genetic resources and protection of associated traditional knowledge.

1. The Foreign Ministers of Brazil, Celso Amorim, of South Africa, Nkosazana Dlamini-Zuma, and of India, Yashwant Sinha, met in Brasilia on June 6, 2003, following ongoing consultations and after the respective Heads of State and/or Government of their countries held conversations during the G-8 meeting, in Evian.
2. This was a pioneer meeting of the three countries with vibrant democracies, from three regions of the developing world, active on a global scale, with the aim of examining themes on the international agenda and those of mutual interest. In the past few years, the importance and necessity of a process of dialogue amongst developing nations and countries of the South has emerged.
3. The Foreign Ministers of Brazil, South Africa and India gave special consideration to the importance of respecting the rule of International Law, strengthening the United Nations and the Security Council and prioritizing the exercise of diplomacy as a means to maintain international peace and security. They reaffirmed the need to combat threats to international peace and security in accordance with the Charter of the United Nations and with the legal instruments to which Brazil, India and South Africa are parties.
4. They agreed on the need to reform the United Nations, in particular the Security Council. In this regard, they stressed the necessity of expanding the Security Council in both permanent and non-permanent member categories, with the participation of developing countries in both categories. They agreed to combine efforts in order to enhance the effectiveness of the General Assembly and the Economic and Social Council of the United Nations.

5. They noted that new threats to security - such as terrorism, in all its forms and manifestations, drugs and drug-related crimes, transnational organized crime, illegal weapons traffic, threats to public health, in particular HIV/AIDS, natural disasters, and the maritime transit of toxic chemicals and radioactive waste - must be handled with effective, coordinated and solidary international cooperation, in the concerned organizations based on respect for the sovereignty of States and for International Law.
6. The Ministers highlighted the priority placed by the three governments on the promotion of social equity and inclusion, by implementing effective policies to fight hunger and poverty, to support family run farms, and to promote food security, health, social assistance, employment, education, human rights and environmental protection. They recalled that social empowerment makes better use of human potentials, contributing to economic development in a significant manner. The Ministers recommended that the exchange of experiences in combating poverty, hunger and disease in the three countries would be of immense use to all of them. They recognized the importance of international effort to combat hunger. The three countries recognized and undertook to explore a trilateral food assistance program.
7. The Foreign Ministers stressed the importance, for equity reasons as well as for development goals, to address issues related to the elimination of all kinds of racial discrimination and to promote gender equality and mainstreaming a gender perspective in public policies.
8. The three Foreign Ministers expressed their satisfaction with the approval of the Convention on Tobacco Control, in the 56th Health World Assembly, and committed themselves to make every effort to ratify the Convention on the shortest period of time. They also committed themselves to promote the main objective of the Convention – to protect present and future generations against the devastating consequences of the consumption of tobacco and against exposure to tobacco smoke.
9. The Foreign Ministers identified the trilateral cooperation among themselves as an important tool for achieving the promotion of social and economic development and they emphasized their intention to give greater impetus to cooperation among their countries. While noting that their societies have diverse areas of excellence in science and technology and offer a broad range of potential opportunities for trade, investment, travel and tourism, they stressed that the appropriate combination of their best resources will generate the desired synergy. Amongst the scientific and technological areas in which cooperation can be developed are biotechnology, alternative energy sources, outer space, aeronautics, information technology and agriculture. Avenues for greater cooperation in defense matters should also be explored.

The Ministers agreed upon putting forward to their respective governments that the authorities in charge of the portfolio for science and technology, defense, transportation and civil aviation, among others, also hold trilateral meetings, aiming at the creation of concrete co-operation projects.

10. The Ministers noted that the new information and communication technologies are transforming the world at a rapid speed, and in a fundamental way. At the same time, a vast digital divide exists between the developed and developing countries, which is adversely affecting the capacity of developing countries to derive optimum benefits from the globalisation process. They agreed to intensify their cooperation in ICT, including in international efforts and initiatives towards narrowing the digital divide.

11. With respect to environmental issues and sustainable development, they recognized that the Rio Conference and its Agenda 21, the Millenium Summit and the Monterrey and Johannesburg Summits, and the Program for the Implementation of Agenda 21, contain fundamental guidelines to orient the action of their governments and cooperation initiatives. They reaffirmed that Agenda 21 identifies the major causes of continuing deterioration of the global environment as unsustainable patterns of consumption and production and call for the necessary action as contained in the Johannesburg Program of Implementation. They also highlighted their concern over the results of atmospheric warming due to the emission of greenhouse gases and encouraged countries having emission reduction goals in the Kyoto Protocol to work to bring them into force and fully implement them, as well as urged the countries which have not signed or ratified the Protocol to do so.

12. They also reiterated their efforts for the effective implementation of the Convention on Biological Diversity, especially the rights of countries of origin over their own genetic resources, as well as the protection of associated traditional knowledge. The fair and equitable sharing of benefits arising from the access to, use and management of genetic resources and associated traditional knowledge must be assured as a way to stimulate social and economic development, as well as the adding of value and the processing of bio-diversity-based resources in megadiverse countries. In this context, they placed special significance on the negotiation of an international instrument on benefit sharing under the auspices of the Convention on Biological Diversity, as agreed at the Johannesburg Summit. They, thus, expressed their Agreement that the activities of the Group of Like-minded Megadiverse Countries, of which Brazil, South Africa and India are founding members, should gain even greater importance. They also emphasised

the need to render the relevant parts of the TRIPS Agreement compatible with the Biological Diversity Convention.

13. While welcoming the expansion of economic growth, employment, and social development, and the accompanying rise in standards of living, in several developing countries as a result of freer movements of trade, capital, and technology, the Foreign Ministers of Brazil, India and South Africa expressed their concern that large parts of the world have not benefited from globalisation. They agreed that globalisation must become a positive force for change for all peoples, and must benefit the largest number of countries. In this context, they affirmed their commitment to pursuing policies, programmes and initiatives in different international forums, to make the diverse processes of globalization inclusive, integrative, humane, and equitable.
14. The Ministers regretted that major trading partners are still moved by protectionist concerns in their countries' less competitive sectors. They stressed the need to fully carry out the Doha Development Program and emphasized how important it is that the results of the current round of trade negotiations provide especially for the reversal of protectionist policies and trade-distorting practices, by improving the rules of the multilateral trade system. They reiterated their expectation that negotiations will gain new political impetus and that it will be possible to overcome deadlocks on issues of fundamental interest to developing countries, before the Fifth Ministerial Conference in Cancun. Furthermore, Brazil, India and South Africa decided to articulate their initiatives of trade liberalisation.
15. The Foreign Ministers noted with concern the increased economic vulnerability of developing countries to fluctuations in global prices of commodities. They affirmed the importance of a predictable, rule-based, and transparent International Trading System, to enable the developing countries to maximise their development, through gains from enhanced exports of goods and services of their competitive advantage.
16. They drew attention to the economic and social impact suffered by many developing countries in recent years, as a result of volatile global financial flows. They agreed to strengthen their cooperation towards making the international financial architecture responsive to development, and towards increasing its effectiveness in preventing and addressing national and regional financial crises.
17. They reiterate their belief that success in globalization with equity requires good governance, both at the national and in particular at the international levels, in recognition of the fact that, as a Result of globalization, external factors have become critical in determining the success or Failure of achieving sustainable development.

18. The Ministers recommended to their respective Chiefs of State and/ or Government the convening of a summit meeting of the three countries. They also decided to further intensify dialogue at all levels, when needed, to organize meetings of top officials and experts responsible for issues of mutual interest.

19. They decided to hold regular political consultations on international agenda items, as well as to exchange information on areas of mutual co-operation in order to co-ordinate their positions on issues of common interest. To give expression to issues discussed and all other matters emerging out of consultations, the Ministers further agreed to establish a Trilateral Joint Commission. The Foreign Ministries will be the focal points of the Trilateral Joint Commission and the meetings will be co-chaired by the three Foreign Ministers. The secretariat facilities will be co-ordinated by the Secretary in charge of this area in the Foreign Ministry of the host country.

20. The Ministers decided to call this group "India, Brazil and South Africa Dialogue Forum" (IBSA). At the invitation of the Indian Government, the next meeting is going to take place in New Delhi, within twelve months.

The Ministers of India and South Africa thanked the Brazilian Minister for convening this first trilateral meeting.

Brasilia,
June 6th, 2003.

❮64❯

New Delhi Declaration Adopted at the International Ministerial Conference on the Dialogue among Civilizations-Quest for New Perspectives, New Delhi (09.07.03)

> Underlining the contemporary relevance of the ancient Indian concept of "Vasudeva Kutumbakkam", the International Ministerial Conference recognized the crucial role of education in promoting a scientific temper and spiritual value system. They resolved to pursue "education for all" and underlined the importance of protecting traditional knowledge systems. They called upon governments to ensure full participation of women and youth to foster dialogue among civilizations.

We, the participants in the International Ministerial Conference on Dialogue among Civilisations -Quest for New Perspectives, held in New Delhi from 9-10 July 2003,

Recognising that all civilizations celebrate the unity in diversity of humankind and are enriched and have evolved through dialogue with other civilizations,

Underlining the contemporary relevance of the ancient Indian concept of *Vasudhaiva Kutumbakkam*, which means that all the world is one family, and that a common humanity unites all civilisations,

Recognising that dialogue among civilisations, which has existed since the earliest stages of history has blurred the frontiers of different civilisations and led to today's multitude of overlapping cultures, which are rich in diversity while preserving the uniqueness of identities,

Noting that while civilisation provides an important source of identity, people have multiple identities deriving from nationality, gender, profession etc,

Emphasising that complementarity of civilisations is strengthened by constant inter-play and exchange of ideas as well as by creativity in science, art, philosophy, ethics and spirituality and allows for the highest attainments of civilisational diversity,

Noting that globalization, while offering great benefits, also presents the challenge of preserving and celebrating the rich intellectual and cultural diversity of humankind and of civilization,

Noting further the threat to equitable social and economic development of all civilisations consequent to problems of poverty, unsustainable patterns of consumption and production and profligate utilisation of the natural resource base of the planet,

Emphasizing that international cooperation, as a key means of promoting dialogue among civilisations, should contribute to enabling everyone to have access to knowledge, to enjoy the arts and literature of all peoples, to share in advances made in science in all parts of the world and in the resulting benefits, and to contribute to the enrichment of social, economic and cultural life.

Convinced of the need to contribute to the Global Agenda and Programme of Action for Dialogue among Civilisations contained in the United Nations General Assembly resolution 56/6 of 21 November 2001.

1. Recognise that tolerance is a fundamental value common to all civilizations and that this includes respect for others, regardless of diversity of belief, culture and language neither fearing nor repressing differences within and between societies but cherishing them as a precious asset of humanity;
2. Underline the need to address and overcome ignorance and prejudice about the ways of life and customs of peoples;
3. Recognise the crucial role of education in promoting a scientific temper and an ethical and spiritual value system which facilitate the use of knowledge and reasoning in understanding other cultures and civilizations;
4. Recognise further that education promotes tolerance, respect for diversity and friendship among peoples and nations;
5. Affirm that the nature and content and quality of education should help to develop knowledge, values, attitudes and skills necessary to ensure a high quality of life for all;
6. Recognise that education is necessary to develop communities and societies rooted in principles of democracy, justice and respect for human rights;
7. Invite governments to also give special emphasis to democratic principles and practices as well as pluralism, including through the teaching and learning at all levels of formal, informal and non-formal education;
8. Encourage all governments to expand their educational curriculam and learning materials in order to promote a better understanding of all cultures and civilizations – especially through the teaching of respect for various cultures and civilizations and their histories and philosophies, human rights education, non-violence and the teaching of languages;

9. Emphasise the importance of knowledge, information and scholarship among governments and civil society in order to promote a better understanding of all cultures and civilizations;
10. Emphasise that the pursuit of the six Education for All (EFA) goals, including especially the fight against gender discrimination in education, is essential to an inclusive approach to dialogue among civilizations;
11. Resolve to take suitable steps to establish in educational institutions a learning environment which will contribute to tolerance, respect and understanding about the diversity and wealth of cultural identities;
12. Urge governments to take full and effective measures to ensure that educational institutions are protected from teachings that promote extremism, intolerance and violence;
13. Reaffirm that all acts of terrorism represent an attack against humanity as the killing of innocent civilians in order to spread terror is despicable to the values of all civilizations;
14. Affirm that in the 21st century, science must become a shared asset benefiting all people serving as a powerful resource for economic transformation and for understanding natural and social phenomena;
15. Recognise that science and technology are major engines of social change which should be guided by ethical and moral perspectives and approaches;
16. Emphasise that social and human sciences should assume a much more proactive role in analysing all the dimensions of social interaction and transformation in a rapidly changing world with a view to ensuring the well-being of the societies and to enhancing global understanding of civilizational dynamics and processes;
17. Underline the importance of traditional and local knowledge systems as dynamic expressions of perceiving and understanding the world and that this tangible and intangible cultural heritage and empirical knowledge need to be protected and preserved;
18. Affirm further that the information and communication revolution offers new and effective means of exchanging scientific knowledge and advancing education and research which promote the economic and social development of all people;
19. Further recognise that information and communication technologies can enhance intercultural communication and mutual understanding, especially through the promotion of cultural and linguistic pluralism, the generation of cross-cultural links, and the sharing of knowledge and information in various forms by networking communities and individuals;

20. Affirm therefore the need for enhanced inter-cultural dialogue through international cooperation in order for all peoples and nations to share with one another their knowledge and skills;
21. Stress the need to develop the various branches of knowledge side by side and, as far as possible, simultaneously, so as to establish a harmonious balance between technical progress and the intellectual and socio-economic advancement of mankind;
22. Affirm that the respect for diversity of cultures, including the protection and promotion of tangible and intangible cultural heritage, values of tolerance and: mutual understanding are fostered through multi-civilisational discourse and are the best guarantors of peace in the world.
23. In the context of the above, the Conference:
    a. Enjoins all governments and civil society to support actively a dialogue within and among civilizations and cultures so that it will become an effective instrument of transformation, a yardstick for peace and tolerance, and a vehicle for diversity and pluralism;
    b. Calls upon governments and civil society to ensure the empowerment and full participation of women and youth in efforts to foster dialogue within and among civilization and to generate equitable, inclusive societies where mutual understanding may flourish and people may learn to live together in peace;
    c. Recommends that UNESCO initiate a broad based collaboration with Member States, organizations of the UN system, civil society, the scientific, academic and artistic communities, the private sector and other partners with a view to translating the various proposals contained in this Declaration into concrete action.

❮65❯

UNSC Resolution 1500 (2003) on Iraq (14.08.03)

Having considered the report of the Secretary General of 15th July 2003 (S/2003/715), the Security Council welcomed the establishment of a broadly representative Governing Council of Iraq on 13 July 2003 and decided to establish the United Nations Assistance Mission for Iraq to support the Secretary General in fulfillment of his mandate under resolution 1483.

The Security Council,

Recalling all its previous relevant resolutions, in particular resolution 1483 (2003) of 22 May 2003,

Reaffirming the sovereignty and territorial integrity of Iraq,

Reaffirming also the vital role for the United Nations in Iraq which was set out in relevant paragraphs of resolution 1483 (2003),

Having considered the report of the Secretary-General of 15 July 2003 (S/2003/715),

1. *Welcomes* the establishment of the broadly representative Governing Council of Iraq on 13 July 2003, as an important step towards the formation by the people of Iraq of an internationally recognized, representative government that will exercise the sovereignty of Iraq;
2. *Decides* to establish the United Nations Assistance Mission for Iraq to support the Secretary-General in the fulfilment of his mandate under resolution 1483 in accordance with the structure and responsibilities set out in his report of 15 July 2003, for an initial period of twelve months;
3. *Decides* to remain seized of this matter.

❮66❯

Statement of Interdiction Principles for the Proliferation Security Initiative, Paris (04.09.03)

The Interdiction Principles called on all-States concerned to "adopt streamlined procedures for rapid exchange of relevant information concerning suspected proliferation activity", strengthen relevant national legal authorities, take action to board and search any vessel in their internal waters or territorial seas and "seriously consider providing consent" for boarding and searching of its own vessels by other states.

The Proliferation Security Initiative (PSI) is a response to the growing challenge posed by the proliferation of weapons of mass destruction (WMD), their delivery systems, and related materials worldwide. The PSI builds on efforts by the international community to prevent proliferation of such items, including existing treaties and regimes. It is consistent with and a step in the implementation of the UN Security Council Presidential Statement of January 1992, which states that the proliferation of all WMD constitutes a threat to international peace and security, and underlines the need for member States of the UN to prevent proliferation. The PSI is also consistent with recent statements of the G8 and the European Union, establishing that more coherent and concerted efforts are needed to prevent the proliferation of WMD, their delivery systems, and related materials. PSI participants are deeply concerned about this threat and of the danger that these items could fall into the hands of terrorists, and are committed to working together to stop the flow of these items to and from states and non-state actors of proliferation concern.

The PSI seeks to involve in some capacity all states that have a stake in non-proliferation and the ability and willingness to take steps to stop the flow of such items at sea, in the air, or on land. The PSI also seeks cooperation from any State whose vessels, flags, ports, territorial waters, airspace, or land might be used for proliferation purposes by states and non-State actors of proliferation concern. The increasingly aggressive efforts by proliferators to stand outside or to circumvent existing non-proliferation norms, and to profit from such trade, requires new and stronger actions by the International community. We look forward to working with all concerned states on measures they are able and willing to take in support of the PSI, as outlined in the following set of "Interdiction Principles."

Interdiction Principles for the Proliferation Security Initiative

PSI participants are committed to the following interdiction principles to establish a more co-ordinated and effective basis through which to impede and stop shipments of WMD, delivery systems, and related materials flowing to and from States and non-State actors of proliferation concern, consistent with national legal authorities and relevant international law and frameworks, including the UN Security Council. They call on all States concerned with this threat to international peace and security to join in similarly committing to:

1. Undertake effective measures, either alone or in concert with other states, for interdicting the transfer or transport of WMD, their delivery systems, and related materials to and from States and non-State actors of proliferation concern. "States or non-State actors of proliferation concern" generally refers to those countries or entities that the PSI participants involved establish should be subject to interdiction activities because they are engaged in proliferation through: (1) efforts to develop or acquire chemical, biological, or nuclear weapons and associated delivery systems; or (2) transfers (either selling, receiving, or facilitating) of WMD, their delivery systems, or related materials.
2. Adopt streamlined procedures for rapid exchange of relevant information concerning suspected proliferation activity, protecting the confidential character of classified information provided by other states as part of this initiative, dedicate appropriate resources and efforts to interdiction operations and capabilities, and maximize coordination among participants in interdiction efforts.
3. Review and work to strengthen their relevant national legal authorities where necessary to accomplish these objectives, and work to strengthen when necessary relevant international law and frameworks in appropriate ways to support these commitments.
4. Take specific actions in support of interdiction efforts regarding cargoes of WMD, their delivery systems, or related materials, to the extent their national legal authorities permit and consistent with their obligations under international law and frameworks, to include:
    a. Not to transport or assist in the transport of any such cargoes to or from States or non-State actors oı proliferation concern, and not to allow any persons subject to their jurisdiction to do so.
    b. At their own initiative, or at the request and good cause shown by another State, to take action to board and search any vessel flying their flag in their internal waters or territorial seas, or areas beyond the territorial seas of any other State, that is reasonably suspected of transporting such cargoes to or from states or non-state actors of proliferation concern, and to seize such cargoes that are identified.

c. To seriously consider providing consent under the appropriate circumstances to the boarding and searching of its own flag vessels by other states, and to the seizure of such WMD-related cargoes in such vessels that may be identified by such States.

d. To take appropriate actions to (1) stop and/or search in their internal waters, territorial seas, or contiguous zones (when declared) vessels that are reasonably suspected of carrying such cargoes to or from states or non-State actors of proliferation concern and to seize such cargoes that are identified; and (2) to enforce conditions on vessels entering or leaving their ports, internal waters or territorial seas that are reasonably suspected of carrying such cargoes, such as requiring that such vessels be subject to boarding, search, and seizure of such cargoes prior to entry.

e. At their own initiative or upon the request and good cause shown by another state, to (a) require aircraft that are reasonably suspected of carrying such cargoes to or from States or non-State actors of proliferation concern and that are transiting their airspace to land for inspection and seize any such cargoes that are identified; and/or (b) deny aircraft reasonably suspected of carrying such cargoes transit rights through their airspace in advance of such flights.

f. If their ports, airfields, or other facilities are used as transshipment points for shipment of such cargoes to or from States or non-State actors of proliferation concern, to inspect vessels, aircraft, or other modes of transport reasonably suspected of carrying such cargoes, and to seize such cargoes that are identified.

‹67›

Draft Resolution on Confidence-Building Measures in the Regional and Sub-Regional Context Sponsored by Pakistan in the 58th Session of the UNGA (15.10.03)

> The Draft Resolution called upon Member States to "refrain from the use or threat of use of force in the settlement of disputes; ...open consultations and dialogue in the regions of tension and conflict without preconditions; ...and urged the maintenance of military balance between States in the regions of tension..."

The General Assembly,

Guided by the purposes and principles enshrined in the Charter of the United Nations.

Recalling its resolution 57/337 of 3 July 2003 entitled "Prevention of armed conflict", in which it calls upon Member States to settle their disputes by peaceful means, as set out in Chapter VI of the Chapter, inter alia, by any procedures adopted by the parties, including the most effective use of the International Court of Justice,

Recalling the Security Council resolutions relating to the prevention of armed conflict, and noting all Security Council Presidential statements related to this matter.

Considering the importance and effectiveness of confidence-building measures taken at the initiative and with the participation of all States concerned, and taken into account the specific characteristics of each region, since such measures can contribute to regional stability.

Convinced that resources released by disarmament, including regional disarmament, can be devoted to economic and social development and to the protection of the environment for the benefit of all peoples, in particular those of the developing countries,

Recognizing the need for meaningful dialogue in the regions of tension to avert conflict,

Welcoming the peace processes already initiated by regions to resolve their disputes through peaceful means bilaterally or through mediation by third parties, regional organization or the United Nations,

Recognizing that some regions have already taken steps towards confidence-building measures at the bilateral, sub-regional and regional levels in the political and military fields, including arms control and disarmament, and noting that such measures have immensely improved peace and security in those regions and have resulted in rapid progress in the socio-economic conditions of their people.

Concerned that the continuation of disputes among States, particularly in the absence of an effective mechanism to resolve them through peaceful means, may contribute to the arms race and endanger the maintenance of international peace and security and the efforts of the international community to promote arms control and disarmament,

1. *Calls upon* Member States to refrain from the use or threat of use of force in the settlement of disputes;
2. *Re-affirms* its commitment to the peaceful settlement of disputes under Chapter VI of the Charter of the United Nation, which calls for the peaceful settlement of disputes, in particular Article 33, which provides for a solution by negotiation, enquiry, mediation, conciliation, arbitration, judicial settlement, resort to regional agencies or arrangements or other peaceful means chosen by the parties;
3. *Calls upon* Member States that have not already done so to open consultations and dialogue in the regions of tension and conflict without pre-conditions;
4. *Urges* strict compliance with bilateral, regional and international arms control and disarmament Agreements to which the contending States are parties;
5. *Urges also*, in the context of confidence-building measures, the maintenance of military balance between States in the regions of tension and conflict in the acquisition, development and development of conventional and strategic weapon systems;
6. *Encourages* the promotion of bilateral and regional confidence-building measures to avoid conflict and prevent the unintended and accidental outbreak of hostilities;
7. *Requests* the Secretary-General to consult with the States of the regions concerned in order,to ascertain their views on the issue and to promote consultations among them with a view to exploring the best possibilities for furthering efforts towards confidence-building measures in the regions of tensions;
8. *Also requests* the Secretary-General to report on the subject to the General Assembly at its fifty-ninth session;
9. *Decides* to include in the provisional agenda of its fifty-ninth session an item entitled "Confidence-building measures in the regional and sub-regional context"

❮68❯

UNSC Resolution 1511 (2003) on Iraq (16.10.03)

The Resolution authorized a "multi-national force under unified command to take all necessary measures to contribute to the maintenance of security and stability in Iraq" and called upon the Coalition Provisional Authority (CPA) "to return governing responsibilities and authorities to the people of Iraq as soon as practicable". It also gave the Governing Council in Iraq until December 15, 2003 to present a time table to the UNSC for drafting a new constitution and holding democratic elections.

The Security Council unanimously adopted a Resolution on October 16, 2003 providing a framework for U.N. and international participation in the political and economic rebuilding of Iraq and maintenance of security.

The Resolution, originally proposed by the United States, was co-sponsored by Cameroon, Spain and United Kingdom.

Adopted under Chapter VII of the U.N. Charter, the Resolution focuses on three main areas: Iraqi leadership and the transfer of power from the Coalition Provisional Authority (CPA) to the Iraqi people; continued security provided by a multi-national force under unified command; and international and United Nations participation in the financing of reconstruction and recovery projects. It also gives the United Nations a greater role in assisting Iraq in the political process and other areas such as human rights, humanitarian aid, and sustainable development.

In a statement to the council following the vote, U.S. Ambassador, John Negroponte noted that the multi-national force would be under "unified United States command."

The resolution recognizes the current Iraqi Governing Council and its ministers as the "principal bodies of the Iraqi interim administration," and gives the governing council two months, until December 15, 2003, to present a time-table to the Security Council for drafting a new Constitution and holding democratic elections under that Constitution.

Determining that "the provision of security and stability is essential to the successful completion of the political process" and the ability of the United Nations to work in the country, the Resolution authorizes a "multinational force under unified command to take all necessary measures to contribute to the maintenance of security and stability in Iraq." The force is to report to the council atleast every six months.

The resolution also calls upon the CPA "to return governing responsibilities and authorities to the people of Iraq as soon as practicable" and asks the authority, the Iraqi Governing Council, and the

U.N. Secretary General to report to the council on the progress being made.

It urges nations to contribute military forces to the multi-national force and calls on member States as well as International Financial Institutions to provide the necessary resources, including a full range of loans and other financial assistance, for the rehabilitation and re-construction of Iraq's economic infrastructure.

In the resolution, the council also "unequivocally condemns" the terrorist bombings in Iraq and calls on nations to prevent the transit of terrorists and the transfer of weapons and financing for terrorist activities into the country.

Following is the text of the Resolution:

Cameroon, Spain, United Kingdom of Great Britain and Northern Ireland and United States of America: Resolution 1511

The Security Council,

Re-affirming its previous Resolutions on Iraq, including Resolution 1483 (2003) of 22 May 2003 and 1500 (2003) of 14 August 2003, and on threats to peace and security caused by terrorist acts, including Resolution 1373 (2001) of 28 September 2001, and other relevant Resolutions,

Underscoring that the sovereignty of Iraq resides in the State of Iraq, re-affirming the right of the Iraqi people freely to determine their own political future and control their own natural resources, reiterating its resolve that the day when Iraqis govern themselves must come quickly, and recognizing the importance of international support, particularly that of countries in the region, Iraq's neighbours, and regional organizations, in taking forward this process expeditiously,

Recognizing that international support for restoration of conditions of stability and security is essential to the well-being of the people of Iraq as well as to the ability of all concerned to carry out their work on behalf of the people of Iraq, and welcoming Member State contributions in this regard under resolution 1483 (2003),

Welcoming the decision of the Governing Council of Iraq to form a preparatory Constitutional Committee to prepare for a Constitutional Conference that will draft a Constitution to embody the aspirations of the Iraqi people, and urging it to complete this process quickly,

Affirming that the terrorist bombings of the Embassy of Jordan on 7 August 2003, of the United Nations Headquarters in Baghdad on 19 August 2003, of the Imam Ali Mosque in Najaf on 29 August 2003, and of the Embassy of Turkey on 14 October 2003, and the murder of a Spanish Diplomat on 9 October 2003 are attacks on the people of Iraq, the United Nations, and the international community, and deploring the assassination of Dr. Akila al-Hashimi, who died on 25 September 2003, as an attack directed against the future of Iraq,

In that context, *recalling and re-affirming* the statement of its President of 20 August 2003 (S/PRST/2003/13) and resolution 1502 (2003) of 26 August 2003,

Determining that the situation in Iraq, although improved, continues to constitute a threat to international peace and security,

Acting under Chapter VII of the Charter of the United Nations,

1. Re-affirms the sovereignty and territorial integrity of Iraq, and underscores, in that context, the temporary nature of the exercise by the Coalition Provisional Authority (Authority) of the specific responsibilities, authorities, and obligations under applicable international law recognized and set forth in resolution 1483 (2003) which will cease when an internationally recognized representative Government established by the people of Iraq is sworn in and assumes the responsibilities of the Authority, inter alia through steps envisaged in paragraphs 4 through 7 and 10 below:
2. Welcomes the positive response of the international community, in form, such as the Arab League, the Organization of the Islamic Conference, the United Nations General Assembly, and the United Nations Educational, Scientific and Cultural Organization, to the establishment of the broadly representative Governing Council as all important step towards an internationally recognized, representative Government;
3. Supports the Governing Council's efforts to mobilize the people of Iraq, including by the appointment of a Cabinet of Ministers and a preparatory Constitutional Committee to lead a process in which the Iraqi people will progressively take control of their own affairs;
4. Determines that the Governing Council and its Ministers are the principal bodies of the Iraqi interim administration, which, without prejudice to its further evolution, embodies the sovereignty of the State of Iraq during the transitional period until an internationally recognized, representative Government is established and assumes the responsibilities of the Authority;
5. Affirms that the administration of Iraq will be progressively undertaken by the evolving structures of the Iraqi interim administration;
6. Calls upon the Authority, in this context, to return governing responsibilities and authorities to the people of Iraq as soon as practicable and requests the Authority, in cooperation as appropriate with the Governing Council and the Secretary-General, to report to the Council on the progress being made;
7. Invites the Governing Council to provide to the Security Council, for its review, no later than 15 December 2003, in cooperation with the Authority and, as circumstances permit, the Special Representative of the Secretary-General, a time-table and a programme for the drafting of a new Constitution for Iraq and for the holding of democratic elections under that Constitution;
8. Resolves that the United Nations, acting through the Secretary-General, his Special Representative, and the United Nations Assistance Mission

in Iraq, should strengthen its vital role in Iraq, including by providing humanitarian relief, promoting the economic re-construction of and conditions for sustainable development in Iraq, and advancing efforts to restore and establish national and local institutions for representative Government;

9. Requests that, as circumstances permit, the Secretary-General pursue the course of action outlined in paragraphs 98 and 99 of the report of the Secretary-General of 17 July 2003 (S/2003/715);
10. Takes note of the intention of the Governing Council to hold a Constitutional Conference and, recognizing that the convening of the Conference will be a milestone in the movement to the full exercise of sovereignty, calls for its preparation through national dialogue and consensus-building as soon as practicable and requests the Special Representative of the Secretary-General, at the time of the convening of the Conference or, as circumstances permit, to lend the unique expertise of the United Nations to the Iraqi people in this process of political transition, including the establish establishment of electoral processes;
11. Requests the Secretary-General to ensure that the resources of the United Nations and associated organizations are available, if requested by the Iraqi Governing Council and, as circumstances permit, to assist in furtherance of the programme provided by the Governing Council in paragraph 7 above, and encourages other organizations with expertise in this area to support the Iraqi Governing Council, if requested;
12. Requests the Secret Secretary-General to report to the Security Council on his responsibilities under this Resolution and the development and implementation of a time-table and programme under paragraph 7 above;
13. Determines that the provision of security and stability is essential to the successful completion of the political process as outlined in paragraph 7 above and to the ability of the United Nations to contribute effectively to that process and the implementation of Resolution 1483 (2003), and authorizes a multinational force under unified command to take all necessary measures to contribute to the maintenance of security and stability in Iraq, including for the purpose of ensuring necessary conditions for the implementation of the timetable and programme as well as to contribute to the security of the United Nations Assistance Mission for Iraq, the Governing Council of Iraq and other institutions of the Iraqi interim administration, and key humanitarian and economic infrastructure;

14. Urges Member States to contribute assistance under this United Nations inundate, including military forces, to the multi-national force referred to in paragraph 13 above;
15. Decides that the Council shall review the requirements and mission of the multi-national force referred to in paragraph 13 above, not later than one year from the date of this Resolution, and that in any case the mandate of the force shall expire upon the completion of the political process as described in paragraphs 4 through 7 and 10 above, and expresses readiness to consider on that occasion any future need for the continuation of the multi-national force, taking into account the views of an internationally recognized, representative Government of Iraq;
16. Emphasizes the importance of establishing effective Iraqi police and security forces in maintaining law, order, and security and combating terrorism consistent with paragraph 4 of Resolution 1483 (2003), and calls upon Member States and international and regional organizations to contribute to the training and equipping of Iraqi police and security forces;
17. Expresses deep sympathy and condolences for the personal losses suffered by the Iraqi people and by the United Nations and the families of those United Nations personnel and other innocent victims who are killed or injured in these tragic attacks;
18. Unequivocally condemns the terrorist bombings of the Embassy of Jordan on 7 August 2003, of the United Nations Headquarters in Baghdad on 19 August 2003, and of the Imam Ali Mosque in Najaf on 29 August 2003, and of the Embassy of Turkey on 14 October 2003, the murder of a Spanish Diplomat on 9 October 2003, and the assassination of Dr. Akila al-Hashimi, who died on 25 September 2003, and emphasizes that those responsible must be brought to justice;
19. Calls upon Member States to prevent the transit of terrorist to Iraq, arms for terrorists, and financing that would support terrorists, and emphasizes the importance of strengthening the cooperation of the countries of the region, particularly neighbours of Iraq, in this regard;
20. Appeals to Member States and the International Financial Institutions to strengthen their efforts to assist the people of Iraq in the re-construction and development of their economy, and urges those institutions to take immediate steps to provide their full range of loans and other financial assistance to Iraq, Working with the Governing Council and appropriate Iraqi Ministries;

21. Urges Member States and International and Regional Organizations to support the Iraq re-construction effort initiated at the 24 June 2003 United Nations Technical Consultations, including through substantial pledges at the 23-24 October 2003 International Donors Conference in Madrid;
22. Calls upon Member States and concerned organizations to help meet the needs of the Iraqi people by providing resources necessary for the rehabilitation and re-construction of Iraq's economic infrastructure;
23. Emphasizes that the International Advisory and Monitoring Board IAMB referred to in paragraph 12 of Resolution 1483 (2003) should be established as a priority, and reiterates that the Development Fund for Iraq shall be used in a transparent manner as set out in paragraph 14 of Resolution 1483 (2003);
24. Reminds all Member States of their obligations under paragraphs 19 and 23 of Resolution 1483 (2003), in particular the obligation to immediately cause the transfer of funds, other financial assets and economic resources to the Development Fund for Iraq for the benefit of the Iraqi people;
25. Requests that the United States, on behalf of the multi-national force as outlined in paragraph 13 above, report to the Security Council on the efforts and progress of this force as appropriate and not less than every six months;
26. Decides to remain seized of the matter.

❮69❯

Iran Declaration between the Iranian Government and Visiting EU Foreign Ministers on Iran's Nuclear Programme (21.10.03)

The Iranian Government decided to sign the IAEA Additional Protocol, commence ratification procedures and "voluntarily suspend all uranium enrichment and processing activities as defined by the IAEA". In return "once international concerns" are fully resolved "Iran could expect easier access to modern technology and supplies in a range of areas".

1. Upon the invitation of the Government of the Islamic Republic of Iran, the Foreign Ministers of Britain, France and Germany paid a visit to Tehran on October 21, 2003.

The Iranian authorities and the ministers, following extensive consultations, agreed on measures aimed at the settlement of all outstanding IAEA [International Atomic Energy Agency] issues with regards to the Iranian nuclear programme and at enhancing confidence for peaceful cooperation in the nuclear field.

2. The Iranian authorities reaffirmed that nuclear weapons have no place in Iran's defence doctrine and that its nuclear programme and activities have been exclusively in the peaceful domain. They reiterated Iran's commitment to the nuclear non-proliferation regime and informed the Ministers that:

   a) The Iranian Government has decided to engage in full co-operation with the IAEA to address and resolve through full transparency all requirements and outstanding issues of the agency and clarify and correct any possible failures and deficiencies within the IAEA.

   b) To promote confidence with a view to removing existing barriers for cooperation in the nuclear field:

      i) Having received the necessary clarifications, the Iranian Government has decided to sign the IAEA Additional Protocol and commence ratification procedures. As a confirmation of its good intentions the Iranian Government will continue to cooperate with the agency in accordance with the protocol in advance of its ratification.

ii) While Iran has a right within the nuclear non-proliferation regime to develop nuclear energy for peaceful purposes it has decided voluntarily to suspend all uranium enrichment and processing activities as defined by the IAEA.

3. The foreign ministers of Britain, France and Germany welcomed the decisions of the Iranian Government and informed the Iranian authorities that:

a) Their governments recognise the right of Iran to enjoy peaceful use of nuclear energy in accordance with the nuclear Non-Proliferation Treaty.

b) In their view the Additional Protocol is in no way intended to undermine the sovereignty, national dignity or national security of its state Parties.

c) In their view full implementation of Iran's decisions, confirmed by the IAEA's director general, should enable the immediate situation to be resolved by the IAEA board.

d) The three governments believe that this will open the way to a dialogue on a basis for longer term cooperation which will provide all parties with satisfactory assurances relating to Iran's Nuclear Power Generation Programme. Once international concerns, including those of the three governments, are fully resolved Iran could expect easier access to modern technology and supplies in a range of areas.

e) They will cooperate with Iran to promote security and stability in the region including the establishment of a zone free from weapons of mass destruction in the Middle East in accordance with the objectives of the United Nations.

❮70❯

Bangkok Declaration of the Asia Pacific Economic Cooperation (21.10.03)

In order to advance the Doha Development Agenda (DDA) and "Bogor Goals" of free trade and investment, the leaders agreed to work towards abolition of agriculture export subsidies, extend support for early accession of the Russian Federation and Vietnam to the WTO, implement the Shanghai Accord and Los Cabos Directives. They also agreed to dismantle trans-national terrorist groups and strengthen efforts to deal with the threat posed by the acquisition of Man Portable Air-Defence Systems (MANPADS) by terrorists.

We gathered in Bangkok for the 11th APEC Economic Leaders' Meeting to combine our diverse strengths to meet the challenges facing our region. In line with APEC's theme for this year, "A World of Differences: Partnership for the Future," and its sub-themes, following our interactive and meaningful exchange of views, we agreed that strong partnership is vital in order to achieve the goals we set out in Bogor. To realize our vision amidst the rapidly changing international environment, we agreed to strengthen our partnership not only to liberalize and facilitate regional trade and investment, but also to protect our peoples and societies against threats to their security, while preparing them to benefit fully from free and open trade. By taking these steps, we can realize the APEC vision, established by Leaders in 1993, of "achieving stability, security and prosperity for our peoples."

1. Promoting Trade and Investment Liberalization

We reaffirmed the primacy of the multilateral trading system, and agreed that the Doha Development Agenda (DDA) offers the potential for real gains for all economies, particularly developing economies, in the areas of agricultural reform, improved market access for goods and services, and clarification and improvement of trade disciplines. We lent our strong support for continuing the valuable work done at the Cancun Ministerial Conference to advance the DDA. We agreed that for global free trade to flourish, regional and bilateral Free Trade Agreements must be consistent with WTO principles, advance WTO objectives and contribute to the Bogor Goals.

To advance the DDA and the Bogor Goals of free and open trade and investment, as well as their supporting conditions, we agreed to:

- Press for an ambitious and balanced outcome to the DDA, reiterating that the development dimension is at its core.
- Re-energize the negotiation process, building on Chairman Derbez's text of 13 September 2003, recognizing that flexibility and political will are urgently needed to move the negotiations toward a successful conclusion.
- Work towards the abolition of all forms of agricultural export subsidies, unjustifiable export prohibitions and restrictions, and commit ourselves to work in the negotiating group on rules in accordance with the Doha mandate.
- Advance free trade in a co-ordinated manner among multilateral, regional and bilateral frameworks so that they are complementary and mutually reinforcing.
- Extend our continued support for the early accession of the Russian Federation and VietNam to the WTO.
- Continue APEC's work on WTO capacity and confidence building in areas where APEC can best add value, while reviewing past performance to improve its effectiveness.
- Instruct Ministers to take concrete steps to make APEC's trade agenda more supportive of the work of the WTO and report on their progress in 2004.
- Work with the APEC Business Advisory Council (ABAC) and the business community to continue to implement the Shanghai Accord and Los Cabos directives to facilitate business activity in the APEC region, including the reduction of transaction costs 5 percent by the year 2006.
- Advance all pathfinder initiatives, including the APEC Sectoral Food MRA and Digital Economy Statement to, e.g., stop optical disk piracy and allow technology choice for business.
- Fight corruption, a major obstacle to social and economic development, by working in 2004 to develop specific domestic actions to combat it. Promote transparency by implementing our general and area-specific transparency standards through our Transparency by 2005 Strategy.

2. Enhancing Human Security

We agreed that trans-national terrorism and the proliferation of weapons of mass destruction pose direct and profound challenges to APEC's vision of free, open and prosperous economies. We agreed to dedicate APEC not only to advancing the prosperity of our economies, but also to the complementary mission of ensuring the security of our people.

We, therefore, committed at Bangkok to take all essential actions to:

- Dismantle, fully and without delay, transnational terrorist groups that threaten the APEC economies.

- Eliminate the severe and growing danger posed by the proliferation of weapons of mass destruction and their means of delivery by strengthening international non-proliferation regimes, adopting and enforcing effective export controls, and taking other legitimate and appropriate measures against proliferation.
- Confront other direct threats to the security of our region.

We pledged to discuss at each Leaders' Meeting our progress toward these security commitments, and to take specific actions in pursuit of them.

We agreed this year to:

- Strengthen our joint efforts to curb terrorist threats against mass transportation and confront the threat posed by terrorists' acquisition and use of Man-Portable Air Defense Systems (MANPADS) against international aviation by committing to: adopt strict domestic export controls on MANPADS; secure stockpiles; take domestic action to regulate production, transfer, and brokering; ban transfers to non-state end-users; and exchange information in support of these efforts. We agreed to continue efforts to strengthen domestic controls on MANPADS and to review our progress next year in Chile.
- Increase and better co-ordinate our counter-terrorism activities, where appropriate, through effective collaboration, technical assistance and capacity building, and cooperation between APEC's Counter Terrorism Task Force, the Counter Terrorism Action Group (CTAG) of the G-8, the United Nations Security Council Counter Terrorism Committee and other relevant international, regional and functional organizations.
- Implement the APEC Action Plan on SARS and our Health Security Initiative to help APEC prevent and respond to regional health threats, including naturally-occurring infectious disease and bio-terrorism. We welcomed the establishment by Singapore and the United States of a Regional Emerging Disease Intervention (REDI) Center. We encouraged the Life Sciences Innovation Forum to complete its strategic plan by 2004.
- Establish a regional trade and financial security initiative within the Asian Development Bank, to support projects that enhance port security, combat terrorist finance, and achieve other counter-terrorism objectives.
- Support implementation of the Advance Passenger Information (API) System pathfinder initiative and efforts to explore development of a regional movement alert system to protect air travellers.
- Accelerate the implementation of the Energy Security Initiative by endorsing its Implementation Plan and, as appropriate, a new Action Plan to enhance regional and global energy security.

3. Using APEC to Help People and Societies Benefit from Globalization

Sustainable economic development requires empowering people and strengthening societies for globalization. In this regard, we welcomed efforts to increase APEC's contribution to this process by: making it more effective; better focusing and strengthening its work on economic and technical cooperation; and increasing its interaction with international financial institutions, the private sector, and other outside organizations. This will make APEC's work more effective in bridging the gap between developed and developing economies.

To create the conditions that allow peoples and societies to make the most of their potential and prepare for the challenges of the future, we agreed to:

- Strengthen efforts to empower people and societies, including women and youth, to integrate into the global economy. We underlined the importance of strengthening small and medium enterprises and micro-enterprises, of social safety nets in promoting sustainable and equitable economic development, and of mainstreaming the informal sector. We welcomed the outcomes of the meetings of APEC Finance and SME Ministers in this regard and instructed Ministers to coordinate on micro enterprise financing and capacity building initiatives, in collaboration with international financial institutions and other relevant parties, in order to leverage resources for implementation of the Micro-Enterprises Action Plan in 2004.
- Step up efforts to build knowledge-based economies. We instructed Ministers to accelerate progress towards the Brunei Goals on expanding Internet access, improvement of intellectual property rights facilitation, protection and enforcement, and implementation of the e-APEC Strategy, in partnership with relevant stakeholders. We voiced support for science and technology innovation, the upgrading of English-language and computer skills among the workforce for effective use of the Internet, advancing cyber-education and ICT capacity building, including for small and micro enterprises.
- Strengthen regional efforts to promote sound and efficient financial systems and fundamentals. We urged further cooperation on development of domestic and regional bond markets, as well as securitization and credit guarantee markets to enhance the efficiency of those markets. We support issuance of new financial products, including long-term, local currency-denominated debt instruments, derivatives and asset-backed securities.
- Accelerate structural reform in the APEC region. We reiterated APEC's strong political commitment to continued structural reform to ensure sustainable economic growth and development in the Asia-Pacific

region. We welcomed the adoption of the APEC Structural Reform Action Plan that includes strengthening economic legal infrastructure as a guiding working program and instructed Ministers to review implementation of this Action Plan and identify future initiatives.

- Strengthen APEC. We discussed the need to make APEC more efficient and responsive to all stakeholders. We instructed Ministers to explore the issue and report on progress by the time we meet in Chile in 2004.

We endorsed in full the conclusions of and the Joint Statement agreed by Ministers at the Fifteenth APEC Ministerial Meeting.

‹71›

The Proposal by the Liberation Tigers of Tamil Eelam on Behalf of the Tamil People for an Agreement to Establish an Interim Self-governing Authority for the Northeast of the Island of Sri Lanka

> The LTTE proposed the setting up of an Interim Self-Governing Authority (ISGA) comprising 8 districts in the Northeast "until a final negotiative settlement is reached and implemented." The ISGA shall consist of members appointed by the LTTE, Government of Sri Lanka and the Muslim community in the Northeast with powers for governance, preparing an annual budget and control over marine and off-shore resources of the adjacent seas.

Consistent with the principles of the rule of law, the human rights and equality of all persons, and the right to self-determination of People,

Determined to bring lasting peace to all persons of the island of Sri Lanka,

Acknowledging with appreciation the services of the Royal Norwegian Government, the Norwegian People, and the international community in attempting to bring peace to the island,

Recognizing that a peaceful resolution is a real possibility, despite the challenging history of the peace process between the Tamil people and the Sinhala people.

Determined to establish an interim self-governing authority for the NorthEast region and to provide for the urgent needs of the people of the NorthEast by formulating laws and policies and, effectively and expeditiously executing all resettlement, rehabilitation, re-construction, and development in the NorthEast, while the process for reaching a final settlement remains ongoing.

Being aware that the history of the relations between the Tamil People and the Sinhala People has been a process of broken promises and unilateral abrogation, by successive Governments of Sri Lanka, of pacts and Agreements solemnly entered into between the Government of Sri Lanka (GOSL) and the elected representatives of the Tamil People,

Bearing in mind that successive Governments of Sri Lanka have perpetrated persecution, discrimination, State violence and State-orchestrated violence against the Tamil People,

Noting that the Tamil people mandated their elected representatives to establish an independent sovereign, secular State for the Tamil people in the elections subsequent to the **Vaddukoddai Resolution** of 1976,

Bearing in mind that the Tamil armed struggle as a measure of self-defense and as a means for the realisation of the Tamil right to self-determination arose only after more than four decades of non-violent and peaceful Constitutional struggle proved to be futile and due to the absence of means to resolve the conflict peacefully,

Recalling that the Liberation Tigers of Tamil Eelam (LTTE) first took measures towards peace by unilaterally declaring the ceasefire in December, 2000 and again in December, 2001, opening highways, facilitating trade and the free movement of people, and entering into peace negotiations in good faith in the hope of creating an environment conducive to the return of normalcy and a just resolution of the conflict,

Taking Note of the political courage of the present GOSL in reciprocating to the 2001 cease-fire,

Realizing that the war in the island of Sri Lanka was principally confined to the NorthEast, resulting in the destruction of the social, economic, administrative, and physical infrastructure of that area, and that the NorthEast still remains the region in the island of Sri Lanka affected by war,

Recognising that the majority of the Tamil People in the NorthEast, by their actions in the general elections held in the year 2000, gave their mandate acknowledging the LTTE as their authentic representative,

Knowing that the LTTE exercises effective control and jurisdiction over the majority of the NorthEast area of the island of Sri Lanka,

Realising that reaching a final negotiated settlement and the implementation thereof is expected to be a long process,

Affirming the necessity for the safe and free return of all refugees and displaced persons and their urgent need for unimpeded access to their homes and secure livelihoods at land and sea in the NorthEast,

Mindful that institutions and services provided by the GOSL have proved to be inadequate to meet the urgent needs of the people of the NorthEast,

Recognising the failure of the Sub-committee on Immediate Humanitarian and Rehabilitation Needs (SIHRN) and other Sub-Committees formed during the peace negotiations, which failure was due to the composition of such Sub-Committees, which repeatedly led to inaction,

Acknowledging the recognition by the GOSL of the necessity for an Interim Authority, as mentioned in its 2000 election manifesto,

Realising that maintenance of law and order is an essential pre-requisite for a just and free society,

Recognising the need for raising revenue to meet the urgent needs for the Resettlement, Rehabilitation, Re-construction and Development of the NorthEast region, which has been devastated by war, and for the carrying out of any function of Government,

Recognising the importance of control over land in resettlement, rehabilitation, re-construction and development,

Mindful that the Tamils did not participate in the making of the 1972 and 1978 Constitutions, which institutionalized discrimination and denied them an effective role in the decision-making process,

Noting the practice in international relations over the last decade of solving conflicts between People through Agreement between the parties to the conflict on terms of equality and through innovative and imaginative measures.

Relying on international precedents for establishing interim governing arrangements in war-torn countries having the force of law based solely on pacts or Agreements between the warring parties recognized by the international community,

Noting that measures such as the Ceasefire Agreement, including the role of the Sri Lanka Monitoring Mission (SLMM), and, the establishment of the SIHRN and the NorthEast Reconstruction Fund (NERF) constitute valid precedents for making such arrangements,

Wherefore, the Parties, namely the Liberation Tigers of Tamil Eelam and the Government of Sri Lanka, hereby agree to the following provisions:

1. Interim Self-Governing Authority

An Interim Self-Governing Authority (ISGA) shall be established comprised of the eight districts namely: Amparai, Batticaloa, Jaffna, Kilinochchi, Mannar, Mullaitivu, Trincomalee and Vavuniya in the NorthEast, until a final negotiated settlement is reached and implemented.

Representatives of the Muslim community have the right to participate in formulation of their role in the ISGA.

2. Composition of the ISGA

2.1. The ISGA shall consist of such number of members as may be determined by the Parties to this Agreement.

2.2. The composition of the ISGA shall be:

2.2.a. Members appointed by the LTTE,

2.2.b. Members appointed by the GOSL, and

2.2.c. Members appointed by the Muslim community in the NorthEast.

2.3. The number of members will be determined to ensure:

2.3.a. An absolute majority of the LTTE appointees in the ISGA.

2.3.b. Subject to (a) above, the Muslim and Sinhala Communities in the NorthEast shall have representation in the ISGA.

2.4. The Chairperson shall be elected by a majority vote of the ISGA and shall serve as the Chief Executive of the ISGA.

2.5. The Chairperson shall appoint the Chief Administrator for the NorthEast and such other officers as may be required to assist in the performance of his/her duties. The Chairperson shall have the powers to suspend or terminate any such appointment.

3. Elections

The provisions of Clauses 2.2 and 2.3 shall continue until elections for the ISGA are held. Such elections shall be held at the expiry of five years of the coming into force of this Agreement, if no final settlement has been reached and implemented by the end of the said period of five years. An independent Election Commission, appointed by the ISGA, shall conduct free and fair elections in accordance with International Democratic Principles and standards under international observation.

4. Human Rights

The people of the NorthEast shall be accorded all rights as are provided under international human rights law. Every law, regulation, rule, order or decision of the ISGA shall conform to internationally accepted standards of human rights protection. There shall be an independent Human Rights Commission, appointed by the ISGA, which shall ensure the compliance with all such human rights obligations. The Commission will seek the assistance of international human rights bodies to facilitate the rapid establishment of an effective regime for protecting human rights. The Commission shall be entitled to receive petitions from any individual person, award compensation to any such affected person, and ensure that such person's rights are restored.

5. Secularism

No religion shall be given the foremost place in the NorthEast.

6. Prohibition against Discrimination

The ISGA shall ensure that there is no discrimination on grounds of religion, race, caste, national or regional origin, age or gender in the NorthEast.

7. Prevention of Bribery and Corruption.

The ISGA shall ensure that no bribery or corruption is permitted in or under its administration.

8. Protection of All Communities

No law, regulation, rule, order or decision that confers a privilege or imposes a disability on any community, which is not conferred or imposed on any other community, shall be made concerning culture or religion.

9. Jurisdiction of the ISGA.

9.1. The ISGA shall have plenary power for the governance of the NorthEast including powers in relation to resettlement, rehabilitation, re-construction, and development, including improvement and upgrading of existing services and facilities (hereinafter referred to as RRRD), raising revenue including imposition of taxes, revenue, levies and duties, law and order, and over land.

These powers shall include all powers and functions in relation to regional administration exercised by the GOSL in and for the NorthEast.

9.2. The detailed modalities for the exercise of such powers and the performance of such functions shall be subject to further discussion by the parties to this Agreement.

10. Separation of Powers

Separate institutions for the administration of justice shall be established for the NorthEast, and judicial powers shall be vested in such institutions. The ISGA shall take appropriate measures to ensure the independence of the judges.

Subject to Clauses 4 (Human Rights) and 22 (Settlement of Disputes), of this Agreement, the institutions created under this clause shall have sole and exclusive jurisdiction to resolve all disputes concerning the interpretation and implementation of this Agreement and any other disputes arising in or under this Agreement or any provision thereof.

11. Finance

The ISGA shall prepare an annual budget.

There shall be a Financial Commission consisting of members appointed by the ISGA. The members should have distinguished themselves or held high office in the fields of finance, administration or business. This Commission shall make recommendations as to the amount out of the Consolidated Fund to be allocated to the NorthEast. The GOSL shall make its good faith efforts to implement the recommendation.

The ISGA will, giving due consideration to an equitable distribution, determine the use of funds placed at its disposal. These funds shall include the NorthEast General Fund, the NorthEast Reconstruction Fund (NERF) and the Special Fund.

The GOSL agrees that any and all of its expenditures in or for the NorthEast shall be subject to the control of the ISGA.

11.1. NorthEast General Fund

The NorthEast General Fund shall be under the control of ISGA and shall consist of:

11.1.a. The proceeds of all grants and loans made by the GOSL to the ISGA and the proceeds of all other loans made to the ISGA.

11.1.b. All allocations by the GOSL from Agreements with states, institutions and/or other organizations earmarked in any such Agreements for the NorthEast.

11.1.c. All other receipts of the ISGA, other than the funds specified below.

11.2. NorthEast Reconstruction Fund

The NERF shall continue to exist in its present form except that control over it will be transferred to the ISGA.

All grants given for the reconstruction of the NorthEast, will be received through the NERF. Utilization of resources from NERF will be directly determined and supervised by the ISGA.

11.3. Special Fund

All loans and any grants which cannot be channeled through the NERF for the specific purpose of RRRD will be received into the Special Fund. As in the case of other Funds, the ISGA shall control the Special Fund.

12. Powers to Borrow, Receive Aid and Trade.

The ISGA shall have powers to borrow internally and externally, provide guarantees and indemnities, receive aid directly, and engage in or regulate internal and external trade.

13. Accounting and Auditing of Funds.

13.1. The ISGA shall appoint an Auditor General.

13.2. All Funds referred to in this Agreement shall be operated, maintained and audited in accordance with internationally accepted accounting and auditing standards. The accounts will be audited by the Auditor General. The auditing of all moneys received from international sources shall be subjected to approval by an internationally-reputed firm appointed by the ISGA.

14. District Committees.

14.1. In the effective exercise of its legislative and executive powers, the ISGA may create District Committees to carry out administration in the districts and delegate to such Committees, such powers as the ISGA may determine. The Chairpersons of such Committees shall be appointed by the ISGA from amongst its members in order to serve as a liaison between the ISGA and the Committees.

14.2. The other members of the Committees shall also be appointed by the ISGA, which shall have the powers to suspend or terminate any such appointment. In appointing such members, due consideration shall be given to ensure representation of all communities.

14.3. The Committees will function directly under the ISGA.

14.4. The Chief Administrator of the ISGA shall appoint Principal Executive Officers in the districts, who shall also function as the Secretaries to the Committees. The Chief Administrator shall have the powers to suspend or terminate any such appointment.

14.5. All activities and functions of the Committees shall be coordinated through the respective Secretaries to the Committees.

14.6. Sub-Committees may also be appointed to facilitate administration.

15. Administration

As part of the exercise of its executive powers the ISGA shall have direction and control over any and all administrative structures and personnel in the NorthEast pertaining to the powers set out in Clause 9 of this Agreement.

The ISGA may, at its discretion, create expert Advisory Committees in necessary areas. These areas will include but are not limited to Economic Affairs, Financial Affairs, Judicial Affairs, Resettlement and Rehabilitation Affairs, Development of Infrastructure, and Essential Services.

16. Administration of Land

Since land is vital to the exercise of the powers set out in Clause 9 (jurisdiction of the ISGA), the ISGA shall have the power to alienate and determine the appropriate use of all land in the NorthEast that is not privately owned.

The ISGA shall appoint a Special Commission on Administration of Land to inquire into and report on the rights of dispossessed people over land and land subject to encroachment, notwithstanding the lapse of any time relating to prescription.

The ISGA shall determine the term of competencies of the Special Commission.

17. Resettlement of Occupied Lands

The occupation of land by the armed forces of the GOSL, and the denial to the rightful civilian owners of unfettered access to such land, is a violation of the norms of international law. Such land must be immediately vacated and restored to the possession of the previous owners. The GOSL must also compensate the owners for the past dispossession of their land.

The ISGA shall be responsible for the resettlement and rehabilitation of displaced civilians and refugees in such lands.

18. Marine and off-shore resources

The ISGA shall have control over the marine and offshore resources of the adjacent seas and the power to regulate access thereto.

19. Natural Resources

The ISGA will have control over the natural resources in the NorthEast region. Existing Agreements relating to any such natural resources will continue in force. The GOSL shall ensure that all monies due under such Agreements are paid to the ISGA. Any future changes to such existing Agreements should be made with the concurrence of the ISGA. Future Agreements shall be entered into with the ISGA.

20. Water Use

Upper riparian users of river systems have a duty to ensure that there is a fair, equitable and reasonable use of water resources by lower riparian users. The GOSL and the ISGA shall ensure that this internationally recognized principle is followed in the use of water resources.

21. Agreements and contracts

All future Agreements concerning matters under the jurisdiction of the ISGA shall be made with the ISGA. Existing Agreements will continue, but the GOSL shall ensure that all proceeds under such Agreements are paid to the ISGA. Any changes to such existing Agreements should be made with the concurrence of the ISGA.

22. Settlement of Disputes

Where a dispute arises between the Parties to this Agreement as to its interpretation or implementation, and it cannot be resolved by any other means acceptable to the Parties including conciliation by the Royal Norwegian Government, there shall be an arbitration before a tribunal consisting of three members, two of whom shall be appointed by each Party. The third member, who shall be the Chairperson of the tribunal, shall be appointed jointly by the Parties concerned. In the event of any disagreement over the appointment of the Chairperson, the Parties shall ask the President of the International Court of Justice to appoint the Chairperson.

In the determination of any dispute the arbitrators shall ensure the parity of status of the LTTE and the GOSL and shall resolve disputes by reference only to the provisions of this Agreement.

The decision of the arbitrators shall be final and conclusive and it shall be binding on the Parties to the dispute.

23. Operational Period

This Agreement shall continue until a new Government for the NorthEast, pursuant to a permanent negotiated settlement, is established. The Parties will negotiate in good faith to reach such a settlement as early as possible.

Provided, however, that at the end of four years if no final Agreement has been reached between the Parties to this Agreement, both Parties shall engage in negotiations in good faith for the purpose of adding, clarifying, and strengthening the terms of this Agreement.

❮72❯

China-Pakistan Joint Declaration on Bilateral Cooperation (03.11.03)

In furtherance of their commitment to further deepen "their all-weather friendship", China and Pakistan agreed to strengthen the role of China-Pakistan Joint Committee on Economic, Trade, Scientific and Technological Cooperation (JAC); promote and standardize border trade; cooperate in areas of mutual interest such as telecommunications, aviation and space technology, computer, electric power, automation, meteorology, IT, medicine & health, non-proliferation and export control.

Chinese President Hu Jintao and Pakistani President Pervez Musharraf signed in Beijing a joint declaration on the directions of bilateral cooperation.

Following is the full text of the declaration:

Joint Declaration Between the People's Republic of China and the Islamic Republic of Pakistan on Directions of Bilateral Cooperation

The People's Republic of China and the Islamic Republic of Pakistan (hereinafter referred to as the "two parties") have similar historical experience and common aspirations for peace, progress in the region and the world. The two parties have developed an exemplary State-to-State relationship on the basis of the Five Principles of Peaceful Co-existence.

Since the establishment of diplomatic relations between the two Parties on May 21, 1951, China-Pakistan good-neighbourly and friendly relations, fostered by the successive generations of leaders of both countries, have been growing from strength to strength and bilateral cooperation remain fruitful. The two parties have already established a future-oriented all-round cooperative partnership. The good-neighborly and friendly relations between the two Parties have been an important and indispensable factor for peace and stability in Asia and have contributed to greater international understanding and amity.

The two countries have developed wide-ranging mutually beneficial co-operation with the aim of promoting socio-economic development and ensuring prosperity and better future for their peoples. The two Parties stress that the relationship between China and Pakistan is based on mutual respect of each other's sovereignty, independence, culture and traditions, mutual trust and mutual support. Such a relationship, with its profound popular basis, great vitality and tremendous potential of growth, should remain dynamic forever and be passed on to the future generations.

The further consolidation and strengthening of the existing good-neighbourly and friendly relations not only serves the fundamental interests of the two countries and the two peoples, but also contributes to regional peace, stability and prosperity. The two parties have firm belief in the centrality of the United Nations in the promotion of world peace and development and will continue to cooperate in this regard. Both countries share common values in the conduct of their international relations and stand for peaceful settlement of international disputes and upholding of the purposes and principles of the UN Charter.

The two parties have maintained close cooperation in the multilateral fora. They have supported each other internationally in pursuit of the common objectives of peace and development. Similarly, the two parties have consistently supported peace initiatives in Asia and efforts aimed at developing and strengthening economic cooperation and activity that would benefit the peoples of the continent. Pakistan supports the *Boao Forum for Asia* (BFA) and commends its efforts to promote and enhance economic activity and regional economic cooperation in Asia and with other countries.

At the beginning of the new century, the two parties are committed to developing closer bilateral relations and further deepening and broadening their all-weather friendship and all-round cooperative partnership. In the spirit of this commitment, the two parties hereby state as follows:

1. The two parties agree to maintain frequent exchange of high-level visits and contacts and strengthen the exchange of visits and communication between their government departments, Parliaments, political Parties, armed forces, non-governmental organizations and local organizations with a view to enhancing mutual understanding and friendship and promoting an all-round, steady and deepened development of the bilateral relations.
2. The two Parties stress the important role of annual diplomatic consultation mechanisms in enhancing bilateral political cooperation and agree to strengthen consultations and exchanges between their Ministries of Foreign Affairs at various levels and in various areas to share views on bilateral relations and regional and international issues of mutual interest, and maintain regular exchanges and co-ordination on various occasions.
3. The two parties agree to build on the current sound basis of co-operation, make full use of their political and geographical advantages and promote cooperation in the realms of economy, trade, investment, agriculture, technology and tourism in accordance with the principles of equality, mutual benefit, efficiency, mutual complementarities, diversity of forms and common development. To this end, the two parties will

   (1) Continue to strengthen the guidance and co-ordination on economic and trade cooperation. Both sides will give play to the

role of China-Pakistan Joint Committee on Economic, Trade, Scientific and Technological Cooperation (JEC) and explore new approaches and channels for mutually beneficial economic and trade cooperation. To further tap the potential of bilateral economic cooperation, the two Parties agree to strengthen the role of China- Pakistan Business Council. The two Parties will also improve related laws and regulations, standardize enterprise behavior, and create favorable conditions and offer necessary facilitation for the economic and trade and investment activities of their companies, enterprises and organizations.

(2) Actively expand bilateral trade and entrust JEC to take appropriate steps in that direction. The two Parties agree to encourage and support two-way investment by their enterprises in accordance with the Agreements on the promotion and protection of investment between the two governments, domestic laws and their respective international obligations. They agree to expand bilateral trade on the basis of the newly concluded preferential trade arrangement with the ultimate goal of establishing a free trade arrangement. The two parties agree to strengthen co-operation in contract labor services, and take necessary measures to further promote bilateral trade.

(3) Promote and standardize border trade. The two parties will take steps to facilitate existing border trade and further take steps to conclude a new Border Trade Agreement so as to promote their economic development and social stability, especially in the border areas.

(4) Guide and encourage their government departments, scientific research institutes, universities and high-tech enterprises to conduct broad technological cooperation in areas of mutual interest such as telecommunication, water conservancy, electric power, aviation and space technology, computer, automation, metallurgy, IT, medicine and health, petrochemistry, biotechnology and peaceful utilization of nuclear power. The two parties will endeavor to promote transfer of know-how and exchange of information. In this context, the two parties will give full play to the guiding and co-ordinative role of the intergovernmental Joint Committee on Scientific and Technological Cooperation. Strengthen cooperation in non-proliferation and export control. The two Parties will consider launching, at an appropriate time, the negotiation and conclusion of a bilateral Agreement on mutually issuing of ultimate consumer and end use certificate.

(5) Promote mutually beneficial cooperation in agriculture, forestry and fishery and make the best of the rich natural resources and

strong complementarities of the two countries to encourage and support enhanced exchanges and cooperation between the relevant enterprises and Departments in agricultural technology, processing of agricultural and forest products, manufacturing of agricultural machineries, offshore fishing and aquaculture.

(6) Promote close cooperation in the industrial sector, including sharing of professional expertise and joint production with raw materials and technologies of both sides and development of industrial zones, industrial harbors, export free zones and human resources, give play to the leading role of large enterprises and enhance cooperation among small and medium enterprises. They agree to encourage and facilitate collaboration between the private sectors of the two countries and promote the establishment of joint ventures, particularly in the field of textile manufacturing.

(7) Strengthen exchanges and cooperation in fiscal and financial areas and in macro-economic control.

(8) Strengthen transport cooperation and promote interflow of personnel and commodities through Karakoram Highway.

(9) Hold more investment and trade fairs and commodity fairs in their major commercial cities to enhance mutual understanding between their enterprises. The key chambers of commerce of both countries (the China Council for the Promotion of International Trade and the Federation of All Pakistan Chambers of Commerce and Industry) will establish a regular exchange mechanism.

(10) Expand cooperation in tourism. Pakistan has been designated as a destination for outbound Chinese tourists. The two Parties will finalize the concrete measures as early as possible, to increase the number of tourists, expand tourism markets and enhance tourism promotion.

4. The two Parties attach great importance to the role of the China-Pakistan Defense and Security Consultation Mechanism in promoting military-to-military exchanges and cooperation. To develop defense co-operation, the two parties should, on the basis of equality and mutual benefit, continue to actively conduct exchanges and cooperation at all levels and in all fields, including exchange of visits, personnel training, armed forces training, culture and sports. In this regard, the efforts of the Sino-Pakistan Joint Committee on Cooperation in Defense Technology and Industry shall be supported to enhance defense industrial cooperation.

5. The two Parties agree to strengthen the exchanges and cooperation in the fields of culture, education, public health, sports, media and

religion. Both agree to strengthen mutual understanding and friendship between the two peoples through exchange of students, teachers, delegations, art performance groups, experts and exhibitions. Special importance will be attached to the friendly exchanges and communication between the youth to enhance their awareness of China-Pakistan traditional friendship, and ensure that they will inherit and develop the friendship, mutual trust and cooperation between the two people. Noting the serious threat facing the world environment, the two Parties agree to cooperate with each other in this field in a joint effort to prevent water and air pollution, soil erosion and unsustainable deforestation. The two parties agree to cooperate on efficient and economical use of energy and on research and development for sustainable management of natural resources and improvement of the environment.

6. The two Parties agree that separatism, extremism and terrorism pose serious threats to regional security and stability. Both sides are resolved to strengthen co-ordination and cooperation under bilateral and multilateral frameworks. They will actively support and facilitate substantive cooperation between their Departments in combating separatism, extremism and terrorism with a view to safeguarding regional peace and stability.
7. The two Parties will promote mutual assistance in criminal and legal matters and law enforcement cooperation between the Departments concerned and build closer ties in the surrender of fugitive offenders, investigation and taking of evidence, sharing of criminal information, crackdown on organized trans-national crimes, economic and other crimes, such as smuggling of drugs, weapons and ammunition, and trafficking in human beings.
8. The Chinese side reaffirms that it respects the independence, sovereignty and territorial integrity of Pakistan, and appreciates and supports the efforts of Pakistan for peaceful resolution of all outstanding issues with neighbours and to safeguard its state sovereignty and independence. The Pakistani side reaffirms that it will continue to consistently adhere to the one-China policy, and recognize the Government of the People's Republic of China as the sole legal government representing the whole of China and Taiwan an inalienable and indivisible part of Chinese territory, and fully support China's cause of peaceful re-unification.
9. The two parties are satisfied with their close and efficient cooperation over the years in international and regional affairs. Both sides share the view that the purposes and principles of the UN Charter, the Five Principles of Peaceful Co-existence and other universally recognized norms governing international relations must be respected by all

countries and that the central role of the UN in international affairs should be maintained and strengthened, especially through faithful implementation of the resolutions of the Security Council. The two Parties agree to continue to strengthen their communication and collaboration in international and regional affairs and commit themselves to enhanced solidarity and cooperation among developing countries and maintenance of their legitimate rights and interests in the process of globalization, enhancement of regional and global peace and security, and to the establishment of a new international political and economic order that is fair and rational.

Both sides agree that the visit of President Pervez Musharraf to China has been an outstanding success and a new milestone in the further strengthening of mutual understanding, trust and the traditionally close friendly cooperation between the two countries. On behalf of the Government and the people of Pakistan, President Pervez Musharraf extended cordial invitations to President Hu Jintao and Premier Wen Jiabao to pay visits to Pakistan at their convenience. The invitations have been warmly accepted. President Pervez Musharraf expressed his appreciation to the Government and the people of the People's Republic of China for their warm and friendly hospitality accorded to him and his delegation.

Done in duplicate at Beijing on November 3, 2003 in the Chinese and English languages, both texts being equally valid.

(Hu Jintao) President of the People's Republic of China

(Pervez Musharraf) President of the Islamic Republic of Pakistan

(Xinhua News Agency November 5, 2003)

❮73❯

The "Agreement on Political Process" signed by the Iraqi Governing Council (IGC) and the Coalition Provisional Authority (CPA) in Baghdad (15.11.03)

The IGC and CPA decided to agree on a "fundamental law" by February 28, 2004 that would lay down the timetable leading to an elected government and principles to be followed until a full constitution is drawn up. After the Transitional National Assembly chosen by 31st May 2004 elects an executive and appoints ministers to make up a Transitional Administration by 30th June 2004, the CPA will disband. A constitution will be drawn up by a constitutional convention that will be elected by the people by 15th March 2005 followed by election for an Iraqi Government by 21st December 2005.

Summary

- The IGC and the CPA will agree on a " fundamental law" laying down the time-table leading to an elected government and principles to be followed until a full Constitution is drawn up. These principles will include provisions for human rights, a federal structure for Iraq and civilian control of the armed forces.

  The fundamental law will be agreed by 28 February 2004.
- There will also be a security Agreement between the IGC and the CPa on the continued presence of coalition armed forces. These will have "wide latitude" to Provide for the safety and security of the Iraqi people."
- After the fundamental law is agreed, a National Committee of selected Iraqis will organise Caucuses, that is meetings of selected delegates, in the 18 governorates around the country.
- These caucuses will choose members of a Transitional National Assembly by 31 May 2004.
- The Assembly will elect an executive and appoint ministers. These will make up the Transitional Administration to be formed by 30 June, 2004. It will assume sovereign powers and the CPA will be disband.
- A Constitutional Convention will be elected directly by the people by 15 March 2005.

- A Constitution will be drawn up by the convention and put to a referendum.
- Elections for an Iraqi government will be held by 31 December 2005 on the basis on the new Constitution.

The Full Text Agreement on Political Process

1. The Fundamental Law

To be drafted by the Governing Council, in close consultation with the CPA. Will be approved by both the GC and CPA, and will formally set forth the scope and structure of the sovereign Iraqi transitional administration.

1. Elements of the Fundamental Law:

Bill of rights, to include freedom of speech, legislature, religion; statement of equal rights of all Iraqis, regardless of gender, sect, and ethnicity; and guarantees of due process.

Federal arrangement for Iraq, to include governorates and the separation and specification of powers to be exercised by central and local entities.

Statement of the independence of the judiciary, and a mechanism for judicial review.

Statement of civilian political control over Iraqi armed and security forces.

Statement that Fundamental Law cannot be amended.

An expiration date for Fundamental Law.

Time-table for drafting of Iraq's permanent constitution by a body directly elected by the Iraqi people; for ratifying the permanent Constitution; and for holding elections under the new Constitution.

Drafting and approval of Fundamental Law to be complete by February 28, 2004.

2. Agreements with Coalition on Security

To be agreed between the CPA and the GC.

Security Agreements to cover status of Coalition forces in Iraq, giving wide latitude to provide for the safety and security of the Iraqi people.

Approval of bilateral Agreements complete by the end of March 2004.

3. Selection of Transitional National Assembly

Fundamental Law will specify the bodies of the national structure, and will ultimately spell out the process by which individuals will be selected for these bodies. However, certain guidelines must be agreed in advance.

The transitional assembly will not be an expansion of the GC. The GC will have no formal role in selecting members of the assembly, and will dissolve upon the establishment and recognition of the transitional administration. Individual members of the GC will, however, be eligible to serve in the transitional assembly, if elected according to the process below.

Election of members of the Transitional National Assembly will be conducted through a transparent, participatory, democratic process of caucuses in each of Iraq's 18 governorates.

In each governorate, the CPA will supervise a process by which an Organizing Committee of Iraqis will be formed. This Organizing Committee will include 5 individuals appointed by the Governing Council, 5 individuals appointed by the Provincial Council, and 1 individual appointed by the local council of the five largest cities within the governorate.

The purpose of the Organizing Committee will be to convene a Governorate Selection Caucus of notables from around the governorate. To do so, it will solicit nominations from political parties, provincial/local councils, professional and civic associations, university faculties, tribal and religious groups. Nominees must meet the criteria set out for candidates in the Fundamental Law. To be selected as a member of the Governorate Selection Caucus, any nominee will need to be approved by an 11/15 majority of the Organizing Committee.

Each Governorate Selection Caucus will elect representatives to represent the governorate in the new transitional assembly based on the governorate's percentage of Iraq's population.

The Transitional National Assembly will be elected no later than May 31, 2004.

4. **Restoration of Iraq's Sovereignty**

Following the selection of members of the transitional assembly, it will meet to elect an executive branch, and to appoint Ministers.

By June 30, 2004 the new transitional administration will be recognized by the Coalition, and will assume full sovereign powers for governing Iraq. The CPA will dissolve.

5. **Process for Adoption of Permanent Constitution**

The Constitutional process and timeline will ultimately be included in the Fundamental Law, but need to be agreed in advance, as detailed below.

A permanent Constitution for Iraq will be prepared by a constitutional convention directly elected by the Iraqi people.

Elections for the convention will be held no later than March 15, 2005.

A draft of the Constitution will be circulated for public comment and debate.

A final draft of the Constitution will be presented to the public, and a popular referendum will be held to ratify the Constitution.

Elections for a new Iraqi government will be held by December 31, 2005, at which point the Fundamental Law will expire and a new government will take power.

‹74›

International Atomic Energy Agency Resolution on Iran regarding Implementation of the NPT Safeguards Agreement (26.11.03)

The Resolution welcomed Iran's decision to "voluntarily suspend all enrichment related and reprocessing activities" and noted with satisfaction Iran's decision "to conclude an Additional Protocol to its Safeguards Agreement". It reiterated that the "urgent, full and close cooperation with the Agency of all third countries is essential" in the clarification of outstanding questions concerning Iran's nuclear programme.

The Board of Governors,

(a) Recalling the Resolution adopted by the Board on 12 September 2003 (GOV/2003/69), in which the Board, inter alia:

- expressed concern over failures by the Islamic Republic of Iran to report material, facilities and activities that Iran is obliged to report pursuant to its Safeguards Agreement;
- decided it was essential and urgent, in order to ensure IAEA verification of non-diversion of nuclear material, that Iran remedy all failures identified by the Agency and cooperate fully with the Agency by taking all necessary actions by the end of October 2003;
- requested Iran to work with the Secretariat to promptly and unconditionally sign, ratify and fully implement the Additional Protocol, and, as a confidence-building measure, to act thenceforth in accordance with the Additional Protocol; and
- called on Iran to suspend all further uranium enrichment-related activities, including the further introduction of nuclear material into Natanz, and any re-processing activities,

(b) Welcoming the Agreed Statement between the Foreign Ministers of France, Germany and the United Kingdom and the Secretary of the Iranian Supreme National Security Council issued in Tehran on 21 October,

(c) Noting with appreciation the Director General's report of 10 November 2003 (GOV/2003/75), on the implementation of safeguards in Iran,

(d) Commending the Director General and the Secretariat for their professional and impartial efforts to implement the Safeguards Agreement with Iran and to resolve all outstanding safeguards issues in Iran, in pursuance of the Agency's mandate and of the implementation, inter alia,of the Resolution adopted by the Board on 12 September 2003 (GOV/2003/69),

(e) Acknowledging that Vice-President Aghazadeh of the Islamic Republic of Iran has re-affirmed his country's decision to provide a full picture of its nuclear activities and has also re-affirmed his country's decision to implement a policy of cooperation and full transparency,

(f) Noting with deep concern that Iran has failed in a number of instances over an extended period of time to meet its obligations under its Safeguards Agreement with respect to the reporting of nuclear material, and its processing and use, as well as the declaration of facilities where such material has been processed and stored, as set out in paragraph 48 of the Director General's report,

(g) Noting in particular, with the gravest concern, that Iran enriched uranium and separated plutonium in undeclared facilities, in the absence of IAEA safeguards,

(h) Noting also, with equal concern, that there has been in the past a pattern of concealment resulting in breaches of safeguard obligations and that the new information disclosed by Iran and reported by the Director General includes much more that is contradictory to information previously provided by Iran,

(i) Noting that the Director General, in his opening statement, indicated that Iran has begun cooperating more actively with the IAEA and has given assurances that it is committed to a policy of full disclosure,

(j) Recognising that, in addition to the corrective actions already taken, Iran has undertaken to present all nuclear material for Agency verification during its forthcoming inspections,

(k) Emphasising that, in order to restore confidence, Iranian cooperation and transparency will need to be complete and sustained so that the Agency can resolve all outstanding issues and, over time, provide and maintain the assurances required by Member States,

(l) Noting with satisfaction that Iran has indicated that it is prepared to sign the Additional Protocol, and that, pending its entry into force, Iran will act in accordance with the provisions of that Protocol,

(m) Noting that the Director General, in his opening statement, reported that Iran has decided to suspend enrichment-related and reprocessing activities,

(n) Stressing that the voluntary suspension by Iran of all its uranium enrichment-related activities and reprocessing activities remains of key importance to rebuilding international confidence,

(o) Recognising the inalienable right of States to the development and practical application of atomic energy for peaceful purposes, including the production of electric power, with due consideration for the needs of developing countries,

(p) Stressing the need for effective safeguards in order to prevent the use of nuclear material for prohibited purposes in contravention of safeguards Agreements, and underlining the vital importance of effective safeguards for facilitating cooperation in the field of peaceful uses of nuclear energy,

1. Welcomes Iran's offer of active cooperation and openness and its positive response to the demands of the Board in the resolution adopted by Governors on 12 September 2003 (GOV/2003/69) and underlines that, in proceeding, the Board considers it essential that the declarations that have now been made by Iran amount to the correct, complete and final picture of Iran's past and present nuclear programme, to be verified by the Agency;
2. Strongly deplores Iran's past failures and breaches of its obligation to comply with the provisions of its Safeguards Agreement, as reported by the Director General; and urges Iran to adhere strictly to its obligations under its Safeguards Agreement in both letter and spirit;
3. Notes the statement by the Director General that Iran has taken the specific actions deemed essential and urgent and requested of it in paragraph 4 of the Resolution adopted by the Board on 12 September 2003 (GOV/2003/69);
4. Requests the Director General to take all steps necessary to confirm that the information provided by Iran on its past and present nuclear activities is correct and complete as well as to resolve such issues as remain outstanding;
5. Endorses the view of the Director General that, to achieve this, the Agency must have a particularly robust verification system in place: an Additional Protocol, coupled with a policy of full transparency and openness on the part of Iran, is indispensable;
6. Reiterates that the urgent, full and close cooperation with the Agency of all third countries is essential in the clarification of outstanding questions concerning Iran's nuclear programme;
7. Calls on Iran to undertake and complete the taking of all necessary corrective measures on an urgent basis, to sustain full co-operation with the Agency in implementing Iran's commitment to full disclosure and unrestricted access, and thus to provide the transparency and openness that are indispensable for the

Agency to complete the considerable work necessary to provide and maintain the assurances required by Member States;

8. Decides that, should any further serious Iranian failures come to light, the Board of Governors would meet immediately to consider, in the light of the circumstances and of advice from the Director General, all options at its disposal, in accordance with the IAEA Statute and Iran's Safeguards Agreement;
9. Notes with satisfaction the decision of Iran to conclude an Additional Protocol to its Safeguards Agreement, and re-emphasises the importance of Iran moving swiftly to ratification and also of Iran acting as if the Protocol were in force in the interim, including by making all declarations required within the required timeframe;
10. Welcomes Iran's decision voluntarily to suspend all enrichment-related and reprocessing activities and requests Iran to adhere to it, in a complete and verifiable manner; and also endorses the Director General's acceptance of Iran's invitation to verify implementation of that decision and report thereon;
11. Requests the Director General to submit a comprehensive report on the implementation of this resolution by mid- February 2004, for consideration by the March Board of Governors, or to report earlier if appropriate; and
12. Decides to remain seized of the matter.

❮75❯

Executive Summary of US National Strategy to Secure Cyberspace

Identifying "public-private engagement as a key component of its strategy to secure cyberspace", the document articulated five national priorities including: a national cyberspace security response system; a national security threat and vulnerability reduction programme; a national awareness and training programme; securing government's cyberspace; and international cooperation.

Our Nation's critical infrastructures are composed of public and private institutions in the sectors of agriculture, food, water, public health, emergency services, government, defense industrial base, information and telecommunications, energy, transportation, banking and finance, chemicals and hazardous materials, and postal and shipping.Cyberspace is their nervous system—the control system of our country.

Cyberspace is composed of hundreds of thousands of interconnected computers, servers, routers, switches, and fiber optic cables that allow our critical infrastructures to work. Thus, the healthy functioning of cyberspace is essential to our economy and our national security.

This *National Strategy to Secure Cyberspace* is part of our overall effort to protect the Nation. It is an implementing component of the *National Strategy for Homeland Security* and is complemented by a *National Strategy for the* Physical Protection of Critical Infrastructures and *Key Assets*. The purpose of this document is to engage and empower Americans to secure the portions of cyberspace that they own, operate, control, or with which they interact. Securing cyberspace is a difficult strategic challenge that requires coordinated and focused effort from our entire society—the Federal Government, State and Local Governments, the Private Sector, and the American people.

The *National Strategy to Secure Cyberspace* outlines an initial framework for both organizing and prioritizing efforts. It provides direction to the Federal Government Departments and Agencies that have roles in cyberspace security. It also identifies steps that state and local governments, private companies and organizations, and individual Americans can take to improve our collective cybersecurity. The *Strategy* highlights the role of public-private engagement. The document provides a framework for the contributions that we all can make to secure our parts of cyberspace. The dynamics of cyberspace will require adjustments and amendments to the *Strategy* over time. The speed and anonymity of cyber attacks makes distinguishing among the actions of terrorists, criminals, and nation states difficult, a task which often occurs only after the fact, if at all. Therefore, the *National Strategy to Secure Cyberspace* helps reduce our Nation's vulnerability to debilitating attacks against our critical information infrastructures or the physical assets that support them.

Strategic Objectives

Consistent with the *National Strategy for Homeland Security*, the strategic objectives of this *National Strategy to Secure Cyberspace* are to:

- Prevent cyber attacks against America's critical infrastructures;
- Reduce national vulnerability to cyber attacks; and
- Minimize damage and recovery time from cyber attacks that do occur.

Threat and Vulnerability

Our economy and national security are fully dependent upon information technology and the information infrastructure. At the core of the information infrastructure upon which we depend is the Internet, a system originally designed to share unclassified research among scientists who were assumed to be uninterested in abusing the network. It is that same Internet that today connects millions of other computer networks making most of the nation's essential services and infrastructures work. These computer networks also control physical objects such as electrical transformers, trains, pipeline pumps, chemical vats, radars, and stock markets, all of which exist beyond cyberspace.

A spectrum of malicious actors can and do conduct attacks against our critical information infrastructures. Of primary concern is the threat of organized cyber attacks capable of causing debilitating disruption to our Nation's critical infrastructures, economy, or national security. The required technical sophistication to carry out such an attack is high—and partially explains the lack of a debilitating attack to date. We should not, however, be too sanguine. There have been instances where organized attackers have exploited vulnerabilities that may be indicative of more destructive capabilities.

Uncertainties exist as to the intent and full technical capabilities of several observed attacks. Enhanced cyber threat analysis is needed to address long-term trends related to threats and vulnerabilities. What is known is that the attack tools and methodologies are becoming widely available, and the technical capability and sophistication of users bent on causing havoc or disruption is improving.

In peacetime, America's enemies may conduct espionage on our Government, university research centers, and private companies. They may also seek to prepare for cyber strikes during a confrontation by mapping U.S. information systems, identifying key targets, and lacing our infrastructure with back doors and other means of access. In wartime or crisis, adversaries may seek to intimidate the Nation's political leaders by attacking critical infrastructures and key economic functions or eroding public confidence in information systems.

Cyber attacks on United States Information networks can have serious consequences such as disrupting critical operations, causing loss of revenue and intellectual property, or loss of life. Countering such attacks requires the development of robust capabilities where they do not exist today if we are to reduce vulnerabilities and deter those with the capabilities and intent to harm our critical infrastructures.

The Government Role in Securing Cyberspace

In general, the private sector is best equipped and structured to respond to an evolving cyber threat. There are specific instances, however, where Federal Government response is most appropriate and justified. Looking inward, providing continuity of government requires ensuring the safety of its own cyber infrastructure and those assets required for supporting its essential missions and services. Externally, a government's role in cybersecurity is warranted in cases where high transaction costs or legal barriers lead to significant co-ordination problems; cases in which governments operate in the absence of private sector forces; resolution of incentive problems that lead to under provisioning of critical shared resources; and raising awareness.

Public-private engagement is a key component of our Strategy to secure cyberspace. This is true for several reasons. Public-private partnerships can usefully confront co-ordination problems. They can significantly enhance information exchange and cooperation. Public-private engagement will take a variety of forms and will address awareness, training, technological improvements, vulnerability remediation, and recovery operations.

A federal role in these and other cases is only justified when the benefits of intervention outweigh the associated costs. This standard is especially important in cases where there are viable private sector solutions for addressing any potential threat or vulnerability. For each case, consideration should be given to the broadbased costs and impacts of a given government action, versus other alternative actions, versus non-action, taking into account any existing or future private solutions.

Federal actions to secure cyberspace are warranted for purposes including: forensics and attack attribution, protection of networks and systems critical to national security, indications and warnings, and protection against organized attacks capable of inflicting debilitating damage to the economy. Federal activities should also support research and technology development that will enable the private sector to better secure privately-owned portions of the Nation's critical infrastructure.

Department of Homeland Security and Cyberspace Security

On November 25, 2002, President Bush signed legislation creating the Department of Homeland Security (DHS). This new cabinetlevel department will unite 22 federal entities for the common purpose of improving our homeland security. The Secretary of DHS will have important responsibilities in cyberspace security. These responsibilities include:

- Developing a comprehensive national plan for securing the key resources and critical infrastructure of the United States;
- Providing crisis management in response to attacks on critical information systems;
- Providing technical assistance to the private sector and other government entities with respect to emergency recovery plans for failures of critical information systems;
- Co-ordinating with other agencies of the federal government to provide specific warning information and advice about appropriate protective measures and counter-measures to state, local, and non-governmental organizations including the private sector, academia, and the public; and
- Performing and funding research and development along with other agencies that will lead to new scientific understanding and technologies in support of homeland security.

Consistent with these responsibilities, DHS will become a federal center of excellence for cybersecurity and provide a focal point for federal outreach to State, Local, and non-governmental organizations including the private sector, academia, and the public.

Critical Priorities for Cyberspace Security

The *National Strategy to Secure Cyberspace* articulates five national priorities including:

I. A National Cyberspace Security Response System;

II. A National Cyberspace Security Threat and Vulnerability Reduction Program;

III. A National Cyberspace Security Awareness and Training Program;

IV. Securing Governments' Cyberspace; and

V. National Security and International Cyberspace Security Cooperation.

The first priority focuses on improving our response to cyber incidents and reducing the potential damage from such events. The second, third, and fourth priorities aim to reduce threats from, and our vulnerabilities to, cyber attacks. The fifth priority is to prevent cyber attacks that could impact national security assets and to improve the international management of and response to such attacks.

Priority I: A National Cyberspace Security Response System

Rapid identification, information exchange, and remediation can often mitigate the damage caused by malicious cyberspace activity. For those activities to be effective at a national level, the United States needs a partnership between Government and Industry to perform analyses, issue warnings, and coordinate response efforts. Privacy and civil liberties must be protected in the process. Because no cyber-security plan can be impervious to concerted and intelligent attack, information systems must be able to operate while under attack and have the resilience to restore full operations quickly.

The *National Strategy to Secure Cyberspace* identifies eight major actions and initiatives for cyberspace security response:

1. Establish a public-private architecture for responding to national-level cyber incidents;
2. Provide for the development of tactical and strategic analysis of cyber attacks and vulnerability assessments;
3. Encourage the development of a private sector capability to share a synoptic view of the health of cyberspace;
4. Expand the Cyber Warning and Information Network to support the role of DHS in co-ordinating crisis management for cyberspace security;
5. Improve national incident management;
6. Co-ordinate processes for voluntary participation in the development of national public-private continuity and contingency plans;
7. Exercise cybersecurity continuity plans for federal systems; and
8. Improve and enhance public-private information sharing involving cyber attacks, threats, and vulnerabilities.

Priority II: A National Cyberspace Security Threat and Vulnerability Reduction Program

By exploiting vulnerabilities in our cyber systems, an organized attack may endanger the security of our Nation's critical infrastructures. The vulnerabilities that most threaten cyberspace occur in the information assets of critical infrastructure enterprises themselves and their external supporting structures, such as the mechanisms of the Internet. Lesser-secured sites on the interconnected network of networks also present potentially significant exposures to cyber attacks. Vulnerabilities result from weaknesses in technology and because of improper implementation and oversight of technological products.

The *National Strategy to Secure Cyberspace* identifies eight major actions and initiatives to reduce threats and related vulnerabilities:

1. Enhance law enforcement's capabilities for preventing and prosecuting cyberspace attacks;
2. Create a process for national vulnerability assessments to better understand the potential consequences of threats and vulnerabilities;
3. Secure the mechanisms of the Internet by improving protocols and routing;
4. Foster the use of trusted digital control systems/supervisory control and data acquisition systems;
5. Reduce and re-mediate software vulnerabilities;

6. Understand infrastructure interdependencies and improve the physical security of cyber systems and telecommunications;
7. Prioritize federal cybersecurity research and development agendas; and
8. Assess and secure emerging systems.

Priority III: A National Cyberspace Security Awareness and Training Program

Many cyber vulnerabilities exist because of a lack of cyber-security awareness on the part of computer users, systems administrators, technology developers, procurement officials, auditors, Chief Information Officers (CIOs), chief executive officers, and corporate boards. Such awareness-based vulnerabilities present serious risks to critical infrastructures regardless of whether they exist within the infrastructure itself. A lack of trained personnel and the absence of widely accepted, multi-level certification programs for cybersecurity professionals complicate the task of addressing cyber vulnerabilities.

The *National Strategy to Secure Cyberspace* identifies four major actions and initiatives for awareness, education, and training:

1. Promote a comprehensive national awareness program to empower all Americans—businesses, the general workforce, and the general population— to secure their own parts of cyberspace;
2. Foster adequate training and education programs to support the Nation's cybersecurity needs;
3. Increase the efficiency of existing federal cybersecurity training programs; and
4. Promote private-sector support for well co-ordinated, widely recognized professional cybersecurity certifications.

Priority IV: Securing Governments' Cyberspace

Although governments administer only a minority of the Nation's critical infrastructure computer systems, governments at all levels perform essential services in the agriculture, food, water, public health, emergency services, defense, social welfare, information and telecommunications, energy, transportation, banking and finance, chemicals, and postal and shipping sectors that depend upon cyberspace for their delivery. Governments can lead by example in cyberspace security, including fostering a market-place for more secure technologies through their procurement.

The *National Strategy to Secure Cyberspace* identifies five major actions and initiatives for the securing of governments' cyberspace:

1. Continuously assess threats and vulnerabilities to federal cyber systems;
2. Authenticate and maintain authorized users of federal cyber systems;
3. Secure federal wireless local area networks;

4. Improve security in government outsourcing and procurement; and
5. Encourage state and local governments to consider establishing information technology security programs and participate in information sharing and analysis centers with similar governments.

Priority V: National Security and International Cyberspace Security Cooperation

America's cyberspace links the United States to the rest of the world. A network of networks spans the planet, allowing malicious actors on one continent to act on systems thousands of miles away. Cyber attacks cross borders at light speed, and discerning the source of malicious activity is difficult. America must be capable of safeguarding and defending its critical systems and networks. Enabling our ability to do so requires a system of international cooperation to facilitate information sharing, reduce vulnerabilities, and deter malicious actors.

The *National Strategy to Secure Cyberspace* identifies six major actions and initiatives to strengthen U.S. national security and international co-operation:

1. Strengthen cyber-related counter-Intelligence efforts;
2. Improve capabilities for attack attribution and response;
3. Improve co-ordination for responding to cyber attacks within the U.S. national security community;
4. Work with industry and through international organizations to facilitate dialogue and partnerships among international public and private sectors focused on protecting information infrastructures and promoting a global "culture of security;"
5. Foster the establishment of national and international watch-and-warning networks to detect and prevent cyber attacks as they emerge; and
6. Encourage other nations to accede to the Council of Europe Convention on Cybercrime, or to ensure that their laws and procedures are at least as comprehensive.

A National Effort

Protecting the widely distributed assets of cyberspace requires the efforts of many Americans. The federal government alone cannot sufficiently defend America's cyberspace. Our traditions of federalism and limited government require that organizations outside the Federal Government take the lead in many of these efforts. Every American who can contribute to securing part of cyberspace is encouraged to do so. The federal government invites the creation of, and participation in, public-private partnerships to raise cybersecurity awareness, train personnel, stimulate market forces, improve technology, identify and remediate vulnerabilities, exchange information, and plan recovery operations.

People and organizations across the United States have already taken steps to improve cyberspace security. On September 18, 2002, many private-sector entities released plans and strategies for securing their respective infrastructures. The Partnership for Critical Infrastructure Security has played a unique role in facilitating private-sector contributions to this Strategy. Inputs from the critical sector's themselves can be found at http://www.pcis.org. (These documents were not subject to government approval.)

These comprehensive infrastructure plans describe the strategic initiatives of various sectors, including:

- Banking and Finance;
- Insurance;
- Chemical;
- Oil and Gas;
- Electric;
- Law Enforcement;
- Higher Education;
- Transportation (Rail);
- Information Technology and Telecommunications; and
- Water.

As each of the critical infrastructure sectors implements these initiatives, threats and vulnerabilities to our infrastructures will be reduced.

For the foreseeable future two things will be true: America will rely upon cyberspace and the Federal Government will seek a continuing broad partnership with the private sector to develop, implement, and refine a *National Strategy to Secure Cyberspace*.

❮76❯

Abuja Communique of the Commonwealth Heads of Government (08.12.03)

> The Commonwealth Heads of Government welcomed the continuing progress in growth of democratic institutions in Pakistan and hoped that "negotiations between the Government and the political parties on the outstanding issues in the Legal Framework Orders (LFO) would be concluded successfully...thus leading to the full restoration of democracy and enabling the lifting of Pakistan's suspension from the Council of Commonwealth."

Commonwealth Heads of Government met in Abuja, from 5-8 December 2003, at the invitation of President Olusegun Obasanjo of Nigeria, the host Head of Government and Chairman of CHOGM. Of the 51 countries that attended the Meeting, 38 were represented by their Heads of State or Government.

2. The Opening Ceremony of the Meeting included an address by Her Majesty Queen Elizabeth II, Head of the Commonwealth.
3. Heads of Government conveyed their deep appreciation to the Government and people of Nigeria for the warm hospitality extended to them and for the excellent arrangements made for the Meeting. They also congratulated President Obasanjo for his leadership in chairing their Meeting.
4. Heads of Government welcomed the new Heads of Government who attended CHOGM for the first time.
5. Heads of Government received the Report of the Expert Group on Development and Democracy and the Report of the Secretary-General, which complemented the CHOGM Theme: "Development and Democracy: Partnership for Peace and Prosperity".
6. Heads of Government adopted the Aso Rock Declaration on the CHOGM Theme and also issued the Aso Rock Statement on Multilateral Trade, which is attached to the Declaration.

Fundamental Political Values

7. Heads of Government re-affirmed their commitment to the fundamental political values of the Commonwealth as set out in the Singapore and Harare Declarations and subsequent CHOGM Communiqués, and

reinforced by the Millbrook Action Programme. They reiterated their commitment to non-racism, international peace and security, democracy, good governance, human rights, rule of law, the independence of the judiciary, freedom of expression, and a political culture that promotes transparency, accountability and economic development.

8. Heads of Government endorsed the recommendations of their Law Ministers on Commonwealth Principles on the accountability of and relationship between the three branches of Government. They acknowledged that judicial independence and delivery of efficient justice services were important for maintaining the balance of power between the Executive, Legislature and Judiciary.

9. Heads of Government expressed their full support for the good office role of the Secretary-General in conflict prevention and resolution, and post-conflict reconstruction and development. They also expressed their continuing support for the Commonwealth Secretariat's work for strengthening democratic institutions, processes and culture. They acknowledged the value of election observation, provision of technical assistance and training and other activities. They welcomed the Secretariat's collaboration with the Commonwealth Parliamentary Association, the Commonwealth Local Government Forum and other relevant organizations to promote best democratic practice.

Commonwealth Ministerial Action Group on the Harare Declaration (CMAG)

10. Heads of Government received the Report of the Commonwealth Ministerial Action Group on the Harare Declaration (CMAG) covering its deliberations in the period since the Coolum Commonwealth Heads of Government Meeting in 2002 and approved its recommendations in regard to Fiji Islands, Pakistan, Solomon Islands and Zimbabwe.

11. Heads of Government welcomed the commitment of the Government of Fiji Islands to abide by the decision of the Fiji Supreme Court on the constitutionality of the formation of Government and in this context looked forward to the Court's Session scheduled for May 2004. They requested the Secretary-General to continue to monitor the situation in Fiji Islands and provide appropriate technical assistance, as required, in pursuance of his good offices role.

12. Heads of Government welcomed the continuing progress in the development and growth of democratic institutions in Pakistan, as evident by the election of the National Assembly, the Senate and Provincial Assemblies, and the formation of Democratic Governments at the National and Provincial levels. They also welcomed the positive measures taken for women's representation in Parliament, the

representation of minorities and the determination to enhance public accountability and to end corruption. They noted that the outstanding issues in the Legal Framework Orders (LFOs) were an obstacle to Pakistan's full return to democracy.

13. Heads of Government hoped that the negotiations between the Government and the political parties on the outstanding issues in the LFOs would be concluded successfully in the spirit of Commonwealth Parliamentary practice and process and a comprehensive package would be passed in Parliament in accordance with the Constitution, thus leading to the full restoration of democracy and enabling the lifting of Pakistan's suspension from the Councils of the Commonwealth. They requested the Secretary-General to continue to monitor developments and provide technical assistance, as might be required, to strengthen democratic institutions.

14. Heads of Government endorsed CMAG's decision to remove Solomon Islands from its agenda but continue to receive Reports from the Secretary-General on developments in that country.

15. Heads of Government re-constituted the membership of CMAG for the next biennium as follows: The Bahamas, Canada, India, Lesotho, Malta, Samoa, Sri Lanka and Tanzania. They further agreed that Nigeria would continue to be a member of CMAG in its capacity as the representative of the Chairperson in Office, as its ninth member.

Zimbabwe

16. Heads of Government adopted a CHOGM Statement on Zimbabwe on 7 December 2003, which is attached.

Belize

17. Heads of Government welcomed the Agreement to establish a Transition Process and Confidence-Building Measures of February 2003, signed by Belize, Guatemala and the Organisation of American States (OAS). They called on all parties involved to honour their commitments under the Agreement, in particular taking the proposals for a just and definitive resolution of the territorial dispute to popular referenda in both countries.

18. Heads of Government reiterated their full support for the sovereignty and territorial integrity of Belize. They commended the Group of Friends of the Process and expressed appreciation for the constructive role played by the OAS in facilitating a peaceful settlement of the dispute. They noted that the proposals for a final settlement contain a provision for the establishment of a development fund to be used for the benefit of both countries and urged member States to contribute to it generously.

19. They mandated the Secretary-General to convene the Ministerial Committee on Belize whenever necessary.

Cyprus

20. Heads of Government welcomed the signing by the Republic of Cyprus of the Accession Treaty to the European Union on 16 April, 2003 and expressed the wish that a solution of the Cyprus problem would be found before 1 May 2004 that would allow a re-united Cyprus to become a member of the European Union.
21. Heads of Government re-affirmed their support for the independence, sovereignty, unity and territorial integrity of Cyprus.
22. They regretted that the latest effort of the United Nations Secretary-General under his mission of Good Offices in Cyprus collapsed at The Hague meeting on 10 March 2003 due to the negative approach taken by the Turkish Cypriot leader.
23. They further regretted that the Turkish Cypriot leader continues to maintain the same negative approach, thus hindering the resumption of negotiations based on the Annan Plan.
24. Recalling and re-affirming previous UN Security Council Resolutions and re-affirming their previous Communiqués on Cyprus, Heads of Government called upon all parties concerned and in particular Turkey and the Turkish Cypriot leadership to cooperate fully with the UN Secretary-General so as to enable the early resumption of substantive negotiations based on the UN Secretary-General's proposals, aimed at the conclusion of a just, lasting and functional settlement consistent with relevant UN Security Council Resolutions.

Guyana

25. Heads of Government re-affirmed their support for the maintenance by Guyana of its territorial integrity and sovereignty and the unimpeded development by Guyana of the natural resources of its entire territory. They noted that the Commonwealth Ministerial Group on Guyana met in September 2003 and recognised the important role of this Group in support of Guyana.
26. Heads of Government expressed satisfaction at the recent meeting between the Foreign Ministers of Guyana and Venezuela with the UN Secretary-General noting that it was a positive indication of the continued commitment by both Guyana and Venezuela to discussions under the aegis of the UN Secretary-General aimed at the peaceful solution of the controversy.

Small Arms and Light Weapons

27. Heads of Government expressed concern at the continued de-stabilising accumulation and proliferation of small arms, ammunition and light

weapons, which had contributed to the intensity and duration of armed conflicts as well as to international terrorism. They noted that many Commonwealth Governments were adversely affected by the uncontrolled flow and misuse of these lethal weapons. They expressed concern that the spread of small arms threatens national, regional and global security and impedes basic social and economic development. They also noted that the challenge posed by the proliferation of small arms involves security, humanitarian, health and development dimensions.

28. Heads of Government supported the adoption of the United Nations Programme of Action on the Illicit Trade in Small Arms and Light Weapons in all its Aspects that emerged from the 2001 UN Conference on Small Arms. They urged member States to support further implementation of the programme at the International, State and Regional levels to curb and prevent their illicit production, trafficking and misuse.

Landmines

29. Heads of Government recalled the progress made in addressing the global landmines problem through the Comprehensive Framework for Mine Action provided by the Ottawa Convention on the Prohibition of the Use, Stockpiling, Production and Transfer of Anti-Personnel Mines and on their destruction. They urged all countries that are in position to do so to accede to the Convention.

International Criminal Court

30. Heads of Government of those member countries that have ratified the Rome Statute establishing the International Criminal Court (ICC) urged other States, which have not yet done so, to accede to the Rome Statute in a timely manner.

Terrorism

31. Heads of Government received the Report of the Commonwealth Committee on Terrorism (CCT) and endorsed its recommendations. They recalled their Statement on Terrorism of 25 October, 2001 and reiterated their strong condemnation of all acts of terrorism, with the consequent tragic loss of human life and damage to political, economic and social stability. They emphasised that terrorism can never be justified and continues to constitute a threat to all countries and peoples, irrespective of religion, nationality, tradition or ideology. They agreed that the war against terrorism cannot be won by military force and that comprehensive measures against terrorism require building bridges within and across communities of diverse faiths and cultures as well as addressing economic and social disparities and injustice.

They agreed that the Commonwealth is ideally positioned to encourage activities to address these issues.

32. Heads of Government decided to work together as a diverse community of nations to individually and collectively take concerted and resolute action to eradicate terrorism.

33. They called upon member States to increase cooperation and assistance through consultation, information sharing, training and capacity building in counter-terrorism activities and to implement measures to prevent the financing of terrorist acts. They also called upon member States to support the early conclusion of the Comprehensive Convention Against International Terrorism.

34. Heads of Government encouraged all member Governments to continue to follow steps outlined in the Commonwealth Plan of Action and to implement the UNSCR 1373. In this context, they also commended the work of the Commonwealth Secretariat in assisting member countries. They agreed that the CCT be maintained as a Standing Committee, which could be convened by the Secretary-General or at the request of member Governments, as and when required.

35. Heads of Government recognized that travel advisories associated with the threat of terrorism have a negative impact on the economies of a number of member States, including the loss of tourism revenue and the burden of increased costs of implementing new security measures. Noting that national travel advisories are issued by certain countries for the protection of their citizens, they urged that the information about the perceived threat should be conveyed in advance to the countries concerned and in cooperation with them, measures should be taken to counteract the threat of terrorism. They noted that those countries which issue such advisories indicate that it is not always possible to consult in advance.

World Economic Situation

36. Heads of Government noted that the global economic recovery continues to be fragile and subject to many risks. In view of the fact that one-third of the Commonwealth's nearly 2 billion people live on less than US$1 per day and nearly two-thirds on under US$2 per day, they stressed that a concerted effort is required for sustainable broadbased growth in all areas to enable countries to achieve the Millennium Development Goals (MDGs) and cope with the challenges of poverty reduction and investment in human development. They underlined the importance of nationally owned poverty reduction strategies and urged that policy action in developing countries be matched by developed countries providing more effective development assistance.

37. In order to support the necessary monitoring of progress and removing impediments to the achievement of the MDGs, Heads of Government stressed the need for action to implement all the elements of the Monterrey Consensus and the related Commonwealth Action Plan, as well as the need to examine constructively all proposals for securing a further increase in aid commitments. In particular, Heads of Government welcomed further elaboration of the initiative for an International Finance Facility (IFF) and looked forward to the consideration of this or other similar options.

38. Heads of Government called for the timely implementation of the Brussels Programme of Action for the Least Developed Countries (LDCs) for the Decade 2001-2010 adopted at the Third UN Conference on LDCs in May 2001.

Multilateral Trade Issues

39. Heads of Government re-affirmed their commitment to a transparent, rules-based multilateral trading system and called for an immediate resumption of the WTO multilateral trade negotiations. They urged all parties to show the flexibility and political will necessary to achieve positive results in the areas of agriculture, non-agricultural market access, special and differential treatment and all other areas mandated in the Doha Development Agenda. They reiterated the need to build up the capacity of developing, and particularly the least developed, small and vulnerable WTO members to negotiate more effectively and to implement their obligations within the WTO system.

Debt Relief

40. Heads of Government called on International Financial Institutions to adopt a broader and more flexible approach to debt relief designed to achieve long-term debt sustainability and release resources particularly for health and education.

41. Heads of Government re-affirmed their commitment to a successful HIPC Initiative, and recognised that some HIPCs, particularly conflict-affected countries, face a continued challenge in reaching decision-point and require a flexible approach to address their special problems. They called on all non-Paris Club creditors that are not yet participating in this initiative to do so. Heads of Government also called for topping up to be applied so that HIPCs achieve a sustainable exit from their debt burden at their completion points.

42. Heads of Government stressed that long-term debt sustainability for poor countries requires sound debt management, improved market access, more financing in the form of grants and consideration of new arrangements for concessionary contingency finance.

Investment

43. Heads of Government stressed the importance of developing the capacity to produce internationally competitive goods and services to take advantage of the opportunities generated by globalisation. They recognised the importance of private capital flows in promoting the development of such capacity and expressed disappointment at the difficulties that poor and vulnerable economies were experiencing in attracting such flows, even when they had implemented wide ranging reform programmes. They called for innovative and cost effective ways of utilising official resources to promote private capital flows to pre-emerging markets.

44. In this connection, Heads of Government noted the progress made by the Commonwealth Secretariat in examining the feasibility of proposals to address the special difficulties faced by small, vulnerable economies and LDCs in attracting investment and welcomed the interest expressed by commercial banks, International Financial Institutions, regional development banks and other development partners in exploring more effective ways to promote domestic and foreign investment in such economies, and in developing a new "Small and Vulnerable Economies Facility", to be launched initially in the Pacific region. They called upon the Secretariat to continue to work towards developing similar cost effective facilities for other regions of the Commonwealth.

Strengthening Financial Systems

45. Heads of Government welcomed the fact that the recent meeting of the OECD Global Forum focused on the issue of a level playing field and stressed that the way forward required a satisfactory resolution of this issue. They emphasised the importance of tax and fiscal sovereignty, transparency and inclusiveness in the dialogue between OECD and international financial centres in non-OECD jurisdictions. They urged the Commonwealth to remain engaged on this issue and requested the Secretariat to support the affected jurisdictions to mobilise assistance to meet international standards, strengthen and deepen their financial sectors and diversify their economies.

Combating Corruption

46. Heads of Government welcomed the recent adoption of the United Nations Convention Against Corruption and requested member states to sign and ratify it. They noted that systemic corruption, extortion and bribery undermine good governance. They called for enhanced mutual cooperation in the repatriation of illegally acquired public funds and assets to the countries of their origin in accordance with the provisions of the Convention. International Economic Cooperation

47. Heads of Government appreciated the need for constructive dialogue and cooperation to achieve sustainable development. They welcomed the outcomes of the International Conference on Financing for Development and urged implementation and follow up to the outcomes of this Conference. New Partnership for Africa's Development (NEPAD)

48. Heads of Government re-affirmed their strong support for the New Partnership for Africa's Development (NEPAD), which was internationally accepted as a socio-economic and political framework to support the development efforts of countries in Africa. They requested the Secretariat to bring its various programmes in Africa within the NEPAD framework and strengthen its partnership with NEPAD, both in the delivery and implementation of its Action Plan for the benefit of African member countries and specifically to promote the achievement of the Millennium Development Goals.

Sustainable Development

49. Heads of Government welcomed the outcomes of the World Summit on Sustainable Development (WSSD) and pledged to work towards the full and effective implementation of Agenda 21, and the Johannesburg Plan of Implementation.

50. Heads of Government stressed that Climate Change is one of the greatest challenges facing Commonwealth member States and the wider international community. They undertook to continue efforts towards the conclusion of effective international approaches to climate change mitigation and re-affirmed Commonwealth support through technical assistance to address the adaptation concerns of small island and other States that are particularly vulnerable to global warming and sea level rise. They also supported the efforts under the Convention to Combat Desertification and the Johannesburg Plan of Implementation to address climate and drought concerns, particularly in Africa.

HIV/AIDS

51. Heads of Government highlighted the devastating impact of HIV/AIDS and the fundamental importance of confronting it in order to meet the Millennium Development Goals. They noted there were promising signs of a reduction in new cases in some countries and welcomed the political commitment and called for increased financial resources including the Global Fund to combat HIV/AIDS and other funds to combat malaria, tuberculosis and other communicable diseases.

52. Heads of Government acknowledged that many developing countries and particularly LDCs, small and vulnerable economies could not provide universal treatment to victims of HIV/AIDS without further access to concessionary financing. They also acknowledged that this goal will

only be achieved if a broad range of partners accelerate and co-ordinate their efforts, and pledge to play their role in these efforts. They welcomed the recent Agreement in the WTO on the manufacturing of life saving generic drugs in the developing countries under certain conditions and circumstances to help ensure the provision and availability of affordable drugs at low cost to poor developing countries.

53. Heads of Government re-emphasised the importance of a broad based and balanced response to HIV/AIDS integrating prevention, care and treatment and impact mitigation. They agreed that progress infighting the global HIV/AIDS pandemic requires enhanced international effort and co-ordination.

Small States

54. Heads of Government received the Report of the Ministerial Group on Small States (MGSS) and endorsed its recommendations.

55. Heads of Government reaffirmed the Doha Mandate to integrate special and differential treatment into the International Trading System. They emphasised the need for access to International Development Finance on concessionary terms to assist the sustainable development programmes of vulnerable and small States. They noted in this regard that there were also other countries that were not small States but whose proportion of world trade was similarly small and with whom small states could seek to find common cause and build partnership.

56. Heads of Government noted further that terrorism and its consequences had placed additional burdens on small States in the form of high costs of security and possible loss of tourism revenue, including the impact on their national budgets in the form of diversion of funds away from the critical areas of development. They cautioned that the current efforts in dealing with terrorism and the significant level of resources, which are being allocated to fight it should not derail their development agenda. Heads of Government, therefore, called on the international community to assist with appropriate additional resources in the context of supporting the global development agenda.

57. Heads of Government noted that small states were increasingly vulnerable to the spread of HIV/AIDS and other communicable diseases. They called on the international community to provide assistance in these areas.

58. Heads of Government stressed the importance of capacity building and its retention in critical areas such as trade-related technical assistance in small States.

59. Heads of Government noted that global warming and climate change were life threatening to small island States and other low lying areas. They confirmed their full support for the Barbados Plan of Action for

the Sustainable Development of Small Island States and looked forward to the contribution of the Commonwealth, the World Bank and other members of the UN system and other regional organisations to the preparations for the Review of Implementation of the Plan of Action to take place at the International Meeting in Mauritius in August 2004. They urged Commonwealth members and other states to prepare for and participate in this Conference.

60. Heads of Government commended the Commonwealth Secretariat for the work done on small States, particularly in implementing the recommendations of the 2000 Commonwealth Secretariat/World Bank Joint Task Force on Small States and the new Agenda for Commonwealth Work on Small states, which was endorsed by them at their last meeting in Coolum in 2002. They called on the Secretariat to continue to strengthen small States' representation in the WTO and continue its work on the OECD initiative. They also called on the Secretariat to strengthen Commonwealth's partnerships and collaboration with individual organisations and institutions to advance the small States' agenda.

61. Heads of Government stressed the importance of market access for the traditional products of small and vulnerable states to enhance their export earnings. In this context they noted the concern of South Pacific States on the economic implications of a ban on KAVA imports by some developed countries and urged that this issue be resolved expeditiously.

Role of Business

62. Heads of Government received the Report of the Commonwealth Business Council (CBC) and the Commonwealth Business Forum and noted the recommendations, particularly for establishing Business-Government Partnerships for Removing Practical Obstacles to Wealth and Job Creation – "The Abuja Manifesto" and for the CBC's Joint Action Plan for Business and Government: Enabling Corporate Citizenship for Sustainable Development.

63. Heads of Government commended the work of the CBC in mobilising investment, removing barriers to trade, promoting good corporate governance, creating a good environment for business and investment, and bridging the digital divide. They particularly welcomed the CBC initiatives for developing an investment index to contribute to significant investment flows to developing countries on a fully commercial and sustainable basis; supporting multilateral trade negotiations on the progressive liberalisation of trade in goods and services in both developed and developing countries; and establishing and developing common standards and codes of ethics for governance and accountability in Government, the private sector and civil society.

Commonwealth Functional Cooperation

64. Heads of Government considered the various aspects of Commonwealth functional cooperation and endorsed the Report of the Committee of the Whole. They also acknowledged the valuable work of other Commonwealth Organisations, which report to them through the COW.

65. They requested the Secretary-General to submit a Report to the 2005 CHOGM on the respective roles of the Commonwealth Partnership for Technology Management (CPTM) and the Commonwealth Business Council (CBC), reaffirming the linkages between CPTM, CBC and the Commonwealth.

66. Heads of Government noted that the role of the Commonwealth Fund for Technical Cooperation (CFTC) in providing technical assistance to member countries was crucial in the delivery of Secretariat's programmes. They stressed that any diminution in the CFTC below £20 million could seriously undermine the Fund.

Commonwealth of Learning

67. Heads of Government received with appreciation the Report of the Commonwealth of Learning (COL) and accepted its recommendations, in particular, the proposal of the Commonwealth Conference of Education Ministers for a Commonwealth Virtual University for Small States. They noted COL's request for resources to finance its three-year Strategic Plan.

Commonwealth Foundation

68. Heads of Government received the Report of the Commonwealth Foundation and commended its work in developing civil society's engagement and partnerships with Governments in the Commonwealth. They expressed appreciation for the positive contribution of civil society in advocacy and capacity building for democracy and sustainable development in member countries. They noted the Foundation's request to review the level of assessed contributions to finance the increasing programme of activities undertaken by the Foundation.

High Level Review Group Recommendations

69. Heads of Government endorsed the report of the Commonwealth Intergovernmental Committee to Review the Mandates of the Commonwealth Organisations (CIC) and urged member countries to implement its various recommendations. With regard to the Commonwealth Partnership for Technology Management (CPTM), Heads of Governments noted CPTM's successful activities in fulfilment of its mandate and its preferred mode of delivery through advisory country-tasks and smart partnership national and international dialogues

in enhancing development, democracy, and prosperity. They recognized CPTM's initiatives in establishing the Endowment Fund and contributions to this Fund from Commonwealth governments and the private sector to enable it to undertake enhanced activities that benefit the Commonwealth.

Meeting of Commonwealth Tourism Ministers

70. Heads of Government encouraged member countries to attend the Meeting of Commonwealth Tourism Ministers in Malaysia from 18-21 March 2004.

Election of the Secretary-General

71. Heads of Government re-elected Rt. Hon Don McKinnon as the Commonwealth Secretary-General for the second term 2004-2008.

Next Meeting

72. Heads of Government accepted the offer of Malta to host the next CHOGM in 2005. They also agreed that the 2007 CHOGM would be hosted by Uganda.

Abuja
8 December 2003

<77>

The EU Security Strategy-Implications for Europe's Role in a Changing World (11.12.03)

> According to Javier Solana security threats "cannot be tackled by purely military means". He stressed the need for "an effective multilateral approach" with well functioning international institutions and emphasized that within this web, "NATO is and will remain key to safeguarding our security". The EU must be ready to act before a crisis occurs and be capable of consolidating relationships with other great partners like Russia, Japan, China, India and Latin America.

We sometimes forget how young is our ambition to build a common foreign and security policy. Let us remind ourselves that we began this task only in 1992. We have achieved a lot in a short time. Much more remains to be done.

Since we began work, events have strengthened the conviction that the Union has an important role to play in the international community. We have seen dramatic changes in the world around us. September 11 has revealed a world more complex and with threats more potent and urgent than we had feared. The Iraq crisis has been a painful and divisive experience for Europe, but one that we are determined to learn lessons from.

It would be wrong to think that the Union has stood impassive as the world around it changes. The imminent enlargement of the Union is itself a response to the contemporary challenges, reinforcing political stability and economic security on our own continent.

Part of the work of the Inter Governmental Conference is based on the same wish for Europe to play a stronger political role. We must also take care to ensure that our political project is well adapted to the new international strategic context.

A restructuring of international relations is taking place. Today, America is the pre-eminent world power. But no single country, however powerful, can deal with all the problems alone. Europe is becoming a more important actor, but our success is uneven. The other great actors on the world stage are also at the cross-roads.

Globalisation brings more freedom and wealth, but if not properly managed it can also generate new frustrations. We must be alive to the prospect of new combinations of threats : terrorism capitalising on the persistence of regional conflicts; criminal organisations acquiring weapons of mass destruction, whether through theft, collaboration with rogue States or the collapse of State structures; collusion between fundamentalists, cyber-terrorists and international criminal organisations.

This new context underlines the need for more effective collective security through a common appreciation of the major challenges facing us. If we identify the threats together, we are better able to deal with them together, to fight together against terrorism, proliferation of Weapons of Mass Destruction, organised crime, violent conflicts and instability in our neighbourhood.

At the same time, we must re-double our efforts to combat the great ongoing challenges of extreme poverty, hunger and the new pandemics, breaking the cycles of insecurity and tackling bad governance, corruption and disregard of rule of Law.

This demands that we develop new and more appropriate strategies at a global level. It is with this aim in view that European Union Heads of State and of Government have asked me to define a security strategy which they will adopt at the end of the year. As the EU grows to encompass 25 countries with some 450 million inhabitants producing one quarter of the world's GDP, we have a duty to assume our responsibilities on the world stage. As a global actor the Union must now face up to its responsibility for global security.

Europe has to be prepared to contribute vigorously to extending the scope of international law, to strengthening the institutions of world governance and to developing closer regional cooperation. Thus, the European Union can make a difference in three areas.

Firstly, we must address threats with effective strategies and on an individual basis with targeted tools and methods. Sometimes these threats may seem distant – think of proliferation in South East Asia or the Middle East – but, they have the potential to gravely affect Europe's security. Threats cannot be tackled by purely military means.

Rather, they require a systematic policy of preventive engagement by the Union which must be ready to use the full panoply of tools - economic, political, military - at its disposal to confront the threats as they emerge. At the same time, we have to bear in mind that our response has to be adapted to the different nature of each threat. Multi-faceted as well as appropriate strategies are needed to ensure comprehensive approaches.

Secondly, we must promote an arc of well-governed States in our neighbourhood with whom we can enjoy close and cooperative relations., creating a circle of good governance on the perimeter of the Mediterranean and on our eastern frontiers – from the Middle East to the Caucasus via the Western Balkans. Enlargement will dramatically change in particular the Eastern border of the Union, which will be to a great part formed by the Polish border with Belarus and the Ukraine. This is a historic step for the entire European continent and presents a unique opportunity to strengthen cooperation with its neighbours to the East.

Thirdly, we must help create a world both fairer and more secure. To do so, we require an effective multilateral approach to international order with well-functioning international institutions and rules that are enforced.

That means that the international order is based on agreed rules, and that we are prepared to ensure the respect of these rules when they are broken. As a Union based on the rule of law we carry a particular responsibility to ensure a rule-based international order, the cornerstone of which is the United Nations Charter.

Regional conflicts as much as injustice and frustration fuel terrorism. The proliferation of weapons of mass destruction is never more dangerous than when the international community is divided. In short, we must be ready to take appropriate action when the principles of the United Nations Charter are scorned. I, passionately believe, that the security of the EU in the face of global threats can only be safeguarded if the fundamental values enshrined in the UN Charter and other international regimes and treaties are woven into an extensive web of multilateral instruments.

Within this web, NATO is and will remain key to safeguarding our security: not as a competitor but as a strategic partner. We have seen in practice in the Balkans how this partnership can generate results in terms of peace and stability.

To achieve these objectives, Europeans will be working along four tracks: being more active, strengthening our military and civilian capabilities, improving the coherence of our resources and developing co-operation with our major partners.

Making a stand first requires being more active. The threats are today dynamic. Left alone, they will become more dangerous. The EU must actively counter these threats. It must be ready to act before a crisis occurs. Preventive engagement can avoid more serious problems. Conflict prevention and threat prevention cannot start too early.

The Union will have to deliver that synergy by better co-ordinating assistance programmes, development funds, military and civilian capabilities, trade instruments, diplomatic relations. A better co-ordination between external actions and those in the field of Justice and Home Affairs will be particularly crucial in the fight against terrorism and organised crime.

Secondly, it requires strengthening our capabilities, both military and civilian. 25 European States spending 160 billion each year on Defence should be able to provide more efficient capabilities. At the same time civilian and diplomatic means are still essential for our success in preventing or managing crises.

Greater coherence is the third track. The European Union is the only regional organisation with such a wide range of political, diplomatic, humanitarian, economic and financial, police and military instruments. Improved synergy in their use is crucial.

But improved consistency and capabilities will not be enough unless Europe strengthens relations with its strategic partners. Better co-operation with them is the key to effective multilateralism. Threats are never more dangerous than when the international community is divided. For this reason in particular, the transatlantic link is irreplaceable. Our security and the effectiveness of the common fight against threats depend on the strength and balance of that relationship.

A stronger Europe with a common strategic vision is also a Europe capable of consolidating relationships with the other great partners – Russia, of course, but also Japan, China, India and Latin America. All are crucial partners in the fight against terrorism and proliferation.

Lastly, this will be a Europe capable of partnership with the other great geographical centres in their quest for stability and development. I am obviously thinking about the Arab world but also of Africa of course.

These are the ambitions behind the preparation of the European Union's security strategy. These are the implications for Europe's role in a changing world. The EU is becoming a global actor. This means that it must also be a pillar of the organisation of a new world, more free and more united, fairer and safer.

‹78›

Declaration of Principles Building the Information Society: A Global Challenge in the New Millennium (12.12.03)

In its desire and commitment to build "a people-centered, inclusive and development-oriented information society", the representatives agreed to improve access to information and communication infrastructure; identified connectivity as a central enabling agent in building the information society; emphasized the need to promote "a global culture of cyber security" and the need to prevent information, resources and technologies to be used for criminal terrorist purposes.

A. Our Common Vision of the Information Society

1. We, the representatives of the peoples of the world, assembled in Geneva from 10-12 December 2003 for the first phase of the World Summit on the Information Society, declare our common desire and commitment to build a people-centred, inclusive and development-oriented Information Society, where everyone can create, access, utilize and share information and knowledge, enabling individuals, communities and peoples to achieve their full potential in promoting their sustainable development and improving their quality of life, premised on the purposes and principles of the Charter of the United Nations and respecting fully and upholding the Universal Declaration of Human Rights.
2. Our challenge is to harness the potential of information and communication technology to promote the development goals of the Millennium Declaration, namely the eradication of extreme poverty and hunger; achievement of universal primary education; promotion of gender equality and empowerment of women; reduction of child mortality; improvement of maternal health; to combat HIV/AIDS, malaria and other diseases; ensuring environmental sustainability; and development of global partnerships for development for the attainment of a more peaceful, just and prosperous world. We also reiterate our commitment to the achievement of sustainable development and agreed development goals, as contained in the Johannesburg Declaration and Plan of Implementation and the Monterrey Consensus, and other outcomes of relevant United Nations Summits.

3. We re-affirm the universality, indivisibility, interdependence and interrelation of all human rights and fundamental freedoms, including the right to development, as enshrined in the Vienna Declaration. We also re-affirm that democracy, sustainable development, and respect for human rights and fundamental freedoms as well as good governance at all levels are interdependent and mutually reinforcing. We further resolve to strengthen respect for the rule of law in international as in national affairs.
4. We re-affirm, as an essential foundation of the Information Society, and as outlined in Article 19 of the Universal Declaration of Human Rights, that everyone has the right to freedom of opinion and expression; that this right includes freedom to hold opinions without interference and to seek, receive and impart information and ideas through any media and regardless of frontiers. Communication is a fundamental social process, a basic human need and the foundation of all social organization. It is central to the Information Society. Everyone, everywhere should have the opportunity to participate and no one should be excluded from the benefits the Information Society offers.
5. We further reaffirm our commitment to the provisions of Article 29 of the Universal Declaration of Human Rights, that everyone has duties to the community in which alone the free and full development of their personality is possible, and that, in the exercise of their rights and freedoms, everyone shall be subject only to such limitations as are determined by law solely for the purpose of securing due recognition and respect for the rights and freedoms of others and of meeting the just requirements of morality, public order and the general welfare in a democratic society. These rights and freedoms may in no case be exercised contrary to the purposes and principles of the United Nations. In this way, we shall promote an Information Society where human dignity is respected.
6. In keeping with the spirit of this declaration, we re-dedicate ourselves to upholding the principle of the sovereign equality of all States.
7. We recognize that science has a central role in the development of the Information Society. Many of the building blocks of the Information Society are the result of scientific and technical advances made possible by the sharing of research results.
8. We recognize that education, knowledge, information and communication are at the core of human progress, endeavour and well-being. Further, Information and Communication Technologies (ICTs) have an immense impact on virtually all aspects of our lives. The rapid progress of these technologies opens completely new opportunities to attain higher levels of development. The capacity of

these technologies to reduce many traditional obstacles, especially those of time and distance, for the first time in history makes it possible to use the potential of these technologies for the benefit of millions of people in all corners of the world.

9. We are aware that ICTs should be regarded as tools and not as an end in themselves. Under favourable conditions, these technologies can be a powerful instrument, increasing productivity, generating economic growth, job creation and employability and improving the quality of life of all. They can also promote dialogue among people, nations and civilizations.

10. We are also fully aware that the benefits of the information technology revolution are today unevenly distributed between the developed and developing countries and within societies. We are fully committed to turning this digital divide into a digital opportunity for all, particularly for those who risk being left behind and being further marginalized.

11. We are committed to realizing our common vision of the Information Society for ourselves and for future generations. We recognize that young people are the future workforce and leading creators and earliest adopters of ICTs. They must, therefore, be empowered as learners, developers, contributors, entrepreneurs and decision-makers. We must focus especially on young people who have not yet been able to benefit fully from the opportunities provided by ICTs. We are also committed to ensuring that the development of ICT applications and operation of services respects the rights of children as well as their protection and well-being.

12. We affirm that development of ICTs provides enormous opportunities for women, who should be an integral part of, and key actors, in the Information Society. We are committed to ensuring that the Information Society enables women's empowerment and their full participation on the basis on equality in all spheres of society and in all decision-making processes. To this end, we should mainstream a gender equality perspective and use ICTs as a tool to that end.

13. In building the Information Society, we shall pay particular attention to the special needs of marginalized and vulnerable groups of society, including migrants, internally displaced persons and refugees, unemployed and underprivileged people, minorities and nomadic people. We shall also recognize the special needs of older persons and persons with disabilities.

14. We are resolute to empower the poor, particularly those living in remote, rural and marginalized urban areas, to access information and to use ICTs as a tool to support their efforts to lift themselves out of poverty.

15. In the evolution of the Information Society, particular attention must be given to the special situation of indigenous peoples, as well as to the preservation of their heritage and their cultural legacy.
16. We continue to pay special attention to the particular needs of people of developing countries, countries with economies in transition, Least Developed Countries, Small Island Developing States, Landlocked Developing Countries, Highly Indebted Poor Countries, countries and territories under occupation, countries recovering from conflict and countries and regions with special needs as well as to conditions that pose severe threats to development, such as natural disasters.
17. We recognize that building an inclusive Information Society requires new forms of solidarity, partnership and cooperation among governments and other stakeholders, i.e. the private sector, civil society and international organizations. Realizing that the ambitious goal of this Declaration—bridging the digital divide and ensuring harmonious, fair and equitable development for all—will require strong commitment by all stakeholders, we call for digital solidarity, both at national and international levels.
18. Nothing in this Declaration shall be construed as impairing, contradicting, restricting or derogating from the provisions of the Charter of the United Nations and the Universal Declaration of Human Rights, any other international instrument or national laws adopted in furtherance of these instruments.

B. An Information Society for All: Key Principles

19. We are resolute in our quest to ensure that everyone can benefit from the opportunities that ICTs can offer. We agree that to meet these challenges, all stakeholders should work together to: improve access to information and communication infrastructure and technologies as well as to information and knowledge; build capacity; increase confidence and security in the use of ICTs; create an enabling environment at all levels; develop and widen ICT applications; foster and respect cultural diversity; recognize the role of the media; address the ethical dimensions of the Information Society; and encourage international and regional cooperation. We agree that these are the key principles for building an inclusive Information Society.

1) The role of governments and all stakeholders in the promotion of ICTs for development

20. Governments, as well as private sector, civil society and the United Nations and other international organizations have an important role and responsibility in the development of the Information Society and, as appropriate, in decision-making processes. Building a people-centred

Information Society is a joint effort which requires cooperation and partnership among all stakeholders.

2) Information and communication infrastructure: an essential foundation for an inclusive information society

21. Connectivity is a central enabling agent in building the Information Society. Universal, ubiquitous, equitable and affordable access to ICT infrastructure and services, constitutes one of the challenges of the Information Society and should be an objective of all stakeholders involved in building it. Connectivity also involves access to energy and postal services, which should be assured in conformity with the domestic legislation of each country.
22. A well-developed information and communication network infrastructure and applications, adapted to regional, national and local conditions, easily-accessible and affordable, and making greater use of broadband and other innovative technologies where possible, can accelerate the social and economic progress of countries, and the well-being of all individuals, communities and peoples.
23. Policies that create a favourable climate for stability, predictability and fair competition at all levels should be developed and implemented in a manner that not only attracts more private investment for ICT infrastructure development but also enables universal service obligations to be met in areas where traditional market conditions fail to work. In disadvantaged areas, the establishment of ICT public access points in places such as post offices, schools, libraries and archives, can provide effective means for ensuring universal access to the infrastructure and services of the Information Society.

3) Access to information and knowledge

24. The ability for all to access and contribute information, ideas and knowledge is essential in an inclusive Information Society.
25. The sharing and strengthening of global knowledge for development can be enhanced by removing barriers to equitable access to information for economic, social, political, health, cultural, educational, and scientific activities and by facilitating access to public domain information, including by universal design and the use of assistive technologies.
26. A rich public domain is an essential element for the growth of the Information Society, creating multiple benefits such as an educated public, new jobs, innovation, business opportunities, and the advancement of sciences. Information in the public domain should be easily accessible to support the Information Society, and protected from misappropriation. Public institutions such as libraries and archives, museums, cultural collections and other community-based access

points should be strengthened so as to promote the preservation of documentary records and free and equitable access to information.

27. Access to information and knowledge can be promoted by increasing awareness among all stakeholders of the possibilities offered by different software models, including proprietary, open-source and free software, in order to increase competition, access by users, diversity of choice, and to enable all users to develop solutions which best meet their requirements. Affordable access to software should be considered as an important component of a truly inclusive Information Society.
28. We strive to promote universal access with equal opportunities for all to scientific knowledge and the creation and dissemination of scientific and technical information, including open access initiatives for scientific publishing.

4) Capacity building

29. Each person should have the opportunity to acquire the necessary skills and knowledge in order to understand, participate actively in, and benefit fully from, the Information Society and the knowledge economy. Literacy and universal primary education are key factors for building a fully inclusive information society, paying particular attention to the special needs of girls and women. Given the wide range of ICT and information specialists required at all levels, building institutional capacity deserves special attention.
30. The use of ICTs in all stages of education, training and human resource development should be promoted, taking into account the special needs of persons with disabilities and disadvantaged and vulnerable groups.
31. Continuous and adult education, re-training, life-long learning, distance-learning and other special services, such as telemedicine, can make an essential contribution to employability and help people benefit from the new opportunities offered by ICTs for traditional jobs, self-employment and new professions. Awareness and literacy in ICTs are an essential foundation in this regard.
32. Content creators, publishers, and producers, as well as teachers, trainers, archivists, librarians and learners, should play an active role in promoting the Information Society, particularly in the Least Developed Countries.
33. To achieve a sustainable development of the Information Society, national capability in ICT research and development should be enhanced. Furthermore, partnerships, in particular between and among developed and developing countries, including countries with economies in transition, in research and development, technology transfer, manufacturing and utilization of ICT products and services are crucial

for promoting capacity building and global participation in the Information Society. The manufacture of ICTs presents a significant opportunity for creation of wealth.

34. The attainment of our shared aspirations, in particular for developing countries and countries with economies in transition, to become fully-fledged members of the Information Society, and their positive integration into the knowledge economy, depends largely on increased capacity building in the areas of education, technology know-how and access to information, which are major factors in determining development and competitiveness.

5) Building confidence and security in the use of ICTs

35. Strengthening the trust framework, including information security and network security, authentication, privacy and consumer protection, is a pre-requisite for the development of the Information Society and for building confidence among users of ICTs. A global culture of cyber-security needs to be promoted, developed and implemented in cooperation with all stakeholders and international expert bodies. These efforts should be supported by increased international cooperation. Within this global culture of cyber-security, it is important to enhance security and to ensure the protection of data and privacy, while enhancing access and trade. In addition, it must take into account the level of social and economic development of each country and respect the development-oriented aspects of the Information Society.

36. While recognizing the principles of universal and non-discriminatory access to ICTs for all nations, we support the activities of the United Nations to prevent the potential use of ICTs for purposes that are inconsistent with the objectives of maintaining international stability and security, and may adversely affect the integrity of the infrastructure within States, to the detriment of their security. It is necessary to prevent the use of information resources and technologies for criminal and terrorist purposes, while respecting human rights.

37. Spam is a significant and growing problem for users, networks and the Internet as a whole. Spam and cyber-security should be dealt with at appropriate national and international levels.

6) Enabling environment

38. An enabling environment at national and international levels is essential for the Information Society. ICTs should be used as an important tool for good governance.

39. The rule of law, accompanied by a supportive, transparent, pro-competitive, technologically neutral and predictable policy and regulatory framework reflecting national realities, is essential for building a people-

centred Information Society. Governments should intervene, as appropriate, to correct market failures, to maintain fair competition, to attract investment, to enhance the development of the ICT infrastructure and applications, to maximize economic and social benefits, and to serve national priorities.

40. A dynamic and enabling international environment, supportive of foreign direct investment, transfer of technology, and international cooperation, particularly in the areas of finance, debt and trade, as well as full and effective participation of developing countries in global decision-making, are vital complements to national development efforts related to ICTs. Improving global affordable connectivity would contribute significantly to the effectiveness of these development efforts.

41. ICTs are an important enabler of growth through efficiency gains and increased productivity, in particular by small and medium sized enterprises (SMEs). In this regard, the development of the Information Society is important for broadly-based economic growth in both developed and developing economies. ICT-supported productivity gains and applied innovations across economic sectors should be fostered. Equitable distribution of the benefits contributes to poverty eradication and social development. Policies that foster productive investment and enable firms, notably SMEs, to make the changes needed to seize the benefits from ICTs, are likely to be the most beneficial.

42. Intellectual Property protection is important to encourage innovation and creativity in the Information Society; similarly, the wide dissemination, diffusion, and sharing of knowledge is important to encourage innovation and creativity. Facilitating meaningful participation by all in intellectual property issues and knowledge sharing through full awareness and capacity building is a fundamental part of an inclusive Information Society.

43. Sustainable development can best be advanced in the Information Society when ICT-related efforts and programmes are fully integrated in national and regional development strategies. We welcome the New Partnership for Africa's Development (NEPAD) and encourage the international community to support the ICT-related measures of this initiative as well as those belonging to similar efforts in other regions. Distribution of the benefits of ICT-driven growth contributes to poverty eradication and sustainable development.

44. Standardization is one of the essential building blocks of the Information Society. There should be particular emphasis on the development and adoption of international standards. The development and use of open, interoperable, non-discriminatory and demand-driven standards that take into account needs of users and consumers is a basic element

for the development and greater diffusion of ICTs and more affordable access to them, particularly in developing countries. International standards aim to create an environment where consumers can access services worldwide regardless of underlying technology.

45. The radio frequency spectrum should be managed in the public interest and in accordance with principle of legality, with full observance of national laws and regulation as well as relevant international Agreements.

46. In building the Information Society, States are strongly urged to take steps with a view to the avoidance of, and refrain from, any unilateral measure not in accordance with international law and the Charter of the United Nations that impedes the full achievement of economic and social development by the population of the affected countries, and that hinders the well-being of their population.

47. Recognizing that ICTs are progressively changing our working practices, the creation of a secure, safe and healthy working environment, appropriate to the utilisation of ICTs, respecting all relevant international norms, is fundamental.

48. The Internet has evolved into a global facility available to the public and its governance should constitute a core issue of the Information Society agenda. The international management of the Internet should be multilateral, transparent and democratic, with the full involvement of Governments, the private sector, civil society and international organizations. It should ensure an equitable distribution of resources, facilitate access for all and ensure a stable and secure functioning of the Internet, taking into account multi-lingualism.

49. The management of the Internet encompasses both technical and public policy issues and should involve all stakeholders and relevant intergovernmental and international organizations. In this respect it is recognized that:

   a) Policy authority for Internet-related public policy issues is the sovereign right of States. They have rights and responsibilities for international Internet-related public policy issues;

   b) The private sector has had and should continue to have an important role in the development of the Internet, both in the technical and economic fields;

   c) Civil society has also played an important role on Internet matters, especially at community level, and should continue to play such a role;

   d) Intergovernmental organizations have had and should continue to have a facilitating role in the coordination of Internet-related public policy issues;

e) International organizations have also had and should continue to have an important role in the development of Internet-related technical standards and relevant policies.

50. International Internet governance issues should be addressed in a co-ordinated manner. We ask the Secretary-General of the United Nations to set up a working group on Internet governance, in an open and inclusive process that ensures a mechanism for the full and active participation of governments, the private sector and civil society from both developing and developed countries, involving relevant intergovernmental and international organizations and forums, to investigate and make proposals for action, as appropriate, on the governance of Internet by 2005.

7) ICT applications: benefits in all aspects of life

51. The usage and deployment of ICTs should seek to create benefits in all aspects of our daily life. ICT applications are potentially important in government operations and services, health care and health information, education and training, employment, job creation, business, agriculture, transport, protection of environment and management of natural resources, disaster prevention, and culture, and to promote eradication of poverty and other agreed development goals. ICTs should also contribute to sustainable production and consumption patterns and reduce traditional barriers, providing an opportunity for all to access local and global markets in a more equitable manner. Applications should be user-friendly, accessible to all, affordable, adapted to local needs in languages and cultures, and support sustainable development. To this effect, local authorities should play a major role in the provision of ICT services for the benefit of their populations.

8) Cultural diversity and identity, linguistic diversity and local content

52. Cultural diversity is the common heritage of humankind. The Information Society should be founded on and stimulate respect for cultural identity, cultural and linguistic diversity, traditions and religions, and foster dialogue among cultures and civilizations. The promotion, affirmation and preservation of diverse cultural identities and languages as reflected in relevant agreed United Nations documents including UNESCO's Universal Declaration on Cultural Diversity, will further enrich the Information Society.

53. The creation, dissemination and preservation of content in diverse languages and formats must be accorded high priority in building an inclusive Information Society, paying particular attention to the diversity of supply of creative work and due recognition of the rights of

authors and artists. It is essential to promote the production of and accessibility to all content—educational, scientific, cultural or recreational—in diverse languages and formats. The development of local content suited to domestic or regional needs will encourage social and economic development and will stimulate participation of all stakeholders, including people living in rural, remote and marginal areas.

54. The preservation of cultural heritage is a crucial component of identity and self–understanding of individuals that links a community to its past. The Information Society should harness and preserve cultural heritage for the future by all appropriate methods, including digitisation.

9) Media

55. We re-affirm our commitment to the principles of freedom of the press and freedom of information, as well as those of the independence, pluralism and diversity of media, which are essential to the Information Society. Freedom to seek, receive, impart and use information for the creation, accumulation and dissemination of knowledge are important to the Information Society. We call for the responsible use and treatment of information by the media in accordance with the highest ethical and professional standards. Traditional media in all their forms have an important role in the Information Society and ICTs should play a supportive role in this regard. Diversity of media ownership should be encouraged, in conformity with national law, and taking into account relevant international conventions. We reaffirm the necessity of reducing international imbalances affecting the media, particularly as regards infrastructure, technical resources and the development of human skills.

10) Ethical dimensions of the Information Society

56. The Information Society should respect peace and uphold the fundamental values of freedom, equality, solidarity, tolerance, shared responsibility, and respect for nature.

57. We acknowledge the importance of ethics for the Information Society, which should foster justice, and the dignity and worth of the human person. The widest possible protection should be accorded to the family and to enable it to play its crucial role in society.

58. The use of ICTs and content creation should respect human rights and fundamental freedom of others, including personal privacy, and the right to freedom of thought, conscience, and religion in conformity with relevant international instruments.

59. All actors in the Information Society should take appropriate actions and preventive measures, as determined by law, against abusive uses of ICTs, such as illegal and other acts motivated by racism, racial discrimination, xenophobia, and related intolerance, hatred, violence,

all forms of child abuse, including paedophilia and child pornography, and trafficking in, and exploitation of, human beings.

11) International and regional cooperation

60. We aim at making full use of the opportunities offered by ICTs in our efforts to reach the internationally agreed development goals, including those contained in the Millennium Declaration, and to uphold the key principles set forth in this Declaration. The Information Society is intrinsically global in nature and national efforts need to be supported by effective international and regional cooperation among Governments, the private sector, civil society and other stakeholders, including the International Financial Institutions.

61. In order to build an inclusive global Information Society, we will seek and effectively implement concrete international approaches and mechanisms, including financial and technical assistance. Therefore, while appreciating ongoing ICT cooperation through various mechanisms, we invite all stakeholders to commit to the "Digital Solidarity Agenda" set forth in the Plan of Action. We are convinced that the worldwide agreed objective is to contribute to bridge the digital divide, promote access to ICTs, create digital opportunities, and benefit from the potential offered by ICTs for development. We recognize the will expressed by some to create an international voluntary "Digital Solidarity Fund", and by others to undertake studies concerning existing mechanisms and the efficiency and feasibility of such a Fund.

62. Regional integration contributes to the development of the global Information Society and makes strong cooperation within and among regions indispensable. Regional dialogue should contribute to national capacity building and to the alignment of national strategies with the goals of this Declaration of Principles in a compatible way, while respecting national and regional particularities. In this context, we welcome and encourage the international community to support the ICT-related measures of such initiatives.

63. We resolve to assist developing countries, LDCs and countries with economies in transition through the mobilization from all sources of financing, the provision of financial and technical assistance and by creating an environment conducive to technology transfer, consistent with the purposes of this Declaration and the Plan of Action.

64. The core competences of the International Telecommunication Union (ITU) in the fields of ICTs—assistance in bridging the digital divide, international and regional cooperation, radio spectrum management, standards development and the dissemination of information—are of crucial importance for building the Information Society.

C. Towards an Information Society for All Based on Shared Knowledge

65. We commit ourselves to strengthening cooperation to seek common responses to the challenges and to the implementation of the Plan of Action, which will realize the vision of an inclusive Information Society based on the Key Principles incorporated in this Declaration.
66. We further commit ourselves to evaluate and follow-up progress in bridging the digital divide, taking into account different levels of development, so as to reach internationally agreed development goals, including those contained in the Millennium Declaration, and to assess the effectiveness of investment and international cooperation efforts in building the Information Society.
67. We are firmly convinced that we are collectively entering a new era of enormous potential, that of the Information Society and expanded human communication. In this emerging society, information and knowledge can be produced, exchanged, shared and communicated through all the networks of the world. All individuals can soon, if we take the necessary actions, together build a new Information Society based on shared knowledge and founded on global solidarity and a better mutual understanding between peoples and nations. We trust that these measures will open the way to the future development of a true knowledge society.

‹79›

Tokyo Declaration for the Dynamic and Enduring Japan-ASEAN Partnership in The New Millennium (12.12.03)

> Japan and ASEAN agreed to promote the development of regional and trans-regional framework, particularly the ASEAN plus three process, ARF and APEC; reinforce the "Comprehensive Economic Partnership"; strengthen political and security cooperation in the areas of counter-terrorism, anti-piracy and other trans-national crimes.

We, the Heads of State/Government of Japan and Member Countries of the Association of Southeast Asian Nations (ASEAN), gathered in Tokyo, Japan on 11 and 12 December 2003, for the Japan-ASEAN Commemorative Summit, note with deep satisfaction that our countries have fostered a close and cooperative relationship over the last thirty years, contributing to peace, stability, development and prosperity of the region;

Inspired by the significant progress made in the Japan-ASEAN relations, encompassing the political and security, economic, social and cultural, and development cooperation areas;

Re-affirming the principles which have guided our relations, which include partnership, shared ownership, mutual respect and benefits;

Appreciating the significant contribution of Japan to the economic development and prosperity of ASEAN countries in the past three decades, in particular, Japan's Official Development Assistance (ODA) to ASEAN, which represented around 30% of Japan's total bilateral ODA in the past ten years and constituted the largest part of its ODA, reflecting the special importance that Japan has been attaching to ASEAN;

Acknowledging the importance of the rich Asian traditions and values that will serve as the rallying point for our determined efforts to tap the opportunities and meet the challenges of the new millennium;

Convinced that the "heart-to-heart" understanding, nurtured among peoples of Japan and Southeast Asian countries and based on mutual trust and respect, has developed into the "acting together, advancing together" partnership which is the foundation for our future relations;

Determined to continue the deepening and broadening of cooperation within Japan-ASEAN strategic partnership to ensure peace, stability and prosperity in the region;

Recalling the Joint Statement of the Meeting of the Prime Minister of Japan and the ASEAN Heads of State/Government, Kuala Lumpur, 7 August 1977, and the Joint Statement of the Meeting of the Prime

Minister of Japan and the Heads of State/Government of the Member States of ASEAN, Kuala Lumpur, 16 December 1997, which laid the groundwork for a comprehensive Japan-ASEAN cooperation and strengthened the resolve to further advance this partnership in the 21st Century;

Considering the Joint Declaration of the Leaders of Japan and ASEAN on the Comprehensive Economic Partnership signed in Phnom Penh on 5 November 2002 and the Framework for Comprehensive Economic Partnership between Japan and ASEAN signed in Bali on 8 October 2003 to minimise barriers and deepen economic linkages, lower business costs, increase intra-regional trade and investment, improve economic efficiency, create a larger market with greater opportunities and larger economies of scale for the businesses of both Japan and ASEAN, and enhance our attractiveness to capital and talent; Signed of Prime Minister and President (photos)

Taking note of the Final Report with Recommendations towards Vision 2020: Japan-ASEAN Consultation Conference on the Ha Noi Plan of Action of October 2002 to facilitate the realisation of the ASEAN Vision 2020 and to promote dynamic and deeper Japan-ASEAN cooperation;

Reiterating full support for the implementation of the Declaration of ASEAN Concord II signed in Bali on 7 October 2003 leading to the formation of a more integrated ASEAN Community comprising the ASEAN Security Community, ASEAN Economic Community and ASEAN Socio-Cultural Community;

Welcoming the Declaration on Accession to the Treaty of Amity and Cooperation in Southeast Asia by Japan, and the accession by other Dialogue Partners of ASEAN, which will further strengthen trust, peace, and stability in Southeast Asia;

Reaffirming that the Japan-ASEAN relationship is forward-looking and actionoriented in respect of advancing, intensifying and deepening the partnership and linkages with Dialogue Partners and the rest of the world for the common good of all;

Hereby adopt the following:

1. Fundamental Principles and Values

- Japan and ASEAN will further deepen and broaden their relationship, natural economic complementarities, social and cultural affinities, including the desire for closer people-to-people contacts and exchanges;
- Japan and ASEAN will enhance their cooperation through closer consultation and adherence to the principles enshrined in the Charter of the United Nations and international law, and commend the purposes, principles and spirit of the Treaty of Amity and Cooperation in Southeast Asia, including respect for national sovereignty and territorial integrity, renunciation of threat or use of force, peaceful settlement of disputes, and non-interference;

- Japan and ASEAN will contribute to the creation of an East Asia region where countries and peoples can live in peace with one another and with the world at large in a just, democratic and harmonious environment;
- Japan and ASEAN will forge common visions and principles, including respect for the rule of law and justice, pursuit of openness, promotion and protection of human rights and fundamental freedom of all peoples in accordance with the Charter of the United Nations, the Universal Declaration of Human Rights, and the Vienna Declaration and Programme of Action, promotion of mutual understanding for cultures and civilisations, and enhancement of mutual benefits of market economy;• Japan, through its development assistance and support programmes, will give high priority to ASEAN's economic development and integration efforts as it strives to realise the ASEAN Community;
- Japan and ASEAN will collectively promote the development of regional and trans-regional frameworks, particularly the ASEAN Plus Three process, ASEAN Regional Forum (ARF), Asia Co-operation Dialogue (ACD), Asia-Pacific Economic Cooperation (APEC), Asia-Europe Meeting (ASEM), the Forum for East Asia-Latin America Cooperation (FEALAC) and sub-regional cooperation schemes in the Southeast Asian region; and
- Japan and ASEAN will address regional and global issues, keeping in mind their special relationship based on equality, mutual respect and mutual benefit.

2. Common Strategies for Action

Japan and ASEAN will harness their collective strengths to pursue expeditiously and substantively common strategies for joint action in the following areas:

(1) Reinforcing Comprehensive Economic Partnership and Monetary and Financial Cooperation

- Reinforce their economic partnership, by strengthening economic linkages and integration under the Joint Declaration of the Leaders of Japan and ASEAN on the Comprehensive Economic Partnership, noting the principle of reciprocity, transparency and mutual benefits;
- Undertake bilateral and regional initiatives under which Japan and any ASEAN Member Country can build a bilateral economic partnership while seeking to realise a Comprehensive Economic Partnership through the measures outlined in the Framework for Comprehensive Economic Partnership to be implemented by 2012 allowing

special and differential treatment to the ASEAN Member Countries and taking into account the economic level and sensitive sectors in Japan and each ASEAN Member Country, including the extension of additional five years for completion by the new ASEAN Member Countries;

- Promote more opportunities for trade in goods and services such as through opening and enlarging markets, progressively eliminating non-tariff barriers including technical barriers to trade, enabling economies of scale for industries, and enhancing cooperation in standards and conformance and mutual recognition arrangements;
- Create a transparent and liberal investment regime through the enhancement of trade-related investment procedures and trade and investment promotion and facilitation measures, conduct of trade and investment policy and business dialogues, improvement of the business environment, facilitation of mobility of business people and skilled labour, cooperation in standards and conformance, and other measures to enhance economic linkages;
- Foster and strengthen financial and monetary cooperation such as capital market development, capital account liberalisation, and currency cooperation;
- Forge cooperation in wide-ranging areas of mutual benefit, particularly in science and technology, including research and development, industrial and tourism sectors and the transport sector, including ensuring safe and efficient transport networks;
- Cooperate in expanding and deepening information and communications networks and flows in Asia through realising mutually beneficial information and communications technology cooperation programmes; and
- Work together on programmes for enhancing the capacity of small and medium enterprises (SMEs) in ASEAN to capitalise on the market access for trade in goods, services and investment and to expand business opportunities of SMEs.

(2) Consolidating the Foundation for Economic Development and Prosperity

- Work together to consolidate the foundation for economic development and prosperity. Japan will continue to give priority to ASEAN Member Countries in its ODA programmes by actively extending assistance to them in response to their actual needs. Given the new challenges facing ASEAN countries, Japan will especially enhance its cooperation in human resource development and related areas to address major issues where Japan's cooperation produces tangible results;

- Strengthen cooperation and support the realisation of ASEAN integration goals by implementing projects, particularly those under the Initiative for ASEAN Integration (IAI);
- Strengthen efforts to support ASEAN's integration by enhancing regional and subregional development including in the Mekong region and Brunei-Indonesia-Malaysia-Philippines East ASEAN Growth Area (BIMP-EAGA) to promote economic and social development, sharpen the competitive edge of ASEAN and improve standards of living;
- Enhance support and cooperation in developing the Mekong region to narrow the gaps between the new Member Countries and the other Member Countries of ASEAN based on the common view that development will contribute to reinforcing regional integration, and lead to self-sustaining economic growth through the integrated approach of economic cooperation and promotion of trade and investment with due consideration to environmental conservation;
- Continue expanding and deepening cooperation in capacity building, particularly in human resource development, developing and strengthening ASEAN institutions, enhancing public health and social security, and imparting skills and management know-how;
- Promote infrastructure development, and strengthen industrial bases and the transfer of expertise and technologies;
- Promote joint efforts for research and development, develop modalities for sharing advanced research and promote intellectual exchanges, to strengthen the economic partnership and co-operation in technology development; and
- Enhance cooperation in energy security, food security and food safety.

(3) Strengthening Political and Security Cooperation and Partnership

- Enhance political and security cooperation and partnership at all levels in order to consolidate peace in the region, and work together towards peaceful settlement of disputes in the region bilaterally and through the ARF and other regional and international fora;

- Enhance cooperation in the areas of counter-terrorism, anti-piracy and in combating other transnational crimes through the ARF, ASEAN Plus Three process, ASEAN Ministerial Meeting on Transnational Crime Plus Three as well as other regional and international fora; and
- Enhance cooperation in the areas of disarmament and non-proliferation of weapons of mass destruction and their means of delivery, and related materials.

(4) Facilitating and Promoting Exchange of People and Human Resource Development

- Foster a sense of togetherness based on mutual trust, respect and understanding of each other's traditions and values among the younger generation and future leaders thereby creating caring societies where people-to-people contact will flourish and human capital can be further developed; and
- Support the aspirations and cooperative spirit of youths by reinforcing partnerships and mutual assistance in education and human resource development, through networking among research institutes, universities and other educational institutions and by promoting youth exchanges to enhance people-to-people interactions.

(5) Enhancing Cooperation in Culture and Public Relations

- Cooperate in identifying and preserving cultural heritage, both tangible and intangible, and in transmitting the cultural values and norms and the rich heritage to their future generations, to instil pride in East Asia; and
- Promote awareness and understanding of Japan and ASEAN and their standing in the international community through cooperation among public information agencies, media and others, and through harnessing greater use of information and communications technology in disseminating information about Japan and ASEAN effectively.

(6) Deepening East Asia Cooperation for an East Asian Community

- Recognise that the ASEAN Plus Three process as an important channel to promote cooperation and regional economic integration networks in East·Asia to attain the goals of sustainable development and common prosperity; and

- Seek to build an East Asian community which is outward looking, endowed with the exuberance of creativity and vitality and with the shared spirit of mutual understanding and upholding Asian traditions and values, while respecting universal rules and principles.

(7) Cooperation in Addressing Global Issues

- Cooperate actively, in addressing global issues, such as the fight against terrorism, intensifying disarmament and non-proliferation of weapons of mass destruction and their means of delivery, enhancing cooperation in United Nations peace-keeping operations, promoting rule-based international frameworks, strengthening the United Nations, reinforcing the multilateral trading system through the World Trade Organisation (WTO), alleviating poverty and narrowing economic disparity, protecting the environment, promoting disaster reductions, combating people smuggling and trafficking in persons, combating infectious diseases, enhancing human security and promoting South-South cooperation, taking into account the strong interconnections among political, economic and social realities and accepting the concept of comprehensive security as having broad political, economic, social and cultural aspects.

3. Institutional and Funding Arrangements for the Implementation of the Declaration

- Japan and ASEAN will implement concrete activities and flagship projects in realising the purposes of this Declaration based on the attached Plan of Action;
- Japan and ASEAN will strengthen the existing funding mechanisms for effective co-ordination and implementation of this Declaration and the Plan of Action;
- Japan and ASEAN are committed to providing requisite resources in accordance with their respective capacity including mutually exploring effective and innovative resource mobilisation to accomplish the various strategies and measures outlined in the Plan of Action;
- The progress made in the implementation of the Declaration and the Plan of Action will be reviewed by the meeting of the Foreign Ministers of Japan and ASEAN and reported to the annual Japan-ASEAN Summit; and
- The Plan of Action will be reviewed periodically taking into consideration the dynamic developments in the region and in the world.

Signed in Tokyo, Japan, this Twelfth Day of December in the Year 2003 in two originals in the English language.

For Japan
Junichiro Koizumi
Prime Minister

For Brunei Darussalam
Haji Hassanal Bolkiah
Sultan of Brunei Darussalam

For the Kingdom of Cambodia
Samdech Hun Sen
Prime Minister

For the Republic of Indonesia
Megawati Soekarnoputri
President

For the Lao People's Democratic Republic
Bounnhang Vorachith
Prime Minister

For Malaysia
Abdullah Ahmad Badawi
Prime Minister

For the Union of Myanmar
General Khin Nyunt
Prime Minister

For the Republic of Philippines
Gloria Macapagal-arroyo
President

For the Republic of Singapore
Goh Chok Tong
Prime Minister

For the Kingdom of Thailand
Dr. Thaksin Shinawatra
Prime Minister

For the Socialist Republic of Viet Nam
Phan Van Khai
Prime Minister

Part 2-B

‹80›

State of the Union Address by President George W. Bush (28.01.03)

President Bush announced the achievements of his Government like the creation of the Department of Homeland Security, commitment of an additional $400 billion to strengthen Medicare, $1.2 billion for research in hydrogen powered automobiles, project bio-shield to guard against bio-terrorism and the development of a Terrorist Threat Integration Centre.

THE PRESIDENT: Mr. Speaker, Vice President Cheney, Members of Congress, Distinguished citizens and Fellow citizens: Every year, by law and by custom, we meet here to consider the State of the union. This year, we gather in this chamber deeply aware of decisive days that lie ahead.

You and I serve our country in a time of great consequence. During this session of Congress, we have the duty to reform domestic programs vital to our country; we have the opportunity to save millions of lives abroad from a terrible disease. We will work for a prosperity that is broadly shared, and we will answer every danger and every enemy that threatens the American people. (Applause.)

In all these days of promise and days of reckoning, we can be confident. In a whirlwind of change and hope and peril, our faith is sure, our resolve is firm, and our union is strong. (Applause.)

This country has many challenges. We will not deny, we will not ignore, we will not pass along our problems to other Congresses, to other presidents, and other generations. (Applause.) We will confront them with focus and clarity and courage.

During the last two years, we have seen what can be accomplished when we work together. To lift the standards of our public schools, we achieved historic education reform — which must now be carried out in every school and in every classroom, so that every child in America can read and learn and succeed in life. (Applause.) To protect our country, we reorganized our government and created the Department of Homeland Security, which is mobilizing against the threats of a new era. To bring our economy out of recession, we delivered the largest tax-relief in a generation. (Applause.) To insist on integrity in American business we passed tough reforms, and we are holding corporate criminals to account. (Applause.)

Some might call this a good record; I call it a good start. Tonight, I ask the House and Senate to join me in the next bold steps to serve our fellow citizens.

Our first goal is clear: We must have an economy that grows fast enough to employ every man and woman who seeks a job. (Applause.) After recession, terrorist attacks, corporate scandals and stock market declines, our economy is recovering — yet, it's not growing fast enough, or strongly enough. With unemployment rising, our nation needs more small businesses to open, more companies to invest and expand, more employers to put up the sign that says, "Help Wanted." (Applause.)

Jobs are created when the economy grows; the economy grows when Americans have more money to spend and invest; and the best and fairest way to make sure Americans have that money is not to tax it away in the first place. (Applause.)

I am proposing that all the income tax reductions set for 2004 and 2006 be made permanent and effective this year. (Applause.) And under my plan, as soon as I sign the bill, this extra money will start showing up in workers' pay cheques. Instead of gradually reducing the marriage penalty, we should do it now. (Applause.) Instead of slowly raising the child credit to $1,000, we should send the cheques to American families now. (Applause.)

The tax relief is for everyone who pays income taxes — and it will help our economy immediately: 92 million Americans will keep, this year, an average of almost $1,000 more of their own money. A family of four with an income of $40,000 would see their federal income taxes fall from $1,178 to $45 per year. (Applause.) Our plan will improve the bottom line for more than 23 million small businesses.

You, the Congress, have already passed all these reductions, and promised them for future years. If this tax relief is good for Americans three, or five, or seven years from now, it is even better for Americans today. (Applause.)

We should also strengthen the economy by treating investors equally in our tax laws. It's fair to tax a company's profits. It is not fair to again tax the shareholder on the same profits. (Applause.) To boost investor confidence, and to help the nearly 10 million senior who receive dividend income, I ask you to end the unfair double taxation of dividends. (Applause.)

Lower taxes and greater investment will help this economy expand. More jobs mean more tax-payers, and higher revenues to our government. The best way to address the deficit and move toward a balanced budget is to encourage economic growth, and to show some spending discipline in Washington, D.C. (Applause.)

We must work together to fund only our most important priorities. I will send you a budget that increases discretionary spending by 4 percent next year — about as much as the average family's income is expected to grow. And that is a good benchmark for us. Federal spending should not rise any faster than the paychecks of American families. (Applause.)

A growing economy and a focus on essential priorities will also be crucial to the future of Social Security. As we continue to work together to keep Social Security sound and reliable, we must offer younger workers a chance to invest in retirement accounts that they will control and they will own. (Applause.)

Our second goal is high quality, affordable health care for all Americans. (Applause.) The American system of medicine is a model of skill and innovation, with a pace of discovery that is adding good years to our lives. Yet for many people, medical care costs too much — and many have no coverage at all. These problems will not be solved with a nationalized health care system that dictates coverage and rations care. (Applause.)

Instead, we must work toward a system in which all Americans have a good insurance policy, choose their own doctors, and seniors and low-income Americans receive the help they need. (Applause.) Instead of bureaucrats and trial lawyers and HMOs, we must put doctors and nurses and patients back in charge of American medicine. (Applause.)

Health care reform must begin with Medicare; Medicare is the binding commitment of a caring society. (Applause.) We must renew that commitment by giving seniors access to preventive medicine and new drugs that are transforming health care in America.

Seniors happy with the current Medicare system should be able to keep their coverage just the way it is. (Applause.) And just like you — the members of Congress, and your staffs, and other federal employees — all seniors should have the choice of a health care plan that provides prescription drugs. (Applause.)

My budget will commit an additional $400 billion over the next decade to reform and strengthen Medicare. Leaders of both political parties have talked for years about strengthening Medicare. I urge the members of this new Congress to act this year. (Applause.)

To improve our health care system, we must address one of the prime causes of higher cost, the constant threat that physicians and hospitals will be unfairly sued. (Applause.) Because of excessive litigation, everybody pays more for health care, and many parts of America are losing fine doctors. No one has ever been healed by a frivolous lawsuit. I urge the Congress to pass medical liability reform. (Applause.)

Our third goal is to promote energy independence for our country, while dramatically improving the environment. (Applause.) I have sent you a comprehensive energy plan to promote energy efficiency and conservation, to develop cleaner technology, and to produce more energy at home. (Applause.) I have sent you Clear Skies legislation that mandates a 70-percent cut in air pollution from power plants over the next 15 years. (Applause.) I have sent you a Healthy Forests Initiative, to help prevent the catastrophic fires that devastate communities, kill wildlife, and burn away millions of acres of treasured forest. (Applause.)

I urge you to pass these measures, for the good of both our environment and our economy. (Applause.) Even more, I ask you to take a crucial step and protect our environment in ways that generations before us could not have imagined.

In this century, the greatest environmental progress will come about not through endless lawsuits or command-and-control regulations, but through technology and innovation. Tonight I'm proposing $1.2 billion in research funding so that America can lead the world in developing clean, hydrogen-powered automobiles. (Applause.)

A single chemical reaction between hydrogen and oxygen generates energy, which can be used to power a car — producing only water, not exhaust fumes. With a new national commitment, our scientists and engineers will overcome obstacles to taking these cars from laboratory to showroom, so that the first car driven by a child born today could be powered by hydrogen, and pollution-free. (Applause.)

Join me in this important innovation to make our air significantly cleaner, and our country much less dependent on foreign sources of energy. (Applause.)

Our fourth goal is to apply the compassion of America to the deepest problems of America. For so many in our country — the homeless and the fatherless, the addicted — the need is great. Yet there's power, wonder-working power, in the goodness and idealism and faith of the American people.

Americans are doing the work of compassion every day — visiting prisoners, providing shelter for battered women, bringing companionship to lonely seniors. These good works deserve our praise; they deserve our personal support; and when appropriate, they deserve the assistance of the federal government. (Applause.)

I urge you to pass both my faith-based initiative and the Citizen Service Act, to encourage acts of compassion that can transform America, one heart and one soul at a time. (Applause.)

Last year, I called on my fellow citizens to participate in the USA Freedom Corps, which is enlisting tens of thousands of new volunteers across America. Tonight I ask Congress and the American people to focus the spirit of service and the resources of government on the needs of some of our most vulnerable citizens — boys and girls trying to grow up without guidance and attention, and children who have to go through a prison gate to be hugged by their mom or dad.

I propose a $450-million initiative to bring mentors to more than a million disadvantaged junior high students and children of prisoners. Government will support the training and recruiting of mentors; yet it is the men and women of America who will fill the need. One mentor, one person can change a life forever. And I urge you to be that one person. (Applause.)

Another cause of hopelessness is addiction to drugs. Addiction crowds out friendship, ambition, moral conviction, and reduces all the richness of life to a single destructive desire. As a government, we are fighting illegal drugs by cutting off supplies and reducing demand through anti-drug education programs. Yet for those already addicted, the fight against drugs is a fight for their own lives. Too many Americans in search of treatment cannot get it. So tonight I propose a new $600-million program to help an additional 300,000 Americans receive treatment over the next three years. (Applause.)

Our nation is blessed with recovery programs that do amazing work. One of them is found at the Healing Place Church in Baton Rouge, Louisiana. A man in the program said, "God does miracles in people's lives, and you never think it could be you." Tonight, let us bring to all Americans who struggle with drug addiction this message of hope: The miracle of recovery is possible, and it could be you. (Applause.)

By caring for children who need mentors, and for addicted men and women who need treatment, we are building a more welcoming society — a culture that values every life. And in this work we must not overlook the weakest among us. I ask you to protect infants at the very hour of their birth and end the practice of partial-birth abortion. (Applause.) And because no human life should be started or ended as the object of an experiment, I ask you to set a high standard for humanity, and pass a law against all human cloning. (Applause.)

The qualities of courage and compassion that we strive for in America also determine our conduct abroad. The American flag stands for more than our power and our interests. Our founders dedicated this country to the cause of human dignity, the rights of every person, and the possibilities of every life. This conviction leads us into the world to help the afflicted, and defend the peace, and confound the designs of evil men.

In Afghanistan, we helped liberate an oppressed people. And we will continue helping them secure their country, rebuild their society, and educate all their children — boys and girls. (Applause.) In the Middle East, we will continue to seek peace between a secure Israel and a democratic Palestine. (Applause.) Across the Earth, America is feeding the hungry — more than 60 percent of international food aid comes as a gift from the people of the United States. As our nation moves troops and builds alliances to make our world safer, we must also remember our calling as a blessed country is to make this world better.

Today, on the continent of Africa, nearly thirty million people have the AIDS virus — including three million children under the age 15. There are whole countries in Africa where more than one-third of the adult population carries the infection. More than 4 million require immediate drug treatment. Yet across that continent, only 50,000 AIDS victims — only 50,000 — are receiving the medicine they need.

Because the AIDS diagnosis is considered a death sentence, many do not seek treatment. Almost all who do are turned away. A doctor in rural South Africa describes his frustration. He says, "We have no medicines. Many hospitals tell people, you've got AIDS, we can't help you. Go home and die." In an age of miraculous medicines, no person should have to hear those words. (Applause.)

AIDS can be prevented. Anti-retroviral drugs can extend life for many years. And the cost of those drugs has dropped from $12,000 a year to under $300 a year — which places a tremendous possibility within our grasp. Ladies and gentlemen, seldom has history offered a greater opportunity to do so much for so many.

We have confronted, and will continue to confront, HIV/AIDS in our own country. And to meet a severe and urgent crisis abroad, tonight I propose the Emergency Plan for AIDS Relief — a work of mercy beyond all current international efforts to help the people of Africa.

This comprehensive plan will prevent seven million new AIDS infections, treat at least two million people with life-extending drugs, and provide humane care for millions of people suffering from AIDS, and for children orphaned by AIDS. (Applause.)

I ask the Congress to commit $15 billion over the next five years, including nearly $10 billion in new money, to turn the tide against AIDS in the most afflicted nations of Africa and the Caribbean. (Applause.)

This nation can lead the world in sparing innocent people from a plague of nature. And this nation is leading the world in confronting and defeating the man-made evil of international terrorism. (Applause.)

There are days when our fellow citizens do not hear news about the war on terror. There's never a day when I do not learn of another threat, or receive reports of operations in progress, or give an order in this global war against a scattered network of killers. The war goes on, and we are winning. (Applause.)

To date, we've arrested or otherwise dealt with many key commanders of Al-Qaida. They include a man who directed logistics and funding for the September the 11th attacks; the chief of Al-Qaida operations in the Persian Gulf, who planned the bombings of our embassies in East Africa and the USS Cole; an Al-Qaida operations chief from Southeast Asia; a former director of Al-Qaida's training camps in Afghanistan; a key Al-Qaida operative in Europe; a major Al-Qaida leader in Yemen. All told, more than 3,000 suspected terrorists have been arrested in many countries. Many others have met a different fate. Let's put it this way — they are no longer a problem to the United States and our friends and allies. (Applause.)

We are working closely with other nations to prevent further attacks. America and coalition countries have uncovered and stopped terrorist conspiracies targeting the American embassy in Yemen, the American embassy in Singapore, a Saudi military base, ships in the Straits of Hormuz and the Straits the Gibraltar. We've broken Al-Qaida cells in Hamburg, Milan, Madrid, London, Paris, as well as, Buffalo, New York.

We have the terrorists on the run. We're keeping them on the run. One by one, the terrorists are learning the meaning of American justice. (Applause.)

As we fight this war, we will remember where it began — here, in our own country. This government is taking unprecedented measures to protect our people and defend our homeland. We've intensified security at the borders and ports of entry, posted more than 50,000 newly-trained federal screeners in airports, begun inoculating troops and first responders against smallpox, and are deploying the nation's first early warning network of sensors to detect biological attack. And this year, for the first time, we are beginning to field a defense to protect this nation against ballistic missiles. (Applause.)

I thank the Congress for supporting these measures. I ask you tonight to add to our future security with a major research and production effort to guard our people against bio-terrorism, called Project Bioshield. The budget I send you will propose almost $6 billion to quickly make available effective vaccines and treatments against agents like anthrax, botulinum toxin, Ebola, and plague. We must assume that our enemies would use these diseases as weapons, and we must act before the dangers are upon us. (Applause.)

Since September the 11th, our Intelligence and law enforcement agencies have worked more closely than ever to track and disrupt the terrorists. The FBI is improving its ability to analyze Intelligence, and is transforming itself to meet new threats.

Tonight, I am instructing the leaders of the FBI, the CIA, the Homeland Security, and the Department of Defense to develop a Terrorist Threat Integration Center, to merge and analyze all threat information in a single location. Our government must have the very best information possible, and we will use it to make sure the right people are in the right places to protect all our citizens. (Applause.)

Our war against terror is a contest of will in which perseverance is power. In the ruins of two towers, at the western wall of the Pentagon, on a field in Pennsylvania, this nation made a pledge, and we renew that pledge tonight: Whatever the duration of this struggle, and whatever the difficulties, we will not permit the triumph of violence in the affairs of men — free people will set the course of history. (Applause.)

Today, the gravest danger in the war on terror, the gravest danger facing America and the world, is outlaw regimes that seek and possess nuclear, chemical, and biological weapons. These regimes could use such weapons for blackmail, terror, and mass murder. They could also give or sell those weapons to terrorist allies, who would use them without the least hesitation.

This threat is new; America's duty is familiar. Throughout the 20th century, small groups of men seized control of great nations, built armies and arsenals, and set out to dominate the weak and intimidate the world. In each case, their ambitions of cruelty and murder had no limit. In each case, the ambitions of Hitlerism, militarism, and communism were defeated by the will of free peoples, by the strength of great alliances, and by the might of the United States of America. (Applause.)

Now, in this century, the ideology of power and domination has appeared again, and seeks to gain the ultimate weapons of terror. Once again, this nation and all our friends are all that stand between a world at peace, and a world of chaos and constant alarm. Once again, we are called to defend the safety of our people, and the hopes of all mankind. And we accept this responsibility. (Applause.)

America is making a broad and determined effort to confront these dangers. We have called on the United Nations to fulfill its charter and stand by its demand that Iraq disarm. We're strongly supporting the International Atomic Energy Agency in its mission to track and control nuclear materials around the world. We're working with other governments to secure nuclear materials in the former Soviet Union, and to strengthen global treaties banning the production and shipment of missile technologies and weapons of mass destruction.

In all these efforts, however, America's purpose is more than to follow a process — it is to achieve a result: the end of terrible threats to the civilized world. All free nations have a stake in preventing sudden and catastrophic attacks. And we're asking them to join us, and many are doing so. Yet, the course of this nation does not depend on the decisions of others. (Applause.) Whatever action is required, whenever action is necessary, I will defend the freedom and security of the American people. (Applause.)

Different threats require different strategies. In Iran, we continue to see a government that represses its people, pursues weapons of mass destruction, and supports terror. We also see Iranian citizens risking intimidation and death as they speak out for liberty and human rights and democracy. Iranians, like all people, have a right to choose their own government and determine their own destiny — and the United States supports their aspirations to live in freedom. (Applause.)

On the Korean Peninsula, an oppressive regime rules a people living in fear and starvation. Throughout the 1990s, the United States relied on a negotiated framework to keep North Korea from gaining nuclear weapons. We now know that that regime was deceiving the world, and developing those weapons all along. And today the North Korean regime is using its nuclear program to incite fear and seek concessions. America and the world will not be blackmailed. (Applause.)

America is working with the countries of the region — South Korea, Japan, China, and Russia — to find a peaceful solution, and to show the North Korean Government that nuclear weapons will bring only isolation, economic stagnation, and continued hardship. (Applause.) The North Korean regime will find respect in the world and revival for its people only when it turns away from its nuclear ambitions. (Applause.)

Our nation and the world must learn the lessons of the Korean Peninsula and not allow an even greater threat to rise up in Iraq. A brutal dictator, with a history of reckless aggression, with ties to terrorism, with great potential wealth, will not be permitted to dominate a vital region and threaten the United States. (Applause.)

Twelve years ago, Saddam Hussein faced the prospect of being the last casualty in a war he had started and lost. To spare himself, he agreed to disarm of all weapons of mass destruction. For the next 12 years, he systematically violated that Agreement. He pursued chemical, biological, and nuclear weapons, even while inspectors were in his country. Nothing to date has restrained him from his pursuit of these weapons — not economic sanctions, not isolation from the civilized world, not even cruise missile strikes on his military facilities.

Almost three months ago, the United Nations Security Council gave Saddam Hussein his final chance to disarm. He has shown instead utter contempt for the United Nations, and for the opinion of the world. The 108 U.N. inspectors were sent to conduct — were not sent to conduct a scavenger hunt for hidden materials across a country the size of California. The job of the inspectors is to verify that Iraq's regime is disarming. It is up to Iraq to show exactly where it is hiding its banned weapons, lay those weapons out for the world to see, and destroy them as directed. Nothing like this has happened.

The United Nations concluded in 1999 that Saddam Hussein had biological weapons sufficient to produce over 25,000 liters of anthrax — enough doses to kill several million people. He hasn't accounted for that material. He's given no evidence that he has destroyed it.

The United Nations concluded that Saddam Hussein had materials sufficient to produce more than 38,000 liters of botulinum toxin — enough to subject millions of people to death by respiratory failure. He hadn't accounted for that material. He's given no evidence that he has destroyed it.

Our Intelligence officials estimate that Saddam Hussein had the materials to produce as much as 500 tons of sarin, mustard and VX nerve agent. In such quantities, these chemical agents could also kill untold thousands. He's not accounted for these materials. He has given no evidence that he has destroyed them.

U.S. Intelligence indicates that Saddam Hussein had upwards of 30,000 munitions capable of delivering chemical agents. Inspectors recently turned up 16 of them — despite Iraq's recent declaration denying their existence. Saddam Hussein has not accounted for the remaining 29,984 of these prohibited munitions. He's given no evidence that he has destroyed them.

From three Iraqi defectors we know that Iraq, in the late 1990s, had several mobile biological weapons labs. These are designed to produce germ warfare agents, and can be moved from place to a place to evade inspectors. Saddam Hussein has not disclosed these facilities. He's given no evidence that he has destroyed them.

The International Atomic Energy Agency confirmed in the 1990s that Saddam Hussein had an advanced nuclear weapons development program, had a design for a nuclear weapon and was working on five different methods of enriching uranium for a bomb. The British government has learned that Saddam Hussein recently sought significant quantities of uranium from Africa. Our Intelligence sources tell us that he has attempted to purchase high-strength aluminum tubes suitable for nuclear weapons production. Saddam Hussein has not credibly explained these activities. He clearly has much to hide.

The dictator of Iraq is not disarming. To the contrary; he is deceiving. From Intelligence sources we know, for instance, that thousands of Iraqi security personnel are at work hiding documents and materials from the U.N. inspectors, sanitizing inspection sites and monitoring the inspectors themselves. Iraqi officials accompany the inspectors in order to intimidate witnesses.

Iraq is blocking U-2 surveillance flights requested by the United Nations. Iraqi intelligence officers are posing as the scientists inspectors are supposed to interview. Real scientists have been coached by Iraqi officials on what to say. Intelligence sources indicate that Saddam Hussein has ordered that scientists who cooperate with U.N. inspectors in disarming Iraq will be killed, along with their families.

Year after year, Saddam Hussein has gone to elaborate lengths, spent enormous sums, taken great risks to build and keep weapons of mass destruction. But why? The only possible explanation, the only possible use he could have for those weapons, is to dominate, intimidate, or attack.

With nuclear arms or a full arsenal of chemical and biological weapons, Saddam Hussein could resume his ambitions of conquest in the Middle East and create deadly havoc in that region. And this Congress and the America people must recognize another threat. Evidence from intelligence sources, secret communications, and statements by people now in custody reveal that Saddam Hussein aids and protects terrorists, including members of Al-Qaida. Secretly, and without fingerprints, he could provide one of his hidden weapons to terrorists, or help them develop their own.

Before September the 11th, many in the world believed that Saddam Hussein could be contained. But chemical agents, lethal viruses and shadowy terrorist networks are not easily contained. Imagine those 19 hijackers with other weapons and other plans — this time armed by Saddam Hussein. It would take one vial, one canister, one crate slipped into this country to bring a day of horror like none we have ever known. We will do everything in our power to make sure that that day never comes. (Applause.)

Some have said we must not act until the threat is imminent. Since when have terrorists and tyrants announced their intentions, politely putting us on notice before they strike? If this threat is permitted to fully and suddenly emerge, all actions, all words, and all recriminations would come too late. Trusting in the sanity and restraint of Saddam Hussein is not a strategy, and it is not an option. (Applause.)

The dictator who is assembling the world's most dangerous weapons has already used them on whole villages — leaving thousands of his own citizens dead, blind, or disfigured. Iraqi refugees tell us how forced confessions are obtained — by torturing children while their parents are made to watch. International human rights groups have catalogued other methods used in the torture chambers of Iraq: electric shock, burning with hot irons, dripping acid on the skin, mutilation with electric drills, cutting out tongues, and rape. If this is not evil, then evil has no meaning. (Applause.)

And tonight I have a message for the brave and oppressed people of Iraq: Your enemy is not surrounding your country — your enemy is ruling your country. (Applause.) And the day he and his regime are removed from power will be the day of your liberation. (Applause.)

The world has waited twelve years for Iraq to disarm. America will not accept a serious and mounting threat to our country, and our friends and our allies. The United States will ask the U.N. Security Council to convene on February, the 5th to consider the facts of Iraq's ongoing defiance of the world. Secretary of State Powell will present information and intelligence about Iraqi's legal — Iraq's illegal weapons programs, its attempt to hide those weapons from inspectors, and its links to terrorist groups.

We will consult. But let there be no misunderstanding: If Saddam Hussein does not fully disarm, for the safety of our people and for the peace of the world, we will lead a coalition to disarm him. (Applause.)

Tonight I have a message for the men and women who will keep the peace, members of the American Armed Forces: Many of you are assembling in or near the Middle East, and some crucial hours may lay ahead. In those hours, the success of our cause will depend on you. Your training has prepared you. Your honor will guide you. You believe in America, and America believes in you. (Applause.)

Sending Americans into battle is the most profound decision a President can make. The technologies of war have changed; the risks and suffering of war have not. For the brave Americans who bear the risk, no victory is free from sorrow. This nation fights reluctantly, because we know the cost and we dread the days of mourning that always come.

We seek peace. We strive for peace. And sometimes peace must be defended. A future lived at the mercy of terrible threats is no peace at all. If war is forced upon us, we will fight in a just cause and by just means — sparing, in every way we can, the innocent. And if war is forced upon us, we will fight with the full force and might of the United States military — and we will prevail. (Applause.)

And as we and our coalition partners are doing in Afghanistan, we will bring to the Iraqi people food and medicines and supplies — and freedom. (Applause.)

Many challenges, abroad and at home, have arrived in a single season. In two years, America has gone from a sense of invulnerability to an awareness of peril; from bitter division in small matters to calm unity in great causes. And we go forward with confidence, because this call of history has come to the right country.

Americans are a resolute people who have risen to every test of our time. Adversity has revealed the character of our country, to the world and to ourselves. America is a strong nation, and honorable in the use of our strength. We exercise power without conquest, and we sacrifice for the liberty of strangers.

Americans are a free people, who know that freedom is the right of every person and the future of every nation. The liberty we prize is not America's gift to the world, it is God's gift to humanity. (Applause.)

We Americans have faith in ourselves, but not in ourselves alone. We do not know — we do not claim to know all the ways of Providence, yet we can trust in them, placing our confidence in the loving God behind all of life, and all of history.

May He guide us now. And may God continue to bless the United States of America. (Applause.)

❮81❯

Speech by Chief UN Weapons Inspector Hans Blix to the UN Security Council on Disarming Iraq (14.02.03)

Mr. Hans Blix informed the UNSC that "in no case have we seen convincing evidence that the Iraqi side knew in advance that the Inspectors were coming", and that on Mustard Gas "the results to date have been consistent with Iraq's declarations. However, he stated that "the Al-Samoud 2 and the Al Fatah could very well represent prima facie cases of proscribed missile systems".

Mr President, Since I reported to the Security Council on 27 January Unmovic [the UN weapons inspection agency] has had two further weeks of operational and analytical work in New York and active inspections in Iraq.

This brings the total period of inspections to eleven weeks. Since then we have also listened on 5 February to the presentation to the council by the US Secretary of State and the discussion that followed.

Lastly, Dr. ElBaradei and I have held another round of talks in Baghdad with our counter-parts and with Vice President Ramadan on 8 February.

Let me begin today's briefing with a short account of the work performed by Unmovic in Iraq.

We have continued to build up our capabilities. The regional office in Mosul is now fully operational at its temporary Headquarters.

Plans for a regional office in Basra are being developed.

Our Hercules L 100 Aircraft continues to operate routine flights between Baghdad and Larnaca. The eight helicopters are fully operational.

With the resolution of the problems raised by Iraq for the transportation of minders into the low-fly zones our mobility in these zones has improved.

We expect increased utilisation of the helicopters. The number of Iraqi minders during inspections had also reached a ratio as high as five per inspector.

During the talks in January in Baghdad the Iraqi side agreed to keep the ratio to about one-to-one. The situation has improved.

Since we arrived in Iraq, we have conducted more than 400 inspections covering more than 300 sites.

All inspections were performed without notice, and access was almost always provided promptly.

In no case have we seen convincing evidence that the Iraqi side knew in advance that the inspectors were coming.

The inspections have taken place throughout Iraq at industrial sites, ammunition depots, research centres, universities, Presidential sites, mobile laboratories, private houses, missile production facilities, military camps and agricultural sites.

At all sites which had been inspected before 1998, re-baselining activities were performed.

This included the identification of the function and contents of each building, new or old, at a site.

It also included verification of previously tagged equipment, application of seals and tags, taking samples and discussions with the site personnel regarding past and present activities.

Missile capability

At certain sites, ground-penetrating radar was used to look for underground structures or buried equipment.

Through the inspections conducted so far, we have obtained a good knowledge of the industrial and scientific landscape of Iraq, as well as of its missile capability but, as before, we do not know every cave and corner.

Inspections are effectively helping to bridge the gap in knowledge that arose due to the absence of inspections between December 1998 and November 2002.

More than 200 chemical and more than 100 biological samples have been collected at different sites.

Three-quarters of these have been screened using our own laboratory analytical capabilities at the Baghdad Centre (Bomvic).

Mustard gas

The results to date have been consistent with Iraq's declarations.

We have now commenced the process of destroying approximately 50 litres of mustard gas declared by Iraq that was being kept under Unmovic seal at the Muthanna site.

One-third of the quantity has already been destroyed. The laboratory quantity of thiodiglycol, a mustard gas precursor, which we found at another site, has also been destroyed.

The total number of staff in Iraq now exceeds 250 from sixty countries.

This includes about 100 Unmovic inspectors, 15 IAEA inspectors, 50 aircrew, and 65 support staff.

Mr President, in my 27 January update to the council, I said that it seemed from our experience that Iraq had decided in principle to provide cooperation on process, most importantly prompt access to all sites and assistance to Unmovic in the establishment of the necessary infrastructure.

This impression remains, and we note that access to sites has so far been without problems, including those that had never been declared or inspected, as well as to Presidential sites and private residences.

In my last updating, I also said that a decision to cooperate on substance was indispensable in order to bring, through inspection, the disarmament task to completion and to set the monitoring system on a firm course.

Such cooperation, as I have noted, requires more than the opening of doors. In the words of resolution 1441, it requires immediate, unconditional and active efforts by Iraq to resolve existing questions of disarmament-either by presenting remaining proscribed items and programmes for elimination or by presenting convincing evidence that they have been eliminated.

South Africa Delegation

In the current situation, one would expect Iraq to be eager to comply.

While we were in Baghdad, we met a Delegation from the government of South Africa.

It was there to explain how South Africa gained the confidence of the world in its dismantling of the nuclear weapons programme, by a whole-hearted cooperation over two years with IAEA inspectors.

I have just learned that Iraq has accepted an offer by South Africa to send a group of experts for further talks.

How much, if any, is left of Iraq's weapons of mass destruction and related proscribed items and programmes? So far, Unmovic has not found any such weapons, only a small number of empty chemical munitions, which should have been declared and destroyed.

Another matter-and one of great significance-is that many proscribed weapons and items are not accounted for.

Credible evidence

To take an example, a document, which Iraq provided, suggested to us that some 1,000 tonnes of chemical agent were "unaccounted for".

One must not jump to the conclusion that they exist. However, that possibility is also not excluded.

If they exist, they should be presented for destruction. If they do not exist, credible evidence to that effect should be presented.

We are fully aware that many governmental Intelligence organizations are convinced and assert that proscribed weapons, items and programmes continue to exist.

The US secretary of state presented material in support of this conclusion.

Governments have many sources of information that are not available to inspectors.

Nerve agent

Inspectors, for their part, must base their reports only on evidence, which they can, themselves, examine and present publicly.

Without evidence, confidence cannot arise.

Mr President, in my earlier briefings, I have noted that significant outstanding issues of substance were listed in two Security Council Documents from early 1999 (S/1999/94 and S/1999/356) and should be well known to Iraq.

I referred, as examples, to the issues of anthrax, the nerve agent VX and long-range missiles, and said that such issues "deserve to be taken seriously by Iraq rather than being brushed aside".

The declaration submitted by Iraq on 7 December, despite its large volume, missed the opportunity to provide the fresh material and evidence needed to respond to the open questions.

This is perhaps the most important problem we are facing.

Although I can understand that it may not be easy for Iraq in all cases to provide the evidence needed, it is not the task of the inspectors to find it.

Iraq itself must squarely tackle this task and avoid belittling the questions.

In my January update to the council, I referred to the Al Samoud 2 and the 'Al Fatah' missiles, reconstituted casting chambers, construction of a missile engine test stand and the import of rocket engines, which were all declared to Unmovic by Iraq.

I noted that the 'Al Samoud 2' and the 'Al Fatah' could very well represent prima facie cases of proscribed missile systems, as they had been tested to ranges exceeding the 150km limit set by the Security Council.

I also noted that Iraq had been requested to cease flight tests of these missiles until Unmovic completed a technical review.

Missile ranges

Earlier this week, Unmovic missile experts met for two days with experts from a number of member States to discuss these items.

The experts concluded that, based on the data provided by Iraq, the two declared variants of the 'Al Samoud 2' missile were capable of exceeding 150km in range.

This missile system is therefore proscribed for Iraq pursuant to resolution 687 and the monitoring plan adopted by resolution 715.

As for the 'Al Fatah', the experts found that clarification of the missile data supplied by Iraq was required before the capability of the missile system could be fully assessed.

With respect to the casting chambers, I note the following-Unscom ordered and supervised the destruction of the casting chambers, which had been intended for use in the production of the proscribed 'Badr-2000 missile system'.

Iraq has declared that it has reconstituted these chambers.

Engine tests

The experts have confirmed that the reconstituted casting chambers could still be used to produce motors for missiles capable of ranges significantly greater than 150km.

Accordingly, these chambers remain proscribed.

The experts also studied the data on the missile engine test stand that is nearing completion and have assessed it to be capable of testing missile engines with thrusts greater than that of the SA-2 engine.

So far, the test stand has not been associated with a proscribed activity.

On the matter of the '380 SA-2 missile engines' imported outside of the export/import mechanism and in contravention of paragraph 24 of resolution 687, Unmovic inspectors were informed by Iraq during an official briefing that these engines were intended for use in the 'Al Samoud 2 missile system', which has now been assessed to be proscribed.

Any such engines configured for use in this missile system would also be proscribed.

I intend to communicate these findings to the Government of Iraq.

At the meeting in Baghdad on 8 and 9 February, the Iraqi side addressed some of the important outstanding disarmament issues and gave us a number of papers, e.g. regarding anthrax and growth material, the nerve agent VX and missile production.

Experts who were present from our side studied the papers during the evening of 8 February and met with Iraqi experts in the morning of 9 February for further clarifications.

Although no new evidence was provided in the papers and no open issues were closed through them or the expert discussions, the presentation of the papers could be indicative of a more active attitude focusing on important open issues.

The Iraqi side suggested that the problem of verifying the quantities of anthrax and two VX-precursors, which had been declared unilaterally destroyed, might be tackled through certain technical and analytical methods.

Staff testimony

Although our experts are still assessing the suggestions, they are not very hopeful that it could prove possible to assess the quantities of material poured into the ground years ago.

Documentary evidence or testimony by staff that dealt with the items still appears to be needed.

Not least against this background, a letter of 12 February from Iraq's National Monitoring Directorate may be of relevance.

It presents a list of 83 names of participants "in the unilateral destruction in the chemical field, which took place in the summer of 1991".

As the absence of adequate evidence of that destruction has been and remains an important reason why quantities of chemicals have been deemed "unaccounted for", the presentation of a list of persons who can be interviewed about the actions appears useful and pertains to co-operation on substance.

I trust that the Iraqi side will put together a similar list of names of persons who participated in the unilateral destruction of other proscribed items, notably in the biological field.

Document search

The Iraqi side also informed us that the commission, which had been appointed in the wake of our finding 12 empty chemical weapons warheads, had had its mandate expanded to look for any still existing proscribed items.

This was welcomed.

A second commission, we learnt, has now been appointed with the task of searching all over Iraq for more documents relevant to the elimination of proscribed items and programmes.

It is headed by the former minister of oil, General Amer Rashid, and is to have very extensive powers of search in industry, administration and even private houses.

The two Commissions could be useful tools to come up with proscribed items to be destroyed and with new documentary evidence.

They evidently need to work fast and effectively to convince us, and the world, that this is a serious effort.

The matter of private interviews was discussed at length during our meeting.

The Iraqi side confirmed the commitment, which it made to us on 20 January, to encourage persons asked to accept such interviews, whether in or out of Iraq.

So far, we have only had interviews in Baghdad.

A number of persons have declined to be interviewed, unless they were allowed to have an official present or were allowed to tape the interview.

Three persons that had previously refused interviews on Unmovic's terms, subsequently accepted such interviews just prior to our talks in Baghdad on 8 and 9 February.

These interviews proved informative. No further interviews have since been accepted on our terms.

New legislation

I hope this will change. We feel that interviews conducted without any third party present and without tape recording would provide the greatest credibility.

At the recent meeting in Baghdad, as on several earlier occasions, my colleague Dr. ElBaradei and I have urged the Iraqi side to enact legislation implementing the UN prohibitions regarding weapons of mass destruction.

In a letter just received two days ago, we were informed that this process was progressing well and this morning we had a message that legislation has now been adopted by the Iraqi National Assembly in an extraordinary session.

This is a positive step.

Mr President, I should like to make some comments on the role of intelligence in connection with inspections in Iraq.

A credible inspection regime requires that Iraq provide full co-operation on "process"-granting immediate access everywhere to inspectors-and on substance, providing full declarations supported by relevant information and material.

Eyes in the sky

However, with the closed society in Iraq of today and the history of inspections there, other sources of information, such as defectors and government Intelligence agencies are required to aid the inspection process.

I remember how, in 1991, several inspections in Iraq, which were based on information received from a government, helped to disclose important parts of the nuclear weapons programme.

It was realised that an international organisation authorised to perform inspections anywhere on the ground could make good use of information obtained from governments with eyes in the sky, ears in the ether, access to defectors, and both eyes and ears on the market for weapons-related material.

It was understood that the information residing in the Intelligence services of governments could come to very active use in the international effort to prevent proliferation of weapons of mass destruction.

This remains true and we have by now a good deal of experience in the matter.

International organisations need to analyse such information critically and especially benefit when it comes from more than one source.

The Intelligence agencies, for their part, must protect their sources and methods.

Those who provide such information must know that it will be kept in strict confidence and be known to very few people.

Unmovic has achieved good working relations with Intelligence agencies and the amount of information provided has been gradually increasing.

However, we must recognise that there are limitations and that misinterpretations can occur.

Intelligence information has been useful for Unmovic.

Useful inspections

In one case, it led us to a private home where documents mainly relating to laser enrichment of uranium were found.

In other cases, Intelligence has led to sites where no proscribed items were found.

Even in such cases, however, inspection of these sites were useful in proving the absence of such items and in some cases the presence of other items-conventional munitions.

It showed that conventional arms are being moved around the country and that movements are not necessarily related to weapons of mass destruction.

The presentation of Intelligence Information by the US secretary of State suggested that Iraq had prepared for inspections by cleaning up sites and removing evidence of proscribed weapons programmes.

I would like to comment only on one case, which we are familiar with, namely, the trucks identified by analysts as being for chemical de-contamination at a munitions depot.

Satellite images

This was a declared site, and it was certainly one of the sites Iraq would have expected us to inspect.

We have noted that the two satellite images of the site were taken several weeks apart.

The reported movement of munitions at the site could just as easily have been a routine activity as a movement of proscribed munitions in anticipation of an imminent inspection.

Our reservation on this point does not detract from our appreciation for the briefing.

Yesterday, Unmovic informed the Iraqi authorities of its intention to start using the U-2 surveillance aircraft early next week under arrangements similar to those Unscom had followed.

We are also in the process of working out modalities for the use of the French Mirage aircraft starting late next week and for the drones supplied by the German Government.

The offer from Russia of the 'Antonov aircraft', with night vision capabilities, is a welcome one and is next on our agenda for further improving Unmovic's and IAEA's technical capabilities.

These developments are in line with suggestions made in a paper recently circulated by France, suggesting a further strengthening of the inspection capabilities.

It is our intention to examine the possibilities for surveying ground movements, notably by trucks.

In the face of persistent Intelligence reports for instance about mobile biological weapons production units, such measures could well increase the effectiveness of inspections.

Unmovic is still expanding its capabilities, both in terms of numbers of staff and technical resources.

On my way to the recent Baghdad meeting, I stopped in Vienna to meet 60 experts, who had just completed our general training course for inspectors.

More time

They came from 22 countries, including Arab countries.

Mr President, Unmovic is not infrequently asked how much more time it needs to complete its task in Iraq.

The answer depends upon which task one has in mind-the elimination of weapons of mass destruction and related items and programmes, which were prohibited in 1991-the disarmament task-or the monitoring that no new proscribed activities occur.

The latter task, though not often focused upon, is highly significant-and not controversial.

It will require monitoring, which is "ongoing", that is, open-ended until the council decides otherwise.

Weapons-related items

By contrast, the task of "disarmament" foreseen in resolution 687 and the progress on "key remaining disarmament tasks" foreseen in resolution 1284 as well as the "disarmament obligations", which Iraq was given a "final opportunity to comply with" under resolution 1441, were always required to be fulfilled in a shorter time span.

Regrettably, the high degree of cooperation required of Iraq for disarmament through inspection was not forthcoming in 1991.

Despite the elimination, under Unscom and IAEA supervision, of large amounts of weapons, weapons-related items and installations over the years, the task remained incomplete, when inspectors were withdrawn almost eight years later at the end of 1998.

If Iraq had provided the necessary cooperation in 1991, the phase of disarmament-under resolution 687-could have been short and a decade of sanctions could have been avoided.

Today, three months after the adoption of resolution 1441, the period of disarmament through inspection could still be short, if "immediate, active and unconditional cooperation" with Unmovic and the IAEA were to be forthcoming.

❮82❯

Excerpts of Speech by President George W. Bush Declaring End to Major Combat in Iraq (01.05.03)

On board the US aircraft carrier Abraham Lincoln, President Bush declared that "in the battle of Iraq, the United States and other allies have prevailed" and that "major combat operations in Iraq have ended". However, he cautioned that "we have difficult work to do in Iraq...and the transition from dictatorship to democracy will take time, but it is worth every effort".

Amid cheers from the 5,000-member crew of the aircraft carrier USS Arabham Lincoln, President Bush declared the battle of Iraq had ended in victory. "Because of you, the tyrant has fallen, and Iraq is free," he told the military.

In a nationally televised address, Mr. Bush sought to cast the conflict in Iraq as one aspect of a broader war on terror. He said Saddam Hussein's defeat "is one victory in a war on terror" that still goes on.

"Major combat operations in Iraq have ended," Mr. Bush said from the deck of the carrier, which has sent thousands of jets into war. "In the battle of Iraq, the United States and our allies have prevailed."

Earlier, Mr. Bush flew to the carrier on a Navy jet and made a screeching stop as his plane was snagged by a cable stretched across the deck. He changed out of his flight suit to address thousands of cheering Navy personnel dressed in yellow, green and power blue crew shirts and crowded abroad the sun-dappled deck to hear their commander in chief.

"The liberation of Iraq is a crucial advance in the campaign against terror," the president said. "We have removed an ally of Al-Qaida and cut off a source of terrorist funding. And this much is certain: No terrorist network will gain weapons of mass destruction from the Iraqi regime because that regime is no more."

Mr. Bush sought to give the nation a closure to the fighting while avoiding a sweeping claim of overall victory. He said much still needed to be done, including bringing order to the country, finding weapons of mass destruction, creating a democratic government and pursuing leaders of the fallen regime, including Saddam.

"The battle of Iraq is one victory in a war on terror that began on Sept. 11, 2001, and still goes on," he said.

"Our mission continues. Al-Qaida is wounded, not destroyed. The scattered cells of the terrorist network still operate in many nations, and we know from daily intelligence that they continue to plot against free people. The proliferation of deadly weapons remains a serious danger. The enemies of freedom are not idle, and neither are we."

Mr. Bush stopped short of declaring victory or an end to the war. Such declarations could trigger international laws requiring the speedy release of prisoners of war, limiting efforts to go after deposed Iraqi leaders and designating the United States as an occupying power.

With the shores of California in sight, Mr. Bush also said dangerous work also remains in Afghanistan. Hours earlier, Defense Secretary Donald H. Rumsfeld said major combat had ended in that country, where U.S. troops had routed the Taliban months ago.

"In the battle of Afghanistan, we destroyed the Taliban, many terrorists, and the camps where they trained," he said. "We continue to help the Afghan people lay roads, restore hospitals and educate all of their children. Yet we also have dangerous work to complete."

"And as I spreak, a special operations task force, led by the 82nd Airborne, is on the trail of terrorists, and those who seek to undermine the free government of Afghanistan. America and our coalition will finish what we began," he said.

The focus on his speech was Iraq.

"We are helping to rebuild Iraq, where the dictator built palaces for himself instead of hospitals and schools for the people. The transition from dictatorship to democracy will take time, but it is worth every effort."

The image the president sought to present, with the splendor of the Lincoln all around him, was that of a commander in chief, fully in charge - an image the White House hopes will be etched in voters minds as Mr. Bush turns his sights on domestic concerns.

Mr. Bush was ferried to the ship, still hundreds of miles off the California coast, by a Navy S-3B Viking, a small four-seat plane used for surveillance missions. The aircraft was dubbed Navy One because of its presidential passenger.

After touching down, Mr. Bush, dressed in a green flight suit, plunged into a crowd of service members aboard the ship, which is headed home from the Iraq war.

"Yes, I flew it!" said the president, who was apparently given a chance at the controls. "Of course I liked it!"

Mr. Bush lingered on deck, shook hands and posed for photos. He pointed a thumb toward the pilots in a tribute to "these heroes."

...... On the landing, a tailhook on the back of the plane caught the last of four steel arresting cables stretched across the moving carrier. The cables stop the aircraft within 350 feet, subjecting passengers to twice the force of gravity, or two G's.

Miliary historians said they thought it was the first time a president had landed on an aircraft carrier in such a way.

The USS Abraham Lincoln has been deployed for more than nine months. Its aircraft, including the S-3B Vikings, have flown more than

16,500 sorties and have made 12,700 takeoffs and landings without incident, said Navy spokesman Lt. Cmdr. Danny Hernandez. The S-3Bs find and attack ships and submarines and are sent on surveillance and refueling missions.

❮83❯

State of the Nation Address by Russian President Vladimir Putin (16.05.03)

Highlighting the achievements of the Russian Federation, President Putin stated that during the last three years the GDP of Russia increased 20 per cent, export of oil, petroleum and gas increased by 18 per cent and there were an estimated 10 million people who use the Internet. Highlighting the economic priorities he stated that Russia should double its GDP in a decade, achieve full convertibility of the Rouble and take steps towards joining the WTO.

Good day, Esteemed Colleagues, Members of the State Duma, Members of the Federation Council, Citizens of Russia.

Today, under the Constitution I submit to you the State of the Nation Address and above all I will sum up some of the results.

Last year's results have largely become the continuation of what was started three years ago. Over this period of three years, we have not only substantially cleared the logjams of problems — and life itself was forcing us to deal with them practically on a daily basis — but we have also accomplished some positive results.

Now, we have to make the next step. And all our decisions, all our actions we must aim at securing Russia a place among strong, economically developed and influential countries in the very near future.

This is a qualitatively new task. A qualitatively new level for the country. A level that we could not reach before for a number of reasons, because of scores of other urgent problems. Now, we have such an opportunity and we must use it.

Russia should be and will be a country with a developed civil society and sustainable democracy, where human rights, civil and political rights will be fully ensured.

Russia should and will be a country with a competitive market economy, a country where property rights are securely protected, and economic freedoms allow people to work honestly and earn without fear or limit.

Russia will be a strong country with modern, well-equipped and mobile armed forces, with an army that is ready to defend Russia and its allies, the national interests of the country and its citizens.

All this must create decent living conditions for people and enable Russia to be an equal member of the community of most developed countries.

People will not only be proud of such a country. They will multiply its wealth, they will remember and respect our great history.

This is our strategic goal.

But to achieve this what is necessary is consolidation, mobilization of intellectual forces, the combined efforts of the bodies of Government, of the civil society, of all the people in the country.

On the basis of understandable and clear goals we have to achieve consolidation to resolve the main national problems that we face.

Why do I consider this to be vital?

Our entire historical experience attests that such a country as Russia can only live and develop within its existing borders if it is a strong power. At every period of the weakening of the country, political or economic, Russia has invariably and relentlessly been faced with the threat of disintegration.

Yes, some achievements of the past years have allowed us to talk about stabilization. Some people even developed a feeling that all our problems have been solved, that the future of Russia is quite predictable and successful and the only question is whether our economy should grow by 4 or 6 percent and how much we should spend. Let me tell you that this is not so. We are confronted with serious threats. Our economic foundation, although it has become noticeably stronger, is still shaky and very weak. The political system is not developed enough. The State apparatus is inefficient and most sectors of the economy are uncompetitive. The size of the population continues to diminish. Poverty is receding very slowly. The international situation remains complicated. Competition in the world economy is not diminishing.

We see around us countries with highly developed economies. Let us face it, they are squeezing out Russia from promising world markets wherever they can. And their visible economic advantages provide a reason for growth of geo-political ambitions.

Nuclear weapons continue to spread in the world. Terrorism is threatening peace and the security of our citizens. Strong and well-armed national armies are sometimes used not to combat this evil but to expand certain countries' zones of strategic influence. Can Russia seriously counter these threats if our society is divided into small groups, if we are concerned only about our own narrow-minded group interests, if parasitic sentiments grow, not subside, and these sentiments are fueled by bureaucracy's complacent attitude toward the fact that the national wealth is not protected and accumulated but often wasted away?

I am convinced that without consolidation, at least around basic national values and objectives, it will be impossible to counter these threats.

I would like to remind you that throughout our history Russia and its citizens committed and commit truly historic deeds for the sake of the country's integrity, for the sake of peace in it and stable life. Keeping the country together on vast expanses, preserving the unique community of peoples, with the strong positions of the country in the world, is not only a strenuous job but also tremendous sacrifices and deprivations of our people. Such is the thousand-old history of Russia, such is the method of its reproduction as a strong country. And we have no right to forget this. We must take this into account as we assess present-day dangers and our main tasks.

That we can solve them is evident from our common results we have achieved jointly in the last three years. Yes, we have already resolved very many problems, including those that until recently seemed simply insolvable.

We have finally — juridically and actually — restored the unity of the country. We have consolidated the state authority, we have brought the federal power closer to the regions. Thanks to restoring a single juridical space, we have been able to closely get down to delimiting the powers between the Centre and the regions. Much still has to be done in this area but at any rate we have got down closely to dealing with it. We have begun building vigorous, well financed authorities at the local level. I am speaking about it quite carefully as you can see. We have just begun this work.

Having adopted the third part of the Civil Code of Russia we have completed a major stage of work of codifying legislation. A new Labour Code has also been adopted. The renewed legislation, the systematic dialogue with the trade unions and entrepreneurs have begun to mold a civilized labor market.

Serious headway has been made in the establishment of a really independent judiciary. We have adopted a new Criminal Procedure, Civil Procedure and Arbitration Procedure Codes, thus ensuring additional guarantees of human rights.

We have perfected the electoral system. Conditions have been established in the country for developing a full-fledged civil society, including for the veritable emergence in Russia of strong political parties.

We have made substantial headway in tax reform. We have begun the military reform. As a result of work that has not been simple we have been able to take off the ground the reform of land relations. I will remind you that this question remained for a whole decade a serious economic barrier on the way toward democracy and market.

The first steps have been made in reforming the pension system, infrastructural monopolies of the housing and utility sector.

We together overcame an absolutely unacceptable situation when some Russian territories were effectively outside the federal jurisdiction. The supremacy of the Russian Constitution and the federal laws, like the duty to pay taxes into the federal treasury have become the norm for all the regions of the Russian Federation. At this point I would like to make an important digression on a topic that is sensitive to all of us. The previous Address spoke of the need to bring the Chechen Republic back into the political and legal space of the country. It spoke about free elections, the creation of effective republican power institutions and let us face it, not many people at the time believed in it.

But a year has passed and reality has confirmed that together we can achieve a great deal. I would like once again to thank all those who have backed this line of the leadership of the country, those who took an active part in this policy and of course those who took an active part in the preparation of the Constitutional Referendum in Chechnya itself.

Today, I offer particular thanks to the Chechen people for their courage, for not allowing themselves to be intimidated, now as in the past, for the wisdom that people who are simple but sensitive to the truth invariably have. People in Chechnya have felt in their hearts their responsibility and their human interest. And finally, the referendum has shown that the Chechens rightly regard themselves to be an inalienable part of the single multi-national people of Russia.

Yes, we have all had to pay a heavy price for restoring the territorial integrity of Russia and we bow our heads in memory of the dead servicemen and civilians in the Chechen Republic, all those who at the cost of their lives prevented the country from being rent asunder and fulfilled their duty to the last.

The Constitutional Referendum that took place in the republic drew a line under the time of troubles, the years when power in Chechnya had been usurped by bandits, when the citizens of the republic found themselves in the Middle Ages in the direct sense of the word, were denied elementary human rights, when public executions were held regularly and demonstratively in the streets of Chechen cities and villages, when thousands of people became live commodities in the hands of slave traders, when neither schools nor institutes nor hospitals worked.

All that has finished.

But for life in the republic to be finally brought back to normal a very great deal has yet to be done. It is necessary, on a democratic basis and in accordance with the Constitution adopted at the Referendum to elect the president and the parliament of the republic, to form the local government bodies, to develop and sign a treaty on delimitation of powers between the federal centre and the republic. And of course to restore the economy of Chechnya.

We also are to hand over to the Chechen militia the organization of law enforcement work in the republic. Besides, as part of the continued process of political settlement jointly with you dear colleagues, preparation is underway for an amnesty. It will create conditions for drawing into peaceful life those people who for various reasons have not done so before, but are ready to do so now.

All this have to be done in complex conditions. Obviously, the remnants of the bandits will try to use threats, murder and terrorist acts to intimidate the citizens of the republic, to disrupt the dynamic political process. And we see that the terrorist acts perpetrated by the bandits are more and more frequently targeted against the civilian population, against the common people.

But we will see this through. People in Chechnya will have a normal human life.

Esteemed Assembly,

Three years ago we decided that the most serious threats to the country were demographic degradation, Russia's economic weakness, and the inefficiency of the State.

Have we succeeded in solving these problems? Yes and no. There are both successes and serious mistakes. We will talk about this frankly today.

The shrinkage of the Russian population was named as one of the most acute problems. This shrinkage is caused first of all by a decrease in the birth rate and an increase in the death rate.

In the last few years the death rate continued to grow and increased 10 percent over the last three years. Projected life expectancy also continued to decline — these are sad figures — from 67 years in 1999 to 64 in 2002. One of the reasons for this is a high rate of illness, deaths caused by accidents, poisoning and injuries. The spread of so-called new epidemics, is aggravating the situation, including drug addiction and AIDS.

However, over the same three years the birth rate increased 18 percent, the rate of death among infants decreased 21 percent and is now at a record low level in the history of our country.

Let me remind you that not so long ago we considered at the State Council a set of issues regarding an accelerated transition to health insurance. I believe this will help strengthen the financial basis of health care considerably. After organizational questions have been worked out in 16 regions of Russia in the second half of this year, health insurance will be offered to pensioners on the entire territory of the country from next year. I do hope that this will give good support to our elderly people.

The national census showed that according to the preliminary data the permanent population of the country is over 145 million. It's almost two million more than current statistics showed. But it is also two million less than in 1989.

What do these figures speak about?

Firstly, that the population of the country continues to diminish, albeit at a slower pace than was shown by current statistics, but it is diminishing.

Secondly, despite a certain increase in birth rates, our population was increasing not thanks to them but rather thanks to the legal immigration. Over the past ten years a total of around seven million people have moved to settle in this country, mainly from the countries of the Commonwealth of Independent States.

It is a very indicative result and it indicates that despite all our difficulties, Russia remains an attractive country for life and work of millions of people.

One of the serious problems mentioned three years ago was the intensifying globalization of the economy and of the entire public life of the modern world. Today, not a single country, whatever its size or wealth, can develop successfully if it is isolated from the rest of the world. On the contrary, success comes to those states that are consciously and intelligently and dynamically integrating into the world economy.

Over the past three years, on the road toward international integration, we have made a number of serious steps.

First and foremost, in June last year Russia was invited to become a full-fledged member of a club of eight most developed States of the world. In it, together with the partners, we are working to safeguard both our national interests and to solve the common problems faced by contemporary civilization. A major example of this is the global partnership in the matter of non-proliferation of weapons of mass destruction. Disposal of these weapons will enable us to restore the health of the ecology of certain regions of Russia.

I would also like to point out that the credit rating of the country has become the highest in the entire history of new Russia. Some of the Russian companies have joined the largest European and world companies. Some of them for the first time over the past ninety years have begun a serious expansion into the world markets. They have become notable participants in international economic relations, serious competitors to foreign firms.

I must say that we have made a significant headway toward joining the World Trade Organization.

And finally, mentioned as a strategic and principled challenge to the country three years ago was the economic weakness of Russia.

What has changed since then?

On the one hand, over the period in question there have appeared signs of changes for the better. Thus, the economic growth continued. During these three years the gross domestic producı of Russia increased 20 percent. Investment into fixed assets — by more than 30 percent. The physical export of goods increased by one-fourth, including the export of machines and equipment and transport vehicles — by more than 70 percent. Not a bad indicator.

For the first time in half a century Russia ceased to be an importer of grain and became its exporter. From 1999 the sales of our food products in foreign markets increased three times.

The export of oil and petroleum products and gas increased by 18 percent. And today Russia is a major exporter of fuel and energy resources in the world.

Information technologies were developing at a high rate. The so-called new economy is growing in Russia. The increase in its output ranged from 20 to 30 percent a year. The standard of telephonization of the country has grown substantially. The number of mobile phone users has been doubling every year and has now reached almost 18 million. An estimated 10 million people in Russia today use the Internet.

These figures show that a balanced growth of the Russian economy, based both on traditional industries and on modern technologies, is possible.

The increased economic potential of the country has improved the lives of tens of millions of people. Thanks to economic growth almost 4 million people during these years have dropped out of the ranks of the jobless. The possibility to work and earn has seriously reduced the scale of strike activity from nearly 900,000 people in 1997 to less than 5,000 in 2002. And this in a situation when the trade unions are becoming more and not less active.

The real incomes of the population have grown by 32 percent. The average pension only three years ago was 70 percent of the living minimum of pensioners, last year it was equal to the living minimum.

And finally, end consumption per capita has increased during three years by almost a third. Last year that indicator exceeded not only the level of three years ago, not only of the crisis year of 1998 and even the pre-crisis 1997, but it hit a record in 2002 in the whole history of Russia.

Such an enumeration of dry figures may appear to be difficult to understand, but not to you. Behind these figures are the large assets that have become available to millions of our citizens. These assets have helped to boost people's well-being, supported their health and made it possible to solve difficult social problems in the country.

And yet, inspite of everything I have said I have to state that the economic results we have achieved are still very very modest.

First, one-fourth of Russian citizens still have incomes below the living minimum. One-fourth of the population of the country!

Secondly, economic growth in the country remains extremely unsustainable. While in the year 2000 industrial production grew throughout the year, in the year 2002 combined growth occurred only during six months. As a result, unemployment began to grow in the last few months.

And finally, the third point. The pace of economic growth is declining. Last year, after 10 percent growth in 2000, the economy grew only 4-odd percent. However, the declining pace of economic growth inevitably slows down social development and makes it impossible to solve many other problems facing the country.

We must admit that economic growth in Russia is owed mainly to a favorable situation on the world markets in the last couple of years. The unprecedented improvement of the terms of foreign trade for our economy gave Russia considerable economic advantages and big additional revenue. Part of this revenue was used to improve the quality of life for our citizens, part was invested in the Russian economy, another part was used to pay the foreign debt, which we have reduced by one-fourth. Finally, this revenue allowed us to augment our reserves. The combined reserves of the Finance Ministry and the Central Bank, and the foreign exchange and gold reserves of the Central Bank have reached an all-time high of 61 billion dollars, while only three years ago they stood at only 11 billion.

I think it's clear that without this, I mean a favorable foreign economic situation, our successes in social and economic development would have been much more moderate. We must remember that such a favorable situation cannot and will not last forever.

In this connection, I would like to draw your attention to yet another problem. The total annual size of the social obligations of the State is at present 6.5 trillion rubles. This is practically twice the consolidated budget of Russia. Both the executive and the legislative branches have over the years given people more promises than the Russian economy is able to deliver. Moreover, under populist slogans and deceiving the citizens of the country, promises that cannot be kept are increasing. Some politicians, unfortunately, seek to build them up even today.

In addition to frustrated hopes, a serious consequence of growing empty promises is the deterioration of the quality of current economic policy. That also leads to disproportions and conflicts in the inter-budgetary relations. With State expenditure growing at a faster rate than the real economy, one can hardly expect anything different.

I think, esteemed members of the two houses of the Federal Assembly and esteemed Heads of the regions, it is high time we all together put an end to this kind of policy. The authorities cannot and must not and have no right to deceive the citizens of their own country. If we have promised something to people, we should fulfill these promises. Otherwise, it is better not to promise and not to do it.

And the last thing. State regulated tariffs for the products of the infrastructure monopolies are increasing faster than prices are growing in the free sector of the Russian economy. As a result, there is growing re-distribution of economic resources in favor of the monopoly sector and its share in the Russian economy is growing. And yet, the monopoly sector is not exhibiting a high level of efficiency. So, the monopolists strangle the competitive sector in our economy. The government should control this more strictly. The continuation of such a policy obviously is the road to stagnation.

The conclusion from the above is evident: given the above-mentioned positive trends and indicators, the favorable external conditions and the stable political situation have not been used — certainly have not been fully used — to achieve our strategic goals.

Esteemed Deputies,

Members of the Federal Assembly,

The last three years also showed what we can achieve if we work jointly to the same end.

They showed that Russia is not a country doomed to live in crises and misery, that Russian people are talented, initiative-driven and industrious, that they can work and deserve a better life, that they can build a better life. Ofcourse, if they are not hindered, at least if they are not hindered. It would be even better if we help.

I believe, the return of Russia to the community of rich, developed, strong and respected countries of the world must be our goal of principle.

But this will happen only when Russia becomes economically strong, when it no longer depends on tips from International Financial Organizations or unpredictable turns in the foreign trade environment.

This can be possible only in conditions of sustainable and fast growth that is based on the use of all factors, internal and external, traditional and contemporary, domestic and foreign.

Finally, fast and sustainable growth can be possible only when competitive goods are made. Everything must be competitive: goods and services, technologies and ideas, business and the state itself, private companies and state institutions, entrepreneurs and public servants, students, professors, science and culture.

In the meantime, the economic growth is sometimes said to be opposed to reform. They say that it is dangerous to spur it up, that it is much more important to pursue structural changes and reforms. I would like to express my own opinion on this score. Such opposing is contentious, to say the least. Reforms for the sake of reforms are not needed. There is no need for a permanent revolution.

It is obvious that the engine of the economic growth is private initiative of both the Russian and foreign business working in the Russian territory. It is also obvious that the Russian business itself must become modern, enterprising, flexible, mobile. It must worthily continue the great traditions of Russian entrepreneurship and patriotism must be added to it for good measure.

I will repeat that the success of the country to an immense extent depends on the Russian entrepreneur.

And finally, the policy of economic growth cannot be opposed to social policy. I would like to stress that the economic growth is necessary for us in the first place for raising the well-being of the citizens. It is directly linked with solving a number of essential problems. These include good quality nutrition and good and comfortable housing, the uninterrupted supply of electricity and hot water. It is also good education and modern health care. It is also protection from accidents and natural cataclysms. Finally, it is also the longer life expectancy.

Some time in the past we said that tough competition was a norm in the modern world. And that is why our ability to compete, the readiness to fight for resources and influence directly determine the situation inside the country and Russia's weight in international affairs.

This approach—the perspective of our development—was heeded within the Russian society and accepted.

The idea that the high competitiveness of the country must become a major goal was accepted by practically all the influential political forces and our citizens. Now we should make sure that this goal is present in the practical activities of the bodies of State power and Local Government.

Meanwhile the Russian bureaucracy proved to be ill-equipped for working out and implementing decisions that meet the modern needs of the country. And conversely, it has become quite skillful in deriving the so-called administrative rent from its position. I spoke about it last year.

And we also spoke about the problem of inefficient State three years ago. We stressed that the weakness of the state nullifies economic and other reforms.

Our bureaucracy still possesses immense powers, but the number of powers in its hands is still not matched by the quality of power. I must stress that a major source of such power is excessive functions of state bodies. In spite of the huge number of bureaucrats in the country there is a dire shortage of personnel at all levels and in all power structures. A shortage of modern managers, efficient people. The above is the background against which the vital administrative reform must be carried out in the country.

As you know, the Government has made an inventory of the functions of Ministries and agencies and it has counted about 5,000. But in the course of this work it was found that almost every agency believes that its own functions should not be curtailed but broadened, sometimes at the expense of the agencies next door.

For all the awareness of the complexity of the tasks and the difficulties that have cropped up, the administrative reform has been dragging on too long.

Apparently the Government needs to be helped. Apparently it needs an additional political impetus. Ofcourse, it will get it.

I believe we must not convince bureaucracy to cut down on its appetite but to impose restrictions upon it through directives.

The functions of State bodies must be cut radically. Ofcourse, everything must be calculated most thoroughly. Otherwise, we may not be able to solve this problem. This must be done on the basis of the inventory that the government commission is finishing and it must be linked to a set of decisions on the delimitation of powers between different levels of government and on their financial autonomy.

At the same time it is necessary to create effective mechanisms for resolving disputes between the citizen and the State by perfecting administrative procedures and judicial mechanisms.

A few words about social and economic priorities. I can often hear that the Russian economy does not need qualitative rises and leaps, that there is no need for major national projects that will generate big growth, that it would be quite enough to be consistent in carrying out the current policy, even though it cannot produce the expected big growth.

I must say that with such an attitude toward business and with such a fear of making a responsible choice — I am not talking, ofcourse, about large-scale projects of the period of stagnation — we shall not be able to go forward quickly and with good quality, but I believe that the problem of choosing a source of growth will arise only if there is a strong need to solve concrete ambitious tasks.

Such a task does exist. It is quite realistic although it is extremely difficult.

We should at least double the gross domestic product in a decade.

The doubling of the GDP is a systemic and ofcourse a large-scale task. It will call for a profound analysis and adjustment of the existing approaches to economic policy. But the main thing that we have to do here and what we will need is, again, the consolidation of political forces, of society. Consolidation of all the branches of Government, the pooling of the best intellectual forces, support of the social and political structures, cooperation between Parliament and Government, joint search for optimum ways of solving the truly strategic, vital, historic task for Russia.

I am convinced that all the conditions for setting and solving such tasks exist in Russia. There is a possibility to start a large-scale building of a modern and strong economy and ultimately forming a state that is competitive in every sense of that word.

Another major task that should be tackled together is achieving full convertibility of the ruble. Not only internal convertibility, but also external convertibility, not only in current, but in capital operations. Let me remind you that in the past Russia had one of the strongest and most respected currencies in the world. The dignity of the gold ruble was equated to the dignity of the power.

Let me tell you that the country needs a ruble that freely circulates in international markets. We need a strong and reliable link to the world economic system.

Russia which has become a full-fledged member of the G-8 of the most developed States in the world is under an obligation to solve this task.

The achievement of that goal will become a factor of Russia's real integration into the world economy. And for the ordinary citizens of this country this will mean in practice that when preparing to travel outside Russia it will be sufficient to take along the passport and Russian rubles.

The basic principles of tax policy must remain the simplicity of tax registration and application of legal norms, the equality of the subjects of taxation and a reasonable level of taxes.

Allow me to say a few words on this topic. The tax reform in Russia is regrettably becoming permanent and continuous. Yes, the measures proposed by the Government to reduce the tax burden are ofcourse movement in the right direction. But the frequency of changes introduced into tax legislation clearly surpasses the permissible level. Let us put it straight: this is the measure of the quality of work, a quality that is not high. This hampers life planning for all: for the State, for the entrepreneurs, for the citizens.

Now in the tax policy, the government has for the first time switched over from annual planning to medium-term. Recently, the program was approved for tax changes for the coming three years. This is ofcourse a correct, important and needed step.

Now it is necessary to move further, to develop the contours of a tax system that would exist in Russia for many, many years to come.

I would also dwell on another, very important topic that affects the interests of very many people, the problem of citizenship.

At the present time over one million people who have come to Russia after the demise of the Soviet Union — and pending the passage of the new legislation on citizenship — found themselves in a most complex life situation. We have quite recently discussed this topic with the leaders of factions of the State Duma.

Those people who came to us lived and worked in Russia, participated in its political life; many of them served in the Russian Army. And now they have found themselves to be stateless in their own country.

The laws passed last year were called upon to bring order to the immigration flows, to make them transparent. What came out of it is not conducive to the solution of the task. Rather, it creates serious problems for a large number of people. I believe it is our duty to rectify this situation. I agree with the leaders of factions on this score. Let us think about it and introduce corresponding adjustments.

What we need ofcourse is not bans and barriers, we need an effective immigration policy that is good for the country and convenient for people, especially for the citizens in the Commonwealth of Independent States, those who are close to us and with whom we understand each other well, with whom we speak the same language. These are people belonging to our common Russian culture.

Esteemed colleagues,

Russia seeks to and will maintain friendly, good-neighborly relations with all the countries of the world, solve common problems with them and protect common interests. The main task of the Russian foreign policy is to promote our national interests. But of course the basic principle remains compliance with the norms of international law.

The events of the past year have brought another proof that in ensuring national interests one needs equally an efficient diplomacy and a reliable defense potential of Russia.

In the modern world, the relations among states are to a large extent determined by the existence of serious world-wide real and potential threats. Among such threats we count International Terrorism, the spread of weapons of mass destruction, regional and territorial conflicts and the narco threat.

And it is extremely important that if a certain threat to the international community as a whole and to individual countries increases, a clear, transparent and generally recognized decision-making mechanism is used. Undoubtedly the most important mechanism of this kind is the United Nations and its Security Council.

Yes, decisions are not adopted always easily at the Security Council, and sometimes they are not adopted at all. Sometimes the initiators of a resolution do not have enough arguments to convince other countries. Not everybody always likes UN decisions. But the international community has no other, let alone more universal, mechanism. Therefore, it must be handled with great care.

Ofcourse it is necessary to modernize international organizations and make them more efficient. Russia is open to discuss these issues.

I believe such approaches toward international affairs are civilized and correct. These approaches are not directed against anyone or in favor of someone else. This is our position of principle, and we will stick to it in the future.

Russia was one of the first countries that encountered the huge threat of International Terrorism. As we all know, not so long ago it threatened the territorial integrity of the Russian Federation. After the terrible tragedies caused by terrorist acts, an anti-terrorist coalition was created in the world with our active participation and cooperation with the United States and other countries, and it proved its high efficiency in combating the threat of terrorism in Afghanistan.

Russia values the anti-terrorist community. It values it as an instrument for co-ordinating interstate efforts in combating this evil. Moreover, successful cooperation within the coalition on the basis of international law may provide a good example of consolidating civilized states in the fight against a common threat.

I will stress again that Russia is interested in a stable and predictable world order. Only this order can ensure the global and regional stability and on the whole — the political and economic progress. It will contribute to the struggle with poverty in the world, which is one of the major tasks.

Our unconditional foreign policy priority remains strengthening the relations with the countries of the Commonwealth of Independent States. These countries are our close neighbors. We are united by many centuries of historical, cultural and economic relations. The interdependence of our development is also obvious. In addition to all else, there are tens of millions of Russians living there.

And I must say it straight that we regard the CIS space as a sphere of our strategic interests. We also proceed from the assumption that for the countries of the Commonwealth Russia is an area of their national interests. Besides, our country is interested in stability and economic progress in the CIS space.

I wish to stress that the uniting economic processes now at work in the CIS are linked with the integration of our countries into the world economy and are helping to implement this integration more dynamically, on conditions more advantageous for all our partners. In the process, we will be consistently deepening our cooperation within the framework of the increasingly effective Eurasian Economic Community.

In addition, the events in the world confirm the correctness and timeliness of the choice we made in favor of establishing the Organization for Collective Security Treaty. In the immediate vicinity of Russia there are quite a few sources of real, not imagined threats of terrorism, transnational crime, narco intervention. Together with the OCST partners, we are obligated to safeguard the stability and security on a significant area of the former Soviet Union.

One major element of our foreign policy is the broad rapprochement and real integration with Europe. Naturally, we are talking there about a complicated and long process. But this is our historical choice. It has been made and it is being consistently implemented, at this stage through more active bilateral relations, the development of strategic partnership with the European Union and active participation in the work of the Council of Europe.

Together, in the interests of the Russian citizens, we have found a political compromise on the problem of transit between the Kaliningrad region and the rest of the Russian territory.

It is equally obvious that our interests and the interests of Greater Europe demand new qualitative steps to meet each other. This is interests of citizens, business, cultural and scientific communities in the European countries and in the Russian Federation. Our proposals on the prospects of the development of all European processes are known. They include free movement of citizens, the formation of a common economic space.

This is not the prospect for the very near term. To achieve these goals one will have to cover a difficult and fairly long road, but the dynamic of all European processes suggests that these are absolutely realistic plans and is actively backed by many of our partners in the European Union.

Now about the modernization of our military organization.

In the military reform the key issues are substantial re-armament, improvement of the principles of recruitment and the very structure of the armed forces.

We need a strong, professional and well-armed army for a happy and peaceful development of the country. This army must be able to defend Russia and its allies and to interact effectively with the armed forces of other countries in the struggle against common threats.

In accordance with the endorsed plans, we will continue to create permanent readiness units in the land forces, airborne troops, and marines on a professional basis. This work must be completed in 2007. In addition, service in the interior and border guard troops will also be professional.

In plain terms (this is not the only result but a very important one) it means the following: only well-trained professional units must be used in trouble spots and local conflicts, if Russia, God forbid, faces such challenges.

I also want to say that sergeants in the armed forces will also be recruited on a professional basis as quickly as possible.

From the year 2008, the length of service for draftees will have to be reduced to one year. During the first six months draftees will master military specialties in the training units. After that they will be allowed to choose between serving the remaining six months in the line units or signing a contract. Those who have served three years on a contract basis should receive certain preferences, including a guaranteed right to higher education with all costs to be paid by the state.

Also a decision of principle has been adopted that it would be expedient to hire citizens from the CIS countries into the Russian armed forces to serve on a professional basis. After three years of service on a contract basis, they will be entitled to fast-track Russian citizenship.

Much of what has been said about will require legislative decisions. In this connection, I hope for your support, for the support of the Federal Assembly.

In the upcoming period, we are to substantially improve the equipment of our armed forces with modern weapons. A corresponding program of rearmament, as you know, has been developed, approved and will be unconditionally fulfilled.

A serious component of the reform of the armed forces will be the strengthening and modernization of the nuclear deterrent.

Besides, I can inform you that at present the work to create new types of Russian weapons, weapons of the new generation, including those regarded by specialists as strategic weapons is in the practical implementation stage. These weapons will ensure the defense capability of Russia and its allies in the long term.

Let me repeat, the country needs a combat capable army, an army with an intellectual officers corps, highly professional junior command and, finally, soldiers who sincerely want to and are ready to serve their country.

Esteemed Deputies,

Esteemed members of the Federation Council,

The prospects of the development of Russia and the solution of many of our problems will to a considerable degree be determined by the outcome of the main political event of the year, elections to the State Duma. I cannot pass over this key event in the country's life. It is an important stage in the evolution of our democracy.

In recent years, the relations between the legislative and executive branches have qualitatively improved. In place of confrontation, there is constructive cooperation based on substantive exchange of opinions, weighed criticism. Interaction has become a reality.

I consider the solidarity demonstrated by responsible politicians on the issues of combating International Terrorism, the preservation of territorial integrity of the country who support our efforts in the foreign policy arena to be a key sign of the improved spiritual health of our society. I am saying it without any exaggeration, I sincerely thank these politicians of different orientation.

I also want to thank representatives of all Deputies' Associations for active joint work. At the same time, some peculiarities of the national political life are a matter of concern to me. First of all, the mechanisms of financing political parties remain a big secret for voters. The market of election and other political technologies is largely one of the sectors of the shadow economy. I hope that in the very near future our joint work will make party life more transparent, give people more objective information, and as a result, more chances to make a correct choice.

Lack of transparency in financial operations in the political scene is often complemented by unclear ideological positions, and sometimes, let's face the truth, certain political insincerity. I will explain what I mean. Sometimes Deputies who claim to be liberals and advocates of progressive economic theories in real life vote for bills that ruin the state budget. And they understand what they do. Those who shamelessly name businessmen robbers and blood-suckers blatantly lobby for big companies.

Parliamentary parties are a part of the State-political machinery and at the same time a part of civil society. I should add that they are the most influential part of civil society and therefore the most responsible one. We are all interested in the deepening of interaction of party structures with the regions of the nation, with citizens and their public organizations.

It is obvious that the active contacts with people cannot and must not be confined to the framework of electoral debates and the campaign deadlines. Only the daily link between the State and society, that the large parties can and must ensure, can save the authorities from making serious political mistakes.

We often talk about the greatness of Russia. But a great Russia is not only a great state. It is above all a modern, developed society which cannot emerge by itself.

The fully developed civil society will emerge only in conditions of a drastic cut in the functions of the State apparatus, of eliminating the mistrust between different social groups.

But the main thing is that this will become possible only in conditions of national unity in assessing the strategic tasks faced by the nation. Creating such conditions without the vigorous participation of political parties is impossible.

I consider the coming election to the State Duma to be yet another stage in the development of our multi-party system, development in the direction of greater openness of intentions, greater effectiveness of action, more responsibility vis a vis the people of Russia.

A strong and responsible authority, based on the consolidation of society, is necessary for preserving the country. Without a strong authority it is not possible to breakthrough into the future.

I would like to stress once again that we are being faced with serious problems and threats. We need to be clever and strong in order to survive in the toughest competitive struggle in the world.

We must not simply survive. We must possess a substantial economic, intellectual, moral, and military advantage. Only in this way, shall we keep our positions among the major powers of the earth.

And that is why among the major objectives — I have already spoken about this today and I will repeat it — I regard the following:

Doubling the Gross Domestic Product; Overcoming poverty; Modernizing of the armed forces.

I believe our society is capable of achieving these results before the year 2010. The consolidation of public forces, the unshakableness of the Constitution of the Russian Federation and guaranteed rights and freedoms of citizens serve as the basis for achieving these goals.

I urge all those who consider the formulated tasks a priority for the country to mobilize intellectual potential, work out common approaches and co-ordinate concrete plans.

I have already said that I support the overall policy of increasing the role of parties in public life. Based on the results of the upcoming elections to the State Duma, I believe it will be possible to create a professional and efficient Government that will have the support of a Parliamentary majority.

As I conclude my speech, I want to say that it is possible to consolidate our efforts if the main political forces have civil responsibility that is needed for joint work.

I am convinced that Russia will most certainly rise to a height that matches its potential.

The consolidation of all our intellectual, Government and moral resources will allow Russia to achieve the most ambitious goals.

The greatest goals that are worth of a great people.

Let us wish each other success.

Thank you very much for your attention.

❮84❯

Prime Minister's Road Map for Myanmar (30.08.03)

The Prime Minister of Myanmar, Gen. Khin Nyunt reviewed the progress made by Myanmar and revealed a "roadmap" for the future. The roadmap outlined seven key steps, including reconvening the National Convention that had been adjourned since 1996, drafting of a new Constitution, holding of free and fair elections for legislative bodies and building a modern, developed and democratic nation.

Shortly after becoming Prime Minister of Myanmar on August 25, 2003, General Khin Nyunt gave a speech in which he reviewed the progress made in Myanmar and revealed a "road map" for the future. The road map outlines seven key steps, including convening a National Convention, writing a national Constitution, and holding elections.

The text of the speech is as follows:

"I would like to first of all wish all the responsible members of the State, Heads of Department and specially invited guests health and happiness.

"In my address today, I shall be explaining about important matters of the State that responsible members of the State and the general public should be aware. The address will be in three parts.

"In the first part, I would be explaining about the all round development achieved in the country from the time of the assumption of responsibilities by our Government, an achievement made possible through day and night efforts of responsible persons and the cooperation of the entire people in keeping with the objective for the emergence of modern and developed State.

"In the second part, I shall be briefly touching on the political developments in the country.

"In the third part, I shall be speaking about the various steps of the political program which will be implemented for the emergence of a modern, developed and democratic State that corresponds to the political, economic and social conditions of the country and is based on Myanmar's historical background and experiences as well as the culture and civilization of the people.

"If I may now turn to the first part of my address. Today, the State Peace and Development Council is endeavoring in all aspects for the emergence of a peaceful, modern and developed State with the aim of transforming our nation into one where the level of development of the country is comparable to those in the international community; where our national economy will be strong; and where the people will enjoy a high standard of living.

"In marching towards this national goal of a peaceful, modern and developed State, we have laid down and are vigorously implementing political, economic and social objectives that would not only yield positive results such as peace and stability, progress and development but will also strengthen national unity spirit and Union spirit that constitute the main pillars for the perpetuation of the Union.

"Peace and stability, economic development, national unity, and perpetuation of the Union are matters that are not only interlinked but are also mutually reinforcing.

"The nation will only be peaceful and tranquil if there is national unity. Likewise, it is only when there is a peaceful environment can there be development of the basic infrastructure for national development. Moreover, it is only through these developments that the national economy will grow with momentum.

"Similarly, sound economic foundation strengthens national unity and perpetuation of the Union as well as contributes to peace, stability and prosperity of the country.

"Therefore, since the time of the assumption of responsibilities by the Tatmadaw Government, it has been systematically striving for national re-consolidation, peace and tranquility and prevalence of law and order as first priority task. It is also simultaneously implementing national projects that would strengthen national economic life and the economic, social and development infrastructure necessary for the emergence of a modern and developed State.

"The national projects for development are being implemented on a pragmatic manner based on the strength of our natural resources; on the strength of our intellectuals, technicians and people; and on the strength of the economic and development infrastructure that are being built or are in the process of being built.

"It can be seen that today, due to the efforts of the Government based on the strength and capabilities of its own national resources and the participation of the entire people, the Union of Myanmar is on the right path for development. Moreover, sound foundation and fruitful results are being attained in respect of the fundamentals for national unity, basic infrastructures for national economic progress, for national development, for social development, as well as in technology.

"I believe everybody will remember that at the time of our assumption of State responsibilities, the economy was in recession and, because of the destruction and looting by destructionists, almost all the basic infrastructure necessary for development, such as factories and workshops were in ruins. Moreover, communication and transportation system in the entire country had broken down and all activities in the country had grounded to a halt.

"Starting from 1986, the economy of the country had declined and in the 1988-89 financial year, the gross domestic product (GDP) of the country was at its lowest at (47141) million kyats.

"After the assumption of responsibilities, the market oriented economic system that encourages the private sector was introduced and the national economic projects that were being implemented were also changed to correspond with the new economic policy.

"At the same time, even while the factories, workshops and the economic infrastructure that had been destroyed or damaged were being repaired and reconstructed, development infrastructures such as roads, river-crossing bridges, dams and reservoirs, universities and colleges as well as hospitals were built throughout the nation.

"Due to the day and night efforts of the Government, the GDP of the nation, which stood at only over (47000) million kyats in fiscal year 1988-89, recovered from its decline and by the 1990-91 financial year reached (50260) million kyats. In the three years period from 1989-90 to 1991-92, the GDP of the nation achieved an average annual growth rate of (5.9) percent.

"At the end of 1992-93 to 1995-96 Short Term Four Year Plan, the GDP of the country grew by an average annual rate of (7.5) percent.

"Next, from 1996-97 to 2000-2001, the Second Short Term Five Year Plan was laid down and implemented.

"During this Second Short Term Five Year Plan, systematic implementation was carried out to ensure that the present sound economic foundations would be further consolidated and that Myanmar's economy will be placed on a path of steady and durable economic growth. As a result, at the end of the Second Five Year Plan, the GDP grew by an average annual growth rate of (8.5) percent.

"The present 2003-2004 fiscal year represents the third year of the current 2001-2002 to 2005-2006 Short Term Five Year Plan. During this Five Year Plan, the planned target is to realize an average yearly GDP growth of (10.7) percent. During the 2002-2003 fiscal year i.e. the second year of the Plan, (11.1) percent GDP growth was achieved. Moreover, at the end of the 2002-2003 fiscal year, per capital GDP had increased to (105940) kyats.

"In addition, in order to diminish unemployment in the country, our Government created employment opportunities by using various methods and means. Consequently, we were able to find employment for nearly 10 million workers and the work force increased from (19) million in 1988 to the present (29) million.

"Let me now turn to the Agricultural Sector. In trying to achieve growth and development with momentum in national economic life, the Government pays special attention for all round development of the country based on an economic policy which calls for taking of agriculture as the basis and development of other economic sectors as well.

"In the initial stage, taking paddy which is the main crop in the country as the basis, the government focused its attention on measures to increase sown acreage, to utilize modern agricultural techniques and high yield seed varieties as well as to use various methods to ensure the availability of adequate water for agricultural purposes.

"At the time, when we first assumed responsibilities, paddy production in the nation was only 654 million baskets a year. Therefore, the government encouraged the farmers to grow paddy not only during the rainy season but also during summer as double cropping and set the target of reaching an annual production of 1,000 million baskets a year. Consequently, paddy production reached over 800 million baskets from 1995-96 to 1997-98 and increased to 965 million baskets in the 1999-2000 fiscal year. The original target of 1,000 million tons had been realized since the 2000-2001 fiscal year.

"As availability of water for agricultural purposes is a main requirement for development of the agricultural sector, the government has constructed dams, reservoirs, sluice gates and implemented water pumping and underground water tapping projects across the country.

"In order to obtain necessary water for agricultural purposes, a network of dams including small and medium size projccts, some coupled with power generation facilities, were constructed across the country. Since 1988, during the time of our Government, (150) dams and reservoirs as well as 265 river water pumping projects in areas where water is scare had been constructed. Due to the projects undertaken for obtaining water, agricultural land increased by more than 2 million acres.

"More than 63,494 million kyats were used from government funds to construct the 150 dams, reservoirs and weirs. Presently, 39 irrigation projects are in the process of being built and there are plans to construct 84 more.

"With regard to the Livestock and Fisheries Sector. Together with the agricultural sector, the government is also focusing on the development of the livestock and fisheries sector as Myanmar's geographical features has made this sector as one of the most economically promising sector.

"Since both the Government as well as the private sector have expanded with great momentum livestock breeding and marine industries, the livestock and fisheries sector achieved an average annual growth rate of (4.6) percent during 1992-93 to 1995-96 First Short Term Economic Plan and (12.7) percent during the 1996-97 to 2000-2001 Economic Plan. In the 2001-2002 fiscal year the sector grew by (12.6) percent and in 2002-2003 by (12.0) percent.

"The production of fresh water and salt water fish and prawns in 1987-88 was only (681,000) tons. However, this has increased to (1,579,000) tons in 2002-2003.

"With respect to the Forestry Sector: Together with the agricultural and livestock and fisheries sector, another great natural resource of our country is the forestry sector. (52.28) percent of our total land area is still covered with forests containing diverse valuable wood and bamboo resources including the internationally renowned teakwood.

"In 1988-89, reserved and protected public forest accounted for (24.8) million acres and protected area system amounted to (1.35) million acres. Due to the preservation and reforestation efforts, by the 2002-

2003 fiscal year, the reserved and protected public forest area has increased to (35.05) million acres and protected area system acreage amounted to (3.36) million acres.

"Moreover, between 1998-99 and 2002-2003 fiscal years, forest plantation including special teak plantations, has been implemented in nearly (1.1) million acres.

"Due to the progress in the forestry sector, wood-based industries have been established and value added wood products are on the increase.

"With regard to the Industrial Sector: In order to achieve economic growth based on modern industrial production during the time of our government, we are endeavouring to increase the capabilities of the state own large industrial enterprises as well as to increase industrial production on the whole. Moreover, to increase the industrial capabilities of the regions and to be able to offer more jobs opportunities, the private sector had set up (18) industrial zones and additional expanded industrial zones in various States and Divisions. At the moment, the private industrial zones are now capable of producing motor vehicles, agricultural machinery and equipment, electronic goods, spare parts needed for large factories. Moreover, there are also small factories such as factories that produced soap and detergents.

"With a view to increase industrial production, to improve the quality of the products as well as to produce import substitution goods, (257) new large, medium and small sized factories have been established in the State sector. On the other hand, the private sector also constructed (24,293) new factories. Therefore, the number of state and private owned factories increased from (27,430) in 1988 to (51,980) at present. These efforts and achievements show the endeavours by both state and private sectors to develop the industrial sector in order to realize the goal of the emergence of the modern industrial country.

"Regarding the developments in the Roads and Bridges Sector: What is contributing effectively to significant achievement in building sound foundations for economic development is the dynamic growth of the transportation infrastructure including roads and river-crossing bridges that is being constructed by the Government all over the country.

"During the time of our Government, river-crossing bridges and major roads have been constructed so that now there is a network linking east and west and south and north of the nation. Thus, all parts of the country including regions like Rakhine State and Ayeyawady Division that are full of rivers and creeks as well as the border areas are now linked by this network.

"In 1988, there were only (461) roads in the country with a total length of (13600) road miles. In the time of our Government, we were able to construct (55) new roads measuring nearly (2000) road miles.

"If we look at the bridges, before 1988, there were only (2) major bridges namely the Sagaing Bridge across the Ayeyawady and the Sittoung Bridge across the Sittoung river. Today, (158) new bridges of more than (180) feet span have been constructed including (7) large bridges spanning across the Ayeyawady river, (2) across the Chindwin river and (3) across the Thanlwin river.

"Presently, (35) new bridges including the Thanlwin bridge (Mawlamyine) which will be the longest bridge in Myanmar and Ayeyawady bridge (Yadanabon) are under construction. Moreover, plans are underway to construct another (23) bridges.

"As for the Rail Transport Sector: New rail lines that would link the important centres of the country have been constructed. These include Nyaungshwe-Yatsauk rail line, Aungban-Pinlong-Loikaw rail line, Namhsan-Mognai rail line, Shwenyaung-Namhsan rail line in the Shan State. Moreover, Chaung Oo-Pakoku-Gangaw-Kalay rail line which would involve the construction of a high standard tunnel as well as a rail line that would circle the Yoma are also being built.

"In 1988, the rail systems in Myanmar consisted of (1976) miles of railroads. In our times, another (1012) miles of railroads have been added and thus the rail system now consists of over (2900) and nearly (3000) miles of railroads.

"As for Aviation and Maritime Transport Sector: With the increased momentum in various economic and development sectors, the Government has systematically implemented measures so that international aviation and maritime transportation as well as internal aviation and inland water transportation would also develop in tandem.

"Due to these efforts to upgrade the air transportation sector, the number of airports in the country has increased to (27) from (21) airports in 1988. Moreover, at that time, there were only (6) airports in the nation where a Fokker F-28 jet aircraft can land. Today, there are (18) such airports.

"Moreover, the runways of the various airports are being lengthened so that larger aircraft can land. In addition to the upgrading of airports, (7) new airports are under construction.

"Similarly, with regard to maritime transportation, international terminals such as International Thilawa Terminal, Thakayta Terminal, Alon Terminal and Myanmar Industrial Terminal as well as modern cargo handling systems and equipment, international standard container terminals testify to the achievements in this sector.

"One development which deserves a special mention in the aviation and maritime transportation sector is the establishment for the first time ever in Myanmar of the Myanmar Maritime University and Myanmar Aerospace Engineering University where international standard marine technicians, architects and engineers as well as aviation technicians, architects and engineers are being trained.

"In the Communication Sector: Efforts to upgrade the communication sector with momentum have been implemented in order to facilitate contacts between the people living in different parts of the nation. Furthermore, it can be seen that there has been a dramatic increase in linkages with the international telecommunication network by using rapidly changing information and communication technology.

"In addition to establishing cellular, CDMA and GSM phone systems in the country, Data Communication, E-Mail, Internet, Intranet facilities are now available through the use of Information and Communication Technology (ICT).

"As Packet Switching System has been installed in both Yangon and Mandalay, it is now also possible to use Data Line and E-Mail.

Regarding the Electricity Sector: With the advancement of the nation and the raising of the standard of living and quality of life of the people, there has been a significant increased in the consumption of electricity. The Government is, therefore, implementing systematic measures to meet the increased demand for electricity.

"In 1988, the consumption of electricity amounted to (2226.45) million units. However, due to the systematic implementation of electricity projects, people are now using up to (5064.20) million units of electricity. In other words, electricity consumption has increased 2.27 times.

"To increase the generation of electricity, the Government has built hydroelectric plants, steam turbine plants, natural gas plants, as well as electricity plants using diesel oil. As a result, the installed capacity increased nearly (2) times to (1219.81) megawatts as compared to (706.82) megawatts in 1988.

"This increase in production of electricity is made possible because the Government constructed (28) Hydro-power Projects and (6) natural gas plants.

"Eleven new Electric Power Projects including Paunglaung Hydroelectric Project that would produce (280) megawatts and Yeywa Hydroelectric Project that would produce (780) megawatts are also under construction. When these (11) projects are completed, additional (1960) megawatts of electricity will become available to the public.

"Turning to the Education Sector: The national task of the education sector is to nurture and develop human resources in all fields in order to maintain and promote for the future the benefits accrued from the advancement of the nation. It must also systematically implement measures so that the rapidly progressing science and technology in international arena will reach and spread in the country.

"The Four Year Special Plan to raise the national education level involves not only the Education Ministry but also Health, Science and Technology and other Ministries concerned with Higher Education.

"In order to provide opportunities for education, basic education schools, universities and colleges have been opened across the country.

"As a result, in 1988 the number of basic education schools amounted to (33,747) schools. However in 2003, this has increased to (40,049) including branch schools and affiliated schools.

"With a view to providing the rural areas with the opportunities to get basic middle school education, (3,800) post primary schools have been opened in the country.

"As the increase in basic education schools requires additional teaching staff, the number of teachers has been increased to (222,000) in 2003 from (173,000) in 1988. In 1988, the number of students attending basic education was over (5.2) million (5,239,878). This has now increased to over (7.5) million (7,550,896).

"There were many illiterate people in our country because of the colonial legacy and the weaknesses of the succeeding periods. Therefore, after we assumed responsibility, adult literacy classes were arranged throughout the nation including the remote border areas in order to decrease the number of illiterates with the eventual aim of totally eliminating illiteracy in the country. Because of these classes, today (500,963) adults are now able to read and write. The literacy rate also increased from (78) percent to (92.2) percent.

"With regard to higher education, universities and colleges have been opened in the (24) special development zones established in (14) States and Divisions with the aim of providing all parts of the nation with opportunities for higher education as well as for human resource development of the region.

"Due to the opening of new universities and colleges, the number of universities and colleges has increased from (32) in 1988 to (154) at present.

"The expanded opening of universities and colleges have provided the people with greater educational opportunities and as a result, the number of students studying at colleges and universities increased from (130,000) to over (890,000) in 2003.

"Similarly, the teaching faculties have also seen great increase. Previously, there were only (5,600) university teachers, ranging from professors to tutors and demonstrators. Today, the number stands at (16,600).

"Moreover, in 1988, it was only possible to study up to a Master Degree. However, in 2003, various universities and colleges under the Education Ministry are providing (150) different post-graduate diploma and degree courses including (18) kinds of Master Researcher Degree, (40) kinds of Master Courses and (20) kinds of Doctorate Courses.

"If we include the (90) different kinds of Master and Doctorate Courses opened by Universities of Medicine, (73) kinds of Master and Doctorate Courses opened by Technological Universities and Universities of Computer Studies, then the number of Post Graduate Diploma and Degree Courses being arranged by Universities and Colleges in Myanmar amounts up to (313).

"In 1988, only (266) students obtained the Master Degree. As the Government has greatly expanded Post-Graduate Master and Doctorate Courses, in a period of (3) years between 2001 and 2003, (9,474) students obtained the Master Degree and (206) received their Doctorates.

"With respect to the Technical Education Sector: In the time of our Government, Science and Technology Universities and Colleges have been opened in all the States and Divisions in the country. Therefore, at present, there are four Universities of Technology, (2) Computer Universities, (1) Myanmar Aerospace Engineering University, (26) Government Technological Colleges, (24) Government Computer Colleges and (9) Government Technical Institutes.

"In previous days, the Technological Universities could only offer Master Classes. Indeed, in 1988, there were only (22) students who received the Master Degree. However, in the time of our Government, it is now possible for students to study in (73) different kinds of Post-Graduate Degree and Diploma Courses including (19) Doctorate Courses and (27) Master Courses. Consequently, from 2000-2001 to 2002-2003, within a space of (3) academic years, (1,424) students obtained their Master Degrees and (128) students received their Ph.Ds.

"Turning to the Health Sector: In endeavouring for the development of the nation, it is necessary for our people not only to have higher standards of education, but also to be healthy and strong. The greatly increased availability of health care and a higher standard of health care reflect the rising social standards of the nation.

"If we look at the progress made in health infrastructure, it can be seen that while in 1988, there were only (617) hospitals including specialist hospitals and general hospitals, in 2003 this has increased to (757) hospitals. Similarly, (84) local dispensaries and (1,414) rural health centres have been established in all parts of the country.

"In addition to (140) new hospitals, existing hospitals are being upgraded. The 25-bed hospitals have been upgraded to 50-bed ones. 100-bed hospitals to 200-bed hospitals and even up to 300-bed hospitals. Altogether (114) hospitals were upgraded.

"In 1988, there were only (4) Universities of Medicine. Today, there are (14) Universities of Medicine under the Ministry of Health. In previous times, only (10) Diploma Classes and (13) Master Classes were available. Today, the Universities of Medicine are offering (28) different Diploma Courses, (26) Master Courses, (7) Dr. Med. Sc. Courses and (29) Ph.D Courses.

"With regard to development of Border Areas Sector: During the time of our Government, we were able to build up unity among our national races; and to restore peace and stability to the border areas. As a result, we are now able to implement, in a systematic manner, projects for the development of border areas and national races. To provide more momentum to border area development works a separate Ministry for Borders was established. Thus, the development of border areas and national races and the raising of the standard of living are being implemented with greater impetus.

"Although, in the initial stage, border area development programmes were carried out only in areas where peace had returned, it has now been extended to cover all the areas in the country that have lagged behind the development.

"Presently, border area development programmes are being carried out in (18) different areas of the country covering (68) Townships in (7) States and (2) Divisions covering (83,415.34) square miles. The population in these areas is over (5.3) million and the Government is providing wide ranging humanitarian assistance to them.

"The sectors in which development activities are being carried out for border area development are ones that directly impact on the backwardness of the region and include roads and bridges, education, health, agriculture, livestock breeding, electricity, communication, mineral exploration etc. and therefore are of great benefit to the people.

"Border area development projects were implemented phase by phase starting from the 1993-94 to 1995-96 First Short Term 3-Year Plan, 1996-97 to 2000-2001 First Five-Year Plan and 2001-2002 to 2005-2006 Second Five-Year Plan. These plans also correspond with the overall national plans.

"As border areas and national races development programmes are being undertaken with momentum, the Government has already spent (45,762.87) million kyats and over US $ (506) million from the time when border area development programmes started in 1989 to the present. Due to these efforts, it can be seen that there have been significant all-round development in the border areas.

"In previous times, border areas such as Panwa in Kachin State, Laukkai, Namtit, Panhsan, Mongla in Shan State were very backward in development. Today, they have been transformed into towns with modern buildings, international standard hotels, department stores, that are comparable to those in the capital city of Yangon. These endeavours, moreover, have strengthened the spirit of national unity and Union Spirit in the country.

"In the Second Part, I will be informing the responsible persons and the people the true facts about the reasons why our Government had to assume responsibilities as well as the political developments after our assumption of responsibilities.

"It is because of the historical necessity that we were compelled to assume State responsibilities on 18 September 1988. It may be recalled at that time there arose a most alarming movement towards chaos and anarchy due to the political influences behind the violent demonstrations in the country. It is because of this situation that we unavoidably had to assume responsibilities.

"Some unscrupulous persons distorted the undeniable historical fact and tried to term the unrest and demonstrations that happened during 1988 as a movement for democracy. However much they try to persuade with sweet words, a careful analysis of the events of 1988 will show that people who tried to get political gain, people who were swayed by instigations and encouragement of western countries and people with leftist views who had donned the cloak of democracy united to deliberately create anarchism among the demonstrators and protesters who had grievances against the previous Government. As the group who were making demonstrations and launching struggles and demands with the aim of getting political gain and the group of people who were waiting for an opportunity to loot and destroy combined to form the majority, anarchism reigned over the nation and the Union was on the verge of disintegration. The people were facing untold hardship and difficulties and the Tatmadaw which has the responsibility for national defense and security of the nation had to unavoidably assume State responsibilities.

"From the time of the assumption of duties of the entire country, the historical task of restoring peace and tranquility to a nation where unrest and instability had spread to the entire nation as well as to transform the future Union of Myanmar into the peaceful modern and developed State was thrust onto our Government. It is our belief that in keeping with the changing political and economic conditions in the world, we should systematically lay down and implement national policy and programmes in keeping with democratic practices so that the Union of Myanmar will become a peaceful, modern, and developed State. In other words, we believe that we must give shape for the emergence of a democratic State that corresponds with our country and our people.

"Therefore, as you all are aware, at the time of the assumption of responsibilities it was declared that elections will be held and that multi-party system will be introduced. Political reforms were carried out step by step for the transformation to a genuine multi-party Democracy System. Our endeavours were not done in a haphazard way but to ensure the best possible future after studying the weaknesses and strength of the Democracy System that had been practiced in the past as well as to treat the historical wounds that have not been healed yet.

"Democracy can only materialize after taking into account the historical background and objective conditions of the country concerned. It is also a truth that democratic practices differ from one country to another. There exist differences between the countries that practice Democracy today and the historical background, geographical conditions as well as the culture and character of the people of our country.

"It is an undeniable fact that because of these differences, we cannot directly copy or import a Democratic System that is being practiced abroad. Neither can such a change be affected overnight.

"Because of the nature of our geography, there are many fast flowing creeks and rivers in the Union of Myanmar. There also exists steeped mountains and dense forests. Therefore, transportation connections between one place and another are inadequate and communication is difficult. Many national races live in the Union of Myanmar. There are slight differences in language and culture between them and they live in all the regions. Because of the transportation and communication difficulties, some regions lagged behind in development.

"Moreover, since the time of the regaining of independence, armed insurrection emerged across the country due to the differences in ideology and thinking, thus greatly hindering internal peace and stability as well as development and progress. This is a reason why we lagged behind in development. Even today, in some parts of the border areas there still exists armed opposition from some national brethren.

"Because of these conditions, because of these difficulties, the border regions and the remote areas where the national races live lagged behind in education, health, social and economic conditions.

"Moreover, it also resulted in the weakening of national unity in the country. Because of the lack of peace and stability in the country, it has to face great difficulties in trying to make the country modern and advanced. As such, it is not surprising that even after fifty years of independence, when compared to other countries Myanmar lagged behind in development and standard of living. Without trying to heal these own injuries and wounds it is very difficult to change overnight into a Democratic State.

"Therefore, from the time that we assumed the responsibilities, we have given priority to the development of the border areas and the national races. It is known to all that if one looks at the first declaration (1/88) issued after the assumption of responsibilities it is clearly stated that we would strive for the restoration of smooth transportation as well as for economic development to meet the food, clothing and shelter needs of the people.

"It is also our belief that consolidation of national unity in the country and emergence of economic foundations for regional development, together with the raising of the standards of living of the people are basic foundations of the Democratic System.

"Even as the Government lays down and rapidly implement the projects for the development of border areas and national races for the sake of re-consolidating national unity, it simultaneously engaged in efforts to restore trust and confidence with the armed groups so that they could return to the legal fold. As a result, 17 armed groups have now returned to the legal fold. Even a casual look can reveal that the task of persuading the armed groups to return to the legal fold represents a very difficult change. It was definitely not easy to overcome from difficult conditions created by more than four decades of national brethren fighting against each other with loss of life on both sides while the people face all kinds of difficulties and sufferings. Our Government has to achieve what had not been possible for the previous successive Governments. This success was due to the fact that there was mutual respect, understanding, confidence and sincerity on both sides. It is heartening to note that the national leaders from these groups are actively participating in the construction of basic infrastructure not only in their regions but for national development as well.

"As the conditions for peace and stability improved in the country and as national unity had been built to a certain extent, efforts were initiated in 1992 for the convening of the National Convention. The National Convention is a convention which tries to find a solution by discussion and deliberation for basic principles required in the drafting of the constitution that would shape the future democratic State. The Convention was not only composed of representatives from the political parties, representatives-elect, representatives from the national races, national races leaders that had returned to the legal fold but also from representatives of intellectuals, public servants and people from various strata in the country.

"In the National Convention, political parties and politicians have the right to take part in official deliberations and to make known their views and wishes. The National Convention, which people from the political field had longed for so long, was convened in a manner that allows all the political forces to participate in the process. The convening of the National Convention is also for the emergence of a modern, developed and democratic State in accordance with the aspirations of all strata of people.

"However, in 1995, one of the above-ground political forces, namely the NLD, decided to ignore the future of the country and placed the attitude and wishes of an individual and the interests of its own party above the national cause, and carried out a plan aimed at destroying the National Convention. Consequently, efforts for political development have now faltered at half way point.

"Instead of systematically participating and cooperating in a political program that needs to be implemented step by step, the NLD continued to intransigently hold on to the results of an election that was held thirteen years ago and launched a political attack based on the convening of the Hluttaw and holding a dialogue for its own political ends. It was they themselves and according to their own decisions that they decided to pay heed to the interests of an individual and a political party and turn their backs on the National Convention that was providing an opportunity for political parties, national races and people from all strata to hold political discussions at the highest level. However, believing that the establishment of mutual understanding and mutual confidence can contribute towards national unity, the Head of State himself with magnanimity met with Daw Aung San Suu Kyi and tried to find ways to smooth out the differences.

"However, it did not develop as we have hoped for. Due to the pressure and embargoes placed by some big nations as well as due to continuous political manipulations in order to bring down the present Government, the transformation process was again retarded. As long as a political force in the country is acting in harmony with the efforts of the collaborators of neo-colonialism from abroad who are trying to find ways to bring down the existing Government and as long as this political force continues to maintain a negative attitude or refuses to change its methods, it will result in a situation where the golden land that we all hope for will remain in the distance.

"On our part, we consider as a strength all national forces that hold true to our own country and our own national interests. Without entertaining prejudice against any person or any faction, we tried to work hand and hand with the NLD and guide it toward political change. However, the NLD turned away from the national political path and took the attitude that it would do whatever it liked. Because of this, Democracy, which was almost at hand, has become distant again.

"It is known to all that at the moment some big nations are siding with the interests of the individual which they desire and believing in one-sided false news, are unjustly pressuring our country without taking into account the interests of the 52 millions people in Myanmar and thus causing all kinds of difficulties to the people. Since the time of our independence, Myanmar has never participated or sided in any world grouping, regional grouping or military pact. However, it has consistently endeavoured to have friendly relations with neighbouring countries, regional countries and friendly nations. In the relations between States, Myanmar has never deceived or hidden anything but has always acted sincerely as befitting a good neighbour. It is also always careful not to become involved or intervened in the internal affairs of other countries or problems between different groupings. In keeping with its independent and active foreign policy, it has acted with honesty and integrity.

"In the sphere of the United Nations and international affairs, it has always respected international law and Agreements. Because Myanmar has constantly acted with integrity, it can be seen that it has contributed towards the peace and stability of regional countries including the neighbouring nations. Whether you look from the ASEAN perspective, East Asia Pacific region perspective or from BIMST-EC perspective, it can be seen that Myanmar is a strategically important country. If a big power practices hegemonism over Myanmar and installs a puppet government, it can be a threat to the existing solidarity among the nations of the region including the neighbouring countries. It will also definitely affect the peace and stability of the region. As an independent and sovereign country, Myanmar has the right to shape its own destiny. Based on the objective conditions of the country, the government and the people must and will act in unity to achieve the best possible and most appropriate results for the people".

Basically, in building a genuine Democratic State,

(1) Human Resource,

(2) Natural Resource,

(3) Capital,

(4) Technology,

(5) Stable Work Environment.

are the main requirements. A stable work environment means political stability. Presently, because we have worked day and night, the positive developments taking place in all the sectors of the country can be clearly seen. This progress was achieved due to the united efforts of the people and the national races, responsible persons from various departments, national economic forces and non-governmental organizations. Our country had to pass through very rough times in our history. We have already encountered experiences which are worse than the sanctions that are now imposed from abroad. If the unity among the national forces in the country is strong, we will be able to overcome any kind of situation. Therefore, we are striving to consolidate our national unity and to do what is necessary for building a genuine Democratic State.

"The facts that I have presented are true representations of the actual work done by the Government. We are constantly endeavouring for correct work and positive efforts in the interests of our country and its people. However, some big nations, acting on false and incorrect information and misled by the fabrications of their collaborators, have adopted a negative approach and are giving all sorts of pressures. Such actions will not contribute towards democracy and will only cause it to become further and further away. The more one pressures, the further it will become. However, as we already have the correct objective, we will work together with the people so that there will be no deviation from the path that we have chosen.

"What I have presented are the true conditions under which the government has to work as well as true events and developments.

"In the third part, I shall now continue to present the political programme that will be undertaken step by step by our Government.

"As the Union of Myanmar is composed of over 100 nationalities that have lived together in unity and harmony for thousands of years, it is a nation that is striving with highest priority to build national unity. Therefore, non-disintegration of the Union, non-disintegration of national solidarity and perpetuation of sovereignty have been laid down as national policy of the country.

"In accordance with this national policy, we are systematically advancing towards the goal of the State by laying down four political objectives, four economic objectives and four social objectives for the emergence of a modern and developed nation.

"At this junction, I would like to reiterate the most important four political objectives, which are:

(1) Stability of the State, community peace and tranquility, prevalence of law and order;

(2) National re-consolidation;

(3) Emergence of a new enduring State Constitution;

(4) Building of a new modern developed nation in accord with the new State Constitution.

"The manner in which the nation will be built can clearly be seen in these four political objectives. Therefore, the emergence of a new enduring State Constitution is the most important key in building a new nation.

"Therefore, the Government will be implementing in a step-by-step and systematic manner the following political program for building the nation.

(1) Reconvening of the National Convention that has been adjourned since 1996.

(2) After the successful holding of the National Convention, step by step implementation of the process necessary for the emergence of a genuine and disciplined Democratic System.

(3) Drafting of a new Constitution in accordance with basic principles and detailed basic principles laid down by the National Convention.

(4) Adoption of the Constitution through national referendum.

(5) Holding of free and fair elections for Pythu Hluttaws (Legislative bodies) according to the new Constitution.

(6) Convening of Hluttaws attended by Hluttaw members in accordance with the new constitution.

(7) Building a modern, developed and democratic nation by the State leaders elected by the Hluttaw; and the Government and other central organs formed by the Hluttaw.

"This is the Road Map of Myanmar"

"In concluding, I would like to summarize that:" The most important factor in building a new, peaceful, modern, developed and Democratic nation is the emergence of a disciplined Democratic System that does not effect the historical traditions of the Union of the national races living in unison and harmony for thousands of years; that does not effect the national prestige and integrity of our people and nation; and that does not effect the national characteristics of our people. Therefore, I would like to urge all the national races to work together with the Government in unity, and the local authorities and the responsible Government departmental personnel to actively render necessary assistance, for the realization of the seven steps in the political programme mentioned above which the Government will continue to implement for the emergence of a new enduring State Constitution and building of a new modern developed nation in accordance with the national policy of Our Three Main National Causes as well as twelve political, economic and social objectives.

"In addition to this, it is very important to advance along the national path without deviation by firmly embracing patriotism, national spirit, spirit of national unity and Union spirit for the perpetuation of the Union in its march towards the national goal of a new peaceful, modern, developed and Democratic State for the long term interest of the State and all the people.

"As the goal of the emergence of a peaceful, modern and developed nation means the strengthening of national economic life and firm establishment of economic infrastructures, we must strive forward by utilizing the natural resources inside the country together with the resources of intellectuals, technicians and the united strength of the people.

"Therefore, in concluding, I would like to urge the Government and all the national races to unitedly work together, for responsible personnel of the Government Departments, local authorities and non-Governmental organizations to endeavour diligently and for all to march on the correct national path in order to reach the goal of a new modern, developed and Democratic Nation which the Union of Myanmar is aspiring for."

‹85›

UN General Assembly Address by President George W. Bush (23.09.03)

In his address to the UN General Assembly, President Bush defended the US action in Iraq. While noting that several countries "disagreed with our action", President Bush appealed to the Assembly to "move forward". He talked at length about the emerging challenges to world peace including the "deadly combination of outlaw regimes, terror networks and weapons of mass murder". He also picked up the theme of "humanitarian crisis" including AIDS, commerce in humans and described the US plan to meet these challenges. He mentioned the US backed "Proliferation Security Initiative" to keep the most destructive weapons away from the US shore.

"Mr. Secretary-General, Mr. President, distinguished delegates, ladies and gentlemen: Twenty-four months ago and yesterday in the memory of America, the center of New York City became a battlefield and a graveyard and the symbol of an unfinished war. Since that day, terrorists have struck in Bali, in Mombasa, in Casablanca, in Riyadh, in Jakarta, in Jerusalem, measuring the advance of their cause in the chaos and innocent suffering they leave behind.

Last month, terrorists brought their war to the United Nations itself. The U.N. Headquarters in Baghdad stood for order and compassion and for that reason, the terrorists decided it must be destroyed.

Among the 22 people who were murdered was Sergio Vieira de Mello. Over the decades, this good and brave man from Brazil gave help to the afflicted in Bangladesh, Cyprus, Mozambique, Lebanon, Cambodia, central Africa, Kosovo and East Timor, and was aiding the people of Iraq in their time of need.

America joins you, his colleagues, in honouring the memory of Senhor Vieira de Mello, and the memory of all who died with him in the service of the United Nations.

By the victims they choose, and by the means they use, the terrorists have clarified the struggle we are in. Those who target relief workers for death have set themselves against all humanity.

Those who incite murder and celebrate suicide reveal their contempt for life itself. They have no place in any religious faith, they have no claim on the world's sympathy and they should have no friend in this chamber.

Events during the past two years have set before us the clearest of divides: Between those who seek order and those who spread chaos; between those who work for peaceful change and those who adopt the methods of gangsters; between those who honour the rights of man and those who deliberately take the lives of men and women and children, without mercy or shame.

Between these alternatives there is no neutral ground. All governments that support terror are complicit in a war against civilization. No government should ignore the threat of terror because to look the other way gives terrorists the chance to regroup and recruit and prepare. And all nations that fight terror, as if the lives of their own people depend on it, will earn the favorable judgement of history.

The former regimes of Afghanistan and Iraq knew these alternatives and made their choices. The Taliban was a sponsor and servant of terrorism. When confronted, that regime chose defiance and that regime is no more.

Afghanistan's president, who is here today, now represents a free people who are building a decent and just society, a nation fully joined in the war against terror.

The regime of Saddam Hussein cultivated ties to terror while it built weapons of mass destruction. It used those weapons in acts of mass murder and refused to account for them when confronted by the world. The Security Council was right to be alarmed.

The Security Council was right to demand that Iraq destroy its illegal weapons and prove that it had done so. The Security Council was right to vow serious consequences if Iraq refused to comply. And because there were consequences, because a coalition of nations acted to defend the peace and the credibility of the United Nations, Iraq is free, and today we are joined by representatives of a liberated country.

Saddam Hussein's monuments have been removed and not only his statues. The true monuments of his rule and his character, the torture chambers and the rape rooms and the prison cells for innocent children, are closed. And as we discover the killing fields and mass graves of Iraq, the true scale of Saddam's cruelty is being revealed.

The Iraqi people are meeting hardships and challenges, like every nation that has set out on the path of democracy. Yet their future promises lives of dignity and freedom and that is a world away from, the squalid, vicious tyranny they have known. Across Iraq, life is being improved by liberty. Across the Middle East, people are safer because an unstable aggressor has been removed from power.

Across the world, nations are more secure because an ally of terror has fallen.

Our actions in Afghanistan and Iraq were supported by many governments, and America is grateful to each one. I also recognize that some of the sovereign nations of this assembly disagreed with our actions. Yet there was, and there remains, unity among us on the fundamental principles and objectives of the United Nations. We are dedicated to the defense of our collective security, and to the advance of human rights. These permanent commitments call us to great work in the world, work we must do together. So let us move forward.

First, we must stand with the people of Afghanistan and Iraq as they build free and stable countries. The terrorists and their allies fear and fight this progress above all, because free people embrace hope over resentment, and choose peace over violence.

The United Nations has been a friend of the Afghan people, distributing food and medicine, helping refugees return home, advising on a new Constitution, and helping to prepare the way for nationwide elections.

NATO has taken over the UN-mandated security force in Kabul. American and coalition forces continue to track and defeat Al-Qaida terrorists and remnants of the Taliban. Our efforts to rebuild that country go on. I have recently proposed to spend an additional $1.2 billion for the Afghan reconstruction effort and I urge other nations to continue contributing to this important cause.

In the nation of Iraq, the United Nations is carrying out vital and effective work every day. By the end of 2004, more than ninety percent of Iraqi children under age five will have been immunized against preventable diseases such as polio, tuberculosis, and measles thanks to the hard work and high ideals of UNICEF.

Iraq's food distribution system is operational, delivering nearly a half-million tons of food per month, thanks to the skill and expertise of the World Food Program.

Our international coalition in Iraq is meeting its responsibilities. We are conducting precision raids against terrorists and holdouts of the former regime. These killers are at war with the Iraqi people. They have made Iraq the central front in the war on terror and they will be defeated.

Our coalition has made sure that Iraq's former dictator will never again use weapons of mass destruction. We are now interviewing Iraqi citizens and analyzing records of the old regime, to reveal the full extent of its weapons programs and long campaign of deception. We are training Iraqi police, border guards, and a new army, so that the Iraqi people can assume full responsibility for their own security.

At the same time, our coalition is helping to improve the daily lives of the Iraqi people. The old regime built palaces while letting schools decay, so we are rebuilding more than a thousand schools. The old regime starved hospitals of resources, so we have helped to supply and reopen hospitals across Iraq. The old regime built up armies and weapons, while allowing the nation's infrastructure to crumble. So we are rehabilitating power plants, water and sanitation facilities, bridges, and airports.

I have proposed to Congress that the United States provide additional funding for our work in Iraq, the greatest financial commitment of its kind since the Marshall Plan. Having helped to liberate Iraq, we will honor our pledges to Iraq. And by helping the Iraqi people build a stable and peaceful country, we will make our own countries more secure.

The primary goal of our coalition in Iraq is self-government for the people of Iraq, reached by orderly and democratic means. This process must unfold according to the needs of Iraqis neither hurried nor delayed by the wishes of other parties. And the United Nations can contribute greatly to the cause of Iraqi self-government.

America is working with friends and allies on a new Security Council resolution, which will expand the U.N.'s role in Iraq. As in the aftermath of other conflicts, the United Nations should assist in developing a Constitution, training civil servants, and conducting free and fair elections. Iraq now has a Governing Council, the first truly representative institution in that country. Iraq's new leaders are showing the openness and tolerance that democracy requires, and also showing courage.

Yet, every young democracy needs the help of friends. Now the nation of Iraq needs and deserves our aid, and all nations of good will should step forward and provide that support.

The success of a free Iraq will be watched and noted throughout the region. Millions will see that freedom, equality, and material progress are possible at the heart of the Middle East. Leaders in the region will face the clearest evidence that free institutions and open societies are the only path to long-term national success and dignity.

And a transformed Middle East would benefit the entire world, by undermining the ideologies that export violence to other lands.

Iraq as a dictatorship had great power to destabilize the Middle East. Iraq as a democracy will have great power to inspire the Middle East. The advance of democratic institutions in Iraq is setting an example that others, including the Palestinian people, would be wise to follow. The Palestinian cause is betrayed by leaders who cling to power by feeding old hatreds, and destroying the good work of others. The Palestinian people deserve their own state, committed to reform, to fighting terror, and to building peace.

All parties in the Middle East must meet their responsibilities, and carry out the commitments they made at Aqaba. Israel must work to create the conditions that will allow a peaceful Palestinian State to emerge. Arab nations must cut off funding and other support for terrorist organizations. America will work with every nation in the region that acts boldly for the sake of peace.

A second challenge we must confront together is the proliferation of weapons of mass destruction. Outlaw regimes that possess nuclear, chemical and biological weapons — and the means to deliver them — would be able to use blackmail and create chaos in entire regions. These weapons could be used by terrorists to bring sudden disaster and suffering on a scale we can scarcely imagine.

The deadly combination of outlaw regimes, terror networks and weapons of mass murder is a peril that cannot be ignored or wished away. If such a danger is allowed to fully materialize, all words, all protests, will come too late. Nations of the world must have the wisdom and the will to stop grave threats before they arrive.

One crucial step is to secure the most dangerous materials at their source.

For more than a decade, the United States has worked with Russia and other States of the former Soviet Union to dismantle, destroy, or secure weapons and dangerous materials left over from another era. Last year in Canada, the G-8 nations agreed to provide up to $20 billion — half of it from the United States — to fight this proliferation risk over the next ten years. Since then, six additional countries have joined the effort. More are needed, and I urge other nations to help us meet this danger.

We are also improving our capability to interdict lethal materials in transit. Through our Proliferation Security Initiative, eleven nations are preparing to search planes, ships, trains and trucks carrying suspect cargo, and to seize weapons or missile shipments that raise proliferation concerns.

These nations have agreed on a set of interdiction principles, consistent with current legal authorities. And we are working to expand the Proliferation Security Initiative to other countries. We are determined to keep the world's most destructive weapons away from all our shores, and out of the hands of our common enemies.

Because proliferators will use any route or channel that is open to them, we need the broadest possible cooperation to stop them. Today I ask the U.N. Security Council to adopt a new anti-proliferation resolution. This resolution should call on all members of the U.N. to criminalize the proliferation of weapons of mass destruction; to enact strict export controls consistent with international standards; and to secure any and all sensitive materials within their own borders. The United States stands ready to help any nation draft these new laws, and to assist in their enforcement.

A third challenge we share is a challenge to our conscience. We must act decisively to meet the humanitarian crises of our time. The United States has begun to carry out the Emergency Plan for AIDS Relief, aimed at preventing AIDS on a massive scale, and treating millions who have the disease already. We have pledged $15 billion over five years to fight AIDS around the world.

My country is acting to save lives from famine as well. We are providing more than $1.4 billion in global emergency food aid, and I have asked the United States Congress for $200 million for a new famine fund, so we can act quickly when the first signs of famine appear. Every nation on every continent should generously add their resources to the fight against disease and desperate hunger.

There is another humanitarian crisis, spreading and yet hidden from view. Each year, an estimated eight to nine hundred thousand human beings are bought, sold, or forced across the world's borders. Among them are hundreds of thousands of teenage girls, and others as young as five, who fall victim to the sex trade. This commerce in human life generates billions of dollars each year, much of which is used to finance organized crime.

There is a special evil in the abuse and exploitation of the most innocent and vulnerable. The victims of sex trade see little of life before they see the very worst of life, an underworld of brutality and lonely fear. Those who create these victims, and profit from their suffering, must be severely punished. Those who patronize this industry debase themselves and deepen the misery of others. And governments that tolerate this trade are tolerating a form of slavery.

This problem has appeared in my own country, and we are working to stop it. The Protect Act, which I signed into law this year, makes it a crime for any person to enter the United States, or for any citizen to travel abroad for the purpose of sex tourism involving children. The Department of Justice is actively investigating sex tour operators and patrons, who can face up to thirty years in prison.

Under the Trafficking Victims Protection Act, the United States is using sanctions against governments to discourage human trafficking.

The victims of this industry also need help from other members of the United Nations. And this begins with clear standards and the certainty of punishment under the laws of every country. Today, some nations make it a crime to sexually abuse children abroad. Such conduct should be a crime in all nations. Governments should inform travellers of the harm this industry does, and the severe punishments that will fall on its patrons.

The American Government is committing $50 million to support the good work of organizations that are rescuing women and children from exploitation, and giving them shelter, medical treatment, and the hope of a new life. I urge other governments to do their part.

We must show new energy in fighting back an old evil. Nearly two centuries after the abolition of the trans-Atlantic slave trade, and more than a century after slavery was officially ended in its last strongholds, the trade in human beings for any purpose must not be allowed to thrive in our time.

All the challenges I have spoken of this morning require urgent attention and moral clarity: helping Afghanistan and Iraq to succeed as free nations in a transformed region, cutting off the avenues of proliferation, abolishing modern forms of slavery. These are the kinds of great tasks for which the United Nations was founded.

In each case, careful discussion is needed and also decisive action. Our good intentions will be credited only if we achieve good results. As an original signer of the U.N. charter, the United States of America is committed to the United Nations. And we show that commitment by working to fulfill the U.N.'s stated purposes, and give meaning to its ideals.

The founding documents of the United Nations and the founding documents of America stand in the same tradition. Both assert that human beings should never be reduced to objects of power or commerce, because their dignity is inherent.

Both recognize a moral law that stands above men and nations which must be defended and enforced by men and nations. And both point the way to peace, the peace that comes when all are free. We secure that peace with our courage, and we must show that courage together.

May God bless you all.

❮86❯

UN Secretary General's address to the General Assembly (23.09.03)

In his fortnight and candid address, the UN Secretary General, in an indirect criticism of the US doctrine of pre-emption, warned that "to use force pre-emptively, even in the territory of other states....represents a fundamental challenge to the principal on which.......world peace and stability have rested for the last 50 years". He described the present moment "no less decisive than 1945 itself". Warning that "history is a harsh judge", the Secretary General exhorted the General Assembly to address the fundamental policy issues facing the UN. He also announced the establishment of a High-Level Panel of eminent personalities to examine the current challenge to peace and security and recommend ways of strengthening the UN.

Thank you Mr. President, Your Majesty, Distinguished Heads of State and Government, Excellencies, Ladies and Gentlemen:

The last twelve months have been very painful for those of us who believe in collective answers to our common problems and challenges.

In many countries, terrorism has once again brought death and suffering to innocent people.

In the Middle East, and in certain parts of Africa, violence has continued to escalate.

In the Korean peninsula, and elsewhere, the threat of nuclear proliferation casts an ominous shadow across the landscape.

And barely one month ago, in Baghdad, the United Nations itself suffered a brutal and deliberate assault, in which the international community lost some of its most talented servants. Yesterday it was attacked again. Another major disaster was averted only by the prompt action of the Iraqi police, one of whom paid with his life.

I extend my most sincere condolences to the family of that brave policeman. And my thoughts go also to the nineteen injured, including two Iraqi UN staff members. I wish them all a rapid recovery. Indeed, we should pray for all those who have lost their lives or been injured in this war – innocent civilians and soldiers alike. In that context I deplore – as I am sure you all do – the brutal attempt on the life of Dr. Akila al-Hashemi, a member of the Governing Council, and I pray for her full recovery, too.

Excellencies, you are the United Nations. The staff who were killed and injured in the attack on our Baghdad Headquarters were your staff. You had given them a mandate to assist the suffering Iraqi people, and to help Iraq recover their sovereignty.

In future, not only in Iraq but wherever the United Nations is engaged, we must take more effective measures to protect the security of our staff. I count on your full support – legal, political and financial.

Meanwhile, let me reaffirm the great importance I attach to a successful outcome in Iraq. Whatever view each of us may take of the events of recent months, it is vital to all of us that the outcome is a stable and democratic Iraq – at peace with itself and with its neighbours, and contributing to stability in the region.

Subject to security considerations, the United Nations system is prepared to play its full role in working for a satisfactory outcome in Iraq, and to do so as part of an international effort, an effort by the whole international community, pulling together on the basis of a sound and viable policy. If it takes extra time and patience to forge that policy, a policy that is collective, coherent and workable, then I for one would regard that time as well spent. Indeed, this is how we must approach all the many pressing crises that confront us today.

Excellencies,

Three years ago, when you came here for the Millennium Summit, we shared a vision, a vision of global solidarity and collective security, expressed in the Millennium Declaration.

But recent events have called that consensus in question.

All of us know there are new threats that must be faced – or, perhaps, old threats in new and dangerous combinations: new forms of terrorism, and the proliferation of weapons of mass destruction.

But, while some consider these threats as self-evidently the main challenge to world peace and security, others feel more immediately menaced by small arms employed in civil conflict, or by so-called "soft threats" such as the persistence of extreme poverty, the disparity of income between and within societies, and the spread of infectious diseases, or climate change and environmental degradation.

In truth, we do not have to choose. The United Nations must confront all these threats and challenges – new and old, "hard" and "soft". It must be fully engaged in the struggle for development and poverty eradication, starting with the achievement of the Millennium Development Goals; in the common struggle to protect our common environment; and in the struggle for human rights, democracy and good governance.

In fact, all these struggles are linked. We now see, with chilling clarity, that a world where many millions of people endure brutal oppression and extreme misery will never be fully secure, even for its most privileged inhabitants.

Yet the "hard" threats, such as terrorism and weapons of mass destruction, are real, and cannot be ignored.

Terrorism is not a problem only for rich countries. Ask the people of Bali, or Bombay, Nairobi, or Casablanca.

Weapons of mass destruction do not threaten only the western or northern world. Ask the people of Iran, or of Halabja in Iraq.

Where we disagree, it seems, is on how to respond to these threats.

Since this Organisation was founded, States have generally sought to deal with threats to the peace through containment and deterrence, by a system based on collective security and the United Nations Charter.

Article 51 of the Charter prescribes that all States, if attacked, retain the inherent right of self-defence. But until now it has been understood that when States go beyond that, and decide to use force to deal with broader threats to international peace and security, they need the unique legitimacy provided by the United Nations.

Now, some say this understanding is no longer tenable, since an "armed attack" with weapons of mass destruction could be launched at any time, without warning, or by a clandestine group.

Rather than wait for that to happen, they argue, States have the right and obligation to use force pre-emptively, even on the territory of other States, and even while weapons systems that might be used to attack them are still being developed.

According to this argument, States are not obliged to wait until there is agreement in the Security Council. Instead, they reserve the right to act unilaterally, or in ad hoc coalitions.

This logic represents a fundamental challenge to the principles on which, however imperfectly, world peace and stability have rested for the last fifty-eight years.

My concern is that, if it were to be adopted, it could set precedents that resulted in a proliferation of the unilateral and lawless use of force, with or without justification.

But it is not enough to denounce unilateralism, unless we also face up squarely to the concerns that make some States feel uniquely vulnerable, since it is those concerns that drive them to take unilateral action. We must show that those concerns can, and will, be addressed effectively through collective action.

Excellencies, we have come to a fork in the road. This may be a moment no less decisive than 1945 itself, when the United Nations was founded.

At that time, a group of far-sighted leaders, led and inspired by President Franklin D. Roosevelt, were determined to make the second half of the twentieth century different from the first half. They saw that the human race had only one world to live in, and that unless it managed its affairs prudently, all human beings may perish.

So they drew up rules to govern international behaviour, and founded a network of institutions, with the United Nations at its centre, in which the peoples of the world could work together for the common good.

Now we must decide whether it is possible to continue on the basis agreed then, or whether radical changes are needed.

And we must not shy away from questions about the adequacy, and effectiveness, of the rules and instruments at our disposal.

Among those instruments, none is more important than the Security Council itself.

In my recent report on the implementation of the Millennium Declaration, I drew attention to the urgent need for the Council to regain the confidence of States, and of world public opinion – both by demonstrating its ability to deal effectively with the most difficult issues, and by becoming more broadly representative of the international community as a whole, as well as the geopolitical realities of today.

The Council needs to consider how it will deal with the possibility that individual States may use force "pre-emptively" against perceived threats.

Its members may need to begin a discussion on the criteria for an early authorisation of coercive measures to address certain types of threats – for instance, terrorist groups armed with weapons of mass destruction.

And they still need to engage in serious discussions of the best way to respond to threats of genocide or other comparable massive violations of human rights – an issue which I raised myself from this podium in 1999. Once again this year, our collective response to events of this type – in the Democratic Republic of the Congo, and in Liberia – has been hesitant and tardy.

As for the composition of the Council, that has been on the agenda of this Assembly for over a decade. Virtually all Member States agree that the Council should be enlarged, but there is no agreement on the details.

I respectfully suggest to you, Excellencies, that in the eyes of your peoples the difficulty of reaching Agreement does not excuse your failure to do so. If you want the Council's decisions to command greater respect, particularly in the developing world, you need to address the issue of its composition with greater urgency.

But the Security Council is not the only institution that needs strengthening. As you know, I am doing my best to make the Secretariat more effective – and I look to this Assembly to support my efforts.

Indeed, in my report I also suggested that this Assembly itself needs to be strengthened, and that the role of the Economic and Social Council – and the role of the United Nations as a whole in economic and social affairs, including its relationship to the Bretton Woods institutions –needs to be re-thought and reinvigorated.

I even suggested that the role of the Trusteeship Council could be reviewed, in light of new kinds of responsibility that you have given to the United Nations in recent years.

In short, Excellencies, I believe the time is ripe for a hard look at fundamental policy issues, and at the structural changes that may be needed in order to strengthen them.

History is a harsh judge: it will not forgive us if we let this moment pass.

For my part, I intend to establish a High-Level Panel of eminent personalities, to which I will assign four tasks:

First, to examine the current challenges to peace and security;

Second, to consider the contribution which collective action can make in addressing these challenges;

Third, to review the functioning of the major organs of the United Nations and the relationship between them; and Fourth, to recommend ways of strengthening the United Nations, through reform of its institutions and processes.

The Panel will focus primarily on threats to peace and security. But it will also need to examine other global challenges, in so far as these may influence or connect with those threats.

I will ask the Panel to report back to me before the beginning of the next session of this General Assembly, so that I can make recommendations to you at that session. But only you can take the firm and clear decisions that will be needed.

Those decisions might include far-reaching institutional reforms. Indeed, I hope they will.

But institutional reforms alone will not suffice. Even the most perfect instrument will fail, unless people put it to good use.

The United Nations is by no means a perfect instrument, but it is a precious one. I urge you to seek Agreement on ways of improving it, but above all of using it as its founders intended – to save succeeding generations from the scourge of war, to reaffirm faith in fundamental human rights, to re-establish the basic conditions for justice and the rule of law, and to promote social progress and better standards of life in larger freedom.

The world may have changed, Excellencies, but those aims are as valid and urgent as ever. We must keep them firmly in our sights.

Thank you very much.

❮87❯

Statement by Mr. Hamid Karzai President of Afghanistan At the 58th Session of the General Assembly of the United Nations (25.09.03)

President Karzai congratulated the ISAF on the "tremendous job of securing the nation's capital" and described NATO's decision to take over command of the ISAF in Kabul as a positive development. He said that the draft constitution would be submitted to a "Loya Jirga" in December and emphasized that "we will never permit our territory to be used against any other country, and expect the same in return".

Mr. President,

Your Excellency the Secretary General, Distinguished guests,
Ladies and gentlemen,

There is no reality more oppressive than the silence of a nation. For too long, Afghanistan was a silenced nation, a country without a voice. After decades of being suppressed to silence, our nation is beginning to have a voice of its own. Recovering from the tragedy of war and destruction, Afghanistan is determined to reverse the effects of the suffering it has long endured.

A lot has changed in Afghanistan over the last two years. But no change is so critical and pervasive than the animated response from the people of Afghanistan to the recent developments in our country. I find no sight more rewarding than the sight of our young girls and boys flocking to schools every morning; I find few things more engaging than the company of elderly representatives who come to Kabul from far-flung provinces of the country to discuss their priorities for reconstruction; and, in the same order, there is nothing more enthusing than the active participation of Afghan men and women in the process of public consultation for the new Constitution.

The people of Afghanistan, we know from the public consultation conducted in connection with the Constitution drafting process, want a modern unitary state that is committed to Islamic values and the preservation of peace and national unity. A state that insures security for all its citizens, enforces justice and the rule of law, and promotes prosperity. Like any post-war society, the need for security and removing the threat of arms and armed factions is a compelling issue for all

Afghans. Our people demand the establishment of truly national and competent institutions, notably the Army and the Police. Afghans want state institutions that are professional and representative; and an administration that is efficient and free of corruption. The Afghan people want tolerance for other religions, protection of human rights, and affirmative actions to promote the rights of women.

Mr. President,

Since I addressed this august assembly in September of last year, Afghanistan has taken significant strides in the path of post-war reconstruction. While total stability may not have been achieved yet, Afghanistan today is more stable and peaceful than at any other period in its recent history. The International Security Assistance Force (ISAF), to the credit of the participating countries, has done a tremendous job of securing the nation's capital. This is partly the reason that people from other parts of the country have demanded that ISAF be expanded to their areas too. We see the NATO's decision to take over the command of ISAF in Kabul as a positive development. The Afghan people have also welcomed the Provincial Reconstruction Teams (PRTs) that are supported by the coalition member states. Reconstruction and security are tied together, and we are absolutely certain that, no matter what flag they fly, forces that ensure stability will be welcomed throughout Afghanistan.

We recognize, however, that providing security to the people of Afghanistan is ultimately our own responsibility. We are grateful to the international community, the United States and Germany in particular, for making a determined effort to help us embark on a process of reforming and rebuilding our security institutions, namely the Afghan National Army and the National Police. After an arduous process of restructuring, we have just completed the Reform of the Ministry of Defense. This step is now paving the way for the implementation of the nation-wide programme on Disarmament, Demobilisation and Re-integration (DDR) which will begin in earnest in mid October with assistance from Japan.

Constitution is the bedrock of the modern state. Under the Bonn Agreement, my government was assigned the historic task of giving Afghanistan its new Constitution. After a broad process of consultation, the commission assigned to the task has just finished the draft constitution. The draft will be submitted for approval to a Constitutional Loya Jirga, or Afghan Grand Council, in December. Work on the reform of the judicial system, and on drafting of new secondary lalaws, has also been continuing with notable outcomes achieved in recent months. The Political Parties Law and the Banking Law have now been officially adopted.

Having started from a below-zero baseline, the 30 percent economic growth rate which Afghanistan enjoyed last year is a promising start. Committed as we are to an open market economy, and seeing the private sector as the true engine for growth, we have moved aggressively to create the legal and financial frameworks for a positive environment to the private sector. Our newly adopted laws that govern investment, banking and property rights, the new stable currency, and the bureaucratic reforms we have enacted, provide a liberal and conducive underpinning to a rapid economic growth. Like never before, Afghanistan is open to business. Once in the past, Afghanistan was at the center of a global threat. Our vision for the future is that Afghanistan should be a center for economic opportunity. We do not call ourselves a landlocked country, we are rather a land-bridging country. Afghanistan connects together South Asia, Central Asia and the Middle East, a fact to which geo-strategists have long been attracted. But it is time that Afghanistan's vast potential for facilitating trade and economic activity is exploited.

Through such nation-wide programmes as the National Solidarity Programme (NSP) the Government aims to take re-construction to the villages and households of Afghanistan. Perhaps no other priority features more widely in the demands of the Afghan people than the provision of education. Today, almost 40 percent of the students and teachers in primary and secondary education are female. This is a huge rise from the close to zero percentage that we inherited from the Taliban. Millions of text books have been published, and schools are being built at a higher pace than ever. However, like in other areas of service provision, the need is much greater than our capacity to deliver.

The struggle against production and trafficking of narcotics continues. We see a direct connection between narcotics and terrorism, and it is in our absolute national interest to fight both. Both are transnational challenges. We in the region and in the international community must make the strategic decision, in the spirit of true partnership, to fight against both menaces.

As we acknowledge that the road ahead of Afghanistan is long and tortuous, we appreciate that significant achievements have been made over the last two years. The people of Afghanistan are grateful to the international community for their crucial support. While countries that have extended friendly hands to Afghanistan are far too many to thank, it would be unfair not to single out the United States, the European Union and Japan for a special mention. The United States of America has led the international community by example in offering support to Afghanistan. The additional assistance provided to us under the Accelerated Success initiative will go a long way towards rebuilding our country. The neighbours of Afghanistan have a special place in our hearts. Our people will always remember the warm welcome they have received from their brothers and sisters in Pakistan and Iran.

Cognizant of our new situation and the emerging opportunities, we are determined to build friendly, civil and constructive relationships with countries of the world. We continue to extend a sincere hand of friendship to Pakistan and all our other neighbours on the basis of the requirements of a civilized relationship. We will never permit our territory to be used against any other country, and expect the same in return. We are deeply concerned about the loss of innocent lives in Palestine and Israel. We support the realization of the right of self-determination for the people of Palestine. We are fully committed to remain a resilient partner with the international community in the fight against terrorism.

Mr. President,

All the achievements I have just noted only amount to a good beginning. Our challenge is to stay the course. This depends not only on the resolute determination of the Afghan people, but also on the continued engagement of the international community.

While achievements are significant, and challenges inevitable, today in this grand forum, I point to what can potentially amount to a critical threat, the ongoing threat of terrorism. The crisis in Afghanistan may well be over, but the forces of violence are still looming. Embodied in various manifestations, from cross-border militant infiltrations to hateful teachings at places disguised as madrassas, terrorism continues to make inroads into the space of peace and prosperity which we want to secure for our nation.

Islam, our universalist religion, has absolutely no place for terrorism. Those apostles of hatred who preach murder in the name of religion; those who abuse the name of Islam and the sanctity of madrassas; are the enemies of Islam. They act against all that Islam teaches-peace, tolerance, compassion, social justice and the good of humanity.

Terrorists aim to harm the nation of Afghanistan; a deeply believing Muslim nation that is averse to extremism. They pose a threat to the process of re-construction in Afghanistan. Terrorists see, in the success of re-construction, their lasting defeat. They are, therefore, maliciously intent on derailing the process.

This must stop! We must defeat the forces and ideas of violence in the region. Today, terrorism is a liability to the governments in the region. Governments must stop using extremism as an instrument of policy. As long as terrorism survives in this part of the world, neither Afghanistan, nor our neighbours, nor indeed the rest of the world can be safe.

Thank you.

❮88❯

Address by Gen. Parvez Musharraf, President of Pakistan, at UNGA (26.09.03)

In an anti-India tirade, President Musharraf stated that India had embarked on a massive build-up of its conventional and non-conventional military capabilities, advanced offensive aircraft, ballistic and cruise missiles, ABM systems, nuclear submarines and an aircraft carrier. He stated that Pakistan would be prepared "to encourage a general cessation of violence within Kashmir, involving reciprocal obligations and restrains on Indian forces and the Kashmir Freedom Movement".

Mr. President,

It is with great pleasure that I extend to you our warmest felicitations on your election. I also congratulate your predecessor, H.E. Mr.Jan Kavan, for his effective leadership during the last Session of the General Assembly.

2. We support Secretary-General Kofi Annan's efforts to infuse a new sense of mission in the United Nations and maintain the centrality of its role in the promotion of global peace and security. We pay tribute to the memory of Mr. Sergio de Mello and the other UN officials who sacrificed their lives in the service of peace.

Mr. President,

3. When the Berlin Wall collapsed, hopes revived for a new age of co-operation and peace, free of ideological confrontations. Sadly, these hopes were dashed:
   - By the ethnic cleansing in Bosnia, and then in Kosovo;
   - By the failure to end the occupation of Palestine, leading to the revived Intifada against Israeli occupation;
   - By the brutal suppression of the Kashmiris demand for self-determination and freedom from Indian occupation;
   - By the unending war in Afghanistan and the international neglect which created a climate in which extremism and terrorism could breed;
   - By the series of international financial crises and the rise of poverty as a consequence of unequal economic globalization.

4. The terrible terrorist atrocity of 9/11 jolted the foundations of the international system. The response has weakened Al-Qaida. But, it has not eliminated its associates. Terrorists have struck repeatedly around the world in Indonesia, Tunisia, Morocco, Saudi Arabia, Russia, Kenya and in my country Pakistan.
5. The tragedy of 9/11 transformed security policies and changed geo-political calculations. Pakistan took a strategic decision, based on the principles of humanity and our national interest, to support the war on terrorism. Our intentions should be in no doubt whatsoever. Our actions speak louder than words. Our capabilities were limited but have been progressively improved. We are acting against Al-Qaida and its associates effectively. We have also acted against other organizations or groups involved in any form of terrorism. Pakistan will remain in the forefront of the war on terrorism.
6. The war against terrorism must be fought comprehensively, on a global front, with vision and understanding. It should "not erode the moral values of our societies. It must not be hijacked by those who seek to use it as an excuse to suppress other peoples. It must not be allowed to engender a clash of civilizations, a clash between Islam and the West."

Mr. President,

Once again, from this august rostrum, I invite India to join Pakistan in a sustained dialogue to resolve the Kashmir dispute. I am convinced that, with goodwill, we can find a just solution which is acceptable to India, to Pakistan and, above all, to the Kashmir people.

I also invite India, jointly with Pakistan, to observe a complete ceasefire along the Line of Control in Kashmir.

Pakistan would also be prepared to encourage a general cessation of violence within Kashmir, involving reciprocal obligations and restraints on Indian forces and the Kashmir freedom movement.

And, may I also add, if India is genuinely concerned about cross-LoC infiltration, we ask that it agree to a viable mechanism to monitor this on both sides of the Line of Control.

The UNMOGIP could be enlarged for this purpose.

Mr. President,

Apart from addressing Kashmir, sustainable security in South Asia requires India and Pakistan to institute measures to ensure mutual nuclear restraint and a conventional arms balance. Unfortunately, India is embarked on a massive build-up of its conventional and non-conventional military capabilities- advanced offensive aircraft, ballistic and cruise missiles, ABM systems, nuclear submarines and an aircraft carrier. This will destabilize South Asia and erode strategic deterrence. Those powers which desire peace, stability and security in South Asia and oppose the proliferation of Weapons of Mass Destruction must review their decisions to offer such major strategic weapons systems to India. They must contribute to maintaining arms restraint and a military balance in South Asia.

Mr. President,

The crises and conflicts of the last decade have enhanced, not diminished, the relevance of the United Nations. The United Nations remains the central forum for dialogue and diplomacy. It must be strengthened. The Security Council must be made more representative by increasing the number of non-permanent members. New permanent members will only expand inequality. States which occupy and suppress other peoples, and defy the resolutions of the Security Council, have absolutely no credentials to aspire for permanent membership of UN Security Council.

Mr. President,

We are on the cusp of a new Millennium. It is a decisive moment in history. We must decide whether to flow with the currents that threaten confrontation and the collapse of our civilization, or muster the collective will to chart the course of history towards a peaceful and cooperative global society. The leaders assembled here bear an enormous responsibility:

- to rescue our world from war and violence, poverty and pestilence;
- to redress inequity and impoverishment which breeds despair and destruction;
- finally to collectively construct a new global architecture of peace and prosperity for all peoples and all nations.

I thank you, Mr. President.

‹89›

Speech by Russian President Mr. Vladimir Putin at the Organization of the Islamic Conference, Putrajaya, Malaysia, (16.10.03)

President Putin described the support of the OIC for developing relations with Russia "not merely as a gesture, but as a long sighted and strategically-oriented decision". He noted that the past decade was a time of revival of the spiritual life of Russia's Muslims and expressed his gratefulness to the OIC and the Arab League for sending observers to the election for the President of Chechnya.

Esteemed Mr. Chairman,

Esteemed Conference participants,

I am sincerely grateful for your invitation and the opportunity to address this forum of such a large and influential international organization.

I would like to especially thank the Chairman of the Summit, the Prime Minister of Malaysia, Mr. Mahathir Mohammad. And, taking this opportunity, I wish to congratulate him on the high assessment that has just been given to him for his contribution to the study and investigation of Islam.

We know that the overwhelming majority of the member countries of the Organization has supported our initiative for developing relations with the OIC. And we regard this not merely as a gesture, but as a long-sighted and strategically oriented decision.

I am convinced-the participation of Russia not only will extend the Organization's vivid palette; it will add to its work new possibilities, will bring the weight and voice of the large Russian Muslim community. A community that no longer separates itself from the world community of Muslims, and is ready to participate fruitfully in its spiritual, cultural and political life.

For centuries Russia as an Eurasian country has been intertwined with the Islamic world by traditional, natural ties. In our country millions of Muslims historically live, and they consider Russia their homeland. The names of the Muslim peoples are present in the geography of the territories which are part of the Russian Federation. And today here in this hall, as members of our delegation, among you are the heads of the subjects of the Russian Federation, in which traditionally the Muslim population constitutes a majority.

I must also note that the past decade was a time of revival of the spiritual life of Russia's Muslims. After many decades of bans on religious education, there are more than 100 madrassas and other religious educational institutions functioning in our country at present. In 1991 Russia had 870 mosques; today their number already exceeds 7,000.

And we are grateful to the OIC countries and other foreign partners-grateful to all who with good intentions and an open heart have helped their fellow believers in Russia, who participated in the construction and renovation of mosques, in the organization of the Haj and carried out educational, cultural and other humanitarian programs in our country.

Esteemed summit participants,

The very history of Russia refutes the still wide-spread perceptions of an insurmountable conflict among civilizations.

You know-throughout the 20th century Russia supported many of your countries in their movement towards national independence. It lent these countries practical assistance within its powers in the formation of an industrial base and a social infrastructure.

Present-day Russia is also actively developing contacts with the majority of the States represented in this hall, essentially keeping up the long-standing, mutually beneficial traditions of cooperation and profound respect for each other.

Esteemed members of the Organization,

We welcome the fact that the OIC builds its activities on universal principles of non-interference in internal affairs and respect for the territorial integrity of sovereign States; that it is against the use of force and for the settlement of conflicts by peaceful means. I would like to note that Russian foreign policy is likewise guided by the above principles.

Russia, just as most of the Islamic States represented here, stands for the consolidation of the system of international law and for the central co-ordinating role of the United Nations in dealing with global problems. And we are convinced that by joint efforts we shall be able to counter the development of events in the world according to adverse scenarios. Scenarios that lead to the appearance of new dangerous dividing lines.

Russia as a permanent member of the United Nations Security Council and many other multilateral institutions-is ready to contribute to such constructive efforts and to seek consistently the affirmation in international relations of the principles of trust, cooperation and mutual understanding.

Almost most dangerous among the multitude of contemporary threats is still the fomenting of inter-ethnic and inter-confessional conflicts. I shall note that attempts to drag the world community into this, essentially artificial conflict exist both in the West and in the East.

Some, using religious slogans as a cover, are actually carrying out armed aggression against their brothers and allies, fighting against lawful authority, provoking separatism and engaging in terrorism.

Others exploit this situation for their selfish aims as an instrument of political pressure to achieve their own aims that have nothing in common with either the interests of Islam or with the protection of human rights or with international law as a whole.

We encounter instances of this kind also at home, in Russia, as shown by the example of the Chechen Republic.

I am grateful to the Organization of the Islamic Conference and the Arab League for sending observers to the election for President of Chechnya. I want to assure those present here in this hall that we shall continue to build on efforts for political stabilization in the republic with the enlistment of all political forces and in the interests of all the inhabitants of Chechnya.

In regard to one of the most serious threats of the contemporary world-terrorism-the position of Russia is consistent and clear: terrorism should not be identified with any religion, cultural tradition or way of life. I must say that, with Russia as an example, attempts by terrorists to provoke xenophobia in our country, at the end of the day, have dismally failed.

I would like before this audience to responsibly declare: for the citizens of our country the Russian Muslims are an integral, full-fledged and full-blooded part of the multinational and multiconfessional people of Russia. And we perceive in that interreligious harmony the strength of the country. We perceive its wealth, prosperity and advantage.

Esteemed Assembly,

Russia-as a unique Eurasian State-has always played a special role in the building of relations between East and West.

And I am convinced that our interaction within the OIC framework can today be a major element of an equitable and secure world as well. It can provide a platform for the conflict-free solution of many international and regional problems.

The addition of our financial, technological and personnel resources can be a real factor of world politics, the start of a breakthrough in many areas of the world economy.

I am certain-this fully corresponds to the interests of our peoples as well as to the humanistic values which all the world religions, including Islam, advocate.

This, I think, is particularly relevant to recall today. In the days when all the Muslims, the entire umma, are awaiting the onset of the sacred month of *Ramadan*.

I want to wish: may it be a time of peace, may it be filled with devout actions, with care of our neighbours and sympathy for those in need.

Thank you for your attention.

❮90❯

Speech by Prime Minister of Malaysia Dr. Mahathir Mohamad at the OIC, Putrajaya, Malaysia (16.10.03)

PM Mahathir Mohamad stated that in view of "disunity and intellectual regression" amongst the Muslim community it is not surprising that the Europeans "should excise Muslim land to create the State of Israel to solve their Jewish problem". He exhorted the Muslims to "stop to think, to assess our weaknesses and strengths, to plan, to strategize and then to counter-attack".

Alhamdulillah, All Praise be to Allah, by whose Grace and Blessings we, the leaders of the Organisation of Islamic Conference countries are gathered here today to confer and hopefully to plot a course for the future of Islam and the Muslim Ummah worldwide...

The whole world is looking at us. Certainly 1.3 billion Muslims, one-sixth of the world's population are placing their hopes in us, in this meeting, even though they may be cynical about our will and capacity to even decide to restore the honour of Islam and the Muslims, much less to free their brothers and sisters from the oppression and humiliation from which they suffer today.

I will not enumerate the instances of our humiliation and oppression, nor will I once again condemn our detractors and oppressors. It would be an exercise in futility because they are not going to change their attitudes just because we condemn them. If we are to recover our dignity and that of Islam, our religion, it is we who must decide, it is we who must act.

To begin with, the Governments of all the Muslim countries can close ranks and have a common stand if not on all issues, at least on some major ones, such as on Palestine. We are all Muslims. We are all oppressed. We are all being humiliated. But we who have been raised by Allah above our fellow Muslims to rule our countries have never really tried to act in concert in order to exhibit at our level the brotherhood and unity that Islam enjoins upon us.

From being a single Ummah we have allowed ourselves to be divided into numerous sects, *mazhabs* and *tarikats*, each more concerned with claiming to be the true Islam than our oneness as the Islamic Ummah. We fail to notice that our detractors and enemies do not care whether we are true Muslims or not. To them we are all Muslims, followers of a religion and a Prophet whom they declare promotes terrorism, and we are all their sworn enemies. They will attack and kill us, invade our lands, bring down our Governments whether we are Sunnis or Syiahs, Alawait or Druze or whatever. And we aid and abet them by attacking and weakening each other, and sometimes by doing their bidding, acting as their proxies to attack fellow Muslims. We try to bring down our Governments through violence, succeeding to weaken and impoverish our countries.

With all these developments over the centuries, the Ummah and the Muslim civilisation became so weak that at one time there was not a single Muslim country which was not colonised or hegemonised by the Europeans. But regaining independence did not help to strengthen the Muslims. Their States were weak and badly administered, constantly in a state of turmoil. The Europeans could do what they liked with Muslim territories. It is not surprising that they should excise Muslim land to create the state of Israel to solve their Jewish problem. Divided, the Muslims could do nothing effective to stop the Balfour and Zionist transgression.

Some would have us believe that, despite all these, our life is better than that of our detractors. Some believe that poverty is Islamic, sufferings and being oppressed are Islamic. This world is not for us. Ours are the joys of heaven in the afterlife. All that we have to do is to perform certain rituals, wear certain garments and put up a certain appearance. Our weakness, our backwardness and our inability to help our brothers and sisters who are being oppressed are part of the Will of Allah, the sufferings that we must endure before enjoying heaven in the hereafter. We must accept this fate that befalls us. We need not do anything. We can do nothing against the Will of Allah.

But is it true that it is the Will of Allah and that we can and should do nothing? Allah has said in *Surah Ar-Ra'd* (verse 11) "He will not change the fate of a community until the community has tried to change its fate itself."

The early Muslims were as oppressed as we are presently. But after their sincere and determined efforts to help themselves in accordance with the teachings of Islam, Allah had helped them to defeat their enemies and to create a great and powerful Muslim civilisation. But what effort have we made especially with the resources that He has endowed us with.

We are now 1.3 billion strong. We have the biggest oil reserve in the world. We have great wealth. We are not as ignorant as the Jahilliah who embraced Islam. We are familiar with the workings of the world's economy and finances. We control 57 out of the 180 countries in the world. Our votes can make or break international organisations. Yet we seem more helpless than the small number of Jahilliah converts who accepted the Prophet as their leader. Why? Is it because of Allah's will or is it because we have interpreted our religion wrongly, or failed to abide by the correct teachings of our religion, or done the wrong things?.

Today, we, the whole Muslim Ummah are treated with contempt and dishonour. Our religion is denigrated. Our holy places desecrated. Our countries are occupied. Our people starved and killed.

None of our countries are truly independent. We are under pressure to conform to our oppressors' wishes about how we should behave, how we should govern our lands, how we should think even.

Today if they want to raid our country, kill our people, destroy our villages and towns, there is nothing substantial that we can do. Is it Islam which has caused all these? Or is it that we have failed to do our duty according to our religion?

Our only reaction is to become more and more angry. Angry people cannot think properly. And so we find some of our people reacting irrationally. They launch their own attacks, killing just about anybody including fellow Muslims to vent their anger and frustration. Their Governments can do nothing to stop them. The enemy retaliates and puts more pressure on the Governments. And the Governments have no choice but to give in, to accept the directions of the enemy, literally to give up their independence of action.

With this their people and the Ummah become angrier and turn against their own Governments. Every attempt at a peaceful solution is sabotaged by more indiscriminate attacks calculated to anger the enemy and prevent any peaceful settlement. But the attacks solve nothing. The Muslims simply get more oppressed.

There is a feeling of hopelessness among the Muslim countries and their people. They feel that they can do nothing right. They believe that things can only get worse. The Muslims will forever be oppressed and dominated by the Europeans and the Jews. They will forever be poor, backward and weak. Some believe, as I have said, this is the Will of Allah, that the proper state of the Muslims is to be poor and oppressed in this world.

But is it true that we should do and can do nothing for ourselves? Is it true that 1.3 billion people can exert no power to save themselves from the humiliation and oppression inflicted upon them by a much smaller enemy? Can they only lash back blindly in anger? Is there no other way than to ask our young people to blow themselves up and kill people and invite the massacre of more of our own people?

It cannot be that there is no other way. 1.3 billion Muslims cannot be defeated by a few million Jews. There must be a way. And we can only find a way if we stop to think, to assess our weaknesses and our strength, to plan, to strategise and then to counter attack. As Muslims we must seek guidance from the Al-Quran and the Sunnah of the Prophet. Surely the 23 years' struggle of the Prophet can provide us with some guidance as to what we can and should do.

We know he and his early followers were oppressed by the Qhuraish. Did he launch retaliatory strikes? No. He was prepared to make strategic retreats. He sent his early followers to a Christian country and he himself later migrated to Madinah. There he gathered followers, built up his defence capability and ensured the security of his people. At Hudaibiyah he was prepared to accept an unfair treaty, against the wishes of his companions and followers. During the peace that followed he consolidated his strength and eventually he was able to enter Mecca and claim it for Islam. Even then he did not seek revenge. And the peoples of Mecca accepted Islam and many became his most powerful supporters, defending the Muslims against all their enemies.

That briefly is the story of the struggle of the Prophet. We talk so much about following the *Sunnah* of the Prophet. We quote the instances and the traditions profusely. But we actually ignore all of them.

If we use the faculty to think that Allah has given us then we should know that we are acting irrationally. We fight without any objective, without any goal other than to hurt the enemy because they hurt us. Naively, we expect them to surrender. We sacrifice lives unnecessarily, achieving nothing other than to attract more massive retaliation and humiliation.

It is surety time that we pause to think. But will this be wasting time? For well over half a century we have fought over Palestine. What have we achieved? Nothing. We are worse off than before. If we had paused to think then we could have devised a plan, a strategy that can win us final victory. Pausing and thinking calmly is not a waste of time. We have a need to make a strategic retreat and to calmly assess our situation.

We are actually very strong. 1.3 billion people cannot be simply wiped out. The Europeans killed 6 million Jews out of 12 million. But today the Jews rule this world by proxy. They get others to fight and die for them.

We may not be able to do that. We may not be able to unite all the 1.3 billion Muslims. We may not be able to get all the Muslim Governments to act in concert. But, even if we can get a third of the Ummah and a third of the Muslim States to act together, we can already do something. Remember that the Prophet did not have many followers when he went to Madinah. But he united the Ansars and the Muhajirins and eventually he became strong enough to defend Islam.

Apart from the partial unity that we need, we must take stock of our assets. I have already mentioned our numbers and our oil wealth. In today's world we wield a lot of political, economic and financial clout, enough to make up for our weakness in military terms.

We also know that not all non-Muslims are against us. Some are well disposed towards us. Some even see our enemies as their enemies. Even among the Jews there are many who do not approve of what the Israelis are doing.

We must not antagonise everyone. We must win their hearts and minds. We must win them to our side not by begging for help from them but by the honourable way that we struggle to help ourselves. We must not strengthen the enemy by pushing everyone into their camps through irresponsible and unIslamic acts. Remember Salah El Din and the way he fought against the so called Crusaders, King Richard of England in particular. Remember the considerateness of the Prophet to the enemies of Islam. We must do the same. It is winning the struggle that is important, not angry retaliation, not revenge.

We must build up our strength in every field, not just in armed might. Our countries must be stable and well administered, must be economically and financially strong, industrially competent and technologically advanced. This will take time, but it can be done and it will be time well spent. We are enjoined by our religion to be patient. *Innallahamaasabirin*. Obviously, there is virtue in being patient.

But the defence of the Ummah, the counter-attack need not start only after we have put our houses in order. Even today we have sufficient assets to deploy against our detractors. It remains for us to identify them and to work out how to make use of them to stop the carnage caused by the enemy. This is entirely possible if we stop to think, to plan, to strategise and to take the first few critical steps. Even these few steps can yield positive results.

The enemy will probably welcome these proposals and we will conclude that the promoters are working for the enemy. But think. We are up against a people who think. They survived 2000 years of pogroms not by hitting back, but by thinking. They invented and successfully promoted Socialism, Communism, human rights and democracy so that persecuting them would appear to be wrong, so they may enjoy equal rights with others. With these they have now gained control of the most powerful countries and they, this tiny community, have become a world power. We cannot fight them through brawn alone. We must use our brains also.

Of late, because of their power and their apparent success they have become arrogant. And arrogant people, like angry people will make mistakes, will forget to think.

They are already beginning to make mistakes. And they will make more mistakes. There may be windows of opportunity for us now and in the future. We must seize these opportunities.

But to do so we must get our acts right. Rhetoric is good. It helps us to expose the wrongs perpetrated against us, perhaps win us some sympathy and support. It may strengthen our spirit, our will and resolve, to face the enemy.

There are many things that we can do. There are many resources that we have at our disposal. What is needed is merely-the will to do it, As Muslims, we must be grateful for the guidance of our religion, we must do what needs to be done, willingly and with determination. Allah has not raised us, the leaders, above the others so we may enjoy power for ourselves only. The power we wield is for our people, for the Ummah, for Islam. We must have the will to make use of this power judiciously, prudently, concertedly. *Insyaallah* we will triumph in the end.

I pray to Allah that this 10th Conference of the OIC in Putrajaya, Malaysia will give a new and positive direction to us, will be blessed with success by Him, Almighty Allah, *Arahman, Arahirn.*

Prime Minister's Office
Putrajaya

‹91›

Statement by Dr. Mohamed ElBaradei, IAEA Director General (16.10.03)

Dr. El-Baradei claimed that "the present nuclear arms control regime is looking battered" and that the rise of terrorist groups makes it essential that "any reform of that regime must begin by conceiving a framework of collective security that does not rely on nuclear deterrence." He suggested limiting the processing of weapon usable material, avoiding the use of materials that may be applied to making nuclear weapons and multinational approaches to the management and the disposal of spent fuel and radioactive waste.

Towards a Safer World

The very existence of nuclear weapons gives rise to the pursuit of them. They are seen as a source of global influence, and are valued for their perceived deterrent effect. And as long as some countries possess them (or are protected by them in alliances) and others do not, this asymmetry breeds chronic global insecurity.

The present nuclear-arms-control regime is looking battered. But any reform of that regime must begin by conceiving a framework of collective security that does not rely on nuclear deterrence. The rise of terrorist groups makes this essential. A nuclear deterrent is clearly ineffective against such groups; they have no cities that can be bombed in reply, nor are they focused on self-preservation. Moreover, their constantly shifting targets and modes of attack demand a more co-operative and flexible international response. The "war on terror" should provide an impetus to work towards a global security culture that will serve the interests of all countries equally, and will make reliance on nuclear weapons obsolete.

Revisiting the NPT Regime

In hindsight, a number of the premises of the 1970 Treaty on the Non-Proliferation of Nuclear Weapons (NPT) seem less than optimal. In a nod to "the early bird gets the nuke", it temporarily legitimised the arsenals of the five countries that had already developed nuclear weapons. It forbade other signatories to develop such weapons, but included no strategy for persuading countries that refused to sign-a loophole which India, Pakistan and, presumably, Israel have used, raising the number of nuclear-armed States to at least eight. And it relied on the promise of the signatories to use nuclear materials for peaceful purposes only. They could use them for health care, agriculture or energy production, but could not divert them to non-peaceful purposes. In fact, however, they have been able to operate very close to a nuclear-weapons capability.

In the climate of the mid-to-late-1960s in which the NPT negotiations took place, this bargain was the best that could be achieved. But the asymmetry it endorsed was never intended to be permanent. The nuclear-weapon States agreed to move towards full disarmament-a commitment renewed "unequivocally" by all five States as recently as 2000-although without a time-table. Some progress on disarmament was made in the late 1980s and early 1990s, but it had nearly ground to a halt by the end of the century, with nearly 30,000 warheads still in existence. The Comprehensive Nuclear Test-Ban Treaty, sought for over four decades as the jewel in the crown of the arms-control regime, was finally concluded in 1996; but seven years after being opened for signature, it still languishes unimplemented. The recent "Moscow Treaty" between the Russian Federation and the United States is encouraging; however, it is not permanent, and it does not address non-operational warheads. And despite volumes of rhetoric on the topic, no progress has been made persuading India, Israel and Pakistan to abandon their nuclear-weapons programmes.

Similarly, on the non-proliferation front, many countries that have signed the NPT have never brought into force the required safeguards Agreement with the International Atomic Energy Agency (IAEA). Fewer than Twenty percent have finalised an additional protocol-endorsed in 1997 after the discovery of Iraq's clandestine nuclear programme-which gives the IAEA the authority to inspect countries more broadly, particularly for undeclared nuclear material and activities.

This sluggish performance on all fronts signals the need for a different approach. Reluctance by one party to fulfill its obligations breeds reluctance in others. Each discovery of a clandestine programme makes us question whether more exist. While I in no way wish to undercut the importance of States' adherence to their NPT obligations, I believe it is time to begin designing a framework more suited to the threats and realities of the 21st century.

In Too Many Hands

Countries with nuclear industries have set up elaborate accounting and protection measures to ensure strong national oversight of their nuclear material. The IAEA inspects regularly to verify the accuracy of what countries report. Export controls restrict the transfer of sensitive technologies that could be misused for nuclear-weapons production.

But controlling access to nuclear-weapons technology has grown increasingly difficult. The technical barriers to designing weapons and to mastering the processing steps have eroded with time. Much of the hardware in question is "dual-use"; for example, it is hard to justify restrictions on exporting "hot cell" technology that could be used for plutonium separation when the same equipment is vital for producing radioi-sotopes used in modern medicine. Changes in political fortunes or economic downturns have at times found nuclear scientists without jobs and reportedly willing to offer their knowledge and services elsewhere. And with the passage of time, the sheer diversity of technology has made it harder to control both procurement and sales. In pre-1992 Iraq, for example, scientists were simultaneously pursuing no fewer than six different technologies to enrich uranium for eventual weapons use, shopping for essential equipment and specialised materials in more than ten countries.

Uranium enrichment is sophisticated and expensive, but it is not proscribed under the NPT. Most designs for civilian nuclear-power reactors require fuel that has been "low-enriched", and many research reactors operate with "high-enriched" uranium. It is not uncommon, therefore, for non-nuclear-weapon States with developed nuclear infrastructures to seek enrichment capabilities and to possess sizeable amounts of uranium that could, if desired, be enriched to weapons-grade.

While high-enriched uranium is easier to use in nuclear weapons, most advanced nuclear arsenals favour plutonium, which can be tailored for use in smaller, lighter weapons more suited for missile warheads. Plutonium is a by-product of nuclear-reactor operation, and separation technology ("reprocessing"), also not proscribed under the NPT, can be applied to extract the plutonium from spent fuel for re-use in electricity production.

Under the current regime, therefore, there is nothing illicit in a non-nuclear-weapon State having enrichment or reprocessing technology, or possessing weapon-grade nuclear material. And certain types of bomb-making expertise, unfortunately, are readily available in the open literature. Should a State with a fully developed fuel-cycle capability decide, for whatever reason, to break away from its non-proliferation commitments, most experts believe it could produce a nuclear weapon within a matter of months.

In 1970, it was assumed that relatively few countries knew how to acquire nuclear weapons. Now, with 35-40 countries in the know by some estimates, the margin of security under the current non-proliferation regime is becoming too slim for comfort. We need a new approach.

My proposal has three parts:

First, it is time to limit the processing of weapon-usable material (separated plutonium and high-enriched uranium) in civilian nuclear programmes, as well as the production of new material through reprocessing and enrichment, by agreeing to restrict these operations exclusively to facilities under multinational control. These limitations would need to be accompanied by proper rules of transparency and, above all, by an assurance that legitimate would-be users could get their supplies.

Second, nuclear-energy systems should be deployed that, by design, avoid the use of materials that may be applied directly to making nuclear weapons. These systems should have built-in features that would prevent countries diverting material to weapons production; prevent the misuse of the facilities and equipment for clandestine manufacture of such materials; and facilitate efficient oversight to ensure continued peaceful use. This is not a futuristic dream; much of the technology for proliferation-resistant nuclear-energy systems has already been developed or is actively being researched. In addition, existing facilities around the world that use high-enriched uranium applications-for example, to produce medical radio-isotopes-should continue, gradually but irreversibly, to be converted to low-enriched processes.

Third, we should consider multinational approaches to the management and disposal of spent fuel and radio-active waste. More than fifty countries have spent fuel stored in temporary sites, awaiting reprocessing or disposal. Not all countries have the right geology to store waste underground and, for many countries with small nuclear programmes for electricity generation or for research, the costs of such a facility are prohibitive.

Considerable advantages-in cost, safety, security and non-proliferation-would be gained from international cooperation in these stages of the nuclear fuel cycle. These initiatives would not simply add more non-proliferation controls, to limit access to weapon-usable nuclear material; they would also provide access to the benefits of nuclear technology for more people in more countries.

The new framework should also "turn off the tap", for all countries, on the production of new material for nuclear weapons. This year marks the tenth anniversary of an historic United Nations resolution calling for a ban on the production of fissile material for weapons use-the so-called Fissile Material (Cut-Off) Treaty-on which little recent progress has been made. This treaty could cap and make public all inventories of fissile material still available, and serve as a starting point for future arms reductions.

I do not have all the answers on what this framework should look like. But it should be inclusive; nuclear-weapon States, non-nuclear-weapon States, and those outside the current non-proliferation regime should all have a seat at the table. The security concerns of all parties should be heard and weighed, and the aim should be to achieve full parity among them under a new security structure that does not depend on nuclear weapons or nuclear deterrence. This naturally should include Agreement on a concrete programme for nuclear disarmament, complete with a time-table.

And lastly, once in force, this new framework should be regarded as a "peremptory norm" of international law-not vulnerable to any nation subsequently withdrawing, based on the whim of a new government or a vote of the latest Parliament. In short, it should be enduring.

A Call for Leadership

In all of human history, no civilisation has ever voluntarily laid down its most powerful weapons. It remains to be seen whether ours can be the first.

We have not yet reached the mid-1960s' prediction of a world of 15 or more nuclear-weapon States, but we are over halfway there. And the trends indicated by recent events should have us all worried.

I worry that, in our collective memories, the horrors of Hiroshima and Nagasaki have begun to fade. I worry about nuclear weapons falling into the hands of terrorists or ruthless dictators. I worry about nuclear weapons already in the arsenals of democracies-because as long as these weapons exist, there is no absolute guarantee against the disastrous consequences of their theft, sabotage or accidental launch, and even democracies are not immune to radical shifts in their security anxieties and nuclear policies.

I worry, but I also hope. I hope that a side-effect of globalisation will be an enduring realisation that there is only one human race, to which we all belong. I hope that dynamic leaders within national governments, international institutions and civil society will step forward with the vision, the integrity and the will to reverse the inertia of fear and insecurity. I hope we can all agree to sit down together, and to start a new.

❮92❯

Speech by President of the People's Republic of China H.E. Hu Jintao at 11th APEC Economic Leaders' Meeting (20.10.03)

President Hu Jintao offered three propositions for strengthening cooperation among APEC members: enhancing mutual trust and stability, striking a balance between economic and social development and opening of markets and improving the multilateral trading system. The APEC Business Travel Card Scheme, according to him, shows what APEC can accomplish if it really wants to be of help.

Prime Minister Thaksin Shinawatra,
Distinguished Colleagues,

It is a great pleasure for me to come to Bangkok and join you in this APEC meeting.Let me begin by expressing my sincere thanks to Prime Minister Thaksin and the Government of Thailand for the thoughtful arrangements in putting this event together.

The international situation has been undergoing profound changes. Peace and development remain the dominant themes of our times and the popular aspirations of people of all lands. But the world we live in is anything but tranquil.Uncertainties that impede peace and development still exist. Local conflicts continue to pose threats to the security and stability of regions and the world as a whole. Non-traditional security concerns such as terrorism and trans-boundary crimes are quite pronounced.Over the past year, the global economy has rebounded somewhat. But burdened by cyclical and structural factors, the recovery is rather slow-paced. It is gratifying to know that our Asia-Pacific region has maintained a sound momentum of economic growth with a positive prospect of further expansion

A part from reviewing the past, we should, more importantly, look to the future and come up with new ideas and new initiatives for jointly promoting economic development in the Asia-Pacific and the whole world and for strengthening cooperation among APEC members.In this connection, I would like to offer three propositions.

First, we should enhance mutual trust and endeavor to make the Asia-Pacific region stable. Stability is a pre-requisite for development. The reason why this region has kept the high growth momentum for decades is because it has basically maintained an environment of peace and stability. We should cherish particularly this peaceful and stable situation that has not come by easily. The Asia-Pacific is a region of rich diversity. Countries are different in history, cultural tradition, political system and economic model, which gives the region its very vigor and vitality. We should increase mutual trust on the basis of mutual respect, seek common ground while putting aside differences, and work to resolve whatever problems there might be through dialogue and consultation in a joint effort to maintain peace and stability in the region. For some time, terrorist attacks have gone on unabated in the Asia-Pacific region, undermining the economic and social development of a number of countries. We should respond to that with closer cooperation and stronger measures to address both the symptoms and root causes of the problem, stand rock firm against terrorism and create a more favourable environment for common development and common prosperity.

Second, we should take effective measures to strike a balance between economic and social development. Only with proper co-ordination can development be long-lasting. Countries in this region should promote regional growth as well as global economic recovery by opting for appropriate macro-economic policies and measures suited to their own conditions. Scientific progress and technological innovation are of vital importance to sustained economic development. To facilitate APEC cooperation in this field, Chinahas proposed the Initiative of Innovative APEC in the hope that certain guiding principles could be formulated for the region's scientific and technological innovation. As a kick-off project, we plan to hold a high-level workshop in February 2004 in Beijingto discuss the issue of science and technology intermediary. All members are welcome to send their representatives when the workshop meets. While pushing for economic growth, we should work hard to promote a co-ordinated development of the economy and society, and of cities and rural areas, and a harmonious co-existence between man and nature so as to rest development on a more solid basis. We propose that APEC reinforce its operations in the field of social development, and in particular, in promoting APEC exchanges in public health, job creation and social security. To promote such cooperation,Chinaplans to sponsor some functions next year on labor and social security.

Third, we should step up mutual opening of markets and improve the multilateral trading system. The world's multilateral trading system is currently facing new challenges mainly in the form of rising protectionism, new trade barriers and frequent trade frictions. This has worsened the difficulties for countries, the developing countries in particular, in their development and hampers global economic recovery and growth. Given such a situation, APEC members should renew their commitment to the Bogor Goals, and at the same time, work together to reject trade protectionism, remove trade barriers and resolve whatever trade disputes they have through dialogues and consultations. A fair and open multilateral trading system serves steady growth of trade at both regional and international levels, contributes to sound economic expansion around the world and conforms with the interests of all parties The fifth WTO Ministerial Conference last month failed to achieve the anticipated progress. The main reason was that the negotiations were not balanced enough to reflect the interests of all parties, particularly the concerns of the developing countries. I hope all parties will demonstrate their political will, take a flexible and pragmatic approach and move ahead the new round of talks to an early fruition. This, in my view, serves the common interests of all.

As the region's important forum for economic cooperation, APEC has done much work and achieved much success in promoting common development. The annual meetings of economic leaders have provided an important venue for leaders to meet regularly and hold in-depth discussions on important issues bearing on regional and global development. Chinahas all along committed itself to Asia-Pacific economic cooperation and actively participated in APEC activities. The new Chinese government will, as always, support and facilitate the APEC process and keep up its mutually beneficial cooperation with other members.

Along with the changes in the regional and international situation, people are thinking more and more about APEC's own future. I believe the following points need to be taken into account in APEC's future development.

The APEC approach, which features respect for differences, equality, mutual benefit, voluntarism and consensus, should be upheld. Facts have proved that such an approach represents an effective vehicle and a right choice for regional cooperation, as it tallies with our region's diversity, accommodates the members' differing needs and helps members to balance their interests.

APEC should embrace reform and innovation by willingly adapting itself to changing circumstances. An organization can maintain its vigor and grow from strength to strength only when it can keep pace with the times and innovate continuously. APEC should act proactively to adapt to new situations, take on new challenges, conduct necessary reform and readjustments to itself and strive to make its activities more timely and relevant.

APEC should gear its multi-faceted cooperation more to the business communities and the general public. The business circle is the main force of economic development. We need to learn more about what they think and what they want and do our best to help them. The APEC Business Travel Card Scheme, which is well received in the business communities, shows what APEC can accomplish if it really wants to be of help. The Chinese government will formally implement this scheme this coming November. We have also adopted a series of trade facilitation measures in customs clearance, inspection and quarantine designed to cut down cost for businesses. APEC should also reach out to the people in our region and conduct more activities that deliver real benefit to as many of them as possible.

Distinguished Colleagues,

Although the sudden onslaught of SARS this year had a negative impact onChina's economy, with hard and persistent efforts, we have moved quickly to get the outbreak under control and sustained the sound growth momentum. We are confident that, on balance, our targets for economic and social development this year will be met. China's development will generate new opportunities for economic growth in the Asia-Pacific region and the whole world. It will offer still broader market for other countries. We will continue to strengthen our friendship and cooperation with other countries and work for peace and development in the Asia-Pacific region and the world at large. China will forever be a force dedicated to world peace and common development.

As a powerful bond that brings the two sides of the Pacific Ocean together, APEC provides its members with an important stage for cooperation. Let us continue to carry forward the community spirit APEC advocates, step up our future-oriented cooperation, and dedicate ourselves to greater economic growth in the Asia-Pacific and the common development and prosperity of all members.

Thank you.

❮93❯

Extracts from LTTE Leader Mr. V. Pirapaharan's Hero's Day Speech (27.11.03)

> The LTTE leader warned that "if the Sinhala chauvinistic ruling elites continue to deny the rights of our people... we have no alternative other than to secede and form an independent state..." He also denied allegations that the recent proposals submitted by his organization constitute the foundation for the creation of a separate state.

Mr Vellupillai Pirapaharan, the leader of the Liberation Tigers of Tamil Eelam (LTTE) in his annual statement commemorating the Heroes' Day has vehemently rejected accusations made by President Chandrika Kumaratunga that his organisation was strengthening its military power and preparing for war. "I wish to deny categorically that there is any truth in these allegations. These false allegations are levelled against us to tarnish the credibility of our liberation organisation and to disrupt the peace process," he said.

The LTTE leader also firmly denied allegations that the recent proposals submitted by his organisation to establish an interim administrative council in the Northeast constitute the foundation for the creation of a separate State.

"Our proposals do not constitute a framework for a permanent final solution. Our draft proposals deal with an interim arrangement. It is true that our proposals for an interim administrative council calls for substantial self-governing authority without which massive programmes for the resettlement and rehabilitation of hundreds of thousands of displaced people and other major development projects could not be undertaken," Mr Pirapaharan explained. He further argued that some of the features of self-governance have been misinterpreted as a project for a separate State.

Characterising the current power struggle in Colombo between the President and the Prime Minister as a typical repetitive historical confrontation between the two major Sinhala political parties, Mr Pirapaharan observed that this phenomenon erupts whenever one party in power attempts to seek a solution to the Tamil ethnic conflict. "This tragic political drama has been continuing for the last fifty years aggravating the plight of the Tamil people," he said.

The LTTE leader also warned that "if the Sinhala chauvinistic ruling elites continue to deny the rights of our people and oppose reconciliation and if the conditions of oppression continue we have no alternative other than to secede and form an independent state invoking the right to self-determination of our people."

Following are extracts from his statement:

"There is no coherent structure in the form a Government in the Sinhala nation. The power of the state is torn between the heads of the two most powerful Sinhala political parties. The Presidency and the Parliament are in conflict with each other. Ranil Wickremasinghe's administration is severely weakened and paralysed following the President's take-over of the Ministries of Defence, Interior and Media. The power struggle between the two leaders has resulted in the de-stabilisation of the state and the peace process has come to a standstill. Frustrated by the confused situation the Government of Norway has suspended its facilitatory role. Because of this sudden development in the south, the conditions of peace are endangered. The peace talks as well as the peaceful resolution of the ethnic conflict are threatened. The Tamil speaking people and the International Governments committed to peace are concerned and disappointed over this crisis.

President Kumaratunga has put forward two reasons for her intervention. One is that the national security and sovereignty of Sri Lanka are threatened as the LTTE has been strengthening is military structure and preparing for war. Secondly, the Government of Ranil Wickremasinghe has provided too many concessions to the Tamil Tigers. I wish to deny categorically that there is any truth in these allegations. These false accusations are levelled against us to tarnish the credibility of our liberation organisation and to disrupt the peace process.

Our organisation, as well as our people do not want war. We want peace and we want to resolve our problems through peaceful means. We are deeply committed to the peace process. It is because of our sincere commitment to peace that we are firmly and rigidly observing ceasefire. It is our organisation that took the initiative of declaring the cessation of hostilities unilaterally and observing peace for the last two years tolerating the provocative actions of the State's armed forces.

There is absolutely no truth in President Kumaratunga's accusation that we are preparing for war by procuring weapons, recruiting on a large scale and strengthening our military machine. We are engaged in the task of maintaining peace but certainly not preparing for war. It is true that we have been recruiting on a small scale since we needed manpower for our administrative structures. The President has distorted and exaggerated this matter and is trying to create fear among the Sinhala people that we are preparing for war.

The ceasefire has not created conditions of peace and normalcy in the Tamil homeland. Oppressive conditions of alien military occupation prevail here. The Sri Lankan armed forces are refusing to fulfil the conditions and obligations of the Ceasefire Agreement. As the military occupation continues in large areas of civilian settlements under the cover of High Security Zones several thousands of people are subjected to enormous suffering, denied the right to return to their homes and villages.

Furthermore, the Tamil civilians continue to suffer harassment and persecution by the occupation army. Though the war has been brought to an end the suffering of our people continues. Our people have not yet experienced total peace and conditions of normal life. Yet, there is total peace and normalcy in the Sinhala nation. There is also improvement in the economic life of the people. While the Sinhala nation enjoys the positive benefits of the ceasefire the tragic oppressive conditions of the Tamils continue. This is the current existential reality.

Our organisation has not rewarded with too many concessions during these two years of ceasefire as accused by President Kumaratunga. Instead, our organisation faced severe losses. During the ceasefire period, two of our merchant ships were attacked and destroyed by the navy in the international waters. Furthermore, several of our fishing trawlers were destroyed. As a consequence of these events we lost twenty-six of our Sea Tiger cadres including senior Commanders. Though these provocative actions pushed us to the brink of tolerance, we maintained calm and observed peace. Such behaviour clearly demonstrates our serious commitment to peace.

The peace talks between our liberation organisation and the Government of Ranil Wickremesinghe, which started in Thailand during September last year, have failed to make any concrete progress. Resolutions and decisions taken during the six rounds of talks that lasted more than six months were not implemented. The sub-committees, which were formed, to deal with the issues of de-escalation and normalisation and for the resettlement and rehabilitation of displaced became defunct. Our efforts to negotiate with the Government to resolve the monumental problems faced by our people became futile. Having ignored the more serious, critical existential issues of resettlement of the displaced, re-construction of the war damaged infrastructure and the re-establishment of normalcy in the Tamil homeland under military occupation, the Government representatives as well as the facilitators devoted their main attention to human values and norms and on guidelines and roadmaps towards a final solution. As a consequence the negotiating process moved in a different direction circumventing the problems and aspirations of our people. In the meantime, Ranil's administration was only interested in projecting the peace process as an ideal model to attract aid and loans from donor countries to build up the economy that collapsed as a consequence of war. At the same time, the Government was also engaged in a plan to set-up an international safety net with the assistance of certain countries. This strategic ploy of Wickremesinghe's Government allowed the space for the increased interest and intervention of several International Governments in the peace initiative as well as in the negotiating process. Some countries have even stipulated parameters within which the Tamil national question has to be resolved. It is because of these international interventions that the peace negotiations became more complex. It was during these circumstances that a crucial meeting of donor countries took place in Washington in April this year marginalizing our organisation. As the main party in conflict enjoying equal status in the peace process, we were disappointed and saddened by such humiliation. It is because of these factors we decided to suspend our participation in the talks and to review the multiple dimensions of the entire peace process.

It is not feasible to find a permanent solution to the Tamil national conflict immediately within a short period. It may take quite a long time. But the existential problems faced by our people are very urgent and they cannot be postponed for longer period. Faced with the urgent humanitarian needs on one side and the issues of resettlement, rehabilitation and re-construction on the other, the immense, complex problems faced by our people necessitates immediate solutions. Having examined these issues in depth, we realised the urgency of setting up an interim administrative authority in the Northeast. We are of the opinion that the proposed interim administrative authority should be an effective mechanism capable of restoring conditions of normalcy in the military occupied Tamil homeland and to undertake the huge tasks of resettlement, rehabilitation and development works efficiently and expeditiously. It is on this basis, we urged the government to submit draft proposals for an interim administrative structure insisting that it should be vested with substantial authority. We also informed the government that we were prepared to resume negotiations if concrete set of proposals were presented to us. I also emphasised the importance of creating an interim administrative set-up with substantial authority when I met the Norwegian Foreign Minister Mr Peterson. I also explained to him the necessity of establishing such an administrative body to re-construct our nation devastated by twenty years of war and to rebuild the shattered lives of our people.

In response to our request, the Government submitted, one after the other, two sets of draft proposals. The interim council envisaged in these proposals were not invested with adequate authority as we suggested. At the same time the role of our organisation was also not clearly defined. The proposals envisaged a development orientated administrative structure with limited powers. Therefore, we rejected these proposals as unacceptable. There after, the government submitted a third set of proposals for our consideration. Though these proposals were unsatisfactory, we did not reject them.

We realised that the Government was hesitant to put forward a concrete set of proposals as expected by our organisation that would satisfy the aspirations of our people. At the same time, we felt that a misconception might arise as if the LTTE was continuously rejecting all the new proposals put forward by the Government. Therefore, we decided not to reject the latest draft proposal out right but to submit our counter proposals to create an interim administrative council with substantial authority. We were not in a hurry to formulate our draft proposal. Since it was the first time we were forwarding our proposals in a written form we wanted to formulate a concrete, practical and original framework though it was an interim set up and might involve time in formulation. We also wanted this framework to have a proper mechanism to find solutions to the complex existential problems of our people. Therefore, we formulated our draft proposals consulting different sectors of people at different levels on a wider scale. We also consulted wider sections of the people of Tamil Eelam, our legal and constitutional experts abroad and international scholars.

There is no need for me to elaborate in detail the draft proposals we submitted to the Government for an Interim Self-Governing Authority. The draft has already been released through the media for everybody's scrutiny and analysis. Though our draft proposals have generated a lot of controversy and confusion, our effort towards a negotiated settlement was welcomed by several countries. Some countries welcomed our attempt, for the first time, to put forward our ideas in writing in a clear and comprehensive form. Ranil's administration did not reject our proposals but rather agreed to resume talks on that basis. But at the same time, the Sinhala racist forces are vehemently opposed to our draft proposals. Sinhala racist political parties and the media are raising critical voices. Critical reviews are coming from the Indian media world and from the Indian political analysts. In a statement released on behalf of the opposition parties, Mr Lakshman Kadirgamar presented a yehement critique of our proposals claiming that Sri Lanka's sovereignty was under serious threat as our draft, according to him, contains elements for a separate State. What surprised us was that within a few days after the release of the draft proposals President Kumaratunga took over three important Ministries that functioned under the Government of Ranil Wickremesinghe. Whatever the reasons she attributes to her actions, it has now become a universal truth that she took this serious action as an immediate response to our draft proposals. As a consequence of her sudden intervention, Ranil's regime has become paralysed without power and the peace process severely endangered.

The allegations levelled against our draft proposals that they aim to create an independent Tamil State or that they contain stepping stones for separation are not true. Our proposals do not constitute a framework for a permanent, final solution. Our draft proposals deal with an interim arrangement. It is true that our proposals for an interim administrative council call for substantial self-governing authority without which massive programmes for the resettlement and rehabilitation of hundreds of thousands of displaced people and other major development projects could not be undertaken. At the same time regional administrative functions i.e. law and order, administration of justice, allocation of funds and distribution of lands also could not be effectively executed. In this context an important factor has to be taken into serious consideration. That is, large areas of the Northeast are already under our effective jurisdiction and efficiently administered by us. I wish to point out that this is the factual reality.

Today, harsh oppressive conditions prevail in the Northeast with the continuous military occupation of our lands and persecution of our people by the armed forces. As normalcy has not returned the suffering of the civilian masses continues. Our people face urgent humanitarian needs as well as serious existential problems. Therefore, we have presented this draft framework as a concrete structure to find just and reasonable solutions to these problems. Our draft framework has progressive, constructive and original elements. This proposed administrative structure is invested with self-governing authority so that the majority Tamils as well as the Muslims and Sinhalese living in Tamil Eelam could promote and enhance their political, social, economic and cultural life. But we regret to note that some forces are attempting to disrupt the peace process by distorting and exaggerating some features of self-governance found in our draft framework and interpreting them as a project for a separate State. We have presented our ideas for an interim administrative authority as a counter programme to the Government's proposals and as a basis for negotiations. Our initiative undertaken with an honest and sincere commitment to the peace process has unleashed a political storm in the south. Sinhalese racist forces are up in arms against us. The power struggle that erupted between the heads of two major political parties of the Sinhala nation has shaken the very foundation of the state structure. Sinhala racism, which has been denying the rights of the Tamils, now stands exposed with its mask torn apart, revealing its true, ugly face to the world.

As a tragic drama without ending, the Tamil ethnic conflict continues forever. Whenever the party in power attempts to resolve the Tamil issue, the party in opposition opposes it and derails the effort. This mode of conflict continues even when the opposition becomes the ruling party and attempts reconciliation. This Sinhala political drama with its typical historical pattern has been staged regularly for the last fifty years. The Directors of this "*bazaar drama*" are the two major Sinhala political parties. Though the main actors have been changing over time the theme of the story is the same. The current political crisis in Colombo is an open enactment of this absurd drama.

As a negative consequence of this chess game, in which the Tamils are used as pawns, several peace efforts have failed; several peace negotiations collapsed, several peace Agreements torn apart and several peace pacts became defunct. As such, the Tamil conflict continues without resolution. The tragic life of our people continues.

We cannot allow the life and potential of our people to be systematically destroyed in the spider web of Sinhala chauvinism. Having renounced violence, we have been making every effort through non-violent means to promote peace and reconciliation. The international community is fully aware of this. But if the Sinhala chauvinistic ruling elites continue to deny the rights of our people and oppose reconciliation and if the conditions of oppression continue, we have no alternative other than to secede and form an independent state invoking the right to self-determination of our people. We urge the Sinhala political leadership not to create the objective conditions that would drive our people to seek this ultimate option," Mr. Pirapaharan declared.

‹94›

Speech By H.E. Mr. Wen Jiabao, Premier of the State Council of the People's Republic of China "Working Together to Write A New Chapter In China-US Relations" (09.12.03)

Mr. Wen Jiabao emphasized the need to handle properly "the sensitive core issue of our bilateral relations i.e. the question of Taiwan." He stated that "we respect the legitimate democratic rights exercised by our Taiwan compatriots, but will absolutely not tolerate the Taiwan Independence forces' attempt to separate Taiwan from China under the sign board of democracy."

It gives me a great pleasure to attend tonight's dinner. I wish to thank the National Committee on US-China relations, the US-China Business Council, the America-China Forum, the Asia Society, the Center for Strategic and International Studies, the Committee of 100, the Council on Foreign Relations, the US Chamber of Commerce and the US-China Policy Foundation for the gracious hospitality. It is delightful to be among friends, both old and new.

In three weeks' time, we shall be celebrating the 25th anniversary of the establishment of diplomatic relations between China and the United States. I was in Hangzhounot long ago, staying in Liuzhuang State Guesthouse where Chinaand the United States negotiated the Shanghai Communiqué. I took a stroll down the West Lake and passed by the Octagonal Pavilion. Gazing at the shimmering ripples of the lake, all sorts of emotions surged within me.

For the last century, China-US relations experienced ups and downs. Our two countries fought together against Fascism at one time, and stood deadly opposed to each other at another.In 1972, the leaders of the two countries, with their outstanding vision and remarkable courage, opened the door of China-US relations that had remained closed for many years. I have boundless respect and admiration for what they have done.

In the past twenty-five years since we established diplomatic ties, our bilateral relations have weathered storms and moved forward. Devoted as you are to Sino-US friendship, you have contributed a great deal to its promotion. Let me take this opportunity, on behalf of the Chinese Government and people, to express our appreciation to all who have contributed to the friendly relations between our two nations.

Where is China-US relations heading? Perhaps this is a subject of greatest interest to you.In fact, when President Jiang Zemin visited your country last year, and President Hu Jintao twice met President Bush this year, they both stated clearly that the Chinese side wished to improve and develop relations with the United States.

A review of the history of China-US relations over the past half century or more since the founding of the People's Republic leads us to three important conclusions.

Conclusion one: China and the United States both gain from peaceful co-existence, and lose from conflicts.

Both China and the US paid a heavy price for their mutual hostility lasting twenty-three years from 1949 to 1971. In contrast, in the thirty-two years since China and the US renewed contact in 1972, both sides have benefited tremendously from our cooperation despite twists and turns. At the time the Shanghai Communiqué was issued in 1972, trade between China and the United States was virtually zero. As a token of friendship toward China, the US Government gave special permission to each traveling American citizen to bring back home 100 US dollars worth of goods made in China. Now, our two-way trade has exceeded 100 billion US dollars.

Conclusion two: Mutual interest serves as the bedrock of our co-operation.

This is, first of all, seen in the win-win and mutually beneficial economic cooperation and trade between our two countries. American companies bring to China their capital, advanced technology and managerial expertise. In return, China's abundant human resources and huge market provide for American companies enormous business opportunities. Furthermore, Chinese enterprises supply US consumers with large quantities of inexpensive and quality consumer goods.

Today, the US has become China's second largest trading partner and the biggest investor in China, whereas for the US, China is the third largest trading partner and the fastest growing export market. Such a significant change is attributable, to a great extent, to China's reform and opening-up.

The reform and opening-up that started in 1978 have brought about fundamental changes to China. We have by and large established a socialist market economy, the GDP has registered an average annual growth rate of 9.4 percent within the past twenty-five years, and the Chinese people are living a relatively well-off life on the whole. China's WTO accession is the landmark of the beginning of all-round opening-up. More than 400 of the world's top 500 multinationals have opened businesses in China.

Accelerated economic growth in China will provide new opportunities and give further impetus to the growth of China-US relations. For instance, the surge of private car sales in China and the growth of the aviation industry prompted by expanding tourism have already brought considerable benefits to American companies. China's import of American agricultural produce such as soya bean, wheat and cotton in large quantities provides a huge market for American farmers. I believe that in the coming twenty years and beyond, it is entirely possible for China to maintain steady and rapid economic growth. Its GDP will quadruple the 2000 volume, exceeding four trillion US dollars by 2020. Just imagine the vast vistas for American investors and companies.

To be sure, there are many other areas of mutual interest that constitute the foundation of cooperation between China and the US.

In short, opening-up is so much better than closing-up. A nation or a country can advance and develop only when it opens up to the outside world.This is the truth that the Chinese people have learned from past experience. However, opening-up is a two-way street.China will open its door even wider to the US, and, hopefully, the US will do the same by opening more sectors to China, including its hi-tech industries.

Conclusion three: China-US cooperation is conducive to stability in the Asia-Pacific region as well as peace and development in the world.

China-US cooperation has played, and will continue to play a positive role in safe guarding stability in the Asia-Pacific region and the world at large. This is a role that cannot be replaced. Terrorism is a common menace to the whole human kind.Chinaand the US have established a mechanism of mid-and long-term anti-terrorism exchange and cooperation based on the principle of "equality, cooperation, reciprocity and mutual benefit". Recently, working together with other parties concerned, China and the US have conducted fruit ful cooperation over a peaceful settlement of the nuclear issue on the Korean Peninsula.

Modern world history tells us that it is the economy and national interests rather than ideologies that under pin the cooperation between big countries. Cooperation between China and the United States, two major countries in the world, shows that countries with different social systems and cultural traditions can co-exist in peace and enjoy common development provided that they set store by their peoples' fundamental interests, and respect and tolerate each other. This will be an example of global significance showing the world how big countries can transcend ideological differences and develop cooperation on the basis of the Five Principles of Peaceful Co-existence. It is possible due to the prevailing trend of the times and the important and profound changes in the international situation.

First, thanks to the advancement of the new global revolution of science and technology as well as economic globalization, there are more interchanges and greater interdependence among various economies. Mutual complementarity grows, which makes their cooperation more mutually beneficial. According to the principle of economic comparative advantages, distribution of industries, the flow of investment and capital and human resources' mobility know no boundary. No country can develop solely on its own in isolation of the world economy.

Second, along with accelerated industrialization and urbanization, environmental pollution, resources depletion, polarization between the rich and the poor, and spread of diseases and narcotics, etc., have become increasingly serious, posing a grave threat to human survival and sustainable development. The solution of these global problems depends on closer international consultation and cooperation, in addition to the efforts of the countries concerned.

Third, at the turn of the century, the international political situation has undergone the most profound change since the end of the Cold War. Ethnic, religious, territorial and resources disputes and regional conflicts keep cropping up. Non-traditional security issues such as terrorism are more prominent. The September 11 incident, not only was a serious shock to the US, but also exerted profound impact on the world.Security interests of countries are increasingly inter-connected. Hardly can any country achieve its security objective on its own. Only by strengthening international cooperation, seeking security through mutual respect and mutual trust and promoting cooperation through equality and mutual benefit can we fundamentally decrease insecure factors.

Fourth, rapid growth of globalized economy and information technology has a great and profound impact on the world cultural development. To increase exchanges and understanding between different cultures so as to promote peace and to avoid conflicts caused by cultural estrangement and discrimination-this will, to a large extent, have a bearing on the fate of mankind in the 21stcentury. In particular, wider access to TV and the Internet allows spiritual and cultural products, healthy or harmful, positive or negative, to spread in the world at an unprecedented pace, directly or indirectly affecting people's mind, values and way of life. It requires, more than ever before, close inter-governmental and non-governmental cooperation to promote the fine culture of every nation and defuse moral crises in the world.

The above-mentioned important changes in the international economic, political and cultural arenas are bound to lead to adjustment in state-to-state relations, particularly relations between major countries.China is the largest developing country while the US the largest developed country. To strengthen China-US cooperation is not only a mutual need but also a responsibility, which our two countries shoulder in the interest of world peace and development. With this understanding of our overall interests and with strategic courage, let us push forward China-US cooperation.

Due to various reasons, there exist estrangements, misunderstandings, and even frictions of one sort or another between China and the United States. In case of differences and contradictions, both sides should keep cool and be sensible. We should try to increase communications, reduce mistrust and seek common ground while shelving differences with a view to properly handling our differences and contradictions. For issues we cannot settle for the time being, let us put them aside and consider them later. The least we want to see is the break of the bond of friendship and co-operation between China and the US. We are friends, not adversaries.

In order to develop China-US constructive and cooperative relations, the Chinese side proposes that:

First, continue high-level visits and strategic dialogue between our two countries;

Second, facilitate mutually beneficial trade and economic cooperation and establish a sound mechanism to address bilateral issues;

Third, intensify co-ordination on major International and Regional issues; and,

Fourth, expand people-to-people exchanges.

The Chinese nation has always cherished peace and harmony. The rise of China is peaceful. It relies on itself for its progress. In foreign relations, we are always in favor of friendship, partnership and co-operation with our neighboring and all other countries.

China is a developing country and will remain so for many years to come. China has a population of 1.3 billion, which is the primary factor of our national conditions.China's GDP ranks the 6th in the world, however, its per capita GNP ranks 111th. China is still faced with such problems as unemployment, poverty and uneven development, which we cannot afford to ignore. These problems are enough to keep us busy.

It calls for arduous endeavours of generations for China to catch up with developed countries. China will never seek hegemony and expansion even when it becomes fully developed and stronger.

Ladies and Gentlemen,

To ensure the healthy and smooth development of China-US relations, we must handle properly the sensitive core issue in our bilateral relations, i.e., the question of Taiwan.

Safeguarding national sovereignty and territorial integrity is the paramount national interest and an unshakable principle for any country.

Our fundamental policy on the settlement of the Taiwan question is "peaceful re-unification" and "One Country, Two Systems". We have all along been doing our utmost to achieve the ultimate re-unification in a peaceful manner.

Recent years have witnessed more frequent people-to-people exchanges and closer economic and trade links between the two sides of the Taiwan Straits. According to statistics, last year, cross-Straits trade reached US$ 44.6 billion, accumulative Taiwanese investment in the Mainland amounted to US$ 35.7 billion. Over three million people travelled back and forth across the Straits each year. In Shanghai alone, 300,000 Taiwan compatriots have settled down, engaging in business or other professions. Before the traditional Chinese New Year, we have to use chartered planes to take them to Hong Kong for transfer back to Taiwan for family reunion. People on both sides of the Taiwan Straits aspire for a peaceful reunification of their motherland as early as possible.

We sincerely hope to see peaceful settlement of theTaiwan question. So long as there is the slightest hope, we will not give up our endeavor for peace. However, our endeavor for peace has time and again been challenged by the Separatist forces in Taiwan. We respect the legitimate democratic rights exercised by our Taiwan compatriots, but will absolutely not tolerate the "Taiwan Independence" Forces' attempt to separate Taiwan from China under the signboard of democracy.

In this regard, American history offers us valuable experiences and lessons. When America was defending the principle that "the Union is perpetual", it was willing to pay a heavy price. It is my belief that the American people would not find it hard to understand our position of resolutely safeguarding the one-China principle and working to achieve national unity.

As you all know, the three China-US Joint Communiqués constitute the basis for China-US relations. The essence of those communiqués is the one-China principle. The separatist activities aimed at "Taiwan Independence" carried out by the Taiwan authorities are seriously undermining the political basis of China-US cooperation and our common interests, and putting peace and stability in the Asia-Pacific region in jeopardy. We hope that the US Government will handle the Taiwan question appropriately and support China's peaceful re-unification.

Ladies and Gentlemen,

Time flies. Twenty-five years is only a short span in the long river of human history. Twenty-five years ago, we could hardly imagine the magnitude and depth of China-US cooperation as we see it today. Now, Chinese people have come to know America better. About 120 million young Chinese are learning English. My little grandson likes Walt Disney's Mickey Mouse and Donald Duck. I am told that American kids enjoy the cartoon Mulan. Young people are the future of a country and the world. I have no doubt that the coming twenty-five years will add more radiance to the blossom of China-US friendship, which will be passed on from generation to generation.

Ladies and Gentlemen,

President Thomas Jefferson once said, "I like the dreams of the future better than the history of the past." Let our two countries and two peoples join hands and work closely together to build a better future for China-US relations.

Thank you.

❮95❯

Speech by Israeli Prime Minister Ariel Sharon to the Herzliyya Institute of Policy and Strategy (18.12.03)

PM Sharon emphasized that "only changing the Palestinian National Authority into a different type of authority will enable progress in the political process". He warned that "if, in another few months the Palestinians are not fulfilling their commitments under the roadmap, Israel will carry out the unilateral security move of disengagement (Hebrew: Hitnatqut) from the Palestinians".

Good evening.

I would like to thank the Organizers of this Conference for the most important and interesting event you have organized here. During the past three days you discussed Israel's situation. I, as Prime Minister, I am responsible for the planning and implementation of moves that will define Israel's path in the coming years.

The mission that we all have is to ensure a Jewish and Democratic Israel: a country in which the burden is distributed equally; in which all sectors have equal rights and obligations through some form of national service; a country with a sound and effective educational system that educates a new generation in values and national pride, and that provides the skills to meet the challenges of the modern world; a country whose economy is in tune with the sophisticated global economy of the 21st Century, where per capita income exceeds 20,000 dollars, and which is equal to the most developed countries of Europe; a country that absorbs new immigrants, that serves as a national and spiritual centre for the entire Jewish world, and that attracts tens of thousands of new immigrants each year. Immigration to Israel is the country's key goal. This is the type of country we want, and in which we want our children to live.

I know that I sometimes have a tendency to concentrate only on Israel's political problems based on the assumption that once Israel's problems with its neighbours, particularly the Palestinians, are solved, all other issues on the agenda will also be solved. I, personally, do not believe this is the case. We face many challenges which must be addressed: the economy, educating the younger generation, absorbing new immigrants, increasing social coherence, and improving relations between Jews and Arabs in Israel.

'Genuine peace'

Like all Israelis, I yearn for peace. I see the utmost importance in taking all possible steps that will lead to a solution of the conflict with the Palestinians. But, in light of the additional challenges we face, if the Palestinians do not make a similar effort to solve the solution I do not intend to wait for them forever.

About seven months ago, the Government which I head approved the road map for peace, which is based on President Bush's speech of June 2002. The road map is a balanced plan for progressing gradually towards peace, which Israel and the Palestinians committed themselves to implement. Full implementation of the road map is the best way to achieve genuine peace. The road map is the only political plan that was accepted by Israel, the Palestinians, the Americans and most of the world. We are willing to move forward in implementing the road map: two states, the State of Israel and a Palestinian State existing peacefully side by side.

The road map is a clear plan, it is also logical. So, it can and must be implemented. The underlying concept of the road map is that only security will bring about peace-and in that order. Without achieving full security, which includes the dismantling of the terrorist organizations, real lasting peace cannot be achieved. This is the essence of the road map. The reverse concept, according to which the actual signing of a Peace Agreement will some how bring about peace, has already been tried and was a failure. This will be the fate of any other plan that follows in the footsteps of this attempt. These are all plans that mislead the public and give them false hope. There will not be peace before terrorism is eradicated.

'Terrorist bodies'

My Government will not compromise on the implementation of all stages of the road map. The Palestinians must root out the terrorist bodies and create a law-abiding society that fights violence and incitement. Peace and terrorism cannot go together. The world is making a firm demand of the Palestinians to stop terrorism and to carry out reforms. Only changing the PNA (Palestinian National Authority) into a different type of authority will enable progress in the political process. The Palestinians must carry out what is required of them. Full implementation will ultimately lead to peace and calm.

We began implementation of the road map in Aqaba, but the terrorist organizations associated with (Palestinian President) Yasser Arafat disrupted the process with a series of cruel terrorist attacks. Together with the demand that the Palestinians eradicate the terrorist organizations, Israel is carrying out-and will continue to carry out-steps to improve conditions for the Palestinian population. Israel will lift blockades and closures and will reduce the number of roadblocks, thereby easing movement by Palestinian traffic, including the passage of goods and people; we will extend the working hours at the international crossing points; we will permit a large number of Palestinian businessmen to conduct normal economic and commercial life with their associates in Israel.

All these steps are aimed at permitting better and freer traffic of the Palestinian population that is not involved in acts of terrorism. In addition, subject to security co-ordination, we will hand over Palestinian cities to Palestinian security control. Israel will make every effort to help the Palestinians and to move the process forward.

Outposts

Israel will comply with its commitments. I assured the President of the United States that Israel will dismantle the unauthorized outposts. I intend to live up to that commitment. Israel is a law-abiding country and the issue of the outposts is not an exception. I understand that the issue is sensitive. We will try to carry out our commitments in a manner that will cause the least pain, but the unauthorized outposts will be dismantled-full stop.

Israel will comply with all its commitments on the issue of construction in the settlements: There will be no construction beyond the existing construction lines, no expropriation of land for construction, no special economic incentives, no construction of new settlements.

I want to use this opportunity to call on the Palestinians and to say again what I said in Aqaba: We have no interest in ruling you. We want you to run your own lives in your own country, a Democratic Palestinian State, a territorially contiguous State in Judaea and Samaria (West Bank), a country with an functioning economy that has normal ties with the State of Israel. Abandon terrorism and let's work together to stop the bloodshed. Let's move forward together towards peace. We want to progress quickly with the implementation of the road map and with our attempts to achieve genuine peace.

'Unilateral security move'

We hope that the PNA will play its part. However, if, in another few months the Palestinians still are not fulfilling their commitments under the road map, Israel will carry out a unilateral security move of disengagement (Hebrew: hitnatqut) from the Palestinians. The aim of the disengagement plan is to keep terrorism at a minimum-as far as this is possible-and to provide Israel's citizens with maximum security. The process of disengagement will improve quality of life and will strengthen Israel's economy.

The unilateral steps that Israel will take as part of the disengagement Plan will be co-ordinated to the maximum with the United States. We must not harm the strategic co-ordination with the United States. These steps will increase the security of Israel's citizens and will make it easier for the IDF and the security forces to fulfil the tough missions they are facing.

The disengagement plan is designed to give maximum security and to create minimum friction between Israelis and Palestinians. We are interested in holding direct negotiations, but we have no intention of making Israeli society hostage to the Palestinians. As I have said, we won't wait for them forever.

Settlements

The disengagement plan will include a redeployment of IDF (Israel Defence Forces) troops on new security lines and a change in the deployment of the settlements, so that the number of Israelis living in the heart of the Palestinian population will be reduced as much as possible. We will draw temporary security lines, and the IDF will deploy on those lines. Security will be provided by the IDF deployment, the security fence, and other physical obstacles. The disengagement plan will reduce the friction between us and them.

The reduction of friction will call for an incomparably hard step: changing the deployment of some of the settlements. I want to repeat what I stated in the past: In a future arrangement, Israel won't remain in all the places where we are today. The relocation of settlements will be done, first and foremost, in order to draw the most effective possible security line, which will create the said disengagement between Israel and the Palestinians.

This security line will not be the permanent border of the State of Israel, but the IDF will be deployed along this line until the implementation of the road map resumes. Settlements to be re-located are those that under any possible format of a future and final arrangement will not be included within the territory of the State of Israel. At the same time, as part of the disengagement plan, Israel will strengthen its control in those parts of Eretz Yisrael that will constitute an inseparable part of the State of Israel under any future arrangement. I know that you want to hear names, but it's better to leave something for later.

Separation barrier

Israel will largely intensify the construction of the security fence. This can be seen fleshing out already today. The speedy completion of the security fence will enable the IDF to remove roadblocks and to alleviate the daily lives of the Palestinian population that is not tainted with terror. In order for the Palestinians to be able to develop their economic and business life and in order for them not to be exclusively dependent on Israel, within the framework of the disengagement plan we will weigh the possibility of enabling, in co-ordination with Jordan and Egypt, freer passage of people and goods through the international crossings as we adopt the necessary security measures.

'Not a political move'. I'd like to emphasize that the disengagement plan is a security move, and not a political one. The steps to be adopted won't change the political reality between Israel and the Palestinians and will not undo the possibility of going back to implementing the road map and of reaching an arrangement through Agreement.

The disengagement plan doesn't preclude the implementation of the road map, but is a step that Israel will take in the absence of any other option in order to improve its security. The disengagement plan will be implemented only in the event that the Palestinians continue to drag their feet and put off the implementation of the map.

Clearly, under the disengagement plan the Palestinians will get far less than they would be able to attain in direct negotiations on the road map. Parts of the disengagement plan designed to provide maximum security to Israel's citizens may be carried out concurrently with the attempt to implement the road map; this, in accordance with the circumstances that will be created.

Call for unity

Ladies and gentlemen, my life experience taught me that attaining peace, just like war, requires broad consensus. We must uphold our unity, even if a poignant debate rages in our midst. In the last three years the Palestinian terror organizations put us to a tough test. Their plan to break the spirit of Israeli society failed. Israel's citizens knew how to stand firm, support each other, stretch out their hand, volunteer, and contribute. I believe that in this way, united, we must continue today as well.

Whether we can make progress in the road map or we have to implement the disengagement plan, experience shows us that together, with broad national Agreement, big things can be done. Let us entertain no illusions: every path will be complicated, fraught with obstacles, and will require the exercise of judgement and responsibility. I am sure that just as we lived up to the challenges in the past, we will stand together and we will succeed also today.

As we proceed, the words of Prime Minister David Ben-Gurion the day after the declaration of Israel's independence will always stand before us-and I quote: These days we must build the State of Israel only with love, faith and Jewish fraternity, and defend it with our souls and with all our might for as long as it is necessary. We are still facing a harsh battle, a dual battle, political and military. Let us not adorn our deeds, certainly not our words, with highfalutin adjectives. Let us be humble. We have come as far as we have with the support of the generations that preceded us, and we have accomplished what we have because we embraced and preserved a precious legacy, the legacy of a small nation that experienced a lot of suffering, but is grand and eternal in spirit, vision, faith, and spiritual values-end of quote.

I am also a great believer in the resilience of this small and courageous nation that experienced a lot of suffering. I am sure that united by the force of faith we'll be able to succeed in any path we choose.

Thank you and a happy Hanukkah holiday.

Index

Notes

Notes

Notes

Notes